CB 351 .S83 v.20

Sources of Anglo-Saxon
culture

CALIFORNIA STATE UNIVERSITY, HAYWARD
LIBRARY

Sources of Anglo-Saxon Culture

The preparation of this volume was made possible (in part) by a grant from the Program for Research Conferences of the National Endowment for the Humanities, an independent federal agency.

Sources of Anglo-Saxon Culture

EDITED BY

Paul E. Szarmach
with the assistance of
Virginia Darrow Oggins

Studies in Medieval Culture XX
Medieval Institute Publications
Western Michigan University
Kalamazoo, MI   1986

Library of Congress Cataloging-in-Publication Data
Main entry under title:

Sources of Anglo-Saxon culture.

(Studies in medieval culture ; 20)
Papers from the Symposium on the Sources of Anglo-Saxon Culture held in conjunction with the Eighteenth International Congress on Medieval Studies at Western Michigan University, May 5-8, 1983.
Includes bibliographies.
1. Civilization, Anglo-Saxon—Congresses.   2. Anglo-Saxon literature—History and criticism—Congresses.
I. Szarmach, Paul E.   II. Oggins, Virginia Darrow.
III. Symposium on the Sources of Anglo Saxon Culture (1983 : Western Michigan University)
CB351.S83   vol. 20   940.17 s   85-21756
[DA152.2]   [936.2]
ISBN 0-918720-67-2
ISBN 0-918720-68-0 (soft)

©copyright 1986 by the Board of the Medieval Institute
Kalamazoo, Michigan 49008

Cover design by Elizabeth King
Printed in the United States of America

Table of Contents

Foreword
Paul E. Szarmach   VII

Part One: Literature

Literary History and Old English Poetry: The Case of *Christ I, II, III*
Thomas D. Hill   3

Source Study as a Trick with Mirrors: Annihilation of Meaning in the Old English "Mary of Egypt"
Colin Chase   23

Evidence for Knowledge of Latin Literature in Old English
Janet M. Bately   35

The Preservation and Transmission of Greek in Early England
Mary Catherine Bodden   53

The Venerable Bede and Hiberno-Latin Exegesis
Joseph F. T. Kelly   65

Towards the Identification of Old English Literary Ideas—Old Workings and New Seams
J. E. Cross   77

Continental Sources of Anglo-Saxon Devotional Writing
Thomas H. Bestul   103

Biblical Style in Early Insular Latin
David R. Howlett   127

Part Two: History, Archaeology, Art History

Celtic and Anglo-Saxon Kingship: Some Further Thoughts
Patrick Wormald   151

Northumbria and Ireland
Rosemary Cramp   185

The Relationship Between Scandinavian and English Art from the Late Eighth to the Mid-Twelfth Century
Signe Horn Fuglesang   203

The Distinctiveness of Viking Colonial Art
James Lang   243

The Imagery of the Living Ecclesia and the English
Monastic Reform
    Robert Deshman   261

Demonic Elements in Anglo-Saxon Iconography
    Louis Jordan   283

The Marvels-of-the-East Tradition in Anglo-Saxon Art
    John Block Friedman   319

Part Three: Interdisciplinary Approaches: *The Dream of the Rood*

The Devotional Context of the Cross Before A.D. 1000
    Sandra McEntire   345

Reflections on the Iconography of the Ruthwell and
Bewcastle Crosses
    Robert T. Farrell   357

Christ over the Beasts and the Agnus Dei: Two Multivalent
Panels on the Ruthwell and Bewcastle Crosses
    Éamonn Ó Carragáin   377

Part Four: Research Tools

The Dictionary of Old English
    Ashley Crandell Amos   407

The Index to Iconographic Subjects in Anglo-Saxon
Manuscripts: A Research Tool
    Thomas H. Ohlgren   415

The Corpus of Anglo-Saxon Stone Sculpture
    Rosemary Cramp   431

A Handlist of Anglo-Saxon Manuscripts
    Helmut Gneuss   433

Dictionary of Medieval Latin from British Sources
    David R. Howlett   437

Abbreviations and Short Titles   439
List of Manuscripts Cited   440
Index   445

Foreword

The papers in this volume are the written record of the Symposium on the Sources of Anglo-Saxon Culture held in conjunction with the Eighteenth International Congress on Medieval Studies at Western Michigan University, May 5-8, 1983. Although the reader will detect the speaking voice in most of the contributions, each writer has revised his or her oral presentation for publication, not only by adding supporting documentation but also by amplifying or extending, when necessary, those arguments abbreviated by the time constraints of the Symposium schedule. The organization of this volume also differs, rather markedly in fact, from the schedule of papers presented over those four days. The nine Congress sessions have become four parts in this book mainly because with revision clearer and more focused issues and topics have emerged. In this regard, "Part One: Literature" shows the most significant divergence from the original order of presentation, for the written versions display a logical movement from papers more theoretical or general in nature to papers more specific. What this volume cannot contain, of course, are the transcripts of those formal and informal discussions that sharpened the oral presentations into their written form. Yet the differences between this written record and the oral performance have not so much altered the original intentions of the Symposium as reaffirmed them. Some consideration of these original intentions is appropriate here.

Within the broad framework of Anglo-Saxon Studies and especially of its continuing development, the original Conference plan sought to focus on three sub-fields in the subject, namely literary culture, iconography, and archaeology. The sub-field of literary culture—the dominant area of interest in North America, and along with history and legal studies the oldest—offered several related topics for discussion. These topics included questions on and developments in methodology, the usefulness and availability of research tools, and advances in manuscript studies. While theoretical issues had to have a natural prominence, the conference plan maintained a steady interest in practical and future results centered around J. D. A. Ogilvy's *Books Known to the English* and Helmut Gneuss' "A Preliminary List of Manuscripts Written or Owned in England up to 1100."[1] The consideration of literary sources implied a thorough consideration of Anglo-Latin contexts. The sub-field of iconography, or more broadly art history, which by comparison with literature and history is a comparatively underdeveloped field in Anglo-Saxon Studies, was a similar focus of interest. The plan for this part of the Symposium had to consider theoretical issues and issues of context, but—equally important—it had to consider questions involving interdisciplinary impact and research tools. Here the focus on practical results meant a discussion of the Index to Iconographic Subjects, which is now at the final stage of development. The sub-field of archaeology posed, essentially, a different set of issues. The rapid and perhaps volatile development of this subject in recent years shifted emphasis to the simple question of "What is going on now?" For the North American audience this simple question is crucial, for there is an information gap that makes it difficult for North Americans to know what is happening: publications in Anglo-Saxon archaeology are hard to acquire in North America, and the publication process itself is so slow that discoveries lose their impact on scholarship.

The various interconnections between and among these three disciplines simply could not be left unmade. Thus, the original plan called for a plenary meeting in discussion format where all participants and attendees could observe, comment, and criticize papers presented, with special reference to future directions in Anglo-Saxon Studies. The plan also called for a "demonstration session," in which literature, iconography, and archaeology could develop an interdisciplinary perspective by concentrating on a single object/text or on a set of closely-related objects/texts. In this book the demonstration session appears as Part Three.

The Symposium plan therefore sought both disciplinary and interdisciplinary interchange within Anglo-Saxon Studies and, if one may use so portentous a term, a "charter" for future research. These two broad goals, most participants seemed to feel, were met. Given the North American audience, whose predominant discipline is literature, the response to the art and archaeology sessions was very positive. More than a hundred participants came to hear the session "Art and Archaeology I," which consisted of papers by Patrick Wormald and Rosemary Cramp. The glance towards future research led to development of a number of general ideas, such as a motif- or theme- index, a catalogue of post-Conquest legal and administrative documents in England, a machine-readable copy of *Domesday Book,* a "Bollandist" presentation of Anglo-Saxon saints' lives, a successor to J. D. A. Ogilvy's *Books Known to the English,* a prosopography for the Anglo-Saxon period, a machine-readable text of the Anglo-Saxon charter corpus, and a corpus of translations from the Latin for students and scholars.

In a real sense the Symposium produced more than was intended. The consensus of the group at the business meeting was that the Symposium should continue over the next several years. In 1984 the Symposium produced six sessions; in 1985 eight sessions; and plans for 1986 are in progress. These continuations reflect the triple-sub-field emphasis of the original 1983 meeting with special attention to problems of literary sources. British participants in the original meeting organized a similar Symposium at Leeds in March, 1984. British and North American scholars have furthermore organized committees of interest to pursue both the general question of literary sources and the specific problem of a successor volume to Ogilvy's *Books Known*. The *Old English Newsletter* regularly reports the activities of the continuing Symposium in its Fall and Spring issues.

This collection of papers, then, ought to mark the beginning of some new directions in Anglo-Saxon Studies. There have been many developments in literary studies in the last generation, but, as Fred C. Robinson writes, "The real frontier in early English studies is the field of pre-Conquest Anglo-Latin, where the language remains largely uncodified."[2] The papers in Part One are to a significant degree a preliminary answer to Robinson's implicit call. Thomas D. Hill and the late Colin Chase begin this section by asking methodological questions about literary history and source study, thus displaying the self-consciousness over methods and approaches that has characterized contemporary analysis. Janet M. Bately and Mary Catherine Bodden introduce new information and new insights on the classical tradition, the former concentrating on classical texts and those post-classical works through which classical themes and references to ancient history and classical myth were transmitted to the early Middle Ages, and the latter working in primary sources for the Greek that Anglo-Saxon authors might have known. Joseph Kelly, J. E. Cross, Thomas H. Bestul, and David R. Howlett consider the Christian tradition. Kelly offers, among other things, up-to-date scholarship from the perspective of Irish Studies. Cross also pursues the Irish connection, but his meticulous analysis of texts with manuscript sources ends with a direct challenge to workers in the field to pursue similar literary riches in the Latin tradition. Bestul presents, in effect, a new category or genre for literary sources, viz., devotional writing, offering an important list of manuscripts as well. Howlett reminds all that style is as much a subject for source analysis as text; he presents a provocative study of Biblical style. In their interest in new methods, the Latin manuscript tradition, and new subject areas in the nexus of Latin and vernacular literature, these essayists suggest that the pursuit of literary sources has an open and bright future with much work to be done.

Similarly, the essayists of Part Two develop issues in other sub-fields of Anglo-Saxon Studies. In a wide-ranging essay which was the O'Donnell Lecture in 1983, Patrick Wormald surveys the state of the question regarding Celtic and Anglo-Saxon kingship. Rosemary J. Cramp continues the Anglo-Celtic theme by reviewing Irish-Northumbrian relations with special reference to art and archaeology. Signe Horn Fuglesang considers the broad range of Anglo-Scandinavian artistic relationships, pointing out some of the stages of artistic development now under special discussion in the field with a view towards establishing criteria for relationships deriving from foreign influence. James T. Lang focuses on sculpture to discuss distinguishing characteristics of Viking colonial art, but his essay weighs in the balance several important governing factors that apply to the whole field of Anglo-Saxon art. Robert Deshman, Louis Jordan, and John B. Friedman consider manuscript art. Deshman shows how Benedictine reformers used a variety of means to express and explain their actions in a propaganda program effective in its imagery. Jordan argues that it was Anglo-Saxon art of the monastic revival and its aftermath that gave the devil his "demonic form" by combining indigenous zoomorphic tradition with Continental iconography, while Friedman traces the Marvels-of-the-East tradition to its Continental roots to show the distinctiveness of Anglo-Saxon artistic representations of the theme.

Part III contains three essays on the *Dream of the Rood* by Sandra McEntire, Robert T. Farrell, and Éamonn Ó Carrigáin. Taken together these essays show how interdisciplinary and cross-disciplinary investigation can illuminate a single artistic object and how this single object in turn requires an interpreter who must be sensitive to the methods and ideas of several disciplines in order to approach its full meaning.

Part Four offers reports on five major projects in Anglo-Saxon Studies that are in various states of completion. These reports and the discussions they inspired constituted the practical business of the Symposium. As indicated above, this business continues as projects for future research in Anglo-Saxon Studies develop.

The Symposium and the Proceedings volume have been the products of cooperation among several institutions and many individuals. The Medieval Institute at Western Michigan University willingly served as host for the Symposium and readily offered its series *Studies in Medieval Culture* as the venue for the Proceedings. For this tangible support, generous indirect financial assistance, and much continuing encouragement, this editor (speaking as well for the participants) thanks Otto Gründler, Director of the Medieval Institute. The Institute staff, specifically Thomas Seiler, Jenny Syndergaard, and Angie Cardozo, made the details of both activities easy and pleasant. The Center for Medieval and Early Renaissance Studies at SUNY-Binghamton joined with the Institute in sponsoring the Symposium and produced the volume by preparing typeset pages ready for the camera. For her editorial work the editor must thank Virginia Darrow Oggins, who did most of the technical editing and styling and gave good advice on other matters. Mario A. Di Cesare, Director and General Editor of Medieval and Renaissance Texts and Studies, which is the publishing program of CEMERS, gave very able and efficient direction to the production process. Before he was editor, the editor was a Project Director under the National Endowment for the Humanities, Division of Research. The NEH provided major funding through its Research Conferences grant program for the Symposium itself and for manuscript preparation. The proposal to the NEH would not have been possible without J. E. Cross, Robert T. Farrell, Thomas Ohlgren, and Thomas D. Hill. These generous colleagues either gave advice, or criticized prose, or organized sessions, or did all of these things. There were other colleagues who assisted: four, remaining anonymous here, reviewed various essays, and the following volunteered to chair sessions: David Yerkes (Columbia University), Cynthia Cornell (DePauw University), F. M. Ahl (Cornell University), Carl T. Berkhout (University of Arizona), Mary Richards (University of Tennessee-Knoxville), Joseph C. Harris (Harvard University), and Joseph B. Trahern, Jr. (University of Tennessee-Knoxville). I also wish to acknowledge with gratitude the support of the British Academy, which funded five participants, and the Government of Norway, which funded Signe Horn Fuglesang. Yet all this network of support would have been hollow had it not been for the participants themselves, whose papers were the substance of the Symposium and the *Proceedings*. It is usually difficult to get twenty-two personal lives and professional careers in synchrony, but the participants have been as one in their cooperation and mutual concern. Our only regret is that Colin Chase cannot share our sense of completion and our anticipation of future developments. Colin died of cancer on October 13, 1984; he taught us much by his scholarship and by his personal example, and we are in great measure diminished.

PAUL E. SZARMACH
Center for Medieval and Early Renaissance Studies
UNIVERSITY CENTER AT BINGHAMTON

Notes

1. J. D. A. Ogilvy, *Books Known to the English, 597–1066* (Cambridge, Mass., 1967), which supersedes his earlier *Books Known to Anglo-Latin Writers from Aldhelm to Alcuin (607–804)* (Cambridge, Mass., 1936); Helmut Gneuss, "A Preliminary List of Manuscripts Written or Owned in England up to 1100," *ASE,* 9 (1981), 1–60.

2. Fred C. Robinson, "Anglo-Saxon Studies: Present State and Future Prospects," *Mediaevalia,* 1, No. 1 (Spring, 1975), 72.

Part One
Literature

Literary History and Old English Poetry: The Case of Christ I, II, and III

THOMAS D. HILL

I

The central problem of Old English literary history is a very simple one. History, as conventionally understood, involves dates, places, and a reasonable (or at least plausible) explanation of the unfolding of events within time. If no explanation is sufficiently plausible, history is still, on the lowest level, an account of events in sequence. Literary history is a subspecies of the larger genre of history and offers special problems; but even so literary history remains very much concerned with chronology and relationships. The scholar who sets out to write a literary history of Anglo-Saxon literature, however, immediately has to face a frustrating and somewhat numbing problem. Those Old English poems which are, by common agreement, the most significant literary monuments of this period are neither dated nor localized. What is even more frustrating, it has not been possible to arrive at a consensus about any very meaningful ordering of the poems within the canon in terms of style, content, or ideological viewpoint. At one point, it seemed possible to date the poems linguistically and to arrive at some agreement about their original dialect. But most of the poetry is apparently either written in a *koine* or reflects an essentially similar development of Anglian originals copied by West Saxon scribes; and it has not proved possible to order the various poems in chronological sequence on the basis of linguistic evidence. Now that full machine concordances exist for the entire corpus of Old English literature, it may be possible to pursue this line of inquiry into chronological sequence more successfully, but at present this possibility has yet to prove fruitful.[1]

Various literary historians have, of course, responded in various ways to this annoyingly intractable problem; but one way of summarizing the discussion is to define two poles toward which most of the scholars who have written on these problems have tended to gravitate. On the one hand, in the nineteenth century and even well beyond it there was a good deal of essentially speculative literary history in which poems were assigned to the school of Cædmon or the school of Cynewulf, and the canon of Cynewulf's poetry was expanded to include a very substantial portion of the corpus of Old English poetry. In reaction to these tendencies, modern literary histories of this period tend to be frankly formalistic and ahistorical. Thus Stanley Greenfield joins together such diverse poems as *Christ I, Christ II,* and *Christ III, Judgment Day I* and *II, The Dream of the Rood, The Descent into Hell,* and *Christ and Satan* in a chapter entitled "Christ as Poetic Hero."[2] Obviously there is no intrinsic relationship among these very diverse poems. But I do not wish to seem to criticize either approach. The tendency to push historical speculation too far was the inevitable excess of an age of great historical discoveries; and a purely formalistic approach is a quite reasonable response to the absence of historical information which would permit historical discourse.

It may be worth attempting to approach this seemingly intractable scholarly problem from a somewhat different perspective. It is the thesis of this paper that the scrupulous study of Old English poetry in relation to its known sources is an essentially new and potentially revealing approach to the problem of Old English literary history. Before we elaborate upon this thesis, it might be worth considering for a moment the particular problems which the history of an early medieval literature such as Old English presents. To begin with, the texts we have were preserved only by chance. The literary historian must therefore be very cautious about assuming any specific relationship between any two given texts. His problem is, in a sense, to arrange and to order this body of material in some meaningful way. The sudden discovery of a list of Old English poets and their published works would be of no real significance unless this list permitted us to make revealing comparisons and see something of the development of this literature as a whole: if the poetry of the early period turned out to be exactly similar to that of the middle and late period, the ability to discriminate between these periods would be a bit pointless. Now the study of Old English poetry in relation to its sources will not necessarily permit us to date or to localize any given poem, but it could permit the literary historian of this period to analyze the relationship of one text to another with much more assurance and objectivity.

The study of the sources of Old English poetry is, of course, a very traditional and well-established branch of Old English literary scholarship.

Whenever an Old English poem is edited or re-edited, it is conventional for the editor to review the problem of its known sources and to contribute whatever new information he can on the topic. There is even a recent anthology of sources in translation to permit the beginning student of Old English literature to compare the Old English texts he may happen to read with their original sources. Yet despite the familiarity and conventionality of source study, there remain current two related (and generally unspoken) assumptions about the project of source study which serve to discourage many potential workers in this field. On the one hand it is felt that, while it is nice to know as accurately as possible the sources of a given poem, this kind of inquiry is, as a practical matter, virtually endless. One could, after all, spend a lifetime attempting to recover the sources of one poem, and at the end of that lifetime the vagaries of manuscript preservation, the limitations of available printed texts, and the imponderables of human memory and poetic imagination could frustrate the zeal of the most dedicated source hunter. Apart from the difficulty of the inquiry, a more deadening assumption is the sense that the quest for more and better sources is not really worth while. Most Old English poetry is explicitly religious in character, and most of these texts are dependent upon one or more Latin sources. These sources are for the most part identified, and have been known for two or more generations. If there is further work to do, it is (or would seem from an unsympathetic perspective to be) that of tidying up the details. And it could be argued, of course, that once we know *in general* what kind of text an Old English poet was working with, we really do not need to know much more.

Both assumptions are intrinsically plausible, and both are obviously true to some degree; but the conclusion to which these assumptions point — that source study is ultimately unrewarding — is fundamentally false. To begin with, while it is true that the study of the sources of any given poem is potentially endless, it is also true that a reasonably close approximation to the sources which a poet used is almost as revealing as discovery of the exact sources would be. The closer the approximation the better, of course, but it is possible to draw some conclusions on the basis of even a fairly rough approximation.[3] Second (and this is, I believe, a crucial point), it is possible to develop a composite image of the way in which a poet worked with the texts in front of him even if some of the details are tentative and problematical. Some poets are meticulously concerned with expressing the verbal detail of the original; others treat their source or sources much more freely; and others have no source in a strict sense at all. Some poets are interested in elaborating a narrative in terms of the figures and diction of Germanic poetry; others are much more restrained in this respect. Obviously this point could be elaborated at some length, but my argument is a simple one. If a poem whose sources are known is of any length, it should be reasonably easy to see how the poet is working with his sources and to acquire a general sense of his approach to his topic.

At this juncture it might be appropriate to raise briefly a logical problem which might seem to inhibit this discussion in a fairly substantive way. In the absence of holograph manuscripts, library inventories, and reading lists, how can we ever be certain that a given feature in a poem is actually original with the poet rather than drawn from some now lost source? Let me offer a specific example to clarify both this objection and my response to it. The main source of *Christ II,* Gregory's Ascension Homily, has been known for over a century now. It is commonplace to observe that Cynewulf Germanicizes his source, embellishing it with figures and rhetoric which echo the conventions of traditional Germanic poetry; and it is customary to ascribe this aspect of *Christ II* to Cynewulf. But it is at least possible that Cynewulf's source was not Gregory's homily as such but a vernacular version of it, either in prose or poetry, which already exhibited the Germanic features which we have attributed to Cynewulf. In this case the innovations which we have ascribed to Cynewulf were actually made by the author of this hypothetical source, and our generalizations thus would seem to be invalid. One immediate response to this objection is to appeal to Occam's razor and insist that when we speak of the "poet" in this context, we simply mean whoever shaped the text as we have it. But to be less defensive, we must also observe that the validity of the comparison is not dependent upon any assumptions about the specific figure responsible for these changes. Whether Cynewulf or some nameless and hitherto unknown predecessor Germanicized Gregory's Ascension Homily, it is a fact that in comparison with its original source *Christ II* is a strikingly Germanic poem. And a literary historian can observe and comment upon this contrast even if he cannot finally be certain who was responsible for it.

Up to this point I have argued that it is possible, within certain limits, to develop reasonable hypotheses about the sources of Old English religious poetry; but at this juncture it is necessary to turn to the more problematical part of my argument—that such study can contribute to our understanding of the development of Old English literary history. The study of sources is, as I have said, a very traditional mode of Old English literary scholarship; but for the most part it has been conducted poem by poem and even passage by passage. It is relatively rare for an editor to consider in any detail a particular poet's use of sources, and even rarer for anyone to compare one poet's usage with another in this respect. And yet there is a great deal of historical information to be gleaned from studying a poet's response to his sources.

The first question to ask, of course, is whether there is a source at all, and if there is, what the poet's choice of this particular text or texts suggests about his educational background and his attitude towards vernacular poetry. There are of course some Old English poems which seem relatively original; but most of the corpus of Old English poetry is dependent upon specific sources or has analogues which can be discerned quite readily. The identification of these sources can in itself tell us a good deal. This point may seem self-evident, but it is important to emphasize that the corpus of Christian Latin literature on which most Old English poems draw is itself a richly varied, complex, and diverse literary heritage. The diversity of this literature has been sufficiently ignored that I would like to digress briefly to characterize it. The primary text, the foundation of Christian culture, is the *sacra pagina,* the Bible, which according to early medieval Christian thought was verbally inspired by God Himself. The fact that the text which medieval European Christians actually possessed was a translation from the original languages and was preserved in manuscripts of dubious authority troubled some early medieval scholars such as Bede, but these problems were for the most part ignored. A more immediate source of sacral literature was the Liturgy, but with some exceptions the Liturgy does not seem to have been as much of an influence on vernacular literature as one might expect. Biblical and Liturgical texts occupied a special position; but in addition to these privileged texts there existed an enormous corpus of Christian Latin literature of very various character. To characterize it briefly in a kind of descending order of sophistication, a significant portion of Christian Latin literature is specifically philosophical or theological in content. The Church Fathers were concerned to reconcile the data, the given events of Biblical history, with late classical philosophical thought. There thus are many texts such as Augustine's *De Trinitate* or the work of Boethius which are concerned with Christian philosophy. One might initially suppose that no aspect of patristic thought would be more alien or inassimilable in a marginally literate, barbarian state in the early Middle Ages, but the fact remains that of the four texts which King Alfred had translated, two, Augustine's *Soliloquies* and the *Consolation of Philosophy,* are both eminently philosophical patristic texts. There also existed a large corpus of exegetical literature. The *sacra pagina* offers many difficulties even to modern Biblical scholarship; to early medieval Christians much of the Bible was either hopelessly obscure or rather disconcerting, and the Fathers devoted a good deal of energy to explaining, and on occasion explaining away, difficult Biblical texts. Biblical exegesis is a controversial subject in Old English literary scholarship, in part because it is consistently associated with allegory and the relevance of allegory to Old English Christian poetry. But a great deal of this exegesis is purely factual and philological—a point which must be borne in mind in considering the problem of its influence.

A natural development of Biblical exegesis is Church history, the continuing story of the people of God in post-Biblical times; and this mode of history leads quite naturally to hagiography, the lives of Christ's saints in the world. Biblical exegesis was on the whole a relatively intellectual genre; hagiography by contrast is more accessible in that it depicts a world in which Christian values are inevitably and immediately triumphant. Hagiography is thus well adapted to popular instruction, and it is not surprising to find that hagiographic texts comprise a very substantial portion of the Old English poetic corpus. Another genre widely attested in patristic literature is the sermon or homily (the technical distinction between the two is not always easy to discern in practice); and these texts, while they can of course be learned and sophisticated, are conventionally thought of as being addressed to the Church as a whole, so that they tend to be less esoteric and demanding than more formal theological literature. Finally, there is a significantly smaller but still substantial corpus, usually only mentioned in passing in the handbooks, which I would call, for want of a better term, Christian imaginative literature. This term embraces Old and New Testament apocrypha, some of the more spectacularly fabulous saints' lives, legends concerning the fabulous prehistory of the True Cross, the account of the eight parts of Adam, visions of heaven and hell, the Fifteen Signs of Judgment, the legend of the anti-christ, and so on. This kind of Christian literature is frankly popular in its appeal and is often dubiously orthodox in its implications. It was explicitly rejected by Ælfric,[4] and some of the most influential texts of this sort were formally condemned in the so-called "Gelasian" Decretal, but these texts remained enormously popular.

To attempt to characterize a body of literature as extensive and diverse as the Christian Latin literature of the first millennium in two paragraphs is manifestly absurd. The *Patrologia Latina,* which is far from being a comprehensive collection, alone contains approximately 120 folio volumes of texts composed during this period. But I do not think it has been clearly recognized how diverse and even discordant Christian Latin literature actually is. The very fact that a given poet chose a specific source gives us some information about the tastes and interests of that particular poet. The *Phoenix*-poet was not only a very good Anglo-Saxon poet himself, but had the good taste and sophistication to choose one of the best and most interesting late Latin poems as his exemplar. In contrast, the *Andreas*-poet had an interest in the exotic and esoteric, and a stronger stomach for fabulous and otherwise unattested miracles than Ælfric seems to have had. Despite the strictures of E. G. Stanley,[5] I like *Andreas* — though I would concede that the *Phoenix* is a better and more sophisticated poem. But there is a real gulf in the taste and learning of these two poets which is suggested simply by the character of the sources they chose to work from.

Another immediate question which source study can answer is whether the poet knew Latin and, if so, whether he was attempting to respect the specific verbal detail of his source. On the whole, the Latinity of the Anglo-Saxon poets seems to have been quite competent — an indication which would support the notion that this poetry was composed in a relatively learned ambiance. The problem of the poet's respect for his source — whether he would attempt to translate fairly closely or not — involves two related questions. Did the poet think of his source as an authoritative text in which the detail of the verbal texture of the original should be respected as far as possible? If not, to what extent did he, as a poetic translator, feel free to expand and elaborate upon his original? Some poets seem to have felt the obligation to respect the textual detail of their source quite strongly; others seem to have felt much freer from such constraints. The *Genesis A* poet, for example, does not translate every line of the first sixteen chapters of Genesis, but, as the recent edition of A. N. Doane reveals clearly by the simple device of putting the relevant texts on the facing page, he was translating verse by verse and was attempting to remain reasonably faithful to his original.[6] By contrast, other Old English Biblical poems are often startlingly free in their rendering of Scripture.

A related question involves the degree to which the poet felt it appropriate to Germanicize his source, and in what contexts. This whole question suffers to some degree from the zeal of the enthusiasts for Germanic antiquity, who have exaggerated and still on occasion do exaggerate the traditional Germanic aspect of this poetry out of all proportion; but after allowances have been made, the fact remains that one of the most striking features of Old English poetry is the fact that Anglo-Saxon churchmen felt authorized by Cædmon's revelation to write vernacular poetry using the figures, diction, and meter of their pagan predecessors. Thus one immediate question which one can raise is what stylistic register a given poet felt to be appropriate for a given subject. Some saints' lives (*Andreas*, for example) are dramatically Germanic in their Old English poetic form; others are much less so. What stylistic choices of this sort poets made and why they made them are important and interesting questions.

A further question involves the problem of the reception of the text — what the poet expected of his audience and what the language of the poetry implies about the shared social world of poet and audience. Thus Dorothy

Whitelock took the single phrase *non dæges* which is used as an indication of time in *Beowulf* as the basis of a cogent argument about a Christian vocabulary which the poet simply assumed.[7] To mention one further and somewhat more complicated example, the whole problem of rank and status can be a very interesting indication of the difficulties which some poets had in reconciling Christian matter and Germanic form. In Christian thought the crucial question of human worth is fundamentally a moral one — whether a man or woman rightly or wrongly orders his or her life in relationship to God. But the Germanic world of the Anglo-Saxons was a profoundly aristocratic one in which kinship and rank were central facts of social life. To cite one example, a poet like the *Genesis A* poet will gratuitously ennoble good Biblical figures such as Abraham, whose social status in the Bible is either ambiguous or frankly plebeian.

Obviously the questions I have raised do not exhaust all the possible issues which a careful comparison of text and source might illuminate. Each case is a separate one, and the more carefully we work with these texts the more we can hope to learn. It is of course true that a good deal of work along these lines has, in fact, already been done: but, as I have already remarked, it has been done poem by poem and often passage by passage; scholars have not attempted to survey the field as a whole. But they should; and what I hope would emerge from this project is a typology in the broad sense, an ordering of Old English poetry on the basis of source study which would be at least reasonably objective and which would permit both new questions and new comparisons.

II

I have been discussing these problems at a fairly comfortable level of generality, and I should now like to turn to a concrete problem to illustrate how the joining of source study and literary history might work in specific detail. The problem I have set myself is a simple one, yet it has remained annoyingly resistant to any definite solution. *The Exeter Book* begins with three separate poems conventionally, though not very happily, entitled *Christ I, Christ II,* and *Christ III*. (The most authoritative retitling, that of the short-title listing for the new *Dictionary of Old English,* avoids the Roman numerals by suggesting A, B, and C in their place; but the fundamental awkwardness remains.) Initially, these poems were thought to be one, and were ascribed to Cynewulf on the basis of the runic signature at the end of *Christ II;* but the consensus of modern scholars is that the poems are in fact separate and that only the second is by Cynewulf. This judgment is not an easy or secure one, however, and the relationship of the three poems to each other remains disputed. Recently, Robert E. Diamond raised the question and attempted a solution on the basis of "formula analysis." He determined that *Christ II* was statistically similar to the other signed poems by Cynewulf in its use of formulaic expressions, but that *Christ I* and *Christ III* were quite different, and he therefore concluded that *Christ II* was indeed a separate poem. But the figures he arrived at for *Christ I* and *Christ III* were quite similar, and so he concluded by raising the "interesting speculation" that these two poems may be "the work of the same poet, who may have sought to provide Cynewulf's poem, *Christ II*, with a setting, much as an artisan might provide a setting for a gem."[8] By contrast, S. A. J. Bradley in his volume of translations of Old English poetry concludes his preface to *Christ III* by saying, "Most [scholars] agree at least that the poem [*Christ III*] is close to Cynewulf."[9] If there is a general consensus that *Christ I, II,* and *III* are indeed three poems, the relationship of the three poems to each other still seems moot.

The fact that I have chosen the *Christ* poems as my example of the importance of source study for Old English literary history is not an accident. In 1900 Albert S. Cook published his monumental edition of these poems as *The Christ of Cynewulf*. The Introduction to that edition is now out of date, and Cook's assumption that Cynewulf wrote all three poems is not now generally accepted. But Cook's one hundred and fifty pages of commentary on these poems remain a fundamental text. Later scholars can and have corrected and emended his work on points of detail; but the edition as a whole still stands as one of the most impressive single monuments of Anglo-Saxon literary scholarship. At any rate, with Cook's edition and with reference to more recent work, one can find the main sources of *Christ I, II,* and *III* quite readily. There are still many problems, and obviously there is more work to be done, but thanks to Cook's edition it is much easier to approach these poems in terms of their sources than most other Old English poems.[10]

A detailed source study of each poem would, of course, be a monograph in itself. I propose, instead, to select a passage from each poem as an example and then to offer some generalizations based upon this example. This has the disadvantage of focusing the argument on single passages, and obviously my examples will prove what I want them to; but I have nothing to say which is terribly novel as criticism of *Christ I, II,* or *III* as specific and individual poems. And, of course, my generalizations can be tested readily enough.

The first example I wish to discuss is from the first of the Advent lyrics in *Christ I:*

```
                        ... cyninge.
Ðu eart se weallstan    þe ða wyrhtan iu
wiðwurpon to weorce.    Wel þe geriseð
þæt þu heafod sie       healle mærre,
ond gesomnige           side weallas
fæste gefoge,           flint unbræcne,
þæt geond eorðb[..]g eall    eagna gesihþe
wundrien to worlde      wuldres ealdor.
Gesweotula nu þurh searocræft    þin sylfes weorc,
soðfæst, sigorbeorht,   ond sona forlæt
weall wið wealle.       Nu is þam weorce þearf
þæt se cræftga cume     ond se cyning sylfa,
ond þonne gebete,       nu gebrosnad is,
hus under hrofe.        He þæt hra gescop,
leomo læmena;           nu sceal liffrea
þone wergan heap        wraþum ahreddan
earme from egsan,       swa he oft dyde.[11] (1-17)
```

These first seventeen lines of *Christ I* are based upon the Advent antiphon "O rex gentium" and are very rich and interesting poetry. Several articles have touched on this passage, and R. B. Burlin devotes a chapter of his book on *Christ I* to it.[12] I wish to make two points. First, although the lyric is based upon a specific Advent antiphon, it has no source in the strict sense. The poet alludes to Psalm 117:22, and the language and imagery of the poem echo other Biblical and patristic texts which Cook duly cites; but the poet, so far as we have been able to determine, is not following any specific Latin or vernacular source. He was steeped in patristic literature, knew the Bible well, and was simply making creative use of religious idiom which was native to him. The second point I would emphasize is that the allegorical meaning of *hus,* which Cook exemplifies with a passage from Ælfric, is relevant and indeed necessary in order to understand this poetry. If one does not happen to know that a *domus* can be understood at the same time as the collective unity of the Church *and* as the *corda et corpora fidelium,* the full meaning of the text is going to escape one. The abrupt shift, from the image of the Church as a ruined temple to the poet's evocation of God the creator of man's body in line fourteen, will simply seem puzzling, not evocative.

The lyrics which comprise *Christ I* are rich and interesting poems, but they are characteristically elliptical and dense. They were written for an audience which shared the Biblical and patristic learning of the poet; without this background they would simply seem opaque and confusing. It is customary in some circles to deprecate the learning of the Anglo-Saxons; one response to this attitude might be to invite such skeptics to read through *Christ I* without the benefit of Cook or any other commentary, to see how much of the Biblical and patristic learning implicit in the poem they could discern for themselves without such help. But though the learned and richly evocative poetry of *Christ I* might violate the expectations of someone who had only read one of the less sympathetic literary histories of the period, it need not surprise us particularly. Monastic and canonical life was centered upon the Bible and the Liturgy; men and women who entered or even simply participated in such a life would have ample opportunity to acquire the kind of learning which would enable them to understand and appreciate *Christ I*. One must wonder, however, how widely this kind of poetry could have been read and appreciated.

One final point about *Christ I* is that the sources and analogues for this poetry which have been identified are either Biblical or drawn from those figures whom Ælfric would identify as the *geleafful fæderas* — the standard patristic authorities whose writings defined the Latin Catholic tradition for the first millennium of Christian thought. The poet is scrupulous in avoiding anything which might seem unorthodox.[13] Thus there are certain salient points which emerge from looking at *Christ I* in terms of its sources. It is a learned poem which draws freely upon a specific tradition of Christian Latin literature. We do not know who wrote it or when or where, but we do know a good deal about the kind of poetry it is, and about the literary tradition of which it is a part, and this information is important for the literary history of this period.

When we turn to *Christ II* we are turning to a different mode of religious thought, and I should emphasize at the beginning that I too consider *Christ II* a good and aesthetically pleasing poem. But it is a quite different kind of poetry from *Christ I*. My illustrative passage is again the beginning lines of the poem, the elaborate rhetorical question which opens the poem as a whole:

>   Nu ðu geornlice   gæstgerynum,
>   mon se mæra,   modcræfte sec
>   þurh sefan snyttro,   þæt þu soð wite
>   hu þæt geeode,   þa se ælmihtiga
>   acenned wearð   þurh clænne had,
>   siþþan he Marian,   mægða weolman,
>   mærre meowlan,   mundheals geceas,
>   þæt þær in hwitum   hræglum gewerede
>   englas ne oðeowdun, þa se æþeling cwom,

> beorn in Betlem.   Bodan wæron gearwe
> þa þurh hleoþorcwide   hyrdum cyðdon,
> sægdon soðne gefean,   þætte sunu wære
> in middangeard   meotudes acenned,
> in Betleme.   Hwæþre in bocum ne cwið
> þæt hy in hwitum þær   hræglum oðywden
> in þa æþelan tid,   swa hie eft dydon
> ða se brega mæra   to Bethania,
> þeoden þrymfæst,   his þegna gedryht
> gelaðade, leof weorud. (440–58)

The initial response of the modern reader to the question in lines 440–50A is likely to be simply one of puzzlement. Ritual and ceremony are not ordinarily a very important part of our lives, and this reading of the Ascension scene which focuses upon the ceremonial implications of an apparently irrelevant detail is likely to seem odd to us. But at any rate, once the modern reader has overcome his puzzlement, he is likely to assume that this poetry is essentially quite similar to *Christ I*. Both poems are Christian; both are concerned with certain specific Biblical events, and there is no radical difference in style and tone between the two. But there is one immediate difference between the two poems: while *Christ I* does not depend upon specific sources, *Christ II* is heavily dependent upon one particular source, Gregory's Twenty-ninth Homily on the Gospels, his Ascension Homily. Cynewulf expanded upon his source on occasion; he seems to have drawn on Bede's Ascension Hymn for certain motifs, and there are other bits in the poem which have no specific source, but which can readily be paralleled in homiletic literature. Colin Chase and other scholars have discussed in some detail how Cynewulf developed and elaborated upon his main source;[14] but Cynewulf did choose to base his poem on a Gregorian homily, and this fact is itself significant for the literary historian. Of the four fathers of the Latin Church, Gregory is conventionally defined as the least philosophical and least intellectual. He is the last of the great patristic teachers; the kind of literary and rhetorical education which he had received was no longer available to his successors, and he was teaching and preaching in a world which was rapidly becoming more and more barbarian. His homilies are thus open, popular, and accessible, and he has a tendency towards the picturesque and extravagant. His analysis of the five "leaps" of Christ in this homily, which Cynewulf reiterates, may serve as a single example of this tendency. Cynewulf was thus choosing a relatively popular, accessible source, and his elaborations on this source do not alter its essential character.

To turn again to the passage I have cited, we have here a long elaborate periodic question which, however, is specifically based on one sentence of Gregory's homily. Cynewulf elaborates upon that sentence — the single phrase *christo nato* becomes the basis for three and one-half lines of Old English — but his elaborations do not significantly affect its purport. Perhaps the simplest way to define the difference between this poetry and that of the *Christ I* poet is to point out that whereas the latter expects his audience to catch allusions and to follow out the implications of typological discourse, Cynewulf himself raises the Gregorian question and then, after a bit of delay to arouse the curiosity of his audience, answers it.[15] As one might expect in a poem based on a homily, *Christ II* is much more open, much more discursive than *Christ I*. Cynewulf explores a variety of quite different topics in *Christ II,* but his characteristic technique is exposition. What is the allegorical significance of the sun and the moon? What comfort did God offer fallen man? In what sense might Christ be likened to a bird? Why are the gifts of wisdom and talent variously distributed? What are the five leaps of Christ? In what way are Christians like voyagers sailing over the sea? A person who read or listened to *Christ II* attentively would be instructed about all of these various matters, but he would not need to know very much beyond the elements of Christian faith to appreciate and enjoy the poem. Another aspect of the poem which accords with this categorization of it is Cynewulf's frequent and extensive use of Germanic imagery and metaphors in expanding upon the relatively brief homily which is its source. One would expect that this kind of imagery would appeal most naturally to a secular Anglo-Saxon audience for whom, for example, the relationship of Christ and his disciples could most readily be imagined in terms of the relationship of thane and lord. And precisely such an audience would benefit most readily from the open and discursive teaching of *Christ II.*

In analyzing *Christ II* in these terms I am not claiming that this text is crude or artistically inept, or even that it reflects "popular Christianity" as this phrase is generally construed. To hazard an analogy, *Christ II* strikes me as similar to the homilies of Ælfric in that both are discursive texts which presume a genuine interest in Christian lore but which do not demand a learned audience. Again, while I have emphasized the very real differences between *Christ I* and *Christ II,* these poems also reflect a shared concern with orthodoxy in that both poems draw on Christian Latin texts which are very much part of the *geleafful,* orthodox tradition.

In turning to *Christ III* we approach a radically different thought-world, one which is easier to exemplify than to define; and so I will cite the passage I have selected and then attempt some definitions. At one juncture in *Christ III,* the poet digresses from his description of Judgment Day itself to the topic of "the witnessing elements," the signs by which insensate nature acknowledged the sufferings of Christ at the Passion. Some of these signs are based upon the Biblical account of the Passion, but the poet expands upon the relatively brief and sober marvels of the synoptic Gospels. One of the marvels which he mentions concerns trees which bled in sympathy with Christ's Passion:

> ge eac beames onbudon   hwa hy mid bledum sceop,
> monge, nales fea,   ða mihtig god
> on hira anne gestag   þær he earfeþu
> geþolade fore þearfe   þeodbuendra,
> laðlicne deað   leodum to helpe.
> Ða wearð beam monig   blodigum tearum
> birunnen under rindum,   reade ond þicce;
> sæp wearð to swate.   Þæt ascegan ne magun
> foldbuende   þurh frod gewit,
> hu fela þa onfundun   þa gefelan ne magun
> dryhtnes þrowinga,   deade gesceafte. (1169–79)

In commenting on these verses Cook quite rightly observes that this motif occurs in 4 Esdras 5:5, and was widely diffused as one of the "Fifteen Signs of Judgment."[16] But while *Christ III* is an eschatological poem, and the trees' bleeding an eschatological sign, Cook's comment does not address a significant anomaly, the fact that in this poem the sign is associated not with the second coming of Christ but rather with His Passion. If the poet had mentioned this motif as a sign of impending judgment, there would be nothing to remark on, other than his predilection for picturesque eschatology. But he apparently thought of the motif as part of the catalogue of witnessing elements, and the fact that he was not simply confused can be illustrated by the fact that this anomaly is paralleled in an Old Irish text, a poem of Blathmac which Carney ascribes to the seventh century:

> To-celt grian a soillsi sain,
> ro-coíni a flaithemain,
> luid diantemel tar nem nglas,
> búiristir rian trethanbras.

> Ba dorchae uile in bith,
> talam fu durbae rochrith;
> oc Ísu uasail aidid
> ro-memdatar márailich.

> Hierosalem taithsloic dian
> marbu a adnacul érchian;
> isind uair hi cés Críst guin
> dlochtae fial in Tempuil.
>
> To-fích sruth folo — ró tinn! —
> combu derg snob cech oenchruinn;
> buí cru for bruinnib betho
> i mbarraib cech prímfedo.
>
> Ba deithbir do dúilib Dé
> muir mas, nem nglas, talam cé
> ce imro-chloítis a ngné
> oc coíniud a ngalgaite.[17]

The sun hid its own light; it mourned its lord; a sudden darkness went over the blue heavens, the wild and furious sea roared.

The whole world was dark; the land lay under gloomy trembling; at the death of noble Jesus great rocks burst asunder.

Jerusalem swiftly released the dead from ancient burial; when Christ suffered slaying the veil of the Temple was rent.

A stream of blood gushed forth (severe excess!) so that the bark of every tree was red; there was blood on the breasts of the world, in the (tree-) tops of every great forest.

It would have been fitting for God's elements, the beautiful sea, the blue heaven, the present earth, that they should change their aspect when keening their hero.

Now in discussing this motif, I would prefer here to ignore the more technical questions of how an eschatological motif came to be associated with the witnessing elements and whether there might be some logic to such an association. The question I would rather raise is what sort of motif this is, and why an Anglo-Saxon poet might have been interested in it. One simple answer is that it reflects a taste for elaborate, fantastic miracles which the spare language of the synoptic account of the Passion does not quite satisfy. In the context of modern Biblical criticism, the marvels at Christ's Passion are problematical in that they seem gratuitous. For the early medieval Christian reader, in the context of the mode of Christianity which *Christ III* exemplifies, the problem was precisely the reverse. There were too few marvels, and those which the Gospels mention are too simple. The specific origin of this particular motif can only be guessed at, but the simplest explanation is that some Christian teacher in the early Middle Ages took it upon himself to improvise more marvels of a sort which would impress a barbarian audience.[18] Given the fact that, so far as I have been able to determine, only two examples of bleeding trees as witnessing elements at the Passion occur, one in an Old Irish and the other in an Anglo-Saxon text, one can speculate that this particular association was made in an Insular Christian context; but until more work is done on the provenance and dissemination of this motif, we can only speculate. One further possible instance of the influence of the motif is the very problematical description of the bleeding Cross in the opening lines of the *Dream of the Rood;* but these lines present special problems of their own.

The motif itself, its relation to the Fifteen-Signs tradition, the dissemination and origin of the latter tradition, and the significance of these striking images, all raise interesting and as yet unsolved questions. Here I should simply like to emphasize one point. While the handbooks sometimes characterize this fascination with exotic and apocryphal lore as typically medieval, this assumption simply ignores an important dichotomy in the early medieval Church. Teachers such as Bede, Alcuin, and of course Ælfric were very cautious about the veracity of this kind of exotic lore. They did not disseminate it themselves, and on occasion they explicitly argued against it. There are clearly at least two modes of Christian thought in the early medieval Insular Church. To turn from Bede to the vernacular or Latin Irish saints' lives or to the *Evernew Tongue* is to move from "Roman" caution, sobriety, and intellectual restraint to an exotic, Insular, imaginative thought-world which is fervently Christian but clearly reflects the imaginative exuberance of the deeply traditional barbarian world in which it existed. The *Christ III* poet was aware of this tradition, and he drew on it for material to enrich his account of the last times without any apparent hesitation.[19] Much of the poet's eschatological lore is conventional in that it can be paralleled in such "geleafful" authorities as Julian of Toledo, but enough of it is drawn from anomalous "Insular" eschatological sources to make the poem quite distinctive in the context of Anglo-Saxon eschatological literature as a whole. In relation to the other two *Christ* poems, then, *Christ III* is similar to *Christ II* and quite different from *Christ I* in that it is open and discursive and requires no excessive learning on the part of its presumed audience. But *Christ I* and *Christ II* are themselves quite different from the *Christ III* poem in that these poems are based upon Latin sources of a specific kind, texts firmly situated in the great tradition of orthodox Christian Latin literature from Augustine to Bede and Alcuin. By contrast, the *Christ III* poet derives much of his lore from apocryphal Insular sources, a very different literary tradition indeed.

I have offered this analysis as an example of literary history based upon the study of sources, and I should like to conclude with some generalizations and suggestions for further investigation. As far as the generalizations are concerned, I would argue that *Christ I, II,* and *III* are very different kinds of poetry, and that their presence together in sequence in the *Exeter Book* is simply the result of the decision of whoever was responsible for the arrangement of the codex. There is no intrinsic reason for these poems to be joined together. One could argue, of course, that they complement each other and that the stylistic and intellectual contrast which they present is aesthetically pleasing. This is a viewpoint which would certainly be difficult to refute and might indeed have some cogency. But to the degree that my arguments hold up — and I am of course aware that I have presented the outline of an argument rather than a fully detailed consideration of each poem in comparison with its sources — I have presented reasons for thinking of these three poems as quite separate. We thus have the beginnings of a typology, in the broad sense of the term, which might define these poems in relation to each other and the rest of the Old English poetic corpus. *Christ I* would thus be related to the most sophisticated and learned poetry in Old English and Anglo-Latin, poems such as the *Phoenix* or *Guthlac B. Christ II,* by contrast, can most readily be compared with Anglo-Saxon homiletic literature, most specifically with the work of Ælfric. And *Christ III* should be considered in relation to the rich and variegated corpus of "Insular" eschatological literature.

As far as *desiderata* in the field are concerned, there are two kinds of work which the larger project I have outlined here would entail. On the one hand, we need to know more about the Latin sources of Anglo-Saxon prose and poetry, and the detailed study of the sources of specific Old English texts needs to be continued; it is particularly important that the wealth of new resources available in the field of patristic studies — new editions, concordances, and scholarly tools of all kinds — be fully exploited by Anglo-Saxonists. At the same time, we should also encourage works of synthesis such as Cook's commentary on the *Christ* poems. One obvious *desideratum* would be a new Cook, an edition which would draw on Cook's work and incorporate the more cogent results of recent scholarship. One wishes we might simply imitate the German scholarly tradition of editing and re-editing a classic edition rather than letting it go out of print. But whoever may edit or re-edit Cook, it is important that the editors continue Cook's practice of citing in full the texts which they believe the poets used. It is simply too easy for readers to ignore a reference; readers need the texts available for immediate comparison. Obviously this kind of historically oriented source-study would involve a very substantial scholarly commitment. But it would be worth while, and of course does not preclude other kinds of scholarship. Linguistic and stylistic analysis, for example, particularly when conducted with machine assistance, might contribute very substantially to our knowledge of the literary history of this period. But scholars have been attempting to work out stylistic and linguistic analyses of Old English poetry for many years, and as yet they have not achieved any generally accepted typology, much less any agreement on dating or localization. In these circumstances, source-study of the sort I have outlined is an important and powerful tool which can elucidate certain historical problems. It would be a pity not to use it.[20]

CORNELL UNIVERSITY

Notes

1. See Ashley Crandall Amos (*Linguistic Means of Determining the Dates of the Old English Literary Texts,* Medieval Academy Books, 90 [Cambridge, Mass., 1980]) for a convenient history and summary of this question.

2. Stanley B. Greenfield, *A Critical History of Old English Literature* (New York, 1965), pp. 124-45.

3. Good examples of the value of even a rather remote analogue are the analogues to Chaucer's "Miller's Tale" printed in *Sources and Analogues of Chaucer's Canterbury Tales,* ed. W. F. Bryan and Germaine Dempster (New York, 1958), pp. 106-23. The closest parallel, the Flemish fabliau "Of Heile of Bersele," is unlikely to have been known by Chaucer, but the comparison between this text and the "Miller's Tale" is very illuminating, and is conventional in Chaucer courses.

4. On this aspect of Ælfric's teaching, see Malcolm Godden, "Aelfric and the Vernacular Prose Tradition," in *The Old English Homily and Its Background,* ed. Paul E. Szarmach and Bernard F. Huppé (Albany, N.Y., 1978), pp. 99-117.

5. E. G. Stanley, "Beowulf," in *Continuations and Beginnings: Studies in Old English Literature,* ed. E. G. Stanley (London and Edinburgh, 1966), pp. 104-41. See, for example, p. 114: "a poetical dunderhead like the poet of *Andreas*"; or p. 138: "Here [in *Andreas*] is a poet who can do the big bow-wow like any man going."

6. A. N. Doane, *Genesis A: A New Edition* (Madison, 1978).

7. Dorothy Whitelock, *The Audience of Beowulf* (Oxford, 1951), p. 6.

8. Robert E. Diamond, "The Diction of the Old English *Christ,*" in *Anglo-Saxon Poetry: Essays in Appreciation (For John C. McGalliard),* ed. Lewis E. Nicholson and

Dolores Warsick Frese (Notre Dame and London, 1975), p. 307. Diamond conveniently summarizes the history of scholarly disagreement on this issue on pp. 301-03.

9. S. A. J. Bradley, *Anglo-Saxon Poetry* (London, Melbourne, and Toronto, 1982), p. 229.

10. Albert S. Cook, *The Christ of Cynewulf*, with a new preface by John C. Pope (1909; rpt. Hamden, Conn., 1964).

11. All quotations of Old English poetry are from the *ASPR*, cited by line numbers.

12. Robert B. Burlin, *The Old English Advent: A Typological Commentary* (New Haven and London, 1968), pp. 58-77. See also *Notes & Queries*, 217 (1972), 84-87.

13. The one exception, the fact that Section VII, which concerns "The Doubting of Mary," is based ultimately upon apocryphal accounts of the birth of Jesus, can be explained quite simply. "The Doubting of Mary" episode was so widely current that it was widely assumed to be canonical, and an Advent antiphon based upon this episode was current in the early English Church. See "A Liturgical Source for *Christ I* 164-213 (Advent Lyric VII)," *Medium Aevum*, 46 (1977), 498-500.

14. "God's Presence Through Grace as the Theme of Cynewulf's *Christ II* and the Relationship of This Theme to *Christ I* and *Christ III*," *ASE*, 3 (1974), 87-101.

15. *Christ II*, ll. 545-56. The lines in which Cynewulf would have answered this question most specifically are unfortunately missing. See John C. Pope, "The Lacuna in the Text of Cynewulf's Ascension (*Christ II*, 556 B)," in *Studies in Language, Literature, and Culture of the Middle Ages and Later* [Rudolf Willard Festschrift], ed. E. Bagby Atwood and Archibald A. Hill (Austin, 1969), pp. 210-19.

16. Cook, p. 200.

17. *The Poems of Blathmac*, ed. James Carney, Irish Text Society 47 (Dublin, 1964), pp. 22-23. I have quoted stanzas 61-65 from Carney's normalized text and translation of *The Poems of Blathmac*. Carney notes this parallel and quotes the OE in translation.

18. The motif itself can only be defined as a naïve elaboration upon the Gospel texts; it is important, however, to note that the *Christ III* poet might have come upon it in a text which seemed to him—and indeed may well have been—authoritative. Eccentric and apocryphal material could easily be assimilated into quite conventional and orthodox texts.

19. A full study of the Insular eschatological material in *Christ III* has yet to be completed. For studies on specific Insular motifs and images see Malcolm Godden, "An Old English Penitential Motif" *ASE*, 2 (1973), 221-39 (*Christ III*, 1292-1305, *et passim*); T. D. Hill, "The Seven Joys of Heaven in 'Christ III' and Old English Homiletic Texts," *Notes & Queries*, 214 (1969), 165-66 (*Christ III*, 1652-60.); "Some Remarks on 'The Site of Lucifer's Throne,'" *Anglia*, 87 (1969), 303-11 (*Christ III*, 900); "Notes on the Eschatology of the Old English *Christ III*," *Neuphilologische Mitteilungen*, 70 (1969), 672-79 (*Christ III*, 947-52); "Further Notes on the Eschatology of the Old English *Christ III*," *Neuphilologische Mitteilungen*, 72 (1971), 691-98 (*Christ III*, 875-880, 892-98, 956-59); "The Old World, The Levelling of the Earth and the Burning Sea: Three Eschatological Images in the Old English 'Christ III,'" *Notes & Queries*, 217 (1972), 323-25 (*Christ III*, 976-88).

20. After I completed this paper in the fall of 1983, Professor Charles D. Wright of Texas Tech University drew my attention to another Insular example of trees — in this instance a tree bleeding at the Crucifixion. In an early Medieval Irish commentary on Matthew erroneously attributed to Jerome in the *Patrologia Latina,* the commentator, in speaking of the Crucifixion, remarks that "hic [i.e., at the sixth hour] stillavit sanguis de ligno" (*PL,* 30:639).

Source Study as a Trick with Mirrors: Annihilation of Meaning in the Old English "Mary of Egypt"

COLIN CHASE

Under sense 4e of the word "source" in *The Oxford English Dictionary* we find: "A work, etc., supplying information or evidence (esp. of an original or primary character) as to some fact, event, or series of these." Further examination reveals that this sense, so appropriate to our collaborative study of "The Sources of Anglo-Saxon Culture," first occurs in the Preface to William Robertson's *History of America* (1778), some four centuries after the now obsolete *sours* of the hawk or the still living *source* of a river. Should it concern us that a concept so fundamental to scholarly method might have seemed foreign or even incomprehensible to the people whose culture we are dedicated to illuminating? Perhaps not, but some of the historical eddies stirred up by such a question are suggested by the further information from the *OED* that the expression "source book" first appeared in print in 1899, as a direct translation from German *Quellenbuch*. Bracketed by these two modern expressions is a whole era of intellectual history, including emergence of belief in the notion of original genius, development of both German and English Romanticism, and the origin and spread of scientific textual criticism, each of which developments can be related in various oblique ways to the meaning and function of "source" as used in modern scholarship.[1] The central question addressed in this study is implicit in the information uncovered in the *OED:* How useful in analyzing and interpreting medieval texts is the radically post-Gutenberg concept of the source or primary text?

There is no contradiction implicit in the application of modern methods to ancient texts. Everyone recognizes that high-powered lenses, infra-red light, and computers often recover for us things that were once clear to our predecessors and even occasionally show us things they would not have suspected. But we must distinguish carefully between technological advance and analytical methodology. In an intellectual climate partially defined by Saussure, Lacan, and Lévi-Strauss and revolutionized by Derrida, de Man, Miller, and Foucault, the value of source study is increasingly at issue.[2] If, as deconstructionists are accustomed to say, the *signe* is semiotically free of the *signifiée,* or if diachronic relations are largely illusory and to be discarded in favor of synchronic ones, or if there is really no context, only "intertext," then clearly *source* in sense 4e has no priority or real explanatory value. We need not become deconstructionists to accept that the questions they have asked bear important implications for our study.

Nor are theirs the only voices calling us to a re-examination of this fundamental methodology. Milman Parry, A. B. Lord, Walter Ong, Eric Havelock, and Marshall McLuhan have shown us that successive alterations in the media of discourse and communication have profoundly altered the way we think about virtually everything, but especially the way we think about the stability of tradition.[3] While most of us find very interesting if highly speculative the thought that oral performance has a kind of fluidity not found in written works, fewer have appreciated the fact that before Gutenberg, chirographic man did not have the sense of the nearly infinite repeatability of a fixed text implicit in such modern ideas as an edition, variants, critical apparatus and, I submit, a textual source. This seems to me important, because behind so many of our habitual attitudes toward the nature and limits of the text lies the belief that prior to this manuscript version or that redaction there seems to hover *a* text which it is the business of the scholar to recover and hand on to posterity. Next to a parallel manuscript witness, a textual source can be, or can seem to be, the surest way of establishing such a text. If, however, neither the author, nor his scribe, nor anyone either of them could imagine reading the work would know what to make of the idea of such a text dwelling in the same realm as Plato's fixed ideas—and transported there for interestingly similar reasons, if we are to believe Havelock and Ong[4]—then of what use is the painful labor of searching out and analyzing sources? Are we to conclude with Ecclesiastes that "in much wisdom there is much grief" and that it is all so much "chasing of the wind"? I think not, finally; for comparison of what I prefer to call variant versions yields insights often attainable in no other way. But such insights are more likely to derive from recognition of contrasts than of congruence, and this is a notion not so far from the slippery and fickle play of *différance* suggested by Jacques Derrida and espoused by his followers.

The *Life of Saint Mary of Egypt* is one of the few non-Ælfrician Lives found in British Library Cotton MSS. Julius E. VII and Otho B. X; a fragment of the Mary *Life* also survives in MS. Gloucester Cathedral 35.[5] The Old English *Life* is closely dependent on a ninth-century version composed by a Neapolitan deacon named Paul.[6] The earliest Latin version was written in the seventh century by an unknown author.[7] But Paul's *Life,* though later, is closer to the Greek text of Sophronius, composed sometime before he died in 638.[8] Sophronius himself was partially dependent on a brief reference to Mary contained in the *Life of St. Cyriacus* composed in the sixth century by Cyril of Scythiopolis.[9] Other Latin versions of the story later than the Old English text appear in the tenth- and twelfth-century poems of Flodoard of Reims (d. 966) and Hildebert of Lavardin (d. 1135), in the *Speculum Historiale* of Vincent of Beauvais (d. 1264) and in the *Golden Legend*.[10] In addition the Mary legend had a very healthy medieval career in Spanish and, particularly, in French vernacular renditions.[11] Such are the main elements, of the Latin tradition especially, and looked at from an Old English point of view: though Peter F. Dembowski concludes his brief discussion of Latin sources by affirming that "the study of the Latin versions of the *Life* and of their classification as well as their precise relationship with the various French versions has still to be done."[12] Yes. But before we do it, perhaps we ought to know why, and of what use such work will be to anyone.

The first problem encountered in this project occurs right here. Today, not many are familiar with the Life of Mary of Egypt, and I am therefore obliged to summarize it. But what do I summarize? Do I visit that Platonic world of really existing, separated, universal forms to find that version of which all others are, in varying degrees, a paler reflection? Or do I seek for the elusive Urtext which must stand behind Julius E. VII and Paul of Naples and Sophronius and which seems to be a variation on the Platonic form? Or do I take a more pragmatic approach, less bedeviled with philosophic abstraction, and simply hand on a version which rehearses the major elements common to all those I am interested in? This last is the path I think we usually take, but it differs from the other two only in being less obvious. At its worst this procedure can be merely a way of setting up a clumsy *petitio circuli* in which I insert into my version whatever I want to emerge from the analytical process; but even at its best, it assumes that there is some way I can abstract *the* version from the various renditions I know.

A good illustration is at hand in the summary which Dembowski provides in his book—a summary which is beyond reproach in its judicious balance and even-handed treatment of the main elements in the tradition.

His summary, which I translate from the French, begins this way:

> In a Palestinian monastery there lived the monk Zosimas who, after fifty-three years of a life of asceticism, feels he has reached the pinnacle of monastic perfection. Still, always looking for a greater spiritual perfection, Zosimas decides to leave his own monastery for another where the customs are even harsher.

Inevitably, just as Dembowski's version belies the one it intends to represent, so does my translation fail to reflect Dembowski's accurately. To avoid weighting the argument too heavily in my favor, I have translated the word *perfectionnement* as 'perfection,' whereas its meaning is more verbal and active than that, suggesting 'improvement' and, I believe, implying that what Zosimas was looking for was a way of life that would be of even more spiritual benefit to him than the one he had been living. The French reads: "Néanmoins, cherchant toujours un plus grand perfectionnement spirituel, Zosime décide de quitter son propre monastère pour un autre où les moeurs sont encore plus sévères."[13] Each word in this summary could be defended, but to me the over-all effect is very different from that of any of the versions — Greek, Latin, Old English, or French — with which I am familiar.

To begin with the Old English, the main focus of concern here, what corresponds to Dembowski's nearly neutral statement that Zosimas "feels he has reached the pinnacle of monastic perfection" ("pense être arrivé au sommet de la perfection monastique") is a passage which explains that after fifty-three years of dedicated asceticism, Zosimus was struck by the thought that he might be perfect in every way and might not need the example of a greater teaching to instruct him, thinking to himself, "hwæðer ænig munuc on eorðan sy . þæt me mage aht niwes getæcan . oððe me on ænigum þingum gefultumian . þæs þe ic sylf nyte."[14] At this point, like Cædmon, "him ætstod sum engel . and him to cwæð": "Ah, Zosimus you have done well till now [here I paraphrase rather loosely], but you still have much to learn. So, [here I am as close to the Old English text as I can get] that you may understand and recognize how great are other paths to salvation, go out of your country and go to the monastery built on the banks of the Jordan." The important phrase here describes the purpose of the journey: "that you may understand and recognize how great are other paths to salvation" ("þæt þu mæge ongytan . and oncnawan hu miccle synd oþre hælo wegas").[15] What is implied here is a whole tradition of ascetic practice, a whole doctrine really concerning the way progress in the spiritual life is taught and learned, involving a master and his (or her) disciple (and the *her* has a special importance in the present context), in which the master's example and personal spiritual authority are the human means to spiritual progress. The importance of what might seem a rather nit-picking distinction becomes clear for us when we read that some months later, in the desert, Zosimus realizes that the master he thought could be found nowhere on earth is a white-haired, reformed prostitute nearing eighty who has spent the previous forty-seven years by herself in the desert. The protagonist of the Old English tale is Zosimus, and the story is the story of his humbling, but in Dembowski's version this dynamic disappears. His Zosimas may be a little vain, but he still has the sense to decide, apparently on his own, to go out and look for greater "perfectionnement spirituel." The result is that more emphasis is placed on the long conversion story which Mary tells to Zosimas and, though this is not a bad place to put it, the tale becomes a different tale with a different protagonist.

The point is not that Dembowski is wrong, or right, or that the Old English version, or mine, ought to be substituted for his in future summaries of the Mary legend. It is rather that even the most careful attempt to summarize, paraphrase, or even translate a work into other words is to alter it essentially. The current deconstructive dictum, that to interpret is to misinterpret, has its useful application here, even in places where interpretation is explicitly eschewed.

My conclusion to the problem of the initial summary, then, is to admit that summary is interpretation and, further, to accept that my interpretation, like Dembowski's or anyone else's, will be misinterpretation, but to plunge ahead on the pretext that it is better to have some starting point, however unreliable:

> Hwæt, we gied-georne   in geardagum
> sancte wifes   sorg gefrunen,
> hu seo ancra   ellen fremede....

Some of the main elements of the story have, in fact, already been rehearsed. After spending several months in the monastery by the Jordan, Zosimus went off, as all the monks did, to spend Lent in solitude in the desert. Walking for twenty-six days "forðan þe he gewilnode swa swa he eft sæde . þæt he sumne fader on þam westene funde . þe hine on sumum þingum getimbrede þæs ðe he sylf ær ne cuðe,"[16] he comes upon the naked, fleeing figure of Mary. Though he is over sixty and she nearly eighty, they run for some time, until she agrees to speak with him if he will lend her his cloak so that she can cover herself. There is a delay while they each insist that the other give a blessing, but they resolve this dilemma when Mary gives the blessing and then tells her story, summarized here in the first person:[17]

I lived with my brother and family in Egypt, but at the age of twelve left home for Alexandria. There I became a prostitute, not because I wanted money (I never charged my clients) but solely because I was inflamed with lust ["onæled mid þære hatheortnysse þæs synlustes"].[18] After living this way, in poverty and passion, for seventeen years, I ended up on a boat bound for Jerusalem to celebrate the feast of the Holy Cross, an expedition I joined for the adventure and because several handsome young men had caught my eye. But in Jerusalem, when I tried to enter the church with everyone else, I was somehow kept out by God's power while the huge throng went in without any difficulty. I tried three or four times, but each time, right at the threshold I was prevented. "Þa onhran soðlice min mod and þa eagan minre heortan hælo andgit" and I began to weep.[19] I prayed to the Mother of God, whose image was there, to let me enter the church if I gave up the life of sin I was living. I entered and prayed at the cross. That same day I washed in the waters of the Jordan and partook of the sacred mysteries of the Lord. Next morning, after praying to holy Mary, I crossed the river and came into this wilderness.

Then, in answer to Zosimus's questions Mary tells briefly of the trials and temptations she met in the desert and how she gradually came to exist virtually without food or clothing and with God as her only teacher. Zosimus leaves after Mary makes him promise to meet her the next year on Holy Thursday with the Body and Blood of Christ. He does this, but it turns out to be their last meeting, for when he goes into the desert in the succeeding Lent he finds her corpse with a note scratched in the earth near by asking him to bury her and explaining that she had died hours after receiving the Eucharist from him the year before. Aided by a friendly lion, he buries the body and returns to the monastery, where he improves the rule according to what he has learned from Mary and serves faithfully for a hundred years.

If we take a moment to examine the difference between the way Dembowski read the story and the way our anonymous Old English homilist did, I think we can note that each is controlled by the presuppositions of his own age. To Dembowski, as to all of us, spiritual development by whatever name — heightened consciousness, deepening sensitivity, growth in openness, etc. — is an essentially interior activity, deeply individual and personal. Earlier ages tended to see such things in a more communal, social way. Thus, Zosimus follows the tradition as he goes to look for a master to instruct him in the spiritual life. A major point of the story, in whatever version, is what later ages have come to take for granted: that the great battles of the spirit are fought interiorly and not in conference. When Zosimus at last finds his master, it is a person without any qualifications but those of Mary Magdalen, a reformed prostitute who has attained high sanctity with no spiritual teacher but God. As the work of scholars such as Walter Ong and Eric Havelock has shown us, the development of a sense of the autonymous psyche in Western man entered with the alphabet and became intensified and even more deeply interiorized under the impact of print technology.[20]

What this suggests is that the culture within which even traditional texts are repeated becomes implicit in their meaning, offering to later generations an invaluable key to understanding. A small instance suggests itself in relation to our Old English text. Think for a moment what sort of guru figure would have replaced Antony and Paphnutius and Zosimas in the latter days of the Benedictine reform, when our text was composed. Perhaps Æthelwold would be an appropriate representative, or even Ælfric himself. Then hear the way in which Zosimas's initial temptation is phrased, first in the seventh century, then in the ninth, and finally in the late tenth or early eleventh century. The seventh-century Zosimas spoke both Latin and Greek but said very similar things in either language, "τῆσ ἑτέρου διδασκαλίασ οὐδαμῶσ προσδεόμενοσ" ('not at all needing the teaching of another') in Greek, and asserting, "aliena doctrina minus egeo" ('I don't need the teaching of anyone else very much') in Latin.[21] In the ninth century he is described as "alterius non indigens in ullo doctrina" ('not requiring another's teaching in anything'), which is closer to Sophronius; but in the days of Æthelwold we are told that "he nanre maran lare bysene ne beþorfte on his mode" ('he did not need the example of any more teaching in his mind').[22] It is perhaps worth speculating on the diction or perceived impact of the expresssion "lare bysene" in the world of Æthelwold, whose reforming spirit touched the monkish scriptorium only less deeply than it did monkish morals, or in the world of Ælfric who, in another context, so fervently urged "on Godes naman, gif hwa þas boc awritan wile, þat he hie gerihte wel be þære bysne" ('that, in the name of God, if anyone should want to copy out this book, he should thoroughly correct it according to the exemplar').[23] The addition of *bysen* in the Old English context, where no exemplum existed in its predecessors, has given a slightly different sense to spiritual discipleship in the Old English Mary story than it had in the earlier versions. The master is an "exemplar" of spiritual doctrine according to whom, one may suppose, the disciple might correct himself. The comparison will seem less apt and less likely to the extent that we fail to see that Ælfric is not talking about preparing an edition in his caveat but only about writing out a copy, and that his *bysen,* though it is a norm, is not a press run but an individual book, subject to the vicissitudes of time like any of its offspring, which—most important—it can father only one word at a time.

This kind of analysis disturbs some of our traditional ways of approaching the relationship between source and text because it obscures the boundaries of the text itself. I have just made a judgment about an Old English text which makes Æthelwold's scriptorium a part of its figurative language. The semantic net that constitutes a text extends beyond its physical boundaries to include the whole culture of which it is a part. The disturbing element is that this net is impossibly complex and even subject to variation according to the way a given text might be understood in different places at the same period. Demonstration of an exclusive reading of a text becomes as impossible as the establishment of the text itself. For instance, the *Vita Mariae* of Paul of Naples begins with a dedicatory preface to Charles the Bald. The fawning character of such a cumulation of superlatives we generally ignore as empty convention, but are we justified in so isolating them from the text they precede? Resounding in the ear, "Domino gloriosissimo ac praestantissimo regi Carolo, sciens gloriosissimam majestatem vestram tam divinis eloquiis, quam sanctorum praecedentium exemplis valde delectari...,"[24] they bring into the story itself a curious tension between the master-disciple relationship and that between courtier and king. When the legend of Mary's progressive spiritual abandonment is proffered explicitly for the delectation of a king, something not insignificant happens to the story itself. In a similar way, the original version of Sophronius can be seen partly as a response to Jerome's *Life of Paul,* which itself can be seen partly as a response to Athanasius' *Life of Antony.* Antony's very fame prompted a question about the possibility of a way of life so holy as to be without any worldly delight at all, including fame. Hence appeared the *Life of Paul,* which describes an anchorite who went to the desert before Antony and about whom no one even knew until his posthumous story was told. Similarly, the *Vita Mariae,* with a friendly lion to match Paul's and a posthumous revelation like his, adds a question about a life so holy as to be without even human spiritual counsel. Part of the meaning of the *Life of Mary of Egypt* is the other two *Lives.* Each tale and each version of the tale is in implicit dialogic relation with the culture of which it is a part, including the living literary tradition. This seems to me so true that Daniel Papebroche's seventeenth-century Latin translation of Sophronius, often cited as a medieval version, can be read as an interesting humanist variant of the legend, part of whose meaning relates neoclassicism to spiritual growth, while Skeat's facing-page translation of the Old English version, complete with "verily's," "eek's," and "thou's," gives us a Zosimus who speaks William

Morris and quotes Scripture according to King James. Where Sophronius began by urging his readers to believe that marvels could happen in the present,[25] Skeat's Gothic diction entices one to delight in the ancient and to admire the pastness of the past as itself a marvel.

That external boundaries to a text are difficult or impossible to identify seems to be part of the familiar idea that meaning is more accurately conceived on the analogy of field rather than particle theory. Any attempt to dissect or isolate constituent elements ends in destroying precisely what is being sought. The same dynamic is evident in the Mary legend. The question which motivates writer, reader, and the central characters of the story is: What is one to do to become perfect? Zosimus wonders if he has already done it, but we know that such an attitude is the substance of his problem. Mary, we sense, has somehow found the answer. And yet, her story at no point reveals anything positive in answer to the question. She renounces sin and does penance, but these are actions which of themselves merely create an emptiness in her. They do not perfect her. The answer to the question remains unexpressed in words in the text, residing in thirty years of desert silence which she barely mentions and cannot describe. They are a remainder, a residue left when one subtracts the seventeen years of trials and temptations in the desert which she *does* describe from the forty-seven years spent there. Everything else in the story is frame or boundary for a meaning which is never stated. Though the meaning is nowhere to be found in this series of nesting frames, remove them and the meaning is gone.

Curiously, what one glimpses at this point is a fleeting resemblance between the most nihilist of modern philosophies and the most traditional of ancient orthodoxies, though the resemblance may in the end be nothing more than a trick with mirrors. Still, at the heart of the desert experience, and of some of the writing which comes from it, just as in the probing questions and reconsiderations of contemporary deconstructionists, one finds — not illumination, presence, pattern, or fulfillment, but — silence, emptiness, denial, and darkness. This need not surprise us, for the *via negativa* has always been a primary response of Christian religious thought, constantly scandalized by its own most treasured definitions and formulations.

For our purpose here, such reflections would discourage a certain view of the text and of the textual sources which I have been calling traditional, a view which seeks to recover a single text and subordinates to it all other versions as false or distorted expressions. In conclusion I should perhaps indicate some of the things such reflection encourages. It encourages the establishment of intertextual analysis, in which texts are not seen so much to influence or derive from one another as to participate in a common cultural dialogue. It encourages us to read and delight not just in one, but in two, three, or five stories. Publication of the Z text of *Piers Plowman* does not seem to me a needless complication of an already impossible textual situation but the addition of another delightful narrative to the stock.[26] It should, therefore, encourage us to edit scribal versions—not diplomatic texts, but readable versions which recognize the radical connection of a text with its culture. Finally, such reflection encourages us to do our best in interpreting texts to avoid abstracting them from their physical and cultural *Sitz im Leben,* realizing all the while that on Parnassus as on Sinai, "Where (mis)interpretations abound, there also do the joys of (mis)understanding the more abound."

UNIVERSITY OF TORONTO

Notes

1. Though the initial signs of these movements can be traced much earlier in the eighteenth century, as in Edward Young's *Conjectures on Original Composition* (1759) and Lewis Theobald's edition of Shakespeare (1734), their full force is experienced only in such work as Coleridge's *Biographia Literaria* (1817) and Friedrich von Schlegel's *Lectures on the History of Literature, Ancient and Modern* (1811).

2. A recent survey of these movements is Vincent B. Leitch, *Deconstructive Criticism: An Advanced Introduction* (New York, 1983).

3. See Albert Bates Lord, *The Singer of Tales* (Cambridge, Mass., 1960); Walter J. Ong, *Ramus, Method and the Decay of Dialogue* (Cambridge, Mass., 1958) and *Orality and Literacy: The Technologizing of the Word* (New York, 1982); Eric Havelock, *Preface to Plato* (Cambridge, Mass., 1963); Marshall McLuhan, *The Gutenburg Galaxy* (Toronto, 1962).

4. Ong, *Orality and Literacy,* pp. 45-46, 79-81, 109.

5. *De Transitu Mariae Aegiptiace,* ed. Walter W. Skeat, in *Ælfric's Lives of Saints,* EETS, OS 94 (London, 1890), pp. 2-53; in EETS rpt. (1966), Vol. II, pp. 2-53. The Gloucester fragment is edited by John Earle in *Gloucester Fragments* (London, 1861), pp. 102-12.

6. Paulus Diaconus Sanctae Neopoleos Ecclesiae (hereafter cited as Paul of Naples) *Vita Sanctae Mariae Aegiptiacae Meretricis,* in *PL,* 73:671-90.

7. *Vita Sanctae Mariae Aegiptiacae,* in Boninus Mombritius, *Sanctuarium seu Vitae Sanctorum* (orig. pub. ca. 1480), ed. A. Brunet (Paris, 1910), II, 134-43.

8. Sophronius Βιοσ Μαριασ "Αιγυπτιασ, in *Acta Sanctorum,* April, Vol. I, Appendix, pp. xi-xviii, and in *PG,* 87, Part III, cols. 3697-725.

9. Cyril of Scythiopolis *Vita Sancti Cyriaci,* in *Acta Sanctorum,* September, VIII, 147-59, esp. p. 157.

10. Flodoard of Reims "De Maria Aegyptiaca et Zozima," Chap. iv of *De*

Triumphis Christi et Sanctorum Palaestinae, in *PL,* 135:541-48; Hildebert of Lavardin, "Paraphrasis Metrica," in *Acta Sanctorum,* April, I, 84-90, and in *PL,* 171:1321-40; Vincent of Beauvais, *Speculum Historiale* (Augsburg, 1474), II, Book 15, Chaps. 65-73, as cited in Peter F. Dembowski, *La Vie de sainte Marie l'Égyptienne: Versions en ancien et en moyen français* (Geneva, 1977), p. 15; the *Life of Mary* appears in any of various editions and translations of *The Golden Legend,* usually as Chap. 56, but sometimes as Chap. 54.

11. See Dembowski, *Vie de sainte Marie.*

12. "L'étude des versions latines de la *Vie,* de leur classement ainsi que de leurs rapports avec les différentes versions françaises reste à faire" (Dembowski, p. 16).

13. Dembowski, p. 13. The first sentence, the English for which is quoted above, reads, "Dans un monastère de Palestine vit le moine Zosime qui après 53 ans d'une vie d'ascèse pense être arrivé au sommet de la perfection monastique."

14. Skeat, p. 4.

15. Skeat, p. 6.

16. Skeat, p. 10.

17. Skeat, pp. 22-36.

18. Skeat, p. 22.

19. Skeat, p. 28.

20. See note 3 above.

21. Sophronius, in *PG,* 87:3700; Mombritius, p. 134.

22. Paul of Naples, in *PL,* 73:674; Skeat, p. 4. Flodoard's version is a 360-line verse summary of the tale, though even his Zosimas is sufficiently proud: "Hoc Zosimas supero ingreditur moderamine ductus / Militia sese reliquos superasse fideli / Dum reputat, Christo cum quis certaret agonem" (*PL,* 135:541).

23. "Ælfric's Preface to Genesis," in Bruce Mitchell and Fred C. Robinson, *A Guide to Old English* (Toronto, 1982), p. 194.

24. Paul of Naples, in *PL,* 73:671-72.

25. "'Ἀλλὰ μηδὲ τοῦτο πρὸσ ἀπιστίαν ἑλκυση τοὺσ ἐντυγχάνοντασ τὸ ἐν τῇ καθ' ἡμᾶσ γενεᾷ θαῦμα τοιοῦτον ἡγουμένουσ γενέσθαι ἀδύνατον" (*PG,* 87:3697).

26. A. G. Rigg and Charlotte Brewer, eds., *William Langland, Piers Plowman: The Z Version* (Toronto, 1983).

Evidence for Knowledge of Latin Literature in Old English

JANET M. BATELY

Even a superficial examination of extant Old English texts, in particular those written in prose, reveals what appears to be an extensive knowledge of Latin literature. Not only are there full-scale translations: there are lengthy excerpts in the vernacular, numerous quotations, allusions, and verbal echoes.[1] Over the last twenty-five years scholars have been assiduous in tracking down the Latin sources used and considering the manner in which material from them has been treated. What has been largely ignored is how this material reached the Anglo-Saxon writers and in what form. As Professor Cross said as long ago as 1972, "the source-hunter's image is still that of continuous reader, not thinker." Yet there are many exciting clues to be followed up, whether in the texts themselves, in extant, sometimes still unedited, Latin commentaries and glossaries, or in surviving manuscripts of the period.

The term "Latin literature" of course covers a very wide range of texts, and that part of the corpus which could have been available to the Anglo-Saxons extends over a no less generous time-span, from the classical period right up to the late tenth and early eleventh centuries. I propose in this paper to concentrate on classical texts and on those post-classical works through which classical themes and references to ancient history and classical myth were transmitted to readers in the early Middle Ages.[2] And I shall as a result mainly be dealing not with ideas and sequences of ideas[3] but with facts. Now the bulk of surviving Old English literature deals primarily with matters religious and provides little or no scope for the display of classical knowledge.[4] The surviving verse, for instance, has as its identifiable source-material almost exclusively Christian Latin (or Biblical) texts. Supposed influence of Apuleius' *Golden Ass* on *Beowulf* can be discounted,[5] while resemblances between *Beowulf* and the *Aeneid* are also too slight to be taken as serious evidence of knowledge of Virgil by the Old English poet. As C. L. Wrenn observes, "It is difficult to be sure of any specific echoes of the *Æneid* in [Beowulf] which can be safely attributed to the *Beowulf*-poet himself."[6] The need for caution in source-hunting may be illustrated by reference to another apparent echo of a classical text in Old English verse, this time in the *Wanderer*. In this poem the speaker refers movingly to the decay of the world and of mortals alike.

>   þes middangeard
> ealra dogra gehwam   dreoseð 7 fealleþ

says the poet, and the veterans too are dead

>   Sume wig fornom,
> ferede in forðwege;   sumne fugel oþbær
> ofer heanne holm;   sumne se hara wulf
> deaðe gedælde;   sumne dreorighleor
> in eorðscræfe   eorl gehydde.[7]

Were it not for recent researches which have unravelled the complex history of the *Ubi sunt* and related themes in post-classical as well as classical Latin texts,[8] it would be tempting to relate these statements by a Christian poet directly to a much older, pre-Christian consolation, Statius' poem on Glaucias, the favorite of Atedius Melior, in *Silvae* II.1.

> Hic finis rapto. quin tu iam vulnera sedas
> et tollis mersum luctu caput? omnia functa
> aut moritura vides: obeunt noctesque diesque
> astraque, nec solidis prodest sua machina terris.
> nam populus mortale genus plebisque caducae
> quis fleat interitus? hos bella, hos aequora poscunt;
> his amor exitio, furor his et saeva cupido,
> ut sileam morbos; hos ora rigentia Brumae,
> illos implacido letalis Sirius igni,
> hos manet imbrifero pallens Autumnus hiatu.
> quicquid init ortus, finem timet. ibimus omnes,
> ibimus....

"It is the end: he is lost to you. Will you not now assuage your pain and lift your grief-sunken head? All that you see is dead or doomed to die; nights and days perish, and the stars, nor does the frame of solid earth avail her. Our race is of mortal kind, and who should bewail the passing of folk whose end is sure? War claims some, the ocean others; some are victims of love, of madness, or fell desire; these winter's freezing breath awaits; those the fierce heat of deadly Sirius, others pale Autumn with rain-bringing jaws. All that has had beginning fears its end. Doomed are we all, ay, doomed."[9]

Late prose is equally unproductive of relevant material, though *Apollonius of Tyre, The Wonders of the East,* and *The Letter of Alexander to Aristotle* all have secular Latin sources,[10] and Ælfric, writing saints' lives or commenting on Biblical texts, not infrequently deals with subject matter relating to Old or New Testament times or to the later Empire.[11] For a demonstration of more general interest in, and knowledge of, classical literature and classical themes we need to turn to the prose literature of the Alfredian period and in particular to four texts: the *Old English Orosius,* Alfred's *Boethius,* Alfred's *Soliloquies* and the *Anglo-Saxon Chronicle.*[12]

Of these four works, three, being renderings of Latin texts, normally only present opportunities for their authors to reveal their classical knowledge when their primary sources are allusive and leave room for explanation — as, for instance, when the author of the *Old English Orosius* tells the story of the Rape of the Sabines, and Alfred that of Orpheus. The fourth, the *Anglo-Saxon Chronicle,* restricts itself by beginning its epitome of world history not with the Creation but (like one of its sources, Bede) in 60 B.C., and then ending it abruptly in the year 110.[13] However, among them the four works include a considerable body of additional material, apparently drawn from a variety of classical and related sources. The task of identifying the material of this type that they incorporate is now more or less complete.[14] The task of ascertaining its full significance remains largely to be performed.

The first and perhaps greatest problem is deciding on the precise source used in a given case: a surprising number of pieces of information could come from more than one Latin text — even from as many as half-a-dozen.[15] One reason for this lack of certainty is the general absence of what may be termed direct quotation. And the latter is not in the least surprising, for sense-for-sense rather than word-for-word translation is the normal practice of both Alfred and the author of the *Old English Orosius,*[16] while the annalistic style of the opening entries of the *Anglo-Saxon Chronicle* is generally extremely terse.[17] A second reason for uncertainty is the frequency with which classical writers and their successors make use of the same information in more or less the same (and sometimes identical) form. Sometimes, of course, it is possible to make informed guesses as to the most likely source used. For instance, given the apparent absence of similar details elsewhere, it is probably safe enough to assume that Sallust is the ultimate source of the *Old English Orosius'* additional information about Marius' expedition against the Numidians at Capsa,[18] and that the four points of contact between the *Old English Orosius'* greatly expanded account of Alexander's attack on an Indian city and that of Quintus Curtius are due to borrowing by the former from the latter, whether at first or at second hand.[19] Again, where there are a number of possible sources for an addition but one has details not found in the others, then it is this one that we may presume to have been the most likely intermediary or immediate source. For instance, in the account of Janus's doors in Book III, Chapter v of the *Old English Orosius* we are told that the structure was a four-doored building, a detail which is found in a number of texts including Augustine *De Civitate Dei* VII.8, Macrobius *Saturnalia* I.ix, and Servius *Aeneid* VII.607; however, the second part of the expansion refers to the Romans hitching up their garments above their knees, and this detail seems most likely to be derived from the comment on the phrase *Gabinus cinctus* which follows immediately afterwards in Servius.[20] However, as Joseph Wittig has demonstrated in his recent paper, even where there is "significant" detail, apparently identifying specific sources, the situation is often a highly complex one. Thus, of the variety of references to the story of Orpheus, the version most likely to have been used by King Alfred in the *Boethius* is that of Virgil in his fourth *Georgic*, with additional details from *Aeneid* VI and Ovid *Metamorphoses* X, and very likely along with a commentary such as that by Servius and "the sort of traditional learning found in an Isidore."[21]

So too with the references to Titus in the *Anglo-Saxon Chronicle* and the *Old English Orosius* as a man who counted that day lost on which he did nothing good:

> Her Titus feng to rice, seþe sæde þæt he þone dæg forlure þe he noht to gode on ne gedyde (*Anglo-Saxon Chronicle*, annal 81);

> Titus ... wæs swa godes willan þæt he sægde þæt he forlure þone dæg þe he noht on to gode ne gedyde (*Old English Orosius* 138/23–139/2).

In the case of the *Chronicle* it seems that this reference, along with others in the same section of this work, is derived from the *Chronicon* of Isidore of Seville; in the case of the *Old English Orosius*, on the other hand, we have to do with a combination of Isidore (either direct or via the *Chronicle*) and Jerome.[22]

However, there remains a substantial body of additions as to whose precise source there is no internal immediate clue. So, for example, in place of two brief allusions to the Rape of the Sabines in Orosius' *History* II.iv.2 and 5 — "Sine more raptas Sabinas, inprobis nuptiis confoederatas maritorum et parentum cruore dotauit," and "Sabinorum, quos foedere ludisque pellexerat, feminas tam inhoneste praesumpsit quam nefarie defendit" — the Old English version (39/5-16) describes in detail how the Romans asked the Sabines for their daughters as wives, and when the Sabines refused the request, obtained the women against their will by treachery,

> asking that they might help them, that they might the more easily sacrifice to their gods. When they granted them this, then they had them as wives and would not give them back to their fathers. Over that there was the greatest war for many years, until they were almost all slain on both sides and they could not be reconciled until the Roman women with their children ran among the combatants and fell at their fathers' feet, asking that for love of the children they should put some end to the battle.

This expansion contains details either found in, or in some way related to, information recorded in a number of Latin texts — for instance, the Romans' request to the Sabines for their daughters as wives and the Romans' seizing of the women when the request was refused. However, two Latin texts, Florus and Livy, do not specify which peoples were initially asked; and Ovid in the *Fasti* does not even name the Sabines. That the intervention of the women in a subsequent battle took place after many years of conflict in which there were heavy casualties on both sides is suggested by Ovid in the *Fasti* (making the first point) and by Augustine in *De Civitate Dei* and the Orosius commentary (making the second). Livy gives no indication of time-scale and no support for the theory that the war lasted "many years." That the women fell at their fathers' feet, on the other hand, appears to be inspired by either Ovid or Augustine, while that they took their children with them is a detail I have so far found only in Ovid and in scholia on Lucan and Juvenal.[23] So a combination of Ovid's *Fasti* and Augustine's *De Civitate Dei* could be responsible for the form that the story takes in the *Old English Orosius,* but other possibilities remain and some of the discrepancies have still to be explained.

Sometimes it is not the presence of certain details from Latin texts that may be significant but their absence; sometimes it is misunderstanding or misapplication or even downright contradiction of source material that may help to reduce the range of possible sources; sometimes it is the presence of variants in textual transmission in the Latin. And occasionally there is no known source at all. The following may serve as illustrations of the complexity of the problem.

1. In commenting on the Nile floods (*OE Orosius* 11/17-20), the author claims that they take place in wintry weather and are caused by the north wind. Most of the potential Latin sources suggest more than one reason for the floods and give the time of year as summer.[24] Presumably, the Old English author's source here took a form such as that in Isidore *Etymologies* XIII.xxi.7: "Aquilonis flatibus repercussus aquis retroluctantibus intumescit et inundationem Aegypti facit," where only one cause is mentioned and the time of year not specified.[25] It may be presumed that the translator then, not unintelligently, proceeded to associate *aquilo* with winter, as in Servius *Aeneid* IV 310: "Mediis Aquilonibus: media hieme, ut per Aquilones 'hiemem' significet."

2. When he expands Boethius' allusion to Busiris as a king who used to put strangers to death until he himself was killed by a stranger, Hercules (*Boethius* II, pr. 6), Alfred explains not only that Busiris was an Egyptian and Hercules son of Jove, but that the manner of death of the strangers (when they tried to leave their host) was drowning in the Nile (*Alfred's Boethius*, 36/29-37/5). According to classical tradition, the strangers were in fact sacrificed on the altars of Busiris' gods, in order to put an end to a nine-year drought. Busiris, king of Egypt, was son of Neptune. Presumably the story reached Alfred (or an intermediary) in a form which was sufficiently imprecise to allow the play of imagination and embroidery on the fact that the major river of Egypt was the Nile and that one of the gods worshipped was presumably Busiris' father, Neptune, the god of water.[26]

3. In its rewriting of the *Chronicle* entry for 60 B.C. the "northern recension" gives the surprising information that Julius Caesar, having had severe losses inflicted on him by the Britons, "forlet his here abidan mid Scottum 7 gewat into Galwalum." The ultimate source of this statement is Bede *Historia Ecclesiastica* I.ii: "Exin Caesar a Britannis reuersus in Galliam, postquam legiones in hiberna misit...." However, the author would seem to have used a Latin manuscript with the reading *hibernia* in error for *hiberna*.[27]

It is in areas such as these where future research is likely to make its most important contribution.

Textual studies have recently been greatly helped and advanced by publication of the Toronto microfiche concordance of materials for the new Anglo-Saxon dictionary. If similar advances are to be made in source studies, then similar aids must be developed. First of all, there is an urgent need for a checklist of all classical additions in Old English texts with details of the Latin texts from which they could have been derived. Then we need a reverse list of those Latin texts, with details of the passages they could have influenced or inspired, and perhaps with cross-references to the range of possible alternative sources. Then finally, I suppose, we need a negative scan: a survey of material in the Latin texts that might have been used but was not, and of the nature of errors that were committed but which should have been avoided if certain works were indeed known. Thus, for instance, as we have seen, Virgil's *Aeneid* and Ovid's *Metamorphoses* have been shown to be the most likely major sources for Alfred's account of Orpheus. However, it is hard to see how the king could have told the story of Ulysses and Circe in the peculiar way he did, with the spell on Ulysses' followers imposed when they attempted to leave their love-lorn lord and return home, if Alfred had read (and remembered) the corresponding account of that episode in Ovid also — which is a pity, since it would be pleasant to be able to conjecture that a misplaced recollection of Ovid's account of the men-animals' fawning on the Greeks in the Ulysses story could account for the detail of Cerberus' fawning on Orpheus as he entered the Underworld.[28]

At the same time, all investigation of potential sources has to be made in the context of possible linguistic expertise. How much of their Latin originals did the writers understand? How familiar might they have been with the vocabulary of their sources?[29] Could they have been helped by Latin-Old English or Latin-Latin glossaries? How far could commentary material have been of use? And lastly, how did the information reach these Old English authors? The list of possible or probable sources is alarmingly long. Were the works of writers such as Virgil, Livy, Sallust, Pliny the Elder, Quintus Curtius, Frontinus, Valerius Maximus, Servius, Suetonius, Ovid, and possibly also Isidore, Eutropius, Florus, and Festus and the *De Viris Illustribus* all available in late-ninth-century England?[30]

From Professor Gneuss' lists it would seem that manuscripts of Orosius, Pliny the Elder, Servius, and Isidore (*Etymologies* and *De Natura Rerum*) were copied in England in the eighth century, while for the ninth century we may add Martianus Capella and a commentary on Capella.[31] And from Ogilvy's studies we may deduce direct knowledge in the seventh, eighth, and ninth centuries also of Claudian, Ovid's *Metamorphoses,* Virgil, and possibly also Horace and Valerius Maximus; but not of Sallust, not Quintus Curtius, not Frontinus, not Valerius Maximus, not Suetonius, Florus, Festus, or the *De Viris Illustribus*.[32]

An additional source of information concerning the presence of Latin texts in England are Latin-Old English glossaries. Thus, for instance, the

Épinal, Erfurt, Leiden, and Corpus Glossaries all have Old English glosses to lemmata from Orosius, while there is also evidence of use of Virgil.[33]

So were these works available to our authors in the late ninth century?[34] And if they were, are we then to assume that the authors consulted them as they wrote, or were so familiar with them that, like Ælfric with patristic texts and homiliaries,[35] they readily recalled details from them? Again there is much scope for research. The evidence of Alfred's works is that his classical knowledge was fairly limited and that he expected some at least of his audience to know even less. Homer, he comments in the *Boethius*, was Greek, and he was the teacher of Virgil, and Virgil was the best among the *Lædenwarum*.[36] And, "we know who built Rome," he says in the *Soliloquies*, but, unlike Augustine *De Videndo Deo*, his source at this point, he does not find it necessary or appropriate to name the builder as Romulus.[37] Alfred may have been slightly better informed than the author of the *Old English Orosius* about Tarquinius Superbus, for when his source refers to the arrogance of the Roman kings as leading to the abolition of the monarchy, he says that "Romana witan on Torcwines dagum þæs ofermodan cyninges for his ofermettum þone cynelican naman of Romebyrig æresð adydon." The author of the *Old English Orosius*, on the other hand, though referring to Tarquin as the proudest and wickedest of a very proud and wicked dynasty, yet can make an extraordinary error in retelling the story of the conflict between the Tarquins and Brutus. Faced by an allusion to Arruns as "Superbi filio," he renders this as "Arrunses sunu ðæs ofermodgan," apparently unaware that *Superbus* is Tarquin. And he goes on to tell how Arruns fought in the stead of Tarquin.[38] Alfred also knows that Seneca committed suicide by having the blood let from a vein in his arm, information which could be derived from Tacitus' *Annals;* however, he appears unaware of the remaining sordid details as set down by Tacitus in two adjoining chapters, and states incorrectly that Seneca asked others to make the incision for him.[39] Alfred also appears to know something of the story of the sword of Damocles, expanding Boethius' statement in Book III, pr. 5: "Expertus sortis suae periculorum tyrannus regni metus pendentis supra uerticem gladii terrore simulauit" ("the tyrant knew well enough the dangers of his position, when he illustrated the fears of kingship by making a sword dangle over his head"). He adds to Boethius' account by describing the sword as suspended by a "smale þræde," but like Boethius he gives no names, merely putting a speech in the mouth of "sum cyning þe unrihtlice feng to rice," presumably either because the names would mean nothing to his audience or he himself had forgotten them, or because he used a source which did not give them.[40] Another place where an alteration or addition could be due to either ignorance or deliberate change is in his rendering of Boethius III, pr. 12. Here Alfred complains, "Me þincð þæt ðu me dwelle 7 dydre, swa mon cild deð; lædst me hidres 7 ðidres on swa þicne wudu ðæt ic ne mæg ut aredian" (*Alfred's Boethius* 100/4–6). In the corresponding section in the *De Consolatione,* Boethius asks Philosophy if she is playing with him, by weaving a labyrinth of arguments from which he cannot find the way out: "Ludisne, inquam, me inextricabilem labyrinthum rationibus texens, quae nunc quidem quo egrediaris introeas, nunc uero quo introieris egrediare" ("At one moment you go in where you'll come out, and at another you come out where you went in"). It is possible, I suppose, that Alfred's rendering could be the result of ignorance of the nature of the labyrinth, just as the author of the *Old English Orosius* is ignorant of the nature of the Minotaur (which he describes as half man, half lion) and of the tribute payable to Crete;[41] however, Alfred could have learned something of the labyrinth from a number of classical and post-classical texts including Isidore and Ovid's *Metamorphoses;*[42] and not only does the metaphor of the wood recall his introduction to the *Soliloquies* but there is evidence elsewhere of his readiness to change details in his source for the sake of clarity and comprehensibility. An example of this is provided by the famous passage where he replaces a reference to Fabricius with a reference to the Germanic Weland: "Hwæt synt nu þæs foremeran 7 þæs wisan goldsmiðes ban Welondes? Forþi ic cwæð þæs wisan forþy þam cræftegan ne mæg næfre his cræft losigan, ne hine mon ne mæg þonne eð on him geniman ðe mon mæg þa sunnan awendan of hiere stede" (*Alfred's Boethius* 46/16–20). The Latin here merely asks:

> Vbi nunc fidelis ossa Fabricii manent,
> quid Brutus aut rigidus Cato? (II, metre 7)

However, Fabricius the *fidelis* was a man renowned in classical sources for his unshakable honesty, and *De Viris Illustribus* 35 says of him: "Ille est Fabricius, qui difficilius ab honestate, quam sol a suo cursu averti posset." It would seem that Alfred used the figure, fully knowing the identity of Fabricius, but changed the name to Weland to bring home his message to his audience with a familiar Germanic reference.[43]

Of course the possibility of immediate reference or recall in a range of instances does not necessarily imply that every added allusion came directly from the source that has been identified for it, even through the author's limited recollection.[44] In the case of King Alfred, recollection by his helpers may have contributed; there may have been available commentaries on the texts which are now lost to us, or the king could have used glossed manuscripts or encyclopedic glossaries. Certainly in the case of the *Old English Orosius,* there is no question of direct access to Ennius for the saying "Aio te, Aeacida, Romanos vincere posse" which appears in *OE Orosius* 84/8-11 in the form "Þu hæfst oþþe næfst." Although this saying is repeated by a number of classical writers, its presence either as a marginal gloss or incorporated in the text of some of the Latin manuscripts of Orosius closest to our translation makes it almost certain that the manuscript used by our translator likewise included it.[45]

Derivation at second hand, whether through marginal gloss or commentary, seems probable in a number of cases—for instance, the surprising claim that Cinna died at Smyrna (*Old English Orosius* 125/12), where information that the poet Cinna wrote a poem called *Smyrna* is transformed into the claim that the soldier Cinna was slain at Smyrna (he was in fact killed near Ancona).[46] A surprising reference in Alfred's *Boethius* to "se foremæra 7 se aræda Romwara heretoga se wæs haten Brutus, oðre naman Cassius" (46/22-23) is paralleled in a ninth-century manuscript containing a commentary on Virgil, and later in Chaucer and Lydgate.[47]

However, surviving commentaries contain very different material from that used by our authors, and where they do deal with the same topics they are sometimes less accurate or less detailed. Thus, for instance, whereas the *Old English Orosius* tells us that Lucretia was wife of (Col)latinus and that she was Brutus' sister (*OE Orosius* 40/6-7), the Orosius commentary (40/8) describes her as wife of Quintus Tricipitinus and makes no reference to Brutus at all. Alfred as we have seen replaces a reference to the labyrinth by a reference to a wood; the commentary in Vatican 3363 tells us that the *labyrinthus* is a house with a thousand walls.[48]

Dependence on material from glossaries is a matter that still needs careful examination.[49] Dependence on encyclopedic texts, however, seems incontrovertible, the main problem being the precise route by which information reached the Old English authors. An example from Alfred's *Boethius* must suffice. Where Boethius (III, pr. 4) comments: "Vnde Catullus licet in curuli Nonium sedentem strumam tamen appellat," Alfred (61/16-21) substitutes a reference to "se wisa Catulus," who "hine gebealg 7 swa ungefræglice forcwæð Nonium þone rican, forðæm he hine gemette sittan on gerenedum scridwæne; forðæm hit wæs ða swiðe micel sido mid Romwarum þæt þær nane oðre an ne sæton buton þa weorðestan...." This rendering must surely be inspired by selective and inaccurate reading of an encyclopedic entry such as that in Isidore *Etymologies* XX.xi.11:

Sella curulis erat in quibus magistrati sedentes iura reddebant. Dictae autem curules, quia apud veteres praetores et consules propter itineris longinquitatem curru forum provehebantur; sellae autem, quae post eos vehebantur, quibus sedentes dicere iura solebant, a curru curules sellae sunt nominatae.[50]

The curule chair was the chair in which magistrates sat when they presided at trials. They were called *curules* because in the old days praetors and consuls were carried to the forum in a chariot, on account of the length of the journey; the seats, which were carried behind them and in which they were accustomed to sit to pronounce the law, are called *curules sellae* from the chariot.

A reference in the *Soliloquies* to Honorius and Theodosius could also be based on information drawn from a source such as Isidore. Augustine is made to comment (p. 88, 1.15) that Honorius is "swiðe god, þeah his feder betere were; he wes swiðe rædfast and swiðe rihte mines hlafordes kynnes, and swa is se (þe) þær gyt lufað" (for "lyfað"). Concerning this reference Carnicelli comments that it is apparently a piece of historical verisimilitude on Alfred's part. Alfred, he says, must have thought that Augustine wrote the *Soliloquies* during the reign of Honorius, since Honorius is mentioned in the dialogue as still being alive; "Actually, the *Sol.* was written during the reign of Theodosius, in 386–387."[51] Honorius and Theodosius were the Roman emperors during most of Augustine's lifetime. The relevant entry in Isidore *Etymologies* V.xxxix.38 is "Honorius ann.xv. Augustinus Episcopus claruit." The previous entry states merely *Theodosius an.iii*. How did Alfred know that Honorius was "the good son of Theodosius, who was even better"? and how did he know that Theodosius was good? Are there other references than Isidore's that could have been Alfred's source?[52] As we have seen, copies of Isidore certainly were available in England at the time. But did Alfred actually use Isidore in composing the *Soliloquies*?

In this paper I have done no more then scratch the surface of what there is yet to be done. There is an urgent need to ask, to look, and to search. But although, like King Alfred, I have never gone to the wood without wanting to bring home more material than I can carry, I must like him urge others with enough strength and more wagons to go there to collect as much as they can of the abundance that is there.

UNIVERSITY OF LONDON
KING'S COLLEGE

Notes

1. For an important statement on this whole subject, see J. E. Cross, "The Literate Anglo-Saxon — On Sources and Disseminations," *Publications of the British Academy,* 58 (1972), 67–100.
2. That is, works such as Orosius *Historiarum adversus Paganos Libri VII,* Jerome's version of Eusebius' *Chronicle,* and Isidore *Etymologies.*
3. See Cross, "The Literate Anglo-Saxon," p. 68.
4. A notable exception are the verse meters of Boethius.
5. See J. D. A. Ogilvy, *Books Known to the English,* 597–1066 (Cambridge, Mass., 1967), p. 75, reporting a suggestion by Donald W. Lee in *A Way to Heorot* (circulated in mimeograph, 1950) and T. J. Brown, "An Historical Introduction to the Use of Classical Latin Authors in the British Isles from the Fifth to the Eleventh Century," *Settimane,* 22 (1975), 273.
6. See *Beowulf,* ed. C. L. Wrenn, 2nd ed., rev. W. F. Bolton (London, 1973), p. 150 and also p. 152. In this connection it is worth noting Antonette diPaolo Healey's comment in *The Old English Vision of St. Paul* (Cambridge, Mass., 1978), p. 52: "We cannot state with any certainty that the *Beowulf* poet knew the *Vision* and drew upon it."
7. *The Wanderer,* ed. T. P. Dunning and A. J. Bliss (London, 1969), ll. 62–63 and 80–84.
8. See J. E. Cross, "On the Genre of *The Wanderer,*" *Neophilologus,* 45 (1961), 63–72; Cross, "The Literate Anglo-Saxon," pp. 86–87; and the editions of *The Wanderer* by Dunning and Bliss and by R. F. Leslie (Manchester, 1966).
9. Translation based on that in Statius, *Silvae,* ed. J. H. Mozley (London, 1928).
10. For an important recent study of the sources and relationships of *The Wonders of the East* see Ann Knock, *Wonders of the East: A Synoptic Edition of "The Letter of Pharasmanes" and the Old English and Old Picard Translations* (Diss. University of London 1982).
11. See, for instance, Ælfric, "Epilogue to Judges," in *The Old English Version of the Heptateuch,* ed. S. J. Crawford, EETS, O.S. 160 (London, 1922), pp. 414–17, with an explanation of Roman customs, and Ælfric on the Old and New Testaments, *OE Heptateuch,* pp. 33–34, with details of the siege and sack of Jerusalem by Titus; also, for the emperor Julianus as once a priest, *The Sermones Catholici or Homilies of Ælfric,* ed. Benjamin Thorpe, 2 vols. (London, 1844, 1846), I, 449.
12. I exclude from consideration here the *Old English Bede* and the *Old English Martyrology.* Although Bede deals with the history of Britain in Roman times, the Old English translator of the *Ecclesiastical History* not only does not add any new material, but actually omits some of the facts that are given and misrepresents others, showing a surprising lack of interest in historical fact. Thus, for instance, Book I, Chapter ii on Caesar's invasion of Britain is cut to a single sentence; and in place of Bede's comment in Book I, Chapter iii that Nero nearly lost Britain, two cities being captured and destroyed during his reign, the Old English makes the claim that "he Breotone rice forlet"; see *The Old English Version of Bede's Ecclesiastical History*

of the English People, ed. Thomas Miller, EETS, O.S. 95, 96 (1890-91; rpt. London, 1959), 30/13-15 and 30; and, for the Latin, *Venerabilis Bedae Historia Ecclesiastica,* ed. C. Plummer (Oxford, 1896). For material relating to the first century A.D. in the *OE Martyrology,* see J. E. Cross, "The Apostles in the *Old English Martyrology,*" *Mediaevalia,* 5 (1979), 15-59.

13. In beginning with 60 B.C., the writer is following Bede: indeed, his material is drawn from the epitome at the end of the *Historia Ecclesiastica.* See Janet Bately, "World History in the Anglo-Saxon Chronicle: Its Sources and Its Separateness from the Old English Orosius," *ASE,* 8 (1979), 177-94. The northern recension, however, adds further details of Caesar's invasion, taken from the body of the *Historia Ecclesiastica.*

14. Perhaps the most fruitful potential area left for source-hunters is that where the Old English authors make what might be termed oblique allusions. See, for instance, *The Old English Orosius,* ed. Janet Bately, EETS, S.S. 6 (London, 1980) (hereafter cited as *OE Orosius*), 25/4-6: "Be þæm Theuhaleon wæs gecweden, swilce mon bispel sæde, þæt he wære moncynnes tydriend, swa swa Noe wæs," beside *Pauli Orosii Historiarum adversus Paganos Libri VII,* ed. C. Zangemeister, CSEL, Vol. V (Vienna, 1882), I.ix.2: "A quo propterea genus hominum reparatum ferunt." Simeon Potter ("Commentary on King Alfred's Orosius," *Anglia,* 71 [1952-53], 390) took the Old English version to be the result of misreading or mishearing of *reparatum* as *repartum* or *reparitum;* however, use of the word *bispell* 'fable' in the *Old English Orosius* suggests knowledge of the myth of Deucalion and Pyrrha, according to which Deucalion became the progenitor of the human race—a story for which there is a number of possible sources: see *OE Orosius,* commentary on 25/4-6. See also the story of Phaethon in *OE Orosius* 26/32-34, with its added reference to "Fetontis forscapunge": "þa hæfdon monige unwise menn him to worde 7 to leasungspelle þæt sio hæte nære for hiora synnum, ac sædon þæt hio wære for Fetontis forscapunge, anes mannes"; compare Orosius I.x.19: "ridiculam Phaethontis fabulam." At the same time some material can be identified for which no source has yet been discovered—for instance, the reference to Ptolemy as arriving "three days later" in the *OE Orosius* 82/22-23, and the description of a second smaller wall outside the moat at Babylon in *OE Orosius* 43/30-31.

15. See, e.g., the references to Caesar's clemency (*OE Orosius* 128/3-4); to Cleopatra as Antony's wife (129/18); to Dido as founder of Carthage (133/9-10); and to the story of Regulus (95/21-96/3), all found in a number of Latin texts, including several apparently used as the source of material elsewhere in the *Old English Orosius.* See my edition, commentary on these lines.

16. See Janet Bately, *The Literary Prose of King Alfred's Reign: Translation or Transformation?* (London, 1980).

17. Additional details in *The Chronicle of Æthelweard* (ed. Alistair Campbell [London, 1962]) do not necessarily derive from a fuller version of the *Anglo-Saxon Chronicle* than those still extant; more probably they incorporate the fruits of Æthelweard's own reading.

18. See Sallust, *Bellum Iugurthinum,* ed. A. Kurfess (Leipzig, 1957), §91, and *OE Orosius* 121/9-15.

19. See *Q. Curti Rufi Historiarum Alexandri Magni Macedonis Libri*, ed. E. Hedicke (Leipzig, 1908), IX.v. 6-20, and *OE Orosius* 73/8-27. Also apparently from Quintus Curtius (VIII.i.20-21 and 43) are the descriptions of Clitus as previously Alexander's father's thegn and of Alexander "leaping up" in anger to kill him (*OE Orosius* 71/18 and 22). Does it follow from this that Quintus Curtius (VIII.i.22 and 43-44) was also the source of the information in 71/19, that Alexander was drunk at the time, information which is found also in other Latin texts such as Justinus, Solinus, and Pliny?

20. See *OE Orosius* 59/3-11; Augustine, *De Civitate Dei*, ed. E. Hoffmann, CSEL, Vol. 49 (Vienna, 1899-1900); *Macrobius*, ed. F. Eyssenhardt (Leipzig, 1893). References to Servius in this article are from *Servii Grammatici qui Feruntur in Vergilii Carmina Commentarii*, ed. G. Thilo and H. Hagen (Leipzig, 1881; rpt. Hildesheim, 1961).

21. Joseph Wittig, "King Alfred's Boethius and Its Latin Sources," *ASE*, 11 (1983), 157-98. References to the Old English text are from *King Alfred's Old English Version of Boethius De Consolatione Philosophiae*, ed. Walter John Sedgefield (Oxford, 1899), hereafter cited as *Alfred's Boethius*.

22. See *OE Orosius* 138/23-139/2; Isidore, *Chronicon*, in *PL*, 83:1042, and *S. Eusebii Hieronymi Interpretatio Chronicae Eusebii Pamphili*, in *PL*, 27:597-98; and for detailed arguments for the use of these sources see Janet Bately, "World History," pp. 185 and 190-91, and *OE Orosius*, p. xc.

23. Augustine *De Civitate Dei* II.xvii and III.xiii; *P. Ovidius Naso Opera*, ed. R. Merkel (Leipzig, 1896), *Fasti* III.189-224; *Adnotationes super Lucanum*, ed. J. Endt (Leipzig, 1909), I.118; *Marci Annaei Lucani Pharsalia*, ed. H. Grotius and C. F. Weber, Vol. III, *Scholiastae* (Leipzig, 1831), I.118; *Scholia in Juvenalem Vetustiora*, ed. P. Wessner (Leipzig, 1931; rpt. Stuttgart, 1967), VI. 163,2; Orosius commentary, Rome, Vatican MS. Reg. Lat. 1650, fol. 7ᵛ; *Annaei Flori Epitomae Libri II*, ed. O. Rossbach (Leipzig, 1896); *Titi Livi Ab Urbe Condita Libri*, ed. G. Weissenborn and M. Muller (Leipzig, 1902, et. seq.), I.ix.

24. See, e.g., *Pomponii Melae de Chorographia Libri Tres*, ed. C. Frick (Leipzig, 1880), I.ix.53; and Bede, *De Natura Rerum*, in *PL*, 90:262.

25. *Isidori Hispalensis Episcopi Etymologiarum sive Originum Libri XX*, ed. W. M. Lindsay (Oxford, 1911).

26. See *Hygini Fabulae*, ed. H. I. Rose (Leiden, 1934), xxxi and lvi; Servius *Georgics* III.5.

27. See *Two Saxon Chronicles Parallel*, ed. Charles Plummer on the basis of an edition by J. Earle (Oxford, 1892; rpt. with notes by Dorothy Whitelock, 1952). The northern recension appears to be using an *m*-type manuscript of Bede, in contrast to the first version which has as its source a *c*-type manuscript. Thus, for instance, the identification of Armenia as the homeland of the Britons goes back to a reading *Armonicano* for correct *Armoricano*, which is typical of *m*-type MSS (though I have also found it occasionally in *c*-type MSS). See Janet Bately, "Bede and the Anglo-Saxon Chronicle," *Saints, Scholars and Heroes: Studies in Medieval Culture in Honour of Charles W. Jones* (Collegeville, Minnesota, 1979), I, 249. The variant *hibernia*, said by Bertram Colgrave and R. A. B. Mynors in their edition of Bede's *Ecclesiastical*

History ([Oxford, 1969], p. 20) to be typical of *c2*-type MSS, I have found also in *m*-type MSS. See further Cross, "Apostles," *passim*.

28. *Alfred's Boethius* 115/12-116/34 and 101/14-15; cf. Ovid *Metamorphoses* XIV, Fable 5, ll. 254-61.

29. For instance, in his translation of the meter on the Golden Age, Alfred apparently misunderstands "classica saeva," relating *classica* incorrectly to *classis* 'fleet' (see *Sweet's Anglo-Saxon Reader,* rev. Dorothy Whitelock [Oxford, 1967], p. 226). Where else might he have met the form *classica* in his reading? What sources might have helped him?

30. For the possible use of some of these in the *Old English Orosius* see my edition, commentary, *passim*, and Introduction, pp. lxi-lxiii.

31. See Helmut Gneuss, "A Preliminary List of Manuscripts Written or Owned in England up to 1100," *ASE,* 9 (1981).

32. See note 5 above. T. J. Brown accepts some 20 items on Ogilvy's list of 40 for the period before 800: see "An Historical Introduction," p. 273; and see also the review of Ogilvy by Helmut Gneuss, *Anglia,* 89 (1971), 129-34.

33. See J[oseph] D. Pheifer, *Old English Glosses in the Epinal-Erfurt Glossary* (Oxford, 1974); W. M. Lindsay, *The Corpus Glossary* (Cambridge, 1921); and *A Late-Eighth-Century Latin-Anglo-Saxon Glossary Preserved in the Library of the Leiden University,* ed. J. H. Hessels (Cambridge, 1906).

34. For possible late-ninth-century dates for the composition of the "first" *Chronicle* and the *Old English Orosius,* see Dorothy Whitelock, *English Historical Documents,* Vol. I, 2nd ed. (London, 1979), pp. 121-22, and Bately, *OE Orosius,* pp. lxviii-lxx.

35. See the articles by J. E. Cross, especially "Ælfric—Mainly on Memory and Creative Method in Two Catholic Homilies," *Studia Neophilologica,* 41 (1969), 152-53.

36. *Alfred's Boethius* 141/11-13: "Omerus se goda sceop, þe mid Crecum selest wæs: se wæs Firg⟨il⟩ies lareow se Frigilius wæs mid Lædenwarum selest"; cf. Boethius V, met. 2.

37. *King Alfred's Version of St. Augustine's Soliloquies,* ed. Thomas A. Carnicelli (Cambridge, Mass., 1969) (hereafter cited as *Alfred's Soliloquies*), 97/5-9; *De Videndo Deo,* in *PL,* 33:598: "unde sciremus esse civitates, ubi numquam fuimus; vel a Romulo conditam Romam, vel, ut de proprioribus loquar, Constantinopolim a Constantino." Alfred omits all reference to Constantinople.

38. See *OE Orosius* 37/19-20 and 40/4 and 26-28, and *Alfred's Boethius* 34/31-35/2. Tarquinius Superbus is of course mentioned in a large number of Latin texts, e.g., Livy, Orosius, and Florus. Boethius (II, pr. 6) merely comments: "Your ancestors wanted to abolish the consulship because of the arrogance of the consuls, just as before that the same arrogance had led them to abolish the title of king."

39. *Alfred's Boethius* 66/23-29, referring to Seneca as "magister 7 fostorfæder"; Boethius III, pr. 5, referring to him as "familiarem praeceptoremque." Tacitus in the *Annals* (*P. Cornelii Taciti Libri qui supersunt,* ed. E. Koestermann [Leipzig, 1969], XV.lxiii) describes Seneca as making an incision in his own and his wife's arms with a single cut, then as cutting his own legs. In Chapter lxiv he is said to drink poison, to take a bath, and then to enter a vapor stove, in which he finally suffocates to death.

40. *Alfred's Boethius* 65/27-66/1. Horace, in the *Carmina* (*Q. Horati Flacci Opera,* ed. F. Klingner [Leipzig, 1959], III.1.17), tells the story without reference to the hair; certain commentaries on Horace, however, are more explicit, as, e.g., Pseudo-Acron: "tyrannus a culmine iussit ligatum seta pendere": see *Acronis et Porphyrionis Commentarii in Q. Horatium Flaccum,* ed. F. Hauthal (Berlin, 1864-66; rpt. 1966). Cicero (*Tusculan Disputations,* ed. J. E. King [London, 1945], V. 21) refers to a horse hair.

41. See *OE Orosius,* 28/13-16. The translator apparently does not know the story of the dispatching in tribute of seven youths and seven maidens, which he could have read in Servius *Aeneid* III.74 among other possible sources. Potter ("Commentary," p. 397) would also convict the author of the *Old English Orosius* of "a flagrantly erroneous addition" in describing Troy as "Creca burg" in 38/31-39/1. However, Troy, or Ilium, was in a part of Alexander the Great's "Creca rice" and subsequently belonged to the Byzantine empire.

42. Isidore, for instance, describes the labyrinth as "perplexis parietibus aedificium, qualis est apud Cretam a Daedalo factus, ubi fuit Minotauro inclusus; in quo si quis introierit sine glomere lini, exitum invenire non valet" (*Etymologies* XV.ii.36), and he goes on to describe the interior of the building; see further below, p. 44.

43. This reading is in MSS of class A. See further the forthcoming posthumous work by Dorothy Whitelock, *King Alfred,* rev. and ed. by Janet Bately and Simon Keynes.

44. And this could have been faulty. For the misattribution of certain stratagems in the *Old English Orosius* see, e.g., the story of the fight between Cyrus and Astyages (33/15-19), where the stratagem described by Justinus (*Iuniani Iustini Epitoma Historiarum Philippicarum Pompei Trogi,* ed. O. Seel after F. Ruehl [Leipzig, 1956], I.vi.10-11) as carried out by Astyages is attributed to Cyrus; and *OE Orosius* 102/18-20, where it appears that details of a stratagem employed by Marcellus, an officer of Marius (fl. 102 B.C.) are attributed to another Marcellus (fl. 216 B.C.): see *Iuli Frontini Strategematon Libri IV,* ed. G. Gundermann (Leipzig, 1888), II.iv.6.

45. See Janet Bately, "King Alfred and the Latin MSS of Orosius' History," *Classica et Mediaevalia,* 22 (1961), 97, and *OE Orosius,* 84/8-11 and commentary. However, the description of the Dead Sea Fruit (*OE Orosius* 23/7-11), an insertion concerning which is found in a number of MSS of Orosius's *History,* but not those closest to the Old English version, may well take its material from Bede *De Locis Sanctis* (in *PL,* 94:1187).

46. See *OE Orosius* 125/12. For Ancona as Cinna the soldier's deathplace, see *De Viris Illustribus* (in *Sexti Aurelii Victoris Liber de Caesaribus,* ed. F. Pichlmayr [Leipzig, 1911; rpt. 1970], 69.4); for Smyrna and Cinna the poet see, e.g., Servius *Bucolics* IX.35 and *Georgics* I.288, and *Catulli Veronensis Liber,* ed. Mauritius Schuster (Leipzig, 1940), *Carmina* XCV.1

47. See H. T. Silverstein, "Chaucer's Brutus Cassius," *Modern Language Notes,* 47 (1932), 148-50.

48. See Fabio Troncarelli, *Tradizioni perdute: la 'Consolatio philosophiae' nell'alto medioevo,* Medioevo e umanesimo, 42 (Padova, 1981). Chaucer in his translation

of Boethius (*Works,* ed. F. N. Robinson, 2nd ed. [London, 1974], pp. 155-57) here writes: "[Thou] hast so woven me with thi resouns the hous of Dedalus, so entrelaced that it is unable to ben unlaced." For arguments that Alfred did not use the commentary in Vatican 3363, see Bately, *The Literary Prose,* p. 16, and Wittig, passim.

49. Alfred would not necessarily have had to look to a commentary on Boethius for his interpretation of *corona* as *heafodbeag gyldenne* (see Josef Kirschner, *Die Bezeichnungen für Kranz und Krone im Altenglischen* [München, 1975], p. 165, n. 106). Glossaries could have provided this information: see *Leiden Glossary* XXI.5: "cum coronis: circulis aureis in capitibus eorum significantes uictoriam eius"; and as compared to Wærferth's Gregory (*Bischof Wærferths von Worcester Übersetzung der Dialoge Gregors des Grössen,* ed. H. Hecht [Leipzig, 1900, 1907; rpt. Darmstadt, 1965], 343/15): "twegen oflæthlafas on beagwisan abacene" (*Dialogues* IV.55 "duas ... oblationum coronas"), see *Leiden* XXXIX.43: "Duas coronas: ii panes pertussos similes corone."

50. Translation mine. It must be remembered that Isidore was frequently used verbatim by later commentaries and glossaries.

51. See *Alfred's Soliloquies,* p. 103; and for descriptions of Theodosius as good see *OE Orosius* 152/20 and 153/25, and Orosius VII.xxxiv.7.

52. Could information linking Augustine with Honorius perhaps be derived from a "Life of Augustine," if such were available in England at the time? See *PL,* 33:44: "... jubente gloriosissimo et religiosissimo imperatore Honorio."

The Preservation and Transmission of Greek in Early England

MARY CATHERINE BODDEN

Why, in their literature, did the Anglo-Saxons preserve the occurrences of a language which few of them professed to know? What was its value to them? And how knowledgeably was it preserved?[1]

The Anglo-Saxons had, actually, a good many reasons for preserving Greek. They knew, in fact, that most of their Latin Biblical and patristic literature derived from Greek sources. Jerome's commentaries on the Old Testament and Augustine's commentaries on the Gospels and the Psalter frequently discuss the Greek terms of the original texts. Next to the Gospels and the Psalter, in fact, commentaries seem to have been among the most valued texts in the Early English monastic curriculum.[2] The Early English collection of canons, the penitentials, and conciliar records all reflect the profound part that the Greek language and in some instances Greek customs[3] had exercised in the early growth of the Church at Rome and later in the English Church. A conciliar record in Trinity MS. B.16.44 (405),[4] for example, preserves a notice that Pope Silvester, through a certain Victor and Vincent, sent to the synod eighty capitula, "namely, forty published by the Greeks in the Greek tongue, and forty published by the Latins in the Latin tongue." This sort of documentation reminds us of the danger of schism courted by the technical differences in Greek and Latin theological vocabularies. One need only consider the terms "filioque" and "ousia" to recall the disastrous consequences which could hang upon a single word. The attention which Jerome, Augustine, and Ambrose lavished upon Greek words in their sources reflects the same concern.[5]

Within the monastic practice itself, the preservation of Greek had several purposes. The Good Friday Liturgy, once bilingual,[6] continued in the tenth century to instruct deacons, standing before the cross, to sing in Greek "AGIOS O THEUS, AGIOS YSCORROS, AGIOS ATHANATOS, ELEYSON YMAS."[7] The schola was to answer in Latin; twice more this Greek and Latin alternation was repeated by the deacons and schola. It may be argued that the pontificals ultimately inherited their ceremonies from the earlier Greek Liturgy used in Rome until the fourth century and that, therefore, they may not accurately reflect an *English* interest in a bilingual Liturgy. However, the chief document of the tenth-century monastic revival in England, the *Regularis Concordia,* calls for the same bilingual ceremony before the cross during the Parasceve Liturgy.[8] In Bodleian MS. Auct. F.4.32, a ninth-century text of Welsh origin but containing tenth-century English interpolations, there are nine folios of bilingual Old Testament readings and Easter lessons. Amalarius of Metz suggests two reasons for the practice of the bilingual Liturgy. He writes: "The Greeks were those among whom the Latin tongue was unknown and the Latins were those among whom the Greek tongue was unknown. The other reason is that the people were one together with each other."[9] This seems to be an embarrassingly simple observation. However, his point is that there was a community of Greeks and Latins neither of whom knew the other's tongue but both of whom required the same ceremony. And evidence of this practice seems deliberately to have been preserved in English manuscripts.

Greek alphabets are literally ubiquitous in Anglo-Saxon manuscripts. They appear written sometimes after a prayer, or squeezed into a margin or alongside a calendar, penned between rows of runes, or scribbled at the end of the codex. They were valued, it seems, by Biblical exegetes who "sought a key to the numerical symbolism of the Apocalypse"[10] or (as in Cambridge, Trinity College MS. O.7.41, a computus by Marian the Scot) were included as numerical values for the names of the pagan gods.[11] Bishops occasionally required the Greek alphabet in the Liturgy for the consecration of a church.[12] Most pontificals, in their directions for the blessing of a church, require inscribing on its pavement the alphabet in the form of the Andreas cross (thus: X).[13] BL Add. MS. 57337, 67ᵛ7f. contains the same direction; but just below these directions, in the bottom margin, is the Greek alphabet—meant, obviously, to be used in the consecration formula.[14] Bernhard Bischoff notes the same procedure in certain Continental manuscripts.[15]

However, it was not solely the example of the Church Fathers, nor the appearance of Greek in their conciliar records and Liturgy, which encouraged the Anglo-Saxons to preserve that language even when the letters frequently seem to have meant nothing to them. They had, in fact, the more immediate example of those educators of the past who figured so largely in their curriculum. Boethius, for example, retained dozens of Greek quotations and phrases in nearly all his translations. Cassiodorus constantly examines Greek words in the *Institutiones,* and Isidore's *Etymologiae* contains Greek words on nearly every other folio. Nor does this brief survey even begin to take note of the work of such writers as Macrobius, Martianus Capella, and Vitruvius, whose works contain hundreds of Greek phrases and terms. Finally, England's own native scholars—Bede, Aldhelm, Alcuin and Byrhtferth—all included generous sprinklings of Greek in their works, especially those by Bede and Byrhtferth.[16]

As to the value of Greek, the Early English had inherited a set of reasons for respecting both the Greek language and those who were proficient in it. In the first place, as we have seen, the Church Fathers bear witness to its value. Augustine, in fact, specifically argues that the meanings of Scripture are much clearer in Greek. In *De Trinitate* (Book I.vi), for example, he distinguishes between "serving" a creature and serving a creator. The intended difference, he points out, is not so clear in the Latin "servire" as it is in the Greek λατρεύω. Many Latin codices, he continues, contain this distinction, though some do not; yet all or nearly all of the Greek sources, he emphasizes, clearly have it. Jerome's constant revision of the Psalter and other books of the Bible reflects the value he assigned to the Greek versions. Eventually, however, as Amalarius of Metz records,[17] Jerome lamented the inadequacies of both Latin and Greek to express the Hebrew original, and he regarded the Psalmist's words "Praise to you Lord, King of eternal glory.... How shall we sing the song of the Lord in a foreign land?" as a comment upon those inadequacies.[18]

Second, Greek was valued because its mastery was considered a sign of great erudition. Vespasian and Hadrian were said to have known Greek; so was Charlemagne, although it is quite unlikely. Paul the Deacon in the *Historia Romana* regards the knowledge of Greek as the sign of great minds and rulers. Even the learning of the Greek alphabet is given an additional moral advantage: in a passage on Theodosius, Paul cites an anecdote about Augustus who, apparently, was easily moved to anger. Because of this failing, a certain philosopher worried lest he make rash decisions in the heat of anger and advised Augustus that whenever he began to become angry, he should repeat by memory the twenty-four letters of the Greek alphabet; with the passage of time his ire would cool.[19] Bede, in the *Historia Ecclesiastica,* particularly notes those early educators who knew Greek; and

Gregory the Great, who seemed almost perversely to love the simple style and the simple-minded, recounts in his *Dialogues* the story of a young boy, simple in mind, who died of the plague and returned to life to visit his master so as to give him the names of those other monks who were to die next of the plague. As proof of the boy's telling the truth, he now spoke in Greek.[20]

On the other hand, "esteem for Greek was not ... a universal heritage throughout the Middle Ages."[21] Gregory, although he had endowed the young boy with "conversational Greek" as a heavenly sign, reverts to self when, as Pope, he states that he neglected to answer a letter because the person who wrote the letter had written it in Greek when, in fact, his native language was Latin: "Quia cum sit latina graece scripsit."[22] And as McGuire records in *Introduction to Medieval Latin Studies,* "In a querulous exchange of letters, Pope Nicolas saw fit to remind the Byzantine Emperor Michael III, that Latin, a language that God made, occupies the first place in the inscription on the Cross."[23]

How knowledgeably was Greek preserved by the Anglo-Saxons? The knowledgeable preservation of any concept and its articulation, or of any language and its grammatical forms, is determined solely through a study of its transmission. The validity of documenting the transmission of any text depends upon there surviving to us several copies of that text. We have preserved to us over a thousand manuscripts known to be of Anglo-Saxon provenance or use or ownership. Surprisingly enough, however, of these thousand manuscripts, apart from the Gospels, Psalter, the works of the Church Fathers (Jerome, Augustine, and Ambrose), and the works of Prudentius, Gregory, Bede, Aldhelm, Alfred and Ælfric, remarkably few of the remaining manuscripts preserve more than one or two copies of individual texts. This situation limits dramatically the field for study of the transmission of texts.

More than five hundred of these manuscripts contain Greek matter. So much, then, for the classicist who, writing about a Greek charm in an early Old English prayerbook, asked, "When a tree falls in the forest when there is no one around to hear it, is there any sound? When a scribe copies Greek in an England that understands no Greek is there any comprehension?"[24] Nevertheless, although we possess such a wealth of manuscripts containing Greek matter, the primary means for studying the transmission of any language requires that there be available a reasonable amount of continuous prose (or poetry). Single words do not really demonstrate the compiler's knowledge of a language; the very individuality of the word renders it impossible to show relationship between words or to reveal the hierarchy of meaning represented by inflection and syntax. Few texts contain continuous Greek prose. Of these, moreover, even fewer are preserved in more than one copy. We have, in fact, only one text which conforms to the two chief conditions for the study of language transmission: namely, that the text survive in a reasonable number of copies, and that within it there be several samples of continuous Greek prose. That text is Boethius' *De Consolatione Philosophiae*. Fourteen Latin copies of Early English provenance remain, and one vernacular version. I have examined eleven of these copies,[25] and have information concerning three others. Not only are they fairly revealing about the problems which the Anglo-Saxons seem to have had in copying Greek, but they offer as well valuable clues to the sort of scribal activity occurring on the Continent and its relationship to English scriptoria.

There are eight instances of continuous Greek "prose" in the text of the *De Consolatione Philosophiae*.[26] Figure 1 shows the first occurrence as it appears in all the English extant Latin copies of the text. It is an excellent example of the mistakes, guesses, changes, and interpolations involved in the written transmission of a literature whose language is unfamiliar to the scribe or to the scholar directing him. The following is a general and deliberately simplified six-step analysis of the corruption involved in the transmission of this Greek sentence.

The first Greek line of the original reads: 'ΕΞΑΎΔΑ, ΜΉ ΚΕΎΘΕ ΝῸΩ, that is, "speak out, do not conceal your thoughts." Of the seven manuscripts containing 'ΕΞΑΎΔΑ, five have acquired the letters NH — a possible duplication of MH? Auct. F.1.15 and BN Lat. 6401 A, originating in the same scriptorium, do not have these letters.

Second, in the first four manuscripts (only one of which is identified as a Canterbury manuscript[27]), which are closely related, in fact, to the Abingdon copy CUL Kk. 3.21 and to CCCC 214, the third word, ΚΕΎΘΕ, has lost its upsilon, and the word ΝΟΩ has lost its first letter, *nu,* becoming somehow ΟΔΥC.

Third, manuscripts six and seven, Bodley Auct. F.1.15 and BN Lat. 6401 A, have kept fairly intact their first three words. In BN Lat. 6401 A, however, the final epsilon has been construed to read *mu,* that is, the early medieval form of *mu* consisting of two inverted parenthesis signs joined by a bar, thus:)─(.

Fourth, the gloss "confitere" must have suggested to a reader (undoubtedly a Continental one) another Greek word meaning "confess," namely, 'ΕΞΟΜΟΛΟΓΈW, or its middle form 'ΕΞΟΜΟΛΟΓΟΎΜΑΙ, whose aorist imperative would be 'ΕΞΟΜΟΛΟΓΟΎ. Majuscule gamma and rho are frequently confused in successive transcriptions and the -oy ending easily lends itself to an omega, particularly when the majuscule upsilon is either broadly written or replaced with an iota, as KOIPΛNOC and BΛCIΛEIC in Figure 2 demonstrate. Minuscule omega, the usual form for patristic and early medieval Greek, was frequently interchanged with omicron. See EΞWMOΛOPW and KOIPΛNWC in Figures 1 and 2, respectively.[28]

Moreover, 'EΞOMOΛOΓΈW had a common liturgical use. It was the opening word for any Greek formulaic confession of faith and the opening word, too, for Greek eucharistic prayers. In monasteries such as St. Gall or Laon, which collected and produced Greek liturgical texts in the eighth and ninth centuries, 'EΞOMOΛOΓΈW might have been as familiar to their scribes as *agios* and *eleyson* would be to us.

Fifth, "mihi" completes the phrase "confitere mihi" and this phrase appears above nearly every manuscript containing the word 'EΞOMOΛOΓO (-ΓW).

Sixth, and finally, EMEN (i.e., ῾HMÍN, 1st pl.d.) replaces the negative particle MḤ, while KAI ("and") and OYΘENOIEN ("ne abscondas" intended?) replace KEŶΘE NOΩ. Thus, the substituted reading now becomes EΞOMOΛOΓOY HMIN, i.e., "confess to us" (as distinct from the Latin gloss: "confess to me").

Of the fourteen English manuscripts, then, ten retain the original EΞAYΔA. Two of these ten, BN Lat. 14380 and El Escorial E.II.1, have glosses reading EΞOMOΛOΓO. Three other manuscripts—Bodmer C.B. 175, Trinity 0.3.7, and BN Lat. 17814—read EΞOMOΛOPW (-PΛ) in their texts. A fourth, BN Lat. 6401, reads EΞOMOΛOΓO. Bodmer, Trinity, and BN Lat. 17814 are, all three, presumed to be Canterbury manuscripts. Bodmer and Trinity are closely related to each other while BN Lat. 17814 appears to be more closely related to the Continental versions.

One manuscript bridges both the English and the Continental groups: Paris BN Lat. 14380. It has the complete EΞAYΔA sentence in its text, and EΞOMOΛOPW in its margin. BN Lat. 14380 is also assigned to Canterbury, Christ Church and slightly postdates Bodmer and Trinity. The fact that its marginal gloss is identical to their texts suggests that its source was either the same Canterbury manuscript or its antecedent from which Bodmer and Trinity were copied.

What does this say about scribal activity? As Figure 1 shows, the Abingdon text, Antwerp MS 190, has picked up in its gloss the text of BN Lat. 6401 A, the manuscript thought to be from Canterbury. In fact, Antwerp is related in several instances to Auct. F.1.15 which is a near-twin of BN Lat. 6401 A. If these texts assigned to Canterbury prove to be un-

MANUSCRIPTS	FOLIO		ἘΞΆΥΔΑ, ΜΉ ΚΕΪΘΕ ΝΌΩ.
1. Antwerp P-M.190 (s.x/xi Abngdon)	7r3	fles? Quid lacrimis manas?	Εzαι ΛΛΙ-ϯ+ΝΗ ΚΗΘΗΟΔΙC *marg. gloss:* εξαγαμηκϝογ:ΗΝΟΔΙC
2. CUL Kk. 3.21 (s.x/xi Abngdon)	6r10	fles? Quid lacrimis manas?	Εzαι ΛΔυ-CΗ+ΝΗ ΚΗ ΘΗΟΔΥC
3. CCCC 214 (s.xi in.)	4r5	"	Εzαι ΛΛυ-CΗΝΗ ΚΑ ΘΗΟΔΥC
4. CUL Gg.5.35 (s.xi med.CaA)	172v3f	"	ΕzΔΙΛΛυ-C+ΝΗ+ ΚΗΘΗΟ:ΔΥC
5. B.N. Lat.14380 (s.x ex. CaCC)	5r14f	"	εzαγ//λα ΤC ΗΝΗ ΚΪΟϒ ΘΗΝΟΔΥC. *marg. gloss:* εzομολορω·εΜΙΝ·και·ογθεΝΟΙεΝ
6. BOD.Auct.F.1.15 (s.x² CaA)	9r15	"	εzΔΥΔΛΛΜΗ ΚεΟϒΘεΝΙΛΙ
7. B.N. Lat.6401 A (s.x ex.CaCC)	6r12	"	εzΔΥΔΛΜΗΚΓΟΥΖ-εΝΟΔΙC.
8. BODM.C.B. 175 (s.x² Ctby?)	7v2	"	εξωμολορω·εΜεΝ·και·ογθεΝΟΙεΝ·
9. TRIN. 0.3.7 (s.x² CaA)	4v7	"	εzομολορω·εΜεΝ·και·ογθεΝΟΙεΝ·
10. B.N.Lat.17814 (s. x ex.Ctby?)	14v8f	"	εΞΟΜΟΔΟΡΔ· εΜεΗ·//και· Ογθ ΕΝΟΕΝ· *marg. gloss:* Εzοογο·/δογω/ΗΛΛΗϒ·και·ογεε ΝΤωC
11. B.N. Lat. 6401 (s. x ex.)	18v25	"	εzομολοτο εΜεΝ·και· ΟϒΘεΝΟΙεΝ·
12. El Escorial E.II.1 (s. x/xi Horton)	14r18	"	ΕΖΛΥΛΜΗ· ΚΕΟΥΘΕ *marg. gloss (doppel):* εzομολορΜ·/εΜΙΝΗ·Κει·οι·Δ/οεΝεΛ
13. Vat.lat. 3363 (s. ix¹ Loire)	4r16f	"	εzαγ· ΛΔrCΗΝΗΚΕΟΥ/ ΘΗΟΔΥC. *marg. gloss:* εzογΛΔΛΝΙ ΤΥΟΥ ΝΟΥ

Fig. 1.

		ΕἿΣ ΚΟΊΡΑΝΟΣ ἘΣΤΊΝ, ΕἿΣ ΒΑΣΙΛΕΎΣ
ANTWERP P-M 190	14r3	εις κοιρανος εςτιν εις και βαςιλεις
CUL Kk.3.21	12r3f.	ΕΙC ΚΟΙΡΑΝΟC ΕC ΤΙΝ ΕΙC ΒαCΙΛΕΙC
CCCC 214	10r5f	εις κοιρανος ες τιν εις / βαςιλεις
CUL Gg. 5.35	174v31	εις κοιρανος ες τινεις βαςιλεις
BOD. AUCT. F.1.15	13v7	εις · κοιρανως · εςτιν · βαςιλεις · εις
B.N. Lat.6401 A	11v16f	εις ·/ κοιρανως · εςτιν · βαςιλεις · εις ·
BODMER C.B. 175	14r1	εις κουρανος · εςτινεις · βαςιλεyς ·
TRIN. 0.3.7	7r17	εις κουραν ος · εςτιν · εις βαςιλεις
EL ESCORIAL E.II.1	21v3f	εις ͜κ ͜οιραλη͡ιος · εςτιν · εις · βαςιλε/εyς
VAT. Lat. 3363	7r22f	εις κοιρανος εςτ ιν εις / βαςιλεyς ·

Fig. 2:

questionably from Canterbury, several conclusions can be drawn: First, Canterbury was an extremely active scriptorium, particularly at the end of the tenth century. Seven out of the ten manuscripts of Boethius's *De Consolatione Philosophiae* are thought to have been produced there, and of the seven, six were copied at the end of the tenth century; the seventh is from the eleventh century. Second, Canterbury seems to have had close contacts with Continental scriptoria. ΕΞΟΜΟΛΟΓΟ originated on the Continent, and of the extant English manuscripts, those from Canterbury alone contain the term in their text. (BN Lat. 6401 may be a Continental manuscript.) Third, Antwerp's relationship with BN Lat. 6401 A, Auct. F.1.15, Bodmer, and Trinity, and especially Antwerp's gloss's unusual identity with the text in BN Lat. 6401 A are strong indications that Canterbury was exporting manuscripts to other English scriptoria.[29]

What other evidence, then, have we of the preservation and transmission of Greek in early England? There are, of course, hundreds of Early English manuscript volumes containing Greek glosses. Glosses can be a secondary means of studying transmission, particularly should any be identical to and derived from apparently unrelated or remotely related texts. They are, in fact, a valuable index to the Greek vocabulary amassed by the Anglo-Saxons. As a systematic indication of Anglo-Saxon knowledge of Greek, however, their value is limited except in instances in which they retain, in translation, the inflection and form of the Greek forms.

In this article, I had intended to examine as well vernacular versions of Latin texts containing Greek matter. The task, however, has turned out to be disproportionate in effort and somewhat paltry in results. It deserves a more thorough treatment later. So far, however, the situation seems to be as follows. There are, of course, Anglo-Saxon works in Latin which contain an occasional Greek word or two. Unfortunately, however, either these works became paraphrased in their vernacular versions, dropping altogether their few Greek phrases, e.g., the Old English version of Boethius' *De Consolatione Philosophiae,* or we have no extant vernacular version at all of many English Latin works containing Greek, e.g., the works of Vitruvius or Macrobius. The vernacular versions of Gregory the Great's *Dialogues* seem to be a compromise; that is, some of the Greek terms are preserved, and some are translated into Old English. In Book III, Par. 35, the Latin, translated, reads, "Among the patients there was one who had lost his mind, a phrenetic, to use the Greek medical term." The Old English renders it: "þa witodlice læg þær sum man on his mode gefangen mid ungewittignesse betwyh þam oðrum soecum mannum, þone swylcne soecne læcas nemniað gewitleasne."[30] Two texts which retain with a fair consistency the Greek terms inherited in their sources are Ælfric's *Grammar* and the Pseudo-Apuleius *Herbarium* along with those texts which usually circulated with it, namely, Dioscorides' *Liber Medicinae* and Sextus Placitus' *Medicina de Quadrupedibus*. But the majority of these terms in Ælfric's *Grammar* are rhetorical and (much as with the medical terms in the treatises) had been Latinized for centuries. A single example in Ælfric is typical of the terms: In the section on conjunctions, he writes: "Sum synd gehatene ENCLITICAE on grecisc, þæt is on leden inclinitivae, and on englisc ahyldenlice"; or when speaking of sentences, he writes, "Sum is gecweden ortographia on grecisc, þæt is on leden recta scriptura and on englisc riht gewrit."[31]

Finally, one of the few instances of Greek which the Anglo-Saxons seem to have made an effort to retain in their vernacular versions is that of the medical charm. What is interesting about Greek charms is that they are often palindromes, i.e., capable of being read backwards and forwards. Apparently, in the Greek East, it has been found, "Palindromic texts are closely associated with magic charms."[32] This makes sense (if magic can be said to make sense) because a palindrome obviously emphasizes the actual physical properties of a word, that is, its visual appearance and its sound, particularly sound at its most elemental. It is that sort of unique perspective about language, namely the interest in its physical features, apart from its communicating components, that unites charms, poetry, and even prayers. I've chosen therefore to end this article with one such Greek charm preserved in BL Royal 2. A. xx (s.viii Worcester) because it reminds one of so many wonderful sense-staggering lines in Anglo-Saxon poetry. Translated, the Greek charm ἀμήσας ἄρδην ὀροφηφόρον ἥδρασα σῆμα[33] reads thus: "Having reaped, I established a lofty-roofed monument"!! How this charm might have cured anyone — Greek or Anglo-Saxon — is an uncertainty with which we will have to live.

MARQUETTE UNIVERSITY

Notes

1. At the moment, there is not available to any student or scholar a single source or collection which discusses in any systematic way the evidence of Greek in Anglo-Saxon manuscripts. There exist, at most, six or seven fine articles on *some* Greek in *some* manuscripts, but these articles span some forty years and occur in a variety

of Continental and North American journals. Below are listed the more recent of these articles: Michael Lapidge, "The Hermeneutic Style in Tenth-Century Anglo-Saxon Literature," *ASE,* 4 (1975), 67-111; Anna Carlotta Dionisotti, "On Bede, Grammars, and Greek," *Revue Bénédictine,* 92 (1982), 111-41; Michael W. Herren, *The Hisperica Famina: I. The A-Text* (Toronto, 1974). Only one brief chapter is devoted to English materials in Walter Berschin's *Griechisch-lateinisches Mittelalter von Hieronymus zu Nikolaus von Keus* (Bern, 1980); Berschin's book tends to be anecdotal (in an informative way) rather than analytical about Greek materials in England and on the Continent. For Continental studies, Bernhard Bischoff ("Das griechische Element in der abendländischen Bildung des Mittelalters," *Mittelalterliche Studien,* 2 [Stuttgart, 1967], 246-74) offers a basic and wide survey of the types of Greek materials in (mostly) Continental libraries. Bernice M. Kaczynski ("Greek Learning in the Medieval West: A Study of St. Gall, 816-1022," [microform] Diss. Yale University 1975) raises some excellent questions about the knowledge of Greek on the Continent; and Edouard Jeauneau ("Jean Scot Érigène et le Grec," *Archivum Latinitatis Medii Aevi,* 41 [1979], 5-50) examines sources available to John Scottus.

2. From the evidence of what remains to us, first from the eighth century in Northumbria, then later at St. Augustine's in Canterbury, and again in the late eleventh century at Durham, Canterbury, Exeter, and particularly at Salisbury, commentaries must have been continuously copied and produced. Between Augustine and Jerome alone, there are nearly fifty surviving manuscripts containing their commentaries; this does not include their theological tracts. See Helmut Gneuss, "Preliminary List of Manuscripts Written or Owned in England up to 1100," *ASE,* 9 (1981), 1-60.

3. For example, in Brussels, Bibliothèque royale MS. 8558-63, 147ʳ10 ff., Greek and Roman behavior as part of Sunday propriety is cited. The Greeks and Romans, it seemed, rowed and rode on Sundays, but the English were allowed to do neither, except to ride to church. As for writing on Sunday, "ne eac grecas nellað openlice writan on ðam dagum, ac gif hwylc nyd þearf bið þonne willað hy digellice writan in heora husum."

4. Cambridge, Trinity College MS. B.16.44 (405) s.xi ex. CaCC, p. 215, ll. 23-25.

5. Augustine *De Trinitate* Bk.I.vi. ed. W. J. Mountain, in CCSL 50 (Turnhout, 1968), p. 43: "ubi iubemur non servire creaturae sed creatori, non eo modo quo iubemur per caritatem servire invicem, quod est graece δουλεύειν sed eo modo quo tantum deo servitur, quod est graece λατρεύειν."

6. On the bilingual liturgy, Ordo XXX B (Ordo of St. Amand), 41 instructs: "Deinde secuntur lectiones et cantica seu oraciones, tam grece quam latine, sicut ordinem habent" (in Michel Andrieu, ed., *Les Ordines Romani du haut moyen âge,* Spicilegium sacrum Lovaniense, 24 [Louvain, 1959], III, 472; note also Ordo XXIII 26, in Andrieu, p. 275. See also Bonifatius Fischer, "Die Lesungen der römischen Ostervigil unter Gregor D. Gr.," in *Colligere Fragmenta: Festschrift Alban Dold,* Texte und Arbeiten hg. durch die Erzabtei Beuron, Abt. I, hft. 2 (Beuron, 1952), pp. 144-59.

7. Rouen, Bibliothèque municipale MS. 1385 (U.107) 27ʳ4 ff.

8. The *Regularis Concordia* is preserved in London, BL Faustina B.iii (the specific lines occur at 184ʳ9 ff.) and in BL Tiberius A.iii (specific lines at 18ᵛ10 ff.).

9. Amalarius is led to this observation while explaining the reason for there being twelve lections in both Greek and Latin. The quote is taken from Cambridge, Trinity College MS. B.11.2(241) 44ʳ ff. Cf. *Amalarii Episcopi Opera Liturgica Omnia*, Vol. II: *Liber Officialis,* ed. John Michael Hanssens, Studi e Testi 139 (Vatican City, 1948), Book II.1.1.

10. Kaczynski, p. 107.

11. Cambridge, Trinity College MS. O.7.41 (1369) 1ʳ12 f.

cccix	cccLiii	dcxii
APNC [APHC]	HP)-(HC	ZHYC

dc ccc xciii		dx
AΦPWΔYΘH		KPW)-(WC

12. Kaczynski, pp. 107 and 109.

13. For example, the Sherborne Pontifical, BN Lat. 943, 13ᵛ24-14ʳ3, the eleventh-century pontifical from Crediton, Rouen B.M. MS. 368 (A.27), 7ʳ10 f., and CCCC MS. 163, 209ʳ.

14. The alphabet in the bottom margin of BL Add. MS. 57337, 67ᵛ7 is in a slightly later hand.

15. Bernhard Bischoff (p. 252 and n. 29) lists MSS. Angers 477 (461) 9ʳ, s.ix, and Paris, BN Lat. 9377, 20ʳ, s.xii in. I have not as yet examined all the extant pontificals in our English collection and cannot therefore give a complete figure for pontificals containing the Greek alphabet.

16. See particularly Bede *De Orthographia* and *De Arte Metrica,* and *De Temporum Ratione;* Aldhelm, *De Laudibus Virginitatis* (prose); Alcuin, *De Orthographia* and *De Dialectica;* and Byrhtferth's *Enchiridion.*

17. *Amalarii Episcopi Opera Liturgica Omnia,* Vol. II, Bk.I.l.16-17.

18. Even in the introduction to his *De Institutione Arithmetica,* Boethius pauses to comment on the value of Greek literature: "sed ea quae ex graecorum opulentia litterarum in romane orationis thesaurum sumpta conueximus" (Cambridge, Cambridge University Library MS. Kk.5.32, 1ʳ7 ff).

19. "... monuit ubi irasci coepisset quattuor atque xx grecas litteras memoria recenseret ut illa concitatio quae momenti est mente alio traducta parui temporis interiectu languesceret melior haud dubie quod est rare uirtutis" (CCCC MS. 276 39ʳ); for further comments on the status of Greek, see also fol. 35ʳ32 ff. The edition — *Pauli Diaconi: Historia Romana,* Fonti per la Storia d'Italia, Vol. 51 (Rome, 1914), Bk.II.5-15 — contains an expanded form of the anecdote.

20. Gregory the Great, *Dialogues,* Bk. IV, §27.

21. Martin R. P. McGuire and Hermigild Dressler, *Introduction to Medieval Latin Studies: A Syllabus,* 2nd ed. (Washington, D.C., 1977). The authors cite *Gregorii I Papae Registrum Epistolarum,* ed. Paul Ewald and Ludwig M. Hartmann, Vol. I (Berlin, 1891-99; rpt. 1957), pp. 224-25, and Gregory, *Epistolae,* Vol. I.

22. Gregory, *Epistolae,* I, 210.

23. *PL,* 112:932A.

24. Lloyd W. Daly, "A Greek Palindrome in Eighth-Century England," *American Journal of Philology,* 103 (1982), 95.

25. Since this article's completion I have seen Oxford, Corpus Christi College MS. 74 whose Greek texts are considerably more corrupt than the other English surviving texts. However, it preserves a mangled form of 'ΕΞΑΫΔΑ although not of the interpolated NH.

26. The two-word phrase, ΕΠΟΥ ΘΕW, has not been included in these eight instances.

27. The provenance and origin assigned to all the English manuscripts are derived from Helmut Gneuss's "Preliminary List."

28. Evangelinus A. Sophocles, *Greek Lexicon of the Roman and Byzantine Periods: B.C. 146–A.D. 1100* (New York, 1958).

29. Of the seventeen Continental manuscripts included in the research, eight contain the 'ΕΞΑΫΔΑ clause, and the other nine contain variations of 'ΕΞΟΜΟΛΟΓΈW with marginal transcriptions showing EΞΟΜΟΛΟΓESE, -ISSE, and so forth. Most of the Continental copies containing 'ΕΞΑΫΔΑ belong to the St. Gall and Munich (Clm) collections; a few are housed in the Bern Burgerbibliothek. The other nine manuscripts containing the 'ΕΞΟΜΟΛΟΓΈW version belong to the BN Lat. and Vatican Lat. collections. Two others belong, again, to Bern. However, these seventeen manuscripts represent only a fraction of the extant pre-twelfth-century texts of the *De Consolatione Philosophiae,* and no conclusion can be drawn from these few geographical details.

30. Gregory the Great, *Dialogues,* Bk. III, §35.

31. *Ælfric's Grammatik und Glossar,* ed. Julius Zupitza (Berlin, 1880), pp. 264 and 291.

32. Daly, p. 96.

33. The words actually appear in BL Royal 2 A XX as AMICO CAPΔINOPO ΦIΦIPON IΔPACACIMO.

The Venerable Bede and Hiberno-Latin Exegesis

JOSEPH F. T. KELLY

Over forty years ago Beryl Smalley pointed out the importance of Bede's exegesis:

> The Venerable Bede was better known for his commentaries on Scripture than for his *Ecclesiastical History of the English People*.... Bede himself put his commentaries on Scripture first in the list of his works; and he was typical.[1]

Ironically, Smalley herself did not treat much of Bede in her book, and few other scholars have followed her suggestion. In a recent article Roger Ray has surveyed the unhappy situation,[2] which, however, is improving, thanks largely to the increasing availability of Bede's commentaries in critical editions from *Corpus Christianorum*.[3] One point at least about Bede's exegesis has never been in doubt: his exegesis is a major point of entry to his thought, even for those concerned primarily with understanding him as an historian. Indeed, for those interested in his sources and the quality of the Jarrow library, it is invaluable.[4]

If the study of Bede's exegesis has been somewhat slow, it has far outpaced the study of Irish or, more accurately, Hiberno-Latin exegesis. This study was founded as a medieval discipline only in 1954, when Bernhard Bischoff published a list of thirty-nine early medieval texts he thought to be Irish or Irish-influenced; of equal importance, he offered a method for tracing Irish works by delineating the *characteristica* from known Irish works and identifying parallels in hitherto unclaimed, usually anonymous, texts.[5] Bischoff did not rely solely upon these parallels but used any available evidence. Although Bischoff discussed some known texts, such as the *De Mirabilibus Sacrae Scripturae* of Augustinus Hibernicus and the *Commentarius in Isaiam* of Iosephus Scottus, the majority of the texts to which he called attention were by anonymous authors and still in manuscript. Most of the texts dated to the eighth and ninth centuries with a few from the seventh century.

In general, scholars accepted Bischoff's conclusions, and further research into these texts has largely validated his initial claims.[6] For generations, the study of Irish Christianity had centered around endless expositions of a limited number of works, such as the Patrician letters, the *opera* of Columbanus, and the metaphysical speculations of John Scotus Erigena. Thanks to Bischoff, a goodly number of new texts are now available for study. These texts offer a much clearer view of the Irish use of the Church Fathers, especially since the Fathers were used in the early Middle Ages primarily for exegesis.[7] The Irish understanding of such terms as *Christus* and *ecclesia* are now clearer, for example.[8] In a recent article, Patrick Sims-Williams discussed the idea of the triad in early Irish literature, and while dealing heavily with vernacular literature, he made use of these texts.[9] Even this brief outline makes obvious the value of these texts for the study of Bede, who grew up in Irish-evangelized Northumbria and would have come into contact with Irish ideas or influences if not an Irish teacher. The Irish who evangelized in Northumbria would have used books, including books written by Irish *magistri*, to teach, and it is quite probable that some of these books would still have been available in Bede's day. These Irish books would have been in Latin, the language which united the English and Irish, since the two peoples were separated by their vernaculars.

The reverse, however, is also true. If the Irish influenced the English via Latin exegesis, the English also influenced the Irish. To be sure, the English came to Christianity and thus to Latin learning later than the Irish, but they produced the leading practitioner of the foremost intellectual discipline of the early Middle Ages in Bede the exegete, and Bede's influence on Irish writings is the second side of this research.

The previous paragraphs have outlined the possibilities of this study; this paragraph must deal with the problems. No one could have given the discipline of Hiberno-Latin exegesis a better start than Bischoff, but even he could not be certain about the dates, origins, and provenances of so many anonymous works. When two texts, one Irish, one not, have parallel passages, it is often difficult to tell in which direction the influence has gone, or even whether there is influence, or whether both are drawing from a common tradition. A second problem is that few Hiberno-Latin texts have been critically edited, whereas the Bedan corpus either has been or will be. Thus the scholar can check to see if a particular passage in Bede has a patristic source and can determine where Bede is original or may possibly be borrowing from a yet-undetected source. (I am not implying that the CCSL editors of Bede have gotten all the sources; a surprising number were overlooked in the edition of the Lukan commentary.) When Irish works have been critically edited, scholars will be able to check the passages unique to the Irish, and then to check them against Bede. In my recent study of "The Venerable Bede and the Irish Exegetical Tradition on the Apocalypse," for example, I used parallel passages to demonstrate that both Bede and the anonymous exegete drew from a common Insular tradition on that Biblical book.[10] Although Bede's commentary is available only in Migne's uncritical edition,[11] at least both works were brief. Such work could not be done with large, unedited texts.

Let us now turn to the specific topic of Bede and Irish exegesis. The starting point is a simple one: locate parallel passages in Bede's works and in the Irish works. These parallel passages will then fall into one of four categories: 1) both Bede and the Irish are citing a known third source, almost always a Church Father; 2) Bede is citing an Irish work; 3) an Irish exegete is citing Bede; 4) both are drawing from a common tradition or a yet-undetected source. We will consider each of these possibilities separately and in two ways: first, for the determination of sources; and second, for their historical value.

The first category of parallel passages seems fairly obvious, both writers citing an identifiable third source; but as is so often the case with the "obvious" in medieval studies, the situation is somewhat complicated. For example, it is quite possible that one early medieval writer's use of the patristic source was the vehicle for the other writer's use, something which can be determined only by examining how the source was used. If both Bede and an Irish writer used Augustine's *De Consensu Evangelistarum* on a regular basis, it is likely that when they agree they are both citing Augustine. If, however, the Irishman uses the work only sporadically and his citations correspond to passages used by Bede, the Anglo-Saxon and not the African may be the source. And, of course, there is the real possibility that one or both were using *florilegia*. In my study on Apocalypse exegesis I found that for one passage (Apocalypse 8:10-11) the use of one word proved that Bede and not Primasius was the source for an Irish exegete.[12]

The second category, Bede's use of Irish writers, is perhaps the most interesting for students of Bede because it offers a new source for his works. There is no doubt that Bede used Irish works. In 1973 the late Robert E. McNally edited two Hiberno-Latin commentaries on the Catholic Epistles.[13] Thanks to references in one commentary to some Irish oral teachers, he could prove that the anonymous Irish exegete composed the commentary in southern Ireland between 650 and 685, considerably earlier than Bede's commentary on the Catholic epistles, which dates ca. 709,[14] and which was long thought to be the oldest Latin commentary on those Biblical books. After establishing the chronological priority of the Irish work, McNally then showed that there were parallel passages between it and Bede's work where there was no patristic source, and he concluded that Bede knew this work, a conclusion which no one has challenged.[15] Using only literary evidence, McNally further argued that the treatment of certain passages shows a development from the first Irish work through the second one (attributed to a Hilarius or, as McNally calls him, Pseudo-Hilary) to Bede. He concluded that Bede knew and used both Irish commentaries.[16]

The problem is more complicated for Gospel exegesis since only one commentary can be safely dated to the seventh century, the *Expositio Quattuor Evangeliorum* attributed to Jerome in the Middle Ages so that scholars refer to its author as Pseudo-Jerome.[17] Both Bruno Griesser[18] and Bernhard Bischoff[19] have argued for its Irish provenance, and Bernard Lambert in his magisterial catalogue of Hieronymian pseudepigrapha also considers it Irish.[20] Its date is usually given as late seventh or early eighth century, but even if the latter is correct, the nature of the work makes it certain that it includes seventh-century material. The *Expositio* has all the appearance of a ready-reference manual — a word or two of Scripture followed by a word or two of allegorizing or moralizing interpretation taken usually from the Latin Fathers. Not all the interpretations, however, are drawn from the Fathers, and some are Irish in origin. The work is an unabashed compilation, and the compiler drew from a variety of earlier sources, so if the work does date to the early eighth century, it still gives us a look at Irish gospel exegesis that antedates Bede's commentary on Luke, written ca. 715, and his commentary on Mark, written ca. 725.

The following citations demonstrate that Bede knew either the *Expositio* or the Irish tradition which stood behind it. Bede deals with Luke 3:17; Pseudo-Jerome with a parallel passage, Matthew 3:12; neither draws from a patristic source.

> *Cuius ventilabrum in manu eius et purgabit aream suam.* Per ventilabrum, id est, palam, discretio iusti examinis per aream vero praesens ecclesia figuratur. (Bede *In Lucam* I. iii. 17)[21]
> *Cuius ventilabrum,* et reliqua: Id est, iustum iudicium; in manu, id est, in potestate; *area,* id est, mundus vel Ecclesia. (Pseudo-Hieronymus *Exp. IV Evv.*)[22]

These citations deal with Luke 19:14.

> *Cives autem eius oderant illum et miserunt legationem post illum dicentes: Nolumus hunc regnare super nos.* Cives impios Iudaeos dicit de quibus alibi protestatur: *Nunc autem et viderunt et oderunt et me et patrem meum.* Qui non solum praesentem usque ad mortem crucis oderant sed etiam post resurrectionem eius miserunt persecutionem apostolis et praedicationem regni caelestis spreverunt. (Bede *In Lucam* V. xix. 14)[23]
> *Cives eius*: Id est, Iudaei. *Miserunt legationem*: id est, occisionem apostolorum. (Pseudo-Hieronymus *Exp. IV Evv.*)[24]

In regard to Bede's Markan commentary, there is tantalizing but inconclusive evidence. In the Pseudo-Hieronymian corpus is an Irish Markan commentary.[25] A ninth-century Gospel primer refers to a Markan commentary by a "novellus auctor nomine Comiano." Bischoff claimed that this Pseudo-Hieronymian commentary was that of Cummianus, and that furthermore this Cummianus was none other than the author of the famous letter to Segene of Iona about the Paschal Controversy (ca. 632).[26] Bischoff offered inconclusive evidence for this attribution, and scholars usually cite the commentary's author as "Cummianus(?)."[27] It is unfortunate that Bischoff was unable to prove this point, because if he is correct, there was a Markan commentary written by an Irish Romanist anywhere from 75 to 100 years before Bede wrote his. Considering Bede's Romanist sympathies, such a commentary would have been an attractive source. Professors Daibhí Ó Cróinín and Maura Walsh are doing an analysis of this commentary.[28] If they verify Bischoff's conclusions, a new source may be available for our understanding of Bede.

Our third category deals with the Irish use of Bede. At least four Irish texts which date no later than 790 use Bede's exegesis, and two may date as early as 750, that is, only fifteen years after Bede's death.[29] Later, i.e., ninth-century, Irish texts regularly make use of Bede, although by that time he was widely accepted as an *auctoritas* in much of Western Europe.[30] An Irish commentary on Luke, dated ca. 785, depends heavily upon Bede's Lukan commentary. This is particularly significant because the two oldest extant manuscripts of Bede's work, one complete, one fragmentary, are both dated to the second half of the eighth century, which means this Irish text is contemporaneous with them.[31] To my knowledge, this Irish commentary represents the earliest known use of Bede's commentary on Luke.

The question may arise as to whether this Irish use of Bede is only apparent, a product of twentieth-century *post hoc, propter hoc* thinking, but the answer must be, "No." Bede's works survive in a large number of manuscripts with a wide geographical range and relatively early dates—mostly of the ninth century. The combination of his authority as an exegete and the distribution of manuscripts of his works makes it inherently likely that the Irish used him. There is also the question of *florilegia*. There can be little doubt that some of his ideas were transmitted in that way; but, again, the number and distribution of manuscripts of his works makes this assumption generally unlikely and certainly unnecessary.

Our fourth category raises the possibility that both Bede and an Irish exegete drew from a common, yet-undetected source and not from one another to arrive at parallel interpretations. At present, this is known only for Apocalypse exegesis where there was a common Insular tradition.[32] But since such a tradition did exist, I am certain that this tradition will appear elsewhere, although only critical editions can finally settle such questions.

For the first part of this paper, we have examined the work to be done on the source criticism of these texts. In the second part, we will examine the historical value of that work.

We return to our first category, passages with a common patristic source. This category must be understood in terms of the general use of the Fathers by Bede and the Irish. Here we can get a good idea of which authors were available to both and, more important, which were used and how. We can determine the nature and quality of the libraries as well as the commentators' intellectual and theological preferences. We may also get an idea of whether or not there was an "Insular" pattern of patristic use or whether national divisions prevailed. For example, the Irish used Pelagius constantly, cited him by name, and even referred to him as "noster Pelagius," something Bede simply would not do.[33] Delineating the availability and use of patristic texts would be a valuable undertaking, and its value cannot be gainsaid.

The study of our second category, Bede's use of Irish writers, has already borne fruit. It proves that Bede used Irish writers. That sounds tautological, but it is a step forward in Bedan studies. Let us consider for a moment the traditional picture of Bede: the firm Romanist, avid supporter of the new order in the English church, and narrator of the Synod of Whitby, which marked the defeat and rejection of the Irish in England. No one questions Bede's Romanism or his support of the new order, but the picture of the Irish in post-Whitby England as one of defeat and rejection must be abandoned.

Henry Mayr-Harting, in *The Coming of Christianity to England,* demonstrated that the Synod of Whitby, far from being an all-England event, was "very much a Northumbrian affair,"[34] and that it was an extension of the Paschal Controversy in Ireland, having been sparked by an Irish Romanist, Ronan. To be sure, the Irish church order had no future in England, but Irish influence continued to be strong down to the Viking period. In the opening chapter of *England Before the Conquest* Kathleen Hughes chronicled the historical relations between the English and Irish churches after Whitby.[35] I have demonstrated the influence of Irish motifs on Anglo-Saxon hagiography after Whitby,[36] while J. E. Cross has proved the influence of Hiberno-Latin exegetical motifs on Old English literature.[37] The importance of Bede's use of Irish writers for his exegesis is now obvious. In addition to helping scholars to understand how he commented on the Bible, it hammers one more nail — and an important one — into the coffin of the old idea that Irish influence in England disappeared after the Synod of Whitby.

As for Bede's actual use of Irish writers, it formed only a minor portion of his exegesis. Like most early medieval monks, he had only the highest respect for the great patristic *auctoritates*. Indeed, in the preface to his Lukan commentary, he felt obliged to explain and to justify why he was even writing such a commentary, since the great Ambrose had written one.[38] From repeated remarks in the *Historia Ecclesiastica,* Bede leaves no doubt that he admired the religious virtues and diligence of the Irish, but there is no way that they could have rivalled the great *patres* as exegetes. In general, Irish exegesis filled in the details or provided an alternate interpretation after the patristic one had been given.

The study of our third category, the Irish use of Bede, will make considerable progress as more Irish texts are edited, but enough have been edited already to provide a general picture. The evidence points to an early and deep appreciation of Bede's work. English sources indicate that Bede was well known and revered in his lifetime,[39] and English missionaries and scribes were certainly the main channels for the spread of his fame and writings.[40] But we should consider the real possibility that the Irish aided in this — I mention again that Irish Lukan commentary which appears to be the earliest known use of Bede's Lukan commentary — and the clue to this is the unaffected Irish willingness to use modern authors in an age dominated by the weight of antiquity. The first Irish commentary on the Catholic Epistles cited five contemporary teachers by name, including four who left no written works. The *De Mirabilibus Sacrae Scripturae,* dated by Paul Grosjean to ca. 655,[41] also cited a contemporary teacher, Manchianus. There is the Markan commentary by the "novellus auctor nomine Comiano." An eighth-century Irish Apocalypse commentary cited Primasius of Hadrumetum who wrote "in modernis temporibus."[42] Columbanus in his letter to Gregory the Great (590-604) on the date of Easter cited Gildas and other, unnamed, sixth-century Insular scholars.[43] The pattern is clear. The Irish—who, of course, also venerated the Fathers—were willing to use contemporary authors, even citing them by name. Their early acceptance of Bede fits this pattern, and it is difficult to doubt that they played some role in the spread of his authority and his works. Bede is another *auctoritas* to be used like Gregory or Isidore. The Irish had no reluctance to use him as they used the older Fathers; they cited him by name and anonymously, as they did for all their sources.

The last category, namely a common Insular tradition from which both Bede and the Irish drew, is similar to the so-called "Q" material of the New Testament, that is, the oral tradition passed along in Christian communities and shaped by frequent use before the composition of the synoptic Gospels. It is certain that the Irish developed their own tradition of oral exegesis, and we know from the *Historia Ecclesiastica* that Northumbrian youths studied with Irish teachers in England and Ireland.[44] Their studies, like all early medieval Christian instruction, would have centered on the Scriptures. We may also safely assume that the English pupils would soon have made contributions of their own. Furthermore, Northumbria was evangelized by preaching, and patristic and early medieval sermons usually have a strong scriptural and even exegetical content, so the oral tradition would have been constantly growing and would have become quite familiar. It would be natural for Bede and the Irish exegetes to draw from this tradition. Isolating this tradition is an involved task, but far from an impossible one. We must acknowledge that elements in the tradition would undergo a transformation in the passage from oral to written form, that we will never be able to determine how much of the oral tradition the recovered material formed, and that it is highly unlikely that we will ever recover an oral tradition in its pristine form. On the other hand, we should be able to recover some of its exegetical content and eventually to form some judgments on its range and depth.

Bede the exegete is still a largely unknown quantity, as Ray has demonstrated,[45] but he will become better and better known. The quality of his exegesis will align him with the patristic tradition, a compliment which would have shocked his humility, but one which we—at a safe distance from his indignation—can pay him. But Bede also stood in another tradition, the Insular one, and to overlook that is to miss an important part of Bede's exegesis. The same is true for the Irish. To study Hiberno-Latin exegesis without reference to Bede is to ignore not only an important source for the Irish exegetes, but also a part of the tradition in which they stood. This new area of research has both potential and value; let us hope it also has practitioners.[46]

JOHN CARROLL UNIVERSITY
CLEVELAND, OHIO

Notes

1. Beryl Smalley, *The Study of the Bible in the Middle Ages,* 2nd ed. (Notre Dame, Ind., 1964), p. xi. (This is a paperback edition of the second edition; the first edition was published in Oxford in 1941.)
2. Roger Ray, "What Do We Know about Bede's Commentaries?" *Recherches de Théologie Ancienne et Médiévale,* 49 (1982), 5-20.
3. The latest CCSL catalogue (January 1983) lists ten of Bede's exegetical works in print and ten more *sub prelo.*
4. M. L. W. Laistner, "The Library of the Venerable Bede," in *Bede, His Life, Times, and Writings,* ed. A. Hamilton Thompson (Oxford, 1935), pp. 237-66; rpt. in Laistner, *The Intellectual Heritage of the Early Middle Ages* (Ithaca, N.Y., 1957), pp. 117-49.
5. Bernhard Bischoff, "Wendepunkte in der Geschichte der lateinischen Exegese im Frühmittelalter," *Sacris Erudiri,* 6 (1954), 189-279; rpt. with some updating in *Mittelalterliche Studien,* Vol. I (Stuttgart, 1966), pp. 205-73. Subsequent references will be to the 1966 version.
6. J. F. T. Kelly, "Hiberno-Latin Exegetes and Exegesis," *Annuale Mediaevale,* 21 (1981), 46-60.
7. See J. F. T. Kelly, "Augustine in Hiberno-Latin Literature," *Augustinian Studies,* 8 (1977), 139-49.
8. Robert E. McNally, " 'Christus' in Pseudo-Isidoriam 'Liber de Ortu et Obitu Patriarcharum,' " *Traditio,* 21 (1965), 167-83.
9. Patrick Sims-Williams, "Thought, Word and Deed: An Irish Triad," *Ériu,* 29 (1978), 78-111.
10. J. F. T. Kelly, "The Venerable Bede and the Irish Exegetical Tradition on the Apocalypse," *Revue Bénédictine,* 92 (1982), 393-406.
11. Bede, *Explanatio Apocalypsis,* in *PL,* 93: 129-206. Thomas Mackay is preparing a new edition of this text for CCSL.
12. Kelly, "Bede and The Irish Exegetical Tradition," pp. 397-99; see n. 10.
13. Robert E. McNally, ed., *Commentarius in Epistolas Catholicas Scotti Anonymi* and Pseudo-Hilarius, *Tractatus in Septem Epistolas Canonicas,* CCSL, 108 B (Turnhout, 1973), pp. 3-50, 53-124.

14. Date given by D. Hurst in his edition of Bede's *In Lucae Evangelium Expositio,* in CCSL, 120 (Turnhout, 1960), p. v, following Laistner.
15. McNally, CCSL, 108 B, pp. xii–xv.
16. McNally, CCSL, 108 B, pp. xiii–xv.
17. Pseudo-Jerome *Expositio IV Evangeliorum,* in *PL,* 30: 531–90 (in some editions, cols. 549–608).
18. Bruno Griesser, "Beiträge zur Textgeschichte der *Expositio IV Evangeliorum* des Ps.-Hieronymus," *Zeitschrift für katholische Theologie,* 54 (1930), 40–87; "Die handschriftliche Überlieferung der *Expositio IV Evangeliorum* des Ps.-Hieronymus," *Revue Bénédictine,* 49 (1937), 279–321.
19. Bischoff, "Wendepunkte," No. 11, pp. 240–41.
20. Bernard Lambert, *Bibliotheca Hieronymiana Manuscripta,* Vol. IIIB (The Hague, 1970), pp. 360–69.
21. CCSL, 120, p. 81, ll. 2457–59.
22. In *PL,* 30: 540B (557C).
23. CCSL, 120, p. 337, ll. 1668–73.
24. In *PL,* 30: 576A (595A).
25. In *PL* 30: 589–614 (in some editions, cols. 609–68).
26. Bischoff, "Wendepunkte," pp. 214–15; No. 27, pp. 257–58. The Gospel primer was edited by Robert E. McNally, CCSL, 108 B, pp. 133–49; the reference to Cummianus appears on p. 142, ll. 309–10.
27. For example, Lambert, *Bibliotheca,* IIIB, 376.
28. A private communication by Prof. Ó Cróinín.
29. *Prebarium* and *Praefacio secundum Marcum,* ed. Robert E. McNally, in CCSL, 108 B, pp. 16–171, 220–24; Anonymus Scottus, *Commentarius in Lucam,* ed. J. F. T. Kelly, CCSL, 108 C (Turnhout, 1974), pp. 1–101; "Reference Bible," unedited, for which see Bischoff, "Wendepunkte," No. 1, pp. 231–36.
30. Alcuin considered Bede a Father of the Church; see *Epistolae Alcuini,* ed. E. Dümmler, *MGH,* Epistolae, 4 (Karolini aevi), 2nd ed., Vol. III (1974), No. 216.
31. For the Lukan commentary, see note 29 above; for Bede's MSS, see D. Hurst, CCSL, 120, pp. v-vii, following Laistner, Bischoff, and E. A. Lowe.
32. See note 10 above.
33. J. F. T. Kelly, "Pelagius, Pelagianism, and the Early Christian Irish," *Mediaevalia,* 4 (1978), 99–124.
34. Henry Mayr-Harting, *The Coming of Christianity to England* (New York, 1972), p. 108; see pp. 103–13 for his discussion of the synod.
35. Kathleen Hughes, "Evidence for Contacts between the Churches of the Irish and English from the Synod of Whitby to the Viking Age," in *England Before the Conquest,* ed. Peter Clemoes and Kathleen Hughes (Cambridge, 1971), pp. 49–67.
36. J. F. T. Kelly, "Books, Learning and Sanctity in Early Christian Ireland," *Thought,* 54 (1979), 253–61.
37. *Inter alia,* see J. E. Cross, "The Influence of Irish Texts and Traditions on the *Old English Martyrology," Proceedings of the Royal Irish Academy,* 81 C (1981), 173–92.
38. Bede *In Lucam,* in CCSL, 120, pp. 6–10.
39. For example, Acca of Hexham was the dedicatee of several of Bede's works

including the Lukan commentary: see CCSL, 120, pp. 5-10; the letter of Cuthbert *De Obitu Bedae* takes Bede's fame for granted. The letter is available in *Bede's Ecclesiastical History of the English People,* ed. B. Colgrave and R. A. B. Mynors (Oxford, 1969), pp. 579-87.

40. Wilhelm Levison, *England and the Continent in the Eighth Century* (Oxford, 1946), pp. 139-48.

41. Paul Grosjean, "Sur quelques exégètes irlandais du VIIe siècle," *Sacris Erudiri,* 7 (1955), 67-98.

42. Text in *PLS,* 4:1850-63; reference in col. 1851.

43. Columbanus, Epistula 1, ed. D. Meehan, Scriptores Latini Hiberniae, 2 (Dublin, 1957, rpt. 1970), pp. 2-13.

44. Bede *Historia Ecclesiastica* III.27; ed. Colgrave and Mynors, pp. 310-15.

45. Ray, "Bede's Commentaries," pp. 6-7.

46. Research for this paper was supported by a grant from the American Philosophical Society.

Towards the Identification of Old English Literary Ideas— Old Workings and New Seams.

J. E. CROSS

At this first meeting of this symposium on "The Sources of Anglo-Saxon Culture" it is appropriate that we should consider more generally our interests and our future needs. In this present group we recognize the value of ascertaining the cultural influences bearing on our Anglo-Saxon writers, or knowing what they read. Within my academic lifetime our understanding of *The Wanderer* and *The Seafarer* has changed, in part because scholars were able to identify the reading and cultural background of the poets within writings of Christians and within the Christian rhetorical mode. More particularly, it is helpful (if possible) to identify the sources of a single text (most probably in prose), because the identified text can then stand as a cultural landmark, to and from which tracks may be plotted, in a period where literary records are comparatively scanty because much has disappeared. At another level also, if an individual text, or a passage within it, is an accurate translation or even a close adaptation of a Latin source, a host of Latin-Old English equivalents may become available to our lexicographers. And whenever we read Latin texts for sources known to some Anglo-Saxons, we are immersing ourselves in their patterns of thought; and these patterns may explain allusions or sequences of thought in other Old English works. All these points are obvious to us who attempt to understand the writings of the Anglo-Saxons. But here I wish to speak mainly of future possibilities. Hence my title, the image being that of coal-mining, a pressing reality of my Forest of Dean birthplace and of my youth. "Old workings" are the results of our remarkable predecessors. Sometimes their findings can be abandoned, but often they have left a rich residue for our use. A miner, however, always hopes to find new seams; and I think that I open one vast new seam of literary ideas for Anglo-Saxon writers, and then suggest how we may find others, by "working at the coal-face," or, in our situation, with unpublished Latin manuscripts.

I begin (in the manner of Charles Lamb in his *Essays of Elia*) with something small, seemingly insignificant, seemingly irrelevant, but an oddity which should alert the source-analyst and should arouse him to possibilities. In an unprinted Easter Day Sermon in Cambridge, Corpus Christi College MS. 162 (pp. 382-91)[1] there is a sentence which reads:

> The seventh heaven he created for himself to sit in, that is then, heaven of the Holy Trinity in which the Almighty God sits.[2]

God sitting in the seventh heaven of the Holy Trinity? The ears of my memory twitched. I recalled Rudolph Willard's monograph on *Two Apocrypha in Old English Homilies*,[3] one of which was "The Apocryphon of the Seven Heavens." Willard, as was his custom, provided as many illustrations as possible, mainly from the Irish vernacular texts in print, and indicated that a tradition existed which named the seven heavens consistently (give or take an error in transmission) and named the seventh, the highest, as Trinity. He had recorded our example in a footnote[4] and published a few lines of the text from Corpus Christi MS. 162. As is my custom when another has made an identification, I took consolation that I was right to prick up my memory at a seventh heaven of Holy Trinity, and thought how helpful it would be for a research student to be able to consult a reference book sub. *Seven*, sub-division *Heavens*, sub-section *Enumeration of*, to find examples of the theme.

Willard's best analogues were from Irish *vernacular* versions of the apocryphon known as *The Evernew Tongue (An Tenga Bithnúa)*,[5] where the tongue is that of the apostle Philip. But it is always likely that a vernacular theme may appear also in Hiberno-*Latin* texts of earlier date. This one does appear in the Latin of Pseudo-Isidore *Liber de Numeris,* now regarded as Irish and reputedly originating in the circle of the Irish bishop, Virgil of Salzburg, in the mid-eighth century.[6] (He is the man whom Boniface of Devon accused of heresy because he was *not* a flat-earth man.) The late Robert E. McNally produced a commentary on the *Liber* in his Munich doctoral dissertation of 1957 and illustrated this section.[7] I have selected the best examples from his work and have added the Old English example from Willard (in Appendix 1). In McNally, however, I noted citations from three unpublished manuscripts — Munich clm. 14276, Vatican Regina lat.

76, and Lyons B.M. 447 (376)—because these three are manuscripts of what Bernhard Bischoff called *The Irish Reference Bible*,[8] either sequential (the Munich and Vatican manuscripts), or a derivative and close relative of this (the Lyons manuscript).

I have now seen these texts, and I now make two points about going closer to the origin of Old English literary ideas: first, that some of us should now read and publish Latin manuscripts of early date, particularly for anonymous works (I will elaborate on this later); second, that we should read and absorb those works which scholars have distinguished as having "Irish symptoms."

I continue with this second point now.

I

Thomas Hill and I collaborated in attempting to identify the ideas in *The Prose Solomon and Saturn* and *Adrian and Ritheus,* now in print (1982). There, on occasion, we drew illustrations from Irish vernacular sources and where possible from early Hiberno-Latin texts in print. But we noted sadly that: "Knowledge of reading contacts depends on continuing source-study and, indeed, still awaits the future publication of identified Hiberno-Latin manuscripts."[9] But *The Irish Reference Bible* provides material which we then lacked, as follows:

Solomon and Saturn 10 reads: "Tell me at what age was Adam when he was created. I tell you he was thirty years of age."[10] Our comment was that this statement derived from the idea that God created Adam in his own image (Genesis 1:27) and that Adam was clearly fully formed at creation.[11] We exemplified from Scripture that thirty appeared to be the age when a man should exercise responsibility or be mature. Our parallels for thirty as the perfect age came from Old English, Middle English, and the Irish vernacular. *The Irish Reference Bible* has the information and gives a common-sense reason: "In what age was Adam created?" it asks, and continues: "that is, thirty, because he had no parents to feed him."[12] That age is also found in another Hiberno-Latin commentary on Genesis, St. Gall MS. 908 (about A.D. 800).[13]

There are analogues for other extra-scriptural information. For Eve's birth from the non-scriptural *left* side, and for the naming of Adam's fruit as a fig (found respectively in *Solomon* and in *Adrian,* with *both* items found in Vercelli Homily 19[14]) we read in *The Reference Bible,* first on Eve: "Why from the rib and not from another bone? Because the rib is near the heart, where is love between men and women,"¹⁵ *and,* a few lines later in two only of the three main manuscripts: "From which side was Eve made? — From the left side, because a rib is lacking there in memory of his work."¹⁶ For Adam's fig we read: "Concerning the fig, some say that Adam ate of the fig and was clothed (covered), and Christ did not find fruit on the figtree and, on a figtree, Christ suffered and Judas hanged."¹⁷ Only two of these concepts are from Scripture.¹⁸ For Eve's rib Hill and I had a more distant analogue in a Coptic account; for Adam's fig, analogues are extant in Greek writings by Pseudo-Athanasius and Isidore of Pelusium¹⁹ and (also for the fig) in the Hiberno-Latin *De Ordine Creaturarum Liber,* which was certainly used by Bede in his *De Natura Rerum* and which was recalled by Ælfric.²⁰

The commentary in *The Reference Bible* has links elsewhere with Old English ideas. The commentator poses a question as to how Eve was able to communicate with the serpent, and answers, in effect, with a testimony — a reference to Scripture which in the Middle Ages was regarded as a proof. "Why more difficult," he says, "for the serpent to speak in human language than the ass or the ox in Rome?"²¹ If Balaam's ass spoke (Numbers 22:28), says the Irishman, why not Eve's serpent? But what about the ox in Rome which the writer clearly expects his readers to know just as well? We know this speaking ox of Rome. It appears in an anecdote in the ninth-century *Old English Martyrology* among a miscellaneous group of portents at Christ's birth, and reads: "An ox spoke to the ploughman in Rome and it said: Why do you goad me? Good wheat will grow this year, but you will not be alive then to eat it."²² The anecdote was also used by Patrick, bishop of Dublin (1074–84) in a Latin sequence of verses "Concerning Signs and Prodigies," and is found in Jerome's version of *Eusebius's Chronicle,* from which it may ultimately derive.²³

We now have five distinctive ideas (and there are more): seven heavens, Adam's age, rib and fig, and the ox in Rome, which are noted in *The Irish Reference Bible* and in Old English texts, and variously in other Hiberno-Latin writings and in Greek and Near-Eastern writings. The common factor for the non-English texts is *The Irish Reference Bible,* which now becomes important to Anglo-Saxonists and not merely to scholars concerned with the contribution of the Irish to European culture. This commentary, as mentioned earlier, is extant in three main manuscripts, Vatican Regina lat. 76 (eighth–ninth century — Genesis incomplete), Munich clm. 14276 (Old Testament) and clm. 14277 (New Testament, ninth century), plus one more: Paris, BN lat. 11561 (Old and New Testaments, late ninth century).²⁴ It is extant in excerpts (useful for variant readings) in other manuscripts such as the Lyons MS. (all noted by Bischoff); and, in answer to a friendly question of mine after I had been reading Stegmüller's *Repertorium*[25] on anonymous commentaries, Bernhard Bischoff was willing to suggest that there were more Irish-linked commentaries among those recorded in Stegmüller. But, most important here, *The Irish Reference Bible* was copied and excerpted in various centers during our period and can be a representative of other Hiberno-Latin commentaries.

Commentaries are normally collections of material to explain scriptural statements. They are normally not very original but make available gathered information. *The Irish Reference Bible* does this, and also names authorities. André Wilmart, however, commenting on Vatican Regina 76 in his catalogue, says: "More often, it appears, writers are not recorded, or they are falsely assigned, or their writings are contracted."[26] This is true but, I think, somewhat unfair. At certain passages which I have known about and in which a name is mentioned, the name is often a lead to the author named, although Augustine may be Pseudo-Augustine, Jerome may be Pseudo-Jerome, and so on. And dim memory of a composer may mislead us on attribution. Memory must be taken into consideration. As Dorothy Whitelock said to me years ago, people who are used to consulting books with indices do not realize how difficult it is to find something we vaguely recall in a manuscript.

In my view *The Irish Reference Bible* is a scholarly commentary within the limits of knowledge for the age. If this view is valid, it means that even where there is no ascription or where the commentator says: "Alii dicunt," the information is transmitted, not original, whether we find a source or not. One case in which no ascription is given is the topos of the Seven Sins of Cain (in Appendix 2), although the commentator elsewhere clearly uses Jerome's letter to Damasus, and the theme derives ultimately from Jerome. Verbal echoes in that topos show that authentic Bede went directly to Jerome; but all the other texts cited are Hiberno-Latin, and all differ slightly from Jerome, including the *Reference Bible*. Perhaps our commentator leaves out Jerome's name here because he is varying Jerome, yet the information is transmitted. One use of *alii dicunt* is a reference to Lamech killing Cain as a result of mistaking him for a stag (*cervus*), a story discussed by Emerson in his paper long ago on the Legends of Cain,[27] and obviously unoriginal in our writer.

But the notable point here is that such Hiberno-Latin commentaries could have disseminated information from various quarters and that they can give us a transmission-point for information which is known elsewhere only in lands far distant from Anglo-Saxon England. We may recall here that George Herzfeld (in 1900) illustrated information on the Days of Creation in the *Old English Martyrology* with parallels in Rabbinic writings and The Talmud;[28] but the martyrologist is actually quoting the Hiberno-Latin *De Ordine Creaturarum Liber*. It is of no account whether the contact occurred in the Insular homeland or on the Continental Mission-field, for the interchange and comradeship of Irish and English have been widely illustrated in both areas. As an example I have chosen an extract on the Cain-Abel story, a topic which has excited Beowulfian scholars, most recently R. E. Kaske and Ruth Mellinkoff (who look to *The Book of Enoch* for traditions)[29] and David Williams writing on *Cain and Beowulf*.[30] I have spotted a few sources but would welcome more, and make some general and a few specific points on the extract and on the topic in *Beowulf*.

Among the sources within the commentary which are established by name and by verbal echo or intricacy of idea are well-known books: Augustine, *De Civitate Dei*; Isidore, *Etymologies*; Gregory on the Gospels and the *Moralia in Job*; Cassian, *Conferences*; and Jerome in a letter which was nevertheless well-used on Cain. Origen is named, but we cannot identify the work. We recall, however, that his books of commentary on Genesis are extant now only in fragments or within those homilies translated by Rufinus; but there is apparently nothing on Cain and Abel.[31] Verbal echoes normally indicate quotation from an open book; and the whole commentary suggests that the writer has a good library. He is willing to quote, but also to adapt (probably as a fluent Latinist) and sometimes to conflate, as with the case of Augustine and Cassian on the origin of the magic arts.

Now we turn to Cain and *Beowulf*. It is clear that the descendants of Cain are misshapen human beings, monsters in the medieval sense — that is, they are ogres (as are Grendel and his mother), not dragons. When Williams attempts to link the dragon with Cain's kin in his chapter ii[32] he is flouting medieval distinction (as Isidore also shows).[33] We see the confusion and alternation of Cain, son of Adam, and Cham (Ham), son of Noah, which is recorded in the literature on *Beowulf*.[34] As to the transmission of magic arts after the Flood, we note in our text their record by Ham on *stone*, although the source Cassian also has these arts inscribed "on plates of various metals."[35] But another Hiberno-Latin text, the *Liber de Numeris*, draws loosely on Cassian and notes Ham's writing "on lead plates and stones."[36] We recall that the inscribed sword which Beowulf brings up from Grendel's lair has been regarded as a reminiscence of this link with the Cain story.[37] As I summarized Ruth Mellinkoff's scholarly papers on *The Book of Enoch* and *Beowulf*, I noted only two points about the ogres which are not in the *Reference Bible*, i.e., the cannibalism, and the ogres' home in the wasteland. The latter, the home in the wasteland, is not found solely in *The Book of*

Enoch. In the curious poem *Maxims II,* in a list of beings and things in their appointed places or with distinguishing qualities, we hear that "A giant (*þyrs*) must dwell in the fen, alone in the land" just as "God must be in heaven" "Courage must be in a nobleman," "A dragon must be in a barrow," and "A door must be in a hall." But I have no wish to oppose the speculation that the ultimate source of these ideas is *The Book of Enoch.* I merely wish to call attention to a reasonable point of dissemination, and I ask that *The Irish Reference Bible* be published,[38] with other Hiberno-Latin commentaries. Who knows what we may find to illuminate rare medieval traditions in Old English literature?

II

But I hasten to Part II — on the necessity for the reading of Latin *manuscripts* generally. My own research over the years has had two strands: identification of sources for the prose (where verbal echoes are discernible), and identification of poetic ideas leading on to explication of some poems (where detailed background is sometimes difficult to ascertain). I began early with the not very original hunch that the poets were of the same intellectual background as the prose writers, and immersed myself in all works then in print. Links began to be seen, and I recommend such general reading. Old English literature is too small in compass to limit oneself to the reading of poetry only.

On the prose I was disconcerted again and again by the uncertainty about the actual texts in print, particularly with anonymous sermons. Recently, however, we have begun to use Latin manuscripts. Pamela Gradon, years ago, at least culled the Bodley and British Library lists for *Elene,*[39] but more recently Janet Bately on *Orosius,*[40] David Yerkes on the Old English version of Gregory's *Dialogues,*[41] Patrick Zettel on Ælfric's Legendary,[42] and others have made real advances; and I have been collecting microfilms of manuscript legendaries from the eighth to the tenth centuries for detailed work on the *Old English Martyrology.*

All of us have asked the question: What are the actual words in Latin which the respective English writers saw? We have not been concerned with a best edition. Individual Anglo-Saxon writers may well have had only one text, and that with scribal errors. What we have looked for is something which careful editors would spurn — a base text with as many variants as possible — and we have weaved our way through the variants to create our author's text. No one hopes to find the actual manuscript seen by a given author. Henry VIII and Oliver Cromwell have obviously had their considerable say about that. But we may, indeed can on occasions find the actual Latin words which an English writer saw.

How do we build up these variant texts? We simply need to go through library catalogues where they are available. I illustrate results from a few examples of homilies.

Some years ago at Kalamazoo Mary Wack spoke on a homily known as *The Three Utterances of the Soul* (at death), published by Willard.[43] This was one of the Rogationtide sermons recently edited or re-edited by Joyce Bazire and me, and we attempted to reconstruct the beautifully balanced Latin homily which was the main source from five Latin manuscripts in print.[44] But on Wack's typescript (which I later saw) she had written titles of other manuscripts. I think I now know where she got these but congratulate her on her postgraduate work.[45] The titles were from Valentin Rose's catalogue of Berlin manuscripts,[46] which is an education in itself. There we find a description of Phillipps MS. 1716 (written about A.D. 800), where, besides the Phillipps MS. itself for our sermon, Rose had noted four more manuscripts of early date. I have recently picked up two more, from Cambrai and St. Omer,[47] so we now have twelve manuscripts of this sermon to collate.

But more—Phillipps 1716 also includes Pseudo-Augustinian sermons printed by Migne without date. The manuscript gives them a date *post quem non*, which is helpful, and one of its sermons certainly was used by a vernacular writer. This was Pseudo-Augustine No. 251 on the Day of Judgment which was used in a homily published by Luiselli Fadda.[48] For my identification of this source in *Anglia* (1982)[49] I used two texts in print, but Rose's catalogue notes ten manuscripts of this sermon besides Phillipps 1716.[50] My suggestions should be refined or even, possibly, confirmed by a collation of manuscripts. Then we can tell the Toronto lexicographers to use Latin equivalents in discussions of words generally, and not merely for translations of the Bible and Bede and in glosses, as in Bosworth-Toller.

One last point which is equally important. Helmut Gneuss has listed manuscripts which were written in England or had a home in England before A.D. 1100.[51] We can use this list and elaborate on it. Recently Christopher Jeffrey wrote a helpful little paper noting variants between two *printed* editions of Gregory's *Dialogues* and *Pastoral Care*,[52] but we now know manuscripts of both these works in England, and David Yerkes has used those on the *Dialogues*. There is no collated edition in print of Gregory's homilies on the Gospels, but there are manuscripts in England whose variants from the printed text should be recorded. These are large named works.

But when manuscripts are called "Legendaries" or "Homiliaries" they need to be analyzed; and I have done the Orleans manuscript[53] as a specimen in Appendix 4. But sometimes a manuscript even in a good catalogue seems to have new and unpublished material, different from variant texts of, say, homilies in print. Such material should be published. One such illustration in Gneuss's list[54] is Cambridge, Pembroke College 25 (written in the second half of the eleventh century in Bury).[55] In M. R. James's catalogue it has 83 items, mainly homilies from Advent to the feast of St. Andrew (Nov. 30); but one item consists of extracts about the office of the Mass attributed to Hrabanus Maurus.[56] I note one small error in James. Items 53–60 are actually one sermon, the influential "Legimus in ecclesiasticis historiis" published in *Traditio,* 33 (1977).[57] In total, and including this item as 8 items, James, who really knew his business, identified only 21 items, i.e., only a quarter of the series in the whole homiliary. Those items identified, apart from the sermon just mentioned, include two homilies of Gregory on the Gospels, two sections from Alcuin's Life of Martin of Tours, one homily of Maximus of Turin, one sermon of Pseudo-Augustine *Ad Fratres in Eremo,* and five sermons from the Appendices to Augustine, including two on Rogations now assigned to Caesarius of Arles. The identified items inform us that this is the *kind* of material which was available early in the Anglo-Saxon period.[58] But, if James is right, the *unidentified* material was *not* in the great homiliaries of Alanus of Farfa and Paul the Deacon, nor in the ninth-century collections of Smaragdus, Hrabanus Maurus, Haymo of Auxerre, etc. Surely we now need to read these unidentified items. Just scanning the catalogue I note that there are two unidentified items on St. Michael[59] and recall that we have one unsourced homily on the archangel recently published by Hildegard Tristram.[60] Who knows?

I hope that in this paper I have persuaded our younger scholars, first, that there is exciting work to be done; but, second and more pointedly, that it is possible to *think* about possible sources: in other words, to be alert to hints and to speculate with profit. A source is not found unless the reading is in the right area. Our predecessors have done much, but there is more to do. Ladies and gentlemen, in terms of my image, let us get our hands dirty at the coal-face of unpublished Latin manuscripts and work such new seams.

UNIVERSITY OF LIVERPOOL

Notes

1. N. R. Ker, *Catalogue of Manuscripts Containing Anglo-Saxon* (Oxford, 1957), Art. 38, no. 32, p. 54. The sermon has been edited by Kenneth Schaefer, "An Edition of Five OE Homilies for Palm Sunday, Holy Saturday and Easter Sunday," Diss. Columbia University 1972, pp. 176–84, with some commentary. The sermon will be re-edited by Clare Lees of Liverpool with detailed commentary on the many ideas and themes of this sermon.
2. "Þone seofoðan heofon he geworhte him sylfum on to sittenne, þæt is þonne þære halgan Þrynnysse heofon on þam sit se Ælmihtiga God...."
3. Rudolph Willard, *Two Apocrypha in Old English Homilies,* Beiträge zur Englischen Philologie, 30 (Leipzig, 1935).
4. Willard, p. 23, n. 113.
5. Willard, p. 7. His one example from Latin, the Reichenau MS. at Karlsruhe (designated K in his table), is, as can be seen, not in the same tradition as regards detailed naming.
6. Robert E. McNally, " 'Christus' in the Pseudo-Isidorian *Liber de Ortu et Obitu Patriarcharum,*" *Traditio,* 21 (1965), 168: and McNally, "Isidorian Pseudepigrapha in the Early Middle Ages," *Isidoriana* (León, 1961), p. 314.
7. Robert E. McNally, *Der irische Liber de numeris: Eine Quellenanalyse des pseudo-isidorischen Liber de Numeris,* Diss. University of Munich 1957, p. 122. The text is published only in part in *PL,* 83:1293–302 (the numbers 1 and 2 and two items of 3), but I have been able to read the whole through the generosity of Professor McNally's literary executors at Fordham University who allowed me to have a photocopy of his preliminary typescript for an edition.
8. Bernhard Bischoff, "Wendepunkte in der Geschichte der lateinischen Exegese im Frühmittelalter," *Sacris Erudiri,* 6 (1965), 189–279. There is a translation of a revised and augmented version of this paper in *Biblical Studies: The Medieval Irish Contribution,* ed. Martin McNamara (Dublin, 1976), where the term "Reference Bible" is created (p. 88) and the texts are discussed (pp. 97–102).
9. *The Prose Solomon and Saturn* and *Adrian and Ritheus,* ed. James E. Cross and Thomas D. Hill, McMaster Old English Studies and Texts, 1 (Toronto, 1982), pp. 9–10.
10. Cross and Hill, p. 26: "Saga me on hwilcere ylde wæs Adam ða he geseapen wæs. Ic þe secge, he wæs on xxx wintra yldo."
11. Cross and Hill, pp. 70–72.
12. "Qua aetate factus est Adam, id est, xxx quia non erant parentes eius (M omits) ut nutrirent eum" Vat. Reg. lat. 76, fol. 47^v; Paris 11561, fol. 15^v col. 2; Munich clm. 14276, fol. 24^v).
13. St. Gall MS. 908, p. 18: "Nam plus credimus quod Deus omnia perfecta creasset; nam et Adam sub una ora (= hora) sub [anno] etatis tricesimae in statura creatus est." On the manuscript see Bischoff in McNamara, p. 104. The 27 pages of the incomplete commentary on Genesis have been transcribed by Clare Stancliffe of Newcastle, and one hopes for publication in a journal.
14. On Eve's manner of birth in *Adrian and Ritheus* 3, see Cross and Hill, pp.

129–30; in Vercelli Homily 19, see *Eleven Old English Rogationtide Homilies,* ed. Joyce Bazire and James E. Cross, Toronto Old English Series, 7 (Toronto, 1982), pp. 7–9. On the fig in *Solomon and Saturn* 16, see Cross and Hill, pp. 128–29, and in Vercelli Homily 19, see Bazire and Cross, pp. 7–9.

15. "Cur de costa et non de alio osse, ideo quia costa prope sit ad cor ubi est dilectio i[n]ter uirum et mulierum" (Vat. Reg. lat. 76, fol. 54^v; cf. Paris 11561, fol. 17^v, col. 1; Munich clm. 14726, fol. 28^r).

16. "De quo latere facta est Eua, de sinistro latere quia ibi deest una costa in memoriam eius operis" (Paris 11561, fol. 17^v, col. 1; Munich clm. 14726, fols. 28^r–28^v; Vat. Reg. lat. 76 omits this statement). It is not thus recorded in the commentary on Vercelli Homily 19 in Bazire and Cross, pp. 7–9, since only Vat. Reg. lat. 76 was available at the time of writing.

17. "De fico alii dicunt quod de fico Adam edit et tectus et in ficulnea (M: ficulneco) Christus fructum non inuenit et in fico Christus passus et Iudas pependit" (Vat. Reg. 76, fol. 57^r; Paris 11561, fol. 18^r, col. 2; Munich clm. 14276, fol. 29^v).

18. Adam's clothing, Genesis 3:7; and Christ's cursing of the barren fig tree, Matthew 21:19; Mark 11:13.

19. See above, note 14.

20. See, for Bede, J. E. Cross, *"De Ordine Creaturarum Liber* in Old English Prose," *Anglia,* 90 (1972), 133 and n. 5; and for Ælfric, J. E. Cross, review of John Pope, *Homilies of Ælfric,* in *Studia Neophilologica,* 43 (1971), 570.

21. "Cur (M: Cum) difficilior (M: difficilius) serpentem loqui humana lingua quam asinus (M: asinum) et bos (M: bouem) in Roma" (Vat. Reg. lat. 76, fol. 56^r; Paris 11561, fol. 18^r, col. 1; Munich clm. 14726, fol. 29^r).

22. "And oxa spæc on Rome to þam ergendum and he cwæð: 'Towhon sticast þu me? God hwæte geweaxeð togeare; ac ne bist ðu þonne ne his ne abitest,'" in *Das altenglische Martyrologium,* ed. Günter Kotzor, Bayerische Akademie der Wissenschaften; Phil.-Hist. Klasse; Abhandlungen; Neue Folge Heft 88:2 [Munich, 1981]), p. 2; cf. George Herzfeld, *An Old English Martyrology,* EETS, OS 116 (London, 1900), p. 2.

23. See discussion in J. E. Cross, *"De signis et prodigiis* in *Versus Sancti Patricii episcopi de mirabilibus Hibernie,"* *Proceedings of the Royal Irish Academy,* 71 C, No. 6 (1971), 247–54.

24. See description by Bischoff in McNamara, pp. 97–102.

25. Fridericus Stegmüller, *Repertorium Biblicum Medii Ævi,* 7 vols. (Matriti, 1940–61), VI, VII: *Commentaria Anonyma.*

26. Andreas Wilmart, *Codices Reginenses Latini* (Bibliotheca Vaticana, 1937), p. 170: "Saepius, ut uidetur, scriptores non referuntur vel falso inscribuntur vel eorum scripta contrahuntur."

27. See the edited extract p. 96, and O. F. Emerson, "Legends of Cain, Especially in Old and Middle English," *PMLA,* 21 (1906), 874–77.

28. Herzfeld, pp. 226–28; for the direct source see above, note 20.

29. Robert E. Kaske, *"Beowulf* and the Book of Enoch," *Speculum,* 46 (1971), 421–31; Ruth Mellinkoff, "Cain's Monstrous Progeny in *Beowulf:* Part I, Noachic

Tradition," *ASE*, 8 (1979), 143-62: "Part II, Postdiluvian Survival," *ASE*, 9 (1981), 183-97.

30. David Williams, *Cain and Beowulf: A Study in Secular Allegory* (Toronto, 1982).

31. See sub *Origines* in *A Dictionary of Christian Biography*, ed. William Smith and Henry Wace, Vol. IV (London, 1887), pp. 104-05.

32. See especially the argument by Williams, *Cain*, pp. 37-38, and now a review by J. E. Cross in *Notes and Queries*, 30 (1983), 446-47.

33. Isidore *Libri Etymologiarum* distinguishes *monstra*, i.e., misshapen humans (lib. XI cap. iii, *PL*, 82:419 et seq.) from *draco* under "De serpentibus" (lib. XII cap. iv, *PL*, 82:442).

34. See, for example, Charles Donahue, "Grendel and the *Clanna Cain*," *Journal of Celtic Studies*, 1 (1949-50), 167-75.

35. "Cham., filius Noe...scelestas artes ac profana conmenta diversorum metallorum lamminis, quae scilicet aquarum conrumpi inundatione non possent, et durissimis lapidibus insculpsit...ac...transmisit in posteros;" *Iohannis Cassiani Conlationes* XXIII, ed. Michael Petschenig, CCEL, 13.2 [Vienna, 1886], p. 240).

36. "Formulas tamen, id est figuras litterarum, Enoc, filius Iareth, nomina novem invenisse ante diluvium legitur, et post eum, Cham, callidus Noe filius, ante diluvium et post diluvium, quia litteras, quas Cham ante diluvium repperit, ne per diluvium delerentur, in lamminas plumbeas et in lapides scripsit. Post vero diluvium litteras scriptas quaesivit et invenit;..." (*Liber de Numeris*, cited from R. E. McNally's typescript).

37. Mellinkoff, *ASE*, 8, 148, n. 5.

38. After this paper was read I was told that M. McNamara (Dublin), with a group of scholars, hopes to edit this text. Mr. McNamara now informs me that he hopes to begin in October 1983 and the first section will be the Commentary on the Psalms.

39. *Cynewulf's Elene*, ed. Pamela O. E. Gradon (London, 1958), p. 16, n. 3; and as used in her discussion of the source, pp. 18-19.

40. *The Old English Orosius*, ed. Janet Bately, EETS, SS 6 (Oxford, 1980), commentary, passim.

41. David Yerkes, *The Two Versions of Wærferth's Translation of Gregory's Dialogues: An Old English Thesaurus*, Toronto Old English Studies, 4 (Toronto, 1979).

42. Patrick H. Zettel, "Ælfric's Hagiographic Sources and the Latin Legendary Preserved in B.L. MS. Cotton Nero E i plus CCCC MS.9 and Other Manuscripts," Diss. Oxford University 1979. But see now Patrick H. Zettel, "Saints' Lives in Old English: Latin Manuscripts and Vernacular Accounts: Ælfric," *Peritia*, 1 (1982), 17-37.

43. Willard, *Two Apocrypha*, pp. 38-57.

44. Bazire and Cross, pp. 115-20.

45. Mary Wack, who was in the audience, smilingly confirmed my speculation after the paper.

46. Valentin Rose, *Die Handschriften-verzeichnisse der Königlichen Bibliothek zu Berlin*, Bd. XII; *Verzeichniss der lateinischen Handschriften*, Bd. I (Berlin, 1893), pp. 72-77. Our sermon is: Primum quidem decet (Phillipps 1716, fol. 16b).

47. Cambrai, Bibliothèque municipale B 822 (727), fols. 107^v–108^v (s.xii); and St. Omer, Bibliothèque municipale 716, tom. VIII, fols. 32–33 (s.xii).

48. *Nuove omelie anglosassoni della rinascenza benedettina,* ed. A. M. Luiselli Fadda (Firenze, 1977), Omelia I, pp. 27–31, ll. 262–313.

49. J. E. Cross, "A Doomsday Passage in an Old English Sermon for Lent," *Anglia,* 100 (1982), 103–08.

50. Rose, p. 73: De die iudicii. O fratres quam tremendus (or: timendus) est nobis dies ille (Phillipps 1716, item 1).

51. H. Gneuss, "A Preliminary List of Manuscripts Written or Owned in England up to 1100," *ASE,* 9 (1981), 1–60.

52. Christopher D. Jeffery, "The Latin Texts Underlying the Old English *Gregory's Dialogues* and *Pastoral Care,*" *Notes and Queries,* 27 (1980), 483–88.

53. Gneuss, No. 869, p. 55. See also Ch[arles] Cuisard, *Catalogue général des manuscrits des bibliothèques publiques de France: Départements,* tome XII, *Orléans* (Paris, 1889), pp. 186–88. This description has a few errors and does not identify the items.

54. Gneuss, No. 131, p. 12.

55. Montague R. James, *A Descriptive Catalogue of the Manuscripts in the Library of Pembroke College, Cambridge* (Cambridge, 1905), pp. 25–29. It should be noted that Pembroke College 23 and 24, designated as versions of Paul the Deacon's homiliary, are from the same house and the same period (Gneuss, Nos. 129 and 130, p. 12).

56. James, *Descriptive Catalogue,* No. 75, p. 29.

57. J. E. Cross, "'Legimus in Ecclesiasticis Historiis': A Sermon for All-Saints and Its Use in Old English Prose," *Traditio,* 33 (1977), 101–35.

58. Some of the identified items, as James notes, are in versions of Paul the Deacon's homiliary.

59. James, *Descriptive Catalogue,* Nos. 51, 52.

60. Hildegard L. C. Tristram, *Vier altenglische Predigten aus der heterodoxen Tradition, mit Kommentar...*, Diss. University of Freiburg 1970, pp. 151–61.

Appendix 1: *Seven Heavens*

	Irish Ref. Bible Vat. Reg. lat. 76 26ʳ-26ᵛ	LIBER DE NUMERIS	PS. BEDE *PL*, 91: 192 B	SALTAIR NA RANN[1] ll. 633-36	CAMBRIDGE, CORPUS CHRISTI COLL. 41[2]
i.	Aer	Aer	Aer	Air	se lyftlica
ii.	Aether	Ether	Aether	Ether	se oferlyftlica
iii.	Olimpus	Olimphus	Olympus	Olympus	se fyrena
iv.	Spacium ignitum	Firmamentum	Spacium igneum	Firmament	se stronga ... þone we 'rodor' hatað
v.	Firmamentum	Caelum Igneum	Firmamentum	Heaven of waters	se egeslica
vi.	Caelum liquatum	Caelum Angelorum	Coelum Angelorum	Heaven of bright angels	engla heofon
vii.	Caelum Trinita[ti]s	Caelum Trinitatis	Coelum Trinitatis	Heaven in which the fair Lord is.	heofon þære halgan Ðrinnesse.

1. Composed 988 A.D.; trans. Fergus Kelly and David Greene (typescript).
2. Willard; *Two Apocrypha*, p. 4.

Appendix 2: *Sins of Cain*

JEROME (*PL*, 22:455)	PS.-BEDE COLLECTANEA (*PL*, 94:556B)	PS.-BEDE PENTATEUCH (*PL*, 91:218)	LIBER DE NUMERIS	Irish Ref. Bible Vat. Reg. lat. 76 63ʳ	BEDE HEXAMERON (*PL*, 91:68C)
non recte diviserit	non recte divisit	male divisit	non recte divisit	non recte divisit etc.	non recte dividebat.
inviderit fratro suo	inviderit fratri suo	inviderit ut: Iratusque est Cain. (Gen. 4:5).	invidit.	invidit ut cur concidit facies tua	fratri invidit.
dolose egerit dicens: Transeamus in campum (Gen. 4:8).	dixerit: Egrediamur foras	tristis fuit ut: concidit vultus eius (cf. Gen. 4:6).	dolose egit	dolose egit ut eamus in agrum	dolose egit dicens: Egrediamur in agrum.
interfecerit.	interfecerit eum	homicidium ut: interfecit eum	Fratrem occisit	interfectio ut consurrexit Cain	interfecit
procaciter negavit, dicens: Nescio etc. (Gen. 4:9).	procaciter negaverit: Nescio	mendacium, ut: Qui respondit: Nescio	Deo mentivit	mentitus est ut nescio	procaciter negavit: Nescio.
se ipsum damnavit, dicens: Maior culpa mea etc. (Gen. 4:13).	seipsum damnaverit, Maior est etc.	* poenitentiam non egerat (=7)	male disperavit	disperavit ut maior est iniquitas mea.	se ipsum damnatus dicens: Major est etc.
		* seipsum desperavit (=6).			
nec damnatus egerit poenitentiam etc.	nec damnatus egerit poenitentiam		Poenitentiam non egit.	non penituit ut vagus (cf. Gen. 4:12).	nec damnatus egit poenitentiam

Appendix 3: *Irish Reference Bible, Cain and Abel*

Base text: V: Vat. Reg. lat. 76 (saec. viii–ix).
Variants: P: Paris BN lat. 11561 (saec. ix med. −2).
           M: Munich Bayerische Staatsbibl. clm. 14276 (saec. ix in).

[The base text is emended only where the meaning may be unclear (but consult variants). Variant spellings are sometimes given where the base text may appear unusual. Abbreviations are expanded and italicized.]

V42ʳ Sciendum e*st* unde sunt monstra ut homo cum uno oculo in fronte et alii plantis uersis re*liqua*. Alii quinquinnis concipiunt. Alii habent cornu in nares. Alii oculos in ceruice. Alii duplicia membra. In oriente homo duplex natus dua capita habens, iiijor oculos, iiijor manus. unus uent*er*, ii pedes. Ag*ustinus* dicit: Haec monstra a Cain nata esse; alii a Ca*m* uel concupuer*unt* enim filii d*e*i filias hominu*m* (cf. Gen. 6:2) inde nati s*unt* gygantes et [monstrosi] homines id est filii Seth concupuer*unt* filias Cain inde nati s*unt* gygantes et monstra ut mulus ex equa et asino, et burdo |42ᵛ| ex equo et asina. Ita in hominib*us* quomodo in animantibus filii enim adulterii declinant in aliud genus. Ite*m* allii a Cain nati s*unt* monstra quia ille suas maicas artes et prestrigias antequa*m* intrauisset in arcam scribsit in lapide quia cognouit suu*m* patrem iustu*m* quod non uoluisset illas maicas 5 10

---

2. V, P: quinquinnis; M: quinquinnes   2. V: habent; M, P: habeat with 'n' superscript   4. V, P: dua; M: duo   5. M: Cham, with 'h' superscript   6, 7. V, P: concupuerunt; M: concupierunt   7. V: monetrosi; M, P: monstruosi (with 'u' superscript)   10. V: adulterii; M, P: adulteri   10. M, P insert Ag*ustinus* before Item   10. V: allii; M, P: alii   10. V, P: Cain; M: Cham   10. V: nati; M, P: nata   10. V, P: quia; M: qui   11. M erases: ille   11. V: maicas; M, P: magicas; (and later)   11. M: introisset   12. M omits: quod

---

1–3. Examples of 'monstra' from Augustine *De Civitate Dei* XVI.viii (cf. Pliny *Nat. Hist.* VII.ii, iii), but last by adaptation.
3. Augustine *D. C. D.* XVI.viii; but this "monster" was reported by Jerome *Epist.* 72 *ad Vitalis* (*PL*, 22:674) as noted by Augustine *Enchiridion* XXIII, cap. 87. Also in *Liber Monstrorum;* see Cross, *Proc. R. Irish Acad.*, 71 C (1971), 252.
5 Augustine *D. C. D.* XV.xxiii; Cassian *Conferences* VIII.xxi; cf. fol. 70ʳ.
10–12. Josephus *Antiquities of the Jews* cap. II notes that sons of Seth, inventors of wisdom concerned with heavenly bodies, wrote on two pillars, one of brick, the other of stone, before the Flood. But John Cassian (named in a repetition of these ideas on fol. 70ʳ) *Conferences* VIII (Abbot Serenus II) cap. xxi has these comments explained as from Ham (Cham).

artes mittere in arcam. Deinde [Cam ueniens] de arca legit omne quod scribsit in lapide et docuit. Deinde p*er* maicam arte*m* uertuntur homines in forma*m* animaliu*m* et bestiaru*m* et, legim*us*, homines in lup[o]s uel in asin[o]s uel in aues ...

5 62ᵛ Et surrexit Cain et int*er*fecit Abel (cf. Gen. 4:8). Cur dicit interfecit cum suffugauit, id est int*er*fectio [nomen] e*st* omnis occissionis. Unde dedicit Cain occidere, id est et animantib*us* se inuice*m* occidentes uel auctor prioris mortis docuit secundum mortem. Strangulauit eu*m* manibus impiis more pecoris suffucati in hostia. Hinc gentiles more*m* suffucati pecoris tenent
10 et inde *Christ*ianis abhominabil[e] est suffugatum et inde peccatu*m* sine confessione clamat ad d*ominum* sicut sanguis Abel.

Hic Abel prim*us* martyr et Cain primus homicida. |63ʳ| Omn[i]s qui occiderit Cain septuplum punietu*r* (Gen. 4:15), id est, vii plagas minatur d*ominus* sup*er* eum qui occiderit Cain ne quis audeat occidere quia non uult
15 dominu*s* mortem peccatoris sed ut conuertatur et uiuat (cf. Ezek. 33:11). *U*el septuplum indicat qu*od* in vii generatione ab Adam occisus e*st* Cain, id est Cain, Enoch, Aidad uel Iareth, Malalael, Matusalem, Lamech qui occidit Cain. In aliis lib*ris* septem uindictas soluet quia p*er* has septim generationes p*ro*fugus erat (profugus, Gen. 4:12) quia Cain septies punitur qui
20 septies peccauit: Id est, prima, non recte diuisit ut si recte non offeras; .ii. inuidit ut cur concidit facies tua; .iii. dolose egit ut eamus in agrum; .iiii. int*er*fectio ut consurrexit Cain; .v. mentitus e*st* ut nescio; .vi. disperauit ut maior est iniquitas mea; .vii. non penetiuit ut uagus.

---

1. V: conueniens; M: Cham ueniens; P: Cam ueniens   3. V, M: formam; P: formas   3. V: et; M, P: ut (before legimus)   3. V: lupus; M, P: lupos   4. V: asinus; M, P: asinos   5. V: Et surrexit; M, P: Consurrexit   6. V: suffugauit; P corr. from suffugauit to: suffocauit; M: suffocauit   6. V: interfectio; M: interfectione (after correction)   6. M inserts: eius after: nominis; V, P: nominis   7. V: occidentes; P underpoints 'es', and superscript: 'ibus'; M: occidentib*us*   8. V: secundum; M: secundam; P illegible   9. V: suffucati; M, P: suffocati   9. P: hostiam   10. V, M: abhominabilis; P: abhominabile   10. V: suffugatum; M, P: suffocatum   12. V: omnes; M, P: oms̄   13. V, P: occiderit; M: occiderint   16. M omits: in, after: quod   16. V, P: occisus est; M: occisus sit   17. V: uel; P: uel, underpointed; M omits   17. V: Malalael; M: Malaleel; P: Malalehel   18. V: septim; M, P: septem   19. V: punitur; M, P: punietur   19. V: qui; M, P: quia   20. P: prima with 'o' superscript; M: primo, after correction

---

16–18. Cf. Jerome *Epist. ad Damasum* §4 (*PL*, 22:454). N.b.: Gaidad (= Aidad) for Irad in another MS (Migne's notes). For this Gaidad, Cassian *Conferences* VIII.xxi has Iaret (= uel Iareth).
20–23. Cf. Jerome *Ad Damasum* §6, and Appendix 2: "Sins of Cain."

Haec sunt septem uindictae sup*er* eu*m*. Prima, interrogatio ut ubi e*st* frat*er* tuus; .ii. maledictio ut maledictus eris; |63ᵛ| .iii. terre sterelitas ut terra non dabit fructum; .iiii. insania ut uagus; .v. ignauia ut p*ro*fugus; .vi. expulsio ut a facie tua; .vii. occissio ut quicumq*ue*. Hier*onimus* dicit: Cain dicit qui inuenerit me me occidit, id est, uidens me homo ex tremore corporis et furiate mentis agitatu*m* me occidit et ieciar a facie tua, id est, conscientia sceleris mei lucem tuam non sustinens abscondar. D*omin*us autem nolens eum conpendio mortis cruciari nec tradens pen[e] qua se ipse dampnauit, ait,: Non sic, id est, non ut estimas, morieris et morte*m* remedium sceleris accipies; Uerum [uiues usque] ad septima*m* generationem et conscientie tuae igne torqueris ita ut qu[i]cumque te occiderit septuplum punietur; secundu*m* duplicem sensum aut in septima generatione uel magno te liberaret cruciatu. Non quo ipse qui p*er*cusserit Cain septim ultionib*us* subiecendus sit sed quo septe*m* uindictas quae in quanto tempore ocurrunt |64ʳ| soluat int*er*fector, occidens eum. Inde Aquila posuit 'septempliciter'; Symachus 'septimanas ulciscitur'. Quaeritur utru*m* uindicabitur in futuro sup*er* Cain sicut in p*re*senti, id est, non uindicat D*omin*us bis in idipsum quod enim semel recepit homo mala in uita sua non eosdem cruciatus parietur post mortem.

Hier*onimus*: 'Ocidi uirum in uulnus meu*m*' re*liqua* usque 'septuagies et

---

3. M inserts: suum, after: fructum   3. P adds superscript: et, above second: ut
4. P adds superscript: eicis me, after: facie tua; M adds superscript: eicis me, above: a facie   4. P adds after quicumque: inueniet me   5. M omits first 'me'; reads: quicumque for: qui   5. V: occidit; M, P: occidet; Jerome: occidet   6. M omits: me   6. P: occidet   6. V, P: ieciar; M: ei.cit   8. V: pena; M: pene (superscript); P: poenae; Jerome: poenae   8. V, P: qua se; M: quasi   9. V, P: estimas; M: times   9. V, P: et mortem; M: sed morte   10. V: uiuisque; P: uiuis (with 'e' superscript over second 'i') usque; M: uiues usque; Jerome: vives usque   11. V, M: torqueris; P: torqueberis; Jerome: torqueberis   11. V: quecumque; M, P: quicumque; Jerome: quicumque   13. V, P: liberaret; M: liberaret with 'ue' superscript after 'a'   13. V, P: quo; M: quod(after correction); Jerome: quod   13. V: septim; M, P: septem   14. V, P: uindictas; M: uindictae   14. V, P: quanto; M: tanto; Jerome: tanto   15. V, P: Aquila; M: Aliqua   17. V: idipsum; P: ipsum, with 'id' added superscript; M: in ipsum   18. V, P: mala; M: mali; Jerome: mala   19. V: parietur; P: patietur; M: perferet; Jerome: patietur in morte   20. V: ocidi; P: occidi; M: occidit   20. M omits: et

---

4-15. Jerome *Ad Damasum* §2 with adaptation and verbal echo.
15-16 Jerome. *Ad Damasum* §4.
17-18. Jerome *Ad Damasum* §5 (*PL,* 22:455).
20-p. 95, l. 8. Jerome *Ad Damasum* §5.

septies' (Gen. 4:23-24) quae sunt septuagies septies uindicte in Lamech exsoluende sunt pro eo quod occidit Cain etiam si non sponte. Dicunt alii lxxvii sunt in genelogia secundum Lucam ab Adam usque *Christu*m sicut enim in septima generatione peccatum Cain desolutum ita peccatu*m*
5 Lamech, id est, totius mundi sanguine *Christ*i soluitur qui tullit peccata mundi. Item Ebrei dicunt quod lxxvii anim[e] ex genere Lamech mortui sunt in diluuio ut in hoc numero de Lamech facta [est] uindicta et sic Ebrei dicunt |64ᵛ| quod ideo clemens d*eu*s donauit longua*m* aetate*m* ad Adam et ad Cain ut saltim malis longeuitate merore conpulsi penetentia*m* agerent
10 et mererentur absolui.

Alii dicunt secundum Petri int*er*rogatione*m* et *Christ*i responsione*m* 'quotiens peccauerit in me frat*er* meus' re*liqua*. (Matt. 18:21). Item 'non dico tibi septies' re*liqua* 'usque septuagies septies' (Matt. 18:22). Peccatum in septima generatione sabatizasse quando Enoch raptus est. lxxii uero in
15 aduentum *Christ*i mortis et peccati aculeum esse confractum.

Signum Cain: quomodo fuit hoc signum, id est, signu*m* predictum ut 'septuplum punietur' (Gen. 4:15) uel 'nequaquam ita' (Gen. 4:15); alii dicunt uagus et p*ro*fugus. Alii dicunt quod habuit barbam p*ro*lixam et saliue in barba*m* cadebant. Hieronim*us*: Alii [in] fronte uel [in] manu dextera
20 ut monogramma erit apud familiam Anti*Christ*i. Hier*on*imus |65ʳ| Uel signum pacis ut Iudas fecit ad *Christu*m.

Cain edificauit ciuitate*m* et uocauit nomine filii sui Enoch (Gen. 4:17). Cur ex nomine filii illa*m* nominauit, ideo quia Enoch stabilitas interp*re*tatur. Inde fecit ciuitatem ut stabilis in ea maneret post instabilitate[m] et uagum.

---

1. M omits: sunt   3. V, P: lxxvii; M: lxxvi   4. V, M: desolutum; P: desolutum, with 'is' superscript over 'e'; Jerome: dissolutum   4. M, P insert: est, after: desolutum   5. V: tullit; P: tulit; M: tollit   6. V: animo; M, P: anime   7. V, M: ut; P: et   8. V: factae; P: facta est   8. M omits: facta ... longuam, inserts: Cain   8. V: longuam; P: longam   8. P erases: ad, before: Adam, and: Cain.   9. P: a malis   9. V, P: longeuitate; M: longeuitatis   9. V, M: merore; P: meroris   10. V, P, M: mererentur (all after correction)   11. P inserts: pro, before: Christi   11. V: quotiens; M, P: quoties; Jerome: quoties   13. M inserts: usque, after: tibi, and reads: sed, for: reliqua, to agree with Scripture   15. V, M: aduentum; P: aduentu   19. V omits: in; M, P: in   21. V, M: ad Christum; P: Christo   24. V: instabilitate; P: instabilem; M: instabilitatem

---

8-10. Jerome *Ad Damasum* §6.
11-15. Jerome *Ad Damasum* §8.

Quomodo potuit unus aedificare ciuitatem et qua causa et cur ex nomine filii sui primogeniti, cum Iudaei non ex Ruben primogenito dicuntur, id est, quis non credat quam multitudo hominum fuerunt super terram quando Cain obiit quia ante diluuium longum tempus uixerunt homines et quia plus de gente Enoch fuerunt ad aedificandam ciuitatem quam de aliis, ideo ex nomine eius nominatur ciuitas et causa gigantum fuit constructa. Et in illo tempore gigantes fortes grandes ideo pauci |65ᵛ| potuerunt edificare ciuitatem. Gregorius: Hic prima ciuitas in mundo.

Cur ex gente Cain prima ciuitas in terra facta et alii artifices uel fabri uel musici et non ex gente Seth, ideo qui enim deferunt altitudinem caeli illi uolunt altius esse in terra. Gens uero sanctorum quantum se separant a cogitacionibus terrenis tantum in caelestibus honorabuntur.

Sciendum est quomodo Cain peccauit septies ita septem uicia principalia ab sua gente inuenta sunt, id est, inuidia, dolus, mendatium, adulterium, uagatio, fuga, homicidium ...

66ᵛ ... Huc usque Origenis dicit. 'Occidi uirum in uulnus meum et aduliscentulum' (Gen. 4:23) in libro meo 'ultio septuplum dabitur de Cain d[e] Lamech uero septuagies septies' (Gen. 4:24). Occidi uox superbiae uirum, id est Cain, ut Hieronimus et Origenis. Sulpicus uero dic[it] quia non de Cain. Hoc dicit 'in uulnus meum', id est, in uindicta eius super me memorans uerbum domini: 'Qui occiderit Cain septuplum ponietur' (Gen. 4:15). Nunc memorat de occisione eius et nesciuit quando occidit quod Cain esset et alii dicunt quod in similitudine cerui occisus est.

Agustinus 'adoliscentulum' quomodo conuenit hoc quia Lamech vii generatione a Cain fuit, id est, quia instabilis et petulans more adoliscentis fuit. Faustus uel 'adoliscen[tu]lum', id est, quia Cain non canus neque senescit ullomodo more |67ʳ| ferrarum non senescentium pro timore. Haec in an-

---

2. V: dicuntur; M, P: dicantur (P after correction)   3. V: quam; M, P: quod   3. M, P: quando Cain obiit; V inserts a second 'quando' after: Cain   4. V, P: quia; M: cum   7. M: fortes et grandes atque pauci   8. V: hic; M, P: haec   9. V, P: ex gente; M per gentem   9. P adds: est after: facta   12. V, P: honorabuntur; M: honorabantur   13. V: ita; P: id est, after erasure; M: item   14. V: ab; M: a; P: ab, with 'b' underpointed   16. V, P: dicit; M: dicet with 'i' superscript over 'e'   17. M: adulescentulum   18. V: da Lamech; M, P: de Lamech   18. M: septuages   19. P: Sulpitius; M: Subpicius   19. V: dic; M, P: dicit   20. V: uindicta; M, P: uindictam   21. V: ponietur; M, P: punietur   24. V: adoliscenlum; M, P: adolescentulum   27. V: ferrarum; M, P: ferarum

---

8 Gregory. *Moralia in Job* lib. VI cap. vi (*PL,* 75:731).

nalibus Ebreorum leguntur de Lamech uero lxxvii ut dominus minatur vii
plagas super eum qui occiderit Cain. Ita Lamech per pena[s] plurimas super
eum qui se occiderit minatur. Cur maior ultio Lamech quam Cain? Quia
ante Cain non factum est homicidium nec correptio nec sententia dura dicta castigauit non sic Lamech uel septuagies septies quia hic numerus de
gente Lamech in diluuio deletus est uel in hoc numero requiescit uindicta.
lxxvii uiri ab Adam usque Christum conpleti sunt et tunc soluetur mundus
et anime hominum requiem inuenient. Uel Hieronimus dicit: Non de occisione alterius dicit Lamech sed de seipso quod occidit se per adulterium
quia ipse primus in mundo diuisit carnem in tres quia .ii. mulieres habuit
inde plus uindicta de occisione trium hominum, ipse et duas mulieres, quam
|67ᵛ| de Cain solo. Hinc Lamech ad uxor[e]s dixit: 'Audite uxores Lamech
reliqua (Gen. 4:23). [Enos] qui primus coepit inuocare nomen domini, id
est, nomen quod est dominus, uel primus adorauit iuxta altare lapidea ubi
Abel obtullit et ignis primitus uenit in terra uel in diebus eius primitus [idola]
facta sunt. Hic est INTERROGATIO. Quis primitus in terra inuocauit
nomen domini et [qua] causa et quis prius adorauit iuxta altare et qualis
fuit primum altare in mundo? Isidorus uero dicit: [Enos] iuxta propriae
linguae uarietate[m] 'homo' uel 'uir' dicitur. Et congrue de eo dicitur: Tunc
enim inicium fuit inuocandi nomen domini. Licet plerique Ebreorum arbitrantur tunc primum in nomine domini et in similitudinem eius fabricata
sunt [idola] ut de forma eius primum idolum in mundum. HUC usque II
PRIME LECTIO. Ambulauit Enoch cum domino reliqua (cf. Gen 5:4), id
est, secundum uoluntatem domini duxit suam aetatem. Ideo specialiter meruit
|68ʳ| ut non apparuit hominibus carnaliter. De isto enim dicitur: 'Consum-

---

1. P omits: dominus   2. V: pena; P: poenas; M: penas, with 's' superscript
4. V: correptio; M, P: correctio   5. P inserts: sunt after: castigauit   7. P:
absoluetur   8. P: inueniunt, after correction   8. M omits: dicit   11. P inserts:
ubi est sui, after: hominum   11. V, P: ipse; M: ipsus   11. M, P: duarum
mulierum, (P after correction)   12. V, P: hinc; M: hic   12. V: uxoris; M, P: ux-
ores   13. V: et nos; P: Enoc; M: Et nos   13. M omits: qui   13. M: prime
14. V, P: altare lapidea; M: aram lapideam. (N.B. 'ara' = altar)   15. V omits:
idola   17. V: quia; M, P: qua   18. V, M: mundo; P: mundum   18. V: et
nos; P: Enoc; M: Enos   19. V: uarietate; P: uarietatem; M: proprietatem. Isidore:
uarietatem   20. V, M: arbitrantur; P: arbitrentur   21. V: tunc; M, P: quod
tunc   22. V: idolora; M, P: idola; Isidore: idola   22. V: mundum; M, P: mundo
24. V, P: ideo; M: inde

5-8. Cf. Jerome *Ad Damasum* §5.
8-10. Cf. Jerome *Epist.* 123 §12 (*PL*, 22:1053) and *Epist.* 79 (*PL*, 22:732).
18-22. Isidore *Etym.* VII.vi.10 (*PL*, 82:275).

matus in breu[i] explicauit tempora longa' (cf. Wisdom 4:13). Gre*gorius*:
Nota quod tres uiri in corpore elati, primus p*er* co[n]iugiu*m* generatus et
generans ut Enoch; Secundus p*er* co[n]iugium generatus nec generans ut
Helias; Tertius ne[c] p*er* co[n]iugium generatus nec generans ut *Christ*us.

Cur Enoch et Elias eleuati sunt, ut in fine mundi resisterent Ante*Christ*o   5
uelut figurant *Christ*um similitudine argentarii primo aliquid formant[i]s
de luto, secundo de stagno uel plumbo, .iii. de argento uel auro, uelut
credamus si non peccauisset Adam eode*m*modo ad caelum ascensuros omnes.

In que*m* loc[um] eleuati sunt D*e*i solius nosse [est]. Alii dicunt in
Paradissum Ade quod non e*st* uerum si enim terrenus in eo habitare non 10
potuit post peccatu*m* Ade, qua[n]tomagis generatus ab eo. Gre*gorius*: in
letis regionibus; Hieronim*us*: in loco requiei ubi om*nes* anime |68ᵛ| expec-
tant usque in iuditiu*m*.

Om*nes* dies Matusalem [dcccc]lxviiii (Gen. 5:26 = 969). [Discussion of
patriarchs' ages; cites AG*USTINUS* as: DIC*IT* IN LIBER DE CIVIT*ATE* 15
D*E*I with extracts from XV, 10; XV, 12: ALSO f. 69ᵛ, N.b.: 'sicut in aliis
libris Grecorum et uno Latino et in uno Syro'.] 69ᵛ Item dicit D*omin*us:
Crescite et multiplicamini r*eli*qua (Gen. 1:22). Sic soluitur |70ʳ| aut enim
serior fuit pubertas quanto uitae p*r*olixitas uel primogeniti filii non com-
memorantur nisi qui ordinem genelogie faciunt.   20

[Enos] qui primus coepit inuocare nomen D*omi*ni, in Ebreo qui sperauit
inuocare nomen D*omi*ni, id est, non q[uod] alii ante non inuocauerunt uel
sperauerunt nomen D*omi*ni ut fuit Abel uel Seth sed p*er* sp*iritu*m prophetiae
dicitur [quia de] genere eius plus sperauit in D*e*o p*er* gratiam sperauit [quam

---

1. V: breue: P: breui; M: breue, corrected to: breuii; Wisd. 4: 13: breui expleuit   1. V, P: explicauit; M: expleuit   2. V: elati; M, P: eleuati   2, 3, 4. V:
coiugium; M, P: coniugium   4. V: ne; M, P: nec   6. V: figurant Christum;
M: figuram Christi; P: figurarent Christum   6. M inserts: in, after: Christum
6. V: formantes; M, P: formantis   9. V: loco; M, P: locum   9. M, P add:
est, after: nosse   11. V: quatomagis; M, P: quantomagis   12. V, P: letis; M:
electis, with 'e' superscript   12. M erases: Hieronimus   13. V: in; P: ad; M
omits   14. V: dccccc; M, P: dcccc   19. V: quanto; M, P: quando   19. V: com-
memorantur; P: commorantur; M: conmimerantur, after correction   21. V: Et
nos; P: Enoc; M: Enos   22. V: q*ui*; M, P: quod   23. P omits: fuit   24. M,
P: quia de; V: quae ad   24. V, P: sperauit; M erases   24. V omits: quam
... sperauit (p. 99, l. 3)

1-4. Gregory *Hom. 29 in Evang.* §6 (*PL*, 76:1217) adapted.
11-12. Cf. Gregory *Hom. 29 in Evang.* §5: Elias ... in secretam quamdam terrae
   regionem.

de aliis; inde interpretatur Enos 'homo' non quod alii homines non fuissent sed pro eo quod non in seipso homine uel in alio homine gens eius per gratiam sperauit] sed in Domino. Hinc dicitur Enos sperauit inuocare [nomen] reliqua. Inde Saulus dicit: 'Omnis qui inuocauerit nomen Domini
5 hic saluus erit' (Rom. 10:13). Item prophetia: 'Maledictus homo qui spem suam ponit in homine' (cf. Jer. 17:5); inde nullus de genere Seth uel Enos mortu[u]s in diluuio fuit sed tantum de gente Cain qu[i] non sperauerunt in Domino. Hinc illi digni pessima repentina morte deleti sunt. Agustinus: Concupuerunt filii Dei filias hominum. Agustinus dicit et Iohannis Cassianus:
10 Cum esset inter ipsos bonos |70ᵛ| de gente Seth et illos malos de gente Cain usque nunc utilis a[c] sanctam diuisio. Uidentes post haec filii Seth, qu[i] filii Dei erant, filias hominum, qu[i] de Cain progenie nascebantur, desiderio pulchritudinis earum acensi acceperunt eas uxores. Hinc dicitur: 'Ego dixi, dii estis et filii excelsi omnes. Uos autem sicut homines moriemini, id est,
15 in diluuio, et sicut unus de principibus cadetis' (Ps. 81:6, 7; Vulgate), id est diabolus. Inde primitus gigantes et magi et omnes artes diaboli de illo adulterio processerunt instinctu diaboli. Hinc [Cam] doctus filius Noe his artibus ante diluui[um] sciens diluuium delere totum mundum et recuperare post diluuium, et nouit suum patrem iustum et sanctum noluisset has artes
20 magicas intrare in arcam, scribsit uel s[cul]psit illas in lapides et post diluuium relegit illas et [docuit] filiis suis. inde hucusque magice [artes] et mal[e] cantationes unde homines uertuntur |71ʳ| in lupos et in iumenta et assinos

---

1. P: Enoc   3. V, M: Enos; P: Enoc   3. P: Inuocare nomen; V: inuocare nomenis; M: et inuocauit nomen domini   4. V: Saulus; M, P: Paulus   5. M erases: hic   7. V: mortuos; M, P: mortuus   7. V: quae; M: qui; P: qui, after correction   9. V: concupuerunt; M, P: concupierunt   9. P: Iohannes   10. V, P: esset; M: seth   11. V: a sanctam; M, P: ac sanctam   11. V: que; M, P: qui, both after correction   12. V: q, P: qui; M: quae; Cassian: qui   14. V, P: autem; M: is   17. V: Cain; M: Cam with 'h' superscript; P: Cam, with illegible superscript   18. V: diluuii; M, P: diluuium   20. V: sclupsit; P: sculpsit; M: 'sc', erasure, 'upsit' with 'l' superscript   20. V, M: lapides; P: lapidibus, with 'ib:' over deletion of 'es'   21. V: Dauid; M, P: docuit   21. V, P: filiis suis; M: filios suos   21. M inserts: sunt superscript before: magice   21. V: aras; M, P: artes   21. V: malas; M, P: male   22. M, P: incantationes

---

4-6. The two scriptural quotations are in Augustine D. C. D. XV.xviii: Jeremias in non-Vulgate wording of Augustine.
9. Seq. John Cassian Conferences VIII (Abbot Serenus II) cap. XXI; cf. Augustine D. C. D. XV.xxiii.
10-15. Cassian Conferences VIII cap. XXI. Adapted but all the ideas.
17-21. Cf. Cassian ibid. — some verbal echoes underlined.

et in aues, ut sunt mult[e] fabule. Sicut legim*us* Circ[e] que socios Ulixis motauit in bestias, et Arcades natantes stagnum conuertuntur in lupos et cum similibus feris p*er* deserta uiuunt. Si uero carne humana non uescuntur iterum post viiii annis eodem stagno renatato reformantur in homines. Si uero homine*m* edat non reuertit iterum in homine. Item Appolleus dicit sibi ips[i] acidisse ut accepto ueneno humano [a]nimo p*er*manente asinus fuit. Item socii Diomedis apparuerunt non suppositis p*ro* eis corporib*us* neque sicut in somnis p*er*dentibus eos ulteribus angelis malis in eas aues qu*ae* pro illis sunt occulte ex aliis locis ubi est hoc genus auium et iterum ad ea loca redeunt. Quod uero Diomedis templo aquam rostris asp*er*gunt et quod blandiunt Grecigenis et aligenas |71ᵛ| p*er*secuntur instinctu demonu*m* faciunt ut deus Diomedis adoratur ab hominibus.

Igit*ur* ex illa inlicita conmixtione filior*um* Seth et filiarum [Cain] nati sunt gigantes crudel[e]s, inorm[es], raptores r*e*l*i*qua. Et non potuit sustinere mala eorum mundus p*ro*pter illos diluuium uenit ut deleret eos. Itaque filii Seth libidine transgresse sunt p*re*ceptum D*omi*ni quod ab initio ingenitum fuit in eis p*er* naturam diu custoditum fuit necesse fuit p*er* literam legis postea recuperari ut filia*m* tua*m* non dabis fili[i]s alienarum uxorem nec de filiab*us* eor*um* accipies filio tuo quia seducant corda uestra ut discedatis a D*e*o uestro ... [cf. Deut. 7:3,4; Exod. 34:16 in Cassian].

---

1. V: multa; M, P: multe   1. V: circamque; M: circamquae; P: circe?mque (after correction); Augustine: Circe qu*ae*   2. V: motauit; M, P: mutauit   2. V, P: conuertuntur; M: conuertit   3. V: carnem humanam; M, P: carne humana, after correction; Augustine: carne humana   5. V, M: reuertit; P: reuertit*ur*   5. V: homine; M, P: hominem   5. V: Appolleus; P after correction: Apuleus; M: Apolleos   6. V: ipse; M, P: ipsi; Augustine: ipsi   6. V: inimo; M, P: animo   8. V, M: ulteribus; P underpoints to delete; Augustine: ultoribus   10. M inserts: auibus superscript after: blandiunt   11. V, P: Grecigenis; M: Grecigeni; Augustine: Grecigenas   11. V: aligenas; P: alienigenas, after correction; M: alienas; Augustine: alienigenas   13. V: Cham; M, P: Cain   14. V: crudelis; M, P: crudeles   14. V, M: inormi; P: enormes   15. M inserts: et, superscript after: mundus   16. V: transgresse; M, P: transgressi   18. V: filis; P: filiis; M omits   18. V: alienarum; M: aligenigenae; P: alienigenarum, both after correction

---

1–4. Augustine *D. C. D.* XVIII.xvii with adaptation and verbal echoes.
5–7. Augustine *D. C. D.* XVIII:xviii. story of Apuleus (Golden Ass), adapted.
7–10. Augustine *D. C. D.* XVIII.xviii with verbal echoes.
10–12. Augustine *D. C. D.,* XVIII.xviii.
13–20. Cassian *Conferences* VIII.xxi, adaptation.

Appendix 4

For the oral delivery of this paper I had analyzed the manuscript Orléans, Bibliothèque municipale 342 (290) since the *Catalogue Général* (see note 51) had not identified the items. But a full description is now available in J(oseph) van der Straeten, *Les Manuscrits hagiographiques d'Orléans, Tours et Angers*, Subsidia hagiographica, 64 (Brussels, 1982), pp. 72-73.

Continental Sources of Anglo-Saxon Devotional Writing

THOMAS H. BESTUL

Numerous Latin manuscript anthologies from the Middle Ages are found in which are gathered prayers, hymns, Biblical extracts, and other matter intended for private devotion as opposed to public or liturgical use. These *libelli precum* are particularly abundant in Anglo-Saxon England. For the purposes of analysis, the Anglo-Saxon collections may be divided into two categories. The first is represented by a relatively small body of manuscripts from the eighth and early ninth centuries which is especially important because it includes the oldest Western examples of the *libellus precum*. The second is made up of a much larger group of manuscripts that began to be numerous from the end of the tenth, and especially in the eleventh, century. The latter group exhibits interesting borrowings from the earlier English tradition and from Continental prayerbooks produced as a result of the monastic reforms of Charlemagne. A study of the sources that inspired both groups, especially those from the Continent, can teach us much about the formation and development of such collections and can contribute to an understanding of Anglo-Saxon culture in general.

The earlier group of Anglo-Saxon prayerbooks consists of five manuscripts, the earliest of which is no earlier than about A.D. 750 and the latest no later than about 825. These are: London, British Library MS. Royal 2 A.xx (s.viii); British Library MS. Harley 2965 (s.viii/ix), known as the *Book of Nunnaminster;* British Library MS. Harley 7653 (s.viii/ix); Cambridge, University Library MS. Ll.1.10 (s.ix), known as the *Book of Cerne;* and Oxford, Bodleian Library MS. Selden Supra 30 (s.viii). The prayers in all of these except the last were printed beginning at the end of the nineteenth century, and since that time have been the object of considerable study, especially those in the British Library Royal manuscript and in the *Book of Cerne*.[1] Harley 7653 is a single quire; Selden Supra 30 has only two prayers. In my discussion I shall concentrate on the three largest collections: Royal, *Cerne,* and *Nunnaminster.* Although the present manuscript of the *Book of Cerne* dates from the ninth century, it has been held with good reason to rest in part, if not wholly, on an earlier collection, possibly compiled under the direction of or for the use of Æthelwold, Bishop of Lindisfarne A.D. 721-740.[2] Thus both *Cerne* and the Royal collection may ultimately date from about the same time, probably the middle of the eighth century; moreover, both share several prayers in common.

These manuscripts have no contemporary Continental analogues, although individual prayers probably intended for private use must have been composed on the Continent and circulated there.[3] As will be seen, the texts of many of the prayers are considerably older than the dates of the manuscripts. Some very early Continental collections of prayers are extant, such as the Spanish *Liber Ordinum,* which probably had its origin in the seventh century; the *Orationale Visigothicum,* also Spanish, from the sixth or seventh century; and the three series of psalter collects, which date from the fifth and sixth centuries.[4] Yet all these compilations are made up of prayers used principally in public worship.

Private prayer and meditation were, of course, an important part of Christian spirituality from the earliest moment. Cyprian distinguishes between public and private prayer as early as 251,[5] and Christian literature from the patristic age has no lack of texts that could have supplied the needs of personal devotion. For example, among the works of Augustine, the *Confessiones,* the *Soliloquia,* and the *De Trinitate* have embedded in them prayers that could be adapted to private use.[6]

The cultivation of private prayer, however, seems to have been especially important in the Irish church, and is best regarded as an indication of the Irish concern for the welfare of the individual soul, the most significant manifestation of this concern being the parallel development of a system of private penance and absolution which was to spread throughout Europe by the ninth century.[7] Columban's *Regula Monachorum* explicitly requires monks to pray privately in their own cells, where Benedict's *Rule* allows for the possibility of private prayer in the oratory.[8] No Irish collections of prayers survive, but some fragments of an Irish devotional tradition can be traced. The one undoubtedly authentic early Irish prayer is the *Lorica* of Laidcenn, who flourished in the middle of the seventh century, and whose prayer was extremely popular and became diffused throughout western Europe as the result of Irish missionary activity.[9] Besides this, we have a series of prayers attributed to Irish authors in later manuscripts; and while the authenticity of the attributions is dubious, at least they reflect an understanding by the compilers of the anthologies that the Irish were likely to have composed private prayers. The prayer attributed to Columban, "Domine deus, destrue quicquid," in Paris, Bibliothèque Nationale MS. lat. 1153, a St. Denis manuscript from the middle of the ninth century, is the most likely to be genuine; much more questionable are the attributions of three prayers in the eleventh-century Vatican MS. Chigi C VI 173 to St. Brendan, and of hymns in the seventh-century *Antiphonary of Bangor* to St. Comgall and St. Patrick.[10]

Edmund Bishop, who was the first to study carefully the sources of the *Book of Cerne* and the Royal collection, concluded that both show signs of very strong Irish influence, not surprising considering the dates of the collections and the part of England where they were probably written.[11] The influence of the Irish church on the English, especially in Northumbria, was great, and although Irish influence is thought to have waned in the eighth century, Kathleen Hughes has shown that it was still active in reduced measure to the end of the century.[12] The English prayerbooks may preserve an Irish core that descends from the seventh century. The *Book of Cerne* and the *Book of Nunnaminster* contain texts of the *Lorica* of Laidcenn, properly attributed; and from a later time, the Royal collection attributes prayers to Hygbald, who is probably the Hygbald mentioned in Bede as abbot in the province of Lindsey, and who visited Ireland some time after 672. The Royal collection also has prayers assigned to Moucan, who is otherwise unknown but who from his name is likely to have been a Celt of some kind, probably a Welshman. Two prayers in the *Book of Cerne* are attributed to Alchfrith, a northern anchorite who flourished about 780 and who seems to have known the sermons of Columban.[13]

Bishop also undertook consideration of the difficult question of Continental influence, and after examining numerous early missals, sacramentaries, and other liturgical texts, of Roman, Gallican, and Spanish origin, he concluded that the patterns he observed in phraseology, epithets for the deity, formulas of invocation, and the like, suggested that the closest affinities of *Cerne* were to Visigothic service books, rather than to Gallican or Roman sources. Bishop thought that these "Spanish symptoms," as he called them, must have reached Anglo-Saxon England indirectly, through the medium of the Irish church, which is thought to have had close contact with the Spanish church of the fifth and sixth centuries.[14] The Gallican or Italian influence on the early prayerbooks was found to be rather slight. Bishop's overwhelming erudition and his careful massing of evidence in detailed tables lends conviction to his hypothesis, but I hope to show that the Latin culture of Northumbria that derived from Italy was equally as important as influences from Ireland or Spain in determining the shape of the English collections.[15]

Before turning to a detailed examination of the Anglo-Saxon anthologies, it is helpful to consider whether they can be placed in a more immediate eighth-century context, or whether they are indeed, as they appear at first, a unique phenomenon. Bede is quite certainly the author of a series of extracts from each of the Psalms, known variously in the manuscripts as the *Collectio Psalterii Bedae,* the *Versus Venerabilis Bedae Presbyteri Collecti de Singulis Psalmis,* or the *Dicta Bedae Presbyteri.*[16] We do not know the purpose for which Bede intended this work, but in all three of the early manuscripts it is part of a devotional anthology, and the incipit of the Tours manuscript of about 850 (Paris, BN MS. lat. 13388) explains that the extracts are "orationibus convenientes cotidianis."[17] Examination of the *Collectio* shows that this is a fair assessment. The phrases from the Psalms are of a form that would allow them to be readily incorporated into prayers with little modification, or such phrases could become the basis upon which private prayers were built. For example, the single phrase chosen from Psalm 90 is "Tu enim es domine spes mea."

The abbreviated psalter seems to be an Insular form: an independent version is found in the *Book of Cerne,* where it is more obviously intended as an aid to devotion, and still another version is in the Irish *liber hymnorum* found in Dublin, Trinity College MS. E 4.2.[18] Although this manuscript is from the eleventh century, its contents appear to be contemporary with the *Book of Cerne,* and sections of it may belong to the eighth century. The Irish version is attributed to Gregory, and the rubric recommends it as a substitute for the whole psalter, if sung with a devout mind.[19]

We also know that Bede wrote or compiled a *liber hymnorum,* as he recounts in the *Historia Ecclesiastica.*[20] While nothing survives that can be identified precisely with this work, a number of his metrical prayers, hymns, and Psalm paraphrases survives, the authenticity of which is probable rather than certain.[21] Bede's intention is again unknown, but to the compilers of the eighth- and ninth-century devotional anthologies in which they are preserved these metrical pieces must have seemed suitable for their purposes. The Royal collection has a partial text of "O deus aeterne mundo," a prayer in elegaic couplets attributed to Bede in the tenth-century prayerbook Orléans, Bibliothèque municipale MS. 184.[22] This text is immediately followed in the Royal manuscript by a metrical paraphrase of Psalm 83, which like the preceding is unattributed, but which is quite possibly Bede's work.[23] After this follows another metrical prayer, attributed in the manuscript to Cuth, probably Cuthbert of Jarrow, Bede's disciple.[24]

The *Book of Cerne* has an unattributed metrical prayer, "Laudate altithronum pueri," which concludes with a passage of ten lines from the *Evangelica Historia* of Juvencus.[25] This prayer, without the passage from Juvencus, is attributed to Bede in a ninth-century manuscript from St. Gall (Stiftsbibliothek MS. 869) and is found with a large number of other metrical pieces by Bede in the tenth-century devotional anthology in Bamberg, Staatsbibliothek MS. B. II. 10.[26]

If we pass from the age of Bede to the era of Alcuin, we can find further evidence pointing to English activity in compiling or composing matter suitable for devotional use. Alcuin himself was the author of two surviving devotional manuals, the *Officia per Ferias* and the *De Psalmorum Usu,* and he addressed a detailed letter to Charlemagne on the cultivation of private devotional life.[27] In 802 he described in a letter a devotional anthology he had copied for Arno of Salzburg that included brief expositions on the Psalms, confessions, hymns, the *Collectio Psalterii* of Bede (Alcuin refers to it as the "psalterium parvum quod dicitur beati Bedae presbyteri"), and Bede's elegaic hymn on Queen Ætheldryd, found in the *Historia Ecclesiastica*.[28] The collection Alcuin made for Arno does not survive, but a very similar anthology, which includes both items by Bede as well as the *Lorica* of Laidcenn, is in Cologne, Dombibliothek MS. 106, written at Cologne about 805.[29] It is a reasonable conjecture that Alcuin carried with him to the Continent familiarity with a type of devotional anthology of which the Royal collection and the *Book of Cerne* are representatives.

Alcuin may have compiled such a collection while he was in England, perhaps following earlier native models, and adding suitable materials of his own selection. In the Bamberg manuscript mentioned above (Staatsbibliothek, MS. B. II. 10) is a large collection entitled "Libri IV de laude dei et de confessione orationibusque sanctorum collecti ab Alchonio levita." Although the manuscript is of the tenth century, Radu Constantinescu, who has made an extensive study of it, believes that it accurately represents a collection made by Alcuin at York about 790.[30] Constantinescu shows quite convincingly that this large anthology was very likely the prototype of a number of Carolingian prayerbooks, such as that in the Cologne manuscript mentioned above, and that it probably rests in part on earlier English exemplars perhaps even dating from the age of Bede. This anthology includes extracts from the Psalter, similar but unrelated to those in the *Book of Cerne;* the text is the *Romanum* as used in eighth-century England.[31] It has a version of the prayer of Polycarp, "Deus dilecti et benedicti," which Alcuin must have taken from the *Historia Ecclesiastica* of Eusebius in the Latin translation by Rufinus, a work known in England from very early times.[32] Another prayer is adapted from one found in the

Vita Julianae, "Domine deus omnipotens, spei insertor"; still another is reproduced almost verbatim from a prayer found in the *Verba Seniorum* as translated by Pelagius, "Misericors et miserator dominus." The anthology also includes extracts from the *Synonyma* of Isidore of Seville, which seems to have inspired a number or English and Carolingian prayers, and has long extracts from the *Soliloquia* and *Confessiones* of Augustine, as well as the prayer found at the end of his *De Trinitate*. A Gloria and Credo are included and twelve hymns and metrical prayers attributed to Bede, along with extracts from the verses of Juvencus, Arator, Fortunatus, Paulinus of Nola, Sedulius, and Aldhelm. The Bamberg manuscript can be viewed as a *florilegium* of material useful in constructing devotional anthologies drawn from Biblical, liturgical, and patristic sources.

The best evidence that the Bamberg anthology may depend on an earlier English model is a fragment of what seems to be a preface to such a collection embedded in a confessional prayer at the end of a prayerbook written at Tours about 850 (Paris, Bibliothèque Nationale MS. lat. 13388), and which is, according to Constantinescu, an abridgment of the Bamberg anthology, although the "preface" is not recorded in the latter:[33]

> Adgrediar pro viribus de pluribus pauca, e maximis modica, de innumerabilibus miraculis metrico carmine contingere aliqua, auctoritate scilicet sanctorum patrum fretus, qui multa in laudibus divinis metrice adplauserunt. E quibus praefulgidorum virorum, Hilarii videlicet Pictavensis episcopi, Sedulii quoque ac Iuvenci presbiterorum, necnon et Aratoris Romane ecclesiae subdiaconi atque Eldelmi et Prosperi discurrens virentia prata, paradisi genas inde sumens comptis floribus herbas, quibusdam flosculis meae inbecillitatis pro viribus locis, et suis oportunitatibus interpolatis, hanc tantillam intexui coronam vernantem.[34]

> For strength, I go to a few things of the many, to a small number of the very large number, to take hold of some of those innumerable miracles in measured song, relying, to be sure, on the authority of the holy fathers, who in divine praises applauded many things in verse. From which most brilliant men — namely, Hilary, bishop of Poitiers; Sedulius and Juvencus, presbyters; as well as Arator, subdeacon of the church at Rome; and Aldhelm and Prosper — I, traversing verdant meadows, the cheeks of paradise, thence taking up herbs from tended flowers, have woven this trifling, verdant garland with certain of those flowering places for strength in lieu of my weakness, places given new form in accordance with their suitability.

The Latinity of the piece, the mention of Aldhelm, and the list of the other authors all would be consistent with an early-eighth-century English origin. As we have seen, the Bamberg anthology includes extracts from Sedulius, Juvencus, Arator, and Aldhelm, and this preface may refer to those extracts. The passage from Juvencus annexed to Bede's "Laudate altithronum pueri" in the *Book of Cerne* may derive from such a florilegium. This preface, together with the metrical pieces by Bede, suggests that the early tradition emphasized verse rather than prose. Indeed, in its original form the *Book of Cerne* may have been primarily a collection of hymns. The "Ympnarius Edilwaldi" Edmund Bishop noticed in a library catalogue from Fulda may refer to *Cerne*.[35]

To turn to the surviving English manuscripts, although certainty is not absolute, it seems they belong to a milieu reaching from the age of Bede through the time of Alcuin in which the collection and promulgation of devotional materials was an active occupation of the monastic culture of the period. This broader literary context, together with an insight into the methods followed by Alcuin and perhaps his predecessors, helps us better to understand the formation of the early Anglo-Saxon devotional anthologies.

The Royal collection begins with Gospel extracts on the Passion and includes canticles, a litany, the Gloria, and a Credo. The Celtic influence on the manuscript has been noted above, as well as the presence of Northumbrian metrical pieces of the kind collected by Alcuin. The book also exhibits its indebtedness to the same Latin heritage that inspired Alcuin a generation or so later, a heritage brought to England from the Continent beginning with the Gregorian mission. The litany is the standard Roman type, and one of the petitions is addressed to St. Gregory; "Sanctus Gregorius pontifex" is invoked in another prayer.[36] The collection includes the prayer based on the *Soliloquia* of Augustine, "Deus universitatis conditor," which is attributed to his authorship, as well as two other prayers attributed to him, "Domine Iesu Christe qui de hoc mundo" and "Deus iustitiae te deprecor," which may be based on the *Confessiones*.[37] The hymn of Sedulius, "A solis ortus cardine," is also properly attributed.[38] The impression left by the Royal collection is that it is a rather learned compilation. It has a short prayer in Greek written in the Roman alphabet, and Greek phrases in Greek characters are found in another prayer.[39] No signs of Greek appear in English prayerbooks again until the Greek litany and Sanctus added to the tenth-century Psalter manuscript British Library Cotton Galba A. XVIII.[40] The series of prayers by Moucan have a Hebrew refrain. The hymn of Sedulius is an abecedarius, as is the hymn immediately following it, "Alma fulget in caelesti," and in the manuscript itself a group of prayers is arranged in this form.⁴¹ All of this reminds us of the literary tastes of the age of Bede, who himself wrote at least one hymn in the abecedarian form.⁴² Aside from the lorica-like prayer "Mane cum surrexero" (which is possibly Irish), the hymn of Sedulius, the hymn "Alma fulget," and the prayers attributed to Augustine, none of the prayers in the Royal collection appears to have been widely circulated. A large core remains, the sources for which are unknown. No doubt some of these prayers, such as those of Moucan, were local products. But a source of inspiration seems likely to have been the same Italian culture which brought patristic learning to England from the sixth century on, a culture with which England remained in contact with some degree of closeness through the seventh and eighth centuries. Bishop showed that the Italian service books, particularly the Gelasian sacramentary, had some influence on the formation of prayers in the *Book of Cerne* and the Royal manuscript, but this influence may have been exercised after the service books had arrived in England.⁴³ Only one shred of evidence suggests that some of the unknown prayers may be ultimately Italian in origin. The prayer in the Royal collection, "Obsecro te Iesu Christe filius dei vivi per crucem tuam," is found elsewhere only in two eleventh-century Italian anthologies, the Psalter of Nonantola (Vatican MS. lat. 84) and the prayerbook of Arnulph of Milan (BL MS. Egerton 3763).⁴⁴ One cannot be certain, but a possible explanation for these seemingly isolated occurrences is that the texts derive from a common Italian source. This derivation seems more likely than influence of English collections on the Italian, especially since we have no Carolingian intermediaries for the two texts.

Thus whoever it was who assembled the Royal collection had access to Irish, Northumbrian, and Roman Latin traditions. It is possible that such a collection could first have been gathered in mid-eighth-century Mercia, where the Royal manuscript was written.⁴⁵ But even though no signs from the manuscript itself indicate that it rests on an earlier exemplar (as can be quite obviously demonstrated in the case of the *Book of Cerne*), the items by Bede and Cuthbert suggest a Northumbrian origin and a somewhat earlier date, with a *terminus a quo* probably Bede's death date.

One may also wonder whether the framework and design of such anthologies may not first have developed in Anglo-Saxon England. Alcuin's procedure suggests that the practice of assembling Biblical passages and culling patristic and hagiographical sources for matter that could be adapted for the purposes of private prayer and meditation was something he learned in England. Constantinescu suggests that Alcuin may have followed the example of Ildefonsus of Toledo (d. 667), but the parallel is not persuasive.⁴⁶ On the whole, it seems safest to assume that the devotional anthology as we have it in the early English manuscripts, and as it was developed in the Carolingian age under the auspices of Alcuin, was an English invention.

The *Book of Cerne,* although in a manuscript of the early ninth century, is a composite volume that appears to rest on an eighth-century compilation. The identity of the "Aedeluald episcopus" spelled out in an acrostic in *Cerne* has been the subject of much controversy, but the arguments of David Dumville that he is to be identified with Æthelwold, bishop of Lindisfarne from about 721 until 740, are convincing. Dumville believes that the existing manuscript is a copy of a compilation put together in Northumbria some time after the death of Æthelwold, and that the original core of the collection was formed primarily of metrical pieces, of which there are some twelve in the present text.⁴⁷

The evidence is strong that both the *Book of Cerne* and the Royal collection are products of the Northumbrian culture of the first half of the eighth century. The *Book of Cerne* has an abbreviated Psalter, as already noted, and Gospel extracts on the Passion, as does the Royal collection, and it includes the Gloria and Te Deum. It shows a similar combination of prose and verse items from Irish, Northumbrian, and patristic sources. The *Lorica* of the Irishman Laidcenn has been mentioned; the Northumbrian characteristics are the acrostic of Æthelwold of Lindisfarne, Bede's hymn "Laudate altithronum pueri," and the three prayers attributed to the Northumbrian anchorite Alchfrith.

The attributions of prayers to Jerome, Gregory, and Ephraim the Syrian are unreliable, but some of the prayers, nevertheless, have their source in the Latin culture of the Continent. The prayer "Succurre mihi domine antequam moriar," here attributed to Jerome, is based on the *Synonyma* of Isidore of Seville, a work excerpted in Alcuin's anthology.⁴⁸ The hymn "Ymnum dicat turba," attributed to Jerome and Paulinus, is assigned to Hilary of Poitiers in the seventh-century *Antiphonary of Bangor,* and the editor of the Bangor book believes that the hymn may indeed be his.⁴⁹ The hymn is quoted by Bede in his *De Arte Metrica,* so we can conclude it was known in England from an early date.⁵⁰ The unattributed hymn "Luce videt Christum" may have been written by Pope Honorius I (625–638) on the basis of attributions in later manuscripts.⁵¹ As in the collection of Alcuin, Latin hagiography provides a source of prayers—the prayer "Salve sancte crux" is from the *Passio Andreae.*⁵² As in the Royal collection, Italian influence, at least indirectly, is likely. Kuypers demonstrated that several of the prayers in the *Book of Cerne* are based on collects in the Gelasian sacramentary.⁵³

The *Book of Nunnaminster* is an early-ninth-century manuscript with passages from the Gospels on the Passion, a series of prayers on the events of the Passion, and several of the prayers found in the *Book of Cerne,* including the *Lorica* of Laidcenn.[54] The *Book of Nunnaminster* also has two prayers which derive from the sources assembled by Alcuin in the Bamberg anthology. The prayer "Deus delicti," attributed to Augustine, is a version of the prayer of Polycarp found therein, and the prayer on the descent into hell "Domine deus spei insertor" borrows its opening phrases from the prayer collected by Alcuin from the *Vita Julianae*.[55] If Alcuin indeed compiled his florilegium while in York about 790, the influence of his collection on the *Book of Nunnaminster* would be possible. The text of the prayer of Polycarp in the *Book of Nunnaminster* is almost identical to that found in the Cologne prayerbook of about 805; both of these probably derive from a common source closer to Alcuin's text than that in the later Bamberg manuscript.[56] The two prayers in the *Book of Nunnaminster* are the sole indication that Alcuin's anthology had influence in England as well as on the Continent.

On the Continent, the great ecclesiastical reforms instituted by Charlemagne and continued by his son Louis the Pious led to a multiplication of new manuscripts, many of which were new collections of private prayers, which fixed the devotional tradition for the whole of Europe for the next three centuries.[57] These collections exist both as independent manuscripts in what may be properly called prayerbooks, similar in design to the *Book of Cerne* except for the absence of Gospel extracts, and, more commonly, in psalter manuscripts, where they usually follow the Canticles. This no doubt reflects the increased emphasis on the psalter resulting from the monastic reforms and the growing recognition, urged by Alcuin himself, of the value of the psalter as an aid to private devotion for laymen as well as clergy.[58] By the end of the ninth century, psalters with private prayers can be found throughout the continent of Europe.

The early English tradition of private prayer undoubtedly had influence on these Carolingian manuscripts, and, as I have suggested, the most likely medium for that influence was Alcuin of York. The presence of Irish *loricae* in Carolingian developments, and the attribution of prayers to Patrick, Columban, and Bede suggest Insular influence. Bede in particular seems to have been esteemed on the Continent as a devotional writer. His hymns and the *Collectio Psalterii* are found in ninth-century prayerbooks, and even if the attributions are not accepted as genuine, they are valuable indications of a common perception. The *Collectio Psalterii* was imitated by Prudentius of Troyes (d. 861), whose *Flores Psalmorum* were explicitly intended for private devotion, and by an Einhard, who may have been the disciple of

Alcuin and biographer of Charlemagne (d. 840), and who in any case directly acknowledges his debt to Bede.[59]

Many prayers from the *Book of Cerne* are found in the Continental collections; in most cases the textual differences are very wide.[60] While one can assume that some of these prayers were Insular compositions that arrived on the Continent as a result of the endeavors of Alcuin, it is also likely that some of the prayers, particularly those from patristic sources, would have been available in Continental manuscripts of which we have no trace. It is hard to believe, for example, that the prayer from Augustine's *Soliloquia*, "Deus universitatis conditor," the oldest text of which is the Royal manuscript, and a much longer version of which is in the *Officia per Ferias* of Alcuin, would not have had some Continental circulation apart from manuscripts of the complete *Soliloquia*, even if it was not part of a formal devotional anthology.[61]

The Benedictine reform movement begun on the Continent reached England very late — not until the tenth century when the political stability finally attained in the reign of Edgar the Peaceable allowed to flourish such reformers or founders of new monastic houses as Dunstan, Æthelwold, and Oswald.[62] After a long period of interruption, during the course of which the leadership in the production and promulgation of devotional prayers had passed from Ireland and England to the Continent, we once again find collections of private prayers being written in England, although these do not belong to the first stages of the reform but for the most part are products of the eleventh century. The new prayerbooks are a direct result of the general quickening of intellectual and ecclesiastical enterprise stimulated by the Benedictine reform. The English manuscripts with devotional prayers are comparatively numerous, and thus have the advantage of providing a field of study adequately broad (see Appendix). The later collections are usually found in psalter manuscripts, following Continental practice.

The question of sources for this considerable outpouring of devotional writing is sometimes thought to be rather simple, but it is on the contrary a complex matter and important to our understanding of the monastic culture of late-Anglo-Saxon England. There are four interconnected questions worth investigating. The first is the extent to which the eleventh-century collections were influenced directly by the earlier Anglo-Irish tradition. The second is the extent to which the later collections may have been influenced indirectly by the same tradition as a result of the Anglo-Irish tradition's being first exported to the Continent and then reintroduced to England under the auspices of the Benedictine reform. The third question for investigation is the extent to which the English devotions are directly influenced by new Continental models, and in particular which Continental monasteries might have provided those models. The fourth is the extent to which late-Anglo-Saxon England contributed something original to the devotional tradition, as opposed to merely transmitting inherited models, whether Continental or native. These questions are subcategories of one of the large questions crucial to our understanding of late-Anglo-Saxon culture—i.e., the degree to which that culture looked toward earlier native precedents, or the measure to which it relied on Continental sources.

The best evidence of direct influence of the early tradition of private prayer is provided by our knowledge that the older manuscripts were actively used in the late tenth and eleventh centuries. Most existing collections of eleventh-century prayers were added to manuscripts written earlier. Several manuscripts from the eighth and ninth centuries were enlarged in the tenth or early eleventh centuries by the addition of new prayers or Old English glosses to existing prayers, a fact which points to their continued use in the later period. Manuscript Royal 2 A.xx has a series of collects added in its margins in the late tenth century; the *Book of Cerne* has one prayer added earlier in the century; and the eighth-century *Vespasian Psalter* has a group of prayers and devotions to the Holy Cross in a new quire written in an eleventh-century hand of Christ Church, Canterbury.[63] Additional material added to the *Book of Nunnaminster* shows that it was used by Alfred's queen Ealhswith early in the tenth century.[64]

The use of earlier English manuscripts in the late tenth and early eleventh centuries is confirmed by the art of the time. J. J. G. Alexander observes that when book production resumed in the tenth century, scribes and artists turned to the earlier surviving manuscripts as natural models. Alexander notes, for example, that the decorated initials of the *Book of Nunnaminster*, which was at Winchester in the tenth century, might have contributed to the subsequent development of the Winchester School of illumination.[65]

Yet it is too simple to assume the later English collections are in a direct line of descent from the English prayerbooks of the eighth and ninth centuries. Analysis of the contents of the later collections reveals a situation more complex. First of all, some of the prayers sometimes cited as borrowings from the earlier collections are found throughout Europe, and by the tenth or eleventh century they belong as much to a European as to an English tradition. Thomas Symons suggests in his discussion of the sources of the *Regularis Concordia* that the series of petitions to the Cross "Domine Iesu Christe, adoro te in cruce ascendentem" may be drawn from the *Book of Cerne*.[66] But these prayers are also in the ninth-century Continental Psalter that King Athelstan presented to Winchester in the tenth century (BL MS. Cotton Galba A. XVIII), and the same prayers are also in two eleventh-century Winchester manuscripts, MS. Cotton Galba A. XIV and Cambridge, Corpus Christi College MS. 391, which show signs of Continental influence.[67] The presence of these devotions in the *Regularis* may be as much a sign of Continental influence as a native survival; or perhaps the revival of native material was legitimated by its presence in so obviously important a Continental manuscript as the Athelstan Psalter.[68]

In other cases direct Continental influence can be documented with some assurance. Cambridge, Corpus Christi College MS. 272 is a psalter manuscript with Latin devotional prayers of the Carolingian type written in northern France in the last quarter of the ninth century and brought to Canterbury probably in the tenth century.[69] This Psalter includes the prayers "Domine deus meus qui non habes dominum" (fol. 178^v), "Domine exaudi orationem meam quia iam cognosco quod tempus meum prope est" (fol. 181^r), and "Clementissime deus qui me inutilem famulum tuum" (fol. 183^r), all of which are found in the early-eleventh-century Christ Church, Canterbury collection in British Library MS. Arundel 155.[70] A comparison of the Arundel texts shows that they are quite close to the versions in this Psalter. Another example of likely Continental influence is the collection of prayers in the eleventh-century Leofric Psalter (MS. Harley 863).[71] This manuscript has a group of prayers found in similar order in two Continental manuscripts, a ninth-century Psalter from Beauvais in Florence, Biblioteca Medicea Laurenziana MS. Ashburnham 10, and Orléans, Bibliothèque municipale MS. 184, a late-ninth-century manuscript from Fleury, a monastic house with which, as is well known, England had close relations during the period of reform.[72]

In other instances later scribes seem to be directly following earlier English sources. The best indication of this is the group of private prayers in the Winchester manuscript Cambridge, Corpus Christi College MS. 391 (known as the *Portiforium* of Wulfstan). This collection has several of the popular prayers of the *Book of Cerne,* but significantly it includes a number of prayers from *Cerne* not found in other anthologies, Continental or English, early or late. The text of these prayers is close to that in the *Book of Cerne.*[73] Such fidelity is more the exception than the rule, since unlike the case of Biblical and patristic texts, scribes usually felt free to alter the texts of prayers, enlarging them or adapting them to the particular needs of individual houses (for example by changing feminine pronouns to masculine, or vice versa). It seems likely that the *Book of Cerne* itself, or collections very similar to it, such as the *Book of Nunnaminster,* which we know was at Winchester from an early time, must have been in active use by the monastic community there during the eleventh century, and the impression is left that at Winchester no special need was felt to change or enlarge upon the inherited models.

In one area, however, Winchester shows unmistakable signs of a strongly innovating spirit. The manuscript Cotton Titus D. xxvi–xxvii, written at the New Minster between 1023 and 1035, has a text of Alchfrith's prayer to the Virgin from the *Book of Cerne,* "Sancta Maria gloriosa dei genitrix" (fol. 83^v), as well as several prayers to the Virgin unique to this manuscript which mark an advance in the Marian devotion of the time.[74] The same manuscript also has a Kalendar recording the earliest Western observance of the Feast of the Conception of the Virgin, and it contains at the same time a drawing, the so-called "Quinity" of Winchester, which is innovative in the iconographic prominence it gives to the Virgin.[75] In this manuscript one of the Carolingian prayers to the Virgin, "Singularis meriti sola sine exemplo," here has the variant, "Singularis *gratiae*" (fol. 82^r), a variant which may reflect a theological understanding of the role of the Virgin more advanced than that of its Carolingian source. The reading "singularis gratiae" is, so far as I can tell, unique to England and probably owes its origin to Winchester. "Singularis gratiae" is found in the somewhat later Winchester manuscript, the *Portiforium* of Wulfstan, and in a psalter manuscript from the second quarter of the eleventh century, Oxford, Bodleian Library MS. Douce 296, of uncertain provenance, but probably from Crowland.[76]

A large number of eleventh-century manuscripts containing prayers can be attributed to Christ Church, Canterbury, with the period 1020–70 being especially productive. These collections, such as that in Arundel 155, from about 1012 to 1023, are heavily influenced by the Continental prayerbooks and draw on a common stock of prayers that must have been in wide circulation by this time; yet there are also prayers found only in the earlier English collections, so the eleventh-century prayerbooks may draw on the native tradition as well. Clear evidence for innovation is also present in the Christ Church collections. The quire added to the eighth-century *Vespasian Psalter* in 1030–40 has five extraordinary prayers to the Holy Cross, unique to this manuscript and presumably composed at Christ Church. These prayers are notable for their intensity of emotion and foreshadow the subjectivism that Anselm of Canterbury was to carry to new heights a generation later.[77]

One Carolingian innovation seems not to have affected eleventh-century England at all, and that is the stress placed by the ninth-century reformers on the cultivation of lay piety, particularly among the nobility. Examples of this abound—Alcuin addressed a letter to Charlemagne, the preface to a collection of prayers, explaining how a layman in active life can yet observe regular times of private prayer ("qualiter homo laicus qui adhuc in activa vita consistit, per dinumeratas horas has Deo supplicare debeat"); Charles the Bald commissioned a prayerbook, which survives; and Prudentius of Troyes sent his *Flores Psalmorum* to a noblewoman, probably the Empress Judith, as an aid in devotion.[78] The best English evidence for the cultivation of devotional life among the nobility is from the age of Alfred, even though no English prayerbooks survive from that time. In the same part of Asser's *Life of Alfred* which contains the well-known story of Alfred's love of Saxon poetry is the less-remarked-upon account of his devotional practices. Asser tells us that Alfred learned the hourly offices, and then certain Psalms and many prayers ("orationes multas"). These were gathered in one book which he had with him in his bosom day and night for the sake of prayer ("orationis gratia"), even among the daily routine of secular life.[79] What Asser describes is almost exactly the model of conduct for a lay person recommended to Charlemagne by Alcuin, and the prayerbook he describes has the standard Carolingian form—Psalms, followed by prayers, in a format small enough to be portable. The rubric to the Prayerbook of Charles the Bald similarly speaks of a series of prayers used daily in Charles's youth which he had ordered to be gathered in one volume ("in unum colligi"). It is commonly recognized that Asser's biography often consciously emulates the Carolingian example, but there is no reason to discredit the account—neither Notker nor Einhard has corresponding passages in his life of Charlemagne. Further, as noted above, there is good evidence that the early-ninth-century *Book of Nunnaminster* was owned by Alfred's Queen Ealhswith. It may be that the development of lay piety was another part of Alfred's program of ecclesiastical reform which owed its inspiration to the Continent and which, like the renewed monasticism, failed to take hold. For the next sign of private devotional life among the nobility, one must turn to Alfred's grandson Athelstan, who gave a psalter manuscript to the Old Minster, Winchester (BL MS. Cotton Galba A. XVIII). Athelstan's Psalter, written in northern France, perhaps at Liège, has a collection of private prayers, including those for the canonical hours, and it is possible that this may have been Athelstan's own book of devotions.[80] We know that Athelstan was no stranger to the Continent and its ways, in part through his tireless efforts to arrange marriages for his sisters.[81] He may have procured for himself, after the fashion of the Frankish royal house, a book to aid him in the practice of private devotion. But after Athelstan's death in 939, there is no evidence for royal ownership of prayerbooks. Archbishop

Wulfstan of Worcester owned a *Portiforium* with private prayers, discussed above, and it seems likely that such private prayerbooks as exist in late-Anglo-Saxon England were used in monasteries or by the lords of the Church rather than by lay magnates or the royal household.

I will conclude by reviewing some approaches to study which may prove fruitful in analyzing the sources of the late-Anglo-Saxon collections of prayers. One begins with the smallest field of inquiry, the text of an individual prayer, and one can reach certain conclusions based on similarities and common variants. This is well-established methodology for the study of textual transmission. To take an example, there are sufficient manuscript versions, both Continental and late-Anglo-Saxon, of the prayer "Deus inaestimabilis misericordiae" to enable us to analyze the text of this prayer with the aim of determining whether surviving copies from both Winchester and Canterbury derive from a common example, are dependent on each other, or derive from separate examples, and to attempt to decide whether the examples are Continental or English.[82] I think it is unlikely that the results of such analysis will lead to the reconstruction of archetypes and elaborate stemmata for such prayers, given the inherent instability of the text and the complexities of transmission, but one can observe the patterns in the variants and make what one can of them, much as one studies the transmission and development of iconographical motifs in art.

It is also well-established methodology to study the provenance of the manuscript as a whole — where it was written and where and when it reached a particular place. Besides the texts of individual prayers and the provenances of the manuscripts containing them, it may prove enlightening to examine units of composition larger than the text of a single prayer and smaller than a whole manuscript. That is, certain prayers are frequently found in rather conventional groupings: an example is the "collectio Effrem" attributed to Ephraim the Syrian.[83] The presence of the same groups of prayers in some manuscripts might be considered evidence of influence or common origin. Surviving collections of prayers seem often to be composites made up of several blocks larger than the individual unit, or prayer. In like manner, it seems that the abstract formal principles organizing these collections are also capable of study and are something that can be borrowed or transmitted as much as an individual text, although it is no easy task to demonstrate the influence of an ordering principle. But to take a simple example, the conventional Carolingian pattern of prayers arranged hierarchically (beginning with God the Father, Son, Holy Ghost, followed by the Trinity, the Virgin, and the saints) can certainly be traced in the English examples, and more refined analysis of such formal characteristics seems possible.

As I have mentioned, a relatively large body of texts exists upon which to test various methodologies.

The late prayerbooks are important for students of literature. The prayers and devotions have an intrinsic interest as the expression of medieval piety and spirituality; and, at the same time, they form an integral part of the literary culture of the period, along with homilies, sermons, histories, poems, hymns, saints' lives, and so on. These prayers belong to the Anglo-Saxon monastic culture of the years from about 975 to 1050. Also products of this culture are the great manuscript anthologies containing the bulk of Old English poetry. A study of the prayers heightens our understanding of the monasticism responsible for the preservation of the corpus of surviving Old English poetry. Moreover, at present a large-scale revision in the dating of Old English poetry is under way, tending to move the dates of poems forward toward the dates of the actual manuscripts.[84] If the revised datings hold, then late-Anglo-Saxon monasticism will assume new significance. To give an example: the origin of the *Vercelli Book* is the subject of controversy, but D. G. Scragg has argued that it is a Kentish compilation;[85] in it is found the *Dream of the Rood,* and while part if not all of that poem is very early, the poem may be considered in the context of the series of prayers to the Holy Cross added to the *Vespasian Psalter* at Christ Church, Canterbury, in the years 1030 to 1040. The *Dream of the Rood* and these prayers may alike be testimony to the cult of the Cross in monasteries of southeastern England in the early years of the eleventh century.

Thus for a multitude of reasons Anglo-Saxon devotional traditions can be a rewarding object of inquiry—comprehension of their sources and transmission enhances our knowledge of Anglo-Saxon culture, both early and late, and throws light on the artistic and literary artifacts that are its fruit.

UNIVERSITY OF NEBRASKA — LINCOLN

Notes

1. The editions are as follows: *The Prayer Book of Aedelualdi the Bishop, Commonly Called the Book of Cerne,* ed. A. B. Kuypers (Cambridge, 1902) (hereafter cited as Kuypers); *An Ancient Manuscript Belonging to St. Mary's Abbey, or Nunnaminster, Winchester,* ed. Walter de Gray Birch, Hampshire Record Society (London, 1889); the prayers from Harley 7653 are in *The Antiphonary of Bangor,* ed. F. E. Warren, Part 2, Henry Bradshaw Society, 10 (London, 1895), pp. 83–86; the prayers from Royal 2 A. xx are in an Appendix to the Kuypers edition of the *Book of Cerne.* For Selden Supra 30, see Falconer Madan, *A Summary Catalogue of the Western Manuscripts in the Bodleian Library at Oxford,* 7 vols. (Oxford, 1895–1953), No. 3418; and E. A. Lowe, *Codices Latini Antiquiores,* Vol. II (Oxford, 1935), No. 257.

2. Kuypers, pp. xi–xiv; Edmund Bishop, *Liturgica Historica* (Oxford, 1918), pp. 192–97.

3. The closest analogue is in Vatican MS. Palat. lat. 67, a collection of penitential psalms with commentaries from the second half of the eighth century, written on the Continent in a center where Anglo-Saxon influence was strong. Prayers were added to the manuscript in the tenth century. See Pierre Salmon, "Libelli precum du VIIIe au XIIe siècles," in *Analecta Liturgica,* Studi e Testi, 273 (Vatican City, 1974), pp. 127–29.

4. *Le Liber Ordinum en usage dans l'église wisigothique et mozarabe d'Espagne,* ed. Marius Férotin, Monumenta Ecclesiae Liturgica, 5 (Paris, 1904); *Oracional Visigotico,* ed. José Vives, Monumenta Hispaniae Sacra, Serie Liturgica, 1 (Barcelona, 1946); *The Psalter Collects from V–VIth Century Sources,* ed. André Wilmart and Louis Brou, Henry Bradshaw Society, 83 (London, 1949). See also Eligius Dekkers, *Clavis Patrum Latinorum,* 2nd ed., in *Sacris Erudiri,* 3 (1961), Nos. 2015–27.

5. Cyprian *Ep.* 15, in *PL,* 4:265; cited in André Wilmart, *Auteurs spirituels et textes dévots du moyen âge latin* (Paris, 1932), pp. 13–14.

6. On early prayers of devotion, see Henri Barré, *Prières anciennes de l'occident à la Mère du Sauveur: Des origines à saint Anselme* (Paris, 1963), pp. 1–11.

7. See Oscar D. Watkins, *A History of Penance* (London, 1920), II, 603–64; Alan J. Frantzen, *The Literature of Penance in Anglo-Saxon England* (New Brunswick, N.J., 1983), pp. 19–121.

8. *Sancti Columbani Opera,* ed. G. S. M. Walker, Scriptores Latini Hiberniae, 2 (Dublin, 1957), p. 130 (*Regula,* c. 7); cf. Benedict *Regula* c. 52.

9. See Kuypers, p. 232; Kathleen Hughes, "Some Aspects of Irish Influence on Early English Private Prayer," *Studia Celtica,* 5 (1970), 51–53. A version of the *Lorica* is in the *Book of Cerne,* ed. Kuypers, pp. 85–88.

10. For the prayer of Columban from the St. Denis manuscript, see *PL,* 101:604; it is printed from an eleventh-century Bobbio manuscript in *Opera,* ed. Walker, pp. lxiii and 214. For the prayers of St. Brendan, see Salmon, *Analecta Liturgica,* pp. 153, 154, 163; Dekkers, *Clavis,* No. 1138. For St. Patrick and St. Comgall, see the *Antiphonary of Bangor,* pp. 14–19.

11. See Bishop's "Liturgical Note" in Kuypers, pp. 234-83; and see Bishop, *Liturgica Historica*, pp. 165-202.

12. Kathleen Hughes, "Evidence for Contacts Between the Churches of the Irish and English from the Synod of Whitby to the Viking Age," in *England Before the Conquest,* ed. Peter Clemoes and Kathleen Hughes (Cambridge, 1971), pp. 49-67.

13. Hughes, "Some Aspects," pp. 57-59; Kuypers, pp. 143-44, 155, 207, 219.

14. See the works of Bishop cited in note 11 above. The matter of Spanish influence on the Irish church is complex and controversial; see J. N. Hillgarth, "The East, Visigothic Spain, and the Irish," in *Studia Patristica,* IV (Berlin, 1961), 442-56; Hillgarth, "Visigothic Spain and Early Christian Ireland," *Proceedings of the Royal Irish Academy,* 62C (1962), 167-94; David N. Dumville, "Biblical Apocrypha and the Early Irish: A Preliminary Investigation," *Proceedings of the Royal Irish Academy,* 73C (1973), 299-338. Henry Mayr-Harting (*The Coming of Christianity to England* [New York, 1972], pp. 127-28) believes Spanish influence on Ireland may be exaggerated.

15. In another arena, Michael Winterbottom has demonstrated the importance of Continental rather than Irish influence ("Aldhelm's Prose Style and Its Origins," *ASE,* 6 [1977], 39-76).

16. *Bedae Venerabilis Opera: Pars IV, Opera Rhythmica,* ed. J. Fraipont, CCSL, Vol. 122 (Turnhout, 1955) (hereafter cited as Fraipont), p. 452; the *Collectio* is edited, pp. 452-70.

17. The early manuscripts, all from the first half of the ninth century, are listed in Fraipont, p. 452. The version from Paris, BN lat. 1153, is in *PL,* 101:569-79; the version from Paris, BN lat. 13388, is in *Precum Libelli Quattuor Aevi Karolini,* ed. André Wilmart (Rome, 1940), pp. 143-59.

18. On abbreviated psalters, see Pierre Salmon, "Psautiers abrégés du moyen âge," in *Analecta Liturgica,* pp. 67-119.

19. See *The Irish Liber Hymnorum,* ed. J. H. Bernard and R. Atkinson, Part 1, Henry Bradshaw Society, 13 (London, 1898), pp. 144-56.

20. Bede, *Historia Ecclesiastica* 5.24.

21. These are edited by Fraipont, pp. 406-51.

22. Kuypers, p. 217 ("Me similem cineri"); the Orléans text (copied mistakenly as two prayers) is in *PL,* 101:1397. See Fraipont, pp. 445-61, and Wilhelm Meyer, "Poetische Nachlese aus dem sogenannten Book of Cerne in Cambridge und aus dem Londoner Codex Regius 2 A.xx," *Nachrichten von der Königlichen Gesellschaft der Wissenschaften zu Göttingen, Philologisch-historische Klasse* (Berlin, 1917), I, 616-18. Meyer was the first to edit the poem correctly.

23. Kuypers, p. 218; Fraipont, p. 449. The attribution is argued for by Meyer, pp. 618-19.

24. Kuypers, p. 218.

25. Kuypers, p. 83; Meyer, p. 598.

26. Fraipont, p. 450; M. L. W. Laistner, *A Hand-List of Bede Manuscripts* (Ithaca, N.Y., 1943), pp. 122-30.

27. Alcuin *Officia per Ferias* and *De Psalmorum Usu,* in *PL,* 101:465-612; the letter to Charlemagne is found in *PL,* 101:509-10. The authenticity of the two treatises

was doubted by André Wilmart, "Le Manuel de prières de saint Jean Gualbert," *Revue Bénédictine*, 48 (1936), 259-69; but a convincing case for their genuineness is made by Pierre Riché, "La Bibliothèque de trois aristocrates laïcs carolingiens," *Le Moyen Âge*, 69 (1963), 87-104.

28. Alcuin *Ep. 156*, in *PL*, 100:407; Bede, *Historia Ecclesiastica* 4.20.

29. For the contents, date and provenance of this manuscript, see Leslie Webber Jones, "Cologne MS. 106: A Book of Hildebald," *Speculum*, 4 (1929), 27-61; the prayers from it are printed by Wilmart, *Precum Libelli*, pp. 49-59.

30. Radu Constantinescu, "Alcuin et les 'Libelli Precum' de l'époque carolingienne," *Revue d'Histoire de la Spiritualité*, 50 (1974), 17-56; on the place and date of composition, for which the evidence is speculative, see p. 56.

31. My discussion of the contents of the Bamberg manuscript depends on Constantinescu, pp. 21-38, 55.

32. See J. D. A. Ogilvy, *Books Known to the English, 597-1066* (Cambridge, Mass., 1967), p. 236.

33. Constantinescu, p. 20.

34. The text is from Wilmart, *Precum Libelli*, pp. 165-66.

35. Bishop, *Liturgica Historica*, pp. 192-96; the likelihood of this supposition is examined by David N. Dumville, "Liturgical Drama and Panegyric Responsory from the Eighth Century? A Re-examination of the Contents of the Ninth-Century Section of the *Book of Cerne*," *Journal of Theological Studies*, 23 (1972), 393.

36. Kuypers, pp. 211-12; 208.

37. Kuypers, pp. 210, 211, 222.

38. Kuypers, pp. 223-24.

39. Kuypers, pp. 221, 223.

40. J. Armitage Robinson, *The Times of Saint Dunstan* (Oxford, 1923), pp. 64-65; Elżbieta Temple, *Anglo-Saxon Manuscripts, 900-1066* (London, 1976), No. 5.

41. Kuypers, pp. 213-17.

42. This is the Hymn to Ætheldryd, *Historia Ecclesiastica* 4.20; the dubious Hymn to St. Peter is also in this form (Fraipont, pp. 428-30).

43. See Kuypers, pp. xxviii-xxx, 283. For the relation of Anglo-Saxon England to the Italian service books, see C. E. Hohler, "Some Service-Books of the Later Saxon Church," in *Tenth-Century Studies*, ed. David Parsons (London, 1975), pp. 60-83.

44. Kuypers, p. 221; for the Vatican MS., see Salmon, *Liturgica Historica*, p. 137; for the Egerton, see D. H. Turner, "The Prayerbook of Archbishop Arnulph II of Milan," *Revue Bénédictine*, 70 (1960), 377.

45. Lowe, *CLA*, Vol. II, No. 215.

46. Constantinescu, p. 18.

47. Dumville, "Liturgical Drama," pp. 393-95.

48. Kuypers, p. 148; Constantinescu, p. 31.

49. Kuypers, p. 167; *The Antiphonary of Bangor*, ed. F. E. Warren, pp. 3, 36-37.

50. Bede, in *PL*, 90:173; Warren, p. 37.

51. Meyer, "Poetische Nachlese," p. 609.

52. Kuypers, p. xxxiii.

53. Kuypers, pp. xxviii–xxix.
54. There are seventeen prayers in common; for a list, see Kuypers, p. xxxii.
55. *Nunnaminster,* ed. Birch, pp. 61, 78; Constantinescu, pp. 24–26.
56. The Cologne text is in Wilmart, *Precum Libelli,* p. 59.
57. See Salmon, *Analecta Liturgica,* pp. 182–94; Barré, *Prières anciennes,* pp. 1–17; for a repertoire of manuscripts, see Salmon, "Livrets de prières de l'époque Carolingienne," *Revue Bénédictine,* 86 (1976), 218–34; 90 (1980), 147–49.
58. See Alcuin's letter to Charlemagne, *PL,* 101:509 and his preface, *PL,* 101:465.
59. Salmon, *Analecta Liturgica,* pp. 72–76.
60. For a list, see Kuypers, pp. xxxii–xxxiii; besides these, versions of prayers in *Cerne*—Nos. 6, 15, 19, 20, 22, 49, 55, 63—are found in the four prayerbooks edited by Wilmart: see *Precum Libelli,* pp. 9, 10, 11, 13, 38, 40, 41, 42, 68, 142.
61. Alcuin's text is in *PL,* 101:580. See G. Raethel, "Das Gebet in den Soliloquien Augustins," *Zeitschrift für Religion— und Geistesgeschichte,* 20 (1968), 139–53.
62. The best account is in David Knowles, *The Monastic Order in England,* 2nd ed. (Cambridge, 1963), pp. 31–82; see also D. A. Bullough, "The Continental Background of the Reform," in *Tenth-Century Studies,* pp. 20–36.
63. See Warren, *The Antiphonary of Bangor,* pp. 97–102 (for the Royal collects); Kuypers, p. 79; T. A. M. Bishop, *English Caroline Minuscule* (Oxford, 1971), No. 25 (for the Vespasian additions). See also N. R. Ker, *Catalogue of Manuscripts Containing Anglo-Saxon* (Oxford, 1957), Nos. 27, 203, 248.
64. Ker, *Catalogue,* No. 237; J. J. G. Alexander, *Insular Manuscripts, 6th to the 9th Century* (London, 1978), No. 41.
65. Alexander, No. 41.
66. Thomas Symons, "The Sources of the *Regularis Concordia,*" *Downside Review,* 69 (1941), 29; printed in *Regularis Concordia,* ed. Thomas Symons (New York, 1953), p. 43.
67. Cotton Galba A. XVIII, fol. 22^r; Cotton Galba A. XIV, fol. 110^r; CCCC 391, p. 609; printed from the last in *The Portiforium of Saint Wulstan,* ed. Anselm Hughes, Part 2, Henry Bradshaw Society, 90 (London, 1960), pp. 18–19.
68. See above, note 40.
69. See M. R. James, *A Descriptive Catalogue of the Manuscripts in the Library of Corpus Christi College, Cambridge* (Cambridge, 1912), II, 29–31.
70. Prayers from the latter manuscript are printed in H. Logeman, "Anglo-Saxonica Minora," *Anglia,* 11 (1888), 115–19; Ferdinand Holthausen, "Altenglische Interlinearversionen lateinischer Gebete und Beichten," *Anglia,* 65 (1941), 230–54; and Jackson J. Campbell, "Prayers from MS. Arundel 155," *Anglia,* 81 (1963), 82–117. See also T. H. Bestul, "St. Anselm, the Monastic Community at Canterbury, and Devotional Writing in Late Anglo-Saxon England," *Anselm Studies,* 1 (1983), 187; Ker, *Catalogue,* No. 135.
71. These prayers are printed in an appendix to *The Leofric Collectar,* ed. E. S. Dewick, Part 1, Henry Bradshaw Society, 45 (London, 1914), pp. 434–54.
72. This is a series of prayers addressed to the Father, Son, Holy Ghost, Trinity, the Virgin, and the Apostles; see Dewick, pp. 449–52; for the Fleury prayers,

see *PL,* 101:1399–1400. The unprinted prayers from the Ashburnham MS. are found in fols. 147ʳ–48ᵛ.

73. These prayers are: "Rogo te beate petre," "O andreae sanctae," and "Obsecro te domine"; see *Portiforium,* pp. 9–11; cf. Kuypers, pp. 144, 160, 161.

74. See Barré, *Prières anciennes,* pp. 136–38, where the prayers are discussed and edited; Ker, *Catalogue,* No. 202.

75. Judith A. Kidd, "The *Quinity of Winchester* Reconsidered," *Studies in Iconography,* 7–8 (1981–82), 21–33.

76. Cf. *Portiforium,* p. 24; Douce 296, fol. 125ʳ. On date and provenance of the latter, see Temple, *Anglo-Saxon Manuscripts,* No. 79.

77. See Bestul, "St. Anselm," pp. 190–92.

78. For the letter to Charlemagne, see *PL,* 101:509; the prayerbook of Charles the Bald was printed by Felicianus, *Liber Precationum Caroli Calvi* (Ingolstadt, 1583); for the text of the *Flores Psalmorum,* see Salmon, *Analecta Liturgica,* pp. 93–119; for the preface, *PL,* 115:1449–52.

79. Asser, *Life of King Alfred,* ed. W. H. Stevenson (Oxford, 1904), p. 21; see also p. 73.

80. See above, note 40.

81. See Bullough, "The Continental Background," pp. 33–34.

82. The prayer is in BL Cotton Vespasian A. I, fol. 156ᵛ; Cott. Galba A. XIV, fol. 53ʳ; Arundel 155, fol. 175ᵛ; and in the eleventh-century Bury Psalter (Vatican MS. Reg. lat. 12); see André Wilmart, "The Prayers of the Bury Psalter," *Downside Review,* 48 (1930), 210–11. For Carolingian examples, see Wilmart, *Precum Libelli,* pp. 21, 56, 73; *PL,* 101:524, 1404.

83. Wilmart, *Precum Libelli,* pp. 14–17.

84. For an example, see *The Dating of Beowulf,* ed. Colin Chase (Toronto, 1981), passim.

85. D. G. Scragg, "The Compilation of the *Vercelli Book,*" *ASE,* 2 (1973), 189–207.

Appendix

A Preliminary Checklist of English Manuscripts Containing
Private Prayers and Other Devotional Materials to 1100
(*Indicates MS written on the Continent)

1. Cambridge, University Library Ff.1.23. s.xi. Psalter. Latin prayers.
2. Cambridge, University Library Gg.3.28. s.x/xi. Ælfric, *Sermones Catholici.* Prayers in Old English.
3. Cambridge, University Library Ll.1.10. s.viii–ix. *Book of Cerne.* Prayerbook.
4. *Cambridge, Corpus Christi College 272. s.ix. Psalter. Latin prayers.

5. Cambridge, Corpus Christi College 391. s.xi. Psalter; *Portiforium* of Wulfstan. Prayers in Latin and Old English.
6. Cambridge, Corpus Christi College 411. s.x. Psalter. Latin prayers.
7. *Cambridge, Gonville and Caius College 144. s.ix/x. "Oratio Prudentii."
8. *Cambridge, Pembroke College 108. s.ix. Justinian, *Edictum de Fide,* etc. Latin prayer.
9. London, British Library Additional MS. 37517. s.x ex. Bosworth Psalter. Latin prayers added s.x/xi.
10. London, British Library Arundel 60. s.xi. Psalter. Latin prayers; others added s.xi, xii.
11. London, British Library Arundel 155. s.xi. Psalter. Latin prayers glossed in Old English.
12. London, British Library Cotton Faustina B. III. s.xi. *Regularis Concordia.*
13. London, British Library Cotton Galba A. XIV. s.xi. Collection of prayers, some in Old English.
14. *London, British Library Cotton Galba A. XVIII. s.ix. Athelstan Psalter. Latin prayers.
15. London, British Library Cotton Julius A. II. s.xii. Metrical prayer in Old English.
16. London, British Library Cotton Nero A. I. s.xi. Ecclesiastical institutes, etc. Latin prayers added s.xi ex/xii.
17. London, British Library Cotton Nero A. II. s.xi. Athelstan's prayer for victory.
18. London, British Library Cotton Tiberius A. III. s.xi. *Regularis Concordia,* etc. Prayers in Latin and Old English.
19. London, British Library Cotton Tiberius C. VI. s.xi. Psalter. Latin prayers.
20. London, British Library Cotton Titus D. XXVI. s.xi in. Latin prayers.
21. London, British Library Cotton Titus D. XXVII. s.xi in. Latin prayers.
22. London, British Library Cotton Vespasian A. I. s.viii. Psalter. Private devotions added s.xi.
23. London, British Library Cotton Vespasian D. VI. s.x. Old English: Kentish Hymn; metrical paraphrase of Psalm 50.
24. London, British Library Cotton Vespasian D. XX. s.x. One OE confessional prayer.
25. London, British Library Cotton Vitellius E. XVIII. s.xi med. Psalter. Latin prayers added s.xii.
26. London, British Library Harley 863. s.xi. Leofric Psalter. Latin prayers.
27. London, British Library Harley 2904. s.x. Ramsey Psalter. Latin prayers.
28. London, British Library Harley 2965. s.viii/ix. *Book of Nunnaminster.* Prayerbook.
29. London, British Library Harley 7653. s.viii/ix. A single quire containing Latin prayers.
30. London, British Library Royal 2 A.xx. s.viii. Prayerbook. New prayers added in margins in s.x/xi.
31. London, British Library Royal 2 B.v. s.x, xi. Psalter. Prayers in Old English.
32. London, Lambeth Palace 427. s.xi. Psalter. Metrical prayer in Old English.

33. Oxford, Bodleian Library Bodley 180. s.xii. Prayer in Old English added to the translation of Boethius, *De Consolatione Philosophiae*.
34. Oxford, Bodleian Library Douce 296. s.xi. Psalter. Latin prayers.
35. Oxford, Bodleian Library Selden Supra 30. s.viii. Acts of the Apostles. Two Latin prayers.
36. Paris, Bibliothèque Nationale lat. 8824. s.xi. Psalter. Latin prayers.
37. Rouen, Bibliothèque municipale A.44 (231). s.xi. Canterbury Psalter. Latin prayers.
38. Salisbury, Cathedral Library 150. s.x. Psalter. Latin prayer glossed in Old English.
39. Vatican Reg. lat. 12. s.xi. Bury Psalter. Latin prayers.

Biblical Style in Early Insular Latin

DAVID R. HOWLETT

When my children recite nursery rhymes like "To market, to market" and "Hickory dickory dock" and "When I was going to St. Ives," or when my fellow parishioners sing Newman's hymn "Praise to the Holiest in the height," they preserve and transmit monuments of what I call Biblical style. Some might say that such a style, if it survives only in children's literature and Christian liturgy, is a marginal feature of our culture. Yet for many centuries this style was the very matrix of British-Latin, Anglo-Latin, and Old English literatures. Modern critics have almost entirely failed to notice it. But by noticing it we acquire a serviceable textual critical tool and, rather better, a window into the minds of our earliest authors. The new view of their works it affords will give new reasons for admiring some old favorites and for revaluing some seriously misprized works.

The "new view" is new only to us. The style is very old indeed, fully developed in the Masoretic text of the Old Testament. It is iterative, that is, it consists in stating an idea and then restating it. The first paradigm is Isaiah 1:10:[1]

```
         a'      b'    c'    d'      e'
προσέχετε νόμον θεοῦ, λαὸς Γομορρας.

       a        b       c          d         e
audite verbum Domini principes Sodomorum

              a'      b'    c'        d'         e'
percipite auribus legem Dei nostri populus Gomorrae

     a        b        c          d         e
Hear the word of the Lord, you rulers of Sodom.

            a'         b'          c'         d'            e'
Give ear to the teaching of our God, you people of Gomorrah.
```

Such a statement followed by a restatement in the same order is a parallelism. An example in nursery rhyme is

> To market, to market, to buy a fat pig;
>   Home again, home again, jiggety jig.
> To market, to market, to buy a fat hog;
>   Home again, home again, jiggety jog.

The second paradigm is Lamentations 1:1:

```
        a2        a1
      הָיְתָה כְּאַלְמָנָה

        b2      b1
       רַבָּתִי בַגּוֹיִם

       b'2     b'1
    שָׂרָתִי בַּמְּדִינוֹת

        a'2     a'1
       הָיְתָה לָמַס׃

      a1     a2
    ἐγενήθη ὡς χήρα

         b1          b2
    πεπληθυμμένη ἐν ἔθνεσιν,

        b'1      b'2
      ἄρχουσα ἐν χώραις

       a'1     a'2
     ἐγενήθη εἰς φόρον.
```

```
                  a1        a2
            facta est quasi vidua

                  b 1       b 2
                domina gentium

                  b′1       b′2
                princeps provinciarum

                  a′1       a′2
                facta est sub tributo
```

```
a     How like a widow has she become,
b         she that was great among the nations.
b′        She that was a princess among the cities
a′    has become a vassal.
```

Such a statement followed by a restatement in reverse order is a chiasmus. An example in nursery rhyme is

```
            When I was going to St. Ives
              I met a man with seven wives.
                Each wife had seven sacks.
                  Each sack had seven cats.
                    Each cat had seven kits.
                  Kits,
                cats,
              sacks,
            and wives,
            how many were going to St. Ives?
```

Newman's hymn is in the same form.

```
            Praise to the Holiest
              in the height,
              and in the depth
            be praise;

            in all His words
              most wonderful,
              most sure
            in all His ways.
```

The third paradigm, Amos 2:14-16, combines parallelism and chiasmus.²

aα	וְאָבַד מָנוֹס מִקָּל
bβ	וְחָזָק לֹא־יְאַמֵּץ כֹּחוֹ
cγ	וְגִבּוֹר לֹא־יְמַלֵּט נַפְשׁוֹ׃
dδ	וְתֹפֵשׂ הַקֶּשֶׁת לֹא יַעֲמֹד
d'α'	וְקַל בְּרַגְלָיו לֹא יְמַלֵּט
c'β'	וְרֹכֵב הַסּוּס לֹא יְמַלֵּט נַפְשׁוֹ׃
b'γ'	וְאַמִּיץ לִבּוֹ בַּגִּבּוֹרִים
a'α'	עָרוֹם יָנוּס בַּיּוֹם־הַהוּא נְאֻם־יְהוָה׃

aα   καὶ ἀπολεῖται φυγὴ ἐκ δρομέως,
bβ   καὶ ὁ κραταιὸς οὐ μὴ κρατήσῃ τῆς ἰσχύος αὐτοῦ,
cγ   καὶ ὁ μαχητὴς οὐ μὴ σώσῃ τὴν ψυχὴν αὐτοῦ,
dδ   καὶ ὁ τοξότης οὐ μὴ ὑποστῇ,
d'α'   καὶ ὁ ὀξὺς τοῖς ποσὶν αὐτοῦ οὐ μὴ διασωθῇ,
c'β'   οὐδὲ ὁ ἱππεὺς οὐ μὴ σώσῃ τὴν ψυχὴν αὐτοῦ,
b'γ'   καὶ εὑρήσει τὴν καρδίαν αὐτοῦ ἐν δυναστείαις,
a'δ'   ὁ γυμνὸς διώξεται ἐν ἐκείνῃ τῇ ἡμέρᾳ, λέγει κύριος.

aα   et peribit fuga *a veloce*
bβ   *et fortis* non obtinebit virtutem suam
cγ   *et robustus* non salvabit animam suam
dδ   et tenens arcum non stabit
d'α'   *et velox* pedibus suis non salvabitur
c'β'   et ascensor equi non salvabit animam suam
b'γ'   *et robustus* corde *inter fortes*
a'δ'   nudus fugiet in die illa dicit Dominus

aα   "And flight shall perish from the swift
bβ   and the strong shall not retain his strength
cγ   and the mighty shall not save his life
dδ   and he who handles the bow shall not stand
d'α'   and he who is swift of foot shall not save himself

c'β'	and he who rides the horse shall not save his life
b'γ'	and he who is stout of heart among the mighty
a'δ'	shall flee away naked in that day," says the Lord.

Note in a and a' the second words, מָנוֹס 'flight' and יָנוּס 'he shall flee'; in b the penultimate word, יְאַמֵּץ 'strengthen', and in b' the first word אַמִּיץ 'strong'; in c and c' the identical concluding phrase לֹא־יְמַלֵּט נַפְשׁוֹ: 'shall not save his life'; in d and d' the similar concluding phrases לֹא יַעֲמֹד 'shall not stand' and לֹא יְמַלֵּט 'shall not save himself'. This makes a clear and consistent chiasmus. But there is also parallelism, as the underlined words make clear. The last word of α, מִקַּל 'from the swift', is echoed by the first word of α', וְקַל 'and the swift'. The first word of γ, וְגִבּוֹר 'and the mighty', is echoed by the last word of γ', בַּגִּבּוֹרִים 'among the mighty'. The chiasmus is partly reproduced in the Septuagint. The editor rejected a variant reading of b', ὁ κραταιὸς οὐ μὴ εὕρῃ, because there is no warrant for the negative in the Hebrew text. The reading is explicable only as an attempt by a Greek-speaking editor or scribe to improve the chiasmus, making ὁ κραταιὸς οὐ μὴ εὕρῃ or εὑρήσει a clearer parallel to ὁ κραταιὸς οὐ μὴ κρατήσῃ. The chiasmus is imperfectly rendered, and the translator of this part of the Septuagint has not reproduced the parallelism at all. But when we look at the Vulgate we see that Jerome has reproduced both. He echoes *a veloce* in α with *et velox* in α', and he repeats *et robustus* in γ and γ'. He also improves the chiasmus with the same device by making the last words of b', *inter fortes,* echo the first words of b, *et fortis.*

From these three paradigms we infer ten rules of Biblical style.

1 and 2. The first two — parallelism and chiasmus — are basic and most common. Scriptural warrant for this statement and restatement is found in Ecclesiasticus 42:25: *Omnia duplicia, unum contra unum, et non fecit quicquam deesse* ("All things are twofold, one opposite the other, and He [God] has made nothing incomplete").
3. Parallelism and chiasmus may be combined, as A 1 2, B 1 2, B'1 2, A'1 2, or exhibited simultaneously, the same passage making both patterns ABCD D'C'B'A' and αβγδ α'β'γ'δ'.
4. The words of parallel members may be wholly or partly identical or synonymous.
5. The nouns of parallel phrases may belong to the same declension and the verbs to the same conjugation, or nouns, adjectives, adverbs, and verbs in one may share the same roots as those in the other.

6. A key word in one member may appear in the same position as its pair in the parallel, or the first word of one member may be echoed by the last word of its parallel.
7. Parallel phrases or clauses may be syntactically similar.
8. Parallel members may be linked by puns or word play or by quotations from or allusions to other texts.
9. Parallel members may be linked by alliteration, assonance, or rhyme.
10. Ideas stated at the beginning of a passage may be restated at both the crux and the end.

An adjunct of Biblical style is composition in mathematically determined forms. Jews and Greeks alike believed that Creation itself had been a mathematical act. The former learned this from Sapientia 11:21: *Omnia mensura et numero et pondere disposuisti* ("Thou hast arranged all things by measure and number and weight"). The latter learned it from Plato's *Timaeus* 31-32.

The elements of Biblical style appear in prose and in verse, in small units such as couplets and quatrains and in large units such as pericopes, chapters, and entire books. They are found in the Law, Historical Books, Major and Minor Prophets, Psalms, Gospels, and Epistles.

British-Latin writers such as Pelagius, Patrick, and Gildas, utterly distinct in every other way, all composed clearly and consistently in Biblical style, as did later Anglo-Latin writers such as Aldhelm, the Monk of Whitby, Eddius Stephanus, Daniel bishop of Winchester, Bede, Boniface, Felix, Alcuin, and Æthelwulf. So also did the Old English compilers of Æthelberht's Law Code, Cædmon, the carvers of the Franks Casket and the Ruthwell Cross, the authors of "The Dream of the Rood," "The Leiden Riddle," "The Ruin," "The Rhyming Poem," and Cynewulf, and all the authors who belonged to the court of King Alfred the Great.

But to make the point briefly let us examine a short work of known authorship which is also widely disseminated. The greatest and most widely revered early English writer, the truly Venerable Bede, taught Cuthbert, who succeeded Hwætberct as Abbot of Wearmouth-Jarrow and fashioned for his teacher a memorial unsurpassed in the literature of the English. When E. V. K. Dobbie edited the *Epistola Cuthberti de obitu Baedae* in 1937[3] he knew of forty-five manuscripts, which he divided into two great recensions, a Continental version attested by twelve manuscripts ranging in date from the ninth century to the sixteenth, most of which contain an Old English poem in Northumbrian dialect, and an Insular version, attested by thirty-

David R. Howlett

three manuscripts ranging in date from the twelfth century to the fifteenth, many of which contain the Old English poem in West Saxon dialect. Dobbie listed the principal characteristics which distinguish these two recensions.[4]

1. The Continental version omits the Salutation at the beginning of the text, marked A below.
2. It gives an incorrect date, *VII Idus Maias,* where the Insular version gives the correct date, *VII Kalendas Iunii,* at C2a'ii.
3. It includes the phrases *in quibus ... admonebat* C5, and *dicens ... corpore* C6a, which the Insular version omits.
4. It specifies the part of St. John's Gospel which Bede translated, at C3'b.
5. It omits the words *Divites autem in hoc seculo aurum et argentum et alia queque preciosa dare student; ego autem cum multa caritate et gaudio fratribus meis dabo quod Deus dederat,* which the Insular version includes after C'3hii.
6. It includes the name of Bede's amanuensis at C'3'a.
7. It includes the sentence marked B'1' below.

Since 1937 another twenty manuscripts have emerged.[5] Of these the most important is a manuscript, probably of the early tenth century, now in the Hague, Koninklijke Bibliotheek, MS. 70 H 7, folios 42–45. It has been published by N. R. Ker[6] and by Colgrave and Mynors, who state:

> It agrees more closely with the 'Continental' text, but in several places offers a good reading found in the English copies, not (it would appear) from any deliberate fusion of texts, but because it descends independently from the common parent of the whole tradition and partakes of the merits of both branches.[7]

Dobbie has given reasons for believing that a manuscript of the eleventh century, now in Bamberg, Staatsbibliothek MS. A.I.47 (MS. Bibl. 22), is the most accurate transcript of the prototype of the Continental version.[8] The following reconstruction of Cuthbert's *Epistola de obitu Baedae* is based upon the Bamberg manuscript, with emendations from other Continental manuscripts marked by italics and emendations from the Hague manuscript and Bodleian MS. Digby 211 (chosen by Dobbie as the best representative of the Insular version) enclosed in square brackets.

Text

```
A  x        Incipit de valitudine et obitu venerabilis Bedae presbiteri.
   1        [Dilectissimo in Christo
   2           collectori
   3           Cuthuuino
   3'          Cuthbertus
   2'          condiscipulus
   1'       in Deo aeternam salutem.]

B  1 a      Munusculum quod misisti multum libenter accepi
     a'       multumque gratanter litteras tuae devotae eruditionis legi
   2        in quibus quod maxime desiderabam missas videlicet et orationes sacrosanctas pro Deo dilecto patre ac
              [nostro] magistro Beda a vobis diligenter celebrari repperi.
   1'       Unde delectat magis pro eius caritate quam fretus ingenio paucis sermonibus dicere quo ordine migraret
              [e] saeculo cum etiam hoc te desiderasse et poposcisse intellexi.

C  1 a      Gravatus est quidem infirmitate
     b        et maxime creberrimi anhelitus
     c        sed tamen pene sine dolore aliquo
   2 a i    ante diem autem Resurrectionis Dominicae
       ii     id est fere duabus ebdomadibus
     b      et sic postea laetus ac gaudens gratiasque agens Omnipotenti Deo omni die et nocte immo
              horis omnibus
     a' i   usque ad diem Ascensionis Dominicae
        ii    id est VII [Kalendas Iunii] vitam ducebat
   3 a i    et nobis suis discipulis cotidie lectiones dabat
       ii     et quicquid reliquum fuit diei in psalmorum cantu
       iii      prout potuit se occupabat
       i'     totam vero noctem
       ii'      laetus in orationibus et gratiarum actione Deo
       iii'       ducere studebat nisi tantum modicus somnus impediret
     b      itemque autem evigilans statim consueta Scripturarum modulamina ruminabat
```

4	a	i	extensisque manibus Deo gratias agere
		ii	non est oblitus.
		iii	Vere fateor quia neminem umquam alium oculis meis vidi
		iii'	nec auribus audivi
		ii'	tam diligenter
		i'	gratias Deo vivo referre.
	b		O vere beatus vir.
	c		Canebat autem sententiam Sancti Pauli Apostoli dicentis
	d		Horrendum est incidere in manus Dei viventis
	e		et multa alia de Sancta Scriptura
5			in quibus nos a somno animae exurgere precogitando ultimam horam admonebat
6	a		et in nostra quoque lingua ut erat doctus in nostris carminibus
			dicens de terribili exitu animarum e corpore
	b	i	Fore thae[m] neidfarae naenig uiuurthit
		ii	thoncsnotturra than him tharf sie
		iii	to ymbhycggannae aer his hiniongae
		iv	huaet his gastae godaes aehtha yflaes
		v	aefter deothdaege doemid ueeorthae.
6'	a		Cantabat etiam antiphonas ob nostram consolationem et suam quarum
			una est
	b	i	O Rex Gloriae Domine Virtutum
		ii	qui triumphator hodie super omnes caelos ascendisti
		iii	ne derelinquas nos orphanos
		iv	sed mitte promissum Patris in nos Spiritum Veritatis
		v	Alleluia.
5'			Cum venisset autem ad illud verbum Ne derelinquas nos orphanos prorupit in lacrimas et multum flebat. Et post horam coepit repetere quae inchoaverat et sic tota die faciebat. Et nos quidem audientes haec luximus cum illo et flevimus; altera vice legimus altera ploravimus immo cum fletu legimus. In tali laetitia quinquagesimales dies usque ad diem praefatum deduximus.
4'	a		Et ille multum gavisus est et Deo gratias referebat
	b		quia sic meruisset infirmari
	c		et saepe dicebat

136   Biblical Style

```
d              Flagellat Deus omnem filium quem recipit
e i               et sententiam Ambrosii
  iiα                Non sic vixi ut me pudeat inter vos vivere
     α'              Sed nec mori timeo quia bonum Deum habemus.
3' a i         In istis autem diebus duo opuscula [multum] memori[a] digna exceptis lectionibus quas cotidie
                   accepimus ab eo
     ii            et cantu psalmorum
     iii           facere studuit
  b           id est a capite Evangelii Sancti Iohannis usque ad eum locum in quo dicitur Sed haec quid
              sunt inter tantos? in nostram linguam ad utilitatem aecclesiae Dei convertit et de libris
              [Rotarum] Isidori episcopi excerptiones quasdam dicens Nolo ut pueri mei mendacium legant
              et in hoc post meum obitum sine fructu laborent.
2'              Cum venisset autem tertia feria ante Ascensionem Domini
1' a         coepit vehementius egrotare
   b            in anhelitu
   c            et modicus tumor in suis pedibus apparuit.
C' 1 a         Totum tamen illum diem docebat et hilariter dictabat et nonnunquam inter alia dixit
     b            Discite cum festinatione quia nescio quamdiu subsistam
     c            et si post modicum tollat me Factor meus.
     b'           Nobis tamen videbatur ne forte suum exitum bene sciret.
     a'           Et sic noctem in gratiarum actione pervigil duxit.
   2 a         Et mane illucescente id est quarta feria praecepit
     b            diligenter scribi quae cooperamus
     c            et hoc fecimus usque ad tertiam horam.
     c'        A tertia autem hora
     b'           ambulavimus cum reliquiis sanctorum
     a'           ut consuetudo illius diei poscebat.
   3 a         Et unus erat ex nobis cum illo qui dixit illi
              [Magister dilectissime]
     b            Adhuc capitulum unum de libro quem dictasti deest et videtur mihi tibi difficile esse plus te
                  interrogare
     d         At ille inquit
```

e		Facile est
f		Accipe tuum calamum et tempera festinanterque scribe
g		Et ille hoc fecit
h	i	A nona hora dixit mihi
	ii α	Quaedam preciosa in mea capsella habeo
	β	id est *piperum* oraria et incensa
	γ	Sed curre velociter
	δ	et adduc presbiteros nostri monasterii ad me
	ε	ut et ego munuscula qualia mihi Deus donavit illis distribuam.
		Et hoc cum tremore *feci*.
j	i	Et presentibus illis locutus est ad eos
	ii	unumquemque monens et obsecrans pro eo *missas et orationes diligenter* facere
	iii	et illi libenter spol[po]nderunt.
	iv	Lugebant autem *et flebant omnes* maxime *autem* in verbo quod dixerat
	v	quia aestimaret quod faciem eius amplius non multo in hoc saeculo essent visuri.
1' a		Gaudebant autem
b		de eo quod dixit
c	i	Tempus est si sic Factori meo videtur ut ad eum modo absolutus ex carne veniam
	ii	qui me quando non eram ex nihilo formavit. Multum tempus vixi
	iii	beneque mihi Pius Iudex
	iv	vitam meam praevidit.
	i'	Tempus absolutionis meae prope est
	ii'	etenim anima mea desiderat
	iii'	Regem meum Christum
	iv'	in decore suo videre.
b'		Sic et alia multa utilitatis causa ad aedificationem nostram locutus
a'		in laetitia
2'		diem ultimum usque ad vesperum duxit.
3' a		Et praefatus puer nomine Uuilberch adhuc dixit
b		Magister dilecte
c		Restat adhuc una [sententia] non descripta.
d		At ille *inquit*
e		*Bene*

	f		scribe
	g	i	Et post modicum dixit puer Modo descripta est
	h	i	At ille Bene inquit
		ii α	Consummatum est
		β	veritatem dixisti
		γ	Accipe meum caput in manus tuas
		δ	quia multum me delectat sedere ex adverso loco sancto meo in quo orare solebam
		ε	ut et ego sedens Patrem meum invocare possim.
	j	i	Et sic in pavimento suae casulae decantans
		ii α	Gloria Patri et Filio et Spiritui Sancto
		β	et caetera
		iii	ultimum e corpore
		iv	exhalavit spiritum
		v	atque sine dubio credendum est quod pro eo quia hic semper devotissimus in Dei laudibus laboraverat ad gaudia desideriorum caelestium anima eius ab angelis portaretur.
		v'	Omnes autem qui audiere vel videre obitum beati *Baedae* patris nostri numquam se vidisse alium in tam magna devotione atque tranquillitate vitam suam finisse dicebant.
	iv'		Quia sicut audisti quousque anima eius
	iii'		in corpore fuit
	ii' α		Gloria Patri
	β		et alia quaedam ad gloriam Dei
	i'		cecinit et expansis manibus Deo gratias agere non cessabat.
B'	1		Scire autem debes quia adhuc multa narrari et scribi possunt de eo
	2		sed nunc brevitatem sermonis ineruditio meae linguae facit.
	1'		Attamen cogito Deo adiuvante ex tempore plenius de eo scribere quae oculis vidi et auribus audivi.
A'	x		[Explicit Epistola Cuthberti de obitu venerabilis Bedae presbiteri.]

David R. Howlett

Translation

A   Here begins "On the illness and death of venerable Bede the priest." For his most beloved fellow lector in Christ, Cuthwine, Cuthbert, his fellow pupil [wishes] eternal salvation with God.

B 1   The little present which you sent I received with much gratitude, and with much pleasure I read your letter of devout erudition,

2   in which I learned what I especially longed for, namely that masses and sacrosanct prayers are being diligently celebrated by you for our father and master, Bede, beloved by God.

1'   Therefore it delights me, trusting more in the love of him than in my own skill, to say in a few words how he passed from this world, especially since I understand that you have desired and requested this.

C 1   He was indeed vexed with illness, and especially with frequent breathlessness, yet almost without any pain,

2   before the day of the Dominical Resurrection, that is, for almost two weeks, and after [Easter] he lived his life cheerful and rejoicing and giving thanks to Almighty God each day and night, indeed every hour, until the day of the Dominical Ascension, that is, the seventh day before the Kalends of June,

3   and to us his pupils he daily gave lessons, and for whatever was left of the day he occupied himself as he could with the chanting of Psalms. And the whole night he diligently passed cheerful in prayers and in giving of thanks to God, unless a short sleep would intervene. But waking up at once he would mull over in the same way the familiar melodies of the Scriptures,

4   and with his hands outstretched he did not forget to give thanks to God. Truly I say that I never saw with my eyes nor heard with my ears any other man give thanks to the living God so diligently. O truly blessed man! For he used to sing the sentence of St. Paul the Apostle, saying, "It is a fearful thing to fall into the hands of the living God," and many other things from Holy Scripture,

5   with which he admonished us to rise up from the slumber of the soul by thinking in good time about our last hour.

6   And in our own language, as he was learned in our poems, speaking about the terrible departure of souls from the body:

> Before that enforced journey   no one becomes
> Wiser in thought   than he may need to be
> For considering   before his going hence
> What for his spirit   of good or of evil
> After his death-day   might be judged.

6'   He used also to sing antiphons for our consolation and his own, of which one is

>   O King of Glory, Lord of Might,
>   Who as a victor today ascended above all the heavens,
>   May you not abandon us as orphans,
>   But send the Father's promised Spirit of Truth to us.
>   Alleluia.

5' But when he came to that word "May you not abandon us as orphans" he burst into tears and wept much. And after an hour he began to repeat what he had left unfinished, and he carried on thus the whole day. And we, hearing these things, mourned with him and wept; at one time we read, at another we cried; really we read weeping. With such joy we passed the quinquagesimal days until the foresaid [Ascension] Day.

4' And he rejoiced much and gave thanks to God because he should so deserve to suffer illness, and he often said, "God scourges every son whom He receives," and the sentence of Ambrose, "I have not so lived that it would shame me to live among you, but neither do I fear to die, since we have a good God."

3' In these days, moreover, he tried to complete two little works very worthy of record, besides the lessons which we daily received from him and the chanting of Psalms, that is, he translated into our language for the profit of the Church of God from the beginning of the Gospel of St. John to the place in which is said "But what are these among so many?" and certain excerpts from the Book of Cycles of Isidore the bishop, saying, "I do not wish that my boys should read a lie and in this respect labor fruitlessly after my death."

2'
1' When the third day [Tuesday] before the Ascension of the Lord arrived he began to worsen seriously in his breathing, and a little swelling appeared in his feet.

C' 1 Nonetheless all that day he continued to teach, and he kept dictating happily, and not a few times he said, among other things, "Learn quickly, for I do not know how long I shall live, nor whether after a little time my Maker may take me away." For it seemed to us that perhaps he might know well the time of his death. And thus he passed the night awake in thanksgiving.

2 And at daybreak, that is, on the fourth day [Wednesday] he ordered the things we had begun to be diligently written, and this we did until the third hour [9:00 A.M.]. From the third hour, however, we processed with relics of the saints, as the custom of that day required.

3 And there was one of us with him who said to him, "Most beloved master, yet one chapter from the book you have dictated is incomplete, and it seems to me to be hard on you to ask you for any more." But he said, "It is easy. Take your pen and mend it and write quickly." And he did this. At the ninth hour [3:00 P.M.] he said to me, "I have some precious things in my little box, that is, pepper, napkins, and incense. But run quickly, and bring the priests of our monastery to me, that I may distribute

	to them such little gifts as God has given me." And I did this tremblingly. And when they were present he spoke to them, urging and begging each one to say masses and prayers diligently for him; and they willingly promised. But they all mourned and wept especially at the word he had said, because he reckoned that they would see his face for not much longer in this world.
1'	But they rejoiced about one thing he said: "It is time, if it should seem fitting to my Maker, that released from my body I should come now to Him Who formed me from nothing when I was not. I have lived a long time, and the Holy Judge has seen to me well my whole life. The time of my release is near, for my soul longs to see Christ my King in His beauty." This and many other profitable things for our edification he said in cheerfulness,
2'	until he came to his last day at Vespers.
3'	And the aforesaid boy, Wilbur by name, said again, "Beloved master, yet one sentence remains not written down." But he said, "Well, write." And after a short while the boy said, "Now it is written." But he said, "Very well. 'It is finished.' You have spoken the truth. Take my head 'into your hands,' because it pleases me to sit opposite my holy place, in which I have usually prayed, so that sitting I may call upon my Father." And thus on the pavement of his cell singing out "Glory be to the Father and to the Son and to the Holy Ghost" and the rest, he breathed out his last breath from his body. And it is to be believed without doubt that because he always worked most devoutly for the praises of God his soul was borne to the joys of heavenly desires by angels. For all who heard or saw the death of Bede our blessed father said that they had never seen another end his life with such great devotion and tranquillity. For as you have heard, as long as his soul was in his body he sang "Glory be to the Father" and other things to the glory of God, and with his hands outstretched he did not cease to give thanks to God.
B'	You ought to know, moreover, that many things can yet be told and written about him, but now the unlearnedness of my tongue makes for brevity of speech. Nonetheless I intend, God helping, to write later more fully about him what I have seen with my eyes and heard with my ears.
A'	Here ends the Letter of Cuthbert about the death of venerable Bede the priest.

Let us consider first the simplest corruptions, distinguished in the text by italics.

	Preferred reading	Bamberg MS.
1. C'1b'	suum exitum	exitum suum
2. C'3hi	A	At
3. C'3hiiβ	piperum	piper

4.	c′3hi′	feci	fecit
5.	C′3jii	missas et orationes diligenter	missas diligenter et orationes
6.	C′3jiv	et flebant omnes	omnes et flebant
7.	C′3jiv	autem	*omits* autem
8.	C′3′d–e	inquit Bene	Bene inquit
9.	C′3′v′	Baedae	Będani

Most of these Bamberg readings are minority, if not unique, readings in the Continental version, and they are easily explained. The first, fifth, sixth, and eighth are simple transpositions. The second may have issued from confusion with the preceding phrases C′3d *At ille* and C′3g *Et ille*. The third is a correct Classical form. The fourth implies that a scribe mistook the subject and object, construing "And he [Bede] did this [distribute gifts]," rather than "And I [Cuthbert] did this [summon the priests]." A scribe omitted the seventh because the same word appears only five words before in the sentence. The ninth is a double inflection, a Latin genitive *-i* added to the Old English genitive form *Bedan*. All the preferred readings except the first and fifth are supported by other manuscripts of the Continental version. The first, third, fourth, fifth, sixth, and eighth are supported by the Hague manuscript of the intermediate version.

The twelve readings enclosed in square brackets are not found in manuscripts of the Continental version. Nine of them are supported by a consensus of Digby and Hague. The remaining three can be confirmed on other grounds. In A Hague reads *Dilectissimo in Christo lectori Cuthuuino Guthbertus diaconus in Deo aeterno salutem*, where Digby reads *Dilectissimo in Christo lectori Cuthwino Cuthbertus condiscipulus in Deo eternam salutem*, although several other Insular manuscripts read *collectori*. In C′3b Digby reads *Magister dilectissime*, where Hague omits this. In A′ Hague gives the Explicit, where Digby omits this.

Biblical style confirms the integrity of the entire composition as well as of the minor details. The *Incipit* Ax and the *Explicit* A′x may not have belonged to the original epistle, but as Cuthbert probably hoped for a wide circulation for his little masterpiece, he may have written them himself. Both contain eight words. The absence of the words *Epistola Cuthberti* from the *Incipit* is explained by the Salutation, which attests the epistolary nature and the authorship of the text. The structure of the entire epistle is the structure of the Salutation writ large, a chiasmus of six parts.

In B Cuthbert thanks Cuthwine for the *litteras tuae devotae eruditionis*. He refers to masses and prayers for Bede at the crux in 2, Cuthwine's gifts to him in 1, and his gift to Cuthwine in 1'. Correspondingly in B' he apologizes for the *ineruditio meae linguae* at the crux in 2 and states in 1 and 1' that more can be written about Bede. The style of reference in B2, *patre ac [nostro] magistro Beda,* is echoed by that in C'3'jv, *Baedae patris nostri.* Cuthbert's preference for the preposition *e* rather than *a* in B1', *migraret* [*e*] *saeculo,* is illustrated by similar constructions in C6a, *de terribili exitu animarum e corpore,* C'1' ci *absolutus ex carne,* and C'3'jiii *ultimum e corpore exhalavit spiritum.*

Cuthbert relates the period of Bede's infirmity from Lent to the penultimate day of his life in C, a chiasmus of twelve parts. He describes Bede's illness in 1 and 1', each comprising three parts. He fixes the period, from Lent to Ascension Day (Thursday, 26 May 735) in 2, a three-part chiasmus, and he alludes to the date again in 2'. He describes Bede's activities in a six-part parallelism in 3a and alludes to them again in a three-part statement in 3'a. He states in 3b that Bede meditated upon Holy Scripture and in 3'b that Bede translated Holy Scripture into English. He mentions in a six-part chiasmus in 4a that Bede gave thanks to God, and he restates this in 4'a. He writes of Bede's blessedness in 4b and his merit in 4'b. He quotes Hebrews 10:31 in 4d and Hebrews 12:6 in 4'd. At the crux in 6 he gives an Old English poem which Bede recited and in 6' a Latin antiphon which Bede repeated. One infers confidently that the text is very nearly as it issued from Cuthbert's pen. The Old English poem consists of five lines and twenty-five words. The Latin antiphon consists of five lines and twenty-five words. From the beginning of the passage at 1a *gravatus est* to 4ai *Deo gratias agere* nothing is out of place. *Deo* is the hundredth word. From the crux of the chiasmus at 6'a *cantabat etiam* to 4'a *Deo gratias referebat* nothing is out of place. *Deo* is the hundredth word. This word count corroborates the witness of the Continental version in including the phrases *in quibus ... admonebat* C5 and *dicens ... corpore* C6a, which the Insular version omits. The former corresponds to C5', and the latter corresponds to C6'a, *ob nostram consolationem et suam;* both these latter appear in the Insular as well as the Continental version, and both are required to bring the total number of words to one hundred at *Deo* in C4'a.

Cuthbert relates the last day of Bede's life in C', a parallelism of six parts. First he reports in 1a what Bede did joyously during the day and in a' what he did during the night. He mentions Bede's death in b and b' and Bede's remarks about his Maker at the crux in c. Correspondingly in 1' he mentions joy in a and a', reports Bede's conversations in b and b', and gives at the crux in c Bede's remarks about his Maker in a parallelism. As in C2 and 2' he refers to the time of these events, Terce in C'2 and Vespers in C'2'. At 3 Cuthbert introduces a climactic paragraph of nine parts. He mentions in a the boy who served as Bede's amanuensis, in b the boy's address to Bede, in c his remark that one chapter of Bede's translation of John remained incomplete, in d Bede's address to him, in e and f Bede's remarks, and in g the boy's response. In h Cuthbert reports Bede's remarks to him in a chiasmus, of which the crux contains five parts. In j he relates Bede's dealings with the assembled priests of his monastery in five clauses. Correspondingly Cuthbert introduces at 3' another paragraph of nine parts. He mentions in a the *praefatus puer nomine Uuilberch,* in b the boy's address to Bede, in c his remark that one sentence of Bede's translation of John remained incomplete, in d Bede's address to him, in e and f Bede's remarks, and in g the boy's response. In h Cuthbert reports Bede's request to the boy in five clauses. In j he relates Bede's death, mentioning his singing in i and i', the *Gloria Patri* in ii and ii', his body in iii and iii', his spirit in iv and his soul in iv', and affirming in v that Bede lived *devotissimus* and in v' that Bede died *in tam magna devotione.* One infers that the text of C' as of C has been transmitted uncorrupt. Bede's speech in C'3hii consists of thirty-two words. His speech in C'3'hii also consists of thirty-two words. This word count confirms the correctness of the omission of the sentence *Divites . . . dederat,* interpolated after C'3hiii in the Insular version. Cuthbert's remarks at C'jv and v' comprise fifty words, twenty-five in v and twenty-five in v'. This word count confirms the authenticity of the Hague readings *atque sine dubio* and *obitum beati Baedae* in preference to Bamberg's *atque ut sine dubio* and *obitum Bedani,* which yield the same total but destroy the symmetry.

Uilberch's address in 3'b, *Magister dilecte,* confirms the authenticity of the address in 3b, *Magister dilectissime.* Uilberch's reference to the incomplete *capitulum* in 3c confirms the authenticity of the reference to the incomplete *sententia* in 3'c. This has troubled many readers. How, they wonder, if Bede's translation had reached only John 6:9 by Tuesday 24 May, could it have reached the last chapter by Terce on the following morning and the last sentence by Vespers on Wednesday evening? The answer is that Bede translated only about the first third of the Gospel according to St. John. That work begins with a chiastic Prologue:

>   In principio
>   erat
>   Verbum
>   et Verbum
>   erat
>   apud Deum

> et Deus
> erat
> Verbum.
> Hoc
> erat
> in principio apud Deum.
>
> Omnia
> per ipsum
> facta sunt
> et
> sine ipso
> factum est
> nihil.
>
> Quod factum est in ipso
> vita erat
> et
> vita erat
> lux hominum.

The narrative of the Gospel moves in a great parallelism, as I hope to show elsewhere. For the present the reader may discover for himself the outlines of this parallelism by comparing the following pairs of verses.

1:12-3:35-36	1:35-37-4:1	1:43-4:43	2:1-4:46a	2:13-5:1
1:15-3:28b	1:41 -4:25	1:48-4:39	2:5-4:51	2:25-5:35, 41
1:20-3:28a			2:11-4:54	
1:28-3:23			2:12-4:46b	

St. John gives no account of the Eucharist at the Last Supper. But the passages given above lead up to the account of the Feeding of the Five Thousand (6:1-14), which both St. John and St. Mark consider as a type of the Eucharist. The Feeding of the Five Thousand, moreover, precedes the first of Jesus' great discourses, *Ego sum panis vitae* (6:35). The incomplete *capitulum* to which Uilberch referred was probably John 6. The last *sententia* which Bede translated was probably *Domine, ad quem ibimus? Verba vitae aeternae habes et nos credimus et cognovimus quia tu es Christus Filius Dei*. Having rendered this into English he may justly have said "*Consummatum est*,"[9] for he had concluded his work at the first great climax of St. John's Gospel.

The order of C'3d–e, *At ille inquit "Facile est"* confirms the order of 3'd–e, *At ille inquit "Bene."* The reversal of original order probably issued from eyeskip, as 3'hi reads *At ille "Bene" inquit,* where that order was necessary to confine the speech in 3'hiii to thirty-two words. Cuthbert's reference to himself in 3hi, *mihi,* confirms the first person singular of 3hi', *feci.* In 3jii the order *missas et orationes* echoes the phrase at the crux of B, *missas videlicet et orationes,* and preserves the alliterative pattern *monens et obsecrans, missas et orationes.*

The text of B and C contains 490 words. The text of C' and B' contains 480 words. The entire text now comprises 997 words, perhaps originally an even 1000 words. But the possible loss of three words does little to impair the beauty of this nearly perfect work.

If we ask why Cuthbert wrote like this, we find the answers both simple and coherent. First, he wrote as he had been taught to write. The most important parts of the Latin Bible are composed thus. Nearly every extant monument of British-Latin and Anglo-Latin literature from the fifth century to the eighth is composed thus. So is nearly all the extant Old English literature which may reasonably be ascribed to the late seventh and early eighth centuries. Wherever Cuthbert looked he must have noted that Biblical style was the traditional and orthodox manner in which to compose.

Second, Cuthbert wrote thus because he knew, as his co-religionists and compatriots had known for centuries, that Biblical style helps to guarantee the integrity of a text. It furnishes aids to the memory through both ear and eye, by parallel and chiastic statement and restatement and mathematically fixed forms, which remain consistent in small units like the Salutation, in larger units like the paragraphs, and in the entire composition. A word, a clause, or a sentence omitted by a careless scribe will be noticed by a perceptive reader unless the scribe should also delete the parallel word, clause, or sentence. Similarly the interpolation of an "improving" scribe or editor will also be noticed unless he adds a parallel interpolation. In a tightly knit composition like Cuthbert's it is very difficult either to omit or to interpolate without doing violence to the syntax and the narrative sequence. But even if one can do this, it is still more difficult not to ruin the mathematical patterns. So the scrupulous weighing and counting of words affords a further indication of textual integrity which confirms all the others. Anyone who had the patience to alter a text like Cuthbert's by omitting or interpolating, but without ruining the parallelism and chiasmus, narrative sequence, and word count would not satisfy himself by tinkering with another man's text. He would adapt and recast the material, as St. Matthew did to St. Mark's Gospel. He would become an author in his own right. But nothing of that sort has happened to Cuthbert's text. The changes from his original words are easily detected by comparison of the variants and the original text easily restored.

I suggest that the Latin Bible affords primary models for literary composition in Anglo-Latin and Old English. By studying the rules of Biblical style from manuscripts of the Latin Bible, which survive in hundreds and thousands, we may apply the rules to emendation of early Insular Latin texts, which survive in scores of manuscripts, and we may begin to consider ways in which the same principles may illuminate our understanding of Old English texts, which often survive in only a few, if not unique, manuscripts.

OXFORD UNIVERSITY

Notes

1. Biblical quotations are taken in Hebrew from *Biblia Hebraica Stuttgartensia*, ed. K. Elliger, W. Rudolph, et al. (Stuttgart, 1967/77); in Greek from *Septuaginta*, ed. A. Rahlfs (Stuttgart, 1935); in Latin from *Biblia Sacra iuxta Vulgam Versionem*, ed. B. Fischer et al. (Stuttgart, 1969); and in English from the Revised Standard Version, 2nd ed.

2. Cf. N. W. Lund, *Chiasmus in the New Testament* (Chapel Hill, N.C., 1942), p. 86. I have made the English translation more nearly literal than the Revised Standard Version.

3. E. V. K. Dobbie, *The Manuscripts of Cædmon's Hymn and Bede's Death Song with a Critical Text of the Epistola Cuthberti de obitu Bedae* (New York, 1937), pp. 49-105.

4. Dobbie, p. 50.

5. M. L. W. Laistner and H. H. King, *A Hand-List of Bede Manuscripts* (Ithaca, N.Y., 1943), pp. 93-112; *Bede's Ecclesiastical History of the English People,* ed. B. Colgrave and R. A. B. Mynors, Oxford Medieval Texts (Oxford, 1969; rpt. 1979), pp. xxxix-lxxvi; K. W. Humphreys and A. S. C. Ross, "Further Manuscripts of Bede's *Historia Ecclesiastica,* of the *Epistola Cuthberti de Obitu Bedae,* and Further Anglo-Saxon Texts of *Cædmon's Hymn* and *Bede's Death Song,*" Notes & Queries, N. S. 22 (1975), 50-55.

6. N. R. Ker, "The Hague Manuscript of the Epistola Cuthberti de Obitu Bedae with Bede's Song," *Medium Aevum,* 8 (1939), 40-44.

7. Colgrave and Mynors, p. 579.

8. Dobbie, pp. 54-55, 61-63.

9. This echoes the Passion narrative of John 19:30. The following phrase C'1'hiiγ may echo the Passion narrative of Luke 23:46.

Part Two
History, Archaeology, Art History

Celtic and Anglo-Saxon Kingship: Some Further Thoughts

PATRICK WORMALD

Not all that long ago, serious scholars believed that, had it not been for the Irish, there would have been no Carolingian Renaissance, and so no European civilization at all. Today, even the Fenians among us would scarcely defend such a view. But it remains common ground that Ireland *was* a "source of Anglo-Saxon civilization." What I wish to do in this paper is to confront a paradox in traditional attitudes towards the early medieval Celts.[1] On the one hand, the so-called "Celtic Church" did far more for the conversion of the Anglo-Saxons and others than the so-called "Roman Church" (and was, besides, much nicer); on the other, Celtic society was quite unlike that with which Celtic missionaries came into contact: so far from being itself transformed by the New Dispensation, it allegedly provides the best evidence there is of what society was like before the legions, let alone the Cross. Of course, one does not have to speak a society's language, literally or metaphorically, in order to change its faith and culture. But it is a reasonable question whether (and if so, why) a civilization whose representatives have widely been believed to have changed the cultural destinies of north-western Europe can itself have been relatively impervious to its own message. Recently, in fact, the revolutionary studies of Donnchadh Ó'Corráin on pre-Norman Irish government, of Michael Lapidge and others on "Celtic learning," of Richard Sharpe on the early Irish Church, and of Charles Doherty on the economy of early medieval Ireland have been tending to qualify the dictum of the late lamented Kathleen Hughes, "Ireland was odd in the early Middle Ages."[2] But my concern here is with an area where Ireland still seems not so much odd as outlandish: in its theory and practice of kingship. My text is taken from Francis John Byrne's fine *Irish Kings and High-Kings,* published ten years ago: "The history of Irish and Anglo-Saxon kingship offers an instructive *study in contrast*" (my italics); my title is my own small tribute to

Daniel Binchy's famous O'Donnell lectures at Oxford in 1968, which first aroused my interest in this subject and which made the definitive case for the unique fascination of secular arrangements among the early Christian Celts.[3] Because Welsh kingship has become the special province of Wendy Davies, it is mainly in Irish kingship that I am interested here, though at the end I shall introduce a third Celtic society which has played a curiously small part in the debate.[4] Conversely, I shall frequently refer to the kingship of the Anglo-Saxons' Germanic cousins, as many other students of the subject have before.

I begin with two points of method. In the first place, when comparing the institutions and cultures of different societies, historians must take account of the balance of the evidence. Not only may we know much more about one society than the other; we may also be confronted with entirely different *types* of evidence, so that the spotlight falls on different corners of what could be essentially similar scenarios. Contrasting types of evidence may, of course, themselves be symptomatic of real social contrasts; I trust that historians a millenium from now will think it significant that the information available for post-1945 Western society is more prolific and less centralized than that available for the East. But before we can be sure that the uneven balance of evidence *is* itself significant, we have to consider the channels of its transmission; it could be that we know different things about our two societies not because they were *then* different but because of contrasts in their subsequent histories. Second, historians of kingship have arguably been too preoccupied by ideology, especially if the ideology is in any way weird. All societies have their political rhetoric, and its study is both legitimate and necessary; but it is never the whole story. What I understand by kingship is the whole nexus of duties, rights, and privileges, expectations both spoken and unspoken, that girt about monarchical government. The observed behavior of kings is as important as the lectures read to them by ideologists. Indeed, one could argue that the best guide to the political ideology of society as a whole, as opposed to that of its more articulate members, is what kings can be seen to have got away with. The only real evidence of a *Widerstandsrecht* in the European Middle Ages is that, just occasionally, kings were withstood by a substantial part of the political nation.

In Binchy's classic presentation, Irish kingship is unmistakably a hangover from the remote Indo-European past. Irish *rí* is etymologically cognate with Latin *rēx* and Sanskrit *rāj*. The many other Indo-European echoes in the terminology, ideology, and myth of the Irish evidence reveal a kingship that steps straight out of the pages of Sir James Frazer's *The Golden Bough*.

Irish kings were inaugurated by an elaborate (and faintly nauseating) ritual, denoting their marriage to the tribal goddess. Their functions were expressed in the concept of the "King's Truth," to which there are Indian and Iranian parallels, and which brought not only victory and peace but also good weather, fertility, and freedom from human and animal disease. Irish legends, which also have parallels elsewhere, imply the ritual sacrifice of kings for failure in these respects, or for breaking the solemn tabus that enshrined their office. In other words, the Irish king was "sacral." But his active functions were severely limited. He was his people's war-leader, but early Irish war was almost a ritual game: by raiding one's neighbors' cattle, one demonstrated one's overlordship, because tribute was paid in cattle; and if one lost one's king, as in chess, one lost the war. The king presided over tribal assemblies on the once-pagan festivals of Beltain, Samain, and so on, but he was not a lawgiver; the law was the province of a specialist lawyer class, the brehons. The limits of a king's administrative rights are brought out by the fact that he had just one court official to enforce them. Thus, an early Irish king was a priestly vegetable; he tells more of the distant past than of the historical development of European monarchy.[5]

The standard picture of Germanic kingship is indeed in marked contrast. True, nineteenth-century views of the subject, like those of Kemble and Stubbs, dwelt on the limitations of royal power;[6] while some, but by no means all, modern historians believe that the early Germanic king was also "sacral," and that his pagan aura lingered on into Christian times.[7] But since the days of Chadwick, historians have stressed the centrality of active and predatory war-leadership for Germanic kings.[8] Royal power was based on the ability to attract heavily armed warriors, and thus on the capacity to reward them with treasure and lands. Only when such resources ran low—as, classically, with Einhard's Merovingians—were kings reduced to powerlessness. More recently, historians have emphasized the transformation of kingly ideology among the post-invasion barbarians.[9] Ruling by "the grace of God," and inaugurated by solemn Christian liturgies, kings were expected to defend not only the Church but also weaker members of society, like widows, orphans, and the poor; to propagate the Faith not only by Crusade and legislation but also by setting their subjects an example of the Christian Life, in charity, sobriety, and (most remarkable) humility. Thus, modern studies of Germanic kingship have a generally healthy respect for royal power, and are inclined to see change rather than continuity in its ideological evolution. Hence Byrne's "study in contrast." On the one hand, we have kingship suffused by the pagan past; on the other, kingship renewed (at least potentially) in the font. On the one hand, there is a king with symbolic status rather than real power; on the other, a king whom St. Augustine might have taken as proof that secular government begins with robber-chiefdoms.[10]

Before we consider this contrast further, we ought to ask why it exists. It seems that, to some extent at least, it is a function of the evidence with which each society has left us — or rather, of the ways in which the balance of the evidence has weighted historical judgment. Our knowledge of Germanic, as of Celtic, kingship begins with classical historians. Scandinavian, like Celtic, saga presents us with a kingship which has suggestively pagan overtones, as we shall see. But otherwise the paths diverge. *Beowulf* may describe remote, if not unreal, events in pagan Scandinavia, but there has long been a consensus that it reflects the social conditions of the poet's own day (whenever that was): I have described it elsewhere as a "window on the thought-world of the Anglo-Saxon aristocracy."[11] Its nearest Irish equivalent, the *Táin Bó Cuailnge,* was memorably epitomized by Kenneth Jackson as a "window on the Iron Age";[12] and while Sutton Hoo notoriously illuminates the world of *Beowulf,* archaeologists have sought in vain for even vaguely contemporary versions of the *Táin*'s chariots.[13] Early Germanic law, as we know it now, was by and large issued by identifiable historical kings attempting to grapple with identifiable historical problems, and its evidence is supported by a very substantial body of charters, showing royal power in action.[14] The tracts of Irish lawyers, the main source for the powerlessness of Irish kings, are important above all because they appear to record customs and institutions reaching right back into the Indo-European past; and there is very little charter material indeed.[15] Finally, the early medieval Western Church produced a very considerable "kingly literature": quite apart from such historical celebrations of kingship as those of Gregory of Tours, Bede, Paul the Deacon, Einhard, and Widukind, there were formal and informal "mirrors of princes," conciliar decrees and coronation liturgies.[16] While it would not be true to say that there is no such Irish evidence, as we shall see, it has tended to be eclipsed by the remarkable, substantially pagan, homilies on kingship that have also survived. In other words, one body of evidence highlights the dynamic, the other the static, elements in kingship and society.

Is this contrast of evidence itself symptomatic of real social contrasts between Germanic and Celtic society? In one respect, it almost certainly is. The most singular, perhaps the most important, feature of early Irish society (one of which there are also hints in Wales) was its class of professional men, learned in secular traditions — men whom it is convenient to call *filid,* although its lawyer-members were usually known (in English spelling) as brehons.[17] This "mandarin class of poets and pedants" (in Byrne's words) corresponds to the Druids described by Caesar and others among the Gauls and to the Brahmans of India; it is itself a feature of remote Indo-European antiquity. In early Christian Ireland, the *filid* were no longer priests, as the Druids had arguably been, but they were guardians of ancient tradition in their capacity as poets, genealogists, historians, prophets, propagandists, and lawyers. Chief poets were protected by an honor-price equal to that of a tribal king, and, unlike even kings, the class's members had full legal rights outwith their native tribes. It was recruited by birth and by rigorous and prolonged training in schools which it itself controlled. And it was this elite that produced the sagas, law-tracts, and statements of kingly principle which have dominated historical understanding of Irish kingship. According to Caesar, however, the Germans lacked Druids, and, on the whole, he seems to have been right.[18] Except conceivably in Scandinavia, there was no Germanic class concerned to nourish ancient tradition, to dam up or at least dilute the onrushing current of Romano-Christian civilization. The Church acquired an effective monopoly of the creation and transmission of written evidence in the early medieval West. Not all Christian churchmen were as scandalized by the pre-Christian past as Bede; but, aside from the reverence which most aristocrats feel for their ancestors, they had no commitment to it *on principle*.

Whatever else our contrasting evidence implies, therefore, it reflects the existence, in one society but not the other, of a class which made a specialty of secular tradition. This does at least raise the possibility that we are faced not with fundamentally different societies as such but with different *images* of society. In this connection, there are three further points to make about the *filid*. First, any elite is liable to be conservative, but the preservation of the past was the entire *raison d'être* of the *filid*. The *filid* did come to terms with one colossal change, their conversion to Christianity. But familiar legends have both St. Patrick and St. Columba endorsing their continuing role in society.[19] By the ninth century, perhaps earlier, the major secular professionals were based in, if not indeed ruling, the greater Irish churches.[20] In the eleventh and twelfth centuries, it was monasteries such as Clonmacnoise, Clonenagh, Glendalough, and Kildare that produced the first great surviving compendia of ancient Irish learning. Thereafter, traditional lore moved out of the monasteries into the custody of learned secular families; and, between the fourteenth and seventeenth centuries, these produced most of what survives of early Irish saga and all that we have of the brehon law-tracts.[21]

As might be expected from this track record, the *filid* showed a knack of adjusting to change, while abandoning as little as possible of fundamental principle and preserving as much as possible of surface appearances. The *filid* in the service of the greater eleventh- and twelfth-century kings wrote cogent propaganda for their masters' ambitions, but dressed much of it up in terms of an immemorial high-kingship based at Tara.[22] Christianity made a considerable impact in the still-formative period of the law-tracts before 750, but much less, on law-tract evidence, than it made in seventh- and eighth-century Europe at large; and substantial elements of ancient custom survived.[23] From the eighth century onwards the solemn texts of brehon law were fossilized, glossed, and annotated in increasing (and ultimately almost total) ignorance of their real meaning. In the period when our legal manuscripts were actually written, cases could be decided on perfectly sensible juristic principles, but not without the rival lawyers competing in the quotation of irrelevant and unintelligible classical law.[24] Similarly, the *Testament of Morand*, the most famous of the substantially pagan Irish "mirrors of princes," is extant only in manuscripts of the 1560's and '70's or later transcripts.[25] If the past could not be preserved in practice, it could always live on in theory. In the face of such a sustained capacity for traditionalism, one is surely entitled to wonder whether, even if what *filid* and brehons say about Irish kingship had once been true, it continued to be true in the historical period. And even at the moment when their views were first committed to writing, did these learned gentlemen describe things as they were, or as they had been (or should have been) and *therefore should still be?* Can a scholastic tradition which appears to have thought the *Testament of Morand* relevant comment in the age of Montaigne be trusted for the age of Adomnán? At the very least, we should allow for the possibility that the contemporary scene was dressed up in the traditional imagery that was a *fili*'s stock in trade.

My second point is that, while a great deal of such evidence survived in Gaelic Ireland from the later medieval and early modern periods, very little else did; and before this survival ratio is taken as symptomatic of pre-Norman conditions, we should consider how much we should know of the early Irish Church if we depended only on manuscripts surviving in Ireland itself. We should have no theology or Biblical commentary, no canon collections or Latin penitentials; there would be no letter of Cummean on the Easter crisis, or correspondence between Lanfranc, Anselm, and the Irish: indeed, we should lack almost all our sources for the twelfth-century reform, the Annals excepted. Apart from the Stowe Missal (which may itself have spent a crucial period elsewhere), we should know little of early Irish liturgy, beyond its corpus of hymns. Even in the hagiographical field, where the three major collections do have Irish provenances, the greatest of Irish saints' lives, Adomnán's *Life of Columba,* is in just one of them (then in the shorter version), and it could hardly be found when Manus O'Donnell was writing his own *Life* in the early sixteenth century; similarly, Continental manuscripts are an essential complement to the precious but incomplete Patrician documents in the Book of Armagh.[26] Other than annals, hymns and saints' lives, what survive are Biblical manuscripts, usually because they had been enshrined.[27] These are the sole source for our knowledge of the Irish charter tradition which, as Wendy Davies has shown, persisted throughout the early Middle Ages.[28] If we depended on texts written into Biblical manuscripts for all our Anglo-Saxon charters, we should have a pathetic fraction of the extant total, and we would be tempted to conclude, as scholars have been in the Irish case, that they began not much more than a century before the Norman Conquest.[29] In the ecclesiastical sphere, it therefore seems that the indigenous channels of transmission, for whatever reason, give an extremely misleading impression of pre-Norman Ireland; and we could hardly expect Continental libraries to do for secular society what they did for the Church. Only the aspects of the secular scene which the *filid* endorsed and treasured stood much chance in Ireland itself. We do then have grounds for suspecting that a possibly distorted image of early Irish society has been given unwarranted prominence by the accidents of subsequent Irish history.

My third and final point is that, although this has hardly registered with his many followers, Binchy himself has always had doubts about the abiding historical relevance of the impression of kingship supplied by *filid* and brehons. In his original lectures, he observed that, however valid this impression was for the petty kingship of the *tuath,* it was not necessarily applicable to the new, more powerful confederacies of the seventh century onwards, notably that of the Uí Néill; he thought that if later Irish lawyers had reflected the conditions of their own day instead of dwelling on traditional patterns, the Irish situation would have looked much more like the Welsh. Recently, in the Introduction to his monumental *Corpus Iuris Hibernici,* he asked:

> How far do these legal records reflect existing conditions? How can the tribal society mirrored in them be reconciled with the testimony of the Annals, and more or less contemporary literary works in which powerful kingdoms and their rulers play such a leading role? Were the earlier jurists, too, like their successors, backward-looking, their gaze still fixed on a dead past?[30]

From the acknowledged master of the hitherto decisive evidence, this challenge to dig beneath the surface of political rhetoric in early Ireland can surely no longer be evaded. It should no doubt be met by a scholar with a better knowledge of Old Irish than mine.

However, a comparative approach, based not on Indo-European analogies but on the ideologies and politics of the early medieval West, may offer as much to the Irish historian as it has to his Anglo-Saxon counterpart. Moreover, some of the most valuable evidence for early medieval Ireland is in Latin. It includes not only the Annals to which Binchy refers, but also important treatises on Christian kingship and a large collection of Irish canon law. This latter material (typically surviving only outside Ireland) makes Irish kingship seem considerably less idiosyncratic than do the vernacular sources, though it has generally been quarried more for traces of the ancient pattern than for hard proof that the pattern was shifting. Before the vernacular sources are permitted to impose their "study in contrast," it is worth seeing whether sources in Latin suggest a seriously different picture in Ireland than elsewhere in post-Roman Europe. Conceivably, the Irish situation from the seventh century onwards was comparable not only with the Welsh but with that of the Anglo-Saxons themselves.

We may begin with "sacral" kingship, and consider first the Celtic and Anglo-Saxon inauguration rituals which apparently stand in such contrast. The ceremonies associated with the making of an Irish king are in some ways more notorious than well-attested, but a hypothetical model might include the following elements. The candidate had intercourse with an animal which was then sacrificed and boiled, and while he bathed in the water, the carcass was shared out among the congregation; so much, at any rate, is attested by Gerald of Wales for the far northwest of Ireland in the late twelfth century, in an account which his Victorian translator not only indignantly repudiated but also (predictably) bowdlerized.[31] More plausibly, the candidate, dressed in white, then either stood barefoot in a footprint carved out of rock, or sat on a stone throne, to be handed his rod of office by a *fili* who recited his genealogy. The standing procedure is recorded for the Lords of the Isles in the fifteenth century, while the seated ceremony has been made famous by the Stone of Scone; and, remarkably, the very same ritual, with a full panoply of esoteric detail, was used to inaugurate the mayor of Brest as late as the eighteenth century.[32] Finally, the traditional sites of the installation of the greater Irish kings—Emain Macha, Tara, Dún Ailline, and Cruachain—were all important prehistoric complexes; while Scone, itself perhaps a prehistoric site, was located (in Archie Duncan's words), "where the salt waters of the sea (and the powers of death who dwell in it) are finally turned back by the living waters of the river" (Tay).³³ What is symbolized by all this is a marriage ceremony between king and tribal goddess; *feis,* the Irish word, has strongly sexual connotations, and sexual symbolism recurs in Irish king-sagas.³⁴

Such evidence may suffice to indicate the survival into historic times of ceremonies which we, but not necessarily (in every respect) the participants, would recognize as pagan. Nevertheless, there are problems. As regards the more outrageous aspects, Gerald was of course closely connected with the Norman conquerors of Ireland and (like some modern historians) was not averse to seeing Normans as harbingers of civilization to backward and barbarous peoples. Indian and Scandinavian analogies suggest that something of the sort may once have happened, but it is a little hard to believe that it was still happening, when Gerald wrote, to a dynasty that supplied Iona with its founder, historian, and first eleven abbots; it seems likely that a renegade *fili* was using his professional memory of ancient custom either to fuel Gerald's prejudices or to pull his leg.³⁵ As regards the inauguration sites, the last annalistic reference to a *feis* at Tara is for 558; at present, the archaeological evidence from all the relevant places suggests no continuity into the Christian period, and, in the case of Emain Macha, a destruction date in the third century B.C.³⁶ But there is also a different consideration here. A variety of evidence, beginning with Gildas, suggests that the unction of kings along Old Testament lines developed at least as early among the Celts as Germans.³⁷ The Irish canon collection begins its chapter on kingship by quoting the relevant passage about Samuel and Saul. By the end of the eighth century, an Uí Néill king could be nicknamed "the Ordained," and even Diarmait mac Cerbaill, holder of the last Tara *feis* according to the Annals, was described by Adomnán as "ordained by God."³⁸ It was the *bishops* that persuaded David I of Scotland to undergo the mysterious "obsequia" traditionally associated with the making of a Scottish king; and the central role in the coronation of Alexander III at Scone in 1249 was played by the bishop of St. Andrews (if we know that Alexander was *not* anointed, we also know why: Henry III of England pressurized the Pope into forbidding it).³⁹ Clergy also figure prominently in the famous account of the inauguration of O'Connor in the later Middle Ages; the role of the *fili* was emphasized by the author, but, given that he was a member of the *fili* family traditionally involved, this is scarcely surprising.⁴⁰ Thus, whatever its originally pagan elements, a Celtic king's inauguration ritual could, and apparently did, acquire Christian elements also. If vernacular sources largely ignore the latter and dwell on the former, we should expect as much. Other evidence surely deserves the same respect.

We can turn now to the Anglo-Saxon rituals, where the position is exactly reversed. The evidence in England and on the Continent is almost wholly clerical, and consists largely of elaborate coronation liturgies. No one denies that these were used (many still are); but, as Janet Nelson has pointed out, it is in the nature of *this* evidence to ignore any *non-ecclesiastical* element in the proceedings. All the same, there are hints in Scandinavian sources that kings were inaugurated on sacred stones; and before the religious ceremony itself, Otto the Great is said to have been enthroned by his nobles outside the Church, *"more suo."*[41] It is a very singular feature of later Anglo-Saxon coronations that they took place at Kingston-on-Thames, which happens, like Scone, to be the highest point of tidal flow on the river.[42] Pre-Conquest English liturgies refer vaguely to an "assembly of elders" as the ceremony begins. We have no full account of this until the fourteenth-century *Liber Regalis,* which says that, on the day of coronation, prelates and nobles shall first assemble in Westminster Palace to consider the "consecration and election" of the king and "the confirmation of the laws of the realm." A "lofty seat" in Westminster Hall was then to be suitably adorned, and the king installed upon it, "after having first bathed, and after being clothed with spotless apparel and shod only with socks." Fifteenth-century sources show that the seat was in fact King's Bench, "the kyngys cheyer or place where alle kyngys ffyrst take possescion" in the words of the *Great Chronicle of London.* The ceremony evidently had considerable significance in the rather special circumstances of the accession of Edward IV, which precluded immediate coronation. It was revived and last performed in the somewhat farcical proceedings of George IV's coronation.[43] We presumably do not conclude from all this that English kingship remained fundamentally pagan and "sacral" even longer than the mayoralty of Brest. But one can hardly stifle the suspicion that, if this were Celtic evidence, it would be well known to historians and used as proof positive of an abiding pagan aura about the kings of England.

The other type of evidence for sacral kingship is what one might call kingly literature: genealogy, saga, and homily. The Irish evidence is here familiar. At least some Irish kings were represented as the descendants of euhemerized deities.[44] The *Testament of Morand* ascribes to the "Prince's Truth" (or "Justice") the rule of great kingdoms, the warding off of plague, successful assault on one's enemies, fair weather for each season, good harvests, a proper growth in population, and (that ultimate Irish desideratum) good fishing.[45] (Correspondingly, a perhaps archaic Welsh poem condemns the "falsehood" of a king.[46]) Irish kings were supposed to be physically perfect and to observe their tabus or *gessa.* As already mentioned, the sagas preserve many echoes of the ritual disposal of kings who failed to live up to the required standards. Diarmait mac Cerbaill (according to saga though not Adomnán) died a triple death, transfixed by his enemy, then drowned in a vat of ale in his blazing house; and the vat *motif* recurs in other prehistoric cases.[47]

We may thus establish that the rhetoric of early Irish politics (at least for certain exponents) had distinctly pagan undertones. It is surely appropriate, however, to ask how far the actual exercise of kingship was affected by specifically pagan values; sacral is as sacral does. It is not easy to find unimpeachable historical evidence of ritual sacrifice, though, given Irish weather, it should have been as common as changes of ministry under the French Fourth Republic.[48] The rather grisly word, *iugulatio,* which the Annals often use of the despatch of kings, might seem to have ritual associations, but it was applied to a Northumbrian king whom we know to have been simply murdered and to a Frankish king who (probably) died in his bed.[49] A law-tract says that a historical king of the Ulaid was deprived of the Kingship of Tara because he was blinded in the eye by a bee-sting and so lost his physical perfection; but, political rhetoric apart, it is legitimate to wonder whether the ever-mounting pressure of the Uí Néill under their first really great king, Domnall mac Aedo, did not have something to do with it — as indeed one set of Annals seems to imply.[50] Moreover, as with inauguration ceremonies, there is another side to the picture. A seventh-century Irishman wrote a Latin tract, *On the Twelve Abuses of the World,* which was later ascribed variously to Cyprian, Augustine, Patrick, and others.[51] The ninth abuse is the Unjust King, and the "pagan" elements here are well known: the unjust king brings not only defeat and disorder but also storms that destroy crops, fruit, and (again) fishing. Predictably less emphasized is that other abuses include the rich man who gives no alms, the contentious Christian, and the negligent bishop. What the tract says of kingship makes it one of the earliest "mirrors of princes" to demand what became the tediously familiar virtues of Christian kingship, including the defense of the Church, the punishment of sin, and the protection of weaker elements in society.[52] On the one hand, the writer is soaked in the fundamental views of Isidore of Seville, and his model for the punishment of unjust kings comes not from Irish saga but from the Old Testament; indeed people who look like *filid* are expressly excluded as royal councilors. On the other hand, this tract was one of the most profoundly influential formulations of Christian political obligation in the entire Middle Ages.[53] Within a century, it was being quoted by English churchmen; it appears (fertility and all) in the tenth-century Mainz pontifical; and Dunstan's coronation admonition was in part translated from it.⁵⁴ It seems, then, that both author and audience were rather less aware of the work's "essentially pagan ethos" than are modern scholars. In the same vein, the considerably more sophisticated Sedulius Scottus is analyzed chiefly for the Insular pagan roots of his *Liber de Rectoribus Christianis;* but a recent discussion also concedes that his was one of the first clear-cut theories of the Crusade.⁵⁵

If, again, we set the Germanic evidence alongside the Irish, we find that descent from gods was frequently a feature of royal genealogies; that Scandinavian sources have the same sort of stories about royal sacrifices (including drowning in a vat) and ominously mysterious encounters; and that these same sources can be equally explicit about the connection between good kings and prosperity, bad kings and famine.⁵⁶ But there is no such Germanic text as the *Testament of Morand,* and historians have generally (though not always) been wary of seeing ritual sacrifice behind every bloody coup. Instead, scholars like J. M. Wallace-Hadrill rightly stress the Old Testament inspiration behind Alcuin's belief that the Viking sack of Lindisfarne was a punishment for vice and disorder among the Northumbrians; and if they detect a pagan element in such views, they ascribe it to Irish influence.⁵⁷ But why is sauce for the Germanic gander not also sauce for the Celtic goose? Why are pre-Christian myths of unfortunate kings any more to the point in Celtic than in Germanic society? Is it any more reasonable to suppose that a king lost power because he lost an eye than that the Vikings sacked Lindisfarne because of "fornications, adulteries and incest ... avarice, robbery, violent judgements, since the days of King Ælfwold"?⁵⁸ Bede and Alcuin drew their new model of kingship from the Bible and the Fathers, and so, presumably in all innocence, produced something not unlike the old model; may we not allow that the author of the *Twelve Abuses* did the same? King Alfred's remarkable writings are taken as the most dramatic of all illustrations of the assimilation of royal and episcopal office in the early Middle Ages; some ninth-century kings of Munster actually *were* bishops: *was* this simply a cynical abuse of power (at least in the case of Cormac mac Cuillennáin)?⁵⁹ Even Ó'Corráin, without whose seminal paper on Irish kingship my own could scarcely have been written, concludes, in the face (it seems to me) of his own evidence: "The attempt to Christianize kingship was never very successful."⁶⁰ If this means that Irish kings of the early Middle Ages were violent and immoral men, it was not just in Ireland that Christianity "failed"; if it means that the theories of the *Twelve Abuses* remained essentially an intellectual construction, exploited by kings only as and when it suited them, it is not clear to me that this is any less true of the letters of Alcuin — or, for that matter, of the *Testament of Morand.*

This brings us to the evidence of kingship in practice with which Celtic and Anglo-Saxon society have left us; and here it is convenient to begin with the Germanic pattern. The normal West and North Germanic word for king is of course a variant on Anglo-Saxon *cyning;* but, while this word was already old, it was almost certainly not "original," because it is unknown in Gothic.[61] The word which Wulfila used to correspond with Greek βασιλεύς was *thiudans,* and his word for Greek ἄρχων was, significantly, *reiks;* Procopius, moreover, implies that *reiks* was what Theodoric was called by his Ostrogoths.[62] *Reiks* may be confined to Gothic, but modern German *reich* is very far from the only instance of words deriving from the same root throughout the Germanic languages.[63] At the risk of sounding simplistic, the fact that the early Germans borrowed the Celtic terminology of kingship from the Gauls (if it was a borrowing rather than an independent inheritance from the common Indo-European stock) at least suggests that primitive Germanic kingship had something in common with Celtic. The point may be confirmed by Peter Sawyer's recent argument that the Icelandic *goði,* usually understood as "priest" because cognate with Gothic *gudja* which does mean priest, may indicate "only that in Iceland, as in Ireland, secular power had archaic religious roots."[64] However this may be, we have already seen some evidence that Germanic kingship was originally "sacral," and the impression of royal power given by Tacitus in his *Germania* is notably "vegetable" — it was, of course, the main basis of the views of Kemble and Stubbs. *Reges* might be "taken" for their *nobilitas* (which *might* imply divine descent), but they were not as such war-leaders: *duces* were "taken" for their *virtus* (say, "qualities of leadership"). Tribal politics was dominated by assemblies of freemen which, like those of the Celts, met on annual religious festivals.[65] The king had little or no law-giving function; as late as the sixth century, when the Frankish "army" still assembled on March 1st, *Lex Salica* was ascribed not to Clovis but to four *rectores* who were not apparently kings whatever else they were.[66] In ninth-century Sweden, a king told St. Anskar that, regrettably, he could not allow him to preach without consulting popular assemblies in different parts of the country;[67] and it is probably a basically sound tradition that attributes some of the colonization of firmly "republican" Iceland to resentment of the growing power of King Harald Finehair of Norway.

Nevertheless, Tacitus highlights significant modifications of the traditional tribal pattern among the first-century Germans, notably the development of the *comitatus* of young warriors, attracted to the service of even a foreign chieftain by the prospect of war and plunder, and pledged in loyalty to their lord up to the point of death.[68] It is of this famous relationship that the heroic literature of the Germans (and others) gives so memorable a picture, justifying in its turn Chadwick's critique of Stubbs. Possession of a warband enabled any leader, whether *rex* or *dux* originally, to solidify his power, and the ceaseless quest of warbands for the plunder which was their social cement inevitably disrupted traditional institutions. Thus, whatever Tacitus says about the theoretical position in the *Germania,* his *Annals* and *Histories* reveal kings who were leaders of miscellaneous tribal remnants, had extensive treasures, and even founded dynasties.[69] It was apparently kings of this sort that led their (often substantially new) peoples into the Roman Empire. And once there, their power was immeasurably increased, at least in the short run, by the landed and movable wealth of Rome; their legal responsibilities were developed by Roman advice or Roman example; and their moral authority was defined by the Church. Clovis could dispose ruthlessly of the other petty kings of the Franks and found a kingdom which soon encompassed all of Roman Gaul and more besides; he was inspired (whatever Frankish tradition said) to produce a Latin statement of his people's law; he was hailed on his baptism as a "new Constantine"; and he was lectured by bishops on his duties to the poor, to strangers, to widows and orphans, even to prisoners.[70] This pattern of development, necessarily oversimplified and drawn from the Germanic world as a whole, has very important implications for Celtic kingship. It shows that, given the right circumstances, a once-powerless and "sacral" tribal kingship might become something very formidable indeed.

In considering whether or not this could also have happened in early Christian Ireland, it is not, I hope, begging the question to concentrate attention on the greater kings in the elaborate regnal hierarchy; for what, after all, is in question is not the one-time existence of petty tribal kingship, but whether the immemorial system was proof against the ambitions of an Irish Clovis. One might begin by observing that to say, with Byrne, that "the tribal king had few governmental duties apart from acting as war-leader" is still to say quite a lot in a society where warfare was evidently endemic.[71] Nor do I see that this warfare can be dismissed as little more than a ritual game, political rhetoric apart; there is nothing necessarily ritual in fighting for tribute and / or revenge, and even if the *Bóruma Laigen* has implausibilities which are lacking in *Beowulf*'s account of the see-saw campaigns of Swedes and Geats, the real-life struggles of Irish kings may not have been so very different from those of the Northumbrians and Mercians in seventh-century England.[72] An army that lost its king was quite likely to be losing the battle anyway, if only because most generals have more sense than Wolfe or Nelson; and the Annals do supply instances of kings fleeing the battlefield.[73] On another tack, Byrne has argued that the coming of Christianity and historical record to Ireland saw the end of the Irish heroic age, as depicted in the Ulster Cycle:

> The brehon laws may depict a peculiarly archaic society, but it is not, primarily, a warlike one. Even the highest grades of the aristocracy are essentially farmers....All freemen, noble and plebeian, have the right and duty to attend the king's hosting, but there is no warrior caste.[74]

One weakness in this argument is that it postulates an actual prehistoric period when the conditions revealed in the *Táin* prevailed; whereas some commentators, archaeologists included, now incline to the view that these conditions, if ever true, are those of the seventh and eighth centuries when the *Táin* was written.[75] Another weakness, more important for us, is that if we went on the evidence of the earliest English law-codes alone, and knew nothing of *Beowulf* and Sutton Hoo, we should perhaps think the same of seventh- and eighth-century England; after all, it is how historians *did* think before Chadwick. Neither in Ireland nor in England are the different impressions given by different kinds of evidence necessarily a reflection of different historical periods.

Above all, one thing that is quite clear about the history of early medieval Ireland is that it saw the rise of new and aggressive dynasties, of which the Uí Néill and the Dál Cais were only the most famous.[76] There is some evidence that Uí Néill power was founded on the sort of plundering raids against Roman Britain that first brought St. Patrick to Ireland.[77] The rise of the Uí Néill irrevocably disrupted the impenetrably ancient fivefold structure of Irish political geography (to which the law-tracts, notwithstanding, remained obstinately loyal), and they aspired to be kings of all Ireland. Though the Uí Néill were never accepted throughout Ireland, their power could be frighteningly real. In 722, the Uí Néill high-king led a large confederation, including three other northern Irish kings, to defeat and death at the hands of the Leinstermen. But his successor was powerful enough, a mere sixteen years later, to avenge this disaster on an equally formidable Leinster confederacy.[78] By the later eighth century, the Uí Néill were wiping out a series of minor tribal kingships, placing the lands in question under lords of their own choosing, exactly as Clovis had done, as Offa of Mercia was doing at the very same time, and as Harald Finehair was to do.[79] When the Vikings appeared in Ireland, it is (for Englishmen) an embarrassing but ineluctable fact that the Uí Néill and other Irish kings did rather better against them than all the English kings except Alfred. In the light of what Alfred Smyth has shown (*I* believe) about the common Viking enemies of England and Ireland, we can hardly say that the threat was less.[80] Yet only once was an Uí Néill king defeated and killed in battle by them; the Annals are studded with a series of spectacular (if, no doubt, exaggerated) victories over them; and the pattern of their Irish settlement, cooped up in a series of coastal enclaves, where eleventh-century kings milked their resources for their own ends, really speaks for itself. In this context, another *parvenu* dynast, Brian Boru, became the first to be acknowledged as supreme in every Irish province, and was entered in the Book of Armagh as *"imperator Scottorum"*: an achievement parallel with, if more ephemeral than, that of Æthelstan in England earlier, and, one might add, that of Gruffudd ap Llywelyn in Wales slightly later.[81] It could be argued, then, that the military power of Irish kings developed along much the same lines as that of their Anglo-Saxon counterparts: from heroic age through dynastic lordship to imperial posture. The differences, such as they are, may be differences of degree rather than kind.

Turning to the more peaceful functions of kingship, we may then ask whether the administrative resources of Irish kings can have been as derisory as the legal sources imply. In some respects, the answer must be yes. Ireland was coinless until ca. 1000, when coin was introduced and largely organized by the Dublin "Ostmen"; and, though foreign coin was probably known in Ireland earlier, there was no question of kings reaping the profits of mintage, as we know that the Carolingians did and may strongly suspect that Anglo-Saxon kings from Offa's time also did.[82] However, O'Corráin has shown that Irish kings from the tenth to the twelfth centuries could raise formidable tributes and had a series of government officers, identifiable in Annals and genealogies as cadets of the royal house or as members of subordinated dynasties, like the *ealdormen* of Anglo-Saxon England; and there is some similar evidence in Wales.[83] As is well known, we have charters of Diarmait Mac Murchada (and of other kings too) from just before the Norman invasion; these are in the contemporary European idiom, and Diarmait had a *"cancellarius."*[84] The chance survival in the central Cistercian archive of a charter dated 1224 shows that, by then, O'Connor had a seneschal, a chancellor, and a notary royal.[85] We should no doubt see foreign influence at work here, though Diarmait's charters do appear to precede his exile, and Connacht was on the whole the least Normanized part of Ireland; the evidence at least raises the possibility of independent Irish development. And, for what the point is worth, the exactions of sixteenth-century Irish chiefs described by hostile English observers look like the traditional levies of early Irish kings, and are presented as very heavy indeed.[86]

But if, by the high Middle Ages, an Irish king's powers may have been as great in peace as in war, how far back did he acquire them? In the lawtract period, the evidence is necessarily indirect, but it can be suggestive. Irish sagas are as eloquent about royal wealth as *Beowulf* itself. In the *Táin*'s "pillow-talk," King Aillil and Queen Medb run through an impressive catalogue of royal treasures in their debate as to who has the greater wealth, before Aillil at last mentions his great bull and Medb launches the *Táin* to get even.[87] This is of course a literary stereotype, and it has been remarked before that Irish sagas are somewhat prone to overstatement;[88] one can no doubt have the same suspicions about the improbably elaborate tributes and counter-tributes listed in the *Book of Rights*.[89] Yet this material, together with the Welsh poems ascribed to Aneirin and Taliesin, shows that there was the same sort of *expectation* of royal wealth in Celtic society as in the "audience of *Beowulf*"; and who would have guessed, before the discovery of Sutton Hoo, that *Beowulf* was not exaggerating? Among the Latin sources, early saints' lives hardly suggest a *fainéant* kingship. Cogitosus refers to the *"thesauri regum"* kept at Kildare (much as those of the Anglo-Saxon King Eadred were entrusted to Dunstan at Glastonbury), and he has an important story about a fortified bridge across a bog, suitable for mounted and wheeled traffic, which a king commissioned "per plebes et provincias quae sub eius erant ditione et iugo."[90] Adomnán shows that one Pictish king also had a treasury, while the Annals record that another had *exactatores* rather than a single court official.[91] One of the striking features of the Irish canons is the anxiety of the Church to escape *census,* or tribute, due to kings. St. Ambrose is quoted to the effect that "the Catholic Church is free from *census,"* and that "if you wish to owe nothing to an earthly king, leave all that is yours and follow Christ"; the significance of these quotations is enhanced by the fact that they apparently come from no known work of Ambrose, and were presumably fathered on him by an Irish source.[92] Freedom from taxation was evidently worth having in seventh- and eighth-century Ireland. It is also a persistent theme (together with the exclusion of royal officials) throughout the "Celtic charter-tradition" which Davies has illuminated.[93] The payments and obligations from which kings like Aed "the Ordained" are said to have freed the Church appear to correspond, like the bridge in Cogitosus' story, to the food-rents and *corvées* from which Aed's Anglo-Saxon contemporaries were also beginning to grant immunity.[94] Given the arguably distorted balance of the evidence, and considering that it is archaeology and numismatics rather than the slender documentary thread which have, quite recently, brought out the real power of Anglo-Saxon kings, we cannot on principle deny the implications of such Irish evidence as there is; and the implications are that, as soon as we have records, Irish royal power was something to be reckoned with.⁹⁵

This leaves the decidedly difficult question of the king's role in the making and enforcement of law, a role denied by the brehon tracts unless the king was himself a qualified lawyer.⁹⁶ Once again, the position had certainly changed by the end of our period. Eleventh-century Annals record elaborate legislative jamborees presided over by O'Brien kings, for all the world like Carolingian emperors; and, though the resulting decrees do not survive, Ó'Corráin points out that we should hardly appreciate the importance of the reforming synods in the twelfth-century Irish Church if all we had to go on was the annalistic record.⁹⁷ Similarly, in a paper severely critical of the relevance of law-tract evidence for the history of later centuries, Doherty argues that kings hanged criminals in twelfth-century Ireland, just as they did in pre-Conquest England.⁹⁸ So, once again, when and how did the legal responsibilities of kings develop? We may note, first, that, although there were no Roman advisers in Ireland to impress upon kings the value of royal lawgiving, as there had been in Continental kingdoms, there were none in Britain either. Like the English, however, the Irish had the Church to make the same point. The *Twelve Abuses* was explicit about royal judgment, demanding that kings prevent theft, punish adultery, condemn parricides and perjurers to death, and appoint just men for the business of the kingdom.⁹⁹ The Irish canons quote from Jerome that "the word of a king is a sword for execution and a rope for binding, condemns to prison, punishes the unjust"; the king is to repress crime, the bishop is to temper the royal wrath, the people are to be terrified of him (as with Ambrose on *"census,"* the quotations are bogus).¹⁰⁰ In the *Vitae,* the justice (or, more often, injustice) of the king in person is a constant concern of saints.¹⁰¹

Against the background of the Latin evidence for a king's executive role in justice, it may be possible to reassess the vernacular sources on his legislative and judicial responsibilities. Not only the *Twelve Abuses* but also the *Testament of Morand* and the *Instructions of Cormac mac Airt* expect a king to be active in pursuit of justice, and other archaic texts condemn royal *"gubreth"* (false judgment).¹⁰² *Crith Gablach* assigns two days in a king's week to "judgments," and the office of king's brehon was of admittedly central importance in the law-tracts.¹⁰³ Legislation was ascribed to Cormac and other prehistoric kings, mythical or otherwise; while an intriguing Würzburg gloss has kings and lawyers collaborating in legislation.¹⁰⁴ Even in legal theory, therefore, the royal presidency of the *óenach* was evidently not purely honorific. Once more, it seems to me that our contrasting impressions of Celtic and Anglo-Saxon kingship in the legal field are functions of contrasting types of evidence. In form and content, Irish law is lawyers' law, emphasizing the lawyer's part in its preservation and enforcement, but sometimes invoking the authority of legendary kings. Welsh law is also lawyers' law, where the king's legislating function is occasionally admitted; in the Welsh case, the original king invoked is the unquestionably historical figure of Hywel Dda, though it is impossible to say how historical his actual contribution was.[105] Anglo-Saxon law is normally recorded in the form of royal decrees, but the extant text of Æthelbert's code is in fact (like *Lex Salica*) anonymous; laws are almost invariably represented as arising from the wisdom of king and councilors in combination; and, from the Norman Conquest onwards (even, as Dafydd Jenkins has recently suggested, before it), records of royal law were made by lawyers.[106] Granted the contrast in types of evidence, and granted also that Irish lawyers constituted a much more self-conscious and articulate class than any Anglo-Saxon equivalents, it is reasonable to wonder how much difference there was in practice between an *óenach* and a *witena-gemot*; especially when the Church's expectations of kings in this respect were as high in Ireland as in England, and when there were kings like the Uí Néill and the O'Briens to exploit them.

In this paper, I have not sought to argue that there were no significant differences between the images and powers of Celtic and Anglo-Saxon kings. I do, however, suggest that the differences were fewer than appears from the balance of the evidence. In formulating this view over recent years, I have been much influenced by a consideration that has hardly featured in the literature hitherto, but which is a final, powerful, reason for revising the received opinion of Celtic kingship. The work of Geoffrey Barrow, of Derick Thomson, and of John Bannerman has taught us that into the high Middle Ages (and for much longer in the Highlands) Scottish society preserved the basic elements of a Celtic polity, including the appropriate learned orders.[107] As such, Scotland supplies clear evidence of that polity's dynamic potential. As we have seen, the Scottish inauguration ceremony fits the traditional Celtic pattern in some respects, but it was firmly directed by the clergy by the time that we know much about it. In the ninth century, a Scottish king and people are said to have renewed the laws of an eighth-century king; and though Marjorie Anderson thinks that the relevant entry in the *Scottish Chronicle* may be an interpolation, one of her main reasons is that "the creation of new laws was not one of the normal functions of Irish assemblies, or of kings either"—and she cites Binchy.[108] Unless it can be proved that the annal is anachronistic, the argument could legitimately be reversed. There is the same sort of evidence in Scotland as in Ireland for royal impositions on the Church, and for an anxiety to be released from them by charter.[109] Above all, the Celtic king as priestly vegetable simply cannot be reconciled with the emergence of Barrow's "warlike and aggressive Scotto-Pictish kingdom," which was to give its big southern brother so many embarrassing moments.[110] If the kingship of the law-tracts could ultimately spawn such *Heerkönige* as Aedán mac Gabráin, Kenneth Mac Alpin, and Malcolm Canmore, could it not have done so in Ireland itself? David I brought Normans to Scotland and is deservedly cherished in Scottish memory. Diarmait mac Murchada did exactly the same in Ireland, and has ever since been thought the arch-traitor. But Diarmait's misfortune (or mistake) was that he was not already in a position to dictate terms throughout Ireland; whereas David inherited (in Duncan's words), "a Celtic realm, remote, moneyless, but with a tradition of submission to one king which, however slender, was no longer fragile."[111] The unity of the Scottish kingdom was a Celtic, not a Norman, achievement. It shows that there was nothing inherent in Gaelic society to doom Diarmait's initiative.

Why, then, have historians been so sure of Celtic (and specifically Irish) backwardness in the early Middle Ages? I have already given one answer: a high proportion of the available evidence was produced by people whose job it was, so far as possible, to show that nothing changed in early Ireland. Another answer is deeply embedded in the history and historiography of Ireland since the twelfth century. The classic statement of Irish "barbarism" was made by G. H. Orpen, whose impressive history was irredeemably flawed by the tormented Victorian experience of Ireland; Freeman, who was perfectly well aware of the linguistic evidence, wished to deny the Celts a place among the ranks of his beloved Aryans.[112] Behind the Victorians lay centuries of an intellectually corrupting colonial regime, which began in Elizabethan times, if not before. In the sixteenth century, it can scarcely be denied that Gaelic Ireland was very "backward" indeed: it is a matter of record that Gaelicized Anglo-French lords gave up using stirrups.[113] Some contemporary commentators, like some modern historians, blamed the *filid* for this situation.[114] Proinsias Mac Cana has recently faced up to the question whether the traditional learned orders could really control the social and political evolution of early Ireland.[115] But his analogy between the curses of the *filid* and ecclesiastical excommunication seems unlikely to impress historians of the later medieval Church with the power of the former, and one is still reminded of Stalin's question, "How many divisions has the Pope?" Obviously, the learned orders enjoyed considerable prestige. One may grant that they could dominate, in fact as well as image, a society threatened and marginalized by external assault. But it was surely quite another thing for them to rein in the ambitions of ascendant *native* kings, like the Uí Néill, the O'Briens and the O'Connors. Whatever the sixteenth-century view, it does not follow that Irish society had always been held in thrall to prehistory by the "men of art."

The first commentators since classical times to describe the Irish as barbarians were twelfth-century ecclesiastical reformers.[116] Their opinion was given a sophisticated twist by Gerald of Wales, whose comments have been illuminated by Robert Bartlett's recent book.[117] Gerald applied the twelfth-century *topoi* of barbarism to the Irish, partly out of self-interest, but also because that is what he thought he saw. One of the most impressively modern things about his account is the way in which he relates Irish society to its economic and geographical context, and in this he may have lessons for modern commentators. If kingship developed along the same lines in Irish as in Germanic society, but (as I readily concede) more slowly and less far, this may have less to do with the innate racial characteristics which obsessed Victorians, or the actual power of the *filid*, as was thought in the sixteenth century, than with the simple fact that there was less movable wealth floating off the Celtic shore. If Alfred Smyth is right about the appalling problems posed by the Irish landscape, a would-be king of all Ireland had a far harder task than King Alfred's descendants. Yet Scotland's geographical and economic drawbacks were scarcely less daunting, and they were triumphantly overcome. Not even economic determinism can preordain Irish backwardness.[118] And in the last resort, the reasons why Irish society so signally failed to impress outside observers from the twelfth century onwards remain intractable. What does seem clear is that these external views all to some extent pre-judge the issue, and are terribly influenced, as historians so often are, by considerations of ultimate "success" and "failure." However backward Ireland was in the sixteenth century, it need not have been so always; one might recall how difficult Rhodesians found it to believe that Shona had built Great Zimbabwe. And it ill becomes an English historian, with all that he now knows of the sophisticated power of the later Anglo-Saxon kingdom, to take the word of the propagandists of ecclesiastical reform and Norman Conquest for Irish conditions.[119]

That said, it seems to me that Irish historiography itself bears some of the responsibility for the image of early medieval Ireland that still prevails. Irish historical scholarship was reborn in the Gaelic League. The League, almost by definition, directed attention towards vernacular sources, with their linguistic challenges and mysterious beauty, rather than to the more mundane Latin evidence that was the staple fare of most European medievalists. Even Mac Neill, a founding father of the League and the greatest Irish historian to date, was an exception that proves this rule: in his attempt to show, as against Orpen, that Ireland was a united and well-organized European monarchy of the normal early medieval type, he was taken in, as Binchy showed, by the very Irish pseudo-historians whose distortions he had himself done so much to expose.[120] Otherwise, rather than compete in Orpen's power-game, Irish scholars have tended, until recently, to fall back on a view of their early history as a sort of Tolkienian "Westernesse": if not a paradise, then at least a place that treasured the most ancient traditions of the Indo-European past, in relative isolation from the world of *realpolitik* elsewhere. And the obsessively loving study of Irish saints and scholarship has served as a substitute for confronting the eccentricities of secular society. One conclusion that I would wish to draw from this paper is that it is sufficient thanks to the *filid* that they have done more than any other written source for our understanding of prehistoric Europe; it is supererogatory to suppose that they kept prehistory alive. A second conclusion to be drawn is that the impact of Irish saints and scholars on English and European culture between the sixth and ninth centuries is best explained by the proposal advanced here: that they came from a society not wholly unlike that in which they moved and settled, and did, metaphorically, speak the same language. My third and final conclusion is that, in times when we are increasingly pressed to defend the "relevance" of history, especially that of such remote periods as the early Middle Ages, one contribution toward the long-overdue reconciliation of Celt and Saxon might be a recognition that their respective histories were not as different as each, for its own reasons, has made them seem.

GLASGOW UNIVERSITY

Notes

1. Versions of this paper were given at the Universities of Durham, Glasgow and St. Andrews, and I have benefited from the comments of their staff and students. The text as it now stands is more or less that of the O'Donnell lecture delivered at Edinburgh on May 20, 1983; like many others, I owe a debt of gratitude to the O'Donnell bequest for the opportunity to clarify and expound my views (even if, like most of them, I fear that I have honored the founder's terms in the spirit

rather than the letter); and I also thank William Gillies for the invitation to give the lecture and for his own helpful comments. Only the first half of the paper was given at Kalamazoo, but I learned much from discussion with other Symposium participants, and I am very grateful to the editor of this volume both for inviting me to contribute and for including the full O'Donnell lecture in the Symposium proceedings. Finally, a number of scholars have given independent assessments of this paper, making many constructive suggestions and saving me from as many errors (though they should not be held responsible for what Irish and Anglo-Saxon historians still find unacceptable): in particular, I thank Francis John Byrne, David Corner, Janet Nelson, Richard Sharpe, Dafydd Walters and Ian Wood; and I owe much, as always, to the intellectual and personal support of Jenny Wormald.

2. Donnchadh Ó'Corráin, "Nationality and Kingship in Pre-Norman Ireland," in *Nationality and the Pursuit of National Independence,* ed. T. W. Moody, Historical Studies, 11 (Belfast, 1978), pp. 1-35; Michael Lapidge, "The Authorship of the Adonic Verses 'ad Fidolium' Attributed to Columbanus," *Studi Medievali,* 3rd ser., 18(2) (1977), 249-314 (and see Michael Herren, "Classical and Secular Learning Among the Irish Before the Carolingian Renaissance," *Florilegium,* 4 [1982], 118-57); Richard Sharpe, "Saint Patrick and the See of Armagh," *Cambridge Medieval Celtic Studies,* 4 (1982), 33-59; and Sharpe, "Some Problems Concerning the Organization of the Early Irish Church," *Peritia,* 3 (1984), 230-70; Charles Doherty, "Exchange and Trade in Early Medieval Ireland," *Journal of the Royal Society of Antiquaries of Ireland,* 110 (1980), 67-89; Kathleen Hughes, "Sanctity and Secularity in the Early Irish Church," in *Sanctity and Secularity: The Church and the World,* ed. Derek Baker, Studies in Church History, 10 (Oxford, 1973), p. 21; and see the comment of Clare Stancliffe, "Red, White and Blue Martyrdom," in *Ireland in Early Medieval Europe: Studies in Memory of Kathleen Hughes,* ed. Dorothy Whitelock, Rosamond McKitterick, and David Dumville (Cambridge, 1982) (hereafter cited as *Ireland in Medieval Europe*), p. 21.

3. Francis John Byrne, *Irish Kings and High-Kings* (London, 1973), p. 29; D[aniel] A. Binchy, *Celtic and Anglo-Saxon Kingship* (Oxford, 1970).

4. Wendy Davies, "Land and Power in Early Medieval Wales," *Past and Present,* 81 (1978), 3-23; Davies, *An Early Welsh Microcosm: Studies in the Llandaff Charters* (London, 1978), pp. 65-107; Davies, *Wales in the Early Middle Ages* (Leicester, 1982), pp. 85-140; and see her forthcoming Oxford O'Donnell lectures for 1983, *Patterns of Power in Early Wales.* For critical comment on one of Binchy's suggestions about Wales in his original lectures, see David Dumville, "The Ætheling," *ASE,* 8 (1979), 1-33.

5. This paragraph is a digest of Binchy, *Celtic and A-S Kingship,* pp. 1-12, 15-21, supplemented by some of his other writings: e.g., "The Linguistic and Historical Value of the Irish Law Tracts," *Proceedings of the British Academy,* 29 (1943), 195-227, rpt. separately and in *Celtic Law Papers: Studies Presented to the International Commission for the History of Representative and Parliamentary Institutions,* Vol. 42 (Aberystwyth, 1971), pp. 73-107; and "The Fair of Tailtiu and the Feast of Tara," *Ériu,* 18 (1958), 113-38 (and esp. pp. 124-25). See also Byrne, *Irish Kings,* pp. 14-27, 30-35, 51-69, 74-78, 94-104, etc.; and Myles Dillon, "The Archaism of the Irish Tradition,"

Proceedings of the British Academy, 33 (1947), 245 ff.

6. John Mitchell Kemble, *The Saxons in England* (London, 1849); William Stubbs, *The Constitutional History of England* (Oxford, 1873-78).

7. Otto Höfler, "Der Sakralcharakter des germanischen Königtums," in *Das Königtum: Seine geistigen und rechtlichen Grundlagen,* ed. Theodor Mayer, Vorträge und Forschungen, 3 (Konstanz, 1956), pp. 75-104, summarizing this scholar's approach and that of others; for the Anglo-Saxons in the same light, see William A. Chaney, *The Cult of Kingship in Anglo-Saxon England* (Manchester, 1970); and, for a subtler approach, J. M[ichael] Wallace-Hadrill, *Early Germanic Kingship in England and on the Continent* (Oxford, 1971), pp. 8-20.

8. Hector Munro Chadwick, *The Origins of the English Nation* (Cambridge, 1907); Chadwick, *The Heroic Age* (Cambridge, 1912); Walter Schlesinger, "Das Heerkönigtum," in *Das Königtum,* ed. Mayer, pp. 105-41; Reinhold Wenskus, *Stammesbildung und Verfassung* (Cologne, 1961), pp. 305-455; Herwig Wolfram, "The Shaping of the Early Medieval Kingdom," *Viator: Medieval and Renaissance Studies,* 1 (1970), 4-9.

9. Eugen Ewig, "Zum christlichen Königsgedanken im Frühmittelalter," in *Das Königtum,* ed. Mayer, pp. 7-73; Walter Ullmann, *The Carolingian Renaissance and the Idea of Kingship* (London, 1969); Wallace-Hadrill, *Early Germanic Kingship;* Wallace-Hadrill, "The *Via Regia* of the Carolingian Age," in *Trends in Medieval Political Thought,* ed. Beryl Smalley (Oxford, 1965), pp. 22-41, rpt. in Wallace-Hadrill's collected essays, *Early Medieval History* (Oxford, 1975), pp. 181-200. For fresh appraisal of the issue see now K. J. Leyser, *Rule and Conflict in an Early Medieval Society* (London, 1979), pp. 75-107; and Leyser, "Some Reflections on Twelfth-Century Kings and Kingship," in his *Medieval Germany and Its Neighbours* (London, 1982), pp. 241-67. See also note 16 below.

10. Peter Sawyer, *Kings and Vikings* (London, 1982), p. x.

11. Ritchie Girvan, *Beowulf and the Seventh Century,* 2nd ed. (London, 1971); Dorothy Whitelock, *The Audience of Beowulf* (Oxford, 1951); Patrick Wormald, "Bede, *Beowulf* and the Conversion of the Anglo-Saxon Aristocracy," in *Bede and Anglo-Saxon England,* ed. Robert T. Farrell, British Archaeological Reports, 46 (Oxford, 1978), pp. 32-95. Despite the arguments of some of the contributors to *The Dating of Beowulf,* ed. Colin Chase (Toronto, 1981), I remain marginally committed to my original dating limits of A.D. 675-875. Two important recent contributions to the debate are David Dumville, "*Beowulf* and the Celtic World: The Uses of Evidence," *Traditio,* 37 (1981), 109-60, and Michael Lapidge, "*Beowulf,* Aldhelm, the *Liber Monstrorum* and Wessex," *Studi Medievali,* 3rd ser., 23(1) (1982), 151-92.

12. Kenneth Jackson, *The Oldest Irish Tradition: A Window on the Iron Age* (Cambridge, 1964).

13. For *Beowulf* and Sutton Hoo, Rupert Bruce Mitford (Appendix to Girvan, *Beowulf and the Seventh Century,* 2nd ed., Chap. iv) states the shortest clear case among many. On chariots and the *Táin,* see David Greene, "The Chariot as Described in Irish Literature," in *The Iron Age in the Irish Sea Province,* ed. Charles Thomas, Council for British Archaeology, Report 9 (London, 1972), pp. 59-73; and now see Stuart Piggott, *The Earliest Wheeled Transport: From the Atlantic to the Caspian Sea* (London, 1983), pp. 235-38.

14. Patrick Wormald, "*Lex Scripta* and *Verbum Regis:* Legislation and Germanic Kingship from Euric to Cnut," in *Early Medieval Kingship,* ed. Peter Sawyer and Ian Wood (Leeds, 1977), pp. 105-38. This article appeared almost simultaneously with the important collection *Recht und Schrift im Mittelalter,* ed. Peter Classen, Vorträge und Forschungen, 23 (Konstanz, 1977), and I was unable to register the many insights in the latter work. I hope to supply a full review of current opinion in this field in *Kingship and the Making of Law in England: From Alfred to Henry I* (Oxford, forthcoming).
15. D. A. Binchy, "Irish History and Irish Law," *Studia Hibernica,* 15 (1975), 27-32. But see note 28 below.
16. J. M. Wallace-Hadrill, "Gregory of Tours and Bede: Their Views of the Personal Qualities of Kings," *Frühmittelalterliche Studien,* 2 (1968), 31-44, rpt. in his *Early Medieval History,* pp. 96-114; Helmut Beumann, *Ideengeschichtliche Studien zu Einhard und anderen Geschichtsschreibern des früheren Mittelalters* (Darmstadt, 1962); Beumann, "Historiographische Konzeption und politische Ziele Widukinds von Corvey," *Settimane di studio del Centro italiano di studi sull'alto medioevo,* Vol. 17: *La Storiografia altomedioevale* (Spoleto, 1970), pp. 875-94; C. A. Boumann, *Sacring and Crowning* (Groningen, 1957); H. H. Anton, *Fürstenspiegel und Herrscherethos in der Karolingerzeit* (Bonn, 1968).
17. Of the very considerable literature on the Irish learned classes and their outlook, I have learned most from (alphabetically): Binchy, "Linguistic and Historical Value," pp. 205-27; Binchy, "The Background of Irish Literature," *Studia Hibernica,* 1 (1961), 10-11; Byrne, *Irish Kings,* pp. 13-16; Byrne, "Senchas: The Nature of the Gaelic Historical Tradition," in *Historical Studies,* Vol. IX, ed. John Barry (Belfast, 1974), pp. 137-59; J. E. Caerwyn Williams, "The Court Poet in Medieval Ireland," *Proceedings of the British Academy,* 57 (1971), 85-135; Dillon, "Archaism of the Irish Tradition," 259-63; Jackson, *Oldest Irish Tradition,* pp. 24-27, 39-40; James F. Kenney, *The Sources for the Early History of Ireland* (New York, 1929; rpt. 1966), pp. 19-26, 34-45; Proinsias Mac Cana, "The Three Languages and the Three Laws," *Studia Celtica,* 5 (1970), 62-78; Mac Cana, "Conservation and Innovation in Early Celtic Literature," *Études Celtiques,* 13 (1972), 61-119; Mac Cana, "Mongán mac Fiachna and *Immram Brain, Ériu,* 23 (1972), 102-42; Mac Cana, "*Regnum* and *Sacerdotium:* Notes on Irish Tradition," *Proceedings of the British Academy,* 65 (1979), 443-79; Brian Ó'Cuív, "Literary Creation and Irish Historical Tradition," *Proceedings of the British Academy,* 49 (1963), 233-62 and nn. 21-24. I owe a special debt to the unpublished Oxford D.Phil. thesis of Hermann Moisl, "Some Aspects of the Relationship Between Secular and Ecclesiastical Learning in Ireland and England in the Early Post-Conversion Period." For reflections of a similar tradition in Wales, see Gerald of Wales "Descriptio Cambriae" i.16-17, in *Giraldi Cambrensis Opera,* Vol. VI, ed. J. F. Dimock, Rolls Series [No. 21] (London, 1868), pp. 194-200 (and see an unpublished paper by Robert Bartlett, "Giraldus: Prophecy"); Kathleen Hughes, "The Celtic Church: Is This a Valid Concept?" *Cambridge Medieval Celtic Studies,* 1 (1981), 13; Moisl, "Some Aspects," pp. 19, 119-20 and nn. 105-06. But Davies is notably reticent on this matter (though see *Wales in the Early Middle Ages,* p. 138).
18. Caesar *De Bello Gallico* vi.21. See Clare Stancliffe, "Kings and Conversion,"

Frühmittelalterliche Studien, 14 (1980), 75-76; Hermann Moisl, "Anglo-Saxon Royal Genealogies and Germanic Oral Tradition," *Journal of Medieval History,* 7 (1981), 236-45.

19. On St. Patrick and the *filid,* see D. A. Binchy, "The Pseudo-Historical Prologue to the Senchas Már," *Studia Celtica,* 10/11 (1975-76), 15-28; Ó'Corráin, "Nationality and Kingship," pp. 13-14; Moisl, "Some Aspects," pp. 228-85. On St. Columba, see Kenney, *Sources,* p. 441; Francis John Byrne, "The Ireland of St. Columba," in *Historical Studies,* Vol. V, ed. J. L. McCracken (London, 1965), pp. 37-58; John Bannerman, "The Convention of Druim Cett," in his *Studies in the History of Dalriada* (Edinburgh, 1974), pp. 157-70.

20. Ó'Corráin, "Nationality and Kingship," pp. 14-16; see also *Annals of Ulster,* Vol. I, ed. William M. Hennessy (Dublin, 1887), s.a. 870, 879, 920, 1003, 1056 (pp. 384-85, 396-97, 440-41, 510-11, and 598-99 respectively). For the argument that the original authors of the written law-tracts were lay *filid* rather than clerics, see Thomas Charles Edwards, rev. of *Corpus Iuris Hibernici,* ed. D. A. Binchy, *Studia Hibernica,* 22 (1982), 144-62.

21. Robin Flower, "Ireland and Medieval Europe," *Proceedings of the British Academy,* 13 (1927), 276; Flower, *The Irish Tradition* (Oxford, 1947), pp. 1-23, 67-106; Kenney, *Sources,* pp. 10-16, 19-26; Proinsias Mac Cana, "The Rise of the Later Schools of *Filidheacht,*" *Ériu,* 25 (1974), 126-46; Alfred P. Smyth, *Celtic Leinster* (Dublin, 1982), pp. 102-04. The manuscripts of Irish law are listed by D. A. Binchy, ed., *Corpus Iuris Hibernici* (Dublin, 1978), p. xxii, and most are fully described in the manuscript catalogues of the British Library, the National Library of Ireland, the Royal Irish Academy, and Trinity College, Dublin. *The Oldest Fragments of the Senchas Már* (ed. R. I. Best and R. Thurneysen [Dublin, 1931]) is a notable facsimile.

22. Binchy, "Fair of Tailtiu," p. 137; Byrne, *Irish Kings,* pp. 269-70; Ó'Corráin, "Nationality and Kingship," pp. 19-21; but the *filid* were capable of "contemporary" propaganda: see Ó'Corráin, "Nationality and Kingship," pp. 31-32.

23. Binchy ("Linguistic and Historical Value," pp. 217-20) on the whole emphasizes Christianity's lack of impact on the law-tracts; for a more positive view, see his *Corpus,* pp. ix-x, and "Bretha Nemed," *Ériu,* 17 (1955), 6; also, Ó'Corráin, "Nationality and Kingship," p. 16; Moisl, "Some Aspects," pp. 285-311.

24. Binchy, "Linguistic and Historical Value," pp. 210-12, 225-27; Gearóid Mac Niocaill, "Notes on Litigation in Late Irish Law," *The Irish Jurist,* N.S. 2 (1967), 279-307. For adverse comment on the abiding "relevance" of the law-tracts, see Byrne, "Senchas," pp. 141-42; Doherty, "Exchange and Trade," pp. 70-71, 84.

25. *Audacht Morainn,* ed. Fergus Kelly (Dublin, 1976), pp. xx-xxvi (but the less archaic text is paradoxically extant in older MSS: see pp. xxvi-xxix); and see also the facsimile *R.I.A., MS. 23 N 10,* ed. R. I. Best (Dublin, 1954).

26. So much emerges from the manuscripts listed throughout Kenney, *Sources.* This masterpiece is, of course, in need of modern revision, but, so far as I know, the point made here still stands. On MSS of the early Brigit *Vitae,* see now Richard Sharpe, "*Vitae S Brigitae:* The Oldest Texts," *Peritia,* 1 (1982), 82-83.

27. Kenney, *Sources,* pp. 627-48; and see E. A. Lowe, ed., *Codices Latini Antiquiores,* Vol. II, 2nd ed. (Oxford, 1971), Nos. 266-77.

28. Wendy Davies, "The Latin Charter-Tradition in Western Britain, Brittany and Ireland in the Early Medieval Period," in *Ireland in Medieval Europe*, pp. 258-80. See also Kenney, *Sources*, p. 5; Binchy, "Irish History and Law"; and now Charles Doherty, "Some Aspects of Hagiography as a Source for Irish Economic History," *Peritia,* 1 (1982), 304-07.

29. Anglo-Saxon charters and legal records in liturgical MSS have not been studied as a corpus. The following, listed in Peter Sawyer, *Anglo-Saxon Charters: An Annotated List and Bibliography* (London, 1968), survive in such a context: Nos. 455, 914, 985-88, 1047, 1090, 1198, 1222, 1229, 1383, 1386, 1389, 1452, 1455, 1462, 1464, 1466, 1469, 1564, 1659-61. The relevant MSS for these and other records are, as listed by Neil Ker, *Catalogue of Manuscripts Containing Anglo-Saxon* (Oxford, 1957): 6, 22, 55, 119, 123, 126, 147, 176, 181, 185, 194, 246, 247, 284, 315, 364, 402. The earliest "charter" and the earliest informal records both appear to date from the reign of Æthelstan, and most are from the eleventh century. As emerges from Davies's discussion ("Latin Charter-Tradition," pp. 258-66), liturgical manuscripts on their own would also give a massively distorted impression of diplomatic history elsewhere in the Celtic West.

30. Binchy, *Celtic and A-S Kingship,* pp. 2, 23, 34, 46; Binchy, *Corpus,* p. xxi.

31. Gerald of Wales "Topographia Hibernica" iii.25, in *Giraldi Cambrensis Opera,* Vol. 5, ed. J. F. Dimock, Rolls Series [No. 21] (London, 1867), p. 169; for the translation see *Giraldus Cambrensis' Historical Works,* trans. T. Forester, rev. T. Wright, Bohn Antiquarian Library (London, 1863), p. 138.

32. Proinsias Mac Cana, "An Archaism in Irish Poetic Tradition," *Celtica,* 8 (1968), 180; John Bannerman, "The Lordship of the Isles," in *Scottish Society in the Fifteenth Century,* ed. Jennifer M. Brown (London, 1977), pp. 224-25; Archibald Duncan, *Scotland: The Making of the Kingdom* (Edinburgh, 1975), pp. 115-16; Léon Fleuriot, *Les Origines de la Bretagne* (Paris, 1980), p. 32.

33. Binchy, *Celtic and A-S Kingship,* pp. 11-12; Byrne, *Irish Kings,* pp. 15-20, 54. See also previous note.

34. Binchy, *Celtic and A-S Kingship,* p. 12; Byrne, *Irish Kings,* p. 17; and see T. F. O'Rahilly, "The Names Érainn and Ériu," *Ériu,* 14 (1946), 7-30; and Proinsias Mac Cana, "Aspects of the Theme of King and Goddess in Irish Literature," *Etudes Celtiques,* 7 (1955-6), 76-114, 356-443.

35. Byrne, *Irish Kings,* p. 18.

36. Bernard Wailes, "The Irish 'Royal Sites' in History and Archaeology," *Cambridge Medieval Celtic Studies,* 3 (1982), 1-29; but note his point (p. 8) that "assemblies and inaugurations may well have left no trace archaeologically."

37. The evidence is deployed by Raymund Kottje, *Studien zum Einfluss des alten Testamentes auf Recht und Liturgie des frühen Mittelalters* (Bonn, 1970), pp. 97-100.

38. *Adomnán's Life of Columba* i.36, ed. A. O. and M. O. Anderson (Edinburgh, 1961), pp. 280-81; *Collectio Canonum Hibernensis* XXV. 1, ed. H. Wasserschleben, *Die irische Kanonensammlung,* 2nd ed. (Leipzig, 1885), p. 76; and see Byrne, *Irish Kings,* pp. 159-60.

39. Ailred of Rievaulx, "Genealogia Regum Anglorum: De Sancto Rege Scotorum David," in *PL,* 195:713-14; *Johannis de Fordun, Chronica Gentis Scotorum,*

ed. William F. Skene, The Historians of Scotland, Vol. I (Edinburgh, 1871), pp. 293-95; and see Duncan, *Scotland,* pp. 552-53. I owe the first reference to Geoffrey Barrow.

40. Myles Dillon, "The Inauguration of O'Conor," in *Medieval Studies Presented to Aubrey Gwynn,* ed. J. A. Watt, J. Morrall and F. X. Martin (Dublin, 1961), pp. 186-202.

41. Erich Hoffmann, *Königserhebung und Thronfolgeordnung in Dänemark bis zum Ausgang des Mittelalters* (Berlin, 1976), pp. 180-85; Janet L. Nelson, "Inauguration Rituals," in *Early Medieval Kingship,* p. 54.

42. This point was made by C. E. Carrington in a talk on "Coronation Stones" (prompted by the abduction of the Stone of Scone), broadcast by the Third Programme of the B.B.C., January 20, 1951; my colleague, Archie Duncan, kindly showed me his copy. It should be noted, however, that the Thames may hardly have been tidal at all in Roman times and, although the tidal range appreciably increased in the "Dark Age" period, it may not have reached its present extent until quite recently. See Anne Akeroyd, "Archaeological and Historical Evidence for Subsidence in Southern Britain," *Philosophical Transactions of the Royal Society,* 272A (1972), 151-69; and G. H. Willcox, "Problems and Possible Conclusions Related to the History and Archaeology of the Thames in the London Region," *Transactions of the London and Middlesex Archaeological Society,* 26 (1975), 285-92. I am indebted to William Kellaway for advice on this subject.

43. *English Coronation Records,* ed. L. G. Wickham Legg (London, 1901), pp. 15, 30, 50-51, 114; for the circumstances of 1461 (and 1483), see C. A. J. Armstrong, "Inauguration Ceremonies of the Yorkist Kings," *Transactions of the Royal Historical Society,* 4th ser., 30 (1948), 51-73.

44. Binchy, *Celtic and A-S Kingship,* p. 9; but, as he points out, Irish royal genealogies make much less of this than those of the Anglo-Saxons.

45. *Audacht Morainn* 12-21 (ed. Kelly, pp. 6-7).

46. Davies, *Wales in the Early Middle Ages,* p. 121; did Asser mean anything more than the obvious when calling Alfred "rege veredico"? (*Asser's Life of King Alfred* 13, ed. W. H. Stevenson [Oxford, 1904; rpt. 1959], p. 12).

47. Binchy, *Celtic and A-S Kingship,* p. 10; Byrne, *Irish Kings,* pp. 59-64, 97-99, etc.; see *Adomnán's Life of Columba* i.36.

48. Binchy, *Celtic and A-S Kingship,* pp. 9-10.

49. *Annals of Ulster,* s.a. A.D. 650, 658 (ed. Hennessy, pp. 110-11, 114-15); or Oswine's fate, see *Bede's Ecclesiastical History of the English People* iii.14, ed. Bertram Colgrave and R. A. B. Mynors (Oxford, 1969), pp. 256-57. Hennessy took the annal for 658 as referring to Chlothar III, and it is interpreted as recording his accession in *A New History of Ireland,* Vol. VIII: *Chronology,* ed. T. W. Moody, F. X. Martin and F. J. Byrne (Oxford, 1982), p. 25; but "Flodubur" (it seems to me) could easily render "Chlodovechus," and for the circumstances of his death in 657 (apparently a "iugulatio," according to the *Annals* as printed), see *Liber Historiae Francorum,* ed. Bruno Krusch, MGH: Scriptores Rerum Merovingicarum, Vol. 2 (Hanover, 1888), p. 316. I thank Paul Fouracre for information on this point.

50. Byrne, *Irish Kings,* pp. 58, 112-13; see Byrne, *The Rise of the Uí Néill and the High-Kingship of Ireland* (Dublin, 1970), p. 17; and "The Annals of Tigernach, Third Fragment," ed. Whitley Stokes, *Revue Celtique,* 17 (1896), 183-84.

51. "De Duodecim Abusivis Saeculi," ed. S. Hellmann, in *Texte und Untersuchungen zur Geschichte der altchristlichen Literatur,* Vol. III. 4(1) (Leipzig, 1910); substantial selections are in *Collectio Canonum Hibernensis* XXV.3-4 (ed. Wasserschleben, pp. 77-78). For comment see, e.g., Ewig, "Zum christlichen Königsgedanken," pp. 38-54; Anton, *Fürstenspiegel,* pp. 67-78.

52. Hellmann, pp. 32, 51-53.

53. Hellmann, pp. 2, 17-18, 51, 53; and see next note.

54. Anton, *Fürstenspiegel,* pp. 74, 103-06, 195-96, 199, 201, 224, 236; *Memorials of Saint Dunstan,* ed. William Stubbs, Rolls Series [No. 63] (London, 1874), pp. 356-57.

55. Anton, *Fürstenspiegel,* pp. 266-71.

56. A recent discussion of Germanic genealogies, with full literature, is Moisl, "Anglo-Saxon Royal Genealogies," pp. 215-36; for more or less unfortunate encounters with the gods, see *Saxo Grammaticus, The History of the Danes,* trans. Peter Fisher and Hilda Ellis Davidson (Cambridge, 1979), pp. 171-72, 225-26, 243, 283; *Heimskringla,* ed. B. Aðalbjarnarson, Islensk Fornrit (Reykjavik, 1941-51), I, 26, 31-32, 38, 47-50, 74, 312-14. For the equation of kingship and luck, see *Saxo Grammaticus, Books X-XVI,* ed. and trans. Eric Christiansen, British Archaeological Reports, Int. Ser. 84 (Oxford, 1980), pp. 90-95; *Heimskringla,* pp. 26, 31-33, 74, 93, 128, 197, 203, 221, 241-43; see also Erich Hoffmann, *Die heiligen Könige bei den Angelsachsen und den skandinavischen Völkern* (Neumünster, 1975), pp. 63-64, and Rory McTurk, "Sacral Kingship in Ancient Scandinavia: A Review of Some Recent Writings," *Saga-Book of The Viking Society,* 19 (1974-77), 139-67. See also, in an entirely different context, the letter of King Sisebut of the Visigoths to King Adaloald of the Lombards, ed. Ernst Dümmler, in MGH: Epistolae, Vol. 3 (Berlin, 1892), p. 672. Some of this material, at least, is much too early to have been affected by the establishment of the relevant Christian *topoi.*

57. Wallace-Hadrill, *Early Germanic Kingship,* pp. 55-57, 105, 119.

58. *Alcuini Epistolae,* 16, ed. Ernst Dümmler, MGH: Epistolae, Vol. 4 (Berlin, 1895), p. 43.

59. Wallace-Hadrill, *Early Germanic Kingship,* pp. 140-50 and see p. 74, n. 6; Kathleen Hughes, *The Church in Early Irish Society* (London, 1966), pp. 192-93; Donnchadh O'Corráin, *Ireland Before the Normans* (Dublin, 1972), pp. 97-99, 113; but see Byrne, *Irish Kings,* pp. 211-29.

60. O'Corráin, "Nationality and Kingship," p. 17. This is a persistent theme for society as a whole in Kenneth Nicholls's remarkable *Gaelic and Gaelicized Ireland in the Middle Ages* (Dublin, 1972), especially as regards marriage: see pp. 3-17, 73-78. But Ferdinand Mount has recently reminded us that the Church had the greatest difficulty in imposing its marriage prescription on English society: see *The Subversive Family* (London, 1982).

61. On the terminology of Germanic kingship see, e.g., Schlesinger, "Das Heerkönigtum," pp. 107-08; Jan de Vries, "Das Königtum bei den Germanen,"

Saeculum, 7 (1956), 291-94; Wenskus, *Stammesbildung,* pp. 69, 308, 320, 345, 359, 419, etc.; Wolfram, "Shaping of the Early Medieval Kingdom," pp. 2-7. I am grateful to my colleague L. W. Collier for help on these matters.

62. *Procopius, Wars* v.1 (26), ed. H. B. Dewing, Vol. III, Loeb Classical Library (1919), pp. 10-11. Herwig Wolfram ("Athanaric the Visigoth," *Journal of Medieval History,* 1 [1975], 259-78) develops the argument of the article cited in the previous note along stimulating lines; but, despite the Procopian evidence, I am unable to see why *reiks* should *always* have meant a warrior leader: this flies against Wulfila's usage, and Athanaric's emphatic rejection of the title surely suggests that it then had rather humble connotations.

63. See Binchy, *Celtic and A-S Kingship,* pp. 4-7.

64. Peter Sawyer, "The Vikings and Ireland," in *Ireland in Early Medieval Europe,* pp. 352-57.

65. *Cornelii Taciti De Origine et Situ Germanorum* 7-12 (ed. J. G. C. Anderson [Oxford, 1938]). For a fuller exposition of the account which follows, see my "Viking Studies: Whence and Whither?" in *The Vikings,* ed. Robert T. Farrell (Chichester, 1982), pp. 145-47. Both accounts owe a great deal to Edward A. Thompson, *The Early Germans* (Oxford, 1965).

66. Wormald, *"Lex Scripta* and *Verbum Regis,"* pp. 108, 137; and see below, note 106.

67. *Vita S. Anskarii* 26-27, ed. D. F. C. Dahlmann, in MGH: Scriptores, Vol. 2 (Hannover, 1829), pp. 711-13.

68. Tacitus 13-15 (ed. Anderson). Though a very great deal has been written in criticism of this famous passage, I do not consider that its broader outlines are tendentious.

69. Schlesinger, "Das Heerkönigtum," pp. 117-18; Wenskus, *Stammesbildung,* pp. 347-73, 482-83, 492-94, 495-97, 508, 541.

70. J. M. Wallace-Hadrill, *The Long-Haired Kings* (London, 1962), pp. 163-85.

71. Byrne, *Irish Kings,* p. 23.

72. Byrne, *Irish Kings,* pp. 144-46; *Beowulf and the Fight at Finnsburg,* ed. Fr. Klaeber, 3rd ed. (Lexington, 1950), ll. 2200-06, 2379-96, 2472-89, 2611-19, 2922-3007; Bede *Ecclesiastical History* ii.20, iii.9, iii.24, iv.12, iv.21-22 (ed. Colgrave and Mynors, pp. 202-03, 240-43, 288-95, 370-71, 400-05 respectively).

73. E.g., *Annals of Ulster, s.a.* 648, 687 (ed. Hennessy, pp. 108-09, 136-37); and see Byrne, *Irish Kings,* pp. 298, 281.

74. Byrne, *Irish Kings,* pp. 49-50; and see pp. 28, 71.

75. See notes 13 and 36 above; and, from a different angle, James Carney, *Studies in Irish Literature and History* (Dublin, 1955), pp. 66-75, 277-313. It is perhaps worth noting that even "traditional" statements on Irish kingship have strikingly aggressive passages about royal warbands: *Audacht Morainn* 15 and 46 (ed. Kelly, pp. 6-7, 12-15); *The Instructions of King Cormac mac Airt,* ed. Kuno Meyer, Royal Irish Academy, Todd Lecture 15 (Dublin, 1909), 1 (pp. 2-3), 3 (pp. 8-9), 6 (pp. 12-13).

76. Binchy, *Celtic and Anglo-Saxon Kingship,* pp. 35-45; Byrne, *Irish Kings,* pp. 70-97, 111-28, 157-62, 203-04, 254-71; Byrne, *Rise of the Uí Néill;* Ó'Corráin, *Ireland Before the Normans,* pp. 114-17, 120-33; for "new" Leinster dynasties, see Smyth, *Celtic Leinster,* pp. 13-20.

77. Byrne, *Irish Kings*, pp. 76–77.
78. *Annals of Ulster*, s.a. 721, 737 (ed. Hennessy, pp. 172–75, 194–97).
79. Ó'Corráin, *Ireland Before the Normans*, pp. 29–32; Ó'Corráin, "Nationality and Kingship," pp. 9–10; and see Wormald, "Viking Studies," p. 147, and below, note 83.
80. Alfred P. Smyth, *Scandinavian Kings in the British Isles, 850–880* (Oxford, 1977); Smyth, *Scandinavian York and Dublin*, Vol. I (Dublin, 1975); Vol. II (New Jersey, 1979); I have sought to defend Smyth's views against severe criticism in "Viking Studies," pp. 141–44. For Irish successes against the Vikings, see Ó'Corráin, *Ireland Before the Normans*, pp. 95–96, 101–04, 106–07; Byrne, *Irish Kings*, pp. 267–69.
81. Davies, *Wales in the Early Middle Ages*, pp. 102–12; and see Michael Wood, "The Making of King Aethelstan's Empire: An English Charlemagne?" *Ideal and Reality in Frankish and Anglo-Saxon Society: Studies Presented to J. M. Wallace-Hadrill*, ed. Patrick Wormald with Donald Bullough and Roger Collins (Oxford, 1983), pp. 250–52, 271–72.
82. Doherty, "Exchange and Trade," pp. 78–83; and see Peter Sawyer, "Kings and Merchants", in *Early Medieval Kingship*, pp. 139–58.
83. Ó'Corráin, "Nationality and Kingship," pp. 22–23, 26–29; Ann Williams, "*Princeps Merciorum gentis*: The Family, Career and Connections of Ælfhere, Ealdorman of Mercia, 956–83," *ASE*, 10 (1981), 143–72; Patrick Wormald, "Bede, the *Bretwaldas* and the Origins of the *Gens Anglorum*," in *Ideal and Reality*, pp. 112–13; Davies, *Wales in the Early Middle Ages*, pp. 129–33.
84. William Dugdale, *Monasticon Anglicanum* (London, 1830), Vol. VI(2), pp. 1133–34, 1137–38, 1138, 1140, 1141–42; and see "Charters of the Cistercian Abbey of Duiske, Co. Kilkenny," ed. C. Butler and J. H. Bernard, *Proceedings of the Royal Irish Academy*, 35(C) (1918), 1–5.
85. Gearóid Mac Niocaill, "A Propos du vocabulaire social Irlandais du bas moyen âge," *Études Celtiques*, 12 (1968–71), 537.
86. Sir John Davies, *A Discoverie of the True Causes why* IRELAND *Was Never Entirely Subdued...* (1612), ed. Alexander B. Grosart, The Fuller Worthies Library (n.p., 1876), pp. 106–10.
87. *The Táin*, trans. Thomas Kinsella (Dublin, 1969), pp. 52–55.
88. Girvan, *Beowulf*, pp. 59–60.
89. Myles Dillon, *Lebor na Cert: The Book of Rights*, Irish Texts Society, 46 (Dublin, 1962), pp. xii–xx; but see Doherty, "Exchange and Trade," pp. 73–74.
90. Cogitosus "Vita Sanctae Brigidae," in *Acta Sanctorum*, Feb., Vol. I, pp. 140, 141; see *Memorials of St. Dunstan*, p. 31.
91. *Adomnán* ii.33 (ed. Anderson, pp. 402–03); *Annals of Ulster*, s.a. 728 (ed. Hennessy, pp. 182–83).
92. *Collectio Canonum Hibernensis* xxv.10 (ed. Wasserschleben, p. 79); see Wendy Davies, "Clerics as Rulers: Some Implications of the Terminology of Ecclesiastical Authority in Early Medieval Ireland," in *Latin and the Vernacular Languages in Early Medieval Britain*, ed. Nicholas Brooks (Leicester, 1982), pp. 86–87.
93. Davies, "Latin Charter-Tradition," pp. 264–66; Doherty, "Some Aspects of Hagiography," pp. 311–12.
94. *Annals of Ulster*, s.a. 803 (ed. Hennessy, pp. 286–89); and see *The Martyrology*

of Oengus the Culdee, ed. Whitley Stokes, Henry Bradshaw Society, 29 (London, 1905), pp. 2-5; Byrne, *Irish Kings,* pp. 159-60; Nicholas Brooks, "The Development of Military Obligations in Eighth- and Ninth-Century England," in *England Before the Conquest: Studies in Primary Sources Presented to Dorothy Whitelock,* ed. Peter Clemoes and Kathleen Hughes (Cambridge, 1971), pp. 69-84.

95. Donnchadh Ó'Corráin, "Irish Regnal Succession: A Reappraisal," *Studia Hibernica,* 11 (1971), 7-39: the whole point of his revisionist thesis, that succession to the throne ultimately depended on proximity to royal patronage, is that the king had ample patronage to bestow.

96. Binchy, "Linguistic and Historical Value," pp. 214-16; Binchy, *Celtic and A-S Kingship,* pp. 15-17; Binchy, "An Archaic Legal Poem," *Celtica,* 9 (1971), 152.

97. Ó'Corráin, "Nationality and Kingship," pp. 22-24; and see Aubrey Gwynn, *The Twelfth-Century Reform,* History of Irish Catholicism, Vol. 2 (Dublin, 1968), pp. 11, 13, 28-29, 56-60.

98. Doherty, "Exchange and Trade," pp. 79, 84.

99. "De Duodecim Abusivis Saeculi" (ed. Hellmann, p. 51).

100. *Collectio Canonum Hibernensis* xxv.17, xxvii.4 (ed. Wasserschleben, pp. 82, 85).

101. Cogitosus "Vita Sanctae Brigidae" (p. 138); Richard Sharpe has advised me on this point.

102. *Audacht Morainn* 6-8, 23, 51 (ed. Kelly, pp. 4-5, 8-9, 14-15); *Instructions of Cormac mac Airt* 1, 2, 6, 14 (ed. Meyer, pp. 2-5, 4-7, 14-15, and 24-25); Moisl ("Some Aspects," pp. 147-79) has a full and judicious discussion of the problem.

103. *Críth Gablach,* ed. D. A. Binchy (Oxford, 1941; rpt. 1970), 41 (p. 21), and see pp. 37, 79.

104. Thomas Charles Edwards, rev. of *Corpus Iuris Hibernici,* p. 156, n. 43; and see D. A. Binchy, "The Date and Provenance of Uraicecht Becc," *Ériu,* 18 (1958), 52; and now Máirín Ní Dhonnchada, "The Guarantor List of *Cáin Adomnáin,*" *Peritia,* 1 (1982), 182, 196-214.

105. On the problems of Welsh law and legislation, see J. Goronwy Edwards, "Studies in the Welsh Laws Since 1928" and other articles in *Welsh History Review: Special Number on the Welsh Laws,* ed. G. Williams (Cardiff, 1963); Edwards, "Hywel Dda and the Welsh Lawbooks," in *Celtic Law Papers,* pp. 137-60; Davies, *Wales in the Early Middle Ages,* pp. 203-04; and see next note.

106. Dafydd Jenkins, "The Medieval Welsh Idea of Law," *Revue d'Histoire du Droit,* 49 (1981), 323-48. The rubric in the *Textus Roffensis,* ascribing the code to Æthelbert in Augustine's day, is clearly not an original feature of the text; and, for other Germanic "non-royal" legislators, see Wormald, "*Lex Scripta* and *Verbum Regis,*" pp. 136-37.

107. Geoffrey Barrow, *The Kingdom of the Scots* (London, 1973), pp. 69-82; Derick S. Thomson, "Gaelic Learned Orders and Literati in Medieval Scotland," *Scottish Studies,* 12 (1968), 57-78; Bannerman, "Lordship of the Isles," passim.

108. Marjorie O. Anderson, "Dalriada and the Creation of the Kingdom of the Scots," in *Ireland in Medieval Europe,* pp. 121-23; and see her edition of the relevant chronicle in her *Kings and Kingship in Early Scotland* (Edinburgh, 1973), p. 250.

109. Anderson, *Kings and Kingship,* p. 251; Davies, "Latin Charter-Tradition,"

pp. 264-65; Duncan, *Scotland,* p. 110; Anderson, "Dalriada," pp. 125-28.

110. Barrow, *Kingdom of the Scots,* p. 150.

111. Duncan, *Scotland,* p. 116, and see p. 111. It has often, of course, been argued that Scotland was different because exposed to external (i.e., English) influence; but this leaves unanswered the question of why one Gaelic society should have been responsive and the other not.

112. G. H. Orpen, *Ireland Under the Normans,* 4 vols. (Oxford, 1911-20); for Freeman's attitude, see J. W. Burrow, *A Liberal Descent* (Cambridge, 1981), p. 191. On much of what follows, see Rhys Davies, *Historical Perception: Celts and Saxons* (Cardiff, 1979).

113. Nicholls, *Gaelic and Gaelicized Ireland,* pp. 84-85; Smyth, *Celtic Leinster,* p. 107.

114. Kenney, *Sources,* pp. 30-36; Sir John Davies, *A Discoverie,* pp. 102-06.

115. Mac Cana, "*Regnum* and *Sacerdotium.*"

116. John Watt, *The Church and the Two Nations in Medieval Ireland* (Cambridge, 1970), p. 2; Watt, *The Church in Medieval Ireland* (Dublin, 1972), p. 17.

117. Robert Bartlett, *Gerald of Wales* (Oxford, 1982), esp. pp. 157-210; and see Michael Richter, *Giraldus Cambrensis* (Aberystwyth, 1972), esp. pp. 61-86.

118. Smyth, *Celtic Leinster,* esp. pp. 21-40. This author's *Warlords and Holy Men* (The New History of Scotland, Vol. 1 [London, 1984]) contains several explicit and suggestive comparisons with Ireland in general and Leinster in particular. On a similar note, one of the things that disturbed Sir John Davies was the persistence of bloodfeud justice in Ireland: see *A Discoverie,* p. 102; but a similar system, under a powerful (though not centralized) crown, was working smoothly in Scotland until the seventeenth century: see Jenny Wormald, "Bloodfeud, Kindred and Government in Early Modern Scotland," *Past and Present,* 87 (1980), 54-97.

119. Francis John Byrne ("Tribes and Tribalism in Early Ireland," *Ériu,* 22 [1971], 155-57) points out that it was the more "advanced" part of Ireland that was occupied by the Normans, and that many of the pre-Conquest trends within this area matched those of contemporary Europe; see also Ó'Corráin, "Nationality and Kingship," pp. 32-34, and his "Aspects of Early Irish History," in *Perspectives in Irish Archaeology,* ed. B. G. Scott (Belfast, 1974), pp. 68-71. In Ireland, as in England, a contemporary explanation of conquest was that it was caused by sin (Watt, *Church in Medieval Ireland,* pp. 35-36); on the evidence available from both societies, and given that the ways of God are by definition inscrutable, the guilty conscience of the colonialist, whether in the twelfth, sixteenth, or twentieth centuries, perhaps deserves no more of the historian's attention than that of the colonized.

120. *The Scholar Revolutionary: Eoin Mac Neill 1867-1945 and the Making of the New Ireland,* ed. F. X. Martin and F. J. Byrne (Shannon, 1973), pp. 3, 24, 30, 43-48, 81-82, 87, 92, 142, 187-88.

Northumbria and Ireland

ROSEMARY CRAMP

Although the Irish were only one of the neighboring Celtic groups encountered by the Angles when they took over that section of northern Britain lying between the Humber and the Firth of Forth and Clyde, the importance of Irish influence on the formation of early Christian Northumbria has been widely acknowledged from the time of Bede onwards. In well-known passages Bede describes the poverty of the Irish Lindisfarne monks and the liberality of the Irish who received the English, "both nobles and commoners," who had left their own country to retire to Ireland either for the sake of religious studies or to live a more ascetic life.[1] As Bede says, some became monks, others preferred to travel round the cells of the various teachers to apply themselves to study. The Irish welcomed them all gladly, gave them their daily food, and also provided them with books to read and with instruction, without asking for any payment.[2] This open-handed hospitality of the Irish contrasted greatly with the hostility and unhelpfulness of the British. Nor can this contrast be explained entirely by the fact that the Britons had seen their land conquered and their religious sites destroyed or desecrated, while they were forced to shrink their territories ever further westwards or to be enslaved. No doubt this provided a partial reason for British hatred of the English;[3] but the English had also subdued the Irish expatriates of Dalriada by force. From the Battle of Degsastan (A.D. 603) until his time, as Bede said, "No Irish king has dared to make war on the English race to this day."[4] Bede specifically equated the greatest power of the Northumbrians with the period when they were at peace with the Irish, and when in A.D. 684 Ecgfrith sent an army to Ireland under his ealdorman Berht, Bede said he "wretchedly devastated a harmless race who had always been most friendly to the English, and his hostile bands spared neither churches nor monasteries."[5] Subsequently the Picts recovered their own land which the English had formerly held, while the Irish who lived in Britain and in some part of the British nation recovered their independence. Recently Alfred Smyth has suggested that Ecgfrith's raid can be explained in terms of a dynastic feud;[6] but it was clearly necessary for any ruler of North Britain to secure his western seaboard. The Irish were as potentially troublesome as neighbors to the newly settled Anglo-Saxons as were the Britons.

How different — both in social and economic terms — were these northern peoples? A considerable insight into the social structure and art of the Irish can be gained from the fact that they had never been conquered by the Romans, although indeed their economy was strengthened and their arts and crafts were enlivened by their raiding and trading with Roman Britain. In the sixth century the Irish were, like the English, recent settlers in mainland Britain; and perhaps, like the Picts — whom neither the Romans nor the English managed to subdue — they understood other barbarians. As a corollary one might guess that the hostility the Britons felt toward the Anglo-Saxons could have developed partly because the latter were heathen, but also partly because they were non-Roman: Anglo-Saxons had made themselves one with the other barbarians in A.D. 387 when the Roman Wall was breached and it was demonstrated that Roman power could be overthrown.

Nevertheless, the "Men of the North" (as the British chiefs called themselves) reshaped the pattern of their society after the Roman withdrawal to a form very close, apparently, to that of the free Celts of Ireland or Dalriada. In this paper I propose to examine in more detail the manner in which the Irish and the Anglo-Saxons supported their craftsmen and maintained production centers for specialized goods. But first, in order to explain the contacts that existed in the post-Roman period, we must look briefly at the Roman period itself.

Early Production Centers

Let us compare the fortunes and relationships of metal working sites on both sides of the Irish Channel during the Roman period. For some time after the Roman invasion, craftsmen — particularly metal workers — retained their repertory of traditional Celtic patterns. Centers for craftsmen such as those which developed during the first century in the north at Traprain Law seem to have turned out quality metal work and trinkets for the Roman army, and also glass artifacts such as bangles. For the craftsmen at Traprain Law, as at other major hill top sites, the resurgence of the northern tribes in the second century seems to have brought to an end their major activities; but such sites did not cease to exist elsewhere in the free Celtic societies of Ireland and the southwest, and these sites served as models and foci for the Celtic chiefdoms of southwest Scotland and Wales in the immediately post-Roman period.

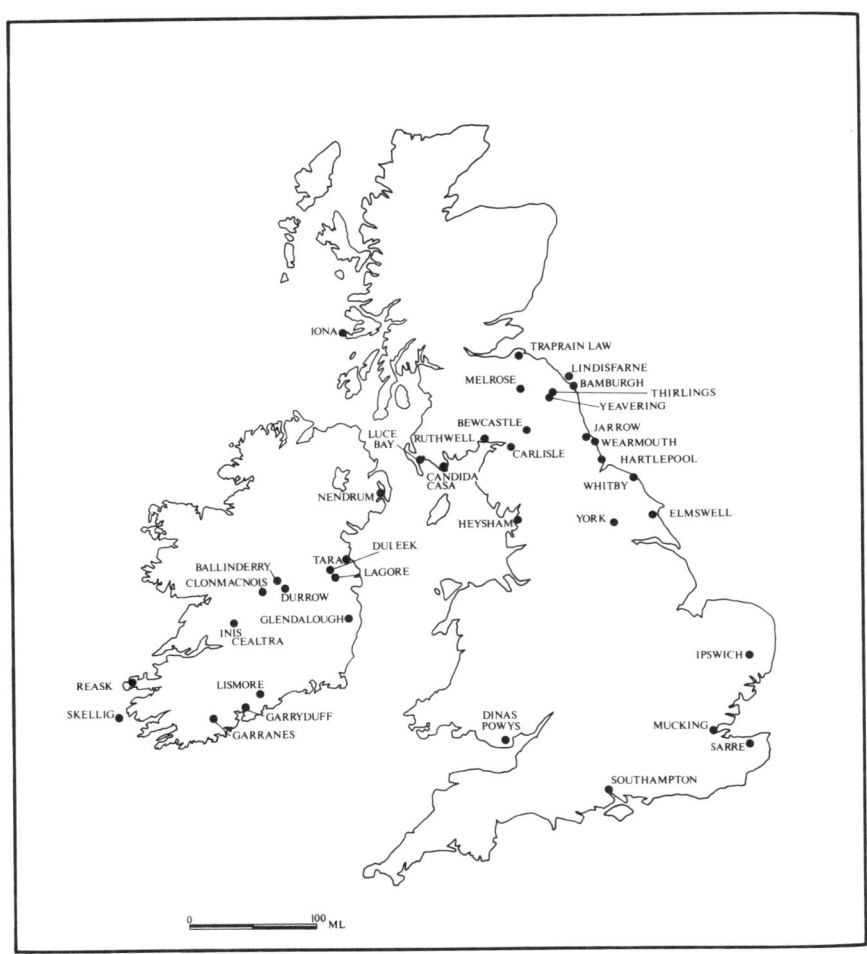

Fig. 1. Sites mentioned in the text.

The site of Elmswell in the East Riding of Yorkshire provides an interesting model both for early links with Ireland and for later links with Anglo-Saxon craftsmen. The quality of work from this settlement, which began in La Tène times and ended in the fifth/sixth century A.D., is reflected in a magnificent piece of first-century repoussé metalwork with an enameled strip along the top which is part of a casket mounting. The first artist/craftsman had developed La Tène curvilinear ornament in a typically northern Romano-Celtic idiom.[7] Artistic productions of such quality did not continue in north Britain under Roman occupation, however. But Irish craftsmen continued to develop the styles of curvilinear ornament, and in Ireland and possibly in parts of Scotland outside the Roman *Limes,* craft workshops flourished uninterruptedly during the Roman period and indeed increased in importance.

The relationships between Britain and Ireland as demonstrated by the archaeological record of the Roman period, and especially of the later Roman/pre-Roman period, have been a popular recent topic for discussion, but there has been little consideration of how Irish craftwork and export of artifacts were organized.

The production of fine metal work is associated with certain types of habitation site, the ring-forts and crannogs (artificial islands) which are a constituent part of non-La Tène Iron Age culture. The origin of these site-types is uncertain, although such a type may derive from Iberia; but they can be paralleled along the Atlantic coast of Scotland.

The massive excavations by Henken, O'Riordan, and O'Kelly have given us in Ballinderry Crannog, Garryduff, Garranes, and Lagore chieftain sites with incredibly rich survivals of which the most intensive occupation was in the seventh/eighth centuries A.D., but which provide evidence as well of more limited occupation during the earlier Iron-Age and the later Viking periods.[8] In summary, this type of site begins in the prehistoric period. At Tara, for instance, the Rath of the Synods includes a metal working site as part of the complex together with an ancient religious burial and assembly place. During the Roman period the community survived, and declined after the fifth century, but revived again in the early Christian period. All these sites throw a brilliant light on the resources and trade or exchange contacts of the Irish chieftains, as well as on the achievements of their craftsmen. It might be considered that some of the sites were occupied by a community of free craftsmen; but it is interesting, if one considers these sites as important centers of resource—including among resources the craftsmen—that the early Christian sites, as opposed to the prehistoric, are heavily enclosed. At Lagore and Garranes the enclosures are massive. This contrasts markedly with the craftsmen's sites of the North Germanic world, which are dispersed settlements—if one can consider sites such as Helgö as typical.[9]

The status of the smiths in both Irish and Germanic society is ambiguous. Françoise Henry says of the smith's work that it enjoyed a position of some importance:

> In the Irish texts the smith is a seer, a man endowed with a prophetic gift. He and the goldsmith belonged to that second class intermediate between the warring aristocracy and the common people which included besides the highest category of craftsmen, the lawyers, the poets, the historians and the clerics.[10]

Nevertheless, the defenses of their settlements imply that the craftsmen were retained in controlled circumstances or had banded together for protection.

At Lagore almost every craft is represented—metalworking in bronze; working with complex twisted iron-work in the Roman manner; and the making of millefiori rods both single and composite. This last craft has considerable relevance for contacts in the post-Roman period, since we also find such rods, outside Ireland, only at Dinas Powys, Luce Bay, and Jarrow on mainland Britain. There are also molds, both in stone and clay, for making glass studs cast within grills; motif pieces for trying out or confirming patterns—some even for taking off repoussé patterns; and there is also evidence for spinning, bone-working, and lathe-turning of wood. The pottery which is found on these sites is imported. Lagore also produced evidence for fine wood production, with a full set of Roman-type carpentry tools; but one may note that in Ireland finds of decorated wood are not common until the Viking period. The motif pieces (or trial pieces as they were once called) which are found at later sites like Garryduff include most of the repertory of Hiberno-Saxon manuscript ornament, with the exception of complex interlace. It is possible, therefore, that we should see some of these sites as working directly to the patronage of the Church, after a brief period of decline at the end of the Roman period.

The sustenance that Irish secular society had been receiving from the Roman-British mainland dried up in the fifth century; and colonies, successful in western Scotland but unsuccessful in Wales, were driven back ca. A.D. 440 by revived British strength. Then came the new impetus to the metal-workers' economy with the introduction of the Christian Church from mainland Britain. The monastery of Nendrum, founded by St. Machaoi from Whithorn in southwest Scotland, was apparently sited in an old ring-fort, and, as will be seen later, this new type of enclosed site—

the monastery—provided a haven for craftsmen in the West.

Most comment and discussion on early medieval Germanic craftsmen has likewise concerned itself with the smith, as Dodwell's recent work has shown.[11] Wilson has also pointed out that the smith was an important figure in Germanic heroic literature;[12] and Weland is known not only from the poem *Deor* but also from the front panel of the Franks Casket. His situation, though, is one of servitude to royal power, for which state by his superior cunning he exacts a terrible revenge. (One wonders indeed if there is not an explicit moral judgment in the juxtaposition of the treatment of the smith by the rulers and the treatment of Christ by the three Magi.)

The few references to the smith's status in Anglo-Saxon society have been often recorded: the reference in the *Laws of Ine* 63 to the provision that a noble, *gesiðcund* man may take with him, if he moves elsewhere, "his reeve, his smith, and his children's nurse"[13] seems to imply a subservient status for some smiths; but the king's smith, like his personal special messenger, is protected by a specified *wergild* in the *Laws of Æthelbert* 7.[14] But, of course, there could have been a major difference between the ironsmith and the bronze- or goldsmith, as later Old English texts imply.

Textual references, at least for the early period, imply then some sort of constraint on the liberty of the smith. No doubt every major group needed a smith, and some could have been retained in lords' households where they would enjoy an enhanced status. Little trace remains of their workshops, however, although there are traces of metal-working residues in several settlement sites of early communities such as Mucking, where the earliest slag base from a shaft-furnace has been found.[15] Of course, the Mucking settlement could have been one of foreign and exploited workers; but the fact that the iron there was worked by a Roman-British type of shaft-furnace could be significant, since the usual Germanic furnaces are the small bowl-type; the superior technology could have been derived from native Roman-British traditions. It is indeed possible that when the Anglo-Saxons gained a firm control over eastern Britain, they took over and stimulated the output of some indigenous metal—workers. Elmswell in Yorkshire we have already noted as a native settlement site occupied from the first century A.D. to at least A.D. 500. There during the later Roman period metal-workers turned from fine bronze-work to iron-working and corn production. There is little evidence for Anglo-Saxon occupation of the site, and one may ask, Did the incomers seize on these smiths and move them to one of their newly established sites? The Roman type of twisted iron-work (as found at Lagore and also at Sutton Hoo), as well as Saxon pottery, combs, and brooches, was discovered at Elmswell.

It seems likely that there were British smiths in areas on the borders of, or even within, Anglo-Saxon-controlled territories who still maintained Roman-British techniques. The short-lived *floruit* of the "quoit brooch style" means that some sort of contact persisted, and not all the Irish/Scottic metalwork in Saxon graves could be loot: some smiths must have been directly employed.

Now what among the Anglo-Saxons are we to set against these production centers in sixth- and eighth-century Britain? The Germanic peoples clearly valued fine metalwork, and in the northern homelands the discovery of production centers such as Helgö has revolutionized our ideas about metalworking output in the sixth to eighth centuries; but how did the English support and retain their craftsmen? It could be suggested that the sunken huts of the Germanic peoples, which appear all over northern mainland Europe from the fifth century onwards, represent an attempt by the new Germanic rulers to harness labor and to develop cottage industries after the wreck of the Roman industrial network. Mucking has produced a mold for a cruciform brooch as well as extensive evidence for bone-working and for spinning and weaving.[16] It is interesting that evidence for weaving is the most frequent feature on these early Anglo-Saxon sites, and the least frequent on the Irish. On most of the sunken-featured hut sites settlement ends, and presumably the inhabitants moved elsewhere, in the late seventh century, so these settlements seem to have been superseded by other sites and even other social structures.

In summary, it is mainly from pagan graves that we see clearly the value that the Anglo-Saxons placed on Celtic works of art. At the highest level of patronage, as demonstrated in the richest Sutton Hoo grave, some metal artifacts such as the great cauldron, the chain, the hanging bowls, the fish in the bowl, even the stag are capable of being seen as having a Romano-Celtic pedigree. Did the Saxon chieftains sweep up into their controlled centers some of the humbler metalworkers like those of the Elmswell group and attract major craftsmen from Gaul and Ireland alike? The complex aspirations of the invading kings to absorb the images of power of their subject peoples and to relate themselves to existing traditions are obviously reflected in the Sutton Hoo burials; but we are concerned with the more northerly Anglian kingdom. Yeavering has provided us with an example of the use by the invading kings of a tribal gathering-place which since Neolithic times had been hallowed for religious assemblies. The great enclosure which dominates the site is paralleled in the native "forts" farther north, and could have served as a tax-gathering or redistributive center — a center which, when it had played its part in linking the new to the old power, was moved to a location with better communications, at Milfield.

Bamburgh, *the* town of the Bernicians, may indeed have been the type of Celtic fortress where crafts could be practiced: like Garryduff, the site has produced a small gold-foil mount.[17] A similar role with respect to Deira could be postulated for York, the urban center of the Roman North. It begins to be clear that only a small section of such Roman towns could have survived with their market-places, and that until the implantation later of monasteries a royal fortress may have been maintained in some as the sole survival of cultural power.

Such ad hoc arrangements could then have been superseded by the establishment of entrepôts or ports of trade—possibly, in England, one major center per kingdom, as, e.g., Southampton for Wessex, Sarre for Kent, or Ipswich for East Anglia. Further, I would consider that these could have been supplemented by other centers before the full development of towns as exchange and production centers.[18]

The Role of the Monasteries

Recent work on Irish monasteries and their social and economic role examines in more detail the nature of the reciprocal exchange between Church and laity and has assembled the literary evidence for trade between Ireland, western Scotland, and Gaul. The Life of St. Philibert describes clothes and footwear brought by Irish ships to Noirmoutier and also discusses the annual fairs or *oenachs* which can be held in monastic centers.[19]

No one imagines today that the typical Irish monastery is the hilltop or stack coastal site, such as Skellig St. Michael—or indeed, that there was a "typical" site. Smyth's recent survey of monastic locations for Leinster covers almost every reasonable location for a settlement. "Irish monasteries were located on major routes as well as on trackways, on borders, and at fording-places on rivers and elsewhere. The vast majority of monasteries, however, owed their existence to serving the local communities."[20]

A comparable pattern can be seen in the English evidence, where monasteries were sometimes twinned with secular settlements as Lindisfarne was with Bamburgh, but where also (as I have tried to demonstrate elsewhere) they played a significant role in the revival of trade by placing an abbott or abbess from the royal kin in what were traditional Roman centers.[21] In Northumbria this applies by the seventh century to Carlisle and York, but also it may be significant that Lindisfarne—the founding monastic center of Celtic Christianity in the north—held land in both these towns and at the ports of entry on both seaboards of Northumbria.

It is unfortunate that at Iona—the most important gateway between Irish and Northumbrian Christianity — excavations conducted by a series of directors have yielded such an incomplete picture of the environment and the life-style of the monastic community at the period when Aidan was sent to Lindisfarne in A.D. 635. The large monastic ditch-and-vallum which surrounded the main complex was a feature in the Irish tradition, but unlike the ditch-and-vallum on most Irish sites, at Iona it was rectangular with rounded corners.[22] Recent surveys have demonstrated also that there were other earthworks of varying dates associated with the enclosure, one of which was curved. Although the massive buildings implied by Adamnán's descriptions of the great hall—the *domus magna*—and the *domus monasterium* have not been found, various workshop areas have been discovered. These have produced molds for manufacturing inlaid glass studs in the Irish manner, a glass rod, and residues of bronze wood, and leather-working.[23] The traditions that Ionan groups brought to Northumbria among others were of close involvement between the ruling kin and the monastic houses — the positioning of bishops in monastic houses rather than in secular courts or urban centers — and a tradition of Christian learning housed in buildings which owed nothing to the Roman techniques of mortared stone. Churches and other ecclesiastical buildings are constantly described as wooden in Irish literature until the later eighth century. The earliest reference to a stone church in Ireland is to Duleek in 724, and this is a site with easy sea contact with Britain and the Continent and, as its link with Pictish-type Annals indicates, in close contact with the Scottish and Pictish mainland. Perhaps we should see this influence from the mainland to Ireland as part of the close Ionan links with Northumbrian monasteries in the eighth century which are discussed below. In the seventh century, as indicated in my introductory quotations from Bede, Ireland was a primary donor of Christian culture to Northumbria.

Only a few Irish monasteries were royal foundations; but in Northumbria a large number of those founded under the direction of the Ionan mission were endowed from royal estates and were ruled by royal kin at least for the first two or three generations. The privilege of founding such establishments was later extended to other landholders who probably provided something like the supporting Irish *manaig* in their endowments of a certain number of households.[24] In both Britain and Ireland there is considerable doubt as to whether all those who worked on the monastic estate and who might be considered as "brethren" were fully committed to the monastic life. At Lindisfarne the famous Gospels were provided with a casing of gold and silver-gilt and jewels by Billfrith the anchorite, who may have been leading a pious life near to, but not in, the community,[25] while at the Whitby/Hackness estate the reference to one of the shepherds of the monastery may refer to a monk or lay associate. Whitby too had a reeve for the monastic estates.[26]

Lindisfarne's pre-Conquest buildings have not been excavated, but Whitby's have — albeit some time ago and in a very inept fashion; and there are some parallels in excavated evidence at Whitby to that of the Irish monastery of Nendrum. Nendrum was founded in an older domestic site — a ring-fort — the church and its surrounding cemetery being sited in the center. It is not possible to distinguish, as on many Irish domestic sites, between those buildings which were for communal and those which were for individual use; but among the peripheral group of circular huts was one rectangular building which its excavator called a "school." It has recently been suggested that the building is best regarded as a workshop for specialized crafts,[27] but perhaps that is only a semantic distinction. The finds from that building — stones with scratched trial designs, styli, knives, needles, a mortar (perhaps for mixing pigments) — suggest a range of skills. One of the circular huts near by produced crucibles, tongs, molds, and residues from bronze-working which, if not on the same scale of deposition as those in the secular ring-forts like Lagore or Garryduff, are nevertheless of the same type.

At Whitby the buildings to the north of the present church likewise resembled the indigenous secular type, and there is some evidence that the site may have been reshaped into a monastery by Saint Hilda. The earliest phase of the site included a circular enclosure like an Irish monastic site, and there are some resemblances to the Irish tradition in the craft residues and artifacts associated with the buildings. There is evidence for bronze- and silver-working from the surviving slags, although there are no molds and crucibles. There are also half-finished and waste products of jet, which occurs in the raw state at Whitby. There is as-yet-unpublished evidence for glass-working on the site in the form of a glass tessera and rod, and there is a glass molded setting and an inlaid glass stud of a type unique in Northumbria but common enough in Ireland. There is also an Irish type of bronze ladle. The 12 styli, 2 vellum prickers, and 123 loom weights are not typical of Irish so much as of Anglo-Saxon secular sites and betray perhaps most clearly the female bias of the site.[28]

The only other excavated monastic sites in Northumbria, those of the twin monasteries of Wearmouth and Jarrow, may well represent a deliberate attempt by their founder to turn away from the close involvement with secular society and even with the housing of bishops that the Irish church had introduced. In contrast, we know very little about how a female double community operated within Anglo-Saxon society. The female founders were, in all the recorded instances which survive, of royal stock, and there seems to have been a determined effort to secure succession through the family by daughter succeeding mother or niece succeeding aunt. In the case of Hilda, of whom it is unknown whether she spent her thirty-three years in secular life as a wife or in the single state, her successor was of the royal kin and could have been related to her. Now it is clear that the male communities retained lay craftsmen and servants, and one wonders whether double monasteries also provided a home for lay females who were skilled in spinning and weaving. Most of the Anglo-Saxon domestic sites provide a great deal of evidence for spinning and weaving. This is not the case in Ireland, where the evidence from sites shows plenty of evidence for spinning but little for weaving. It is possible that no monastic site was self-sufficient, and I have noted elsewhere that there is evidence that some female abbesses were granted royal remission of tolls for their ships, which implies some interest in overseas trade.[29] I have also indicated how monasteries in the early years of the foundation of the network could in the Irish manner have provided secure centers for trade or exchange.

In an earlier article on Monkwearmouth and Jarrow I made, in passing, reference to the founding ideals described above and to their reflection in the archaeological record.[30] Since that time, evidence excavated from the two sites has not been significantly augmented save in the riverside workshops at Jarrow, but there have been both a considerable increase in commentary on the textual background of both English and Irish monasteries, and additional publications on specific sites, such as that on Reask in Ireland.[31]

In earlier articles I searched for parallels for the monastic buildings and layout in Gaul, a reasonably obvious area in which to look since we are told that is where the builders came from, and that Benedict wished to build in the Roman manner. We have already looked at the "Irish manner," and evidence from Wearmouth and Jarrow of painted and plastered walls of mortared stone, concrete floors, stone and slate roofs, and glazed windows surely justified the belief that here was something very different from the buildings one would have expected to see at Lindisfarne. It is true that the shapes and layouts of the major types of stone building were easily seen to be comparable with the halls at Yeavering, just as the smaller structures at Wearmouth or Whitby can be compared with smaller Northumbrian timber buildings such as have been recently excavated at Thirlings. Moreover, such building plans are now known throughout Anglo-Saxon England in Mercia, East Anglia, and Wessex. The Wearmouth/Jarrow buildings could therefore be seen as a direct translation into stone of Germanic timber structures (see figure 2).

Having provided some English and Gaulish parallels, I felt it sufficient to dismiss the Irish example. However, this is to fall into a trap easily sprung by archaeologist and historian alike, namely that the satisfaction of creating one "fit" for two types of evidence precludes the necessity of looking for another. It is very difficult to untangle a multiplicity of influences, or even changing attitudes and functions, when studying archaeological sites.

I have named the buildings at Jarrow according to artifacts discovered in them. The church is obvious and is surrounded by its cemetery in the Celtic manner. At Monkwearmouth the position of the church is similar and there are small scattered buildings in the Whitby manner, although a long gallery linking the monastic buildings to the church has some affinity with building plans derived from Roman prototypes on the Continent: perhaps this gallery is some form of *porticus*. At Jarrow I have more boldly named the major buildings according to their associated artifacts and their plans. Building A I consider to be a refectory, with a dormitory above and a possible kitchen added at a later date in its life-history. Building B I interpret as a general purpose room for assemblies and possibly for some writing, and its form—one large room with a high seat at one end and an independent two-roomed suite beyond—can well be compared to the plans of the royal halls at Yeavering. Alongside the river at the perimeter of the monastery is what could have been a guest-house which later developed into a range of workshops (fig. 2).

Despite their difference in character these buildings are not fused into an organic whole as are later monastic buildings, and Aidan Macdonald's recent analysis of monastic buildings mentioned in the *Annals of Ulster* makes an interesting comparison with Jarrow and the possible function of its buildings. He identifies the Abbot's House, which stands on its platform; the *Tech Mor,* the great house or principal building, as Adamnán describes it at Iona. Then there was the *Proindtech*—the eating house or dining hall, and the *Cucann*—the kitchen. The lack of reference to a dormitory could have resulted from the fact that there was no one central sleeping-place and monks slept in groups in their cells. The domestic buildings and craft huts were perhaps too inconsiderable architecturally for special mention. At Wearmouth and Jarrow Bede is at pains to point out that the early abbots did not have their own special houses, and both at Lindisfarne and the Bedan sites there were common dormitories. Nevertheless we could see Buildings A and B as the *Proindtech* and the *Tech Mor*.

The riverside complex at Jarrow is difficult to relate to any (excavated)

JARROW 1976

Saxon

C E M E T E R Y

building tradition. The finds have something in common with those from Irish workshops in the small bronze tools, the palette, stone lamps and bowls, and the evidence for glass-working, which includes working with millefiori rods. The foundations of the buildings, however, are massively constructed of reused Roman stones. There is some evidence from Jarrow that in the ninth century the craftsmen's huts spread over a wider area of the site. We must expect, however, that in the eighth century, which was indeed the period of England's greatest impact on the Continent, the Irish links became rather irrelevant for some centers, notably those in Yorkshire. Nevertheless, some northern monasteries such as Jarrow maintained their links, those with Iona being particularly strong in the first half of the eighth century. It is no doubt significant that it is from the mid-eighth century onwards that such contacts bear fruit in the eclectic styles of metal-work and sculpture which have recently been discussed by Isabel Henderson.[32]

Craftsmen of different races working together in the same monastic milieu in Northumbria are described in the literary sources. In the Northumbrian monastery celebrated in *De Abbatibus* there is a famous calligrapher, Ultan, who is Irish and a priest and who could ornament books with fair markings. The smith, Cwicwine, was devout in his fasts and devotions, but when matins was finished his hammer could be heard beating out vessels for the tables of the brothers.[33] He was a more devout member of the community than the drunken smith of Lindisfarne whose morals were below monastic standards but whose standard of craftsmanship was high. Chapter xx of *De Abbatibus* describes the interior of the church, softly lit through its glass windows: torches and hanging bowls give light; there are icons or plaques; books are jewelled with gold; altars are glittering with glass, golden chalices and silver patens. To achieve this splendid environment many craftsmen would have been employed for many years, and when the monasteries were sacked and abandoned in the late ninth century, no doubt the craftsmen found patrons elsewhere.

By the tenth century the importance of York as the major manufacturing and trading center, as well as the only mint in Northumbria, was significantly increased by the Dublin/Chester/York trading axis which could link the North Sea and the Irish Channel. We have already noted that the western seaboard of Northumbria could have seen a constant traffic between the Celtic West and the Germanic North. Then, as now, the short crossings from southwest Scotland or Morecambe Bay were no doubt the most frequented; and the traffic was certainly not all one way. If Northumbria could not have developed into its distinctive form without the Irish dimension, neither could the Irish kingdoms have developed without the stimulus from the larger island to the east. Nevertheless, to shake the Irish into real change and to diversify distinctively their settlements into town-like production and trading centers, it needed an invasion of their country by an alien group — the Vikings. Their presence and implanted settlements produced notable artistic and social changes, transforming the previous traditions.

I hope that in this brief review I have not given the impression that Northumbria was uniquely dependent on Ireland for its distinctive development. It is clear that all the English kingdoms looked south for their models of Christian life as well as for trade. For most of this period the most frequent sea traffic on both coasts seems to have been north and south rather than east and west.

However, I wished to stress that for some periods — namely the immediately post-Roman period; the last half of the seventh century to the foundation of the English see of Whithorn in ca. A.D. 731; and again during the Viking period — identity of interest and political federation made Northumbria firmly part of the Irish Sea province. Not all sections of society were equally influenced, however; and with the rise of power in Mercia and Wessex, Northumbria's external contacts became more straitened. The Scandinavian settlements in Yorkshire and Cumbria drove a wedge for some time between old Bernicia, north of the Tees, and Deira, or southern Northumbria. The Lindisfarne community never forgot its Irish roots, however, and when under the threat of renewed Scandinavian raids in the mid-ninth century the community left Lindisfarne, taking with them part of their dependent lay community — (like an Irish *manaig*) — they tried to go back to Ireland. However, they found a haven in the old Roman fort at Chester-le-Street and later, after A.D. 995, on the newly fortified peninsular site of Durham. The community had to come to terms with the Vikings both as landowners and tenants, and their art-styles were clearly affected by this contact. Nevertheless, in their northern territories Anglo-Celtic art still flourished; and a cross from Alnmouth provides the only name of a Northumbrian stone carver for this period. His name, *Myredah,* is an Anglicized form of the Irish *Muirdach.* He thus takes his place in the long and distinguished tradition of Anglo-Irish craftsmen — most of whom are anonymous.

UNIVERSITY OF DURHAM

Notes

1. Bede *Ecclesiastical History of the English People* III.26, 27, ed. Bertram Colgrave and R. A. B. Mynors (Oxford, 1969) (hereafter cited as *HE*), pp. 308–09, 312–13.
2. Bede *HE* III.27 (ed. Colgrave and Mynors, pp. 312–13).
3. Bede *HE* I.23 (ed. Colgrave and Mynors, pp. 68–69).
4. "Ex eo tempore quisquam regum Scottorum in Britanniam adversus gentem Anglorum usque ad hanc diem in proelium venire audebat" (Bede *HE* I.34 [ed. Colgrave and Mynors, pp. 116–17]).
5. Bede *HE* IV.26 (ed. Colgrave and Mynors, pp. 426–28).
6. A. P. Smyth, *Celtic Leinster* (Blackrock, Co. Dublin, 1982), pp. 120–21.
7. H. E. Kilbride Jones, *Celtic Craftsmanship in Bronze* (London, 1980), pp. 66–68. The Elmswell mount was first discussed by P. Corder and C. F. C. Hawkes, "A Panel of Celtic Ornament from Elmswell, East Yorkshire," *Antiquaries Journal,* 20 (1940), 338–57.
8. H. O'N. Hencken, "Lagore Crannog, An Irish Royal Residence of the Seventh to Tenth Centuries A.D.," *Proceedings of the Royal Irish Academy,* 53 (1950), Section C, 1–248; S. P. O'Riordan, "The Excavation of the Large Earthen Ring-Fort at Garranes, County Cork," *Proceedings of the Royal Irish Academy,* 47 (1942), Section C, 77–150; M. J. O'Kelly, "Two Ring-Forts at Garryduff, County Cork," *Proceedings of the Royal Irish Academy,* 63 (1962), Section C, 17–125. This article contains a useful résumé of the dating of other sites of this type from Ireland.
9. W. Holmqvist, *Excavations at Helgö, IV: The Workshop, Part I* (Stockholm, 1972); and W. Holmqvist, "Helgö: An Early Trading Settlement in Central Sweden," in *Recent Archaeological Excavations in Europe,* ed. R. L. S. Bruce-Mitford (London and Boston, 1975), pp. 111–32.
10. F. Henry, *Irish Art in the Early Christian Period to A.D. 800* (London, 1965), pp. 66–67.
11. C. R. Dodwell, *Anglo-Saxon Art, A New Perspective,* Vol. III of *Manchester Studies in the History of Art* (Manchester, 1982), pp. 58–79.
12. D. M. Wilson, "Craft and Industry," in D. M. Wilson, *The Archaeology of Anglo-Saxon England* (London, 1976), pp. 253–81; and see also H. Loyn, *Anglo-Saxon England and the Norman Conquest* (London, 1962), pp. 103–06.
13. "The Laws of Ine (688–694)," in *English Historical Documents,* Vol. I, ed. D. Whitelock (London, 1955), p. 371.
14. "From the Laws of Ethelbert, King of Kent (602–603?)," in *Eng. Hist. Doc.,* Vol. I, ed. Whitelock, p. 357.
15. M. U. Jones and W. T. Jones, "The Crop-Mark Sites at Mucking, Essex, England," in *Recent Archaeological Excavations in Europe,* pp. 133–87.
16. Jones and Jones, pp. 161–62, n. 9.
17. Both Milfield and Yeavering have been discussed by Brian Hope-Taylor in Great Britain, Department of the Environment, *Yeavering: An Anglo-British Centre of Early Northumbria,* Archaeological Reports, No. 7 (London, 1977). The site of Milfield has been recently resurveyed from the air and the findings could indicate

an associated settlement of sunken huts (see note 18).

18. I have discussed the changing patterns of Northumbrian settlement and their functions in "Anglo-Saxon Settlement," in *Settlement in North Britain 1000 B.C.-A.D. 1000,* ed. J. C. Chapman and H. C. Mytum, *British Archaeological Reports,* British Series, 118 (1983), 263-97.

19. This was first discussed by H. Mayr-Harting in *The Coming of Christianity to Anglo-Saxon England* (London, 1972), pp. 84-86, and has been subsequently developed by Charles Doherty, "Exchange and Trade in Early Medieval Ireland," *Journal of the Royal Society of Antiquaries of Ireland,* 110 (1980), 76-78.

20. Smyth, *Celtic Leinster,* pp. 27-30.

21. Cramp, "Anglo-Saxon Settlement," pp. 279-81.

22. An up-to-date summary of the evidence on Iona is to be found in Great Britain, Royal Commission on the Ancient and Historical Monuments of Scotland, *Argyll,* Vol. IV (London, 1982).

23. *Argyll,* IV, 15.

24. This lay support group has been discussed by many scholars, but a recent clear discussion may be found in Kathleen Hughes and Ann Hamlin, *The Modern Traveller to the Early Irish Church* (London, 1977).

25. T. D. Kendrick et al., *Codex Lindisfarnensis,* II (London, 1960), 5.

26. I have discussed Whitby fully in "Monastic Sites," in *The Archaeology of Anglo-Saxon England,* ed. D. M. Wilson (London, 1976), pp. 223-99.

27. Hughes and Hamlin, pp. 75-76, n. 26.

28. Nevertheless, although we tend to think that the loom was a female attribute, it is at least possible that, as in the division of labor described among the West Highland group of St. Kilda, the women spun and sewed but the men wove: see D. A. Quine, *St. Kilda Revisited* (Frome, 1982).

29. Cramp, "Monastic Sites."

30. Cramp, "Monkwearmouth and Jarrow," in *Famulus Christi,* ed. G. Bonner (London, 1976), pp. 10-17.

31. T. Fanning, "Excavation of an Early Christian Cemetery and Settlement at Reask, County Kerry," *Proceedings of the Royal Irish Academy,* 81 (1981), Section C, 3.

32. I. Henderson, "Pictish Art and the Book of Kells," in *Ireland in Early Medieval Europe,* ed. D. Whitelock, R. McKitterick, and D. Dumville (Cambridge, 1982), pp. 79-105.

33. *Aethelwulf De Abbatibus,* ed. A. Campbell (Oxford, 1967), ll. 208 and 282-305 (Cwicwine).

The Relationship Between Scandinavian and English Art from the Late Eighth to the Mid-Twelfth Century

SIGNE HORN FUGLESANG

When discussing Viking and Insular art, we normally tend to emphasize the aspect of reciprocal influence.[1] This is only natural, since both written and archaeological sources testify to frequent and close contacts between the two areas, and a number of deep-going changes, particularly in North-English art are presumed to result from the Viking settlements of the second half of the ninth century and later.

There are, however, countless obvious contrasts between the art of the two areas. Some are contrasts only to be expected when one region was old Christian and the other still pagan-to-neophyte-Christian. But there are differences also in fields where a common heritage existed in Germanic Migration art — namely, in the animal ornament. Such differences should probably be ascribed to separate artistic developments, as embodied in the craftsmen and their training. There are also similarities which may be attributed not to reciprocal influence but to parallel and independent indigenous evolutions and innovations. This whole spectrum of independent differences and similarities complicates the task of comparison because such similarities and differences create uncertainty as to what actually may be taken to constitute proof of influence by one area on another.

In a brief paper I cannot of course discuss the methodological aspects of the problem as well as give some factual information on the material. What I hope to do in the following pages is to point to some of the stages of artistic development in England and in Scandinavia which are now being discussed by archaeologists and art historians with a view to developing criteria for establishing foreign influence. This is, by the way, not merely an interesting scholarly game. The aim and importance of such discussions is to gauge the validity of the visual arts as a historical source for this period.

The decades preceding the attack on Lindisfarne in A.D. 793 seem to have been a period of vigorous artistic innovation and output both in England and in Scandinavia. The narrative art surviving on the picture stones on the island of Gotland shows up at a glance one of the major differences between the two areas (Plate 1). Against the Anglo-Saxon Christian pictures and stone crosses stands the world of Norse mythology, an iconography which apparently often had an eschatological significance. The gods and their home of Valhalla are Scandinavian, but pan-Germanic myths such as those involving Wayland Smith and King Niðuðr also occur on the Gotlandic stones.

Another contrast between the two areas is to be found in the field of animal ornament. If we compare the Anglo-Carolingian ribbon-shaped animals on the Lindau book-binding (Plate 2) with the same motif in Scandinavian style E (Plate 3), the differences of form are obvious. Among major differences are the Scandinavian preferences for sinuous shape, openings within the body, loop compositions, and frond-like limbs. Compared with the S-shaped animals on the disc-on-bow brooch from Gumbalda on Gotland, the ribbon-shaped beasts on the Lindau book-binding can almost be termed naturalistic.

Such differences of form may also explain why Northumbrian metalwork of the eighth and early ninth centuries (presumably largely loot from the early raids) does not seem to have been copied by Scandinavian craftsmen. In spite of the fairly high number of such imports recovered from Norwegian graves, there is so far little evidence that they served as models for indigenous craftsmen.[2]

But at the same time, semi-naturalistic birds and mammals were introduced into Scandinavian art through English or French models. These new motifs underwent a thorough stylization with the same kind of openings, loops, fronds, and sinuous bodies which distinguish the Scandinavian ribbon-shaped animals, and consequently it is difficult to establish their precise area of origin. They may be exemplified by the gilt bronze mounts from Broa on Gotland, works of high artistic quality (Plate 4). One motif which was not treated in this manner is the so-called gripping beast (Plate 5). It too was introduced from abroad, but maintained its solid body with angular twists, squat proportions, spread-eagled limbs, frontal head, and gripping feet. In 1937, Holger Arbman identified a number of examples of gripping beasts from Scandinavian finds as imports, and he suggested Carolingian art as the source of the motif.[3] Later, Günther Haseloff analyzed

Plate 1. Picture stone from Tjängvide, Gotland, Sweden. (Photo: Nils Lagergren, Antikvarisk-topografiska arkivet, Stockholm.)

Plate 2. Book-binding from Lindau. (Photo: Pierpont Morgan Library, New York.)

Plate 3. Disc-on-bow brooch from Gumbalda, Gotland, Sweden. (After B. Salin, *Die altgermanische Thierornamentik* [1904].)

the Anglo-Saxon and Anglo-Carolingian material, and he held that the gripping beast originated in the Northumbrian inhabited scroll (Plate 6) but that the beast had been stylized in Anglo-Saxon metalwork and introduced into Scandinavia through this medium (Plate 7).[4] This view appears to have become generally accepted and offers a satisfactory solution to the problem of the origin of the motif.[5]

In the decades around 800 there is no indication that Scandinavian art made any impact in England, nor did the succeeding Oseberg style of the first half of the ninth century. Even during this stylistic phase, influences from England and France seem to have made themselves felt in Scandinavia. It is, however, difficult to evaluate the relative importance of England and France as countries of origin, since the innovations of the Oseberg style lie mostly in elements of form. In the Oseberg style, Scandinavian ornament was reshaped into a carpet-pattern play of light and shade through the numerous squat animals which are rendered in relief on many planes (Plate 8). Similar stylistic tendencies were current in Carolingian and Anglo-Saxon ornament; the latter is here exemplified by a fragmentary cross-shaft from Croft-on-Tees (Plate 9). When this rendering of an Anglo-Saxon inhabited scroll is compared with wood carvings of the so-called Baroque

Plate 4. Gilt bronze mount with two juxtaposed animals, from Broa, Gotland, Sweden. (Photo: Antikvarisk-topografiska arkivet, Stockholm.)

Plate 5. Gilt bronze mount with gripping beasts, from Broa, Gotland, Sweden. (Photo: Antikvarisk-topografiska arkivet, Stockholm.)

Plate 6. Detail of cross-shaft at Jedburgh, Roxburghshire, Scotland. (Photo: T. Middlemass, Durham University.)

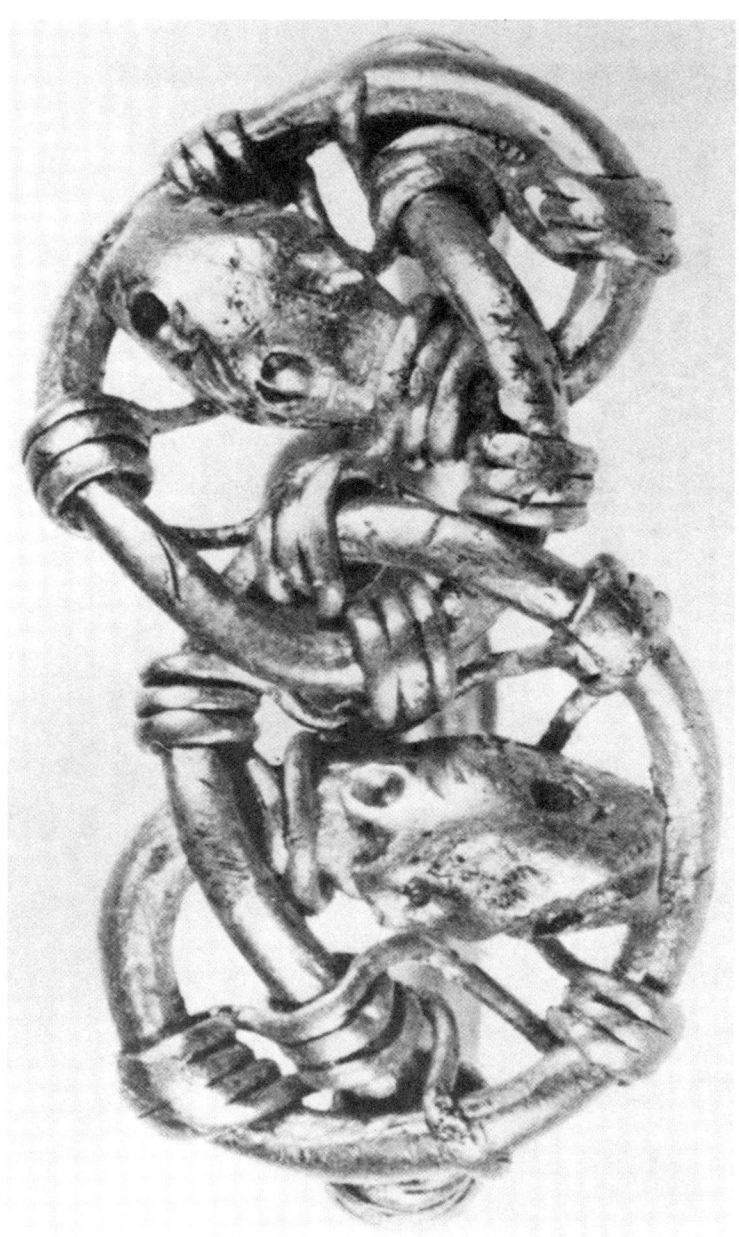

Plate 7. Gold finger-ring from Dorchester, Dorset, England. (After D. A. Hinton, *Anglo-Saxon Ornamental Metalwork in the Ashmolean Museum* [1974].)

Plate 9. Cross-shaft at Croft-on-Tees, Yorkshire, England. (Photo: T. Middlemass, Durham University.)

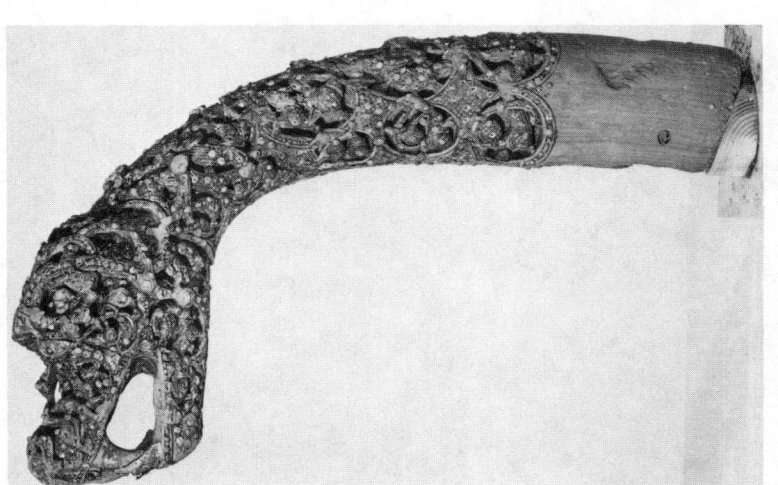

Plate 8. Animal-head post by "The Baroque Master" from Oseberg, Vestfold, Norway. (Photo: Universitetets Oldsaksamling, Oslo.)

Plate 11. Trefoil brooch with vine scroll, animal heads and masks, from Jørstad, Oppland, Norway. (Photo: Universitetets Oldsaksamling, Oslo.)

Plate 10. Gilt bronze mounts from Borre, Vestfold, Norway. (Photo: Universitetets Oldsaksamling, Oslo.)

Master in Oseberg, one can see similarities in composition and form. But whether these similarities reflect Anglo-Saxon influence in Scandinavia or whether they are fortuitous parallels remains an open question.

Not until the Scandinavian phases of the Borre and Jellinge styles is there evidence that Viking art was introduced into England.[6] Borre style ornament in Scandinavia is traditionally characterized by its ribbon motifs which frequently terminate in animal heads. The ribbons themselves are normally made up of equilateral geometrical shapes — squares, circles and triangles — which are interlinked (Plate 10). The so-called ring-chain is a leitmotiv. But the Borre phase in Scandinavia was also a period of eclecticism and experiment, when metalworkers copied Carolingian acanthus leaves and Anglo-Saxon or Carolingian vine scrolls although these motifs were never properly incorporated into the general Scandinavian repertory (Plate 11). Furthermore, the separate spiral or pair of spirals which did acquire significance in Scandinavian art was adopted during this phase (Plate 12). Whether France or England provided the model is not yet established, but David Wilson and C. E. Blunt have convincingly demonstrated that the origin of the spirals lay in vine-scroll motifs.[7] Borre style ornament in Scandinavia is generally considered to have developed at some time in the second half of the ninth century. It occurs on jewelry from hoards of the second quarter of the tenth century, which by the way are the earliest Scandinavian ornament to be datable on coin evidence.[8]

In the British Isles, the Borre style is best represented in Cumbria and on the Isle of Man. It may have been brought to Cumbria by Norse Vikings coming from Ireland just after A.D. 900.[9] The Gosforth Cross is the most famous manifestation of the Borre style in England because of its monumentality as well as its ornament and its narrative representations (Plate 13). The ribbon interlace is of the Borre style, including the ring-chain of a two-strand variety which is rare in Scandinavia; and although David Wilson has demonstrated that the motif does occur there, he regards the Cumbrian as a local Anglo-Norse version.[10] The animal heads at the end of the Gosforth ribbons may reflect corresponding terminals on Scandinavian metalwork, but on the Cross they are intended as monsters. The narrative scenes on the Gosforth Cross show the coexistence of Christian and pagan themes. There is one panel with a Crucifixion. The other scenes are unframed, in accordance with Scandinavian practice, and not all of them can be interpreted. Those that can be identified with reasonable credibility, however, are connected with the Scandinavian myth of Ragnarok, the pagan equivalent of the Last Judgment, and an *interpretatio Christiana* seems indicated.[11] Other Cumbrian carvings illustrate different

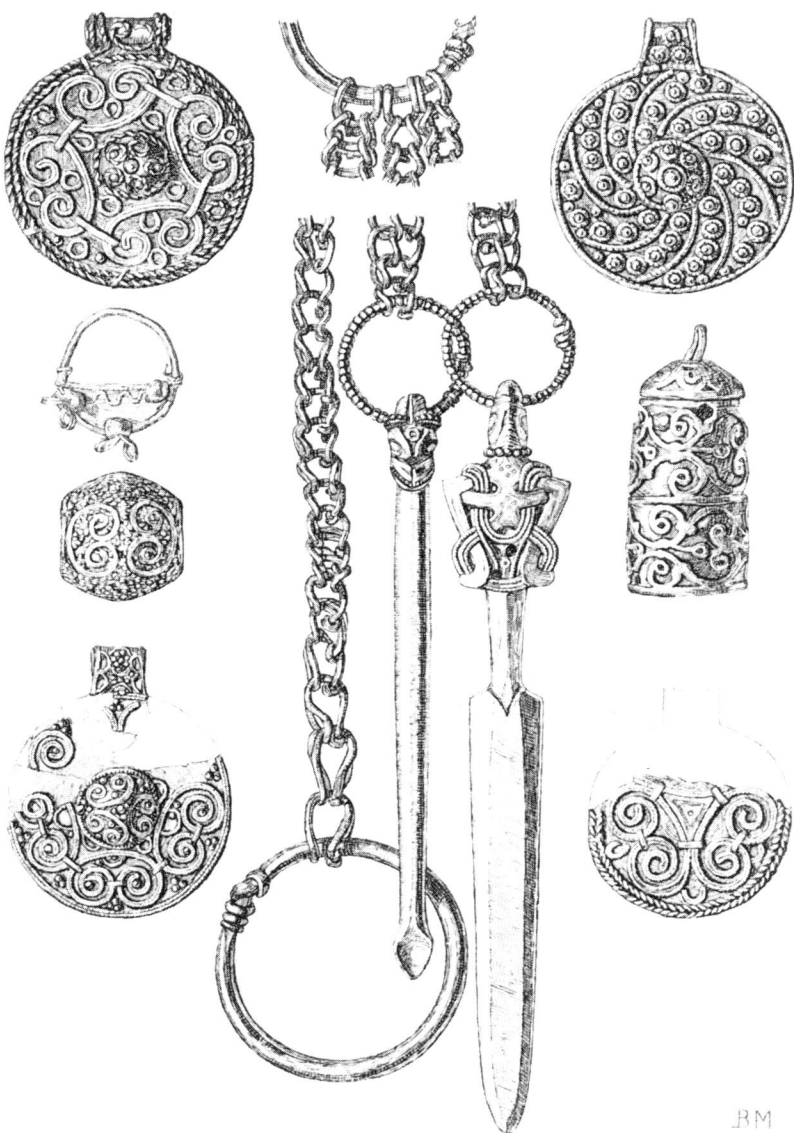

Plate 12. Objects from the hoard from Terslev, Zealand, Denmark.
(After Friis Johansen in *Aarbøger for Nordisk Oldkyndighed og Historie* [1912].)

Plate 13. Cross at Gosforth Church, south face, Cumberland, England. (Photo: T. Middlemass, Durham University.)

Norse myths. On the Great Fishing Stone in Gosforth, for instance, is a representation of Thor's fishing expedition. Skaldic verse of the mid-ninth century includes this theme among the mythical representations which were painted on Scandinavian shields of the period.[12]

The bound figure is a motif which occurs in decorative contexts in Scandinavia. On the fragmentary wood carving from Tune, Norway, a number of identical small men are enveloped in a ribbon ornament (Plate 14). The motif seems to have been adopted and invested with an iconological meaning in England. On the cross from York Minster, for instance, one bound man has been given a prominent position (Plate 15). This transformation of the motif presumably reflects the Christian, Anglo-Saxon tradition of human representations.

In the Danelaw, east of the Pennines, pagan myths seem to have been less common in figure sculpture.[13] Instead, new secular and religious iconographic themes were invented. It is difficult to decide how much of this process is attributable to Viking influence. On the one hand, the process seems to have as part of its background the breakdown of monasticism and the settlements of the last quarter of the ninth century which gradually led to a mixed Anglo-Danish society in the area.[14] On the other hand, no monument with figure representations stylistically comparable with, e.g., the Middleton Cross has survived in Scandinavia. What does survive there strongly suggests that the Scandinavian norm was to render mythical themes with a variety of small figures in an apparently haphazard composition (Plate 1). We find this type of representation on the Cumbrian and Manx crosses (Plate 13), and when this manner of representation occurs in England a Scandinavian influence is probable whatever the subject-matter. But the dominant size and frontal posture of the Middleton warrior are foreign to what remains of Scandinavian art of this period, and it seems to me that the Middleton warrior is best explained as a secularization derived from Christian, Anglo-Saxon art (Plate 16).[15]

The Middleton cross brings us to the Jellinge style and the problems raised by this term. The side-faces of two Middleton crosses are decorated with ribbon ornament of types normally connected with the Borre style. But on the backs of the crosses are S-shaped animals of a type which is attributable to the Jellinge style as the term is commonly used (Plate 17).[16] However, the phrase "Jellinge style" poses special difficulties, since it has become largely a term of convenience applied to S-shaped and ribbon-shaped animals. Before a new definition of the term can be agreed on, the major Scandinavian finds must be studied anew, and in the following paragraphs I shall only sum up the problem as I see it now.

Plate 15. Fragment of cross-shaft from Kirkby Stephen, Westmorland, England. (Photo: T. Middlemass, Durham University.)

Plate 14. Fragment of woodcarving from Tune, Østfold, Norway. (Photo: Universitetets Oldsaksamling, Oslo.)

Plate 16. Cross B in Middleton Church, Yorkshire, England. (Photo: Alan Wiper, Durham University.)

Plate 17. Cross B in Middleton Church, Yorkshire, England. (Photo: Alan Wiper, Durham University.)

It seems probable that with a full survey of the Scandinavian material it will be possible to identify distinct forms of Viking ribbon-shaped animals associated with ornament of (respectively) the Oseberg, the Borre, and the Mammen styles. Moreover, ribbon-shaped animals appear to have been given slightly different form according to the type of object they were used to decorate. In the Borre style, for instance, the ribbon-shaped animal is elongated and has wide openings of the body when it occurs on tongue-shaped pendants (Plate 18). On trefoil brooches, on the other hand, the body can be solid and form double loops (Plate 19). What seems at present to be the Jellinge animal proper, and the one which is important for the relationship with Anglo-Saxon art, is the sleek S-shaped animal such as those on the Jelling cup (Plate 20). As David Wilson has pointed out, this S-shaped animal had been used earlier in Scandinavian art on the Oseberg cart of the first half of the ninth century.[17] But it has so far been difficult to find intermediary stages between this early example and the S-shaped animals of the Jellinge type of the first half of the tenth century. Important for dating of the latter are the silver beaker which was placed in the grave at Jelling ca. A.D. 948,[18] and a pendant in the hoard from Vårby, Sweden, which was deposited ca. A.D. 940 and which contains contemporary pendants with Borre-style motifs from the same workshop (Plate 21).

Dating of the Scandinavian S-shaped animal is important in discussing relative chronological priority. For the West Saxons also revived the ribbon-shaped animal in a new S-shape at the time of the Danish settlements in the last quarter of the ninth century (Plate 22). And the question is — and still remains — whether animals like the one at Ramsbury in Wiltshire represent an indigenous Anglo-Saxon innovation as Thomas Kendrick and recently Rosemary Cramp argue,[19] or whether this type of stone-carving design should be regarded as evidence of a sub-Viking style, as David Wilson has suggested.[20] (There is also a third possibility, namely that the S-shaped animal both in Oseberg and Wessex may have resulted from separate adaptations of earlier Anglo-Carolingian ornament of the types used, for instance, on the Lindau book binding.[21]) Cramp's dating of the development of the S-shaped animal in Wessex to the last quarter of the ninth and first quarter of the tenth centuries would in terms of date open the possibility of influence from the Scandinavian colonies.[22] Moreover, there does not seem to be an Anglo-Saxon tradition for this particular motif in the area settled by the Danes. Earlier sculpture such as the Lindisfarne slab (Plate 23) shows ribbon-shaped animals which descend in style from Northumbrian manuscript decoration. On the other hand, most of the tenth-century carvings with S-shaped animals in Yorkshire have details of indubitably

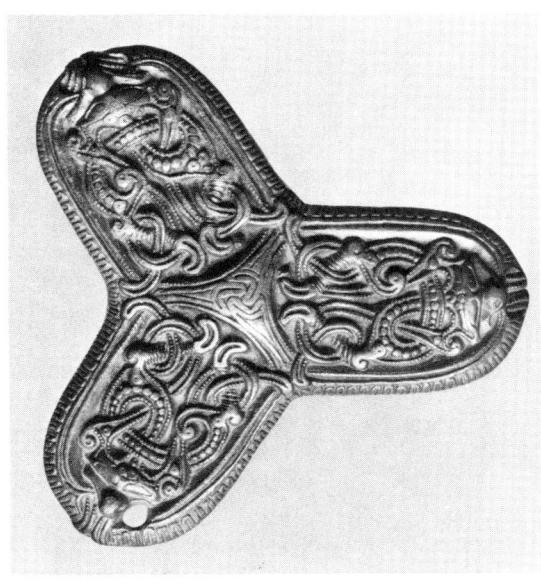

Plate 19. Trefoil brooch from Blaker, Oppland, Norway. (Photo: Universitetets Oldsaksamling, Oslo.)

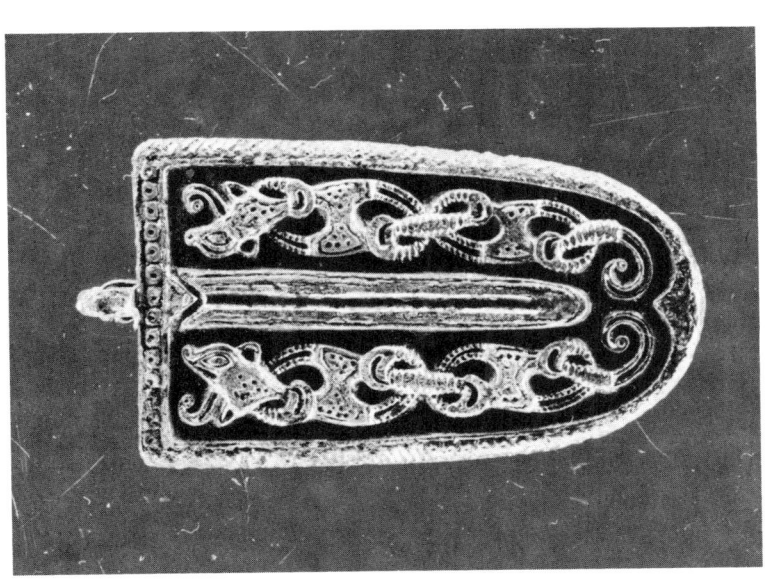

Plate 18. Tongue-shaped pendant from Skemo, Aust-Agder, Norway. (Photo: Universitetets Oldsaksamling, Oslo.)

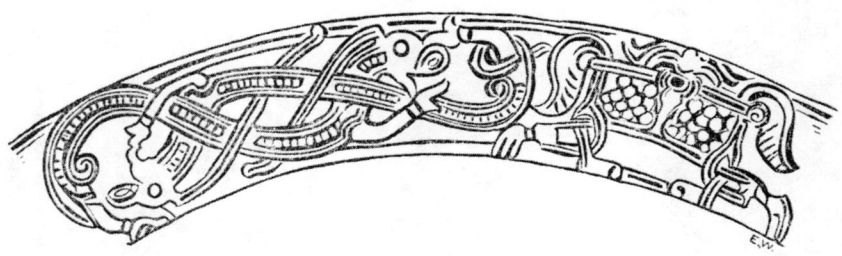

Plates 20a & 20b. Silver beaker from Jelling, Jutland, Denmark. (Photo: Nationalmuseet, København. Drawing: Eva Wilson, London.)

Signe Horn Fuglesang

Plates 21a & 21b. Two silver pendants from Vårby, Södermanland, Sweden. (Photo: Antikvarisk-topografiska arkivet, Stockholm.)

Plate 21c. Silver pendant from Vårby, Södermanland, Sweden.
(Photo: Antikvarisk topografiska arkivet, Stockholm.)

Scandinavian origin, e.g., the jaws and hip-spirals of the animal on the slab from Newgate in York (Plate 24).

In order to solve the problems concerning the S-shaped animal, it is necessary to break down the group referred to as Jellinge-style animals into different categories. Only when the formal elements of different types of these animals have been analyzed can we hope to place them in their appropriate stylistic groups. And it is very likely that in this process the term "Jellinge style" may have to be redefined.

Recent excavations in York have proved the town to be a major center for Anglo-Scandinavian stone carving.[23] Evidence for metalworking is not as numerous and varied, but is quite as important. The die which Else Roesdahl has identified proves that silver crosses of the so-called Hiddensee type were manufactured in York. Other such dies have been found in Hedeby on Jutland, and in surviving hoards this cross type has mainly a Baltic distribution.[24] A mold for a trefoil brooch is further evidence for the production of Scandinavian-type ornaments in York.[25] Important in this connection is also the Scandinavian influence, however limited, which David Wilson has demonstrated in Anglo-Saxon metalwork of this period, and his survey of the evidence for a reciprocal English influence in Scandina-

Plate 22. Cross-shaft at Ramsbury, Wiltshire, England.
(Photo: Rosemary Cramp, Durham.)

Plate 24. Cross-shaft from Newgate, York, England. (Photo: Yorkshire Museum.)

Plate 23. Cross-shaft at Lindisfarne, Northumberland, England. (Photo: T. Middlemass, Durham University.)

vian metalwork.²⁶ It must be emphasized, however, that the Scandinavian influence in the tenth century seems to be limited to the North, i.e., the area in which the Viking settlements had taken place.

To sum up: during the Borre and Jellinge phases of the last decades of the ninth and the first half of the tenth century strong Scandinavian influence can be distinguished very clearly in Yorkshire and Cumbria. It was, however, assimilated by the indigenous traditions into what became an innovative and vigorous hybrid. New types of monument unknown in Scandinavia, such as the hogbacks, and new iconographical schemes resulted. The relative importance of Scandinavian and Anglo-Saxon influence in the development of North-English animal ornament is as yet difficult to determine. That Viking raids and invasions brought with them a coarsening of Anglo-Saxon sculpture is well documented in the monuments. The positive side of the Viking raids, namely, that the Viking invasions also led to innovation, has always been recognized, but only with the work of the Durham team on North-English stone carving is such innovation being analyzed and placed in perspective.

The next important phase is marked by the Ringerike style in the first half of the eleventh century. This was the period of a Danish dynasty in England, and the historical situation was auspicious for close Anglo-Scandinavian intercourse. The semi-naturalistic lion, the bird, and the scrollwork were motifs which had been introduced into Scandinavian art from western Europe in the second half of the tenth century, presumably by way of recently converted Denmark.²⁷ In the Ringerike style, the plant motifs are given new shapes and are fused with animals in a manner which is altogether new in Scandinavian art. On the Heggen vane, for instance, the striking bird has wings shaped in an alternate tendril-and-lobe pattern (Plate 25). This is a composition scheme which the Scandinavian artists seem to have borrowed ultimately from border ornament of the Winchester style, whereas another compositional feature—that of intertwining offshoots in clusters—seems to be of Reichenau/Trier origin.²⁸ Although King Cnut may have been a staunch patron of Anglo-Saxon art and culture, a number of finds (particularly those from London) indicate that the Danes, Norwegians, and Swedes who served or traded under Cnut were patrons of workshops producing Ringerike ornament. The finds include most types of object, from everyday bone pins which may have been carved by any handy man or woman to gracefully executed gilt mounts and the grave marker from St. Paul's with its splendid animal and Scandinavian runic inscription (Plate 26). Finds from northern England are much sparser, although the fragmentary and atypical stone from Otley in Yorkshire testifies that the style was known there.

This is also the phase when Scandinavian art occurs in Anglo-Saxon illumination, although to a very limited extent. The best known and most important example is the Psalter at Cambridge (University Library MS. Ff. 1. 23) (Plate 27). Here, Ringerike-style elements are used not only for the famous animal-shaped initial but also as details in other, Anglo-Saxon types of initial and even in some border motifs.[29] It must be emphasized, however, that by far the larger part both of initials and of border ornament even in this manuscript is without Scandinavian influence. The Ringerike type of animal head must have appealed to English illuminators, because it is found also in two other Winchester-style manuscripts of this period. In the Bury St. Edmund Psalter (Bibliotheca Vaticana MS. Reg. lat. 12), it is used as terminal for a ship and a drinking horn, and in Ælfric's Pentateuch (British Library MS. Claudius B. IV) it appears as the terminal of Noah's Ark.[30] In both cases the head type stands out as an isolated Scandinavism in Winchester-style manuscripts of very high quality. Thomas Kendrick in 1949 saw in a number of Winchester-style manuscripts of this period a "... Saxon approach to something like a Ringerike manner ..."[31] and later scholars have had a tendency to exaggerate the claim for Scandinavian influence in English manuscripts and other ornament of this period. However, as more studies have been published and as we get to know the Winchester style and its development and vagaries better, such claims seem less and less to be substantiated. It rather appears that in contrast with the earlier Borre and Jellinge styles, which really contributed to artistic innovation in northern England, the influence of the Ringerike style is normally restricted to the use of a few Scandinavian models in what is otherwise a pure Winchester-style setting.

The Urnes style was a Scandinavian innovation of the second quarter of the eleventh century, so that the Ringerike and the Urnes styles overlap chronologically. Although plant motifs are not foreign to the Urnes style, animals dominate the repertory, and ribbon-shaped animals and snakes are requisite for the construction of the interpenetrating multi-loops and figures-of-eight which dominate the construction of these designs (Plate 28). The Urnes style has yielded the highest number of monuments in Scandinavia, ranging from the more than a thousand runic memorial stones in Uppland to stave-church ornament and to decorated household goods and furniture.[32]

However, the Urnes style did not die with the Viking period. On the contrary, it formed a vital tradition which hybridized with the Romanesque and has left a number of distinguished monuments from all the Scandinavian countries of the first half of the twelfth century.[33] In connection

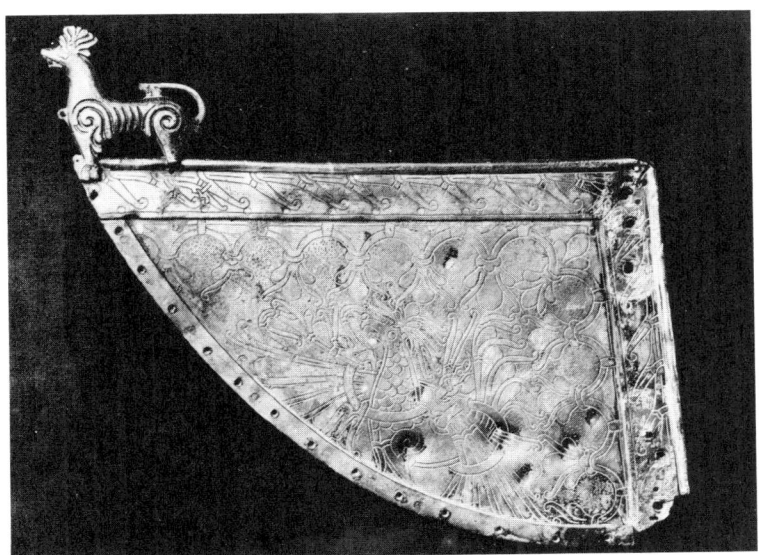

Plate 25. Vane from Heggen, Buskerud, Norway.
(Photo: Universitetets Oldsaksamling, Oslo.)

Plate 26. Grave marker from St. Paul's Churchyard,
London. (Photo: Guildhall Museum, London.)

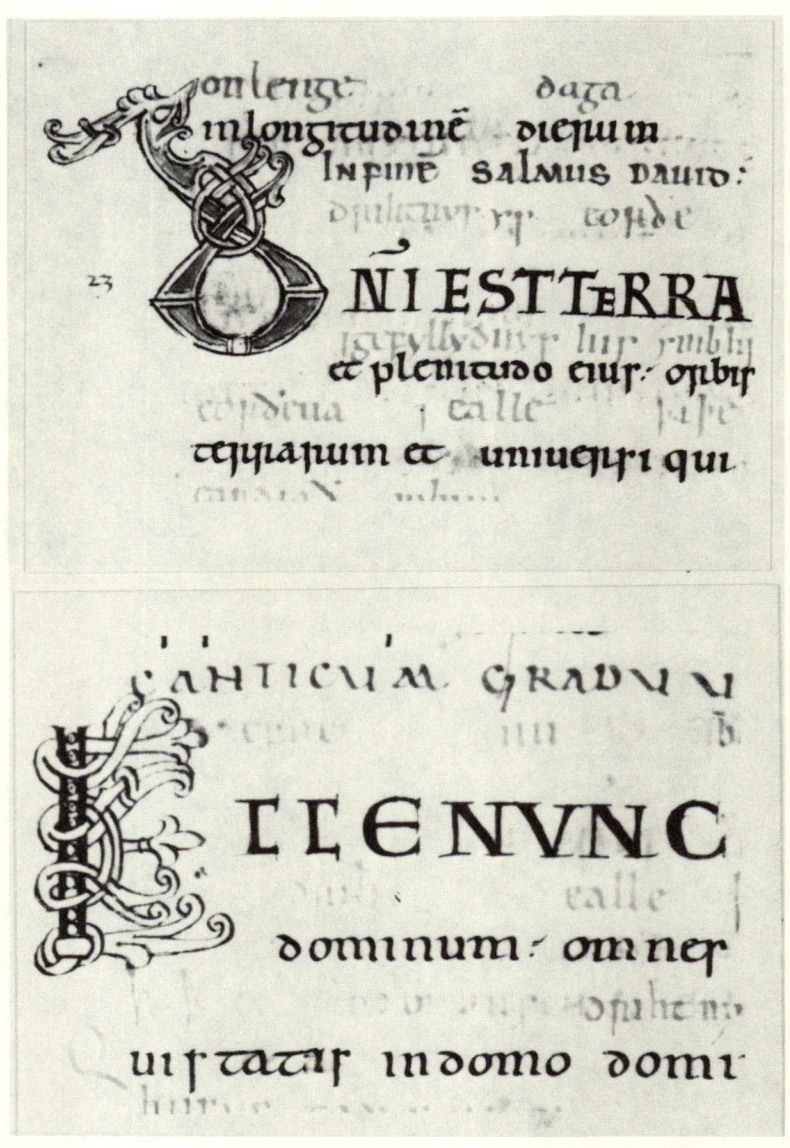

Plate 27. Initials in Cambridge University Library MS. Ff. 1. 23.
(Photo: Cambridge University Library.)

Plate 28. Doorway in Urnes Church, Sogn, Norway. (Photo: Per Maurtvedt, Universitetets Oldsaksamling, Oslo.)

with our questions the metal fittings of the Danish Lisbjerg Altar may be particularly mentioned (Plate 29). Here it can be seen how one eminent workshop used on the same monument Urnes-style motifs in Urnes-style form, Urnes-style form for Romanesque motifs, and Romanesque motifs untouched by the Urnes manner.[34] It is noteworthy that the figure style belongs to the last category.

The English Urnes style divides into the same two major categories as the Scandinavian: Viking Urnes and Urnes/Romanesque. To the Viking-Urnes style belongs, for example, the important carving at Jevington church in Sussex where the highly sculpted, late Ottonian figure of Christ is flanked by two flat but fiery Urnes beasts (Plate 30). To a hybrid Urnes-Saxon category can be ascribed the metalwork originating in the Midlands,[35] whereas the crozier from Durham (which Olwyn Owen, following David Wilson's criticism of the old attribution, has recently taken away from Flambard and attributed to Carileph or Walcher of the late eleventh century) is more consonant with the Scandinavian Urnes style (Plate 31).[36]

The Urnes/Romanesque style can be seen in some Anglo-Norman architectural ornament, such as the tympana at Southwell and at Hoveringham in Nottinghamshire, and the carved stones at St. Nicholas in Ipswich.[37] It may be a coincidence (but I rather think not) that in all three instances St. Michael and the dragon are shown, and the Urnes elements are confined to the looping of the dragon's tail and the shape of its head. Again, we seem to be up against not a general stylistic influence, but the copying of some specific details for use in a particular motif. On the other hand, the boar on the contemporary tympanum at St. Nicholas—for which there is no parallel motif in Scandinavia—clearly shows Urnes-style elements in outlines, shape of body, eye, etc.[38] So it does not do to be dogmatic about English monuments. Of much higher quality is the capital from Norwich Cathedral cloister of ca. A.D. 1125–30, with its two interlinked figure-of-eight-shaped animals in a looped scrollwork (Plate 32).[39] This capital is one of nineteen surviving, and none of the others shows any trace of Urnes-style influence. Again it seems to be a case less of Urnes-style influence or tradition than of a particular model which had been chosen for copying, in the case of the Norwich capital possibly a metal ornament similar to the Pitney brooch.[40]

There are other groups of architectural ornament, mainly in Yorkshire and Herefordshire, for which an Urnes-style tradition has sometimes been claimed.[41] The question is a complicated one since there are as yet no certain means of ascertaining the cause for local stylistic deviations. Slightly atypical elements of form may with equal logic be ascribed to a lingering

Plate 29. Altar front from Lisbjerg Church, Jutland, Denmark. (Photo: Nationalmuseet, København.)

Plate 30. Detail of carving in Jevington Church, Sussex, England. (After T. D. Kendrick, *Late Saxon and Viking Art* [1949].)

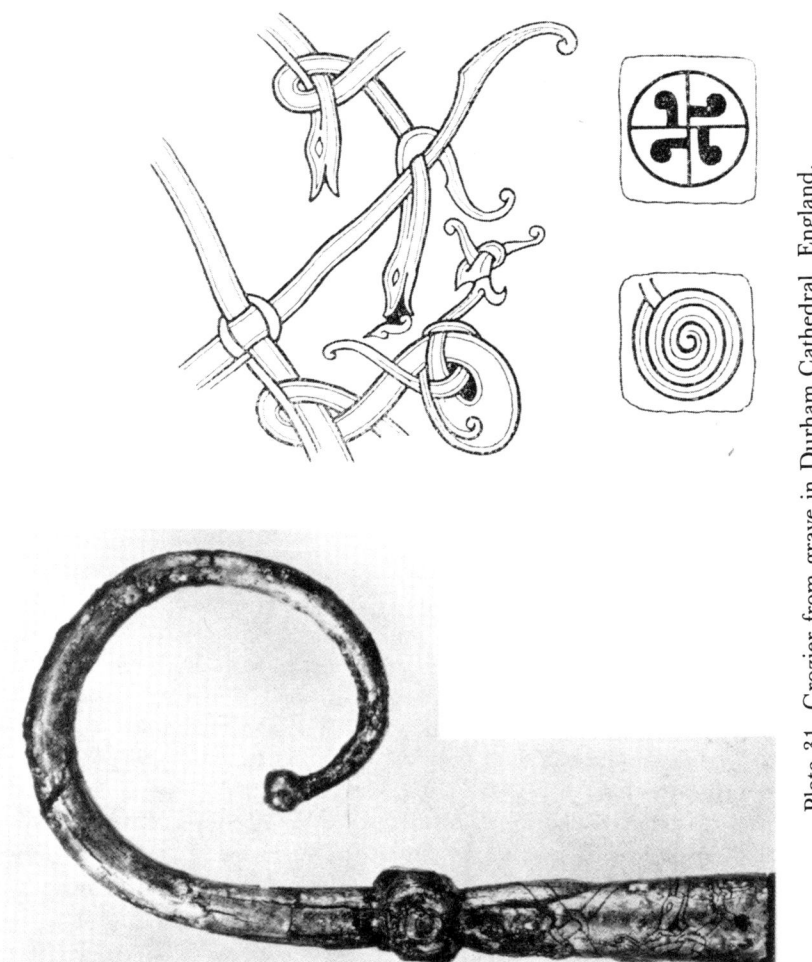

Plate 31. Crozier from grave in Durham Cathedral, England. (After T. D. Kendrick, *Late Saxon and Viking Art* [1949].)

tradition maintained in wood carving now lost, as to spontaneous inventions attributable to a particular master or workshop. But from a Scandinavian point of view, it is difficult at present fully to subscribe to an Anglo-Scandinavian background for these carvings. Two main stylistic criteria have been taken to indicate such a background, namely the juxtaposition of broad and thin ornament lines, and the tendency to loop compositions. However, both elements occur also in indubitably Anglo-Norman contexts, and definitely diagnostic elements of the Urnes style such as the interpenetrating multi-loop compositions are absent (Plate 33). Nor is the presence of snakes in these carvings a sure indicator of a Scandinavian heritage. The origin of the semi-naturalistic snake in Anglo-Norman stone carving has in fact not yet adequately been traced. The motif is fairly normal in England, and on the Continent both winged dragons and wingless snakes are found in several carvings.[42] Again, the snakes at, e.g., Shobdon and Kilpeck are of a fleshy and longitudinal type which is completely at variance with the elegant, slim, and multi-looped varieties of the Urnes and Urnes/Romanesque styles in Scandinavia (compare, e.g., Plates 28 and 29 with Plate 33). Although final judgment must be reserved, I would at present tend to regard the atypical elements in Yorkshire and Herefordshire carvings as spontaneous, local variations on Anglo-Norman themes.

The contrast with Irish ornament of the same period is instructive. There, Urnes-style compositions and animal types were taken over towards the end of the eleventh century.[43] These Scandinavian elements were made symmetrical and fused with the indigenous style, but without losing their multi-loop form and abstract stylization. The Urnes style became a vital force in Irish Romanesque in the first half or three-quarters of the twelfth century, much in the same way as the Borre and Jellinge styles had contributed to the North-English innovations of the tenth century. As compared with the Irish material, the paucity of diagnostic Urnes-style elements in the Anglo-Norman art of England becomes even more striking.

Let me attempt a summing-up of these cursory surveys. First, if it is acceptable that innovations of motif do not always coincide with innovations of form, and I cannot see how that conclusion can be avoided, we get an interesting pattern for the influences flowing between England and Scandinavia. In the second half of the eighth century, i.e., before the Viking raids began, there is a strong influx of West-European motifs in Scandinavian ornament, apparently largely of English origin. During the first period of Viking onslaughts, innovations in Scandinavia consist mostly of new elements of form, and whether this reflects an indigenous process or can be ascribed to foreign influences remains an open question. Scandina-

Plate 32. Capital from Norwich Cathedral, East Anglia, England. (After *Medieval Sculpture from Norwich Cathedral* [1980].)

Plate 33. Detail of doorway of Kilpeck Church, Herefordshire, England. (Photo: Signe Horn Fuglesang.)

vian influence in England cannot be demonstrated until the late ninth or early tenth century. During the periods when the Borre and Jellinge styles flourished — periods which cannot yet be separated properly in the material and which together cover the time from about A.D. 850 to 950 — there were very strong reciprocal influences between northern England and Scandinavia.

For the second half of the tenth century the situation is difficult to gauge, partly because of the many uncertainties surrounding the Jellinge style. There seems to be a lull in Scandinavian influence in northern England in this period, and if this decline in artistic influence is substantiated, it may reflect the political situation in the area after the Scandinavian kingdom in York was overthrown in A.D. 954. The next stage of demonstrable artistic interchange occurs with the Ringerike style of the first half of the eleventh century. In this phase, the Scandinavian ties appear to be predominantly with southern England. Again there is two-way contact, which is normally explained within the framework of English missions in Scandinavia and the Anglo-Danish dynasty. Finally, in the late eleventh century and in the first half of the twelfth century there seems to be mainly one-way contact, with English craftsmen copying some specific Urnes-style animal details on monuments which have no obvious connection with Scandinavian ethnic groups. As David Wilson aptly observes, whatever hand lifted the Durham crozier, it was that of a Norman bishop to a politically very important Norman see.[44]

In the area of methodology, there are two points I should like to emphasize. First, analyses of form are indispensable to comparative studies, although it has not been possible to demonstrate it in this short paper. Second, corpus publications of all available material form an indispensable basis for scholarly discussion. Our evaluation of (among other things) the interaction between Scandinavian and Insular art will in the last instance depend on the information to be gleaned from a full array of catalogue publications. Such catalogues are tools comparable with critical editions of literary texts, and far too few have been published. The corpus of North-English stone carving will be a major contribution in the field.

UNIVERSITETETS OLDSAKSAMLING, OSLO

Notes

1. Important contributions to the question of Scandinavian influence on English art are found in the following works: Johannes Brøndsted, *Early English Ornament* (London, 1924); T. D. Kendrick, *Anglo-Saxon Art to A.D. 900* (London, 1938); Kendrick, *Late Saxon and Viking Art* (London, 1949); David M. Wilson and Ole Klindt-Jensen, *Viking Art* (London, 1966; rpt. 1980); James T. Lang, "Continuity and Innovation in Anglo-Scandinavian Sculpture," in *Anglo-Saxon and Viking Age Sculpture*, ed. J. T. Lang, British Archaeological Reports, 49 (Oxford, 1978), pp. 145-55; Richard N. Bailey, *Viking Age Sculpture in Northern England* (London, 1980). For terms and definitions of the Scandinavian stylistic groups see Wilson and Klindt-Jensen, *Viking Art*; Signe Horn Fuglesang, "Stylistic Groups in Late Viking and Early Romanesque Art," *Acta ad Archaeologiam et Artium Historiam Pertinentia, Series in 8°*, 1 (1981), 79-125; Fuglesang, "Early Viking Art," *Acta ad Archaeologiam et Artium Historiam Pertinentia, Series in 8°*, 2 (1982), 126-73.

2. For such imports see Egil Bakka, "Some English Decorated Metal Objects Found in Norwegian Viking Graves," *Årbok for Universitetet i Bergen* (1963), 4-66; Jan Petersen, *British Antiquities of the Viking Period Found in Norway*, Vol. V of *Viking Antiquities*, ed. H. Shetelig (Oslo, 1940).

3. Holger Arbman, *Schweden und das karolingische Reich* (Stockholm, 1937), pp. 116-46.

4. Günther Haseloff, "Zum Ursprung des nordischen Greiftierstils," in *Festschrift für Gustav Schwantes* (Neumünster, 1951), pp. 202-11.

5. Sverre Marstrander, "Om gripedyrstilen og dens opphav," *Viking*, 28 (1964), 89-116.

6. Wilson and Klindt-Jensen, pp. 114-15; David M. Wilson, "The Dating of Viking Art in England," in *A-S and Viking Age Sculpture*, pp. 136, 138, 140-42.

7. David M. Wilson and C. E. Blunt, "The Trewhiddle Hoard," *Archaeologia*, 98 (1961), 75-122.

8. Wilson, in Wilson and Klindt-Jensen, pp. 92-93; Fuglesang, "Early Viking Art," p. 157.

9. Wilson, in Wilson and Klindt-Jensen, p. 107; Bailey, pp. 34-36, 229-30.

10. Wilson, in Wilson and Klindt-Jensen, p. 108.

11. Knut Berg, "The Gosforth Cross," *Journal of the Warburg and Courtauld Institutes*, 21 (1958), 27-43.

12. Hallvard Lie, "Billedbeskrivende dikt," *Kulturhistorisk leksikon for nordisk middelalder* (1956-78; rpt. 1980), Vol. I, cols. 542-45.

13. But see Bailey, pp. 125-34.

14. Rosemary Cramp, *Anglian and Viking York*, Borthwick Institute for Historical Research, University of York, Borthwick Papers No. 33 (York, n.d.), pp. 14-21; Lang, "Continuity and Innovation," pp. 11-20.

15. Alan Binns recognizes the singularity of the iconography but interprets it as the depiction of a Norse burial in his seminal paper, "Tenth Century Carvings from Yorkshire and the Jellinge style," *Årbok for Universitetet i Bergen* (1956),

16-18. See further James T. Lang, "Some Late Pre-Conquest Crosses in Ryedale, Yorkshire: A Re-appraisal," *Journal of the British Archaeological Association,* 36 (1973), 16-25; Richard N. Bailey, "The Chronology of Viking-Age Sculpture in Northumbria," in *A-S and Viking Age Sculpture,* p. 178; and see Bailey, *Viking Age Sculpture,* pp. 209-10.

16. Binns, figs., 4, 8; Wilson, in Wilson and Klindt-Jensen, pp. 103-04.
17. Wilson, in Wilson and Klindt-Jensen, p. 97.
18. Else Roesdahl, "The Northern Mound: Burial Chamber and Grave Goods," in "Jelling Problems: A Discussion," *Medieval Scandinavia,* 7 (1974), 213.
19. T. D. Kendrick, *A-S Art,* pp. 211-12, Pl. 100; Rosemary Cramp, "The Anglian Tradition in the Ninth Century," in *A-S and Viking Age Sculpture,* p. 10.
20. Wilson, in Wilson and Klindt-Jensen, pp. 105-06.
21. Jean Hubert, Jean Porcher, and Wolfgang Fritz Volbach, *Carolingian Art* (London, 1970), pp. 209-13.
22. Cramp, "Anglian Tradition," p. 10.
23. James Graham-Campbell, *The Viking World* (London, 1980), illustration, p. 100; James T. Lang, "Anglo-Scandinavian Sculpture in Yorkshire," in *Viking Age York and the North,* ed. R. A. Hall, CBA Research Report 27 (London, 1978), pp. 11-20.
24. Else Roesdahl, *Viking Age Denmark* (London, 1982), p. 217, Pl. 50.
25. Arthur MacGregor, "Industry and Commerce in Anglo-Scandinavian York," in *Viking Age York and the North,* p. 42, fig. 24:8.
26. David M. Wilson, *Anglo-Saxon Ornamental Metalwork 700-1100* (London, 1964), p. 42; Wilson, in Wilson and Klindt-Jensen, pp. 115-17.
27. Signe Horn Fuglesang, *Some Aspects of the Ringerike Style,* Medieval Scandinavia Monograph Series (Odense, 1980), pp. 92-96, 98-118.
28. Fuglesang, *Aspects,* pp. 103-05, 111-18.
29. Fuglesang, *Aspects,* pp. 70-75, Pl. 70.
30. Fuglesang, *Aspects,* Pls. 69, 72.
31. Kendrick, *Late Saxon and Viking Art,* pp. 103-04.
32. Fuglesang, "Stylistic Groups," pp. 89-96 and refs.
33. Fuglesang, "Stylistic Groups," pp. 96-117.
34. Poul Nørlund, *Gyldne altre,* 2nd ed. (Århus, 1968), pp. 73-98.
35. Kendrick, *Late Saxon and Viking Art,* p. 116; Wilson, *A-S Metalwork,* p. 51; Wilson, in Wilson and Klindt-Jensen, p. 154.
36. Wilson, *A-S Metalwork,* p. 7, n. 2; Olwyn A. Owen, *A Catalogue and Re-evaluation of the Urnes Style in England,* M.A. thesis, Department of Archaeology, University of Durham, 1979.
37. Kathryn J. Galbraith, "Early Sculpture at St. Nicholas' Church, Ipswich," *The Proceedings of the Suffolk Institute of Archaeology,* 31:2 (1968), 172-84 and refs.
38. Galbraith, Pl. XXV.
39. *Medieval Sculpture from Norwich Cathedral,* Exhibition Catalogue, Sainsbury Centre, University of East Anglia (Norwich, 1980), Cat. No. 3 (p. 12).
40. Wilson, *A-S Metalwork,* Cat. No. 60 (p. 160).
41. Kendrick, *Late Saxon and Viking Art,* pp. 140-41; George Zarnecki, *Later English*

Romanesque Sculpture 1140-1210 (London, 1953), pp. 9-15; Wilson, in Wilson and Klindt-Jensen, p. 160.

42. See, e.g., the Nuit des Temps series: *Poitou roman* (1957), fig. 24:2; *Touraine romane* (1957), fig. 17; *Rousillon roman* (1958), fig. 9; *Lombardie romane* (1978), figs. 26, 50, 91; *Champagne romane* (1981), fig. 25.

43. Françoise Henry, *Irish Art in the Romanesque Period* (Ithaca, 1970), esp. pp. 94-117; Fuglesang, "Stylistic Groups," pp. 112-14 and refs.

44. Wilson, in Wilson and Klindt-Jensen, p. 154.

The Distinctiveness of Viking Colonial Art

JAMES LANG

The Viking settlements in the West during the late ninth and early tenth centuries were not an expression of a centralized Scandinavian empire's expansionism. When the ornamented artifacts and monuments of areas such as Northumbria are explored, we should not imagine, even for the Viking heyday, either that Insular art succumbed to a dominating court taste in the Carolingian vein or that Christian Anglian traditions were submerged beneath Northern barbarism.

Three factors govern any scrutiny of Viking colonial art. First, the geographical range of Scandinavian settlement in Britain and Ireland is wide: Orkney, Shetland, the Western Isles, Man, Cumbria, Ireland, York. These distinct colonies, while topographically discrete, are easily within reach of one another, particularly those using the Irish Sea as a thoroughfare. They were also areas with a long tradition of Insular craftsmanship, much of it idiosyncratic or locally distinctive. Second, at the time of Ivarr's conquest of York in 867 and during the period of the *floreat* of the York-Dublin axis in the tenth century, Scandinavia was pagan, while the Celtic West was Christian and York even had its archbishop. The paucity of pagan graves in the Viking areas of England points up the differences in religion and burial practices which existed between Scandinavia and the Northumbrian colony.[1]

Third, the Viking dominance in northern England was very short-lived indeed, running from Ivarr to the death of Eric Bloodaxe, 867 to 954. The degree of displacement of Anglian culture in what is less than a century can be exaggerated. Similarly, notions of Viking "impact" on Insular art can be inflated into a cultural watershed when at best there is *some* decorative and iconographic influence upon an uninterrupted native art.

Scandinavian settlement of Northumbria was accomplished in two phases. The first was "Danish," stemming from the capture of York and Halfdan's subsequent settlement in 876. The second, in the early decades of the tenth century, was "Hiberno-Norse," and seems to have been peacefully achieved from the West. If the ethnic labels are tentative, it is because in terms of the art of the colony the traditions are thoroughly mixed. The second settlement is of particular importance not only because there was a renaissance of stone sculpture with Celtic features, but also because there occurred a migration not from a homeland to a colony but from one colony to another. It is probable that the population was ethnically diverse and, given the Vikings' propensity for cultural assimilation, their Scandinavian culture may well have been restricted to their language.

If this paper dwells upon the sculpture of this colony rather than its artifacts in other media, it is because the nature of stone monuments tends to fix the object in or very near to its place of production. Provenance of sculpture gives a safe indication of local style, and the balance between Scandinavian and Insular traits can be related to particular, often narrowly focused regions. For example, the pre-Conquest graveyard discovered by Derek Phillips under York Minster yielded a series of highly decorative tombstones which reflected the prestige associated with the most important cemetery in the city.[2] One of its shafts has a profile animal which possesses all the features of the Jellinge style, in both motifs and layout (Plate 1).[3] Such ornament might easily be regarded as diagnostically "Viking" because of the Scandinavian associations of that style. On an adjacent face, however, is a highly modeled portrait head with a dished halo—a work in the local Anglian style which had progressed without interruption from eighth-century pieces such as those at Otley.[4] The term "Anglo-Scandinavian" is fitting for a monument which presents the two traditions side by side in such pure forms. It implies, too, that the Anglian tradition was not submerged during the Viking era.

Yet how far motifs and stylistic details actually denote Scandinavian impact is, I believe, now an open issue. Take, for example, the Gosforth Cross in Cumberland (Plate 2), the figure carving of which has long been recognized as representing Ragnarok, that distinctively Scandinavian event where the Norse gods perish.[5] Nothing could be more "Viking" than the figurative panels, but the *form* of the monument is thoroughly Insular. The wheel-head cross is a Celtic type from the West, and the shaft form, cylindrical below and squared above a swag, derives from local late Anglian monuments. The eclecticism of the Gosforth Cross is therefore threefold: Scandinavian, Anglian, and Celtic. The rounded section of the shaft is covered with a mesh of trilobate vertebral elements which have often been referred to as a reflex of the Scandinavian Borre style's ring-chain and looped

Plate 1: Shaft from York Minster. (Photo: A. Wiper.)

Plate 2: The Gosforth Cross. (Photo: T. Middlemass.)

lozenge.[6] The only other Anglo-Scandinavian monument to carry the netlike form of the motif is a hogback at Cross Canonby, not far from Gosforth on the coastline of the Irish Sea.[7] Since hogbacks are established Norse colonial tombstones, it is natural to see the pattern as Scandinavian, yet when it is compared with the eponymous Borre mounts,[8] the distinctiveness of the Cumbrian pattern becomes apparent. The branched Y-shaped ring-chain is not exclusively Viking; it is found on Romano-British tesselated pavements and modern Irish sweaters. Lennart Karlsson has recently demonstrated the range of the motif in terms of both chronology and distribution.[9]

When the ring-chain appears on the Ballinderry gaming-board it arrests scholars' attention so forcefully that it is given pride of place in Viking exhibitions — and the adjacent Insular patterns of fret and interlace are ignored, though they provide its context.[10] I would argue that the Ballinderry board could be totally Irish in its decoration, its patterns being exclusively from the Insular repertory, including the ring-chain, for the latter motif is found in two of the corners of the Soiscel Molaise, a thoroughly Insular ecclesiastical object and one where one would least expect a borrowing from Scandinavian folk patterns.[11] The even more distinctive version on the Gosforth Cross might be more closely related to the wheel-head than to the Viking figure carvings. The mesh form, in which the elements extend laterally as well as longitudinally, does occur on Irish ecclesiastical metalwork — for example on the capping of St. Conall's bell, now in the British Museum.[12] It also appears on the hitherto unpublished crozier ferule from the River Bann in Northern Ireland (Plate 3),[13] yet another typically Irish artifact whose form and function to a large measure determine the choice of its decoration. With such an embellished pole in mind, its bindings highly ornamented with appliqués, the Gosforth Cross seems more like a skeuomorph of a wooden-and-metal model, writ large in stone.

In Ireland wooden crosses are less putative than they used to be, and in England the round-shafts (or staff roods as Collingwood called them) were already standing in Cumbria and the North Midlands at the time of the colonists' arrival. The type continued, with a Scandinavian overlay in the ornament, through the Viking period and expanded its range east of the Pennines. The ornament of the Anglo-Scandinavian derivatives such as the cross from Lastingham in North Yorkshire (Plate 4)[14] is a vestigial echo of functional rope-and-metal bindings common on the wooden prototypes, so their decorative layout has nothing to do with reflexes in relation to Scandinavian art, but everything to do with borrowing from Insular ecclesiastical artifacts. The pendant triangular panels on the Bromp-

Plate 4: Shaft at Lastingham, North Yorkshire. (Photo: J. Lang.)

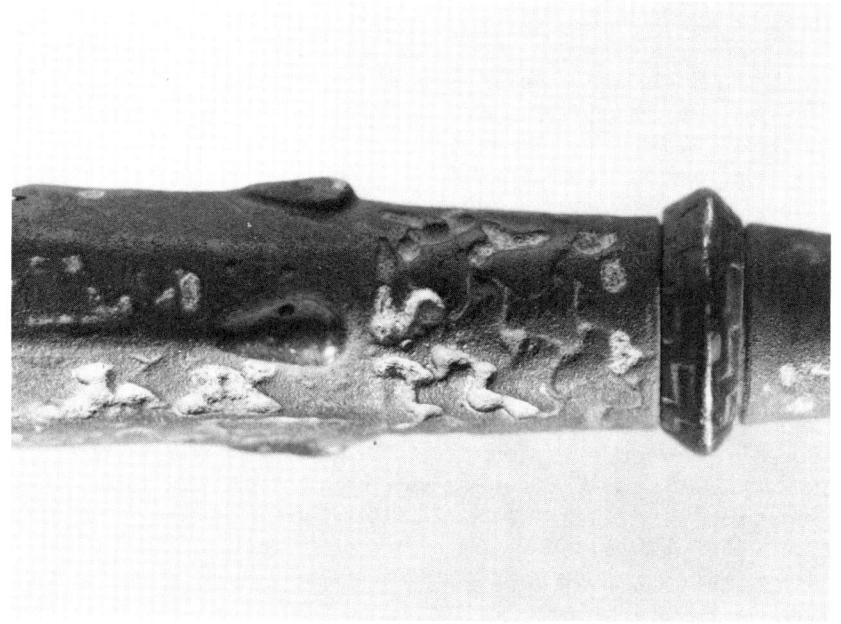

Plate 3: Crozier ferule from the River Bann. (Photo: courtesy of Ulster Museum, Belfast.)

ton and Lastingham shafts (Fig. 1)[15] must derive from the metal van Dyck applied to lengthy wooden objects like the Kells crozier as strengtheners or as fastenings of sections.[16] It is tempting to imagine the bindings on a wooden standing cross as concealing a carpentry joint, the feature surviving decoratively in the stone skeuomorph.

The connection between Anglo-Scandinavian sculpture and Insular metalwork is firmer than one might expect. One of the hogback tombstones at Gosforth closely resembles in shape and decorative layout small metal reliquary shrines such as the one from Lough Erne,[17] even to the reflection of the metal strips used to bind the edging. The treatment of the roof ridge of both shrines and hogback is almost identical.[18] To be fair, a casket is a casket whatever its provenance, and it is equally possible to argue for an alternative source in Scandinavia when the Aspatria hogback is compared with the Cammin casket.[19] This paper's intention, however, is not to establish sources for particular artifacts, but to turn eyes accustomed to Scandinavia toward Britain and Ireland, if only to survey the possibilities.

The Gosforth hogback in question is undeniably a Christian memorial, for it bears a Crucifixion on its gable end, but it is an unfinished carving. The surface has been blocked out initially in rectangles prior to detailed figure-cutting — exactly the same technique employed on the unfinished cross at Kells in Ireland (Plate 5).[20] Sculptural method is borrowed as well as motif and style, an awkward factor in establishing the twin chronologies of the Irish and English carvings. The art historian's usual comparison of like with like, with insertion of a time-lag to accommodate the copying, may not be valid. Recent studies for the British Academy's *Corpus of Anglo-Saxon Stone Sculpture* have concentrated on cutting and design techniques rather than on typology, and the following example concerning the Allertonshire atelier in North Yorkshire illustrates the rapid changes in interpretation taking place in this field.

Some five years ago Professor Richard Bailey convincingly demonstrated the use of templates in late pre-Conquest sculpture from Durham, Middleton, and Allertonshire.[21] This was an important breakthrough in establishing ateliers on (at last) a measurable basis rather than by reliance on an informed eye. Carvings of profile warriors bearing helmets and spears were found to correspond at three sites all within a ten-mile radius — at Brompton, Sockburn-on-Tees, and Kirkleavington.[22] The size and shape of the semicircular helmet were found, by happy accident, to correspond to the pot-bellies of bird motifs at Brompton and Kirkleavington, so the template was assumed to be a basic geometrical shape, a half-moon, rather than a stencil for a naturalistic feature.

James Lang

Fig. 1: Pendant motifs from Brompton and Lastingham.

However, elsewhere in Yorkshire the rubbings taken to determine products of a particular workshop revealed a remarkable degree of detail embodied in the templates, or at least a correspondence of detail and of its precise placing in the carvings themselves. As a result of disquieting speculation on the form and material of the suggested templates, I returned to the Sockburn warrior to measure the portrait in fine detail (Plate 6). The first discovery was that the diameter of the shield had the same measurement as the distance from the upper shield-rim to the helmet crest, and as the distance from the lower shield-rim to the rear foot. This threefold register accounts for the odd foreshortening of the figure. Second, it was found that the radius of the shield matched the horizontal distance from the forward rim of the shield to the inner edge of the arris molding. From this it was possible to postulate a grid system governing the limits of the figure of the warrior (Fig. 2). Smaller units, all equal divisions of the larger measurements taken, began to appear, so that toes, points of kirtles, and hands all touched intersections of a grid of squares. The unit of measure, after considerable metric measurement, was revealed to be one imperial inch (2.5 cm.).

The radius of the crested helmet and its angle are of particular interest. The arc, just over a semicircle, is centered on a grid line and an intersecting diagonal drawn, not from corner to corner of a square, but to the cor-

Plate 5: Gosforth hogback. (Photo: H. Schmidt.)

James Lang

Plate 6: Shaft at Sockburn. Photo: T. Middlemass, copyright R. Cramp.)

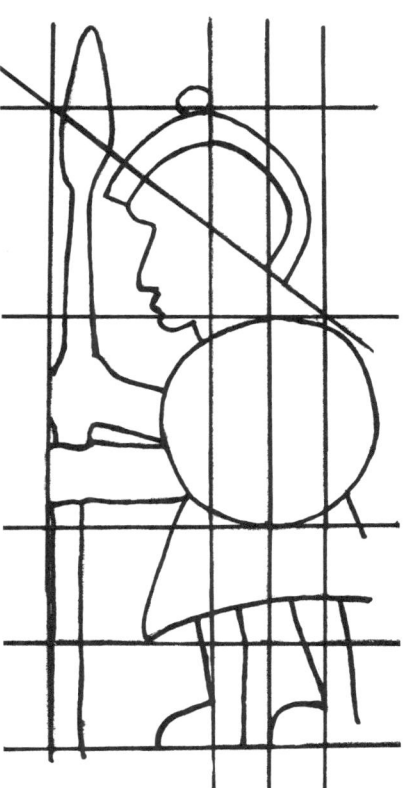

Fig. 2: Sketch of Sockburn warrior showing grid system.

ner plus one unit. The front edge of the kirtle maddeningly did not conform to the grid or its possible diagonals, but Mr. Tom Middlemass' excellent photograph shows that the sculptor was responding to the grain of the stone in that line. The small pellet surmounting the helmet crest is probably not a naturalistic feature but a filler dictated by the shortfall of the gridded figure from the transverse panel molding.

In order to verify the findings implied by Richard Bailey's template research, it was necessary to employ fine measurement on the related Brompton shaft. The bird panels (Plate 7) are constructed on a one-inch-square grid, despite the optical illusion created by the tapering stone. Above the helmeted head, the vine scroll has pointed leaves whose sharp tips mark the stages of regular registers ten inches in length (Plate 8). The angle of the undulating stem conforms to the diagonals of these rectangular registers. This layout technique was used on the vine scroll of an eighth-century Anglian shaft at Otley[23] and its use in the Allertonshire atelier in the tenth century is a surprising survival of native artistic tradition. The choice of motif might have been prescribed by the secular Viking patron, but its manner of execution reaches back to Insular roots.

An adjacent face of the Brompton shaft depicts a cleric holding a maniple and wearing a winglike cloak. Oblique lighting across the surface of the stone reveals drilled holes, some of them aligned vertically, and even some ruled scratches which served as the fix-points for the laying-out of the grid. These would have been concealed by the coating of gesso and pigment which we know originally adorned such carvings. Similar geometrical construction lines have been found on three pieces by the "York Master" and on the Nunburnholme cross,[24] indicating that the method was not confined to a single workshop or craftsman.

This method of blocked layout on grids with a unit of measure of one inch is also found in Ireland, only thirty miles from the Viking city of Dublin. At Castledermot in Kildare there is a whole range of connections between the high crosses there and the Allertonshire workshop. The links are stylistic, technical, and iconographic. One panel on the North Cross at Castledermot, for example, showing Daniel between four lions, is worked on exactly the same principles and units as the shafts at Kirkleavington. The influence was reciprocal, for Castledermot possesses Ireland's only hogback, and the side of the North Cross carries a ring-twist pattern which is unique in Ireland but ubiquitous in North Yorkshire.[25]

It is in the Isle of Man, however, that this method of analysis begins to affect the almost Linnaean classification of Viking-Age art styles. In 1977 Signe Horn Fuglesang pleaded that the definition of these styles should not

Plate 8: Shaft at Brompton. (Photo: T. Middlemass, copyright R. Cramp.)

Plate 7: Shaft at Brompton. (Photo: T. Middlemass, copyright R. Cramp.)

be based exclusively upon motif,[26] yet at Kirk Michael the famous cross slab signed by Gaut has been regarded as "Viking" not only on account of its runic inscription in Old Norse but because its ornamental repertory has been labeled Borre or Jellinge because of particular motif elements such as the ring-chain or the half-moon nick under the hook of the crozier-like tendril (Plate 9).[27] Those semicircular nicks in the edge of the tendril happen to be confined to the outer edge of the monument, and this is always the case when this feature appears in the Isle of Man. The nicks are spaced at regular, equal intervals, and the lessons of the Brompton shaft teach one to regard them as fix-points for the horizontal lines of the grid. When horizontals are extended from the half-moon nicks, they pass through crucial parts of the design, such as interlace crossing-points, edges of registers, and points where the decorative line changes direction abruptly. Hence the nicks are in reality disguised fix-points, not diagnostic features of a style.

Though Gaut wrote in Old Norse, it does not follow that his ornamental repertory was equally Norse. The tendril pattern, or crozier hook with semicircular nick, appears on the primary phase of decoration of St. Mura's bell,[28] and, as in the Manx carved slabs, the nicks are always on the outside edge of the panel. They may have served as fix-points; but in cast metalwork they may originally have been the slots for mold sprigs, the pattern being accommodated to them. This, I suspect, also applies to the Jellinge-style crests of the Søllested horse yokes from Denmark and may well cast doubt on the half-moon nick's being a decorative detail at all, let alone a Jellinge motif.

Constructional analysis of this kind is clearly likely to cause repercussions in the assessment of zoomorphic styles. Profile ribbon quadrupeds should not be dubbed "Jellinge beasts" too hastily. If the conditioning to Scandinavian stylistic labels can be laid aside and an innocent eye cast on the two animals in Figure 3, it is difficult to distinguish their provenance: one is from an Irish shrine, the Soiscel Molaise,. and the other from an Anglo-Scandinavian shaft at Otley. General impression might make one cautious enough, but scrutiny of the motifs and their relationships with the disposition of the design does challenge the notion of a particular repertory of details necessarily indicating an exclusive style. The definition of the Jellinge style, in terms of motif and layout, would include features such as parallel double edges to the animal's body, extended appendages serving as fetters, scrolled leg-joints, nose-folds, and symmetrical interlocking of identical beasts about a horizontal axis. A sense of *horror vacui* and disciplined interlacing produce a typical Jellinge frieze. The strip of animal ornament in Figure 4 would conform in nearly all respects to this definition

Plate 9: Gaut's cross-slab, Kirk Michael, Isle of Man. (Photo: R. T. Jellicoe.)

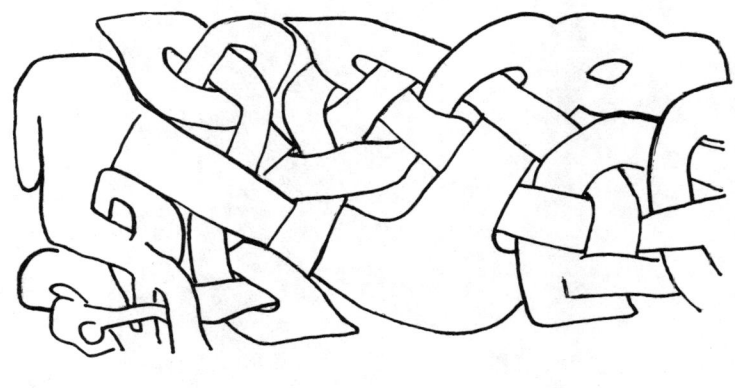

Fig. 3: Profile beasts from Otley sculpture and the Soiscel Molaise.

Fig. 4: Detail from the MacRegol gospels.

of a tenth-century Scandinavian style. It is confusing, therefore, when one realizes that Figure 4 is an uncolored reproduction of part of a page of the Macregol Gospels, an Insular manuscript of the ninth century.[29]

There are indeed small but significant deviations from pure Jellinge in this example: the nose, the shape of the eye perhaps. The similarities outweigh the differences, however, and it is with some pleasure that one can turn back to Shetelig after the assertions of Scandinavian purity in Jellinge uttered in recent decades:

> But the Jellinge style by far becomes a direct imitation of the Irish style. Scandinavian art rejects the logical construction, the intricate maze of geometrical interlacings, and sticks to the animal patterns as a familiar and well-known ornamental form. The whole composition becomes freer, more open, with a wider range of individual variations, very different from the law-bound design in Irish decorations.[30]

A comparison of the Jellinge animals of the Søllested yokes and the Macregol Gospels would confirm Shetelig's distinction. The beasts of the Macregol manuscript lie on the diagonals of a regular grid, and the scrolls, crossing-points, and direction changes lie on the verticals. It is this system which lies behind the Viking colonial carving of Yorkshire.

What, then, of the beast-chains of Anglo-Scandinavian Northumbria, such as one from a York Minster shaft shown in Plate 10?[31] The posture, angles, scrolls, crossings and direction of line all rely upon the grid. The design is rigidly symmetrical; and it is this quality, I believe, which is the chief distinguishing trait of *colonial* Viking art as opposed to that of the homelands. The discovery of this basis for design may well support Shetelig's view that the Jellinge style emerged in the Western colonies,[32] but that is to persevere in the evolutionary view of stylistic progression. The Macregol and York creatures look the way they

Plate 10: Shaft at York Minster. (Photo: A. Wiper.)

do because they are constructed on a grid, not because one is copying the other a century later.

The habit of constructing designs on stone in this way reaches far back into the Hiberno-Saxon period, many of the inhabited scrolls of the eighth century being laid out in gridded registers. The Viking-Age sculptors perpetuated the method, wherever they had learnt it, and combined with the Insular repertory of patterns discussed above it demonstrates an unquenched source of artistic practice. Their reasons for adopting the method could have simply been a matter of taste: a fix-point can be disguised in any number of ways, a panel covered with any kind of animal, so why (as Professor Rosemary Cramp pointed out to me) choose a spiral and a ribbon-beast? Style ultimately depends upon choice.

A second reason, however, may have been more compelling to the pragmatic Viking. In Dublin and York, the twin colonial cities of the tenth century, bone motif pieces have been found, the Irish series being particularly numerous.[33] Formal and zoomorphic motifs are sketched out, sometimes on a geometric base, in miniature, perhaps for future metalwork designs. Consider a large stone shaft under the hand of the sculptor and how essential it would be to ensure the correct proportions of a design several feet in length, expensively and irrevocably cut in stone. The trial piece for such an artifact could easily have been a plank of wood, the design drawn out on a half- or quarter-unit grid. The transfer of the pattern to the stone would have been facilitated by scaling up the grid; and this may have been the *raison d'être* of the method.

To test the validity of the thesis that geometrical construction is a distinguishing characteristic of colonial Viking art as against that of Scandinavia itself, a comprehensive analysis of all the decorative artifacts will have to be undertaken, on both sides of the North Sea. Lennart Karlsson has already begun to re-examine the continuity of motifs in Scandinavia, and his injunction concerning the Viking donation to *English* culture is worthy of note: "The picture is less clear in England, where the Scandinavian contribution is but a very small portion of the enormous whole."[34] An analysis of Insular motifs and styles is perhaps the starting-point for refining out the Viking elements. The connections between Irish metalwork and Northumbrian sculpture with the grid system are hopefully a beginning. Perhaps here we have found not only the distinctiveness but also the conservatism and sense of inherited tradition which is typical of colonials the world over.

UNIVERSITY OF DURHAM

Notes

1. David M. Wilson, "Archaeological Evidence for the Viking Settlements and Raids in England," *Frühmittelalterliche Studien,* 2 (1968), 295.
2. James T. Lang, "Continuity and Innovation in Anglo-Scandinavian Sculpture," in *Anglo-Saxon and Viking Age Sculpture and Its Context,* ed. J. T. Lang, British Archaeological Reports, 49 (Oxford, 1978), pp. 145-53.
3. Ian Pattison, "The Nunburnholme Cross and Anglo-Danish Sculpture in York," *Archaeologia,* 114 (1973), Pls. 46c and 47d.
4. Rosemary Cramp, "The Position of the Otley Crosses in English Sculpture of the Eighth to Ninth Centuries," *Kolloquium über Spätantike und Frühmittelalterliche Skulptur* (Mainz, 1970).
5. K. Berg, "The Gosforth Cross," *Journal of the Warburg and Courtauld Institutes,* 21 (1958), 27-43 ; Richard Bailey, *Viking Age Sculpture in Northern England* (London, 1980), pp. 125-31.
6. Bailey, *Viking Age Sculpture,* pp. 54-55.
7. William S. Calverley, *Notes on the Early Sculptured Crosses, Shrines and Monuments in the Present Diocese of Carlisle* (Kendal, 1899), pp. 103-04.
8. David M. Wilson, *Viking Art* (London, 1966), Pl. 27.
9. Lennart Karlsson, *Romansk Träornamentik i Sverige* (Stockholm, 1976), p. 206.
10. James Graham-Campbell, *Viking Artefacts* (London, 1980), p. 23.
11. Adolf Mahr, *Christian Art in Ancient Ireland,* Vol. I (Dublin, 1932; rpt. New York, 1976), Pl. 57.
12. Mahr, Pl. 124.
13. Françoise Henry, *Irish Art During the Viking Invasions* (London, 1967), p. 194.
14. W. G. Collingwood, "Anglian and Anglo-Danish Sculpture in the North Riding of Yorkshire," *Yorkshire Archaeological Journal,* 19 (1907), 357-59.
15. Collingwood, pp. 300-01, e.
16. Máire Mac Dermott, "The Kells Crozier," *Archaeologia,* 96 (1955), Pl. 34. See also the Baile Dinghbhait Cross.
17. Françoise Henry, *Irish Art in the Early Christian Period to A.D. 800* (London, 1965), Pl. 20.
18. Bailey, *Viking Age Sculpture,* Pl. 26.
19. Calverley, pp. 15-17; Wilson, *Viking Art,* Pl. 55.
20. Henry, *Irish Art During the Viking Invasions,* Pl. 7.
21. Richard Bailey, "The Chronology of Viking-Age Sculpture in Northumbria," in Lang, *A-S and Viking Age Sculpture,* pp. 179-85.
22. Bailey, *Viking Age Sculpture,* pp. 246-56.
23. Cramp, "Position of Otley Crosses," Pl. 42, 2.
24. James Lang, forthcoming; James Lang, "The Sculptors of the Nunburnholme Cross," *Archaeological Journal,* 133 (1976), 76.
25. James Lang, "The Castledermot Hogback," *Journal of the Royal Society of Antiquaries of Ireland,* 101 (1971), 154-58.
26. Signe Horn Fuglesang, "Stylistic Groups in Late Viking Art," in Lang, *A-S and Viking Age Sculpture,* p. 205.

27. Wilson, *Viking Art,* pp. 108-109.
28. Mahr, Pl. 81.
29. Samuel Hemphill, "The Gospels of Mac Regol of Birr; A Study in Celtic Illumination," *Proceedings of the Royal Irish Academy,* 29 (1912), Pl. 1.
30. Haakon Shetelig, *Classical Impulses in Scandinavian Art from the Migration Period to the Viking Age* (Oslo, 1949), p. 133.
31. Lang, *A-S and Viking Age Sculpture,* Pl. 8.14.
32. Shetelig, p. 132.
33. Uaininn O'Meadhra, *Motif-Pieces from Ireland* (Stockholm, 1979).
34. Karlsson, p. 202.

The Imagery of the Living Ecclesia and the English Monastic Reform

ROBERT DESHMAN

Our understanding of the complex culture of the Anglo-Saxons is often limited by the fences separating academic fields. Art historians study the art, literary critics the prose or the poetry, and so on. Though inevitable and often essential, such specialization can sometimes pick apart the strands of an originally unified cultural fabric. During the second half of the tenth century (the period of the monastic reform), art, literature, and religious and political life were all tightly interwoven. To illustrate this, I should like to follow one theme, the concept of the living Church, across disciplinary boundaries in an effort to understand how the monastic reformers utilized a variety of different means to express their ideology and to explain their actions.

We begin with the miniature of Saint Swithun (Plate 1) in the Benedictional made at Winchester about 973 for Bishop Æthelwold, one of the leaders of the reform.[1] Beneath an arch-like baldachine supported on two slender golden columns, the saint stands upon the base of a central column whose shaft and capital are completely hidden behind him. The hard vertical contours of Swithun's golden tunic are assimilated to the geometric shape of a column, and two small arches, which presumably rest upon a hidden capital, almost seem to spring from the saint's nimbed head. This assimilation of the human body to a column created a pleasing decorative unity between the figure and the framework, but the architectural character of the saint was motivated by symbolism as much as by aesthetics. The Winchester Liturgy for the Mass for Swithun's translation, the feast the picture illustrates,[2] described Swithun as an "Olympic column of shining glory" and compared him to "one of the apostles."[3] This architectural symbolism[4] had its roots in the Bible. Galatians 2:9 metaphorically described three of the apostles as *"columnae,"* and on the basis of this and other Biblical texts medieval commentators commonly likened the apostles and their successors, the doctors and preachers of the faith, to symbolic columns supporting and strengthening the spiritual edifice of the Church with their firm faith, upright deeds, and illustrious preaching. Like the Liturgy, the Benedictional's miniature characterized Saint Swithun as a successor of the apostles and a symbolic column of Ecclesia.

This Anglo-Saxon image is part of an older and broader medieval pictorial tradition.[5] In a late eighth-century Gospels from Flavigny, for example, the figures of the Evangelists and John the Baptist are assimilated to column bases and the figures of Christ and the Evangelist symbols to column capitals (Plate 2).[6] In the Benedictional the particular way in which the human form is equated to a column anticipates by almost two centuries the best known examples of such symbolic living architecture, the column statues on the façades of Gothic cathedrals.[7]

In the Benedictional, architectural symbolism is not limited to the miniature of Swithun; it can also be detected in the manuscript's image of the Nativity (Plate 3), although this emerges only upon consideration of the unusual position of Christ and the elaborate form of his crib. Christ is rather incongruously shoved beneath the Virgin's bed. This contrasts with the more normal central position of Christ between Mary and Joseph in medieval images such as the one on the Carolingian ivory casket from Metz now in Brunswick (Plate 4).[8] It has long been known that the Benedictional copied a prototype closely related to this ivory,[9] and so we can be quite certain that one of the changes the Winchester artist introduced into his copy was to move Christ in the crib as well as the adoring animals to a bottom corner. Why should the artist have turned the Lord into a footnote to his mother? The explanation is linked to the appearance of Christ's crib. To judge from the Brunswick casket, the crib in the Carolingian model was a simple if misshapen box; but in the Anglo-Saxon miniature the crib was given an elaborate architectural appearance which assimilated it to an altar. In medieval art altars were often decorated with architectural motifs such as columns and window-like openings.[10] Moreover, in the Benedictional the Christ Child does not lie in the crib so much as on it, and this too suggests the equation of Christ on the crib with the Eucharist on the altar. The immediate textual source of this symbolism was the Christmas blessing that the picture prefaces. This text says that the Lord made Christ, "the bread of the angels, to be the food in the crib of the Church of the faithful animals,"[11] thus giving an Eucharistic significance to the newly born Christ and implicitly identifying the crib with the church altar. The

Plate 1. St. Swithun. London, British Library, MS. Add. 49598, fol. 97ᵛ. (Photo: Trustees of the British Library.)

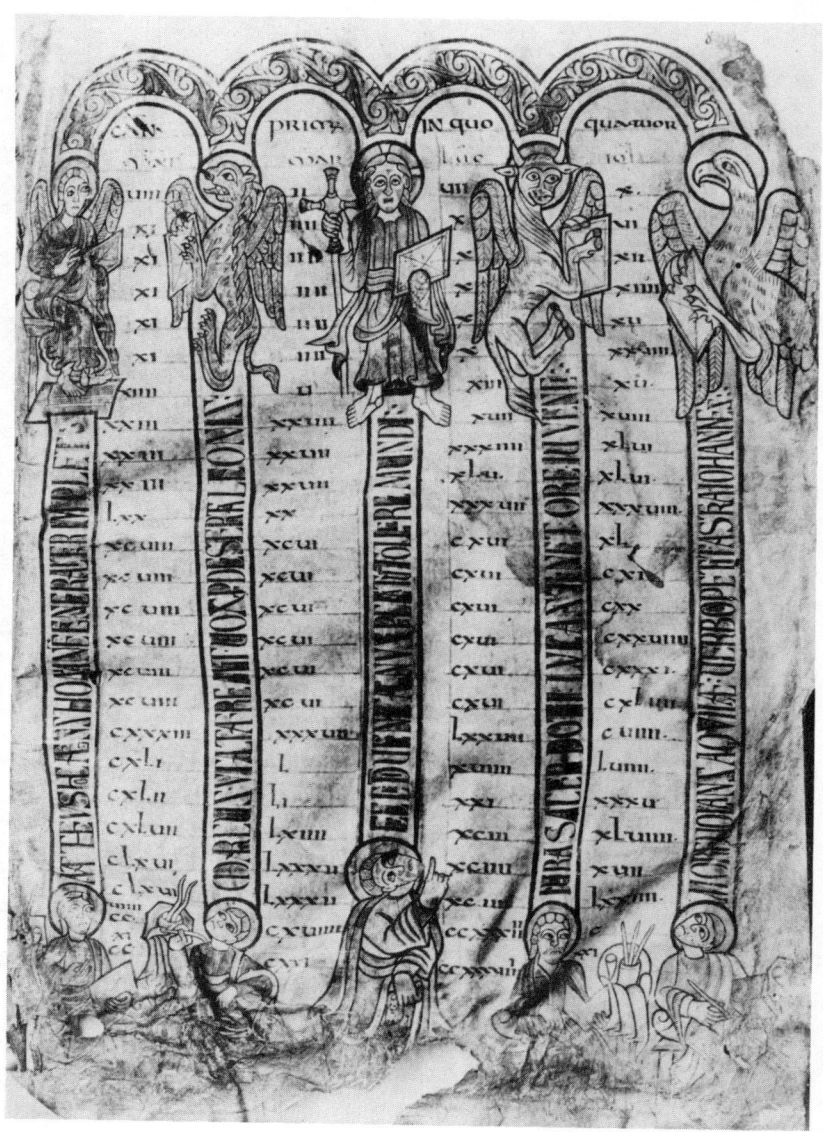

Plate 2. Canon table with columnar figures. Autun, Bibliothèque Municipale, MS. 4, fol. 8. (Photo: Bildarchiv Foto Marburg.)

Plate 3. Nativity. London, British Library, MS. Add. 49598, fol. 15ᵛ.
(Photo: Trustees of the British Library.)

Plate 4. Nativity. Brunswick, Herzog Anton Ulrich-Museum, ivory casket. (Photo: Herzog Anton Ulrich-Museum; after Goldschmidt.)

"faithful animals," the ox and the ass who normally feed from the manger crib, are the symbols of the faithful of the Church who partake of Christ as the Eucharist at the altar.

The association of the crib with the altar was an old and common symbolic concept in Christian thought, and some earlier representations of the Nativity had already visualized this by the portrayal of an altar-crib.[12] Although the primary, Metz model of the English miniature apparently did not include this symbolic motif, the Winchester artist must have known of another, earlier scene that did.[13]

What really makes the crib in the Benedictional so unusual, however, is the degree to which it is architectural. Not only does it have openings like window and doors, it even has towers, a feature seldom if ever found in even the most architectural of altars. If we compare the crib to the actual buildings above the dome in the Benedictional's Annunciation scene (Plate 5), the resemblance is so pronounced that we must wonder whether the artist really did mean to suggest a miniature building as well as a crib and an altar. Probably this is just what he did intend. Some corroboration is found in a representation of the Nativity in the mid-eleventh-century Bury St. Edmunds Psalter in the Vatican (Plate 6).[14] The crib here is unmistakably a building which, like the one in the Benedictional, has several towers. Since the Psalter is an Anglo-Saxon creation, it is reasonable to assume that this rare feature stemmed from an earlier tradition of English iconography, a tradition that in all probability originated in the Nativity picture of the Benedictional itself.

The key to the motif's meaning is contained in the previously quoted text of the Benedictional that described Christ as "food in the crib of the Church of the faithful animals." The phrase "crib of the Church" can be understood in two slightly different senses: either that the crib is *in* the church or that the crib *is* the Church itself. This ambiguity was quite deliberate. In England and elsewhere the altar was traditionally believed to be a symbolic microcosm of the universal Church.[15] The blessing text thus intentionally implied that Christ's crib symbolized both the altar and the universal Church. When medieval artists wished to represent Ecclesia, they often depicted a building.[16] For example, the miniature added by Winchester artists in the second quarter of the tenth century to a small Carolingian manuscript, the Athelstan Psalter in the British Library, depicts the choirs of the saints adoring Christ who rests his feet upon a small building (Plate 7).[17] This structure symbolized Ecclesia, which consisted of its head, Christ, who is enthroned above, and its body, the universal body of believers or all saints who surround Christ. After its illumination, the Athelstan Psalter remained at Winchester, and so it is highly likely that this very miniature with its architectural symbol of the living Ecclesia was known to the later Winchester artist of the Benedictional. In a sense what this artist did was to transfer a traditional symbol of Ecclesia, the building, into the new and unusual iconographic context of the Nativity. He illustrated the symbolic nuances of his liturgical text in an original fashion by representing the crib as both the altar and the Church itself.

To understand the apparently demeaning placement of such an important ecclesiological symbol in the composition of the Benedictional, we must first understand a related feature of the miniature in the Athelstan Psalter; for here the building of Ecclesia was placed, if not at the foot of the composition, then beneath the feet of Christ. This latter motif also occurs in a twelfth-century German ivory recently acquired by the Cloisters in New York (Plate 8).[18] Christ, who hands Peter the keys and Paul the law, stands upon the building of Ecclesia. This motif illustrates what the Lord had said to Peter on this occasion: "Thou art Peter; and upon this rock I will build my church" ("Tu es Petrus et super hanc petram aedificabo ecclesiam meam" Matt. 16:18). Peter's equation to the foundation of the Church was a pun upon his name, Petrus, and *petra,* the Latin for rock. But medieval exegesis also connected Christ's words to the many New Testament texts that likened Christ himself to the foundation and the cornerstone of the spiritual edifice of Ecclesia. For example, Ælfric, who was educated at Winchester by Bishop Æthelwold, said that Peter received his name because he had attached himself through firm faith to Christ, who is the "stone" (1 Cor. 10:4) and "foundation" (1 Cor. 3:10–11) of all the fabrics of his own Church. "All God's churches," Ælfric wrote, "are accounted as one congregation, ... constructed of chosen men, not of dead stones; and all the building of those living stones is founded upon Christ."[19] Thus the building beneath Christ's feet in the ivory and in the Athelstan Psalter symbolized not only Christ himself as the cornerstone and foundation of Ecclesia, but also those chosen men, whether Peter or the choirs of the saints, who as living stones are built upon Christ into one Church.[20] Influenced by the earlier Athelstan Psalter, the artist of the Benedictional found another way to indicate visually that Christ was the cornerstone and the foundation of the Church: he placed Christ on the building of Ecclesia literally in a bottom corner of the composition.

The Benedictional's Christmas text makes no mention of the cornerstone. Why, therefore, did the manuscript's artist incorporate cornerstone symbolism into the depiction of the altar-crib in the Nativity miniature? The illuminator must have been fully aware that the concept of the cornerstone was closely associated with the theme of sacrifice. This association is ap-

Plate 6. Nativity. Rome, Vatican, Biblioteca Apostolica, MS. Regina lat. 12, fol. 93 (Photo: Courtauld Institute of Art.)

Plate 5. Detail of Annunciation. London, British Library, MS. Add. 49598, fol. 5ᵛ. (Photo: Trustees of the British Library.)

Plate 7. Christ and choirs of saints. London, British Library, MS. Cotton Galba A. XVIII, fol. 21. (Photo: Trustees of the British Library.)

Plate 8. Christ presenting keys to Peter and law to Paul. New York, Metropolitan Museum, The Cloisters, ivory plaque.
(Photo: The Metropolitan Museum of Art, The Cloisters Collection, 1979.)

parent in the picture in the Athelstan Psalter where the figure of Christ is enthroned upon the "cornerstone" and at the same time holds a crossstaff and bares his wounds, reminders of his earlier sacrificial death during his first coming. This iconography illustrates New Testament concepts most clearly stated in 1 Peter 2:4–10. Christ first came as a "living stone" which men rejected, but later "chosen and made honorable by God," he became the "head of the corner," and so now believing mankind can be "also as living stones built up, a spiritual house, a holy priesthood, to offer up spiritual sacrifices, acceptable to God by Jesus Christ."[21] Such Biblical ideas also explain why the Christian altar was symbolically equated to the cornerstone and the foundation of the Church as well as to the Church itself in the Anglo-Saxon Liturgy for Ecclesiastical Consecration.[22] Hence the inherent relationship between the cornerstone and sacrificial offering in the New Testament, the Liturgy, and the imagery of the Athelstan Psalter opened the way for the Benedictional's artist to represent the altar-crib of Ecclesia as the cornerstone.

The painter, like the poet of the Old English Advent lyrics in the near contemporary Exeter Book,[23] must have also been influenced by two references to the cornerstone in the Liturgy of the Office about the time of Christmas. A verse on or near Christmas Day states: "The stone which the builders rejected, the same has become the head of the corner."[24] An antiphon a few days before says: "O King of the peoples and their desire and the cornerstone, you who made the two one; come, save man...."[25] This antiphon is based in part upon Ephesians 2:11–22, which applied the cornerstone metaphor to the controversy about whether the Gentiles could join the Church without their literal adherence to Jewish Old Testament laws. Christ was the "foundation" and the "cornerstone" which removed the barrier or partition of the Old Law for the Gentiles and thereby peacefully joined the two walls, that is, the Gentiles and the Jews, into the living edifice of the Church. Since the Gentiles and the Jews together constitute the faithful of the Ecclesia, it is important to remember that, according to the Benedictional's own text, the animals adoring Christ in the miniature are symbols of the faithful. Although this text does not actually specify that the animals are the believing Jews and Gentiles, this was well established in medieval exegesis. Pseudo-Jerome, a seventh- or eighth-century Irish commentator, said, for example, that the ox and the ass at Christ's crib symbolized respectively the Gentiles and the Jews communicating at the altar.[26] In the miniature, the depiction of the two faithful animals at Christ's manger and the representation of the manger as the altar, the cornerstone, and the building of Ecclesia were all complementary symbolic motifs. The location of the crib and the animals in the bottom corner of the composition was anything but a demotion for Christ — it was an ingenious visualization of the symbolic concept that Christ was the very foundation of the Church, the cornerstone of Ecclesia whose advent at the Nativity had cemented the Gentiles and the Jews into the one living Ecclesia.[27]

Both this miniature of the Nativity and that of Saint Swithun drew a symbolic equivalency between the architectural components of the material church and the faithful who with Christ constitute the spiritual edifice of the Church. Though they use very different visual means, these two pictures basically express the same theme of the living Ecclesia. Furthermore, at least seven more of the miniatures in the Benedictional use quite an extraordinary range of iconographic devices to pictorialize the ecclesiological concept of living architecture.[28] In this respect the Benedictional's miniature cycle is the pictorial counterpart of the Advent lyrics, a cycle of distinct but related poems which imaginatively play upon a variety of symbolic architectural motives such as the cornerstone, the key, and the door, and so on.[29]

Why were the Anglo-Saxons in the later tenth century so preoccupied with the theme of the living Ecclesia? The answer lies in the historical background of Swithun's cult and in the biographies of the monastic reformers.

In 971 Bishop Æthelwold translated Swithun's relics into Winchester cathedral, and his subsequent rebuilding and extension of the western part of the church was probably done to provide the relics with a fitting architectural setting. A second translation, perhaps in 974, might have marked the placement of the relics in the new portion of the cathedral.[30] The equation of Swithun with a column of the church in both the miniature and the Liturgy of the feast of his translation commemorated the saint's literal incorporation into the cathedral. Contemporary Winchester sources emphasized that Swithun's career as a popular cult figure and miracle worker was virtually non-existent until the time of Æthelwold. The bishop seems deliberately to have propagated the saint's cult through the translations and also through the image in the Benedictional.[31] Æthelwold's promotion of Swithun was not entirely disinterested, as is clear in a passage from the cantor Wulfstan's late-tenth-century Life of the bishop:

> Æthelwold ... was ... prevailing nobly in word and deed, dedicating churches in many places and preaching the Gospel of Christ everywhere.... His preaching was greatly assisted by Saint Swithun who at that time was declared by heavenly signs and translated and fitly buried beneath the temple. Therefore twin lamps shone at the same time in the house of God...: because what Æthelwold preached by the salutary teaching of words Swithun wonderfully adorned by the display of miracles.... And thus it was brought to pass ... that monasteries were founded everywhere among the English people.[32]

In this text Æthelwold's preaching of the Gospel should be regarded as synonymous with his advocacy of monastic reform; for Benedict had recommended the Gospels to monks as an alternative to his own *Rule*,[33] and monasticism was considered to be the evangelical way of life par excellence.[34] Thus, as Daniel Sheerin has recently suggested, Æthelwold manipulated Swithun's cult so that the saint's unexpected rise from obscurity and his sudden spate of miracles during Æthelwold's reign became signs of heavenly approval for the bishop's monastic reforms.[35] Such celestial support was most welcome because Æthelwold's reforms had included controversial actions such as the forcible replacement of the secular canons of the cathedral with monks.

What has previously escaped attention is the important symbolism that contemporaries attached to the very act of translating the saint. Originally Swithun had been buried in what was probably a prominent site outside the west entrance to the cathedral,[36] but the importance of this site was deliberately played down in a contemporary account of the translation by Lantfred, a monk of Winchester. At the end of the second chapter Lantfred wrote that Swithun's humility caused him to choose to be

> buried outside the church like a vile, scorned and unworthy sinner ... [but] revealed through many miracles and signs, [he] was brought back into this same church, exalted, venerated and renowned. We see in this ... the word of our Lord...: "Because every one that exalteth himself shall be humbled; and he that humbleth himself, shall be exalted."[37]

The first revelation of Swithun in his old tomb had been to a smith who was to deliver a message to a certain Eadsige, explicitly identified as one of the expelled canons who still bore a grudge against Æthelwold and the monks who had replaced him. Eadsige was to go to Æthelwold to relay the message that Saint Swithun wanted to be brought inside the church.[38] Clearly in this incident Swithun was used to bolster the authority of Æthelwold and the reformers. For two years Eadsige refused to carry out this unwelcome mission, but finally he relented. Not only did Eadsige deliver the message, but, in Lantfred's words, "this same cleric who recently had been secular ... became a devout monk much beloved of God.... Blessed be the omnipotent God who pardons sinners, who redeems those who trust him, who casts down the mighty and who raises up the meek!"[39] This passage ends the first chapter and purposely anticipates the previously quoted conclusion of the next chapter which compares Swithun's translation into the church to the redemption of a lowly sinner formerly outside the church but now exalted within it. Lantfred thus deliberately draws a parallel between Eadsige and Swithun, who were both brought into the church physically and spiritually. Later Lantfred re-enforces the parallelism when he tells us that the new monk Eadsige became the keeper of Swithun's new shrine within the cathedral.[40]

Lantfred carefully counterbalances the exaltations of the humble saint and the lowly sinner with the casting down of the mighty and the humbling of the exalted, clearly references to the wicked, impure canons who had been expelled from the cathedral. The unmistakable implication is that Swithun asked to come into the church just because the canons had been expelled from it. Cleansed of these defiling canons and now housing pure monks, the church had become a fitting dwelling for God and his holy saint. Swithun's translation and miracles within the cathedral demonstrated that monasticism had literally sanctified Ecclesia once more, and the rebuilding of the cathedral to house the relics was an external sign of the internal moral renewal of the Church by monasticism. Thus Swithun's new physical and spiritual presence in the cathedral legitimatized the monastic reformers' controversial seizure of physical and spiritual control of Ecclesia. In contemporary Winchester art and liturgy the emphatic association of Swithun with the column, a physical part of the church, must be understood as another way to propagandize the view that the monks and their saintly ally were the only rightful possessors, indeed, the very embodiment of Ecclesia.

In his narrative of one of the preliminary miracles through which Swithun made known his desire to be translated, Lantfred used the column as a symbol of the saint,[41] and on the evidence of prose style Lantfred probably also wrote the Winchester Liturgy which equated the saint with a column.[42] But in neither the narrative nor the Liturgy did Lantfred go so far as to link the column explicitly with monasticism. Nevertheless, the late-tenth- and eleventh-century *Vitae* of the leaders of the monastic reform leave no doubt that the column and, significantly, the cornerstone too were understood in this period as specifically monastic as well as ecclesiastic symbols. Byrhtferth, the probable author of the *Vita Oswaldi,* described Oswald's monastic devotions at Fleury in these words: "He was, as is fitting for friends of God, supported by two columns, that is, by the love of God and the love of fellow men, to which five [columns] were wisely added, which [columns] firmly supported his house so that it was unshaken by the wind...."[43] In this passage the columns are the monastic virtues which literally edify Oswald, making him a sound spiritual house of wisdom. The imagery here derived both from Proverbs 9:1, which describes wisdom's house of seven columns, and from Matthew 7:24–25: "Whosoever hears these words of mine and does them is like a wise man who built his house upon rock, and the rain fell, and the floods came, and the winds blew and beat against the house, but it did not fall: it was founded on rock." Benedict himself had given this Gospel text a monastic interpretation when he quoted it in the prologue of his *Rule*.[44] Since Matthew twice mentioned that this spiritual house is founded on rock, it is not surprising to find in the *Vita Oswaldi* another, related passage that used the metaphor of the cornerstone rather than that of the column to characterize the literally constructive consequences of Oswald's monastic devotions. His chanting and prayers at Fleury earned him, his biographer wrote, "the forgiveness and the grace ... of Jesus. They were the precious stones placed in the corners of his own holy house, which [stones] supported it firmly, so that it was not in a condition to fall, so that not one [stone] was able to be shaken by the most dire force of wind."[45] This monastic interpretation of the Biblical concept of living stones was probably inspired in part by Carolingian monastic writings. In the *Diadema Monachorum* by Smaragdus, a ninth-century treatise well known to the English reformers, a whole chapter was devoted to the theme that monks through their virtuous way of life should become living stones built upon Christ into a spiritual temple.[46]

The two related symbols of the cornerstone and the column were applied not only to Oswald but also to Dunstan, the founder of the monastic reform. Dunstan's early-eleventh-century biographer Adelard termed him "a most solid cube of faith and truth" and "a cornerstone fixed to stone [and] unable to be moved."[47] Adelard also called Dunstan a "column of light" and a "column of God."[48] But most revealing is Adelard's account of Dunstan's foundation of the first reformed monastery at Glastonbury:

> First eliminating whatever offended the eyes of the heavenly Inspector, he, having been made monk and abbot, the first one, began firstly to establish a school of monks. By his zeal in that place holy religion so increased in such a short time that, just as I said that the lamps of others throughout the entire church were kindled from a lamp..., so through him the column of monastic religion spread from this place throughout the whole land of the English.[49]

This account of the reform at Glastonbury has analogies with Lantfred's description of events at Winchester. After being cleansed of impurity displeasing to God (presumably non-monks), the house of God, the church, is occupied by fittingly pure monks and also, in the case of Winchester, by a saintly supporter of the monks. The holy monastic way of life of these new occupants allows them to become, like Dunstan or Swithun, "the column of monastic religion," that is, to build themselves into the living spiritual edifice of the monastic Ecclesia.

From these literary sources it is manifest that the cornerstone and column imagery in the Benedictional was only part of a widely diffused propaganda campaign to identify monasticism spiritually and materially with Ecclesia itself. Probably it was Æthelwold himself who originally conceived this monastic propaganda, for it first appeared in his personal book some two decades before the Lives of the other leaders of the reform were written.[50] Of course, the Anglo-Saxons did not invent the idea that monasticism was a means of constructing a sound spiritual house in Christ — this was derived from earlier monastic writings. But in Anglo-Saxon hands this traditional metaphor for the inner moral effects of monasticism assumed a new level of polemical and even practical political significance: it became a religious rationale legitimatizing the monks' wresting physical, economic, and spiritual control of the churches and the monasteries from the secular canons and their powerful lay allies.[51] In short, internal edification became a pretext for external expropriation.

This propaganda program embraced a number of different media to create the medieval equivalent of a multi-media advertising blitz. Art, liturgy, and hagiographic biography all played their part. In conclusion, one might wonder whether the reformers also pressed into service one other literary genre, Old English poetry. It has already been mentioned that in its preoccupation with various symbols of living architecture the picture cycle of the Benedictional has a literary counterpart in the cycle of Advent poems in the approximately contemporary Exeter Book. It seems something more than coincidence that the Benedictional's Nativity miniature and the first Advent lyric were both influenced by the very same cornerstone texts of the Liturgy, and there are also other correspondences that cannot be pursued in this study. Certainly the poems can be understood on the level of non-monastic Christian spirituality and exegesis, but this is also true of the art and does not preclude the existence of other levels of topical monastic meaning. Until we know whether the Advent lyrics were originally composed or merely copied during the age of the monastic reform we cannot hope to know whether the author intended a monastic interpretation. In the face of this uncertainty, the example of visual art is instructive. In the case of the Benedictional, Æthelwold superimposed monastic meaning on iconography drawn from earlier Carolingian and Anglo-Saxon sources which were probably unconnected to monasticism. Whatever the intentions of the original author of the poems, the prevalent monastic interpretation of cornerstone imagery in late-tenth-century English art and hagiographic literature makes it likely that to contemporary monastic readers of the Exeter Book the cornerstone and perhaps other architectural metaphors of the Advent lyrics would have carried some monastic connotations.

But whether or not this interpretation is accepted, I hope that I have at least shown that the effort of climbing over disciplinary fences to explore several academic fields can sometimes enrich our understanding of the flourishing culture of the Anglo-Saxons.

UNIVERSITY OF TORONTO

Notes

1. Otto Homburger, *Die Anfänge der Malschule von Winchester im X. Jahrhundert*, Studien über christliche Denkmäler, NS 13 (Leipzig, 1912), p. 24; George Frederick Warner and Henry Austin Wilson, *The Benedictional of St. Æthelwold* (Oxford, 1910), pp. xxviii; and see Pl. on fol. 97^v; Francis Wormald, *The Benedictional of St. Ethelwold* (London, 1959), p. 12; Robert Deshman, "The Medieval Images and Cult of Saint Swithun," in *The Cult of Saint Swithun*, ed. Michael Lapidge, Winchester Studies, 4/2 (in press).
2. The picture and its text might also have served for the feast of the anniversary of Swithun's death (July 2); see Warner and Wilson, *Benedictional*, p. lvi.
3. *The Missal of the New Minster*, ed. Derek H. Turner, Henry Bradshaw Society, 93 (Leighton Buzzard, 1962), pp. 125, xxiv, n. 6: "Tu [Deus] idem quoque columnam rutile claritatis olimpicam sanctum pontificem suuithunum ... contulisti; O felicem anglorum gentem cui dominus rerum talem concessit patronum: ut merito ad predictarum populis gentium colatur quasi unus apostolorum."
4. Bruno Reudenbach, "Säule und Apostel: Überlegungen zum Verhältnis von Architektur und architekturexegetischer Literatur im Mittelalter," *Frühmittelalterliche Studien*, 14 (1980), 310-51.
5. Reudenbach, "Säule und Apostel," pp. 337-51; Günter Bandmann, *Mittelalterliche Architektur als Bedeutungsträger* (Berlin, 1951), pp. 64-66; Joseph Sauer, *Symbolik der Kirchengebäudes und seiner Ausstattung in der Auffassung des Mittelalters*, 2nd ed. (Freiburg im Breisgau, 1924), pp. 134-35; Wilhelm Messerer, "Säule," in *Lexikon der christlichen Ikonographie*, Vol. IV (Rome, 1972), cols. 54-56.
6. *Karl der Grosse: Werk und Wirkung* (Aachen, 1965), p. 268, No. 439, Fig. 67; Frans Carlsson, *The Iconology of Tectonics in Romanesque Art* (Hässleholm, 1976), pp. 62-64, Fig. 25.

7. E.g., the transept sculpture of Chartres cathedral; see Willibald Sauerländer, *Gothic Sculpture in France 1140-1270* (London, 1972), Fig. 120.
8. Adolph Goldschmidt, *Die Elfenbeinskulpturen*, Vol. I (1914; rpt. Berlin and Oxford, 1969), pp. 52-53, No. 96, Pl. 45c.
9. Homburger, *Anfänge*, pp. 8-10.
10. Wolfgang Braunfels, *Die Welt der Karolinger und ihre Kunst* (Munich, 1968), Figs. 272, 295.
11. Warner and Wilson, *Benedictional*, p. 5: "Et qui [dominus] eum qui panis est angelorum. in praesepi ecclesiae cibum fecit esse fidelium animalium...."
12. Kurt Weitzmann, "*Loca Sancta* and the Representational Arts of Palestine," *Dumbarton Oaks Papers*, 28 (1974), 36-39; Adolf Katzenellenbogen, *The Sculptural Programs of Chartres Cathedral* (New York, 1959), pp. 12-15; Alphons A. Barb, "Krippe, Tisch und Grab," *Mullus: Festschrift Theodor Klauser*, Jahrbuch für Antike und Christentum, Ergänzungsband 1 (Münster, 1964), pp. 17-27; Ursula Nilgen, "The Epiphany and the Eucharist: On the Interpretation of Eucharistic Motifs in the Mediaeval Epiphany Scenes," *Art Bulletin*, 49 (1967), 311-16.
13. This source was undoubtedly the earlier tenth-century Winchester miniature of the Nativity in the Athelstan Psalter, a manuscript which, as we shall see below, influenced the Benedictional in other ways. See Robert Deshman, "Anglo-Saxon Art After Alfred," *Art Bulletin*, 56 (1974), 183-86, 197, Fig. 15; Elzbieta Temple, *Anglo-Saxon Manuscripts 900-1066, A Survey of Manuscripts Illuminated in the British Isles*, 1 (London, 1976), pp. 36-37, No. 5, Fig. 30.
14. Temple, *Anglo-Saxon Manuscripts*, pp. 100-02, No. 84.
15. Joseph Braun, *Der christliche Altar* (Munich, 1924), I, 751-52. For Anglo-Saxon England see the Winchester rite for the dedication of the church which sometimes uses the phrase "altare vel eclesia," in *The Benedictional of Archbishop Robert*, ed. Henry Austin Wilson, Henry Bradshaw Society, 15 (London, 1903), p. 89; see also below, note 22.
16. Wolfgang Greisenegger, "Ecclesia," in *Lexikon der christlichen Ikonographie*, Vol. I (Rome, 1968), col. 568.
17. See above, note 13.
18. Hermann Schnitzler, "A Romanesque Ivory in the Arthur Sachs Collection," *Bulletin of the Fogg Art Museum*, 2 (1932), 13-18; The Metropolitan Museum of Art, New York, *Notable Acquisitions 1979-1980* (New York, 1980), p. 22.
19. "Ealle Godes cyrcan sind getealde to anre gelaðunge, and seo is mid gecorenum mannum getimbrod, na mid deadum stanum; and eal seo bytlung ðæra liflicra stana is ofer Criste gelogod" (*The Homilies of Ælfric*, trans. Benjamin Thorpe, Vol. I [London, 1843], p. 369). Ælfric continues an older tradition of exegesis; e.g., Rabanus Maurus *Commentariorum in Matthaeum* V. 16, in *PL*, 107:991B-C. For the concept of the cornerstone see Ursula Maiburg, "Christus der Eckstein," in *Vivarium: Festschrift für Theodor Klauser zum 90. Geburtstag*, Jahrbuch für Antike und Christentum, Ergänzungsband, 11 (Münster, 1984), pp. 247-56; Gerhart B. Ladner, "The Symbolism of the Biblical Corner Stone in the Mediaeval West," *Mediaeval Studies*, 4 (1942), 43-60; Ernst Günther Schmidt, "Antike und mittelalterliche Schlusssteinsymbolik," *Das Altertum*, 14 (1968), 31-37; Pius Sciascia,

Lapis Reprobatus, Studia Antoniana, 13 (Rome, 1959); Arnold Ehrhardt, "Vir Bonus Quadrato Lapidi Comparatur," *Harvard Theological Review,* 38 (1945), 177-93; Joseph C. Plumpe, "Vivum Saxum, Vivi Lapides: The Concept of 'Living Stone' in Classical and Christian Antiquity," *Traditio,* 1 (1943), 1-14.

20. Two of the choirs of the saints and the saints in general are specifically linked to Christ the cornerstone in the text of Ephesians 2:19-20. The New Testament (Matt. 21:40-44; Mark 12:6-11; Luke 20:13-18; 1 Cor. 3:10-18) also ascribed an eschatological significance to Christ the cornerstone and the foundation, and thus this iconographic motif reinforces the theme of the Last Judgment in the picture of the Athelstan Psalter; see Deshman, "Anglo-Saxon Art After Alfred," pp. 181-82.

21. "[E]t ipsi tamquam lapides vivi superaedificamini / domus spiritalis / sacerdotium sanctum / offerre spiritales hostias / acceptabiles Deo per Iesum Christum." See also Ephesians 2:13-22, where the Christological cornerstone is associated with both the blood of Christ and the Cross.

22. See the prayer over the newly anointed altar in the Benedictional of Archbishop Robert, a late-tenth-century Winchester manuscript (*Benedictional of Archbishop Robert,* ed. Wilson, p. 84).

23. Robert Burlin, *The Old English Advent,* Yale Studies in English, 168 (New Haven, 1968), pp. 56-66; Jackson J. Campbell, *The Advent Lyrics of the Exeter Book* (Princeton, 1959), pp. 7-8, 11-13; Albert S. Cook, *The Christ of Cynewulf* (Boston, 1900), pp. 1, 73.

24. *Corpus Antiphonalium Officii,* ed. René-Jean Hesbert, 6 vols. (Rome, 1963-79), IV, 63, No. 6251A: "Lapidem quem reprobaverunt aedificantes, hic factus est in caput anguli."

25. *Corpus Antiphonalium,* ed. Hesbert, III, 376, No. 4078: "O Rex gentium et desideratus earum, lapisque angularis, qui facis utraque unum; veni, salva hominem...."

26. *PL,* 30:569B. He is repeated in a commentary on Matthew doubtfully ascribed to Walafrid Strabo (*PL,* 114:896C); see also Gregory the Great (*PL,* 76:458-59) and Jerome (*PL,* 24:27B-C).

27. The symbolism of the cornerstone and the foundation also explains the related depiction of the crib as the building of Ecclesia in the Bury Psalter (Pl. 6) where the drawing illustrates Psalm 86:5: "Shall not Sion say: *This* man and *that* man is born in her? and the Highest himself hath founded her." Commentators such as Augustine (*Enarrationes in Psalmos* LXXXVI. 2-5, CCSL, Vol. 39 [Turnhout, 1956], pp. 1199-1203) sometimes related the mention of the founding of Sion in this Psalm to Christ the cornerstone, Ecclesia, and also heavenly Jerusalem.

28. I shall treat this fully in a monograph on the Benedictional now in preparation.

29. Burlin, *Old English Advent,* passim.

30. For the translations and the cult of Swithun see Roger N. Quirk, "Winchester Cathedral in the Tenth Century," *Archaeological Journal,* 114 (1957), 31-59; Martin Biddle, "Excavations at Winchester, 1969: Eighth Interim Report," *Antiquaries Journal,* 50 (1970), 317-21; idem, "*Felix Urbs Winthonia*: Winchester in the Age of Monasticism," *Tenth-Century Studies: Essays in Commemoration of the Millennium of the*

Council of Winchester and Regularis Concordia, ed. David Parsons (London and Chichester, 1975), pp. 136-38; Daniel J. Sheerin, "Dedication of the Old Minster, Winchester, in 980," *Revue Bénédictine,* 88 (1978), 266-77; Deshman, "Images and Cult of Saint Swithun," in press.

31. Deshman, "Images and Cult of Saint Swithun," in press; Sheerin, "Dedication of the Old Minster," pp. 266-77.

32. Wulfstan *Life of St. Ethelwold* 25-27, in *Three Lives of English Saints,* ed. Michael Winterbottom (Toronto, 1972), pp. 48-49: "Erat ... Adeluuoldus...sermone et opere magnifice pollens, in plerisque locis aecclesias dedicans et ubique aeuangelium Christi predicans....Huius predicationem maxime iuuit sanctus antistes Suuithunus, eodem tempore caelestibus signis declaratus et infra templi regiam gloriosissime translatus ac decenter collocatus. Ideoque gemina simul in domo Dei fulsere luminaria...quia quod Adeluuoldus salubri uerborum exhortatione predicauit, hoc Suuithunus miraculorum exhibitione mirifice decorauit.... Sicque factum est ... monasteria ubique in gente Anglorum ... constituerentur...." See also the almost identical passage in Ælfric's *Life of St. Ethelwold* 18, in *Three Lives,* ed. Winterbottom, p. 25.

33. *Benedicti Regula* 73, ed. Rudolf Hanslik, CSEL, Vol. 75 (Vienna, 1960), p. 164.

34. Jean Leclercq, *La Vie parfaite,* Tradition Monastique, 1 (Paris and Turnhout, 1948), pp. 109-13.

35. Sheerin, "Dedication of the Old Minster," pp. 266-77; Deshman, "Images and Cult of Saint Swithun," in press. See also Jean Leclercq, "La Réforme bénédictine anglaise du Xe siècle vue du continent," *Studia Monastica,* 24 (1982), 107-10.

36. Biddle, *"Felix Urbs,"* p. 136; Sheerin, "Dedication of the Old Minster," pp. 268-69.

37. "[P]resul idem sanctissimus, qui humilitatis uirtute tactus extra templum est sepultus quasi uilis et contemptus preuaricator atque indignus, uirtutibus ac signis declaratus plurimis ad eandem reduceretur sublimis, uenerandus, ac precluis. In quo sermonem Dominicum indubitanter cernimus... 'Omnis qui se exaltat humiliabitur, et qui se humiliat exaltabitur' [Luke 14:11; 18:14]" (Lantfred *Translatio et Miracula Sancti Swithuni* 2, ed. and trans. Michael Lapidge, in *The Cult of Saint Swithun,* in press).

38. Lantfred *Translatio* 1.

39. "[I]dem clericus qui nuper erat biotticus... factus est coenobita religiosus multumque Deo dilectus....Benedictus omnipotens Deus qui peccatores iustificat, qui in sese sperantes saluat, qui superbos humiliat, qui humiles exaltat!" (Lantfred *Translatio* 1).

40. Lantfred *Translatio* 20.

41. Lantfred *Translatio* 3; see also the related passage in the metrical version of Lantfred's text by Wulfstan, *Narratio Metrica de Sancto Swithuno* 3, in *Frithegodi Monachi Breuiloquium Vitae Beati Wilfredi et Wulfstani Cantoris Narratio Metrica de Sancto Swithuno,* ed. Alistair Campbell (Zurich, 1950), p. 108, ll. 690-93, 703-04. See Deshman, "Images and Cult of Saint Swithun" (in press), regarding the column symbolism in this miracle.

42. Private communication from Michael Lapidge.

43. *Vita Oswaldi,* ed. James Raine, in *The Historians of the Church of York and Its Archbishops,* Rolls Series [No. 71] (London, 1879), I, 416: "Erat enim, ut sanctis et veris amicis Dei usuale est, binis fulcitus columnis, id est dilectione Dei et proximi, cui erant quinque sagaciter adjunctae, quae firmiter domum suam sustentabant ne a vento quassaretur...."

44. Benedict *Regula,* ed. Hanslik, p. 6. The Latin text reads, "Omnis ergo qui audit verba mea haec et facit ea / adsimilabitur viro sapienti qui aedificavit domum suam supra petram / et descendit pluvia / et venerunt flumina / et flaverunt venti / et inruerunt in domum illam et non cecidit / fundata enim erat super petram."

45. *Vita Oswaldi,* ed. Raine, p. 419: "veniam et gratiam ... Jhesu.... Fuerunt in angulis sanctae domus suae lapides pretiosi positi, qui eam ne cadere valuisset sustentabant firmiter, ut nullus [lapis] vis [? vi] pessimorum ventorum agitari posset."

46. Smaragdus *Diadema Monachorum* 40, in *PL,* 102:656D-57. Two late-tenth-century Anglo-Saxon copies of this text survive: Cambridge, Corpus Christi College 57, probably from Abingdon, and Cambridge, University Library Ff. 4. 43, probably from Christ Church, Canterbury. See Helmut Gneuss, "A Preliminary List of Manuscripts Written or Owned in England up to 1100," *ASE,* 9 (1981), 6, 8 (Nos. 8 and 41 respectively); Willibrord Wittiers, "Smaragde au moyen âge: la diffusion de ses écrits d'après la tradition manuscrite," *Etudes ligériennes d'histoire et d'archéologie médiévales,* ed. René Louis (Auxerre, 1975), pp. 367-68.

47. *Epistola Adelardi ad Elfegum Archiepiscopum de Vita Sancti Dunstani* 8, 12, in *Memorials of Saint Dunstan,* ed. William Stubbs, Rolls Series [No. 63] (London, 1874), pp. 62, 67: "Dunstanum fidei et veritatis cubum ... solidissimum;" "Dunstanus ... ut lapis angulari lapidi affixus, moveri non potuit...."

48. *Epistola* 6, 11 (ed. Stubbs, pp. 59, 66): "columnam lucis;" "columnam Dei." See also below, note 50.

49. *Epistola* 3 (ed. Stubbs, p. 56): "Unde primum eliminato quicquid oculis superni Inspectoris offendebat, monachus et abbas effectus, monachorum ibi scholam primo primus instituere coepit. Cujus ibi studio sic in brevi sancta excrevit religio, ut sicut dixi de lampade ... caeterorum per omnem ecclesiam lampades accensas, ita per eum ex hoc loco columen religionis monasticae toto Anglorum orbe diffusum sit."

50. It should also be noted that Winchester sources—the two Lives of Æthelwold written by Ælfric and Wulfstan—also refer to Dunstan during his long reign as archbishop of Canterbury as "an immovable column" ("columpna immobilis") (*Lives,* ed. Winterbottom, pp. 21, 42). Wulfstan also used another metaphor, the lamp, to identify Æthelwold and Swithun with the material Ecclesia; see above, note 32, and also note 49.

51. In regard to the great economic and political ramifications of the reform, see Eric John, "The King and the Monks in the Tenth-Century Reformation," *Orbis Britanniae,* Studies in Early English History, 4 (Leicester, 1966), pp. 154-80.

Demonic Elements in Anglo-Saxon Iconography

LOUIS JORDAN

It has long been recognized that demonic imagery played an important role in Romanesque art. During this era devils and demons were frequently represented on church portals, as at Conques and Autun; on capitals, as at Vézelay; and in numerous manuscript illuminations, as in the Winchester Psalter (British Library MS. Cotton Nero C. IV, fols. 38ʳ and 39ʳ). In these works the devil was usually portrayed with an animal body, taloned feet, horns or pointed ears, flaming hair, and a tail, and as a fallen angel he often had wings. These elements served to emphasize the perception of the devil as a powerful and evil being.

However, when Romanesque devils are compared with representations of devils from earlier periods many important differences can be seen. In the fresco of Christ's descent into hell from the lower church of San Clemente in Rome (dated to the eighth century) we see the devil portrayed merely as a small human figure. His only distinguishing feature is his dark skin. There is a similar dearth of iconographic attributes in many areas during the Carolingian period, as in the Temptation of Christ scenes from the Drogo Sacramentary (Bibliothèque nationale MS. Lat. 9428, fol. 41ʳ) and on an ivory book cover (Frankfurt am Main, Stadtbibliothek Cod. Ausst. 68), both from the school of Metz and dated to ca. 850. In these scenes the devil is simply portrayed as a man, although in the Drogo Sacramentary he is given the mildly sinister attributes of a beard and ragged dress. Some later examples include the second temptation of Christ on the ciborium of Arnulf from Reims, ca. 890 (Munich, Schatzkammer der Residenz) and the Last Judgment miniature in the Bamberg Apocalypse from Reichenau, ca. 1000 (Bamberg, Staatsbibliothek, Bibl. 140 [A. II. 42], fol. 51ʳ), where we again see the devil with a fully human form.[1]

These observations lead to the question, What are the sources of the demonic elements so prominent in representations of the devil since the

Romanesque period? In answering this question I believe there are basically three different elements that led to the distinctive iconography of the devil: first, the Anglo-Saxon contribution; second, the Spanish contribution through the dissemination of illuminated manuscripts such as the Beatus Apocalypse Commentaries; and third, the influence of a combination of classical and Byzantine elements that were assimilated into some areas of Carolingian art.[2] In this paper I shall discuss the importance of Anglo-Saxon contributions to the iconography of the devil and make brief mention of some Carolingian elements.

The earliest surviving representation of the devil in Insular art is found in the famous *Book of Kells* (Dublin, Trinity College Library MS. A. I. 6, fol. 202^v), written and illuminated in the late eighth or early ninth century, probably at Iona.[3] In the scene depicting the third temptation of Christ from the Gospel of Luke (Plate 1) the devil is portrayed as a dark, slender, winged figure with a pointed nose and a long tongue. This figure, unique in Insular art, bears a close resemblance to demons found in early Byzantine manuscripts, as in the illumination of Psalm 6 from Vatican MS. graec. 752, fol. 28^r, a Psalter dated 1059.[4] The possibility of Byzantine influence was also suggested by Françoise Henry because the temptation was a popular Byzantine motif, the most notable examples being the scenes from the twelfth-century mosaics of both San Marco in Venice and Santa Maria la Nuova in Monreale. For these reasons it has been suggested that the scene in the *Book of Kells* was modeled either directly from a pre-iconoclastic Byzantine work or indirectly through a Western copy of such a work.[5]

The only other extant representations of devils in early Insular art are from the Irish High Cross of Muiredach at Monasterboise and the High Cross of Scriptures at Clonmacnois. The more elaborate of the two is the Cross of Muiredach, dated ca. 850.[6] On the crossing of the east side there is a Last Judgment with Christ in Glory (Plate 2). To the right of Christ is David playing a harp, followed by an angel playing a trumpet and another angel holding an open book, the *Liber Vitae;* behind the latter are the elect facing toward Christ. To the left of Christ is a figure playing a reed pipe, possibly the Erythrean Sibyl mentioned by Augustine in the *City of God* (XVIII.23) as a prophet of the Last Judgment. Next is a devil wielding a shield and a pitchfork, followed by an enigmatic figure that appears to be kneeling with its legs awkwardly spread out. This figure has been variously interpreted as either a female grotesque, a devil, or even two lovers in an embrace.[7] Next, another devil holds an open book (probably the *Book of the Devil* mentioned in some Irish texts[8]) while he kicks damned souls into hell. On the panel below, the archangel Michael weighs a soul and impales

Plate 1: Detail from the Temptation of Christ. *The Book of Kells*. Dublin, Trinity College Library. MS. A. I. 6, fol. 202ᵛ. Reproduced with permission.

Plate 2: The Last Judgment. Crossing on the east side. The High Cross of Muiredach at Monasterboise. Reproduced with permission.

a devil who is attempting to tip the scale in his own favor.

The Cross of Scriptures at Clonmacnois, also called Flann's Cross, is roughly contemporary with the Muiredach Cross and is thought to be from the same workshop.[9] On the crossing of the east side there is an abbreviated Last Judgment (Plate 3). A trumpeting angel and the elect are to the right of Christ, while on his left is a figure accompanied by the damned. This figure looks similar to the pipe-player interpreted as a sibyl in the previous work, but in this example he is certainly a devil. On the lowest panel on the north side there is a figure thought to represent Christ, Michael, or Saint Patrick, spearing a devil.[10] In both these crosses the devils are portrayed as small humanlike figures with few demonic attributes.

It is generally held that the iconography for scriptural scenes on Irish crosses came from Continental ivories. In fact, it has been suggested that the scenes may have been copied from the original ivories onto small ivory strips which were then affixed to miniature wooden crosses that were used as models in carving the sandstone high crosses.[11] Continental origins for the iconography of the two Last Judgment crosses under discussion are quite likely. Françoise Henry has discovered that the Monasterboise Cross contains the only Irish representation of the Apostle Thomas putting his finger into Christ's wound, a motif frequently found in Carolingian art.[12] Continental influence is also likely in the demonic iconography. Except for the *Book of the Devil* and the sibyl, which may be original Irish elements, the figures essentially conform to the Continental tradition of portraying devils in the form of men.

Thus the few surviving Insular examples indicate that representations of devils in early Insular art were derived from foreign sources, the *Book of Kells* from Byzantine and the Irish crosses from Continental iconography.

Although images of devils were rare, demonic forces were frequently represented in early Insular art. As in the other northern cultures, these forces were personified as fierce animals. From the Sutton Hoo treasure hoard of a seventh-century East Anglian king (London, British Museum) there is a purse-lid depicting two monsters attacking a man (Plate 4).[13] A similar motif is found on a fifth-century silver handle from Nydam Bog (Schleswig, Schleswig-Holsteinisches Museum), on a sixth-century silver fibula from Galsted, Schleswig (Copenhagen, Nationalmuseet) (Plate 5), and on a sixth-century bronze die from Torslunda, Oland, in Sweden (Stockholm, Statens Historiska Museum).[14] These depictions are probably related to a motif found on a seventh-century Frankish gravestone from Niederdollandorf (Bonn, Rheinisches Landesmuseum) which shows a pair of two-headed serpents attacking a man (Plate 6). In this last example we

288 Demonic Elements

Plate 4: The Sutton Hoo purse lid. London, British Museum. Reproduced with permission.

Plate 3: The Last Judgment. Crossing on the east side. The High Cross of Scriptures at Clonmacnois. Reproduced with permission.

Plate 6: Obverse of a Frankish gravestone from Niederdollandorf. Bonn, Rheinisches Landesmuseum. Reproduced with permission.

Plate 5: Silver fibula from Galsted, Schleswig. Copenhagen, Nationalmuseet. Reproduced with permission.

are fairly certain that the voracious animals represent demons of death.[15] Other examples of animals as demons are the heads placed on the prows of Viking ships such as those excavated at the Oseberg burial site dated ca. 850.[16] The animal head was considered to have so much demonic power that according to the *Book of Settlements* (*Landnámabók,* 95) it had to be removed when sailing toward a friendly land so as not to frighten benevolent spirits.[17] During this early period demonic iconography was closely associated with beasts and monsters.

Along with representations of demonic forces we find some literary descriptions of demons, most notably the fierce beast Grendel in the eighth-century epic *Beowulf.*[18] There are also some early descriptions of devils, as in the eighth-century poem *Juliana,*[19] but the more graphic descriptions come from the ninth century. The most extensive is from *Christ and Satan,* probably written in West Mercia during the mid-ninth century.[20] In this poem Satan parallels earlier demons: in fact, the word *æglæca* used in *Beowulf* to refer to Grendel is used here as a synonym for Satan.[21] Satan has a horrible face, emits sparks of fire and poison, and is bound in heavy fire chains. There are dragons, snakes, surging fire, and savage fiends with torment, affliction, and misery everywhere in his dark and sinful abyss.[22] A similarly grotesque description of Satan is found in the contemporary Old Saxon poem *Genesis B* which survives in an Old English version. The main distinction between the two is that *Genesis B* emphasizes Satan's role as a defiant adversary, while *Christ and Satan* accentuates Satan's misery and wretchedness.[23]

These poems, along with the Bible and the writings of Gregory the Great, influenced the works associated with the monastic reform initiated by Saint Dunstan. In the *Life of Saint Guthlac* Satan is equated with various wild animals, including a roaring lion with bloody teeth, a bellowing bull, a bear gnashing its teeth, a howling wolf, a whinnying horse, a belling stag, and a hissing serpent.[24] Ælfric, abbot of Eynsham, and Wulfstan, archbishop of York, use many similar images in their homilies. Ælfric even goes on to say that monstrous creatures were created for the punishment of evil deeds.[25] It is in this milieu that we find the first Anglo-Saxon pictorial representations of Satan.

Significantly, the earliest and most striking portrayal comes from the cornerstone of the Reform movement, the abbey of Glastonbury. In the calendar and computation section of the Leofric Missal (Oxford, Bodleian Library MS. Bodley 579, fols. 49ᵛ–50ʳ), done at Glastonbury in the 970's, there is an illustration of Satan-Mors, Death as the Devil (Plates 7 and 8).[26] The figure is part of a chart called the *Sphaera Apulei* or the Sphere of Life and

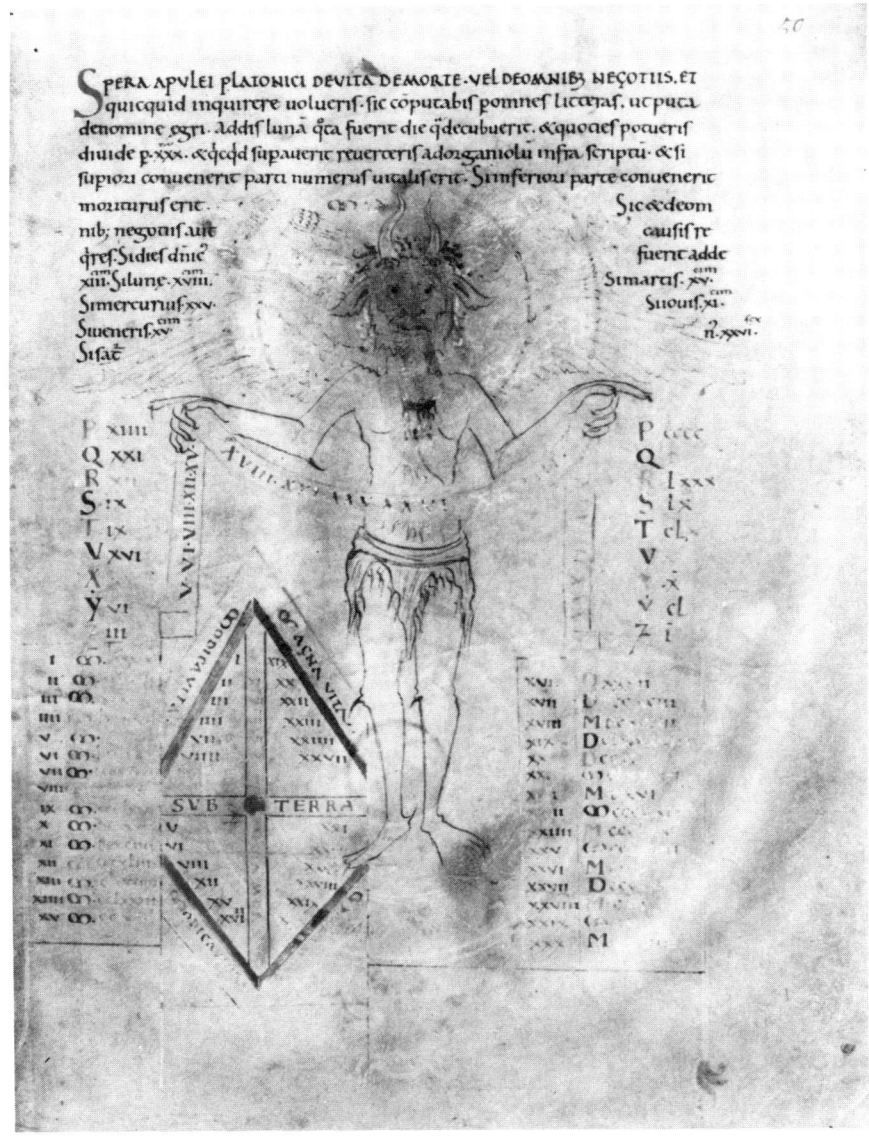

Plate 7: Satan-Mors. *The Leofric Missal*. Oxford, Bodleian Library MS. Bodley 579, fol. 50ʳ. Reproduced with permission.

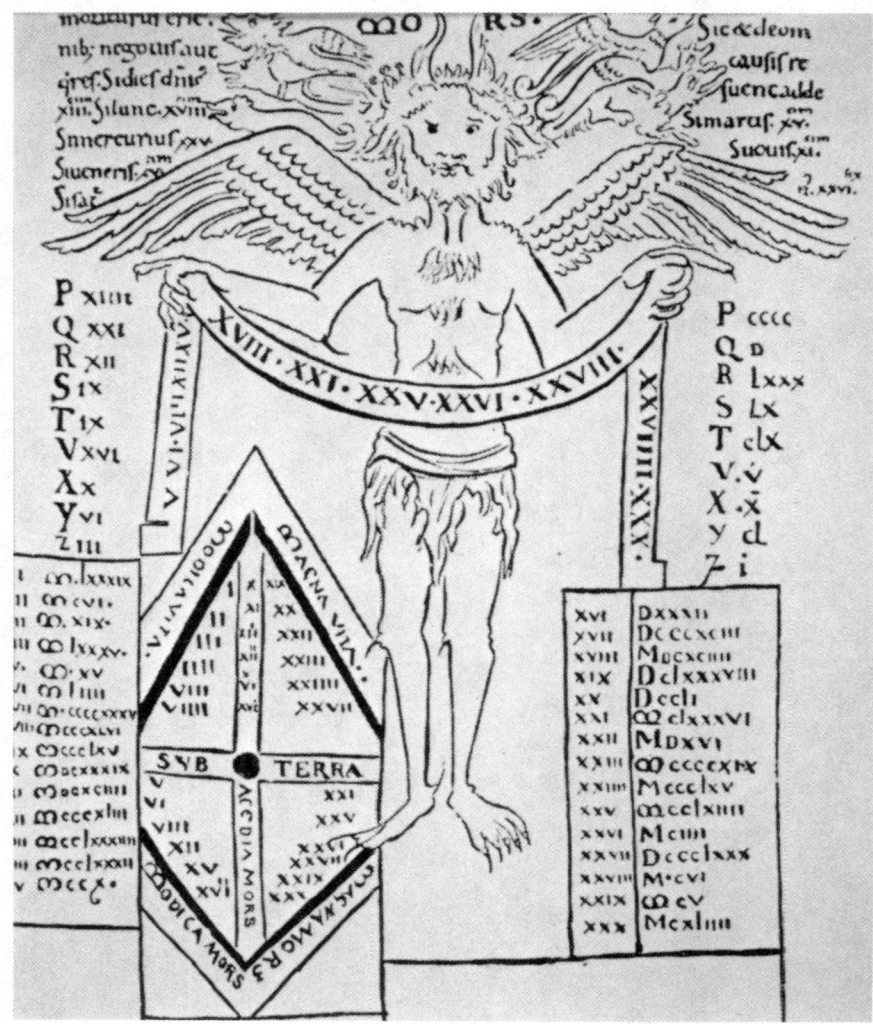

Plate 8: Reconstructed drawing of Satan-Mors. From Frederick Warren, *The Leofric Missal* (Oxford, 1883), p. 45.

Death, which was used in the following manner. When visiting a sick person, the priest would add the numerical equivalents of the letters in the patient's given name with the day of the moon on which the patient fell sick and divide the total by thirty. If the remainder from this answer appeared on the scroll held by Satan-Mors the priest would administer extreme unction; if the number was held by the adjacent crowned figure of Christ-Vita (Plate 9) no special preparations were necessary, for the patient would live.[27]

In the Leofric Missal the figure of Satan-Mors has a beastly face with long pointed ears, horns, and massive wings. These demonic attributes are further accentuated by the hairy chest, spurs protruding from the elbows, knees, and heels, the taloned hands and feet, and the ragged loincloth. Six winged dragonlike demons issue from his head. In 1962 Francis Wormald, without elaboration, suggested the possibility that the six demons may represent the vices with the central figure as *superbia*.[28] Without textual or iconographic evidence this interpretation is highly questionable. It disregards such contemporary portrayals of the vices as those found in the *Psychomachia* manuscripts[29] and depends on twelfth-century illustrations of the tree of vices where *superbia* is the root and the other vices are branches.[30] Adelheid Heimann in 1966 suggested that the figures could represent the six sons of Death mentioned in an early apocryphal Coptic text, *The Resurrection of Christ*.[31] However, there is no evidence that the work was ever known in the West during the Middle Ages.[32] Possibly a better solution is that the figures represent Satan's demonic companions. Some evidence for this interpretation is to be found in the works of the eighth-century Anglo-Saxon monk Aldhelm. In his riddle entitled "Lucifer" Aldhelm has Lucifer say:

> Once I was happy observing the law of God the Thunderer! But alas, after this, bold and proud in mind, I fell; And with vengeance he overthrew the wretched foe. Hence, six companions ascend the sky with me as the expert reader is able to explain through books.[33]

Unfortunately, the passage does not explain the rationale for the companions; but in relation to the Leofric illustration it does account for the number of demons and the fact that they issue forth from Satan towards the sky.

The Leofric Satan combines the Insular tradition of beastly demonic imagery with various Carolingian elements. One of the most striking elements is the horned animal head, an image derived from Pan, the pagan half-goat forest deity.[34] The earliest surviving examples of a goat-headed figure

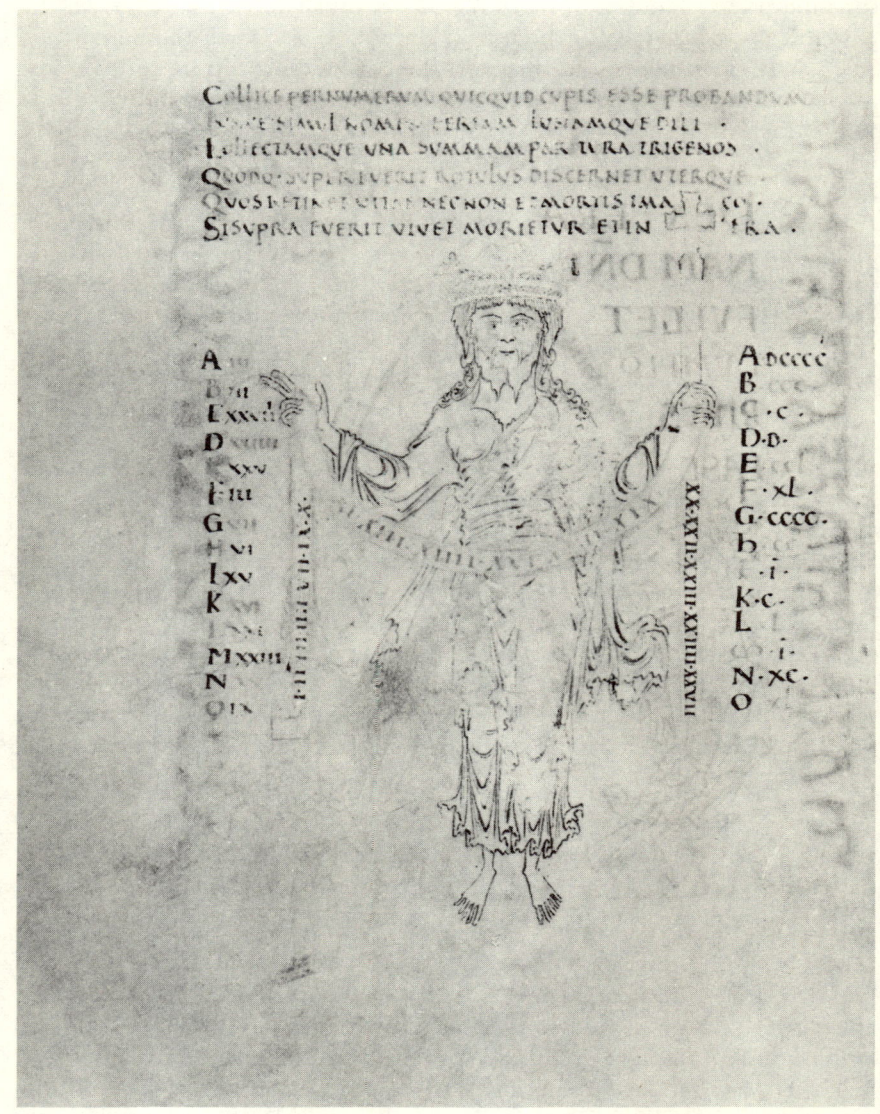

Plate 9. Christ-Vita. *The Leofric Missal*. Oxford, Bodleian Library MS. Bodley 579, fol. 49ᵛ. Reproduced with permission.

of Satan are from the early-ninth-century Trier Apocalypse (Trier, Stadtbibliothek MS. 31, fols. 66ʳ and 67ʳ) and the tenth-century copy done at Cambrai (Cambrai, Bibliothèque municipale MS. 386, fols. 38ʳ and 39ʳ) (Plate 10).[35] The Leofric Satan has borrowed this element,[36] but has transformed the image from a simple goat-headed figure into the most dramatic portrayal of Satan as a powerful enemy in all of early medieval art.

The use of feathered wings may also derive from Carolingian sources. They symbolize Satan as a fallen angel, and are often found in early medieval art, as in the Byzantine-inspired devil from the *Book of Kells* previously discussed. Since Satan was so often portrayed with wings, any number of sources could have influenced the Leofric artist. Possibly an early Christian cycle was consulted such as was used for the Cædmon manuscript. Another possible source, either directly or indirectly, is the Utrecht Psalter (Utrecht, Rijksuniversiteit MS. 32), composed at Reims in the 820's or 830's and known to have been in England by the end of the tenth century.[37] Throughout the manuscript, as in the illustration of Psalm 6 on folio 3ᵛ (Plate 11), we find demons with large feathered wings similar to those in the Leofric drawing. Also, like the Leofric monster, these demons are partially nude, covered only by a ragged loincloth. The iconographic similarities suggest either a direct link or at least a common ancestry for the Utrecht and Leofric demons.

However, although the Anglo-Saxons were influenced by Carolingian iconography, they were not mere copiers. In the Leofric drawing they created a new image of Satan by incorporating Carolingian elements into their zoomorphic tradition. By accentuating the beastly qualities and adding taloned hands and feet[38] and spurs, they produced a figure that was far more menacing than its predecessors. The Anglo-Saxon tendency to emphasize beastly attributes in personifications of demonic figures can also be seen in the Harley Psalter (British Library MS. Harley 603). This is a fairly close copy of the Utrecht Psalter created by four artists during the early eleventh century at Christ Church, Canterbury.[39] However, as Dimitri Tselos has noted, the iconography of the demons differs substantially from the model.[40] As has been seen in the illustration to Psalm 6 of the Utrecht Psalter (Plate 11), the devils are four winged men wielding spears, of whom two wear loincloths and two are nude. But in the copy, done by hand A of the group of four artists,[41] we see the addition of numerous beastly features (Plate 12). The two demons on the left have pendant breasts; each has a human right hand and a taloned left claw, and one has an animal head. The two on the right have animal heads with long snouts, pendant breasts, and large taloned claws for feet. Their nudity exposes male genitalia.

Plate 10. Satan. *The Cambrai Apocalypse.* Cambrai, Bibliothèque municipale MS. 836, fol. 36ʳ. Reproduced with permission.

Plate 11: Detail of devils. *The Utrecht Psalter*.
Utrecht, Bibliotheek der Rijksuniversiteit
MS. 32, fol. 3ᵛ. Reproduced with permission.

Plate 12. Detail of devils. *The Harley Psalter*. London, British Library MS.
Harley 603, fol. 3ᵛ. Reproduced with permission.

These hermaphroditic demons are far more beastly than their Carolingian models and clearly illustrate how the Anglo-Saxons adapted their sources to create a unique image.

This acquisition of beastly qualities, or, if you will, "iconographic demonization" is also found in another Canterbury work, the Cædmon manuscript of ca. 1000 (Oxford, Bodleian Library MS. Junius 11), which contains illustrations for *Genesis A* and *B*.[42] It is based on a lost early-Christian cycle reflecting the tradition of the Cotton Genesis, but again the artist did not make an exact copy of his model. Illustrations were modified and occasionally entire scenes were created so as closely to follow and explicate the written text. Thomas Ohlgren suggests that the shackling of Satan is a modification, for it is mentioned in the text but there is no evidence that Satan had ever previously been portrayed in chains in a Genesis cycle.[43] Another added element is the hell-mouth, which was used in this manuscript in the scenes depicting the fall of the rebel angels (on pages 3 and 16).[44] The hell-mouth is an indigenous Anglo-Saxon creation first found on a late-eighth- or early-ninth-century ivory, and replaces the open pit or human-head entrance used in early Christian art.[45] Although the hell-mouth is not specifically mentioned in the text, the artist incorporated this popular Anglo-Saxon image in his work. As to the figure of Satan himself, the artist seems to have followed the early Christian tradition of portraying him as a nude man, sometimes bearded and sometimes clean-shaven as on page 36 (Plate 13).[46] But we also find some non-traditional elements. In one example on page 20 (Plate 14) Satan has flaming hair, an attribute often associated with the vices,[47] while in another drawing on page 16 (Plate 15) he has clawed feet and a tail, as do some of his cohorts. Since the model for this work is lost we cannot have conclusive proof, but I suspect these demonic elements were not found in the model; rather, they were added by the artist as in the other Canterbury example, the copy of the Utrecht Psalter. This suggestion is reinforced by another but very different image of Satan by the same artist, found in the scene from *Genesis A* on page 3 which depicts the fall of the rebel angels (Plate 16). The strip-narrative character of the page suggests a late antique model, but like so many other scenes in the manuscript it was adapted to explicate the text. In the bottom frame the close integration of Satan with the Anglo-Saxon elements of the hell-mouth and the binding chains suggests that the figure was created for this scene rather than derived from an earlier Christian model. The iconography of Satan also supports this hypothesis. The taloned hands and feet, the wild or flaming hair, and the hairy, beastly body differ radically from the other portrayals of Satan in the manuscript. Again, I

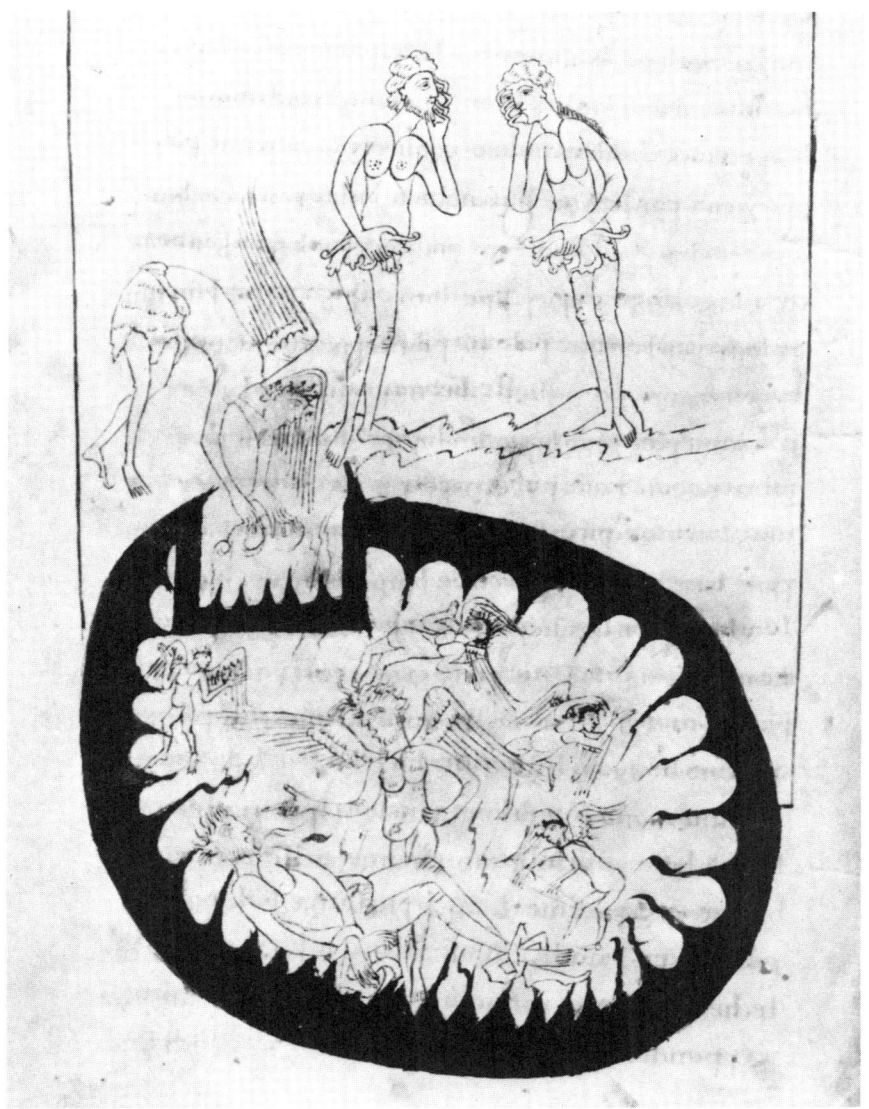

Plate 13: A Devil Reports to Satan. *The Caedmon Manuscript*. Oxford, Bodleian Library MS. Junius 11, p. 36. Reproduced with permission.

Plate 14: Detail of Satan. *The Caedmon Manuscript*. Oxford, Bodleian Library MS. Junius 11, p. 20. Reproduced with permission.

Plate 15: Satan and the Fall of the Rebel Angels. *The Caedmon Manuscript*. Oxford, Bodleian Library MS. Junius 11, p. 16. Reproduced with permission.

302 Demonic Elements

Plate 16: Satan and the Fall of the Rebel Angels. *The Caedmon Manuscript*. Oxford, Bodleian Library MS. Junius 11, p. 3. Reproduced with permission.

believe this figure to be an Anglo-Saxon adaptation reflecting the same demonizing tendencies found in the copy of the Utrecht Psalter and the Leofric Missal.

So far I have examined the tendency toward iconographic demonization at Glastonbury and Canterbury during the era of the millennium. This process continued throughout the Anglo-Saxon period, with some of the more important examples originating at the great manuscript center in Winchester. There is a demonized devil in a well-known illustration from the *Liber Vitae* (London, British Library MS. Stowe 944, fol. 7ʳ) from New Minster, Winchester (Plate 17), done in or shortly before 1031.[48] The central register depicts St. Peter hitting a devil on the head with a key in order to rescue a soul. The saved soul is to be presented to an angel on the left holding an open book, the *Liber Vitae,* while on the right a winged demon takes two condemned souls away. In the center of this register stands a devil with flaming hair. He holds an open book in his left hand, probably the *Book of the Devil* as on the Monasterboise High Cross. Presumably this book lists the names of the damned just as the *Liber Vitae* lists the elect. Like the Leofric and Canterbury demons, he has taloned hands and feet, wears a ragged loincloth, and has a beastly appearance, as does his comrade below who avidly shoves condemned souls into the mouth of hell. There is another devil by the same artist, although in smaller proportions, in a drawing representing the defeat of the devil. This scene was adapted from a motif in the Utrecht Psalter and is commonly known as "The Quinity" (London, British Library MS. Cotton Titus D. XXVII, fol. 75ʳ).[49] Here the devil is nude and has his wrists and legs tied together in such a way that Christ can use him as a footstool as described in Psalm 109:1.[50] However, even in this defeated state the devil is given attributes of demonic power. He has flaming hair, and like the Leofric Satan he has spurs protruding from the heels of his taloned feet, as does the devil in the lower register of the *Liber Vitae* drawing.

Another Winchester example of a demonized devil comes from the Tiberius Psalter (British Library MS. Cotton Tiberius C. VI), dated ca. 1050.[51] This work was certainly influenced by the Leofric Missal. The *Sphaera Apulei* in the Psalter is based on the earlier work, but the figure of Death is no longer closely equated with Satan, for many of the demonic attributes are missing.[52] However, we do find these attributes in the representations of Satan in the manuscript. He is portrayed in the scene of the third temptation of Christ on folio 10ᵛ (Plate 18). This beastly figure has taloned claws and feet, wears a ragged loincloth, and has flaming hair.[53] Satan is again portrayed four folios later, in a scene of the harrow-

Plate 17. Struggle for a Soul. *The Liber Vitae*. London, British Library MS. Stowe 944, fol. 7ʳ. Reproduced with permission.

Plate 18. The Temptation. *The Tiberius Psalter*. London, British Library MS. Cotton Tiberius C. VI, fol. 10ᵛ. Reproduced with permission.

ing of hell (Plate 19). This time in addition to the previously mentioned attributes, he is bound and has an animal face. As in the Leofric Satan, he also has the highly unusual feature of spurs protruding from his heels, knees, and elbows.

These examples from the 1030's and 1050's show the effectiveness and popularity of the demonizing tendencies in Anglo-Saxon iconography. Satan and his followers are portrayed in several other English manuscripts of the period, and so far as I have been able to determine they all have demonic attributes similar to the ones I have discussed (Plates 20–23).[54]

The final Anglo-Saxon example of the devil is found on an ivory cross in the Copenhagen Nationalmuseet carved for Gunhild, daughter of King Swend Estriden and niece of Cnut, shortly before her death in 1076.[55] The artist, Liutger, was probably an Anglo-Saxon or at least strongly influenced by English work. On the reverse of the cross is a Last Judgment (Plate 24). In the center is Christ in Judgment surrounded by angels, to his right are the elect facing toward him, and to his left are the damned facing away. The upper medallion shows Lazarus in the bosom of Abraham surrounded by the blessed, while the lower medallion shows a damned soul in hell. Part of this scene is damaged, obscuring the body of the devil and the flames of hell on the left side of the medallion. But fortunately the central figures are very clear. The devil has regained his horns and pointed ears; he also has the hairy body of a beast and large three-toed hoofs.

With this figure the devil has completed his metamorphosis. Until the Carolingian period he was usually depicted in a human form. Occasionally demonic features were added, as in the goat-headed Satan from the Trier Apocalypse; but it was not until the Anglo-Saxon artistic revival during the monastic reform, or more precisely during the century from the 970's to the 1070's, that we see a consistent development. By combining their indigenous zoomorphic traditions with Continental iconography the Anglo-Saxons transformed the devil into a truly demonic creature. This figure influenced twelfth-century demonology, not only in Anglo-Norman England but throughout the Continent.[56]

By focusing on the transformations in iconographic sources I have tried to emphasize the original and creative elements in Anglo-Saxon demonic iconography. I have also tried to integrate literary sources with the iconography, but clearly my focus has been on the art rather than the literature. A systematic investigation of demonic imagery in the vernacular and Latin literatures of Anglo-Saxon England and their sources is still needed. Through the use of concordances I have been able to check Anglo-Saxon poetry for demonic imagery, but I was not able to make a similar check

Plate 19. The Harrowing of Hell. *The Tiberius Psalter*. London, British Library MS. Cotton Tiberius C. VI, fol. 14^r. Reproduced with permission.

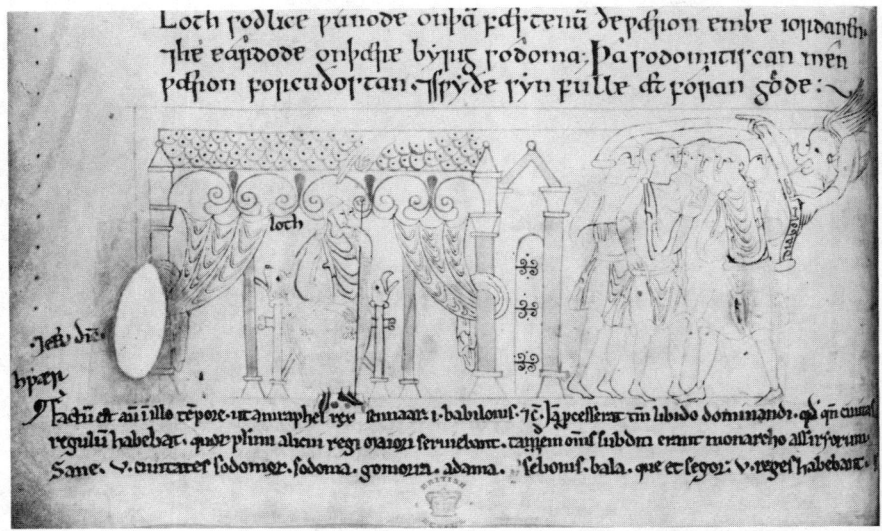

Plate 20. Lot in Sodom. *The Ælfric Paraphrase*. London, British Library MS. Cotton Claudius B. IV, fol. 23ᵛ. Reproduced with permission.

Plate 21. Hell. *The Marvels of the East*. London, British Library MS. Cotton Tiberius B. V, fol. 87ᵛ. Reproduced with permission.

Plate 22. Scenes from the Life of Saint Lawrence. *The Hereford Troper*. London, British Library MS. Cotton Caligula A. XIV, fol. 25ʳ. Reproduced with permission.

Plate 23. Scenes from the Life of Saint Martin. *The Hereford Troper*. London, British Library MS. Cotton Caligula A. XIV, fol. 29ʳ. Reproduced with permission.

Plate 24. Reverse. The Gunhild Cross. Copenhagen, Nationalmuseet. Reproduced with permission.

of the sermon literature, which I believe would be especially fruitful. I also suspect a detailed literary investigation could help to clarify Irish influence on Anglo-Saxon demonology. As a result of this symposium I hope we more fully realize that owing to the relatively small quantity of surviving Anglo-Saxon art and literature, parallel investigations are essential for a more accurate understanding of this unique civilization.

MEDIEVAL INSTITUTE
UNIVERSITY OF NOTRE DAME

Notes

1. For these and other examples of devils in medieval art see Gertrud Schiller, *Ikonographie der christlichen Kunst,* Vol. I (Gütersloh, 1966), pp. 153-55 and plates 389-400, and Vol. III (Gütersloh, 1971), pp. 41-66 and plates 99-162; Beat Brenk, "Teufel," *Lexikon der christlichen Ikonographie,* Vol. IV, ed. Engelbert Kirschbaum (Freiburg im Breisgau, 1972), pp. 295-300; and Beat Brenk, *Tradition und Neuerung in der christlichen Kunst des ersten Jahrtausends: Studien zur Geschichte des Weltgerichtsbildes,* Wiener Byzantinistische Studien, Band 3 (Vienna, 1966), pp. 172-213. On the Bamberg Apocalypse, which is not illustrated in the above works, see Ernst Harnischfeger, *Die Bamberger Apokalypse* (Stuttgart, 1981).

2. On the Spanish contribution to the iconography of the devil, see J. Yarza, "Diablo e infierno en la miniatura de los Beatos," in *Actas del simposio para el estudio de los codices del "Comentario al apocalipsis" de Beato de Liebana,* Vol. II (Madrid, 1980), pp. 229-58. On the Byzantine and classical elements see Brenk, *Tradition.*

3. Jonathan J. G. Alexander, *Insular Manuscripts: 6th to the 9th Century,* A Survey of Manuscripts Illuminated in the British Isles, Vol. 1 (London, 1978), pp. 71-76.

4. Brenk, *Tradition,* p. 196 and plate 26.

5. Françoise Henry, *Irish Art During the Viking Invasion 800-1200 A.D.* (Ithaca, 1967), p. 81 and Documentary Plate 6. See also Henry, *The Book of Kells* (New York, 1974), pp. 189-90 and plates 68 and 110; and Alexander, *Insular Manuscripts,* p. 74.

6. Eric H. L. Sexton, *A Descriptive and Bibliographical List of Irish Figure Sculptures of the Early Christian Period* (Portland, 1946), pp. 223-35; Henry, *Irish Art,* pp. 138-39, 172-73, and plates 83 and 106-07; and Peter Harbison, Homan Potterson, and Jeanne Sheehy, *Irish Art and Architecture* (London, 1978), pp. 62-64 and Pl. 47.

7. See Sexton, *Irish Figure Sculptures,* p. 229, for a variety of interpretations.

8. On *The Book of the Devil* see Brian Ó Cuív, "Some Early Devotional Verse in Irish," *Eriu,* 19 (1962), 6, Stanza 14; 20, n. 14a; and 24, Addendum.

9. Sexton, *Irish Figure Sculptures,* pp. 105-14; Henry, *Irish Art,* pp. 173-74 and

Pl. 110; and Harbison, *Irish Art,* pp. 63-64.

10. Henry, *Irish Art,* Pl. 95; for the various attributions, see Sexton, *Irish Figure Sculptures,* p. 111.

11. Harbison, *Irish Art,* pp. 59-61.

12. Henry, *Irish Art,* pp. 158 and 161.

13. Rupert Bruce-Mitford, *The Sutton Hoo Ship Burial,* Vol. II (London, 1978), pp. 478-522, figures 156, 164, 355-85, and plates 13-14; and see also Bruce-Mitford, *The Sutton Hoo Ship Burial: A Handbook,* 3rd ed. (London, 1979), pp. 110-11 and figures 80 and 84.

14. In addition to Bruce-Mitford, see Hans Weigert, "Demonology: The Barbarian World," *Encyclopedia of World Art,* Vol. IV (New York, 1961), pp. 322-23 and Pl. 176; and David M. Wilson and Ole Klindt-Jensen, *Viking Art,* 2nd ed. (Minneapolis, 1980), pp. 43, 75, and Pl. 3a. For another point of view and additional illustrations, see Karl Hauck, "Zum zweiten Band der Sutton Hoo-Edition," *Frühmittelalterliche Studien,* 16 (1982), 351-62, figures 29, 31, and plates 50-51. For a Continental example see Brenk, *Tradition,* figure 23; and for a general discussion of demonology from the early Germanic period through the Anglo-Saxon era see Diana Walzel, "The Sources of Medieval Demonology," Diss. Rice University 1974, pp. 105-51.

15. Kurt Böhner, "Der fränkische Grabstein vom Neiderdollendorf am Rhein," *Germania: Anzeiger der Romisch-Germanischen Komission der Deutschen Archäologischen Instituts,* 28 (1944-50), 63-75 and Table 13. See also Louis E. Jordan, "The Iconography of Death in Western Medieval Art to 1350," Diss. University of Notre Dame 1980, pp. 26-27, 186, and figures 6 and 7.

16. The Oseberg artifacts, collected near Tönsberg, Norway, are now in the Universitetets Oldsaksamling och Vikingskipshusets in Oslo. See Wilson and Klindt-Jensen, *Viking Art,* pp. 48-70, with various animal-head posts illustrated in figure 21 and plates 11, 12, 14, and 16c. For another view of the demon from Gustafson's sledge see Wiegert, "Demonology," Pl. 176, left side.

17. On the *Landnámabók,* a chronicle about early Viking settlements in Iceland, see Gwyn Jones, *The Norse Atlantic Saga* (London, 1964), pp. 114-42 and 224-25; see also Wiegert, "Demonology," p. 322.

18. *Beowulf,* ed. E. V. K. Dobbie, in Vol. IV of *ASPR* (New York, 1953), esp. ll. 86-114 and 710-836. On the description of Grendel and on a variety of monsters found in early Norse sagas, see Nora K. Chadwick, "The Monsters and Beowulf," in *The Anglo-Saxons: Studies in Some Aspects of Their History and Culture Presented to Bruce Dickins,* ed. Peter Clemoes (London, 1959), pp. 171-203. See also John B. Friedman, "The Marvels-of-the-East Tradition in Anglo-Saxon Art," below.

19. There are a variety of brief descriptions of Satan in *Juliana,* in *ASPR,* ed. G. P. Krapp and E. V. K. Dobie, Vol. III (New York, 1936), ll. 236-258.

20. Charles R. Sleeth, *Studies in Christ and Satan,* McMaster Old English Studies and Texts, Vol. 3 (Toronto, 1982), pp. 27-48.

21. *Beowulf,* ll. 159, 433, 592, and 816; and Robert E. Finnegan, *Christ and Satan: A Critical Edition* (Waterloo, Ontario, 1977), ll. 60 and 578. For these and additional examples see Jess B. Bessinger, ed., *A Concordance to the Anglo-Saxon Poetic*

Records (Ithaca, 1978), p. 1005; and Charles Abbetmeyer, "Old English Poetical Motifs Derived from the Doctrine of Sin," Diss. University of Minnesota 1903, p. 33.

22. For the images mentioned here, see *Christ and Satan,* ed. Finnegan, ll. 61, 78–79, 39–40, 97–98, 102, 27, 103 and 41–42 respectively. For a recent translation, see Robert E. Finnegan, "MS Junius XI *Christ and Satan* and the Latin Vernacular Prose Homiletic Traditions," Diss. University of Notre Dame 1969, pp. 241–71.

23. *Christ and Satan,* ed. Finnegan, pp. 42–49. For references to Satan in other Anglo-Saxon poems, see Bessinger, *Concordance,* p. 1005.

24. Felix, *The Life of Saint Guthlac,* ed. Bertram Colgrave (Cambridge, 1956), p. 114; and Joyce R. Galpern, "The Shape of Hell in Anglo-Saxon England," Diss. University of California at Berkeley 1977, p. 145.

25. Ælfric, *The Homilies of the Anglo-Saxon Church: The First Part Containing the Sermones Catholici or Homilies of Ælfric,* ed. Benjamin Thorpe (London, 1844–46), Vol. I, p. 103. Satan is described as a wolf (I, 241); a dragon (II, 177); and a lion (II, 449). For these and other examples see the excellent discussion in Galpern, "The Shape of Hell," pp. 144–45.

26. Elżbieta Temple, *Anglo-Saxon Manuscripts 900–1066, A Survey of Manuscripts Illuminated in the British Isles,* Vol. 2 (London, 1976), pp. 44–45 and Pl. 56. On Death and the Devil and the Leofric Missal, see Jordan, "Iconography," pp. 28–40, 225–26, and figures 9–11.

27. Henry E. Sigerist, "The Sphere of Life and Death in Early Medieval Manuscripts," *Bulletin of the History of Medicine,* 11 (1942), 292.

28. Francis Wormald, "An Eleventh-Century English Psalter with Pictures," *The Walpole Society,* 38 (1960–62), 8. Wormald is discussing the Tiberius Psalter (BL MS. Cotton Tiberius C. VI), but he also refers to the Leofric illustrations.

29. See Cambridge, Corpus Christi College MS. 23; BL MS. Cotton Cleopatra C. VIII and Additional MS. 24199. All are discussed in Temple, *Anglo-Saxon Manuscripts,* pp. 69–72 and Pl. 155–66.

30. See Salzburg, Studienbibliotek MS. Sign. V. I. H. 162, fol. 75^v. For other examples, see Adolf Katzenellenbogen, *Allegories of the Virtues and Vices in Medieval Art,* trans. J. P. Crick (London, 1939).

31. Adelheid Heimann, "Three Illustrations from the Bury St. Edmund Psalter and Their Prototypes," *Journal of the Warburg and Courtauld Institutes,* 29 (1966), 39–46.

32. The Old Saxon and Old High German magical charms footnoted by Heimann from A. A. Barb ("Animula Vagula Blandula ... Notes on Jingles, Nursery Rhymes and Charmes with an Excursus on Noththe's Sisters," *Folk-Lore,* 61 [1950], 26–30) mention Nesso the Demon of Disease and his family of nine. Such references do not prove any knowledge of the *Book of Resurrection.* Further, Mütherich discards Heimann's explanation of the illumination for Psalm 90 of the Stuttgart Psalter (fol. 107^r). She prefers to interpret the figure as the "Noonday Demon" (*demonio meridiano*) mentioned in the Psalm. See Florentine Mütherich, "Der Inhalt der Bilder," in *Der Stuttgart Bilderpsalter,* ed. Bernhard Bischoff, Bonifaz Fischer, Florentine Mütherich et al. (Stuttgart, 1965–68), II, 121.

33.   O felix olim servata lege Tonantis!
        Heu! post haec cecidi proterva mente superbus;
        Ultio quapropter funestum perculit hostem.
        Sex igitur comites mecum super aethera scandunt,
        Gnarus quos poterit per biblos pandere lector.

(from James Hall Pitman, *The Riddles of Aldhelm,* Yale Studies in English, Vol. 67 [New Haven, 1925] pp. 48-49). My translation is adapted from his more poetic rendering. For a critical text and references to parallel passages in other *aenigmata* collections, see "Aenigmata Aldhelmi," in *Collectiones Aenigmatum Merovingicae Aetatis,* ed. Fr. Glorie, CCSL, Vol. 133 (Turnhout, 1968), pp. 498-99, Riddle 81.

34. Reinhard Herbig, *Pan: Der Griechische Bockgott* (Frankfurt am Main, 1949), with numerous plates.

35. Richard Laufner and Peter Klein, *Trierer Apokalypse* (Graz, 1975), pp. 43-44, 93-97, 147-48. The devil on fol. 7^v is a later drawing over an erasure (see p. 7). Illustrations 19 and 34 show Satan from the Cambrai copy.

36. The artist was also possibly influenced by the Kynokephalos (or Cynocephalen), a mythical creature with a dog's head and a human body. See Laufer and Klein, *Trierer,* pp. 95-96 and Illustrations 38-39; and see Otto Schmitt, ed., *Reallexikon zur Deutschen Kunstgeschichte,* Vol. VI (Munich, 1973), cols. 766-73.

37. Dimitri Tselos, "English Manuscript Illustration and the Utrecht Psalter," *Art Bulletin,* 41 (1959), 137-49. On the vast literature concerning this Psalter see Suzy Dufrenne, *Les Illustrations du Psautier d'Utrecht* (Paris, 1978).

38. There is much emphasis on Grendel's taloned claws in *Beowulf;* see especially ll. 980-90. See also Chadwick, "Monsters," p. 173.

39. Temple, *Anglo-Saxon Manuscripts,* pp. 81-83.

40. Tselos, "English Manuscript Illumination," p. 139 and Illustrations 1 and 3.

41. This drawing is on fol. 3^v. On the artists see Francis Wormald, *English Drawings of the Tenth and Eleventh Centuries* (London, 1952), pp. 69-70. He also discusses later additions to the manuscript.

42. Temple, *Anglo-Saxon Manuscripts,* pp. 76-78.

43. Thomas H. Ohlgren, "The Illustrations of the Cædmonian Genesis," *Medievalia et Humanistica,* NS 3 (1972), 204.

44. The manuscript is paginated rather than foliated. On the scenes of hell see Galpern, "The Shape of Hell," pp. 29-43.

45. In London, The Victoria and Albert Museum: see John Beckwith, *Ivory Carvings in Early Medieval England* (New York, 1972), pp. 118-19 and Illustrations 1 and 16. See also Galpern, "The Shape of Hell," pp. 119-54. She has discovered another example which may predate the ivory (BL MS. Cotton Tiberius C. II., fol. 5^r).

46. On early representations of Satan see note 1 above.

47. As in the late-tenth-century Prudentius manuscript from the same scriptorium at Christ Church, Canterbury (BL MS. Cotton Cleopatra C. VIII). See Temple, *Anglo-Saxon Manuscripts,* pp. 70-71 and Illustrations 159-60 of the vice *ira.*

48. This drawing is often called a Last Judgment, as in David Talbot Rice, *English Art 871-1100* (Oxford, 1952), pp. 217-18; Wormald, *English Drawings,* p. 73; and

Temple, *Anglo-Saxon Manuscripts,* pp. 95-96 and Illustrations 247-48; but this is contested by Galpern, "The Shape of Hell," pp. 120-23, because Christ is not sitting in judgment. Because of the minor position of Christ it is probably more correct to refer to the drawing as a struggle between St. Peter and the devil for a soul, with heaven in the upper register and hell below.

49. Temple, *Anglo-Saxon Manuscripts,* pp. 94-95 and Illustration 245, and Ernst Kantorowitz, "The Quinity of Winchester," *Selected Studies* (New York, 1965), pp. 100-20 and figure 1. For a different view see Galpern, "The Shape of Hell," pp. 167-71.

50. For a miniature of Christ using Death as a footstool see Paris, Bibliothèque arsenal MS. 610, fol. 55^v, discussed in Jordan, "The Iconography of Death," pp. 58-59, 229-30, and figure 30.

51. Temple, *Anglo-Saxon Manuscripts,* pp. 115-17.

52. On the changes in the representation of Death see Jordan, "Iconography of Death," pp. 19-67.

53. The devil has a rather oddly placed set of wings filled with eyes. They are probably copied either from a representation of the four living creatures described in Apocalypse 4:8 as having three sets of wings filled with eyes, or from a cherub, the grade of angel usually depicted with this type of wing because of its association with the apocalyptic image. See Pseudo-Dionysius *On the Celestial Hierarchy,* Chap. vi.

54. These include the Ælfric Paraphrase of the Bible from Canterbury (BL MS. Cotton Claudius B. IV), which depicts Lucifer with a tail and his associates with ragged loincloths in the scene of the fall of the rebel angels (fol. 2^r: see Temple, *Anglo-Saxon Manuscripts,* Illustration 265). In a scene from Chapter xiii of *Genesis* (fol. 23^v) there is a winged dragonlike demon (plate 20) resembling the followers of Satan in the Leofric Missal. In a Marvels-of-the-East manuscript possibly from Winchester (BL MS. Cotton Tiberius B. V. fol. 87^v) there is a variety of monsters in the portrayal of hell (plate 21). Another manuscript, which unlike the above two is not based on an antique source, is the Hereford Troper (BL MS. Cotton Caligula A. XIV), possibly from Canterbury rather than Hereford, which includes demonic creatures in a scene from the life of St. Lawrence on fol. 25^r and in another scene from the life of St. Martin on fol. 29^r (plates 22-23). Other devils are found on the Godwine seal (see Beckwith, *Ivory Carvings,* plate 78); on a fragment from Bristol Cathedral (see Schiller, *Ikonographie,* Vol. III, plate 143); and in Paris, BN MS. Lat. 8824, fol. 6^r (see Robert M. Harris, "An Illustration in an Anglo-Saxon Psalter in Paris," *Journal of the Warburg and Courtauld Institutes,* 26 (1963), 255-57 and plate 31b.

55. Beckwith, *Ivory Carvings,* pp. 57, 127, and figures 82-87; see also Jordan, "Iconography of Death," pp. 51-52, 196-98.

56. The propensity for the demonic in Anglo-Norman art and the possibility of its influencing Continental art was discussed long ago: see Adolph Goldschmidt, "English Influence on Medieval Art of the Continent," in *Medieval Studies in Memory of A. Kingsley Porter,* ed. Wilhelm Koehler, Vol. II (Cambridge, Mass., 1939), pp. 719-22. However, specific examples are just beginning to be investigated. In

fact, since I wrote this paper it has been suggested that the Last Judgment tympanum of Ste. Foi in Conques was dependent on an English manuscript closely related to the Winchester Psalter (BL Cotton Nero C. IV): see Don Denny, "The Date of the Conques Last Judgment and Its Compositional Analogues," *Art Bulletin*, 66 (1984), 7–14.

The Marvels-of-the-East Tradition in Anglo-Saxon Art

JOHN BLOCK FRIEDMAN

Secular subject-matter in Anglo-Saxon illustrated manuscripts is quite rare, and when it does appear is often of a practical kind, such as herbal illustrations, or labors-of-the-months miniatures, or astronomical pictures. It is surprising, therefore, to find three luxurious Anglo-Saxon programs of secular illustration which do not have utilitarian reasons for their existence and which treat pagan subject-matter without the justification of didactic intent. These three manuscripts, collectively known as the Marvels-of-the-East or *Mirabilia* group,[1] provide us with one of the most lavish presentations of secular subject-matter to survive from early English art; they testify, as well, to an intense Anglo-Saxon interest in wonders and monsters and help to elucidate the aesthetic milieu of the poem *Beowulf*, which is, in fact, contained in one of the manuscripts. Not only are they representative of Anglo-Saxon secular iconography, they could be said to embody it and, like many forms of religious art of the place and period, they show an interesting mixture of native and imported motifs and styles.

Though the subject-matter of the *Mirabilia* group is ultimately classical in inspiration and their style classicizing, the peculiar emphasis or focus of presentation in the program of illustration seems to be English, and the fusion of these two elements, subject-matter and treatment, is a fascinating topic for study. Yet, to my knowledge, the attitude expressed by the *Mirabilia* artists towards their subjects has not attracted the attention of art historians, or of the recent editors of one manuscript of the group,[2] even though a literary source for it is extant.

At first glance, the *Mirabilia* manuscripts attest to the pervasive power of the Alexander legend in Europe,[3] for the travels of that conqueror through exotic lands filled with sights that Westerners had not seen and peoples of whom they had only heard play an important role in its transmission. An apocryphal letter of Alexander to Aristotle on the wonders of India called *Epistola Alexandri*[4] was a late imperial rhetorical exercise; it was translated into several European languages, and an Anglo-Saxon version of it is bound together with *Beowulf* in one of the *Mirabilia* manuscripts, British Library Cotton Vitellius A. XV. It tells of Alexander's campaign against Porus and his encounters with many marvels — vegetable, animal, human and sometimes a mixture of all three — while he was in India. Though its contents seem to lend themselves readily to a program of narrative illustration, no such illustrations have survived.

Closely related to the *Epistola Alexandri* in form and intention is another apocryphal letter, that of Pharasmanes to the emperor Hadrian;[5] it too seems to have been a rhetorical exercise. Alexander figures only marginally in this work, which concentrates more upon the monstrous races of men to be found in India than upon military exploits. In the process of translation into Anglo-Saxon, the Letter of Pharasmanes lost its epistolary structure and became more or less a *catalogue raisonnée* of eastern wonders. This translation gave rise to the pictures which concern us here. Though we have no surviving illustrations from the late antique manuscripts of the Letter, such must have existed and served as the ultimate source for the tenth-century Anglo-Saxon translation of the Letter with twenty-nine miniatures which forms part of Cotton Vitellius A. XV.[6] What appears to be an indirect copy of the Vitellius cycle survives in an early-eleventh-century codex with especially fine illustrations, now British Library Cotton Tiberius B. V.[7] This manuscript was in turn copied ca. 1120–40 by a much less accomplished artist in Oxford, Bodley 614.[8]

That a good deal of interpretation on the part of the artists who illustrated the *Mirabilia* manuscripts took place has occasionally been remarked on, but the precise nature and direction of that interpretation[9] and the ways in which it differs from artist to artist have yet to be explored. It is the purpose of the present paper to distinguish among these artists and their differing responses to their material and to suggest a literary source for the responses of the painter of Tiberius B. V.

The term catalogue raisonnée is a useful one to borrow from the art historian here because such catalogues traditionally record what the viewer might see in a gallery, but do not usually judge the works or present the beholder with a strong attitude towards their subject. And such is, in the main, the character of the *Mirabilia*-text descriptions of the many monstrous races of men to be found in the East. Typical entries would be: "Across the Brixon are tall men with giant limbs; they eat whomever they catch"; "The Donestre live on their own island in the Red Sea. They are partly human, speak various languages and entice men to them whom they eat, but they mourn the heads of their victims."[10] The *Epistola Alexandri* is more combative, but the tone is much the same. In the *Epistola*, Alexander does not merely observe marvelous creatures as part of the exotic landscape; he kills them when they try to resist his incursions into their land or captures them like rare fauna to bring home to an admiring populace. His contacts with these races are chiefly military in nature, for these creatures are obstacles to the conqueror's movement. Though most of his contacts are with animal rather than with human creatures, he does have a few with monstrous men. For example, he says, "Then we saw men and women hairy in the manner of beasts, who when we wished to approach nearer, threw themselves into a river." At another point in his journey, he observes, "Then we found a wood full of enormous Cynocephali, who, trying to provoke us, fled, shooting arrows."[11] We cannot know, of course, how artists might have responded to Alexander's words, but we would expect the *Mirabilia* artists to present the marvelous or frightening activities of these strange races of men with an impersonality similar to that of the words they are illustrating. But they do not. In varying degrees, these three artists take an attitude towards monsters — one of ethnocentric and rhetorical fear and distaste — which is very similar to that shown in *Beowulf* towards the Grendel family.

It has been suggested recently that the *Beowulf* poet knew another literary work concerning monstrous races of men and monstrous animals,[12] and I should like to argue that it was an acquaintance with this book which also affected the artist of at least one of the *Mirabilia* manuscripts, the painter of Tiberius B. V. This text was the *Liber Monstrorum*, compiled in England in the 740's, but which quickly migrated to the Continent. This treatise in three parts catalogues and describes human monsters, monstrous animals, and serpents, taking much of its information from the Letter of Pharasmanes tradition and the *Epistola Alexandri*, but also drawing upon Virgil and other Roman authors for monsters from classical mythology. The five known manuscripts of the work range in date from the ninth through the eleventh centuries and are found in England, Switzerland, Germany, and the Netherlands.[13] They are all unillustrated, but nothing precludes there having been an illustrated version of the work available in England in the tenth or eleventh century. The peculiar Latinity and learning of this work are such that it is hard to imagine any group outside of that of Aldhelm and his circle with the skill and sensibility to have composed it.[14] Interestingly, one thirteenth-century writer, Thomas of Cantimpré, the Dominican encyclopedist, quotes in his *De Naturis Rerum* from both the *Liber Monstrorum* and the riddles of Aldhelm, saying that both these works were composed by a certain learned man called Adelinus.[15] Adelinus is a Latinized form of Aldhelm, and at least three ecclesiastical calendars of the twelfth through the fifteenth centuries give his name in that form.[16] Though an Aldhelmian authorship for the *Liber Monstrorum* is an attractive idea, it must however remain only a tantalizing conjecture until further evidence is found.

My interest in the *Liber Monstrorum* is not in the problem of its authorship but in the possible influence on artists of its extreme hostility towards exotic races of men. No catalogue raisonnée this. Nor is the author's aversion a tactical attribute such as we find in the *Epistola Alexandri* where the races the conqueror encounters are seen as obstacles to Western imperialism. Rather, the Carolingian compiler describes unusual races of men in terms of a natural animosity between men and monsters much like that which we find in *Beowulf*. The style of rhetoric he employs plays on the idea of monstrosity, identifying it with Asianism—that is, excess, violence, and disorder—and describing unfamiliar peoples in terms which will heighten these qualities, in contrast to the Aristotelian moderation of ordinary, that is, Western, society. For example, giants in the *Liber* are described by words like these: "mirae magnitudinis," "mole vastissima," "immensis corporibus," and "immensis corporum magnitudinis." The innocuous pygmies of the *Mirabilia* tradition are called "invisum" or hostile, and the six-fingered men are called "bellicosissimi." By attributing to many of these races either cannibalism or the practice of eating raw meat, the author seems to go out of his way to stress the deviation of these beings from the norms of civilized humanity. Even in speaking of the scarcity of monsters, whom he believes to have been greatly reduced in number by the Flood, he evokes their violent nature by his choice of words like "eradicata," "subversa," and "revulsa."[17] One gets the strong impression from these verbs that a just God wished to eliminate monsters from the world.

Let us now look at some Anglo-Saxon pictures of these monstrous men, beginning with several from the earliest codex in the *Mirabilia* group, Vitellius A. XV, a manuscript whose provenance is unknown, but whose figure types are very like those of the earliest "Winchester" school,[18] such as we see in the donation scene of Æthelstan and St. Cuthbert in Cambridge, Corpus Christi College MS. 183, made about 937 (Plate 1).[19] Earlier I used the term catalogue raisonée to describe the *Mirabilia* texts, and perhaps this term is one which applies to the pictures in Vitellius as well. Certainly they are the most emotionally neutral of the *Mirabilia* group. The artist presents the fabled races of India in what we might call generic portraits, quite remote from involvement with the narrator or viewer. This can be made clear from

Plate 2: Cynocephalus. Marvels of the East, British Library Cotton Vitellius A. XV, fol. 100, c. 1000. Courtesy Trustees of the British Library.

Plate 1: Æthelstan presents his book to St. Cuthbert. Cambridge, Corpus Christi College MS. 183, fol. 1, Winchester, c. 937. Courtesy Corpus Christi College.

several of the better-preserved miniatures in the cycle, a dog-headed man (Plate 2); a Blemmyae, or man with his face on his chest (Plate 3); a Panoti — there seems not to have been a singular of this word — or man with giant ears (Plate 4); and finally a Hostes, or a kind of animal-headed giant (Plate 5), races of whom were believed to live in India. The figure of the Blemmyae is placed well within his frame in a static pose, standing, as does the dog-headed man, on a small mountain or crag; these landscapes play no significant role in the miniatures. Somewhat more dramatic are the Panoti and the Hostes. The former's ear and feet emerge from the frame which surrounds him. This is a strongly classicizing technique quite in keeping with the subject-matter of this portion of Vitellius A. XV, and it can be well studied in Anglo-Saxon Prudentius manuscripts[20] made under Continental influence, such as Cambridge, Corpus Christi College MS. 23 (Plate 6). The tapered legs in the Vitellius pictures are reminiscent as well of Prudentius *Psychomachia* drawings. The Hostes, whose name means literally "the enemy," appears as a black giant, holding a human limb. He shares his frame with a Lertex, a wonderful sheep-fleeced, donkey-eared, bird-footed beast, and a shepherd, who is apparently present because of the sheeplike aspect of the Lertex. Though the Hostes shows a certain degree of energy in his arm gesture and the limb he holds suggests that he is dangerous to man — "cito comedunt," says the text — he gets only a small percentage of the frame. His black coloring, however, does make him stand out a bit from the other figures done in blues, brown ochre, and yellow.

On the whole, the artist of Vitellius seems to have viewed his figures passively. There is little suggestion of the kind of interaction between Eastern and Western peoples that is described elsewhere in the *Mirabilia* texts, the *Epistola Alexandri,* and *Beowulf,* if we assume that these works were all together in the codex at the time the artist painted his *Mirabilia* pictures. In the *Epistola,* as we have seen, monstrous men run from Alexander's soldiers or attack them, while *Beowulf* makes the monstrous Grendel family a menace to the Danes on their own ground, penetrating the sleeping and dining quarters of Hrothgar's court. The figures in Vitellius, however, are presented with little attempt at narrative or drama and stand like curious statues on display.

A considerable change in attitude is evident in the work of the artist of Tiberius B. V, which one scholar attributes to Winchester[21] and its most recent editors to Christ Church, Canterbury, because of the emphasis within other portions of the manuscript on Sigeric and his pilgrimage and on Canterbury matters in the genealogies.[22] Tiberius B. V was made about 1050 and shows a striking awareness of late antique and Continental style

Plate 4: Panoti. Marvels of the East, fol. 104r.

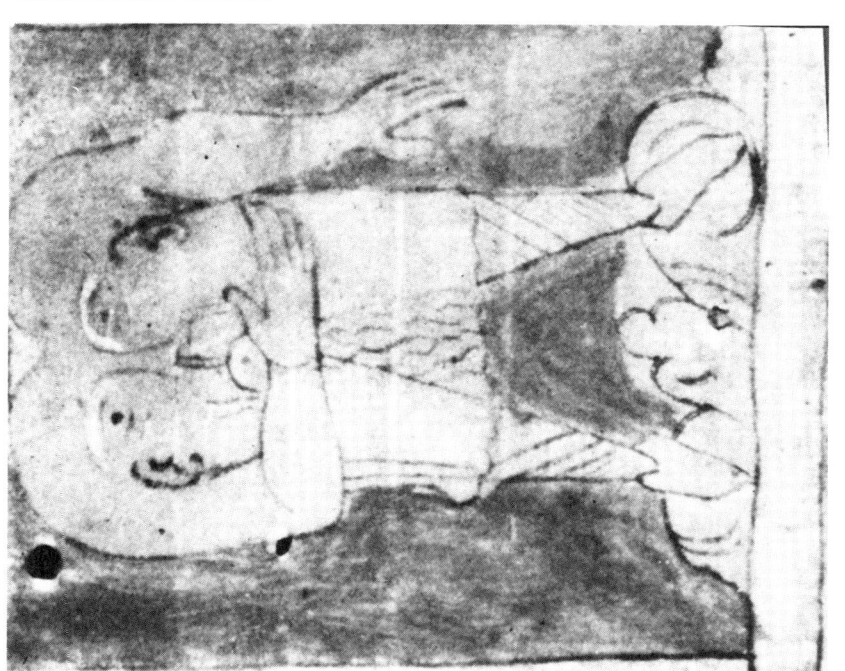

Plate 3: Blemmyae. Marvels of the East, fol. 102v.

Plate 5: Hostes. Marvels of the East, fol. 102ʳ.

Plate 6: Story of Lot and Abraham. Prudentius, *Psychomachia*, Cambridge, Corpus Christi College MS. 23, fol. 2, c. 975. Courtesy Corpus Christi College.

by way of such works as the Utrecht Psalter[23] and the Berne *Physiologus*.[24] The artist's fondness for nudes, moreover, and his ability to handle classical subject-matter suggest that he was acquainted with Alexandrian art as it might have been passed on in ivory carving (Plate 7)[25] or in manuscripts like the Paris Psalter (Plate 8).[26] Another classicizing touch is the fact that the manuscript offers to the reader both the original Latin and the Anglo-Saxon translation of the *Mirabilia* text immediately below.[27]

Let us consider some pictures from this handsome codex which represent the same races we saw in Vitellius A. XV, as well as a few new ones. Here are a Cynocephalus (Plate 9); a Panoti (Plate 10); a Blemmyae (Plate 11); a Donestre (Plate 12); and a Hostes (Plate 13), in company with a Homo dubius (Plate 14) and a "Wife-giver" (Plate 15). It can be seen that in each miniature the artist makes use of both vertical and lateral compression of the figure by its frame, such as we associate with Hiberno-Saxon pocket Gospels like the Book of Mulling,[28] where the inhabitant seems uneasy in the frame or oversteps the frontiers of the frame to create drama and a feeling of danger to the onlooker. In the cases of the Homo dubius and the Panoti, Cynocephalus, Hostes, and the Blemmyae, we find mountain tops or crags and rather plain borders similar to those in Vitellius A. XV, but there is a changed relation between backgrounds and borders and inhabitants. The tiny crags of Vitellius A. XV have in Tiberius become the sketchy, nervous crags inclined to the right which we recognize from the Utrecht Psalter[29] and its English copies (Plate 16) and from the Berne *Physiologus* (Plate 17). The Blemmyae's hands grip the frame as if to force it outward, and his feet come out of pictorial space, much as do the finger of the Homo dubius, the Donestre's foot, and the crown of the Panoti's head. There is, as well, a strong feeling of vertical compression in the Tiberius miniatures of the Blemmyae, Cynocephalus, and especially of the Hostes, contributing to a sense of the figures being confined by a frame; the visual metaphor of their stepping into the viewer's world suggests the possibility of actual confrontation. Similar compression is evident in the scene of Jacob and the lion in the Berne *Physiologus*.

We recall, too, that the Vitellius-artist dressed his figures in classicizing costume, while the Tiberius-painter makes them naked in order to reveal fully the anatomical oddity of races like the Blemmyae and the hybridization of human and animal in such figures as the Cynocephalus and Homo dubius. Certain miniatures make an interesting use of costume and nudity. A striking ethnocentrism appears in the miniatures of the Wife-givers and the Donestre. The Wife-givers, who have no name in the text, present wives to any Western traveller who comes in contact with them. Here we

Plate 8: David and Melodia. *Paris Psalter*, BN Gr. Coislin 139, fol. 16, c. 750. Courtesy Bibliothèque Nationale.

Plate 7: Orpheus and the animals. Ivory pyx, Abbey of San Colombano, Bobbio, c. A.D. 400.

Plate 10: Panoti. Marvels of the East, fol. 83ᵛ.

Plate 9: Cynocephalus. Marvels of the East, British Library Cotton Tiberius B.V, fol. 80ʳ.

330   *The Marvels of the East*

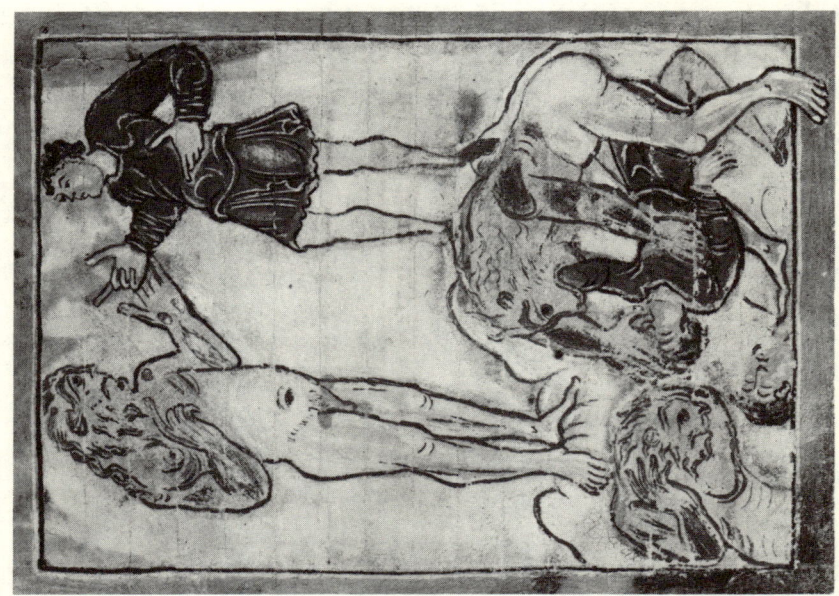

Plate 12: Donestre. Marvels of the East, fol. 83ᵛ.

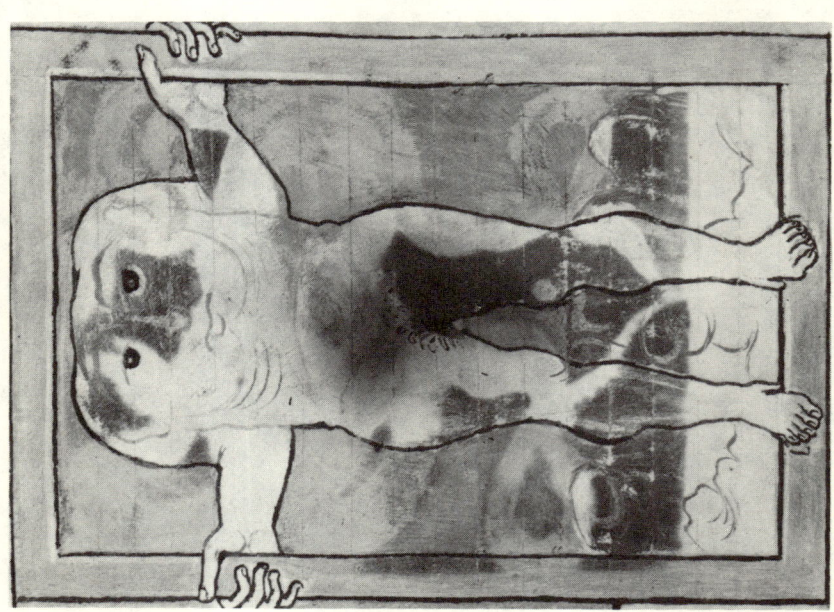

Plate 11: Blemmyae. Marvels of the East, fol. 82ʳ.

Plate 14: Homo dubius, Marvels of the East, fol. 82ᵛ.

Plate 13: Hostes. Marvels of the East, fol. 81ᵛ.

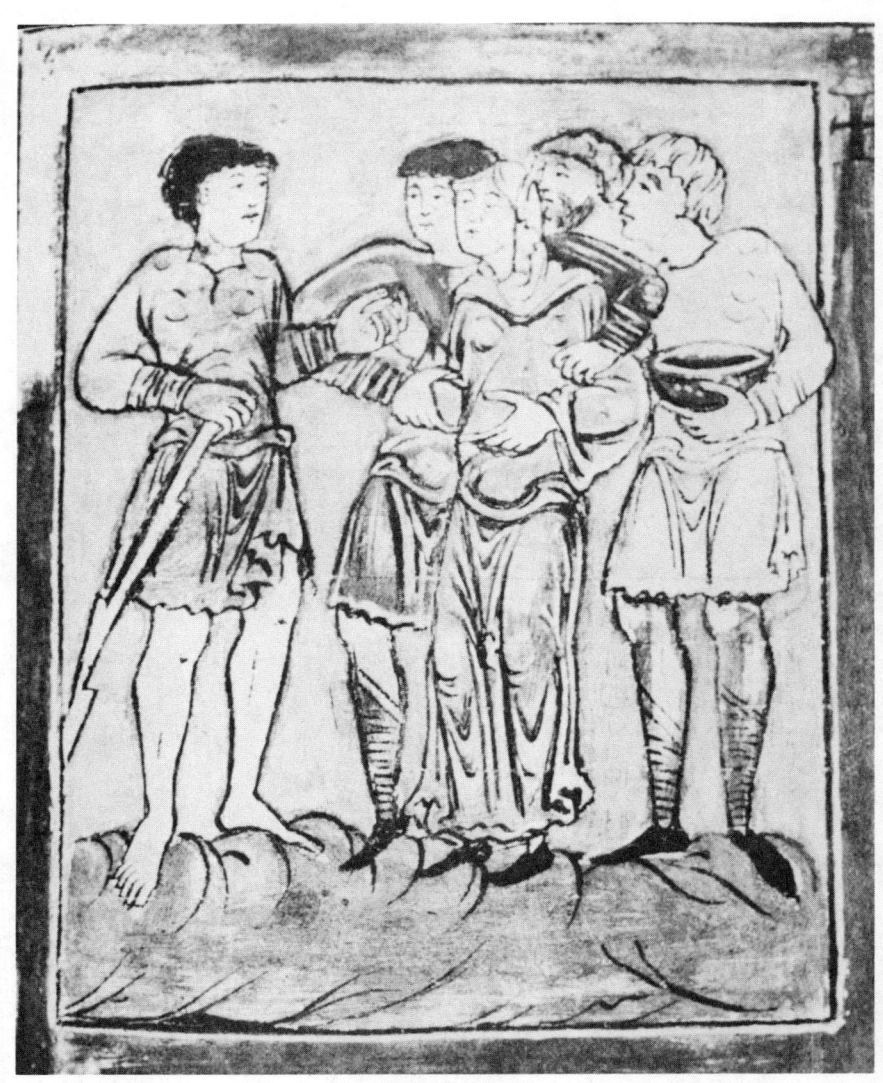

Plate 15: "Wife—givers," Marvels of the East, fol. 86ʳ.

Plate 16: Group with martyr's palms and mountain, Psalm 3, *Utrecht Psalter*, Utrecht, Universiteitsbibliothek MS. 32, fol. 2, c. 800.
Courtesy Utrecht University Library.

Plate 17: Jacob and Lion, *Physiologus*, Berne Municipal Library MS. 318 fol. 7^r, c. 800.
Courtesy Municipal Library, Berne.

see a wife looking reluctant as a Westerner appears ready to claim her. These people, of course, have no anatomical peculiarities, and so the Tiberius-artist paints them fully dressed and looking much as does their guest. Only the elbow of the figure on the left, which protrudes from the frame, and the crag on which the group stands hint at their connection with other monstrous races. They come the closest to "normal" behavior and so their costume echoes this. Rather more is made of the contrast between East and West in the miniature of the Donestre, who is naked and of far greater size than his victim, who is dressed in classicizing Western attire. The scene is a type of narrative with the various elements of the text portrayed sequentially.[30] In the lower right, the Donestre reveals his true savagery as he straddles his victim with his leg and foot coming out of pictorial space into the border.[31] Such scenes indicate by implication Western weakness or defenselessness in contacts with these monstrous races.

The handsome borders of Tiberius are then used for good effect; their plainness helps to focus our attention on the parts of monstrous anatomy which protrude from pictorial space, which would be more difficult if the borders were typical "Winchester" borders with ornate corner pieces.[32] It seems probable that the Tiberius-painter has borrowed his borders from the Berne *Physiologus*. The brick-red, wide border with black inner lining of the Berne miniatures is common in Tiberius A. XV, though the Anglo-Saxon manuscript uses white outlining and it is the blue and green forms of these borders for the *Mirabilia* pictures which are picked out in black. The green and red borders of Tiberius are echoed by alternating green and red initials for the texts below.

The third of the *Mirabilia* group is a more-or-less-direct copy of the second. Bodley 614 drops the Anglo-Saxon translation of the *Mirabilia* text, and shows, in addition to the hand of a less skilled artist, other evidences of simplification and cost-cutting. For the miniature of the Hostes (Plate 18), for example, there is no attempt at a naturalistic background, and some scholars would attribute the slight vertical compression to the more generally horizontal layout of the pages,[33] perhaps to make more economical use of the membrane.

The crags and mountains which we saw depicted by the Tiberius-painter indicate the essential savagery and incivility of the monstrous races, because mountains were regarded in the Middle Ages with fear and loathing.[34] Indeed, mountains of all sorts were taken as examples of God's anger at sinful man as late as the eighteenth century. It is worth noting that the Tiberius-painter's two most likely sources for his illusionistic mountains, the Utrecht Psalter and the Berne *Physiologus,* rarely depict people on their mountains.

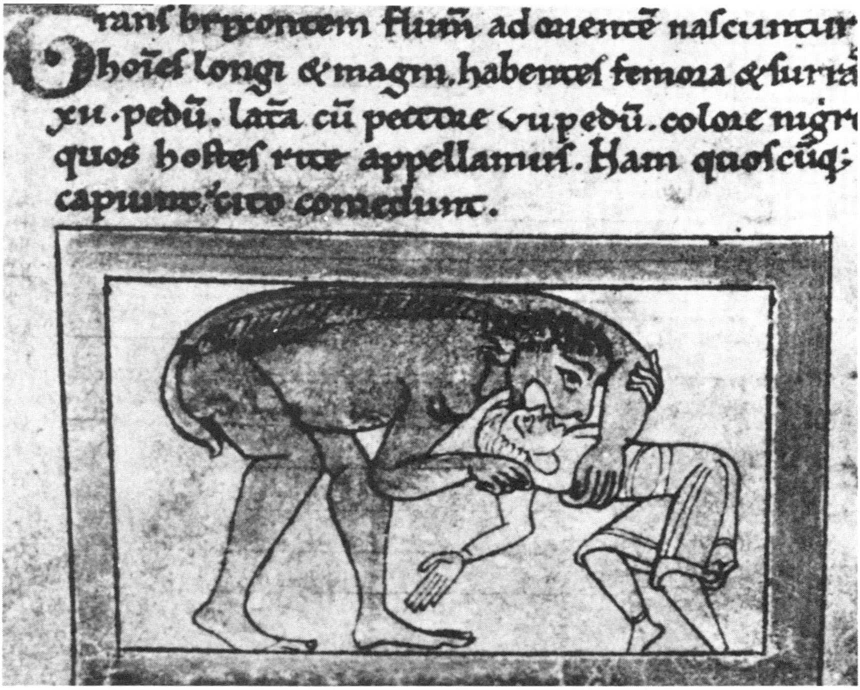

rans br prontem flum ad oriente nascuntur
homines longi & magni, habentes femora & surra
xu. pedu. lata cu pectore v. pedu. colore nigri
quos hostes uoc appellamus. Nam quoscuq;
capiunt cito comedunt.

Plate 18: Hostes, Marvels of the East, Oxford, MS. Bodley 614, fol. 40ᵛ, c. 1120–40.
Courtesy Bodleian Library, Oxford.

In the Berne miniature, for example, Jacob and the lion stand on a grassy sward in front of a backdrop of mountains. Utrecht and its copies place Moses on a mountain to receive the Law (fol. 86ʳ) but otherwise have persons on hills or in valleys, but very infrequently on mountains.

We find such fear and hostility to mountains clearly expressed in the *Liber Monstrorum*, for the fiction with which the author begins his work — that his treatise was written to answer certain questions posed to him by an unnamed patron — allows him to describe the sorts of landscapes peculiarly hospitable to monstrous men:

> You have asked about the hidden parts of the earth and if truly there were as many species of monstrous beings as have been reported in the hidden corners of the earth, beyond the deserts and islands of Ocean, and in the remote hiding places of the furthest mountains. You have desired me specifically to speak of the monsters that strike mankind with the maximum of awe and terror such as the monstrous progeny of men.[35]

Thus "remote hiding places of the furthest mountains" are important to this author's conception of monstrosity and of the emotions it engenders. In his constant use of mountains and crags as important adjuncts to his figures, the Tiberius-artist seems to share in this view of mountains. In one case, that of the miniature containing black men who live in mountains which cannot be reached because they are always burning (Plate 19), which is not based on the *Mirabilia* text but added from Isidore of Seville, the figures themselves are dwarfed by the red (burning?) mountains on which they stand; the mountains appear to be the main characters of the scene and the men are not even black, which further minimizes their dramatic force.

It is possible that these attitudes of extreme hostility towards monstrous races of men present in the *Liber Monstrorum* influenced the artist of the Tiberius miniatures, or alternatively that there were extant in England manuscripts of the *Liber* with accompanying illustrations which reflected the attitudes of its compiler, and that these miniatures served as the source for some of the attitudes we have seen in the Tiberius pictures. Either Winchester or Canterbury could have had such a manuscript of the *Liber Monstrorum;* these libraries were known to have possessed classicizing works of art in the Carolingian Tours or Reims style[36] which may have influenced the Tiberius-painter's use of color, costume, and the relationship of inhabitant to border. We know, moreover, that the Tiberius-painter had access to a Carolingian Aratus manuscript with miniatures which he copied

Plate 19: Black men on burning mountains,
Marvels of the East,
British Library Cotton Tiberius B.V, fol. 87ʳ.

Plate 20: Orion, Cicero's translation of *Aratea*,
British Library Cotton Tiberius B.V, fol. 39ʳ.

in another part of the codex.[37] It too must have been very much a tour de force of late antique style to judge from the Tiberius-artist's adaptation of it (Plate 20). In short, the *Liber Monstrorum* may have provided a rhetorically manipulated and heightened sense of man's dramatic interactions with monsters for the Tiberius-artist, who could have heard the *Liber* read at one of these two great centers of learning or have seen there an illustrated copy of Continental origin.

The demonic energy which the author of the *Liber* sensed about the monstrous races, which made them ever ready to burst into the world of Westerners, was translated from word to picture as we have seen. But it was also an energy which seemed to have had an iconographic birth, flowering, and senescence within the period in which the *Mirabilia* group was created. Of the 29 miniatures illustrating marvels in Cotton Vitellius A. XV, 15 depicted monstrous races of men. The Tiberius and Bodley versions, though apparently following different archetypes, increase this number, even going outside the *Mirabilia* text to do so. Tiberius has 38 miniatures, of which 18 show monstrous men. All of these, as we have seen from a group of representative examples, are sensitively and imaginatively treated. Bodley 614 has 39 colored drawings for the section on marvels of which 26 are monstrous men. The attitudes which we have seen had perhaps begun to fall out of favor by the twelfth century; with the rise of Crusader contacts with the East and the growth of missionary zeal for conversion, monstrous creatures of all sorts began to appear in favorable contexts in European art as part of the mysterious extremes of the universe which could be reached by the power of the Word, as we see in the Vézelay tympanum, with its collection of some of the same races presented in the Anglo-Saxon miniatures, but who stand here in attitudes of contemplation listening to the Word.[38]

In a larger sense, of course, my investigation into the Marvels-of-the-East tradition will, I hope, remind all Anglo-Saxonists, particularly those working more or less exclusively in literature, that we can learn much about verbal images and their contexts from studying contemporary visual images and their backgrounds. We may not always — or often enough at any rate — be able to affirm or deny a particular connection, or to settle a question regarding direct or indirect sources. But more often than not in the study of Anglo-Saxon art and in the pursuit of visual sources, be they Continental or Insular, Christian or classical, we can find those relationships that explain and illuminate the broader tradition, the deeper texture, and the wider significance of a culture whose achievements have not yet had their final description. I can add another voice to the call given above by J. E. Cross: What indeed are we waiting for?

UNIVERSITY OF ILLINOIS
AT URBANA-CHAMPAIGN

Notes

1. Until recent years, the standard edition and study of these manuscripts and illustrations has been M. R. James, ed., *The Marvels of the East* (Oxford, 1929). Now the texts have been re-edited by J. D. Pickles, "Studies in the Prose Texts of the *Beowulf* Manuscript," Diss. Cambridge University 1971 and Paul Alan Gibb, "Wonders of the East: A Critical Edition," Diss. Duke University 1977.

2. See P. McGurk et al., eds., *An Eleventh-Century Anglo-Saxon Illustrated Miscellany (British Library Cotton Tiberius B. V Part I)*, EEMF, Vol. 21 (Copenhagen, 1983).

3. The best study of this subject is that of D. J. A. Ross, *Alexander Historiatus* (London, 1963). See also W. J. Aerts et al., eds., *Alexander the Great in the Middle Ages* (Nijmegen, 1978).

4. This text has been edited by W. W. Boer, *Epistola Alexandri ad Aristotelem* (rpt. Meisenheim am Glan, 1973). See also Vincent Dimarco and Leslie Perelman, eds., *The Middle English Letter of Alexander to Aristotle* (Amsterdam, 1978).

5. See H. Omont, "Lettre à l'Empereur Adrien sur les merveilles de l'Asie," *Bibliothèque de l'Ecole des Chartes*, 74 (1913), 507-15, and Edmond Faral, "Une Source latine de l'Histoire d'Alexandre: la lettre sur les merveilles de l'Inde," *Romania*, 43 (1914), 199-215, 353-70.

6. This manuscript has been described by Elżbieta Temple, *Anglo-Saxon Manuscripts 900-1066*, Vol. II of J. J. G. Alexander, ed., *A Survey of Manuscripts Illuminated in the British Isles* (London, 1976), p. 72, No. 52.

7. See note 2 above.

8. This manuscript is discussed by Otto Pächt and J. J. G. Alexander, *Illuminated Manuscripts in the Bodleian Library Oxford* (Oxford, 1966-73), Vol. III, No. 156, and by C. M. Kauffmann, *Romanesque Manuscripts 1066-1190,* Vol. III of J. J. G. Alexander, ed., *A Survey of Manuscripts Illuminated in the British Isles* (London, 1975), p. 77, No. 38.

9. McGurk, for example, would argue that the "impression is of closeness to a Rheims model and it is unlikely that many significant variations or alterations were introduced by the [Tiberius] artist" (*An Eleventh-Century Anglo-Saxon Illustrated Miscellany*, p. 99).

10. For texts, see McGurk et al., eds., *An Eleventh-Century Anglo-Saxon Illustrated Miscellany*, fols. 81^v and 83^v.

11. *Epistola Alexandri*, ed. Boer, pp. 32-33.

12. See Leslie Whitbread, "The *Liber Monstrorum* and *Beowulf*," *Mediaeval Studies*, 36 (1974), 452.

13. The work has been edited and a *stemma codicum* presented by Corrado Bologna as *Liber Monstrorum de Diversis Generibus* (Milan, 1977). The discovery of a new manuscript of the work, at St. Gallen, is discussed by Ann Knock, "The 'Liber Monstrorum': An Unpublished Manuscript and Some Reconsiderations," *Scriptorium*, 32 (1978), 19-28.

14. Whitbread, pp. 455-61.

15. This problem is more fully discussed, with documentation, in my study *The Monstrous Races in Medieval Art and Thought* (Cambridge, Mass., 1981), pp. 248-49, n. 43.

16. These manuscripts are University of Illinois Library De Ricci MS. 140, Horae, Sarum use, fol. 5^v; Munich, CLM 835, Psalter with calendar, Gloucester use, fol. 3; and Notre Dame University Library MS. 4, Horae, ca. 1470. On this last item, see James A. Corbett, ed., *Catalogue of the Medieval & Renaissance Manuscripts of the University of Notre Dame* (Notre Dame, 1978), p. 32.

17. These quotations are drawn from *Liber Monstrorum*, ed. Bologna, pp. 38, 40, 54.

18. Temple, *Anglo-Saxon Manuscripts*, p. 12, No. 17.

19. This manuscript is described by Temple (pp. 37-38, No. 6).

20. On this subject see Richard Stettiner, *Die illustrierten Prudentius-Handschriften: Tafelband* (Berlin, 1905), and Helen Woodruff, *The Illustrated Manuscripts of Prudentius* (Cambridge, Mass., 1930).

21. Temple, *Anglo-Saxon Manuscripts*, pp. 104-5, No. 87.

22. McGurk et al., *An Eleventh-Century Anglo-Saxon Illustrated Miscellany*, pp. 108-9.

23. See F. Wormald, *The Utrecht Psalter* (Utrecht, 1953), p. 12.

24. See Christoph von Steiger and Otto Homburger, eds., *Physiologus Bernensis, voll-Faksimile* (Basel, 1964), pp. 32-33, and Helen Woodruff, "The Physiologus of Bern: A Survival of Alexandrian Style in a Ninth Century Manuscript," *Art Bulletin*, 12 (1930), 226-30.

25. On this general subject, see A. Goldschmidt, *Die Elfenbeinskulpturen* (Berlin, 1926); W. F. Volbach, *Elfenbeinarbeiten der Spätantike und des frühen Mittelalters* (Mayence, 1952); and Danielle Gaborit-Chopin, *Ivoires du moyen âge* (Paris, 1978). For the Bobbio pyx and a group of other ivories of obvious Alexandrian influence, see Joseph Natanson, *Early Christian Ivories* (London, 1953), pp. 24, 28-29, 30, and figures 3, 22, 23, 24, 26, 27, 30, 32-34.

26. See H. Buchthal, *The Miniatures of the Paris Psalter* (rpt. Nendeln, Liechtenstein, 1968) and Kurt Weitzmann, "Der Pariser Psalter," *Jahrbuch für Kunstwissenschaft*, 6 (1929), 178-94.

27. This translation is discussed in McGurk et al., *An Eleventh-Century Anglo-Saxon Illustrated Miscellany*, pp. 94-95.

28. See, for example, Carl Nordenfalk, *Celtic and Anglo-Saxon Painting* (New York, 1977), pp. 126-27, figure 48.

29. See Suzy Dufrenne, *Les Illustrations du psautier d'Utrecht* (Paris, 1978), pp. 201-5;

and, generally, F. Bucher, "Medieval Landscape Painting: An Introduction," in *Medieval and Renaissance Studies: Proceedings of the Southeastern Institute of Medieval and Renaissance Studies*, ed. J. M. Headley (Chapel Hill, 1968), pp. 119–69.

30. See Otto Pächt, *The Rise of Pictorial Narrative in Twelfth-Century England* (Oxford, 1962).

31. A concise discussion of the space in miniatures of this period can be found in John White, *The Birth and Rebirth of Pictorial Space* (Boston, 1967), pp. 219–35.

32. See, for instance, the Benedictional of St. Ethelwold, BL Add. MS. 49598, in Temple, *Anglo-Saxon Manuscripts*, pp. 51–52; and for a variety of examples, F. Wormald, *The Benedictional of St. Ethelwold* (London, 1959). The remark by Ernst Kitzinger (*Early Medieval Art* [Bloomington, Ind., 1964], p. 62) that "the frames in the early Winchester manuscripts ... are much more than a mere border for a figure scene; they form an essential part of the composition" can justly be applied to the work of the Tiberius-painter.

33. McGurk et al., *An Eleventh-Century Anglo-Saxon Illustrated Miscellany*, p. 98.

34. See Marjorie Hope Nicolson, *Mountain Gloom and Mountain Glory* (New York, 1963).

35. *Liber Monstrorum*, ed. Bologna, Book I, Prologue, p. 34: "De occulto orbis terrarum situ interrogasti et si tanta monstrorum essent genera credenda quanta in abditis mundi partibus per deserta et Oceani insulas et in ultimorum montium latebris nutrita monstrantur, et precipue de his tribus orbis terre generibus respondere petebas, que maximum formidinis terrorem humano generi incutiunt, ut de monstruosis hominum...."

36. Fleury has also been noted as a source of classicizing influence on Anglo-Saxon painting. Woodruff has suggested that Berne 318 may have come from Fleury ("The Physiologus," p. 233). For the connections between Fleury and Anglo-Saxon monasticism, see H. Dauphin, "Le Renouveau monastique en Angleterre au Xe siècle et ses rapports avec la réforme de saint Gérard de Brogne," *Revue Bénédictine*, 70 (1960), 177–96; F. M. Stenton, *Anglo-Saxon England* (Oxford, 1971), pp. 447–51; and F. Wormald, "Continental Influence of English Medieval Illumination," *Transactions of the Fourth International Congress of Bibliophiles* (1967), pp. 4–16.

37. On the Aratea material of Tiberius B. V see McGurk et al., *An Eleventh-Century Anglo-Saxon Illustrated Miscellany*, pp. 67–78.

38. See Adolph Katzenellenbogen, "The Central Tympanum at Vézelay: Its Encyclopedic Meaning and Its Relation to the First Crusade," *Art Bulletin*, 26 (1944), 141–51.

Part Three
Interdisciplinary Approaches: The Dream of the Rood

The Devotional Context of the Cross Before A.D. 1000

SANDRA McENTIRE

In order to understand the milieu out of which arose crosses such as those at Ruthwell and Bewcastle and poems in Old English such as *The Dream of the Rood* and *Elene* in the Vercelli Codex, it is useful to sort out as clearly as possible the various elements of devotion, theology, and liturgy which provided the background and possible inspiration for these works. Several writers have already drawn attention to the monastic devotional traditions of the Anglo-Saxon period which influenced poetic literature and the iconography of the crosses.[1] Some have elucidated the links between the theology of judgment and eschatology and the literary and sculptural arts.[2] In the quest for an understanding of the broad devotional background which informed the spiritual milieu of the Golden Age of Northumbria, this study will focus on three additional elements. These include, first, a reconsideration of the personal devotion of the Sign of the Cross; second, a preliminary investigation of the motif of the Cross as a cosmological symbol; and, third, a brief examination of the theological and devotional meaning of pilgrimage as it relates to the Cross. The primary historical event against which this study is cast is the arrival and subsequent veneration of pieces of the True Cross in Anglo-Saxon England. I shall draw from Cross poetry and sculpture for topical examples.

In the last hundred years, scholars have provided summaries of the historical events surrounding the cult of the Cross.[3] One of the events which gave rise to a particularly popular tradition was the discovery of the Cross attested by such Church Fathers as Chrysostom and Cyril.[4] The discovery of the "true" cross of the three, its miraculous healing power, and its translation are all part of the fervently accepted tradition. Liturgical commemoration soon followed. According to the journal of Aetheria,[5] a document which describes a fourth-century journey to the holy places, Holy Cross day was already being celebrated in 335, less than ten years after the finding. The important point about the festival celebrated in Jerusalem is that it immediately drew scores of pilgrims from all over the Christian world. The pilgrim Aetheria says that they came

> not only from Mesopotamia and Syria, from Egypt and the Thebaid, where the monks are numerous, but from all other places and provinces. In fact, there is no one who would not go to Jerusalem on this day for such solemn liturgy and for such a splendid feast.[6]

Various details taken from other manuscripts of fifth-and sixth-century itineraria indicate how fervent was the devotion to the Cross.[7] Pilgrimage to the holy places was widespread and popular. The give-and-take between East and West was generous and enthusiastic. The itineraries of travelers also give us information concerning the liturgies surrounding the Cross. Veneration of the Wood of the Cross on Good Friday and attendant details with regard to the possible origin of cross reliquaries are described, again by Aetheria:

> The gilded silver casket containing the sacred wood of the cross is brought in and opened. Both the wood of the cross and the inscription are taken out and placed on the table. As soon as they have been placed on the table, the bishop, remaining seated, grips the ends of the sacred wood with his hands, while the deacons, who are standing about, keep watch over it. There is a reason why it is guarded in this manner. It is the practice here for all the people to come forth one by one, the faithful as well as the catechumens, to bow down before the table, kiss the holy wood, and then move on. It is said that someone (I do not know when) took a bite and stole a piece of the holy cross. Therefore, it is now guarded by the deacons standing around, lest there be anyone who would dare come and do that again.[8]

We can thus see that the liturgical feast of the Dedication and the devotion of the Veneration of the Wood of the Cross were already established by the mid-fourth century. Furthermore, gilded and jeweled containers for pieces of the cross functioned not only as receptacles for the sacred object but undoubtedly as vicarious objects of devotion themselves. According to the *Anglo-Saxon Chronicle,* Pope Marinus sent Alfred a piece of the true cross in 883 and another in 885. We also know that praying to the Rood had already been widely encouraged. One homily of Ælfric encourages this devotion: "forðan ðe we nabbað ða ðe he on ðrowade, ac hire anlicnys bið halig swa-þeah, to ðære we abugað on gebedum symle to ðam Mihtigan Drihtne, þe for mannum ðrowade" (For although we have not that on which He suffered, its likeness is, nevertheless, holy, to which we ever bow in our prayers to the Mighty Lord, who suffered for men; and the rood is a memorial of his great passion, holy through him.... We ever honour it for the honour of Christ").[9] The arrival on English soil of an actual piece of the true cross undoubtedly heightened dramatically the efficaciousness of this sentiment. Miraculous healings with the wood could only confirm it. When we recall that the great hymns to the Cross written by Venantius Fortunatus were inspired by relics of the true cross arriving at Poitiers in 569, we can justifiably infer that the response of the English was likewise enthusiastic. Bruce Dickins and Alan Ross suggest that the arrival of the fragment of the cross in England in the eighth century occasioned the revision of the Ruthwell Cross poem.[10] It is also worth remembering that the cross reliquary now in Brussels served not only as a receptacle for a piece of the true cross, but that like the Ruthwell Cross it is inscribed with phrases distinctly parallel to the "Rood" poem: "Rod is min nama; geo ic ricne cyning bær byfigynde blode bestemed" (Rood is my name; in times past I shaking carried the powerful king, drenched with blood). Dickins and Ross suggest that this reliquary was the actual work which contained the second of the pieces Pope Marinus sent to Alfred in 885.[11] In any event, the first sections of *Elene* describe the process of decorating crosses as a part of Constantine's revelatory experience. The poet tells us that Constantine had seen the Cross in his dream "frætwum beorht ... golde geglenged, (gimmas lixtan)" (bright in trappings ... decked with gold, [gems shining]).[12] He then commanded that a token be wrought like the Cross he had seen in the heavens. *The Dream of the Rood* also recalls the decorated and bejeweled Cross in the dream vision of the narrator:

> Þuhte me þæt ic gesawe   syllicre treow
> on lyft lædan,   leohte bewunden,
> beama beorhtost.   Eall þæt beacen
> wæs begoten mid golde;   gimmas stodon
> fægere æt foldan sceatum,   swylce þær fife wæron
> uppe on þam eaxlegespanne.[13]

The personal devotion which correlates with these events is the so-called "Sign of the Cross." In the third century Tertullian had encouraged the use of the sign of the Cross, saying, "Ad omnem progressum atque promotum, ad omnem aditum et exitum, ad calciatum, ad lavacra, ad mensas, ad lumina, ad cubilia, ad sedilia, quaecumque nos conversatio exercet, frontem crucis signacula terimus" ("At every forward step and movement, at every going in and out, when we put on our clothes and shoes, when we bathe, when we sit at table, when we light the lamps, on couch, on seat, in all the ordinary actions of daily life, we trace upon the forehead the sign [of the cross]").[14] Cyprian and Cyril likewise proclaimed that the sign of the Cross had supernatural power.[15] The sign itself was originally a simple gesture marking the forehead by the thumb or forefinger. From the third century on it became an extremely widespread devotion, marked at times by almost magical fervor. And, indeed, the events described in the early *Life of Antony*, written in 357 by Athanasius, provide examples of the efficacious power of the sign. For Antony the use of the sign was not only an act of faith in the Redemption of Christ but a visible means of doing battle against the wiles of the devil. Antony says, "We need not fear [the devils'] apparitions, for they are nothing and disappear quickly—especially if one fortifies himself with faith and the sign of the cross."[16] Furthermore, at this time crosses appear not only on coins, but in the graffiti of the caves and meeting places of the Christians.

The devotion to the Cross as a "signum" to be used in the Christian war against the devil and subsequently as an exorcism reached Britain quite early. That the sign was a widespread devotion is implied in Bede's recommendation to Bishop Egbert to remind the members of his flock "quam frequenti diligentia signaculo se dominicae crucis, suaque omnia adversum continuas immundorum spiritum insidias, necesse habeant munire" ("with what frequent diligence to use the sign of the Lord's cross and so to fortify themselves and all they have against the continual snares of unclean spirits").[17] Alcuin recommends the sign of the Cross as the first act upon awaking in the morning.[18] Ælfric, too, comments on the gesture, saying, "Ne beo ge afyrhte þurh his gesihðe, ac mearciað rode-tacen on eowrum foreheafdum, and ælc yfel gewit fram eow" ("Be ye not afraid at the sight of him [the devil], but mark the sign of the rood on your foreheads, and every evil shall depart from you").[19] But the Irish monks of the eighth-century reform movement known as the Célí Dé were the ones who translated the small sign into a broad bodily gesture. The practice of the Cross-Vigil, also known as the Breastplate of Devotion, was the devotion of praying with arms extended, as a representation of the form of the Cross.[20] This "beacna selest" may well be the same sign, physically represented, which the dreamer in *The Dream of the Rood* is encouraged to bear in his breast as a hope for salvation.[21]

The shift from the sign of the Cross as a weapon in one's personal warfare against the attacks of the devil to a miraculous means for healing others is also attested by Bede. John of Beverley's cure of the dumb boy is an example. "... iussit ad se intrare pauperem; ingresso linguam proferre ex ore ac sibi ostendere iussit, et adprehendens eum de mento, signum sanctae crucis linguae eius inpressit."²² Whereas previously the actual pieces of the true cross had been widely understood to have such miraculous power, we see here that the gesture, accompanied by authoritative command, heals those who have faith.

The next element of devotional import I should like to consider has to do with the motif of the cosmological Cross. From the early Church Fathers we have the description of the Cross characterized by its form, that is, by the four directions of the wood itself: its arms extend to the ends of the earth; its top touches the heavens; its lower extremity penetrates the abyss below.²³ The image of the cosmological Cross also includes the concept of Christ on the Cross embracing the whole world and taking it home to the Father. *The Dream of the Rood* poet may well have been suggesting the resonances of just such theology in the "foldan sceatum" of line 8.²⁴ The concept is widespread. Borrowing from Augustine, Bede, Alcuin, and Ælfric explain the parts of the cross as stretching out toward the four quarters of the world, east and west, north and south, because Christ by his passion thus draws all people to him.²⁵ We see here that the Cross has not only a cosmological redemptive significance, but that the very form of the Cross contains a deeply theological allegorical meaning. Within this context we see the importance of such a detail as that the four dimensional stone crosses are specifically situated with their sides facing the four directions, north, south, east and west. The making and placing of crosses therefore marks a specifically public devotion. The Bewcastle Cross' principal side, for example, faces west, a detail which had to have had significance, perhaps as a sign to the travelers going from the West to the East. Ruthwell, too, must have originally had a directional focus.²⁶ Furthermore, the devotional practice of the Cross Vigil mentioned earlier was at times also practiced "facing the four cardinal points and also facing the ground and the heavens."²⁷ O'Dwyer's interpretation of this practice is that it is a prayer "for God's help for the four corners of the earth, for the dead and finally, in the hope of an eternal reward," turning toward heaven.²⁸ This interpretation may be only partially correct. Facing the four cardinal points does indeed recall the universality of the redemption; however, facing the ground and then the heavens may well represent instead the vertical beam of the Cross, which thus completes the cosmological implications.

A further parallel to this cosmological approach can be found in the so-called boundary crosses. Archaeology has given us evidence of sites where crosses were placed facing the four directions, probably as boundary markers.²⁹ The very placing of the boundary crosses for monastic properties and cemeteries strongly argues for a consciousness of cosmological theology. For example, at the consecration of the Canterbury cemetery, the cross was erected, together with smaller ones at each of the four corners of the plot, corresponding to the point of the compass, to mark the boundaries. In the consecration service, the bishop began by making the circuit of the grounds with his clergy, chanting the litany. Then he read a portion of the service at the eastern cross, did the same at the southern, western, and northern, and concluded at the cross in the center.[30] Thus the act of establishing boundaries for hallowed property contained within it the repetition of a cosmological devotion which was specifically signified liturgically.

R. E. Kaske has convincingly established that the cosmological motif is an important one in his reading of two poems from the Exeter Book, in which he also includes comments on *The Dream of the Rood*.[31] Thomas D. Hill has shown that the concept of the cosmological Cross also provides the rationale for two Anglo-Saxon cattle-theft charms.[32] A full survey of the motif, however, remains undone and would be well worth undertaking.

Closely allied to cosmological theology, however, is the importance of pilgrimage for the early Church in Ireland and Britain. We recall that the monks left home and friends as an ascetic exercise, to preach the Gospel to those who still had not heard it, traveling, at least initially, by boat. The attitude of the monks to travel, whether within the countryside of Ireland and northern England or across the sea to the Continent, was universal in character. They made, as Robin Flower puts it, the "whole world of Europe in their day into their monastery."[33] The image of the "navis crucis" — the Cross as a ship — is noteworthy. Inspired by the ark of Noah, the Church Fathers saw a ship as a figure of the Cross, carrying the chosen to salvation. The Cross is a vehicle, or instrument, by which an individual is saved. *The Dream of the Rood* poet is capturing this sense precisely when he says at the end of the poem:

>   ic wene me
> daga gehwylce   hwænne me Dryhtnes rod,
> þe ic her on eorðan   ær sceawode,
> on þysson lænan   life gefetige
> ond me þonne gebringe   þær is blis mycel,
> dream on heofonum....[34]

Here the Cross is the vehicle of salvation. The link to the ark of Noah is attested iconographically on several of the high crosses, especially the Armagh Cross and the broken cross at Kells. A parallel reminder of the symbolic interconnection between the Cross, pilgrimage, and the protection of Christ is found when the author of *Genesis A,* another Northumbrian poem, says that God "segnade" the door of the ark closed.[35] In this instance the signing distinctly evokes the image of the sign of the Cross.

Perhaps an even stronger representative iconographical depiction of Cross and ship can be found in an Anglo-Saxon manuscript illumination, dated by E. A. Lowe to the second quarter of the eighth century, where a stylized crucified Christ is shown above the hull of a ship in which are seen several passengers, including one central figure and another at the helm.[36] The iconography could well be the imaging of the commentary of Cassiodorus on Psalm 106, where he describes the ship which crosses the sea as having Christ as the pilot, the rowers as the apostles, and the holy pontiffs as select passengers.[37] It is in the light of just such theological and spiritual contexts that a detail in *The Dream of the Rood* should perhaps be seen. In line 91 the term "holmwudu," sea-wood, may be, not a scribal error, but the poet's attempt to capture in an Old English compound the "navis crucis" concept.[38]

The image of the ark and the Church as it signifies to the importance of preaching and admonishing the Christian faithful is widespread. Another look at the manuscript illumination indicates that the central figure in the boat is in fact Christ preaching. And we are immediately reminded that the vision of *The Dream of the Rood* dreamer is not for his own edification or spiritual growth alone. The tree commands him to proclaim what he has seen:

>   Nu ic þe hate,   hæleð min se leofa,
>   þæt ðu þas gesyhðe   secge mannum,
>   onwreoh wordum   þæt hit is wuldres beam,
>   se ðe ælmihtig God   on þrowode
>   for mancynnes   manegum synnum
>   ond Adomes   ealdgewyrhtum.[39]

This injunction parallels the urgency of proclamation in the first-person interpolation at the end of *Elene*: "mægencyning amæt ond on gemynd begeat ... bancofan onband, breostlocan onwand, leoðucræft onleac, þæs ic lustum breac, willum in worlde."[40]

The relationship between catechesis and pilgrimage needs no further emphasis here. But the role of the universal Cross, a Cross perceived as a ship which reaches all mankind, north, south, east and west, would be particularly appropriate to the whole Insular spirit.

The first millennium culminates in great artistic and literary representations of the cult of the Cross. It becomes increasingly evident that stone crosses such as those at Ruthwell and Bewcastle and poetry such as *The Dream of the Rood* and *Elene* are clear and representative expressions of a devotion, spirituality, and theology having roots in a universal awareness which was being constantly renewed by historical event, personal experience, and theological development. The use of the sign of the Cross, the significance of the Cross as a cosmological symbol, and the related importance of pilgrimage all deserve further separate study. This paper presents little new material as such: rather, it proposes a direction for further consideration of the subject. The sign of the Cross, physically represented, was widely encouraged and popularly practiced in this age; what is the relationship between making the sign of the Cross on or with one's body and erecting stone crosses? We find evidence of the motif of the cosmological Cross in literature, stone sculpture, and archaeology; how universal was the understanding of this motif? The Cross is a vehicle of salvation; how do we understand the tension between the Cross taking the believer to heavenly glory and the cross reminding the believer to proclaim to the earthly community the event of the Crucifixion and its attendant redemption? Although the answers to these questions remain uncertain, we can be sure that devotion to the Cross and the expression of the Sign of the Cross were widespread from the eighth to the tenth centuries.

ITHACA, N.Y.

Notes

1. See, for example, Robert B. Burlin, "The Ruthwell Cross, *The Dream of the Rood,* and the Vita Contemplativa," *Studies in Philology,* 65 (1960), 23–43; John V. Fleming, "*The Dream of the Rood* and Anglo-Saxon Monasticism," *Traditio,* 22 (1966), 43–72; Fritz Saxl, "The Ruthwell Cross," *Journal of the Warburg and Courtauld Institutes,* 6 (1943), 1–19; Meyer Schapiro, "The Religious Meaning of the Ruthwell Cross," *Art Bulletin,* 26 (1944), 231–45.

2. See John Canuteson, "The Crucifixion and the Second Coming in *The Dream of the Rood,*" *Modern Philogy,* 66 (1969), 293–97; Christopher Chase, "'Christ III,' *The Dream of the Rood,* and Early Christian Piety," *Viator,* 11 (1980), 11–33; Eleanor Simmons Greenhill, "The Child in the Tree, A Study of the Cosmological Tree in Christian Tradition," *Traditio,* 10 (1954), 323–71 and esp. 331–38; Éamonn Ó Carragáin, "How Did the Vercelli Collector Interpret *The Dream of the Rood?*"

in P. M. Tilling, ed., *Occasional Papers in Linguistics and Language Teaching,* 8 (1981), 63-104.

3. Fernand Cabrol and Henri Leclercq, eds., *Dictionnaire d'archéologie chrétienne et de liturgie* (Paris, 1907-1953), III, 3131-39, v. "croix"; George Willard Benson, *The Cross, Its History and Symbolism* (New York, 1976); William Wood Seymour, *The Cross in Tradition, History and Art* (New York, 1898); William O. Stevens, "The Cross in the Life and Literature of the Anglo-Saxons," in William O. Stevens, *The Anglo-Saxon Cross* (1904; rpt. Hamden, Conn., 1977), pp. 11-103.

4. Chrysostom *In Joannem Homiliae* LXXV, in *PG,* 59:459-60; Cyril *Catechesis* IV.10, in (*PG,* 33:467-70).

5. For the Latin text of Aetheria's journal see CSEL, Vol. 39 (Vienna, 1898), pp. 37-101. See also *Ethérie: Journal de Voyage,* ed. and trans. Hélène Pétré, Sources Chrétiennes, 21 (Paris, 1948). English translations include *The Pilgrimage of St. Silvia of Aquitania to the Holy Places,* ed. John Bernard (London, 1891), and *Egeria: The Diary of a Pilgrimage,* trans. George Gingras (New York, 1970).

6. *Egeria,* trans. Gingras, p. 127; "Nam ante plurimos dies incipiunt se undique colligere turbae non solum monachorum vel aputactitum de diversis provinciis, id est tam de Mesopotamia vel Syria vel de Egypto aud Thebaida, ubi plurimi monazontes sunt, sed et de diversis omnibus locis vel provinciis; nullus est enim, qui non se eadem die in Ierusolima tendat ad tantam laetitiam et tam honorabiles dies" (*Ethérie,* ed. Pétré, p. 264).

7. See the fourth- and fifth-century accounts of pilgrimages in Titus Tobler and Augustus Molinier, eds., *Itinera Hierosolymitana et Descriptiones Terrae Sanctae* (Geneva, 1879).

8. *Egeria,* trans. Gingras, p. 111; "Stant in giro mensa diacones et affertur loculus argenteus deauratus, in quo est lignum sanctum crucis, aperitur et profertur, ponitur in mensa tam lignum crucis quam titulus. Cum ergo positum fuerit in mensa, episcopus sedens de manibus suis summitates de ligno sancto premet, diacones autem, qui in giro, custodent. Hoc autem propterea sic custoditur, quia consuetudo est, ut unus et unus omnis populus veniens, tam fideles quam cathecumini, acclinantes se ad mensam osculentur sanctum lignum et pertranseant. Et quoniam nescio quando dicitur quidam fixisse morsum et furasse de sancto ligno, ideo nunc a diaconibus, qui in giro stant, sic custoditur, ne qui veniens audeat denuo sic facere" (*Ethérie,* ed. Pétré, p. 234).

9. *The Sermones Catholici or Homilies of Ælfric,* ed. and trans. Benjamin Thorpe (London, 1846), Vol. II, p. 307. See also the edition by Malcolm Godden, *Ælfric's Catholic Homilies: The Second Series,* EETS,S.S. 5 (London, 1979), p. 175 with differing punctuation and capitalization.

10. Bruce Dickins and Alan S. C. Ross, eds., *The Dream of the Rood* (London, 1963), p. 19.

11. "It is very probable that the Brussels Cross preserves the fragment of the True Cross sent to Alfred by Pope Marinus" (Dickins and Ross, p. 15). This conclusion had earlier been reached by S. T. R. O. D'Ardenne ("The Old English Inscription on the Brussels Cross," *English Studies,* 21 [1939], 145-64, 271-72). Annemarie E. Mahler has recently taken up the question in "*Lignum Domini* and the

Opening Vision of *The Dream of the Rood:* A Viable Hypothesis?" *Speculum,* 53 (1978), 441-59.

12. George Philip Krapp, ed., *The Vercelli Book,* ASPR, Vol. 2 (New York, 1932), p. 68, ll. 88, 90.

13. Michael Swanton, ed., *The Dream of the Rood* (Manchester and New York, 1970), p. 89, ll. 4-9;

> I beheld, borne up on high, methought,
> a wondrous rood, bewound with light,
> the brightest of beams. That beacon was all
> overlaid with gold; lovely stood the gems at the
> ends of the earth, and up on the crossing
> were five gems more....

(trans. Kemp Malone, *Ten Old English Poems* [Baltimore, 1941], p. 3).

14. Tertullian, *De Corona Militis* III, in *PL,* 2:80; trans. Peter Holmes, *(The Writings of Quintus Sept. Flor. Tertullianus,* Anti-Nicene Christian Library, Vol. 11 (Edinburgh, 1869), p. 336.

15. Cyprian, *De Lapsis* 2, CSEL, Vol. 3, Pt. 1 (Vienna, 1868), p. 238, and *Epistle LVIII,* CSEL, Vol. 3, Pt. 2 (Vienna, 1871), p. 664; Cyril, *Catechesis* XIII.36, in *PG,* 33:815.

16. *Athanasius: The Life of Antony and the Letter to Marcellinus,* trans. Robert G. Gregg (New York, 1980), p. 48. See also *PG,* 26:835-976.

17. *Venerabilis Bedae Opera Quae Supersunt Omnia,* ed. J[ames] A. Giles, (London, 1843), Vol. I, pp. 134-35.

18. "Cum a somno evigilas, et crucis signum depingis in labiis, tertio repete: 'Domine, labia mea aperies, et os meum annuntiabit laudem tuam'" (Alcuin, *De Psalmorum Usu Liber I,* in *PL,* 101:468).

19. Ælfric, *Homilies,* ed. and trans. Thorpe, I, 467.

20. Peter O'Dwyer, *Célí Dé: Spiritual Reform in Ireland 750-900* (Dublin, 1981), pp. 108 ff.

21. Swanton, p. 95, and see p. 131, n. 118. Robert B. Burlin says: "Whether 'in breostum' points to a literal crucifix 'on his breast' or a metaphorical one 'in his breast' is beside the point, for by this time it is evident that in terms of this vision the symbol and its spiritual value are indistinguishable" ("The Ruthwell Cross, *The Dream of the Rood,* and the Vita Contemplativa," p. 32).

22. *Bede's Ecclesiastical History of the English People,* ed. and trans. Bertram Colgrave and R. A. B. Mynors (Oxford, 1969), p. 458, trans. p. 459: "... he ordered the poor man to come in to him and then he told him to put out his tongue and show it to him. Thereupon he took him by the chin and made the sign of the holy cross on his tongue."

23. See, for example, Augustine, *In Joannis Evangelium* CXVIII, CCSL, Vol. 36 (Turnhout, 1954), pp. 654-58.

24. See the note in Dickins and Ross, p. 102, and their discussion of this equation on pp. 50-51.

25. For Bede see *In S. Joannis Evang. Expos.* XIX, in *PL,* 92:913; Alcuin, *Liber*

de Divinis Officiis XVIII in *PL*, 101:1208; Ælfric, *Homilies,* ed. Thorpe, II, 254.

26. See Swanton, p. 13, n. 1: "Originally no doubt, as at Bewcastle, where the cross still stands erect, the principal face looked west so as to be seen by worshippers conventionally approaching from that direction."

27. O'Dwyer, p. 109.

28. O'Dwyer, p. 109.

29. Stevens, p. 61; Françoise Henry, *Irish High Crosses* (Dublin, 1964), p. 20.

30. John Lingard, *History and Antiquities of the Anglo-Saxon Church,* Vol. II (London, 1845), p. 52, n. 2.

31. R. E. Kaske, "A Poem of the Cross in the Exeter Book: 'Riddle 60' and 'The Husband's Message,'" *Traditio,* 23 (1967), 41–71.

32. Thomas D. Hill, "The Theme of the Cosmological Cross in Two Old English Cattle Theft Charms," *Notes & Queries,* 25 (1978), 488–90.

33. Robin Flower, *The Irish Tradition* (Oxford, 1947), p. 66.

34. Swanton, p. 96, ll. 135–40;

> ... and everyday I hope
> the time has come when the cross of my Lord,
> which here on earth I beheld long ago,
> shall fetch me away from this fleeting life
> and bring me then where bliss is great,
> to the happiness of heaven

(trans. Malone, *Ten OE Poems,* p. 7).

35. A. N. Doane, *Genesis A: A New Edition* (Madison, 1978), p. 145, l. 1365. In his note on p. 264, Doane further relates the image to baptism.

36. *Codices Latini Antiquiores,* Vol. IX (Oxford, 1950), p. 52, Pl. 1424. The illumination is reprinted in Paul Thoby, *Le Crucifix, des origines au concile de Trente* (Nantes, 1959), Pl. XI, and in Bernard F. Huppé, *The Web of Words* (Albany, 1970), facing p. 42.

37. "'Qui descendunt mare in navibus, facientes operationem in aquis multis.' Cum dicit, 'descendunt mare,' significat sacerdotes qui saeculi istius procellosa descendunt. Nam cum dicit, 'descendunt,' ostendit inferiora loca esse saeculi, ad quae 'descendi' posse testatur. 'In navibus' autem (ut saepe diximus) ecclesias significat, quae ligno crucis mundi istius tempestates enavigant. Sic enim mare descenditur atque transitur, si tutissimus navibus insidatur, ubi gubernator est Christus, ubi remiges apostoli et sanctorum pontificum beata collectio. Sequitur, 'facientes operationem in aquis multis.' Adhuc in eadem comparatione persistit. Sacerdos sunt enim qui operantur in aquis multis, id est praedicant populis christianis" (Cassiodorus, *Expositio Psalmorum,* CCSL, Vol. 98 [Turnhout, 1958], pp. 979–80). ("They go down to the sea in ships, doing the business in many waters." When he says, "they go down to the sea," he means the priests who go down to the stormy sea of this world. For when he says, "they go down," he reveals the lower places to be of this world to which he asserts it is possible to go down. "In ships," however [as we have often said], means the churches, which sail away from the storm of this world by the wood of the cross. For thus one is brought down

to the sea and brought across, if he is most safely placed in the ships where the pilot is Christ, where the oarsmen are the apostles, and the blessed gathering of the holy pontiffs. "Doing the business in many waters" follows. Still he remains in the same comparison. For the priests are those who work in many waters, that is, they preach to the Christian nations [my translation].)

38. See, in particular, the approach to the *hapax legomenon* by Carl Berkhout in "The Problem of Holmwudu," *Mediaeval Studies,* 36 (1974), 429-33.

39. Swanton, p. 95, ll. 95-100:

> "Now I lay it upon thee, my beloved child,
> that thou tell this sight to the sons of men,
> the tale unfold of the tree of glory
> that God Almighty gave his life on,
> to save mankind from the sin of old Adam,
> and many works of wickedness"

(trans. Malone, *Ten OE Poems*, pp. 5-6). Swanton includes a summary of the critical commentary on p. 128, n. 91.

40. Krapp, *Vercelli Book,* p. 100, ll. 1247-50; The King of power taught me and poured [grace] into my mind ... unbound my body, opened my heart, unlocked skill in song. This I have used gladly, with pleasure in the world.

Reflections on the Iconography of the Ruthwell and Bewcastle Crosses

ROBERT T. FARRELL

The early Anglo-Saxon cross at Ruthwell, Dumfriesshire, is arguably the most important object to have come down to us from Anglo-Saxon England. The carving is of very high quality, both with respect to figural sculpture and vinescroll, and the runic inscriptions are of very great interest not only for the history of the language and philology in the broader sense, but also because we have on the cross fragments of a poem which strongly resembles a text in the Vercelli Book known as *The Dream of the Rood*. The Ruthwell Cross is now under study by scholars in England, Ireland, and America, and publication of their conclusions can be expected in the near future.[1] This brief and provisional account of the iconography of the cross is an interim statement, until the full-scale study is completed. The views presented here are my own; they are very much subject to revision, and do not necessarily represent the views of my colleagues.

The Bewcastle Cross is dealt with both in this report and in the larger publication because it has long been associated with Ruthwell, and because two of the sculptural panels on the west face of the Bewcastle shaft are virtually identical with two on Ruthwell. This relationship will be discussed in detail below.

The History of the Ruthwell Cross in Modern Times

Paul Meyvaert has pursued this subject in a recent article,[2] with particular stress on the period from 1607, when the cross first was mentioned in writing by Nicholas Roscarrock, to 1802, when the Reverend Henry

Duncan reassembled the cross in a garden next to the churchyard at Ruthwell. Meyvaert made use of the comparatively recent history of the cross to bolster his interpretation of a single panel, but the broader implications of his work are equally significant. When the cross was struck down in the mid-seventeenth century, its fragments seem to have been widely scattered, both within the church and in the churchyard. Some were described by Nicolson in 1704 as having been "thrown under through-stones in the church yard."[3] Some fragments would appear to have been buried, since they were recovered from a grave dug deep enough for two, which may mean in excess of two meters. Given this history, it should surprise no one to discover that a close examination of the cross as it exists today shows it to be very seriously damaged indeed. This point needs to be stressed because both the photographs and drawings of the cross that are most readily available *favor* the cross, with shadow obscuring the damaged portions in the photographs, and silent "emendation" being characteristic of the drawings. These observations are *not* intended as attacks or slurs on those who have produced these illustrations of the cross, but rather as a comment on how very difficult it is to deal with the cross as it is currently re-erected in Ruthwell church.[4] The extent of the damage is dramatically clear when one examines the panels with figure sculpture. In its original state, the cross had a sequence of five smaller subjects on each broad face of the cross-head, and five larger-scale panels on the original east and west faces. Of the twenty original panels, *none* has survived without extensive surface damage. In the cross-head sequence, we have only four of the original panels left, all heavily damaged. Though a fragment now bolted to the rail of the cross-pit at Ruthwell *may* be part of the cross-arm, as Professor Cramp proposed in 1978, there is nothing left of the horizontal cross-arms save this fragment, so that six of the original panels in this small sequence are effectively lost.[5]

Of the ten larger panels, one is completely lost (the lowermost on the west face [Plate 1a]), while the Crucifixion (lowermost on the east face [Plate 1b]) is at best a ghost. The two topmost panels are reconstructed from fragments, modern stone, and mortar, and almost every panel has been cut back, or effaced, in some cases to a depth of 5 to 8 cm. (This is most clearly seen in the Annunciation panel.) Figure 1 is a schematic of the east and west faces, with breaks indicated, and modern inserted stones and mortar expunged.[6] Even the casual observer will agree that we have about *half* the original sequence left to us.

Plate 1a: Ruthwell west face, lowermost panel: subject unrecoverable. Durham University Series 1982, No. 2/7. Photographed by Tom Middlemass.

Plate 1b: Ruthwell east face, lowermost panel: Crucifixion. Durham University Series 1982, No. 7/4. Photographed by Tom Middlemass.

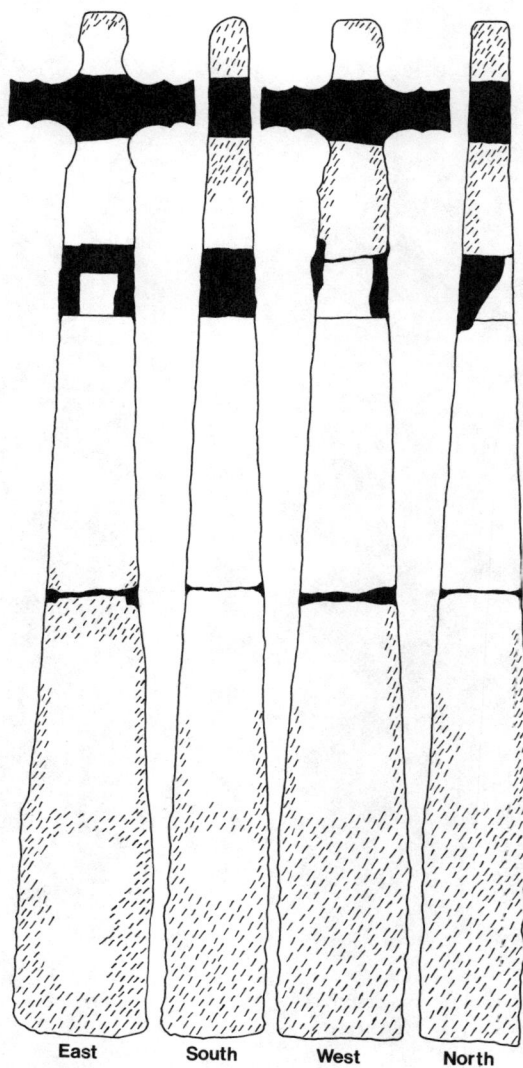

Fig. 1: Losses, fragments of Ruthwell, on sculpture and vinescroll faces.

Construction and "Deconstruction" of the Cross

The cross appears originally to have been composed of two tapering monoliths, the lower circumscribed on the north and south faces by the text of an Anglo-Saxon cross-poem in runes. The upper stone is fragmentary, and the cross-arm is a modern reconstruction. Those who struck down or perhaps more accurately hacked down the monument under the authority of General Assemblies of the Church of Scotland held in 1640 at Aberdeen and in 1642 at St. Andrews[7] appear to have cut downward through the northwest corner of the upper stone at a point about one-third the way up its height. This is the most fragmented and heavily damaged part of the cross, and indeed the cut continues into the northeast corner of the *lower* monolith (Plate 2). A second cut was made through the lower stone, at about mid-height (Plate 3). In addition, the surface of the stone was cut back on almost every panel, with the greatest damage of this sort found at the lowermost part of the column.

The extent of the loss the cross has suffered in this surface destruction can best be appreciated by a study of one aspect of the carver's technique. It is usual to have the figures in high relief, as can be seen by an examination of such panels as the Christ with Magdalene (Plate 4), and Christ with the Man Born Blind (Plate 5). In the latter instance, the left hand of Christ is almost free of the background, and we have completely lost the right hand and arm, almost certainly because it had been cut so far free of the ground that it was struck off entirely in the destruction. On the uppermost fragment of the cross, the leg of the eagle clutching a branch of foliage is entirely free of the ground — one can pass a finger behind it. Such traces as are left on the Flight panel indicate that the beast on which the Virgin and Child are seated was also in part free of the ground. Turning to the Annunciation panel, we have the clearest evidence of yet another kind of damage, the removal of facial and bodily features. The faces in this instance were simply sheared off both the Angel and Mary (Plate 6), and though weathering has obscured the break it is virtually certain that both Christ with the Beasts and the figure with the Agnus Dei above have had similar extensive damage to hand and forearm (Plate 7). Insofar as possible, the plates and illustrations both in this brief piece and in the more extensive publication on the crosses will *not* gloss over this extensive damage. Any realistic appraisal of the fragments we have left to us must tend to a rather sobering conclusion: while we do have remains of slightly more than *half* of the original sculpture panels, most of them have suffered very substantial injury, so that the re-erected monument now in Ruthwell church

Plate 3: Ruthwell Cross, lower monolith: 17th-century cut through the stone. (Note reduction of surface ca. 6 cm. on right of panel, and similar damage in profile on left.) Durham University Series 1982, No. 2/1. Photographed by Tom Middlemass.

Plate 2: Ruthwell Cross, upper monolith: damage from 17th century. Durham University Series 1982, No. 9/8. Photographed by Tom Middlemass.

Plate 5: Ruthwell Cross east face: detail of Christ healing man born blind. Note parallel gestures with hands. Oxford Series 1969, No. 16:V. Courtesy Christopher Ball.

Plate 4: Ruthwell Cross east face: *Magdalene at feet of Christ*. Note depth of carving (8 cm. at bottom), and detail of Christ's garments seen from below. Oxford Series 1969, No. 17:V. Courtesy Christopher Ball.

Plate 6: Ruthwell east face: side view of Annunciation, showing faces sheared off and extensive reduction of carving (ca. 8 cm. at bottom of stone). Durham University Series 1982, No. 1/4. Photographed by Tom Middlemass.

Plate 7: *Christ on the Beasts* (JUDEX AEQUITATIS), and heads of Paul and Anthony. Durham University Series 1982, No. 7/1. Photographed by Tom Middlemass.

represents only a small part of the cross as it looked when it left the remarkably skilled craftsmen and artists who conceived, designed, and executed it.

An Incongruous Fragment

It is possible and in my view probable that at least one fragment of carving incorporated into the cross as we now have it does not belong with the others. I refer to a piece incorporated into the east face of the cross at the bottom of the panel, showing two confronted figures, which has been interpreted as the Visitation. A review of the reconstruction of this entire section of the cross is necessary at this point in the discussion, because it is a serious matter to call into question a fragment which has been so long accepted as a part of the original composition. Even the casual viewer must have questions about the *whole* of the upper monolith as we now have it, for there are glaring errors. If one examines the nimbed figure holding a lamb on the west face, both the proportions and the alignment of the figure are not right. The lowest section is very much out of line, and is displaced to the viewer's left. This error is most easy to see in the left border, which is made up with modern mortar for the middle third of its length; the made-up section takes a sudden jog to the left in order to join the upper and lower borders together (Plate 8a). This displacement is caused by the two large stones inserted to the right of the figure, which are not in accord with the size of the border on the rest of the panel. These stones extend through the entire breadth of the north face of the cross, and fill the lower left of the border on the east face. It is only when one turns to the east face that the reason for the odd dimension of these inserted stones can be understood, for they *are* in proportion with the border of the lowermost fragment of the Visitation scene (Plate 8b). The decision of the nineteenth-century mason who re-erected the cross was to follow the fragment now incorporated as the bottom fragment of the Visitation scene. The choice was unfortunate, for the small area of border in this fragment does not agree with *any other section of border on the cross*. It is unusual in another respect, for it is the only section of border which has no trace whatever of any inscription, either Latin or in runes—the rule elsewhere on the cross. The feet shown in this fragment are also unique in that they appear to be shod in footwear resembling sabots; again, this feature is not seen elsewhere on the cross, and indeed cannot be readily paralleled in Anglo-Saxon carving. Finally, a somewhat impressionistic argument must be put forward. While the in-

Plate 8a: Ruthwell west face, upper monolith: fragmented figure holding a lamb. Oxford Series 1969, No. 35:V. Courtesy Christopher Ball.

Plate 8b: Ruthwell Cross east face, upper monolith: fragmentary confronted figures: the *Visitation*. Durham University Series 1982, No. 5/8.
Photographed by Tom Middlemass.

serted figure on the west face (i.e., *through* the cross) gives an impression of being dumpy and foreshortened, the two confronted figures on the east face appear overly long from the waist downwards,[8] by the insertion of yet another nineteenth-century filler stone which substitutes for the body just below the waist to just above the ankle.

While none of these arguments on the fragment with the broad border is conclusive in and of itself, it seems that the *sum* of the arguments is strong enough at least to call this fragment into question, if not to exclude it. Is it possible that there was another cross or crosses at Ruthwell? Many an early medieval religious house was possessed of more than one cross,[9] and the wording of the acts under which the Ruthwell Cross was struck down has been interpreted on occasion as referring to more than one "idolatrous" monument at Ruthwell, though Meyvaert makes it clear that the closest and most significant document uses the singular.[10] Even if the fragment that I have called into question is an anomaly, it would be over-reaching the evidence to posit another cross; but in view of finds elsewhere of Anglo-Saxon sculpture it would hardly be over-interpreting to hold that some other source was the point of origin for this piece. It should be understood that even if this fragment is rejected, no greater complexity or uncertainty of iconographic interpretation arises, for we still have two confronted figures, and the basic composition remains unchanged.

The Iconographic Sequence at Ruthwell

The question of the iconographic sequence at Ruthwell — the way in which all the panels can be put into series — is one of the most difficult aspects of the study of the cross, and an extended discussion of the sequence would be improper here. Éamonn Ó Carragáin studies some possibilities in his contribution to this volume, but in this piece it is important to start with very basic material: How do the scenes on the cross fit in with general uses in the early Church? Some are in common use throughout, some are of limited distribution, and several are problematic either because they are unusual, or not in accord with general tradition. The cross-head sequence has already been addressed in a recent study by Rosemary Cramp.[11] Her conclusions were that while the Ruthwell cross-head sequence is "unique in that portraits and symbols [of the Evangelists] occur together,"[12] this group of panels serves to stress an apocalyptic significance, a use which is confirmed by later Anglo-Saxon examples. On the Ruthwell Cross, the association of the apocalyptic image is confirmed by placing the Evangelist series over the Christ as Judge and Saviour.[12]

The ten large-scale panels on the shaft can be roughly characterized in this way:
1. Scenes in fairly common use throughout the early church:
   a. West face: None
   b. East face: Visitation; Christ healing Man Born Blind; Annunciation; Crucifixion
2. Scenes in limited distribution:
   a. West face: Paul and Anthony Breaking Bread; the Flight into (or out of) Egypt[13]
   b. East face: Magdalene at the Feet of Christ
3. Scenes which are problematic:
   a. West face: Standing figure with lamb, usually identified as John the Baptist with the *Agnus Dei*;[14] Christ on the Beasts
   b. East face: None.

A few remarks are in order on the Ruthwell use of each classification.

1. *Scenes in common use*. Even when a traditional subject is treated at Ruthwell, the iconography is often adjusted — or perhaps it is more accurate to say stripped down — to suit the medium in which the carver is working. Space permits attention to only one panel — the Annunciation — as an example. Ruthwell has the Virgin standing on the right; she draws back from the angel who approaches from the left. Her stance indicates awe, or fear, as she is as far drawn back as she can be, and her hands clutch her garments. The angel is shown leaning toward the Virgin, and he is shown in profile, with one foot ahead of the other, to indicate motion. As Michael Swanton has pointed out, the only Anglo-Saxon parallel, the tenth-century Hovingham slab, shows her seated, as is the case with the Ravenna throne or Adana medallions.[15] Many early representations show Mary seated, holding a spindle, or distaff and spindle, while Gabriel has a staff. At this point, the closest parallel I have found for the Ruthwell composition is in Etschmiadzen Monastery MS. 299, folio 228^v, a Gospel book,[16] but even this example differs from Ruthwell in that Gabriel carries a staff in his left hand. However, the stance and hand positions of the two figures are close to the Ruthwell example.

2. *Scenes of limited distribution*. Christ with the Magdalene, Paul and Anthony breaking bread, and the Egypt flight are not generally popular in Early Christian art. The major parallels for Paul and Anthony are found in Irish or Insular contexts, and both this scene and Christ with the Magdalene are important in the Irish Church, in iconography, liturgy, commentary, or some combination of these contexts. Saxl long ago demonstrated

the importance of Paul and Anthony as early hermits in the Irish Church,[17] and Schapiro independently commented on the same practices in the Anglo-Saxon Church.[18] The Eucharistic importance of the rite of *Cofractio Panis* is also important here, and this ground is covered well by Saxl.

As for the Magdalene at the Feet of Christ, an Irish tradition of the *Ecclesia Primitiva* which drew both on general patristic commentaries and on Bede and pseudo-Bede in particular saw the Magdalene as a type of the Church as it was received of the gentiles. While this is no absolutely *new* use in the early Church, Glenn W. Olsen shows how this interpretation had a particular importance in Irish schools of thought on the Continent.[19] It is all the more important to note that this scene appears to have no parallel in Anglo-Saxon sculpture, and that no Early Christian example is extant, though Saxl has pointed out that the scene was known in fifth- and sixth-century eastern contexts.

The purpose, nature and significance of the "Egypt Flight" panel is now very much open to discussion, because George Henderson in a recent paper has directed a good deal of attention to this panel. His first point is that such examples as have come down to us of the Flight *into* Egypt have the figures moving from left to right, while the Ruthwell scene depicts a progression from right to left. The Flight *out of* Egypt is shown as moving as the Ruthwell Flight does. Henderson associates the Flight out of Egypt with the scene of Christ as "Saviour and Nourisher of his Chosen People, first Israel, then the Church."[20] It is not possible to give Henderson's views the attention they deserve in this brief survey, but it is hoped that before long his careful and stimulating paper will be available in print as a contribution to lively debate about the cross.

3. *Panels difficult to interpret*. The third category of the iconography at Ruthwell is extremely interesting and important, for it is clear that the Christ on the Beasts and the figure holding a lamb just above the panel are of crucial importance. At this point the relationship between the Ruthwell and Bewcastle crosses must be considered, for the two upper panels of figure sculpture on the Bewcastle Cross are virtually identical with those at Ruthwell. Dealing with the parallels is problematic, but the Ruthwell and Bewcastle crosses must be studied together for a number of reasons. Though present boundaries put Ruthwell in Scotland and Bewcastle in England, both are in relation to the line of Hadrian's wall, and both can be associated with the traditions of Jarrow and a series of other religious centers of the north, Jedburgh, Rothbury, and Otley among them. (See Fig. 2.) Ruthwell and Bewcastle are the most ambitious examples of stone crosses left to us

Fig. 2: Schematic of England, Solway Firth to Tyne.

from the Anglo-Saxon period; both are conceived on a grand scale, both have very ambitious schemes of decoration, and both have long runic inscriptions, which appear to be very early in date.[21] All the complexities of the relation between the Ruthwell and Bewcastle crosses cannot be dealt with in this brief overview, so I put forward only one argument, dealing with the question of priority, in which Ruthwell precedes Bewcastle.[22] It is generally agreed that the figure of Christ standing upon two beasts is derived from the standard iconography of Psalm 90:13, but forty years ago Saxl proposed that the Ruthwell version was a distinctive Northumbrian variant, derived from a common Mediterranean formula. The most distinctive aspect of the Ruthwell example was in Saxl's view the attitude of the beasts (swine?) which Saxl claims have their paws raised and crossed in "a gesture of adoration."[23] This question of attitude and gesture is taken further by Schapiro, who saw Christ on the Beasts as a survival of the Messianic harmony of Christ with all nature, an interpretation "abandoned by the triumphant church of the fourth century, which ... survived through the Middle Ages among the hermit monks and the independent religious spirits, like St. Francis, who were possessed by a more spontaneous and lyrical Christianity and took as their model the Christ of the desert or the open country and streets."[24]

The crux of the argument here is the interpretation of the attitude and kind of the beasts: Can they, necessarily or even readily, be accurately described as adoring, *without* turning to the inscription that surrounds the panel on the Ruthwell Cross? — i.e., JUDEX AEQUITATIS; BESTIAE ET DRACONES COGNOVERUNT IN DESERTO SALVATOREM MUNDI.

Saxl made a very useful survey of the illustrations of Psalm 90:13 and concluded that we have a distinctive Northumbrian variant at Ruthwell; in other words, he held that even if the number of beasts were reduced from the asp, basilisk, lion, and adder, early illustrations were more closely associated with the beasts as numbered and described. He sees the beasts we have at Ruthwell as two representatives of a single species, swine (?). I must confess that I cannot see the basis for this conclusion, as the beasts on Ruthwell have heads which are triangular, and they are differentiated from one another. The beast on the right has an ear shaped like a figure eight, the bottom loop being larger than the upper, while the beast on the left has ears in the shape of rounded triangles,[25] which can indeed be interpreted as pig- or dog-like. There are clear indications of toes on the paws. (See Plate 7.) A survey of early examples of the illustration of Psalm 90 shows that even in the Early Christian period, the beasts associated with Christ have drifted considerably from the four specific creatures mentioned in Psalm 90:13. This subject is a commonplace on terra-cotta lamps, where a figure treads on a single beast (as on a serpent, from a lamp in Carthage)[26]; or the beasts may be multiplied, as on another lamp published in Cabrol,[27] where the Christ stands on the back of a singularly unsubmissive dog- or pig-like creature with floppy triangular ears, and three or perhaps four serpents are found in the composition, one of them circling around the back of the human figure with its head at about the level of Christ's ankles. The two closest parallels I have so far found for the Ruthwell/Bewcastle composition are in a manuscript from Einsiedeln (apparently of the tenth century) and on a book cover now in Paris.[28] The first example has two Latin inscriptions, Psalm 90:13, and RIGAT OMNES ACTUS [sic] VESTROS ARBITER SUMMUS. The Christ stands on a lion and a serpent-like creature whose bodies are twisted and appear to be pressed heavily downwards by the weight of Christ. One very significant detail is that the snake-like creature has pointed ears, and the lion, rounded ears. If one accepts the notion I have put forward above, that the Ruthwell iconographies were stripped because of the constraints of the medium, and if one blocks out the Einsiedeln manuscript page so as to parallel the Ruthwell panel, the resemblance of the *heads of the beasts* in both compositions is striking. As for the Paris book cover, it depicts a standing Christ with cross-standard and a scroll (?); Christ treads on a basilisk (?) and a lion. If this composition is compared with the Ruthwell panel, the resemblance is all the more striking. It must be remarked that I have not as yet come upon a parallel for the crossed paws at Ruthwell and Bewcastle in what might be termed the common "adversarial" illustrations of Psalm 90:13, but in view of the comparative evidence it is perhaps valid to question the interpretation of this posture as adoring, *without* calling on the Ruthwell inscription in order to draw such a conclusion.

We may then propose that the *natural* association of Christ standing on two beasts is a fairly common variant of the iconography of Psalm 90, verse 13, and that the Ruthwell inscription leads us explicitly to Christ as Judge, and to the less evident and extremely rare Christ with the Beasts.[29] The attitude of the beasts as adoring is established *only* when the inscription is called upon. It would seem, therefore, that if the Bewcastle panel showing Christ on the Beasts is to have the meaning of Christ as Judge being recognized by the beasts in the desert, it can have this meaning only if such an association had been established at Ruthwell. There is no strong probability that an inscription like that on the Ruthwell Cross could ever have had a place on the Bewcastle sculpture, for the borders on the latter are cut into bands by incised lines. I would argue that since the whole composition of the Bewcastle panel is so similar to that of the Ruthwell Cross, and unparalleled outside of these two contexts, it is likely that the Ruthwell Cross established a tradition on which the Bewcastle sculptor then drew.

Conclusions

This paper has been an attempt to give an indication of the current state of study of the crosses. Sandra McEntire's paper is a contribution towards the understanding of the spirituality of the crosses, a subject addressed and carried further in Ó Carragáin's contribution to this volume. As can easily be seen by even a quick reading of our respective contributions, we have still more questions than answers, and we have much to settle within the larger publication, in terms of dating, priority of evidence, and the like. We all hope that the notions we have put forward here will be scrutinized and questioned by other scholars before the larger-scale study is completed. As a first point, it should be made clear that while we hope to do a broadly based study of all aspects of the crosses, we do not expect to reach unanimity of opinion or interpretation on all points. It would be unrealistic to suppose that these magnificent and problematic monuments will be "solved" in any single work of scholarship.

CORNELL UNIVERSITY

Notes

1. The current list of contributors includes Christopher Ball, Master of Keeble College, Oxford; Gerald Bonner, Reader in Theology at Durham; Rosemary Cramp, Professor of Archaeology at Durham; Éamonn Ó Carragáin, Professor of Medieval English and English Language at Cork; Ray Page, Fellow of Corpus Christi College at Cambridge; and myself.
2. Paul Meyvaert, "An Apocalypse Panel on the Ruthwell Cross," in *Medieval and Renaissance Studies,* ed. Frank Tiro, Proceedings of the Southwestern Institute of Medieval and Renaissance Studies (Durham, N.C., 1982), pp. 3–32.
3. As cited by Meyvaert, p. 5. (The source from which Meyvaert quoted is not at present available to me.)
4. The cross is sunk into a stone-lined pit not quite two meters deep in the floor of the church; the major face, with Christ on the Beasts central, faces the wall of

the specially constructed apse and is therefore impossible to photograph in its entirety. The cross is lit by a series of skylights which cause a light-fall that confuses the eye. It is in some ways far easier to study the cross at night, by artificial light.

5. Rosemary Cramp, "The Evangelist Symbols and Their Parallels in Anglo-Saxon Sculpture," in *Bede and Anglo-Saxon England,* ed. R. T. Farrell, British Archaeological Reports, 46 (Oxford, 1978), pp. 118–30.

6. The orientation of the cross as it is currently displayed is unlikely, and almost certainly wrong. The panel showing Christ standing on two beasts is almost certainly the major panel on the cross, as it is the largest. Since the crosses are so similar, and since the sequence "a) figure with Agnus Dei, b) Christ in Majesty" appears on both crosses, it seems reasonable to accord Ruthwell and Bewcastle. Bewcastle seems to have been undisturbed since it was erected, and has Christ in Majesty on the west face, coming out of the East.

7. See further Meyvaert, pp. 4–5.

8. No other human figures on the cross are so elongated; if one examines the panel with Christ Healing the Man Born Blind, it appears that the lower part of that panel has been left blank, perhaps to avoid elongation of the figures.

9. Sandra McEntire has discussed instances of this in her paper in this volume.

10. Meyvaert, p. 5.

11. See note 5 above.

12. Cramp, p. 122.

13. George Henderson makes a case for the scene showing the flight *out of* Egypt in a lecture given at Durham in May, 1982: I am much indebted to him for a copy of this excellent contribution to our knowledge of the cross; the paper is to be published.

14. Meyvaert makes a very cogent argument for the figure with the lamb's being an Apocalyptic (Meyvaert, n. 22), but his conclusions are called into question in Henderson's unpublished lecture. Space does not permit a full-scale discussion here of this lively debate, but it will be taken up in the larger study.

15. *The Dream of the Rood,* ed. M. J. Swanton (Manchester, 1970), p. 18.

16. F. Macler, *Evang. Armenien* (1920), fol. 228^v (reference cited from Index of Christian Art at Princeton; I have yet to see it).

17. Fritz Saxl, "The Ruthwell Cross," *Journal of the Warburg and Courtauld Institutes,* 6 (1943), 1–19.

18. Meyer Schapiro, "The Religious Meaning of the Ruthwell Cross," *Art Bulletin,* 26 (1944), 231–45.

19. Glenn W. Olsen, "References to the *Ecclesia Primitiva* in Eighth Century Gospel Exegesis," *Thought,* 54 (1979), 303–12.

20. George Henderson, unpublished lecture; see note 13.

21. See R. Page, *An Introduction to English Runes* (London, 1973).

22. I have discussed scholarship on this point in a recent introduction to A. S. Cook's *Some Accounts of the Bewcastle Cross...,* re-issued under the title *The Anglo-Saxon Cross* (Hamden, Conn., 1967 [*recte* 1977]).

23. Saxl, p. 13.

24. Schapiro, pp. 235–36. Schapiro also points out that the subject is virtually

unrepresented in the early Middle Ages. See further Robert Eisler, "Jesus Among the Animals by Moretto da Brescia," *Art in America,* 23 (1935) 137–40.

25. It is interesting to note that the "figure-eight" ear is used by the sculptor to represent the human ear, as is seen in the Paul-Anthony panel directly below Christ with the Beasts.

26. See *Rev. Art Chrét,* III (1892), fig. p. 135 (citation as in Princeton Index of Christian Art).

27. F. Cabrol, *Dict.* III^2 (1914), fig. 3090 (reference as in Princeton Index of Christian Art).

28. See Ernest T. DeWald, "The Art of the Scriptorium of Einsiedeln," *Scripta Helvetica,* 5 (1943), Plate XI.

29. Book cover, Paris, BN MS. lat. 10514.

Christ over the Beasts and the Agnus Dei: Two Multivalent Panels on the Ruthwell and Bewcastle Crosses

ÉAMONN Ó CARRAGÁIN

Gerald Bonner and I are committed to write, for the forthcoming study of the Ruthwell and Bewcastle crosses, a joint chapter entitled "The Spirituality of the Crosses." The question which our chapter will try to answer is, "In what ways do the iconographic programs of these crosses provide evidence of the spiritual life of the communities which erected the crosses?" In the present paper, I shall discuss one of the problems which need to be faced in any attempt to approach this question.[1]

A chapter on "the spirituality of the crosses" must build upon iconographic and stylistic studies. For example, any theories about the spirituality of the crosses must be very tentative indeed until Rosemary Cramp and Robert T. Farrell arrive at their conclusions about how the fragments of the Ruthwell Cross should be reconstructed, and about the artistic and historical relationships between the Ruthwell and Bewcastle crosses. On the Bewcastle Cross, a panel apparently representing John the Baptist bearing the Agnus Dei occurs above a panel representing Christ being adored by beasts. Between the two panels there is a runic inscription, "gessus kristtus,"[2] which could refer to either panel or to both. On the Ruthwell Cross, as at present reconstructed, a similar panel, apparently representing John the Baptist bearing the Agnus Dei,[3] is likewise placed above a panel representing Christ being adored by beasts. Does the Bewcastle Cross, in which the "Agnus Dei" panel is clearly placed above that representing Christ over the beasts, provide us with valid confirmatory evidence that the present reconstruction of the Ruthwell Cross is the true one? It is not impossible that the Ruthwell "Agnus Dei" panel, on a separate stone from the panel representing Christ adored by the beasts, should originally have been reversed. It may originally have stood above the panel (placed on the other side of the cross as it is now reconstructed) which represents the penitent sinner washing the feet of Christ.[4] Such a rearrangement of the cross could not but have a drastic effect on our interpretation of the spiritual themes of the Ruthwell Cross. The juxtaposition of the "Agnus Dei" panel and that representing Christ adored by beasts on the west side of the Bewcastle Cross suggests nevertheless that the present reconstruction of the Ruthwell Cross is, in this particular, correct. I shall in this paper proceed on the assumption that at Ruthwell, as at Bewcastle, the "Agnus Dei" panel stood from the beginning above the "Christ over the Beasts" panel. However, only the technical studies of Cramp and Farrell can provide the detailed evidence needed to decide such matters.

Our chapter must therefore logically come later in the study than, and be dependent on, the chapters on the archaeology of the crosses and on the stylistic relationships of the Ruthwell and Bewcastle crosses. But an effort to assess the spirituality of the crosses must cope with problems distinct from those of the archaeologist or the art historian. I propose briefly to examine one of these problems. Our ruminations on such matters are still very much "work in progress." However, even the effort to state the problem may be useful, in that it may prompt other scholars to restate the question in a more searching form, or to arrive at more convincing conclusions.

The problem I wish to raise is that the communities which had the monuments erected may well have related a panel to their spiritual lives in several different ways at once. One spiritual use need not in any way preclude other uses; and if in the end we go so far as to state that one spiritual use was primary, it would be wise to do so in the clear awareness that early medieval monks are likely to have been not at all exclusive in such a matter. The reverse, in fact, was probably true: they are likely to have valued figural representations which were relevant to as many facets of their lives (individual and communal) as possible. In a famous passage, St. Gregory the Great wrote that a commentator on Holy Scripture should take every opportunity of digressing from his main theme so as to incorporate other edifying material into his commentary where he felt that such a digression would provide material of spiritual value to his readers or hearers. Gregory used the image of a river, always ready to wander from its course to fill up any neighboring valley which might present itself.[5] Gregory's idea is clearly relevant, *mutatis mutandis,* to the planning of an important religious monument. The concerns of an early medieval monastic patron are likely to have differed markedly from those of a modern scholar anxious to set forth a single coherent theme which can be abstracted from a series of figure-sculptures and to present that as the "iconographic program" of the series. The monastic patron may have been much less interested in any single theme which can be seen to run from panel to panel, and much more interested in how the various panels, and the Cross as a whole, could be seen by members of his monastery to reflect and inspire some of the most important aspects of their community life.

Panels, in short, may have been intended to be "multivalent" — to relate simultaneously to several aspects of the spiritual life of an individual or of a community. I wish to consider the two panels common to the Ruthwell and Bewcastle crosses, because they seem to me to be "multivalent" in this way. The people who erected the crosses are likely to have felt that these panels referred at once to several different scriptural texts and to several different liturgical ceremonies and seasons. I shall argue that the people who erected the crosses would not have seen one interpretation of these panels as excluding other, equally relevant ones.

I. The Principle of Multivalence in the "Christ over the Beasts" Panels on the Ruthwell and Bewcastle Crosses

The "Christ over the Beasts" panel occupies a central position on the west side of the Bewcastle Cross. I would agree with Robert T. Farrell, who argues that the similar panel which occupies a central position on the north side of the Ruthwell Cross originally faced west also: as Farrell points out, this would have meant that on both crosses the figure of Christ would originally have been presented as "coming out of the East" (see Farrell, above, Note 6). The Ruthwell panel was provided with an inscription which indicates how the Ruthwell community felt the panel should be interpreted: "IHS XPS IVDEX AEQVITATIS: BESTIAE ET DRACONES COGNOUERVNT IN DESERTO SALVATOREM MVNDI" ("Jesus Christ the judge of equity. The animals and serpents recognized the Saviour of the world in the desert").[6] The inscription directs our attention to three important themes: (a) Christ as "judge of equity"; (b) the recognition of Christ as "the Saviour of the world"; (c) the "beasts and dragons" who recognize Christ in the desert.

Fritz Saxl and Meyer Schapiro have fully explored the importance of "life in the desert" (a *topos* seen as particularly relevant to the monastic life) as a theme on the Ruthwell Cross: the theme is emphasized, for example, in the panel immediately below "Christ over the Beasts," which represents the Egyptian monks, Saints Paul and Anthony, breaking bread in the desert, and is inscribed "scs pavlvs et antonivs fregervnt panem in deserto."[7] Saxl and Schapiro have also set forth the verbal parallels in the psalter and in the Acts of the Apostles to the phrase "ivdex aeqvitatis."[8] Meyer Schapiro, in particular, has emphasized that the theme of the recognition of Christ by the beasts has its origin in visions of Messianic harmony between the human and natural worlds which go back to the prophecies of Isaiah.[9] Recent research has suggested that there may have been an early monastic enclosure at Ruthwell.[10] In any effort to understand the part the "Christ over the Beasts" panel (and its inscription) may have played in the spiritual life of a community at Ruthwell, two scriptural texts become preeminent, because they were given particularly prominent and relevant liturgical uses. Such liturgical uses must have affected the way in which the Ruthwell monks imagined the "Christ over the Beasts" panels on their cross.

My argument in this paper will depend on the assumption that because the liturgy constituted *the* work of a monastery, liturgical texts were by their nature very different from literary texts. The importance of the liturgy is indicated by the names used for it: *officium divinum* or *opus Dei;* and an immediate indication of its central role in monastic life can be gained by considering how many of the chapters of the Benedictine Rule (and other monastic rules, earlier and later) are devoted to prescribing what texts should be sung, and when.[11] Literary texts (say, patristic commentaries on Scripture) were used primarily for private meditation, *lectio divina:* a detail in them might have meant a lot to one man; but they could have hardly meant as much to every member of a community. Liturgical texts, on the other hand, were communally sung; those sung daily or weekly, or on great feasts such as Good Friday, must have been seen as familiar landmarks, spacing out a monk's life in the community. It was by the liturgical services that a monk counted the hours: these services were as regular as clockwork, or at least as regular as could be managed in a world without clocks. Thus individual liturgical texts literally shaped the life of a monk. It is difficult to find appropriate analogies in modern secular life: perhaps, *mutatis mutandis,* the morning drive to work, or the recurrence of an important lecture one day each week, or the firm's annual stock-taking exercise, are the closest available. It follows that the significance or connotation of a liturgical text must have been determined by its liturgical uses as well as (and almost as much as) the literal denotations of its words.

The most relevant guides to the meaning of a given liturgical text are (a) the other texts used with it that day; and (b) the liturgical actions which accompanied the singing of the text. Liturgical performance is for literary scholars a particularly fascinating phenomenon, because it continually involved the deconstruction and reconstruction of scriptural texts: deconstruction, in that texts were taken out of their original contexts, so that their meaning was thereby altered, often drastically (Old Testament texts, for example, were placed in new contexts which made it impossible to read them except as prefiguring Christianity); reconstruction, because texts were recombined into varied new conjunctions, controlled by the shape of the liturgical year. As we shall argue, a monk or a nun would have seen references to Christ in the desert from the perspective of the Lenten season, when the Church each year symbolically accompanied Christ into the desert to fast, pray, and overcome temptation. This spiritual aspect of the Lenten season may be one reason for the emphasis on the "IN DESERTO" theme on the north side of the Ruthwell Cross. Because liturgical performance was central to the life of a monk or a nun, scriptural events would have merged in his or her imagination with the ways in which the community publicly re-enacted these events each year, each month, each week and perhaps each day. Liturgical performance gave to each liturgical text a dramatic context which must never be forgotten when considering its meaning.

With these considerations in mind, let us consider the two texts whose liturgical uses make them of primary importance for the "Christ over the Beasts" panels at Ruthwell and at Bewcastle. The first text is Verse 13 of Psalm 90 (Latin numbering): "Super aspidem et basiliscum ambulabis et conculcabis leonem et draconem" ("Thou shalt walk upon the asp and the basilisk: and thou shalt trample under foot the lion and dragon").[12] All scholars agree that the panel (whatever its other associations) represents Christ during his sojourn in the desert at the beginning of his public ministry — the episode summarized in St. Mark's Gospel as follows: "And he was in the desert forty days and forty nights, and was tempted by Satan. And he was with beasts: and the angels ministered unto him" (Mark 1:13). The primary reference of the phrase "IN DESERTO" in the inscription to the panel is clearly to Christ's sojourn in the desert. But Christ's forty-day fast in the desert would have been re-enacted yearly, in the liturgical life of the Ruthwell and Bewcastle communities, in forty days of Lenten fasting. At the beginning of this season, on the first Sunday of Lent, St. Matthew's account of Christ's fast in the desert and of his victory over the devil's temptations was read at Mass (Matthew 4:1-11). In this lection, Psalm 90:12 is quoted by the devil in his second temptation, when he urges Christ to cast himself down from the pinnacle of the Temple: "For it is written: 'That he hath given his angels charge over thee, and in their hands shall they bear thee up, lest perhaps thou dash thy foot against a stone'" (Matthew 4:6–7). Patristic commentaries, both on the Gospel accounts and on Psalm 90, naturally interpreted the following verse of Psalm 90, in which the Messiah tramples on the beasts and dragons, as a prefiguration of the way in which Christ rejected this temptation.[13]

In 1944, Meyer Schapiro pointed out that St. Matthew's account of Christ's temptations in the desert was used as a Lenten reading, and Robert T. Farrell, in a paper published in 1978, brought out the importance of this idea.[14] The practical relevance of Christ's sojourn in the desert would have been made clear to the Ruthwell community by the fact that Matthew 4:1–11 was read at Mass on the first Sunday in Lent. The first Sunday in Lent, *Dominica in Caput Quadragesimae,* was of primary importance: the liturgical readings and responsories for that day established both the rationale and the atmosphere for the ensuing season. The other scriptural texts adduced by Saxl and Schapiro are indeed relevant to the panels; but because Psalm 90 was actually quoted in the liturgical lection which described Christ's desert ordeal, a monastic community would have been particularly sensitive to any visual or verbal reference to it. It is not at all that Psalm 90 would exclude reminiscences of the other texts; but its liturgical prominence must have given that psalm a special place in the imagination of a monastic community. The sung texts (introit psalm, gradual, tract, offertory and communion) for the first Sunday in Lent were all taken from Psalm 90: it must have been very difficult for a monk or nun to imagine Christ in the desert without thinking also of the psalm so closely united with Matthew 4:1–11 by the liturgy.[15] Reminiscences of texts which had less prominence in the liturgical life of the community would have, as it were, clustered around the texts which had the greatest liturgical importance. The relevance of other texts would indeed have been appreciated; but they would hardly have had quite the same resonance for monastic audiences as those texts which were central to their communal life.

In the life of a monk or nun, Lent had a greater significance than any other liturgical season. St. Benedict had laid down that "the life of a monk ought at all times to be Lenten in its character."[16] It is relevant therefore to point out that Psalm 90 was prescribed by the Benedictine Rule for compline every evening of the year.[17] If the Ruthwell and Bewcastle communities followed the Rule of St. Benedict, or the Roman custom, in this particular, they would have sung Psalm 90 each evening as part of their preparations against "the terror of the night" ("non timebis a terrore nocturno" [Psalm 90:5]); they would therefore have been reminded, nightly, of the fulfilment of Psalm 90, in Christ's victory over temptation in the desert. It is therefore interesting that representations of Christ over the beasts (Psalm 90:13) often occur, as Professor Farrell has pointed out above, on terra-cotta lamps: the lamps were presumably used at night-prayers, during which Psalm 90 would have been recited, or to light the way to bed immediately afterwards. Monks or nuns would each night have been reminded of their kinship, as individuals and as a community, with Christ who had withdrawn from the world to fast and pray "IN DESERTO." A monastic community must therefore have been particularly ready to respond to any association between Psalm 90 and a scene in which Christ was victorious in the desert.

But it is unlikely that the sculptors at Ruthwell and at Bewcastle intended Psalm 90, important as it was, to be the only association in the minds of those who looked at the "Christ over the Beasts" panels on their crosses. While clearly referring, in both panels, to visual representations of Psalm 90:13, the sculptors fundamentally altered the appearance and so the significance of the "Christ over the Beasts" panels on both crosses. If the sculptors were familiar with representations of the verse in which Christ, sometimes clad in armor, often bore the Cross as his weapon and trampled on a lion, a dragon, an asp, a basilisk or some combination of these beasts,[18] then it is highly significant that the sculptors completely avoided such heroic details and represented Christ on each cross with his right hand raised in blessing and with a scroll in his left hand. As Robert T. Farrell has pointed out above, the beasts at Ruthwell and Bewcastle may or may not have their paws raised in prayer or adoration. But it is highly interesting that they cannot definitely be identified as asps, basilisks, lions, or dragons—nor even, as Farrell has correctly emphasized, as swine. In the light of Farrell's discussion, it would seem that the sculptors at Ruthwell and Bewcastle were not concerned to suggest particular species of animals; in each case, their primary concern seems to have been to represent, simply, "two animals."

This brings us to the second text which, I wish to argue, the Ruthwell and Bewcastle sculptors wanted their communities to recall when they looked at the "Christ over the Beasts" panels. As long ago as 1944, Meyer Schapiro suggested that the Old Latin version of Habbakuk, Chapter 3 might be relevant to the "Christ over the Beasts" panel at Ruthwell.[19] But, apparently not realizing the liturgical importance of Habbakuk, Chapter 3, he simply listed this text in a footnote along with other texts, and so the importance of the passage for the interpretation of the panels was not realized. The Old Latin version of the Canticle of Habbakuk was sung every Friday morning at lauds. Bede wrote a commentary on the canticle for an unnamed nun: in it he naturally follows the Old Latin text, and begins by emphasizing the symbolic significance of singing it every Friday:

> Canticum prophetae Abacuc, quod tibi exponi petisti, dilectissima in Christo soror, sacramenta dominicae passionis maximo pronuntiat. Vnde et consuetudine sanctae universalis et apostolicae ecclesiae sexta sabbati, qua eadem passio conpleta est, solet in laudibus matutinis per singulas ebdomadas sollemniter repeti.[20]

> The canticle of the prophet Habbacuc, of which, beloved sister in Christ, you asked for an exposition, prophesies above all the sacred events of the Lord's Passion. Therefore, and by the tradition of the holy, universal and apostolic Church, on the sixth day from the Sabbath [Friday], on which that same Passion was brought to completion, it is customary to repeat it solemnly each week, at the morning service of praise [lauds].

I quote the beginning of the canticle from the Vespasian Psalter:

> Domine audivi auditum tuum et timui:
>   Consideravi opera tua et expavi.
> *In medio duorum animalium innotesceris:*
>   Dum adpropiaverint anni *cognosceris;*
>   Dum advenerit tempus ostenderis in eo.
> Dum conturbata fuerit anima mea in ira,
>   misericordiae memor eris.
> Deus a Libano veniet,
>   et sanctus de monte umbroso et condenso.
> Operuit caelos majestas ejus
>   et laudi ejus plena est terra.

> Lord, I have heard your voice and been afraid:
>   I have considered your works and been terrified.
> *In the midst of two animals you will be recognized:*
>   When the years come to pass *you will be known;*
>   When the time comes, you will be revealed in it.
> When my soul is totally shaken in [your?] anger,
>   you will remember mercy.
> The Lord will come from Lebanon,
>   and the holy one from a shaded, thickly-wooded hill.
> His majesty has overspread the heavens,
>   and the earth is filled with his praise.[21]

At Ruthwell and at Bewcastle, the sculptors have encouraged reminiscence of the Canticle of Habbakuk in various ways. They used the verb "cognoscere" in the inscription (COGNOUERVNT IN DESERTO). As Robert T. Farrell has demonstrated in his article, it is uncertain whether the animals adore Christ or pray to him; but their attitude certainly suggests that they recognize him. The sculptors seem to have tried to make them as unspecific as possible — simply "two animals." The sculptors presented Christ, not as trampling down upon, but as recognized by the animals. On both crosses, the heads of the animals converge: their bodies are represented as sloping inwards towards each other, and fill the outward corners of the bottom of each panel. Thus the sculptors have suggested that the bodies of the animals extend outward, on either side of the towering figures of Christ who is, to this extent, "in medio duorum animalium." A more obvious representation of the animals on either side of the figure of Christ on each cross would have had two serious disadvantages. As the crosses were so slender, each figure of Christ would have had to be made unacceptably thin or small. Second, and more important, the multivalence of the panels would have been destroyed. It was by presenting the two animals below the feet of Christ yet recognizing him that the sculptors managed to combine a reference to Psalm 90 with a reference to the Canticle of Habbakuk.

Both Psalm 90 and the Canticle of Habbakuk were used together during one very important ceremony — the ceremony of readings on Good Friday. On Good Friday, Mass was not celebrated. Instead, at the ninth hour (3 P.M.), the hour at which, according to the synoptic Gospels, Christ died on the Cross, there began a service of readings and solemn prayers; this ceremony ended with the veneration of the Cross. During the eighth century, a communion service, the "Mass of the Presanctified," began to be added to the original "aliturgical" service of readings, after the veneration of the Cross.[22] The first reading in this solemn ceremony was an Old Testament prophecy of the Passion (Hosea 6:1-6); and this was followed by the singing of responsories based on the opening verses of the Canticle of Habbakuk.[23] Thus, writing about A.D. 394, St. Jerome stated that the common people saw the phrase "in medio duorum animalium innotesceris" as referring to Christ, who is recognized between two thieves on the Cross; Jerome himself, as we shall see, preferred more learned interpretations of the phrase.[24] This popular association of the canticle with the Crucifixion probably indicates that the canticle was, already in the fourth century, intimately associated with the Good Friday liturgy.

What for Jerome was merely a popular tradition was for Bede of central importance. Bede gives far more prominence than Jerome had done to the idea that "in medio duorum animalium innotesceris" refers to Christ on the Cross, and so interprets the phrase primarily in the light of its liturgical use (on Good Friday and on every other Friday). Bede relates the phrase to two episodes: the Transfiguration, in which the three disciples (Peter, James and John) had recognized Christ in the midst of Moses and Elijah; and the Crucifixion itself, in which Christ was recognized between two thieves. Bede emphasizes that these two episodes were related: at the Transfiguration, Christ revealed to the disciples that he was to suffer, die and rise again, while the voice from heaven revealed to them that Christ was the Son of God. Likewise, the Crucifixion is seen by Bede as a revelation of Christ's twofold nature as man and God:

> Potest etiam in medio duorum latronum non inconuenienter accipi, inter quos crucifixus moriendo innotescebat, quia homo erat. Obscurato autem sole, terra commota, et ceteris quae euangelium narrat circa crucem facta miraculis, innotescebat quia Deus erat. Interpellando ipse patrem pro interfectoribus suis, quam pius esset innotescebat.[25]

> Indeed, [the phrase] can be not unsuitably taken as "in the midst of two thieves"; for by dying on the Cross between those, he made known that he was a man. However, by the darkening of the sun, the earthquake, and the other miracles which the Gospel narrates as performed about the Cross, he made known that he was God. He made known how merciful he was, when he himself interceded with his Father for his executioners.

The crucial factor uniting Transfiguration to Crucifixion in Bede's imagination is that both scenes involve an audience of the faithful. For Bede, the important element in each scene is not Moses and Elias or the two thieves, but the onlookers to whom, in each scene, Christ's twofold nature is revealed. As we shall see, this is important both for the interpretation of the "Christ over the Beasts" panel, and for that of the neighboring panels on the same side of the Ruthwell Cross. At this stage, the important point to note is that Bede's emphasis on the Crucifixion as an epiphany of Christ's nature is quite consistent with, and indeed was probably suggested by, the liturgical uses of the canticle.

In the Good Friday liturgy, the Habbakuk responsory was followed by the second Old Testament reading, the divine commands to Moses about how the Paschal lamb was to be prepared and eaten (Exodus 12:1–11). In all the surviving antiphonaries, this second reading is followed by the tract

"Eripe me" (from Psalm 139); but up to the end of the eighth century the tract after this second Old Testament reading was none other than the "Qui habitat," Psalm 90. This tract was later transferred to the first Sunday in Lent, a Sunday on which, as we have already seen, the antiphons of the Mass were already dominated by Psalm 90.[26] After the "Qui habitat" came the solemn reading of the Passion according to St. John, and the adoration of the Cross.

It would seem, therefore, that in presenting their "Christ over the Beasts" panels as multivalent images which recall at once the Canticle of Habakuk and Psalm 90, the Ruthwell and Bewcastle sculptors intended a direct reference to the Good Friday liturgy. A monk or nun of the Ruthwell community would probably have recited Psalm 90 each evening, and the Canticle of Habakuk every Friday morning: but the image on the Ruthwell Cross would have reminded them of the ceremony in which both texts were sung by the community directly after one another (for in a monastery the whole community would have participated in the responsories, while the Old Testament lections would have been assigned to a single lector) — the commemoration of the moment of Christ's death on Good Friday.

On both the Ruthwell and Bewcastle crosses, Christ is represented as facing out towards the spectator, his right hand raised in blessing and his left hand grasping a scroll. Such a presentation of Christ may be influenced by the Canticle of Habakuk. The scroll can possibly be interpreted in the light of St. Jerome's commentary on "in medio duorum animalium." The central theme of Jerome's commentary on the phrase is the way in which God, and the mystery of the Trinity, was progressively revealed in Scripture, first in the Old Testament, then in the New. Having surveyed the relevant Old Testament texts (in particular the way in which God used to speak to Israel "de medio duorum cherubim," over the ark of the covenant [Exodus 25:22]), Jerome briefly refers to the popular interpretation of the phrase as referring to Christ on the Cross between the two thieves. But Jerome saw the phrase primarily in ecclesiological terms. Thus the climax of his interpretation relates the phrase to the way Christ was made known, in the life of the primitive Church, by the combined testimony of the Old and New Testaments:

> Qui autem melius, hoc dicunt, quod in prima Ecclesia quae de circumcisione fuit, et de praeputio congregata, duobus populis se hinc inde cingentibus, intellectus sit Saluator et creditus. Sunt qui duo animalia, duo intellegant testamenta, nouum et uetus, quae uere

animantia sint, quae uitalia, quae spirent et in quorum medio Dominus cognoscatur.[27]

But those who [understand the matter] better, say that the Saviour is to be understood and believed in the primitive Church, which was brought together both from the circumcised and from the uncircumcised — the Saviour surrounding himself, on the one side and on the other, by two peoples. There are those who interpret the two animals as the two Testaments, Old and New, which can be said to be truly life-giving and full of life, to breathe [the Spirit], and in the midst of which the Lord may be known.

What is common to Bede's and to Jerome's interpretations is their readiness to interpret the two animals as referring to human beings (Bede's use of Moses and Elias and of the two thieves, and Jerome's use of the Jews and Gentiles, whose coming together constituted the Church). The scroll in Christ's left hand, in each panel, seems designed to suggest that the animals below are to be taken as standing for the ways in which Christ was to be known through the Church's teaching (as in Jerome's commentary). The upraised paws of the animals, if indeed they *could* be gestures of prayer or adoration, would also reinforce this symbolic level of meaning.

The right hand of Christ, raised in blessing, is another significant detail in each of the two "Christ over the Beasts" panels. The inscription on the Ruthwell Cross combines, as we have seen, three ideas: Christ as judge, the recognition of Christ as Saviour, and his recognition by animals in the desert. In the Canticle of Habbakuk, these three ideas are strikingly combined. Not only does the canticle present Christ as revealed between two animals; throughout the canticle the ideas of judgment and salvation, of advent and eschatology, are repeatedly juxtaposed. In the opening verses, quoted above, the prophet moves from fear at "the Lord's voice" ("auditum tuum") to trust that he will remember mercy ("misericordiae memor eris"). This progression is repeated throughout the canticle: both the canticle and the panels on the two crosses are concerned with the interrelationship of fear and trust, and of judgment and blessing.[28]

The association of the Canticle of Habbakuk with lauds, the office sung at daybreak, is interesting. As we have seen, Robert T. Farrell has argued (see above, Note 6) that the "Christ over the Beasts" panels on both crosses originally faced west, as the one at Bewcastle still does. But this would have meant that a monk at Ruthwell or Bewcastle, when he left the monastic church after lauds on Friday morning, would have seen the rising sun behind the "Christ over the Beasts" panel. He could hardly fail to be reminded of such verses in the canticle he had just sung as

> Operuit caelos majestas ejus,
>   et laudi ejus plena est terra.
> Splendor ejus sicut lumen erit,
>   cornua sunt in manibus ejus:
> ibi confirmata est virtus gloriae ejus,
>   et posuit claritatem firmam fortitudini suae.[29]

> His majesty has óverspread the heavens,
>   and the earth is filled with his praise.
> His glory will be as a radiance,
>   there are horns in his hands:
> there is the power of his glory established,
>   and there has he set a powerful light for his valour.

It may not be a coincidence that the corresponding panel on the opposite side of the Ruthwell Cross depicts the healing of the blind man, and that the inscription to this panel quotes the beginning of the appropriate lection, John 9:1–38. If Robert Farrell's theory about the orientation of the Ruthwell Cross is correct, this panel would have occupied the central position on the east side of the cross. It would then have been seen daily against the setting sun, and the Ruthwell community might possibly have been reminded of the importance in that lection of images of light and of approaching darkness:

> Me oportet operari opera eius qui misit me, donec dies est: venit nox, quando nemo potest operari: quamdiu sum in mundo, lux sum mundi.[30]

> I must work the works of him that sent me, whilst it is day: the night cometh, when no man can work. As long as I am in the world, I am the light of the world.

Again, the multivalence of the symbolism embodied in the panels should be emphasized. What we might term "orientational" symbolism would not have interfered with the other symbolic patterns to which these panels contribute; but it would have helped the Ruthwell community, and those who looked at the Bewcastle Cross, to relate to their daily or weekly lives any wider symbolic significance which the panels had. If monastic life was shaped and marked out by the hours of the divine office, we should not be surprised to find references on the crosses to the hours at which canticles were sung, or to find Gospel lections represented in positions which brought out the symbolic importance of temporal references within them.

Indeed, if the Ruthwell Cross was oriented in the way Farrell has suggested, there may have been a practical liturgical purpose behind such orientation. If at certain times it was thought proper to erect a temporary altar at the cross, it would have been placed against the west side. In this way, the celebrant could correctly face east during Mass. Such an altar would have covered the "Return from Egypt" panel; immediately above it, however, the "Paul and Anthony" panel would have been at least partially visible; and the celebration of Mass or the distribution of the Eucharist (for example, during the "Mass of the Presanctified" on Good Friday, a ceremony which I shall discuss in relation to the two crosses in a forthcoming article), would have given a very practical application to the "eucharistic triptych" (Paul and Anthony/Christ over the Beasts/Agnus Dei).

The orientation suggested by Farrell may have facilitated the liturgical use of the crosses; it would certainly have enriched the devotional associations of the "Christ over the Beasts" panel on each cross. It has long been recognized that these panels refer to Messianic harmony between men and beasts; and the earthly paradise was known to have existed in the East. The Ruthwell inscription gives an eschatological interpretation to the panel; and Scripture foretold that Christ would come like lightning from the East ("sicut enim fulgur exit ab oriente" [Matthew 24:27]) to judge the world. On both crosses, this truth is presented with a noble fusion of urgency and confidence: Christ may be represented as judge, but his right hand is raised to bless the onlookers on whom he gazes so majestically. This confident faith, movingly represented on both crosses, has at Ruthwell been also recorded in words. The Ruthwell community waited in the desert to recognize Christ as "IVDEX AEQVITATIS."

On the Bewcastle Cross, the "Christ over the Beasts" and "Agnus Dei" panels would also, as at Ruthwell, have been visible above a temporary altar. If Mass was ever celebrated at the cross, the theme of "recognizing Christ," which as we shall argue unites both panels, would have been made plain by liturgical action.[31] It is possibly in such practical liturgical use of the Ruthwell and Bewcastle crosses that an explanation may be found of the close correspondence between the upper parts of the two monuments, while the lower panels are different on each cross. When a temporary altar was placed before each cross, the monument would have functioned as a reredos for the altar. Over the altar, at both Ruthwell and Bewcastle, the iconography would have been the same: and we shall see that in each case it would have been clearly eucharistic.

II. The Principle of Multivalence in the "Agnus Dei" Panels on the Ruthwell and Bewcastle Crosses

On both the Ruthwell and the Bewcastle crosses, the panel directly above "Christ over the Beasts" represents a human figure bearing a lamb, presumably the Lamb of God (Agnus Dei). There are at least four possible spiritual contexts for the panels:

(i) The first is that of private devotion: Edmund Bishop long ago pointed out that the words "Agnus Dei, qui tollis peccata mundi, miserere nobis" came to England as part of the Litany of the Saints, and seem to have been used as a private prayer from about the year 700.[32] Such a devotion would have been reflected with particular appropriateness on a monument associated with Good Friday: we have seen above how, in the Good Friday readings, Christ's sacrifice on Calvary was associated with the paschal lamb of Exodus.

(ii) The second possible context is baptism: it was at the Jordan, where he was baptizing converts, that John the Baptist acclaimed Christ as the Lamb of God. It is only in St. John's Gospel that John the Baptist is described as acknowledging Christ as the Agnus Dei; and in that Gospel, John the Baptist is not described as baptizing Christ. Nevertheless, the scene takes place in Bethania across the Jordan, "where John was baptizing" (John 1:28). St. John's Gospel used material in this scene which clearly corresponded to the synoptic accounts in which the Baptist baptized Jesus. Thus, the account of the Baptist hailing Christ as the Lamb of God in John's Gospel was universally harmonized with the synoptic accounts of the baptism of Jesus.

(iii) A third possible context for the "Agnus Dei" panel is the Eucharist: Pope Sergius I introduced the words "Agnus Dei, qui tollis peccata mundi, miserere nobis" into the Mass; they were chanted at the moment of the breaking of bread for Communion.[33] The importance of this innovation has been emphasized by Michel Andrieu:

> On sait combien, dans l'ancienne liturgie romaine, les prières directement adressées au Christ sont rares. Dans le Canon de la messe et dans l'oraison dominicale, c'est le Père tout-puissant, et lui seul, qu'invoque le célébrant, par les mérites et l'intercession du Sauveur. Brusquement, avec l'*Agnus Dei,* la prière prend une autre orientation: c'est vers la victime sainte que sont maintenant dirigées les supplications de l'assemblée.[34]

In the canon and communion of the Mass, during which prayers were almost entirely addressed directly to God the Father *through* Christ his Son, this direct petition to Christ was a striking innovation. This innovation in public worship is perhaps the most likely context for the single word which still survives of the inscription around the "Agnus Dei" panel, the plural verb "ADORAMVS."[35]

(iv) A fourth possible context is eschatological: in the fifth chapter of the Apocalypse of St. John, the triumph of the slain but risen Christ is celebrated in the symbol of the Lamb being adored by a multitude of the blessed.

Which of these contexts is most relevant to the crosses? The fact that the Agnus Dei prayer was used in private devotion suggests that certain members of the Ruthwell congregation may have responded to the panel in isolation, without reference to neighboring panels, as a devotional object in its own right. Such a response could have validly coexisted with baptismal, eucharistic or eschatological interpretations of the panel. The baptismal associations of the Agnus Dei are also very appropriate to the context of the panel on the Ruthwell Cross. The recognition of Christ as the Agnus Dei comes from the Gospel of St. John ("Ecce agnus Dei, ecce qui tollit peccatum mundi" [John 1:29; cp. John 1:36]). St. John has transformed the synoptic accounts of Jesus' baptism into a threefold proclamation, by John the Baptist, of the divinity of Jesus:

> sed qui misit me baptizare in aqua, ille mihi dixit: Super quem videris Spiritum descendentem, et manentem super eum, hic est qui baptizat in Spiritu sancto. Et ego vidi: et testimonium perhibui quia hic est Filius Dei. Altera die iterum stabat Ioannes, et ex discipulis eius duo. Et respiciens Iesum ambulantem, dicit: Ecce agnus Dei. (John 1:33-36)[36]

> But he who sent me to baptize with water said to me: He upon whom thou shalt see the Spirit descending and remaining upon him, he it is that baptizeth with the Holy Ghost. And I saw: and I gave testimony that this is the Son of God. The next day again John stood and two of his disciples. And beholding Jesus walking, he saith: Behold the Lamb of God.

The scene in the Gospel of St. John in which John the Baptist acknowledges Jesus as the Lamb of God combines a meditation on Christian baptism with a solemn declaration that Jesus is the Son of God. But the recognition of Christ's true nature seems to be an important devotional concern of the panels under discussion. On both crosses, the panel just below the Agnus

Dei emphasizes that even the "bestiae et dracones" recognized Christ as the Saviour of the world. At Ruthwell, as we shall see, this devotional theme is carried even further, by the "Paul and Anthony" and the "Return from Egypt" panels.

Bede wrote a whole homily on the lection from St. John's Gospel in which Christ is recognized as "the Lamb of God" by John the Baptist (John 1:29-34). The homily was intended for use on the Sunday after the Epiphany, the Sunday on which Christ's baptism was commemorated. The opening paragraph of this homily is an extended meditation on the various meanings of the title "Agnus Dei," and this passage is surely the *locus classicus* for understanding how an eighth-century monastic audience would have interpreted the Ruthwell and Bewcastle "Agnus Dei" panels.[37] What is very revealing is the relative space Bede devotes to the various interpretations of the title, and so the relative emphasis he places on each possible devotional perspective. Bede first contrasts the innocence of Christ, the second Adam, with the sin of the first (ll. 5-7). This leads naturally to the idea of the lamb (especially the lamb among wolves) as a symbol of threatened innocence (ll. 8-11). Bede begins the central part of his exposition (ll. 11-28) with the idea that Christians have been washed in the blood of the lamb (he quotes 1 Peter 1:18-19 and Apocalypse 1:5). In this passage, Bede fuses images of baptismal washing with images of Christ's sacrifice on Calvary; and mention of Calvary brings Bede to his central point: the daily re-enactment of Calvary in the Mass. The importance of this passage for the Ruthwell panel is very great. It shows that in Bede's mind the idea of the Agnus Dei, and the very idea of baptism, was intimately associated with the eucharistic sacrifice. This passage has, indeed, been adduced by G. G. Willis to show that Bede used the "Agnus Dei" chant (with its variant "peccata mundi," instead of St. John's "peccatum mundi") daily at the breaking of bread for communion:

> Non solum autem lauit nos a peccatis nostris in sanguine suo quando sanguinem suum dedit in cruce pro nobis uel quando unusquisque nostrum mysterio sacraesanctae passionis illius baptismi aqua ablutus est uerum etiam cotidie tollit peccata mundi lauatque nos a peccatis nostris cotidianis in sanguine suo cum eiusdem beatae passionis ad altare memoria replicatur cum panis et uini creatura in sacramentum carnis et sanguinis eius ineffabili spiritus sanctificatione transfertur sicque corpus et sanguis illius non infidelium manibus ad perniciem ipsorum funditur et occiditur sed fidelium ore suam sumitur in salutem.[38]

Not only did he wash us from our sins in his blood when he gave his blood for us on the Cross, or when each one of us was washed in the water of baptism through the mystery of his sacred Passion: but indeed he daily takes away the sins of the world, and washes us from our daily sins in his blood, when the memory of his blessed Passion is re-enacted at the altar, and when what was created bread and wine is transformed into the sacrament of his body and blood, through the ineffable hallowing of the spirit. And in this way his body and blood is no longer spilled and slain by the hands of infidels to their damnation, but is received by the mouths of the faithful to their salvation.

Bede then rounds off his exposition of the title "Agnus Dei" by referring to the sacrifice of a paschal lamb yearly in the Old Law (to commemorate the paschal lamb of Exodus) as a figure of Calvary (ll. 28-32). But this leads him back finally to his central theme: how such Old Testament rites were fulfilled when Christ, the priest according to the order of Melchisedech, offered himself to his Father under the form of bread and wine (ll. 32-36).[39]

If devotion to the Agnus Dei was primarily seen by Bede in the context of the Eucharist, this seems also to be the context primarily in the minds of the Ruthwell sculptors. In the context they provided for their "Agnus Dei" panel, eucharistic associations predominate. On the same side of the cross as the "Agnus Dei" panel, we have the figures of Saints Paul and Anthony, identified by the inscription as having "broken bread in the desert"; while between the "Paul and Anthony" panel and the "Agnus Dei" panel on Ruthwell, there is the figure of Christ recognized by the beasts. Anyone able to read the Ruthwell inscriptions would have recognized in the "fregerunt panem" of the "Paul and Anthony" panel a reference to the "fractio panis," the technical term for the breaking of bread for Communion at Mass.[40] Similarly, such a reader of Latin inscriptions would have been likely to recognize, in both the "fregerunt panem" phrase and in the phrase "cognoverunt ... Salvatorem mundi," attached to the panel of "Christ over the Beasts," the echo of the episode in St. Luke where the disciples on the road to Emmaus "recognize" the anonymous Christ "in the breaking of bread":

> accepit panem, et benedixit, ac fregit, et porrigebat illis. Et aperti sunt oculi eorum, et cognoverunt eum: et ipse evanuit ex oculis eorum.[41]

> [H]e took bread and blessed and brake and gave to them. And their

eyes were opened: and they knew him. And he vanished out of their sight.

This scriptural passage is referred to during the Communion ceremony in the Stowe Missal, in a passage which makes perfectly clear that in eucharistic contexts there was an important connection between "knowing" the Lord ("cognoverunt") and the "fractio panis": "cognoerunt dominum. alleluia. in fractione paniş. alleluia"[42] ("they knew the Lord. Alleluia. in the breaking of bread. Alleluia").

George Henderson has provided convincing evidence that the Ruthwell community is likely to have seen eucharistic significance in all of the surviving panels on this side of the cross. He has pointed out that the representation of the so-called "Flight into Egypt," below the "Paul and Anthony" panel, is more likely to have been seen as illustrating the prophecy quoted by St. Matthew apropos of Christ's sojourn in Egypt: "Out of Egypt I have called my son."[43] The panel can therefore be seen to represent the Christ Child re-enacting the crossing of the desert during the Exodus, when the Jews were fed with manna from heaven. Christ himself was the heavenly food which the manna of the Exodus had prefigured.

What of the fourth, eschatological, context which I have suggested for the "Agnus Dei" panel? Eschatological ideas are evident in the panels which apparently flanked the "Agnus Dei" panel on the Ruthwell Cross. As Rosemary Cramp suggested in 1978, there was probably an apocalypse scene on the crosspiece of the transom (directly above the "Agnus Dei" panel). She argued that at the crosspiece there was a representation of the apocalyptic Lamb, or perhaps of a *Majestas Domini*. This central figure would have been surrounded by the four Evangelist symbols, of which two still survive (St. John and his eagle above,[44] St. Matthew and his angel below). The scene would have represented the passage in the Apocalypse of St. John in which the Lamb and the throne are adored by the beasts and elders.[45] An eschatological perspective is also clearly implied by the inscription around the figure of Christ, "IVDEX AEQVITATIS," adored by the beasts.

George Henderson has pointed out that the probable existence of the apocalypse scene above the "Agnus Dei" panel would have made it unlikely that the "Agnus Dei" panel itself represented the same scene.[46] It is, however, important to note how natural would have been the transition from an "Agnus Dei" panel to the crosspiece which may have represented the adoration of that Lamb (or of Christ in majesty) by the beasts in the Apocalypse. The "Agnus Dei" chant was, as we have seen, from the late seventh century on sung in the Roman Mass while the consecrated bread was being broken for distribution in the Eucharist. But from the earliest days of Christianity, the Eucharist had been seen to have eschatological implications. As the Eucharist had been prefigured by the feeding of Israel with manna in the desert, so the Eucharist itself was seen as a symbol of the complete communion of the Church with Christ which would only be realized with the second coming; while the failure to distinguish Christ's presence in the bread and wine would bring judgment upon the person who received the Eucharist in such an unworthy way:

> Quotiescumque enim manducabitis panem hunc, et calicem bibetis, mortem Domini annuntiabitis *donec veniat*. Itaque quicumque manducaverit panem hunc, vel biberit calicem Domini indigne, reus erit corporis et sanguinis Domini.... Qui enim manducat et bibit indigne, *iudicium sibi manducat et bibit: non diiudicans corpus Domini.*[47]

> For as often as you shall eat this bread and drink the chalice, you shall shew the death of the Lord *until he come*. Therefore, whosoever shall eat this bread, or drink the chalice of the Lord unworthily, shall be guilty of the body and of the blood of the Lord.... For he that eateth and drinketh unworthily *eateth and drinketh judgment to himself, not discerning the body of the Lord.*

This passage from 1 Corinthians comes directly after the classic description by St. Paul of the institution of the Eucharist (1 Corinthians 11:23–25). Verse 26, quoted above, is paraphrased in the words added by the scribe Moelcaich at the end of the formula of consecration in the ninth-century Irish Stowe Missal. Moelcaich expands the Pauline verse so as to bring out the eschatological significance of St. Paul's "donec veniat":

> in mei memoriam faciatis passionem meam predicabitis resurrectionem meam adnuntiabitis aduentum meum sperabitis donec iterum ueniam ad uos de celis.[48]

> You should do this in memory of me; you will proclaim my passion; you will announce my resurrection; you will hope for my coming until I come again to you from the heavens.

St. Paul implies that it will not be long before Christ returns in judgment; and it is clear that he sees the fate of the Christian at the Judgment as depending on whether he has recognized or discerned Christ in the Eucharist. The Ruthwell sculptors were evidently thinking along similar lines when they placed a panel depicting "IHS XPS IVDEX AEQVITATIS" directly above the panel in which Saints Paul and Anthony recognize Christ in the breaking of bread. If Rosemary Cramp's theory about the iconography of the missing crosspiece is correct, the sculptors planned the upper part of this side of the cross so as to represent, in a different symbolic form, the same sequence of ideas. For the second time on this side of the cross, they linked a scene with eucharistic significance directly to an eschatological scene: they placed the panel in which John the Baptist recognizes Christ in symbolic form, as the Agnus Dei, directly under the crosspiece, in which the four evangelist-beasts of St. John's Apocalypse may have been represented as adoring the same Agnus Dei, now revealed in glory at the Last Judgment. The liturgical significance of the linking of the two panels would have been equally clear whether Christ was represented on the missing crosspiece as a glorified Agnus Dei, or "in propria figura" as the *Majestas domini*.

We may suggest, therefore, that while eucharistic associations are dominant in the context provided for the "Agnus Dei" panel on the Ruthwell Cross, all of the four main devotional uses of the Agnus Dei are relevant to the panel. Any one of them may have been important at various times to such members of the Ruthwell community as were in the habit of using their cross as an aid in their devotional lives. The Ruthwell sculptors seem to have intended their cross primarily for devotional use by a community. The way in which they conceived of the people who would use the cross as forming a community can be seen by examining the ordered progression which they embodied in the wording of the inscriptions on this side of the cross. Coming out of Egypt, the Christ Child is carried by "MARIA ET IO[SEPHVS]"—the inscription clearly referring to a pair of figures; another pair, "PAVLVS ET ANTONIVS," break the eucharistic loaf directly above. In this second panel, Christ is already recognized between two figures: and it is significant that the two animals who recognize Christ are placed just above the heads of (and thus visually related to) the figures of St. Paul and St. Anthony. But although a single pair of animals is represented in the "Christ over the Beasts" panel, the inscription refers to them in the plural as "BESTIAE ET DRACONES." The significance of the progression from singular to plural is made clear by the verbal reminiscence which, as Elisabeth Okasha has pointed out, probably lies behind the wording of the inscription:

> Glorificabit me bestia agri, dracones et struthiones: quia dedi in deserto aquas, flumina in invio, ut darem potum populo meo, electo meo.[49]

> The beast of the field shall glorify me, the dragons and the ostriches: because I have given waters in the wilderness, rivers in the desert, to give drink to my people, to my chosen.

By referring to the "BESTIAE ET DRACONES" in the plural, the sculptors recall, through them, "my people, my chosen" ("populo meo, electo meo") whom Christ feeds in the desert. No less an authority than Gregory the Great referred to "all the faithful" as "holy animals" fed by Christ in the Eucharist with his own body ("ut fideles omnes videlicet sancta animalia, carnis suae frumento reficeret").[50] The inscription for the panel directly above carries the pattern we have been examining one step futher, and completes it. The "ADORAMVS" which remains from the "Agnus Dei" inscription is not merely plural but in the first person. It seems to refer directly to the liturgical actions of the Ruthwell community. The inscription around the "Agnus Dei" panel possibly referred openly to the eucharistic significance of the Agnus Dei, and so to the eucharistic theme of "recognizing Christ" expressed in symbolic ways by the panels below. It was just such references to the presence of Christ in the Eucharist, after all, which would have attracted the most diligent attentions of seventeenth-century iconoclasts out to destroy "idolatrous monuments"; ironically enough, it is possible that the "Agnus Dei" chant itself had been introduced at the moment of the breaking of bread as a practical refutation of iconoclastic tendencies in seventh-century Byzantium.[51] Like Paul and Anthony in the desert, the Ruthwell community would have adored Christ, the Agnus Dei, at the breaking of bread. Indeed, a community which saw the Eucharist as their daily spiritual bread could very aptly have summed up their liturgical life in the words "COGNOUERVNT IN DESERTO SALVATOREM MVNDI."

It will be our task, in examining the spiritual uses to which the Ruthwell and Bewcastle crosses may have been put, to be faithful to the fact that, in monastic spirituality, one devotional perspective could coexist quite naturally with another, and indeed with several others. The primary artistic virtue of the monastic tradition was the ability to weave around any theme a rich web of scriptural associations. For monks or nuns, it was not a tangled web. The shifting patterns of association may seem confusing to us, but for a monastic audience the liturgy itself would have controlled, articulated, and organized the various devotional perspectives. Monastic writers like Bede seem to have rejoiced precisely in the variety of perspectives available to them at any one time. They could do so without fear of their readers' being confused: the liturgy itself determined which perspective should be the dominant one, at any particular season, in the devotional life of their readers. The liturgical year was an ordered unity: from the perspective of any part of it, the reader could fittingly be reminded of the riches of the other seasons and their scriptural associations. Modern scholars are trained in a positivistic university tradition preoccupied with what can be shown to be the single correct solution, and with excluding all else as false. But such training can make us unsympathetic to the very different aims and methods of the art of early medieval monasticism. We must indeed remain faithful to our responsibility to be clear and consistent, and to discriminate between associations which are more important and those which are less so; but we should also be careful not to foist our more cut-and-dried forms of thinking onto a culture whose artistic achievements depended on cultivating different virtues.

UNIVERSITY COLLEGE, CORK.

Notes

1. I wish to thank scholars who read various parts and versions of this paper and made valuable suggestions as to how it should be improved, especially my colleagues at Cork, Jennifer O'Reilly and Terence O'Reilly; and, at Oxford, Malcolm Parkes and David Howlett. I also wish to thank the Blackfriars Community, Oxford, for allowing me to use their excellent theological library.

2. See R[aymond] I. Page, "The Bewcastle Cross," *Nottingham Medieval Studies,* 4 (1960), 36–57 (at p. 38).

3. Paul Meyvaert has recently argued that the Agnus Dei is borne, in this panel (and perhaps also on the Bewcastle Cross), not by John the Baptist but by God the Father, the *Majestas Domini:* "An Apocalypse Panel on the Ruthwell Cross," *Medieval and Renaissance Studies: Proceedings of the Southeastern Institute of Medieval and Renaissance Studies, Summer 1978,* ed. Frank Tirro (Durham, N. C., 1982), pp. 3–32. This interpretation has been convincingly challenged by George Henderson in lectures at Cambridge and in a forthcoming paper, "The St. John the Baptist Panel on the Ruthwell Cross." I am grateful to Dr. Henderson for allowing me to read a typescript of this paper before publication.

4. Such a suggestion was made by Paul Meyvaert in a lecture given at Oxford in November 1980 and subsequently given at Cork.

5. Gregory, *Moralia sive Expositio in Job, Epistula Praevia ad Leandrum Hispalensem,* in *PL,* 75:509–16, at column 513.

6. Text and translation adapted from Elisabeth Okasha, *Hand-List of Anglo-Saxon Non-Runic Inscriptions* (Cambridge, 1971), p. 110.

7. Text adapted from Okasha, p. 110; see F[ritz] Saxl, "The Ruthwell Cross," *Journal of the Warburg and Courtauld Institutes,* 6 (1943), 1–19 (at pp. 1–2 and p. 5); and Meyer Schapiro, "The Religious Meaning of the Ruthwell Cross," *Art Bulletin,* 26 (1944), 232–45 (at pp. 232–36).

8. Schapiro, p. 233, and Saxl, p. 1.

9. Schapiro, pp. 234–35; the close and suggestive verbal parallel in Isaiah 43:20 for "bestiae et dracones ... in deserto," identified by Elisabeth Okasha (p. 110), is discussed in the second part of this paper.

10. I rely on the evidence adduced by Paul Meyvaert, in the unpublished lecture already referred to.

11. *The Rule of St. Benedict,* ed. and trans. Justin McCann (London, 1952); and *La Règle de Saint Benoît,* ed. and trans. A. de Vogüé and J. Neufville, 6 vols., Sources Chrétiennes (Paris, 1971–72).

12. Quotations from the psalter and canticles throughout this article are taken from the Vespasian Psalter, ed. Henry Sweet, in *The Oldest English Texts,* EETS, O.S. 83 (London, 1885), pp. 183–420; other Biblical quotations are from *Biblia Sacra iuxta Vulgatam Clementinam,* ed. Alberto Colunga and Laurentio Turrado (Madrid, 1965). All translations from Scripture are from *The Holy Bible* (Douay version) (London, 1914). Unless otherwise indicated, other translations are mine.

13. See Schapiro, p. 233 and n. 5; Saxl, p. 2.

14. Schapiro, pp. 238–39; Robert T. Farrell, "The Archer and Associated Figures on the Ruthwell Cross — A Reconsideration," in *Bede and Anglo-Saxon England,* ed. Robert T. Farrell, British Archaeological Reports, 46 (Oxford, 1978), pp. 96–117 (at pp. 105–07).

15. In 1978, Farrell stated that he could not prove that Psalm 90 was liturgically used on the first Sunday in Lent in Bede's day, although he felt it to be "highly probable" that it was (p. 107). He was surely right in so thinking: verses from Psalm 90 are prescribed for the first Sunday in Lent in the earliest surviving Roman Mass-antiphonaries: see René-Jean Hesbert, ed., *Antiphonale Missarum Sextuplex* (Brussels, 1935), No. 40, pp. 52–55; see the discussion in Hesbert's Introduction, pp. l-lii, of the role of Psalm 90 in the successive chants assigned to the first Sunday in Lent. Matthew 4:1–11 is likewise found as the pericope for the first Sunday in Lent in all the earliest Roman lectionaries: see Theodor Klauser, ed., *Das römische "Capitulare Evangeliorum,"* Liturgiewissenschaftliche Quellen und Forschungen, 28 (Münster, Westphalia, 1935), pp. 19 (No. 56); 65 (No. 64); 107 (No. 60); 146 (No. 73); and 175 (No. 64). As Farrell points out, Matthew 4:1–11 is also given for the first Sunday in Lent in the *capitula lectionum,* of Neapolitan origin, found in the Lindisfarne Gospels: see Stefan Beissel, *Entstehung der Pericopen des Römischen Messbuches* (Freiburg-im-Breisgau, 1907), p. 112. It is likely that Bede made use of this lectionary: see D. Hurst, ed., *Bedae Venerabilis Homiliarum Evangelii Libri II,* CCSL, Vol. 122 (Turnhout, 1965), pp. viii, ix-xvi; and G. G. Willis, "Early English Liturgy from Augustine to Alcuin," *Further Essays in Early Roman Liturgy,* Alcuin Club Collections, 50 (London, 1968), pp. 189–258 (at p. 215). For further examples of the early use of this lection, see Farrell, p. 107 and n. 29.

16. "Licet omni tempore vita monachi Quadragesimae debet observationem habere" (*Rule of St. Benedict,* Chap. 49; ed. McCann, pp. 114–15).

17. "Ad Completorios vero cotidie iidem psalmi repetantur: id est, quartus, nonagesimus, et centesimus trigesimus tertius" (*Rule of St. Benedict,* Chap. 18; ed. McCann, pp. 64–67). Benedict here was following the Roman order for singing

the psalms: see the note in Vogüé and Neufville, at Chapter 18, verse 19 (Vol. II, pp. 532-33).

18. On the traditional visual representation of Psalm 90:13, see Robert T. Farrell, above. It is interesting to speculate on how an Anglo-Saxon monk, who did not have an illustrated psalter, would have imagined the beasts of Psalm 90:13. The Vespasian Psalter (ed. Sweet, p. 320) glosses "aspidem" as "nedran," "basiliscum" as "fagwyrm," "leonem" as "leon" and "draconem" as "dracan."

19. Schapiro, p. 235, n. 21.

20. *Expositio Bedae Presbyteri in Canticum Abacuc Prophetae,* ed. J. E. Hudson, CCSL, Vol. 119B (Turnhout, 1983), pp. 376-409 (at p. 381); cf. *PL,* 91:1235-54 (at cols. 1235-37).

21. Text from the Vespasian Psalter, where the canticle is given the rubric "sexta feria" (Friday) (ed. Sweet, p. 407). Translation mine. On the liturgical use of the canticle, see *The Vespasian Psalter,* ed. David H. Wright, EEMF, Vol. 14 (Copenhagen, 1967), pp. 52-53; James Mearns, *The Canticles of the Christian Church, Eastern and Western, in Early and Medieval Times* (Cambridge, 1914), pp. 51-53; Dom Fernand Cabrol in *Dictionnaire d'archéologie chrétienne et de liturgie* (Paris, 1907-53) (henceforth cited as *DACL*), Vol. II, pt. 2, cols. 1975-94, under "Cantiques." For commentary on the canticle see, in addition to Bede, Jerome *Commentarium in Abacuc Prophetam ad Chromatium,* in his *Commentarii in Prophetas Minores,* ed. M. Adriaen, CCSL, Vol. 76A (Turnhout, 1970), at pp. 618-54 (cf. *PL,* 25:815-1578); and the fragmentary commentary by Verecundus Iuncensis, *Commentarii super Cantica Ecclesiastica, VI, Habbacuc,* in *Verecundi Iuncensis Opera,* ed. R. Demeulenaere, in CCSL, Vol. 93 (Turnhout, 1976), pp. 124-47 (the beginning is missing, including the commentary on Verses 1-3).

22. John Walton Tyrer, *Historical Survey of Holy Week, Its Services and Ceremonial,* Alcuin Club Collections, 29 (Oxford, 1932), pp. 118-42. For the time of the service at Rome, from the seventh century onwards, see the Gelasian Sacramentary, in Leo Cunibert Mohlberg, ed., *Liber Sacramentorum Romanae Aeclesiae Ordinis Anni Circuli,* Rerum Ecclesiasticarum Documenta, Series Maior: Fontes, 4 (Rome, 1960), p. 64, par. 395. The ceremony was held at the ninth hour, at Rome, from the seventh to the fifteenth centuries: see Ludwig Eisenhofer and Joseph Lechner, *The Liturgy of the Roman Rite* (Edinburgh and London, 1961), p. 197; earlier, it had been held at the third hour (9 A.M.), the time at which, according to St. Mark (15:25) Jesus was nailed to the Cross (Tyrer, p. 120). For the ninth hour as the time of Christ's death in the synoptics, see Matthew 27:46; Mark 15:34; Luke 23:44. The third, sixth and ninth hours were traditional Jewish times for prayer; and it has been argued that the indications of time in the Passion narratives themselves originated in the earliest Christian liturgies commemorating the Passion. As Michael D. Goulder has put it, "the Gospel was born from the womb of the liturgy" (*The Evangelists' Calendar: A Lectionary Explanation of the Development of Scripture* [London, 1978], pp. 296-305 [at p. 297]); see also Etienne Trocmé, *The Passion as Liturgy: A Study in the Origin of the Passion Narratives in the Four Gospels* (London, 1983).

23. Tyrer, p. 120; Michel Andrieu, *Les Ordines Romani du haut moyen âge,* 5 vols.,

Spicilegium Sacrum Lovaniense, Vols. 11, 23, 24, 28, and 29 (Louvain, 1931-61), Ordo XXIII, Nos. 17-18 (Vol. III, p. 271) and Ordo XXIV, No. 24 (Vol. III, p. 292). For full texts of the Good Friday responsories, see René Hesbert, No. 78a, pp. 94-95.

24. Jerome *Commentarium in Abacuc*, p. 621; cf. *PL*, 25:1309D. For the date of Jerome's commentary on Habbakuk, see J. N. D. Kelly, *Jerome: His Life, Writings and Controversies* (London, 1975), pp. 159 and 163.

25. Bede *Expositio . . . in Canticum Abacuc*, p. 383; cf. *PL*, 91:1238.

26. Hesbert, p. lix. This use of Psalm 90 on Good Friday is attested by the older Roman *ordines:* see Andrieu, Ordo XXIII, No. 18 (Vol. III, p. 271). Amalarius of Metz, who did not himself use the *Qui habitat* in the Good Friday ceremonies, nevertheless recorded that its use on Good Friday was "iuxta morem antiquum Romanae ecclesiae" (*De Ordine Antiphonarii*, Chap. 7 [cf. *PL*, 105:1260A]), as quoted by Andrieu, Vol. III, p. 271, note.

27. Jerome *Commentarium in Abacuc*, p. 621.

28. Verses 8-9 of the Canticle of Habbakuk, and their interpretation by Jerome and Bede, seem of the greatest relevance for understanding why, on the south side of the Ruthwell Cross, an archer is depicted directly over the heads of Saints Martha and Mary. I develop this idea in a forthcoming paper on the spiritual program of the south side of the cross. The phrase "in medio duorum animalium" seems to be referred to widely (usually in eucharistic contexts) in Pictish and Irish high crosses: see my forthcoming paper, "The Meeting of St. Paul and St. Anthony: Visual and Literary Uses of a Eucharistic Theme (on the Ruthwell Cross, Pictish and Irish Monuments; in the *Navigatio Sancti Brendani* and Adomnán's *Vita Columbae*)," in *Keimalia: Studies in Archaeology and History in Memory of Tom Delaney*, ed. Gearóid Mac Niocaill and Patrick Wallace (Galway: Galway University Press, 1985).

29. Vespasian Psalter, ed. Sweet, p. 407.

30. John 9:4-5.

31. See *DACL*, Vol. XII, Pt. 2, cols. 2665-69, under "Orientation"; the earthly paradise and Christ coming from the East in judgment are discussed at col. 2667; Louis Gougaud, "Eastward Position in Prayer," *Devotional and Ascetic Practices in the Middle Ages* (London, 1927), pp. 44-50. For recent bibliography, see Frank Leslie Cross and E. A. Livingstone, eds., *The Oxford Dictionary of the Christian Church*, 2nd ed. (Oxford, 1978), p. 1008, under "Orientation."

32. E. Bishop, "The Litany of the Saints in the Stowe Missal," *Liturgica Historica* (Oxford, 1918), pp. 137-64, at pp. 143, 147-48. On the various devotional perspectives within which the "Agnus Dei" can be seen, see Elisabeth Okasha and Jennifer O'Reilly, "An Anglo-Saxon Portable Altar: Inscription and Iconography," *Journal of the Warburg and Courtauld Institutes*, 47 (1984), 32-51. I am grateful to these scholars for allowing me to consult this article before its publication.

33. See É. Ó Carragáin, "Liturgical Innovations Associated with Pope Sergius and the Iconography of the Ruthwell and Bewcastle Crosses," in *Bede and Anglo-Saxon England*, ed. Farrell, pp. 131-47, at pp. 134-37.

34. Andrieu, Vol. II, p. 49; on the Syrian origin of such devotion, and hence the importance of the Syrian Pope Sergius I in its introduction into the Roman

liturgy, see Josef A. Jungmann, *The Place of Christ in Liturgical Prayer* (London and Dublin, 1965), pp. 259-63. In my "Liturgical Innovations" article (p. 139) I incorrectly stated that Sergius was appointed "prior cantorum" before he became pope. This was based on a misunderstanding of the *Liber Pontificalis,* which in fact states that Sergius had been placed under the direction of the Prior (for instruction in chant): "et quia studiosus erat et capax in officio cantelenae, priori cantorum pro doctrina est traditus" (Louis Duchesne, *Le Liber Pontificalis,* with additions and corrections by Cyrille Vogel, 3 vols. [rpt. Paris, 1981], I, 371).

35. Okasha, p. 110.
36. For the three stages of the proclamation, see John, 1:19 ff., 29 ff. and 35 ff.
37. Bede *Homiliarum Evangelii Libri II,* Book I, Homily 15 (ed. Hurst, pp. 105-10). Hurst points out (note on p. 105) that Bede is here following the Romano-Neapolitan use reflected in the Lindisfarne Gospels, in which John 1:29-35 is the lection for the first Sunday after Epiphany.
38. Bede *Homiliarum Evangelii Libri II* (ed. Hurst, pp. 105-06, ll. 18-28). See Willis, p. 221. In the "Agnus Dei" chant, the plural variant "peccata mundi" was modeled on the *Gloria* chant, which has the phrase, "qui tollis peccata mundi, miserere nobis"; see *DACL,* Vol. I, col. 966, under "Agnus Dei."
39. This passage, and other eucharistic references in Bede, are discussed by X. le Bachelet, "Le Vénérable Bède témoin de la foi eucharistique dans l'Eglise anglo-saxonne," *Proceedings of the Nineteenth International Eucharistic Congress* (London, 1909), pp. 311-26.
40. See Louis Gougaud, "Les Rites de la consécration et de la fraction dans la liturgie celtique de la Messe," *Proceedings of the Nineteenth International Eucharistic Congress* (London, 1909), pp. 348-61, at pp. 352-53.
41. Luke 24:30-31.
42. G. F. Warner, ed., *The Stowe Missal,* 2 vols., Henry Bradshaw Society, Vols. 31-32 (London, 1906-15), I, 34^r; II, 17.
43. Matthew 2:15, which refers to Hosea 11:1; see Henderson, forthcoming paper.
44. On the Ruthwell Cross as at present reconstructed, this figure has been reversed mistakenly, and is now on the south side.
45. See Rosemary Cramp, "The Evangelist Symbols and Their Parallels in Anglo-Saxon Sculpture," in *Bede and Anglo-Saxon England,* ed. Farrell, pp. 118-30.
46. As suggested by Meyvaert, "An Apocalypse Panel"; but see Henderson's forthcoming paper.
47. 1 Corinthians 11:26-29. 1 Corinthians 11:26-32 is given as a reading for Mass in the Stowe Missal, ed. Warner, Vol. I, fol. 15^{r-v}; Vol. II, p. 5. Saxl (p. 4) has already emphasized how relevant to the Ruthwell iconography are the eschatological dimensions of the Eucharist.
48. Stowe Missal, ed. Warner, Vol. I, fol. 28^{r-v}; Vol. II, p. 13.
49. Isaiah 43:20; Okasha, p. 110.
50. Gregory *Homiliarum in Evangelia Libri Duo* I.8, in *PL,* 76:1104B. Gregory is commenting on the ox and the ass at the manger in Bethlehem, in a sermon for Christmas morning. See also Bede, *Homeliarum Euangelii,* ed. Hurst, pp. 41-42.
51. Ó Carragáin, "Liturgical Innovations," p. 135.

Part Four
Research Tools

The Dictionary of Old English

ASHLEY CRANDELL AMOS

Dictionaries and indices, bibliographies and lists, catalogues and concordances are research tools, instruments for the study and preservation of the language, texts, objects, and culture which they record. As tools they are not ends in themselves, and they should be undertaken and assessed in the context of the knowledge they document and the research they make possible. The Dictionary of Old English now under way in Toronto will itself be a basic research tool, but it could not be prepared without the excellent research tools already available for work in Old English.

The Dictionary of Old English is intended to take its place with the *Middle English Dictionary* and the *Dictionary of the Older Scottish Tongue* as one of the period dictionaries complementing the *Oxford English Dictionary*. The Dictionary project developed out of two planning conferences in Toronto in 1969 and 1970. It was founded and directed by Angus Cameron, was funded by the Canada Council (now the Social Sciences and Humanities Research Council of Canada) and the University of Toronto, and will eventually be published by the University of Toronto Press. From the beginning the Dictionary was intended to be comprehensive in its coverage; in fact, because of the convenient size of the Old English corpus, it has been possible to make the coverage exhaustive.

The first research tools essential for the preparation of the Dictionary were catalogues — catalogues of extant manuscripts, diplomas and charters, inscriptions, and texts. N. R. Ker's *Catalogue of Manuscripts Containing Anglo-Saxon* (1957; Supplement 1976) was complemented by P. H. Sawyer's *Anglo-Saxon Charters* (1968); by H. Marquardt's *Die Runeninschriften der Britischen Inseln*, Vol. I of *Bibliographie der Runeninschriften nach Fundorten*, (1961), R. Derolez' *Runica Manuscripta: The English Tradition* (1954), and R. I. Page's *An Introduction to English Runes* (1973); and by Elisabeth Okasha's *Hand-List of Anglo-Saxon Non-Runic Inscriptions* (1971).[1] Using these lists and the excellent annual bibliographies of work in Old English, Cameron prepared a list of all Old English texts and their most useful modern editions which was published in *A Plan for the Dictionary of Old English* in 1973.[2] Cameron's list was organized generically and listed with alphanumeric codes (the Cameron numbers) in an open-ended system which has made it possible to add texts easily. Perhaps twenty or thirty such additions have been made over the past decade, including texts newly discovered and texts or manuscripts overlooked in the early list. A few texts intentionally omitted from the early list deserve attention because they suggest the great influence a work of reference can have. Ker purposely omitted twelfth-century manuscripts like British Library Harley 6258B, the *Peri Didaxeon,* from his *Catalogue:* he felt, on paleographical grounds, that they could not be considered Old English.[3] Cameron intentionally followed Ker in omitting these texts in order to avoid material that could only dubiously be considered Old English, and the *Peri Didaxeon* and a few similar texts are excluded from the Old English corpus. When our first entries were read with the corresponding entries of the *Middle English Dictionary* and the *Oxford English Dictionary,* it became clear that the interesting and useful evidence of the twelfth-century texts was not always fully represented. These texts are now being added to the corpus; their evidence will be cited, with some warning marker indicating that it is late, in the Dictionary.

Catalogues and lists can, to an extent, influence, and perhaps even control, ideas of what is Old English and what is not, but they have also made it possible to consider the full range of surviving texts in Old English. It is no accident that, after a century of work concentrating preponderantly on Old English poetry, there has been a recent surge of interest in the prose and the glosses, in homilies and medical recipes and translations. The works of Ker, Sawyer, and Cameron, along with the new bibliographies, chief among them that by Greenfield and Robinson, have shown us where to look, and shown how much more there is in Old English than we had thought.[4]

As he drew up his list of Old English texts and editions Cameron collected and pre-edited the best editions of all the texts and built up a machine-readable corpus of Old English. The corpus consists only of the Old English texts; emendations are marked, but neither manuscript readings nor variants are given, nor are notes of any kind. The texts are identified by Cameron numbers (which proved ideally suited to computer use), and the Latin of the glossed texts is included, marked by special delimiters. The corpus in this form occupies approximately 30 megabytes of computer storage; although it has been proofread twice, a number of errors remain which are corrected as they are discovered. The corpus was prepared, like other research tools at the project, for internal use in writing the Dictionary—it was the essential first step toward the production of concordances and slips. In some respects it is therefore rough and idiosyncratic in format. Nevertheless there are now over thirty copies in use throughout the world, and a score of researchers are using or have used the corpus. They have investigated linguistic features including vocabulary, spellings, and syntax, run concordances, and done word counts. How do editorial sentences begin or end in Old English? Does the character string *sh* ever appear as a spelling for *sc?* Where outside the saints' lives are saints mentioned? How does sentence length, or word length, vary with genre? What texts use particular collocations, or treat particular motives? These are the sorts of question which can be investigated with the machine-readable corpus of Old English.

The texts of the Old English corpus were concorded, one by one, at the University of Wisconsin at Madison in the mid-seventies under the direction of Richard L. Venezky. These concordances were printed as dictionary slips, and each slip contained its headword and the full sentence in which that word occurred. Venezky and one of the Dictionary's editors, Antonette diPaolo Healey, produced a merged form of the concordance to the corpus on microfiche in 1980: the concordance filled over 400 fiches and documented 2,994,750 Old English words.[5] The handful of high-frequency spellings excluded from the main concordance have also been concorded; their concordance, a complement to the first and almost as big, was produced by Richard Venezky and another of the Dictionary's editors, Sharon Butler, and became available in 1984.[6] We could not write dictionary entries without these concordances. The concordance acts as a record of any slips which may have miscarried on their way to the files, as a check that odd spellings and odd forms have been considered, corrected if necessary, and included in the proper entry, and, with the list of reverse spellings, as a means of finding all the compounds formed from a given word. The concordance is an unpolished working document, a finding list, and scholars should cite Old English from the editions the microfiche concordance refers to, not from the concordance itself. But, granted that proviso, the concordance makes a versatile research tool. One can consider the use of a word within a single text or across the Old English corpus, look for collocations, idioms, and formulas, compare spellings to identify texts similar in dialect or date, look for compounding or syntactic patterns — or just find an epigram or a usable reference to an Old English sentence cited by an early scholar in a confusing and obscure form. Reading through the concordance reinforces the impression conveyed by the catalogues of manuscripts and texts — that the Old English corpus is rich and strange, with much that is interesting but not often consulted.

Both the machine-readable corpus and the concordances are in one sense incomplete: they do not contain every instance of every surviving word of Old English. In general, texts which survive in more than one manuscript copy are present in the corpus only in one form, the text prepared by their editor, which may be a composite or a single manuscript text. Apart from the charters, fewer than four hundred Old English texts survive in more than one manuscript; and, of those that do, some important texts have several versions included in the corpus — both the Hatton and Corpus manuscripts of *Gregory's Dialogues* are included, for example, as are three versions of *Bede's Death-Song* and two of *Cædmon's Hymn*. But there is a range of material, including both unique spellings and unique words, which is not available in the concordance. A list of lexical variants from texts with multiple manuscripts is now being compiled, and although there are no plans to publish the list of lexical variants before the Dictionary is complete, the material from the list will be included in the Dictionary and will be available for consultation in our Toronto offices when it is complete. The lexical variants provide particularly striking evidence about the use of language, since they may represent cases where a scribe replaced, whether deliberately or by force of habit, the reading of his exemplar with a word of his own choosing (presumably of his dialect or *Schriftsprache*).

Some of the material most helpful in writing the Dictionary entries comes from the individual work of previous scholars — good notes, glossaries and editions, and the bibliographies that help us find them. The bibliographic work of A. G. Kennedy, Stanley Greenfield and Fred Robinson, Carl Berkhout, and others has been essential. A brief bibliography of word studies compiled from the Dictionary collections has just appeared; it provides a guide to major semantic discussions of Old English words and also includes a number of more minor references, including some amusing exchanges between scholars skeptical about one another's work.[7] Bruce Mitchell has generously made his work on Old English syntax available to the Dictionary in draft, and has courageously offered to tackle the entries for the syntax words with us.[8]

Such are the research tools necessary in writing the Dictionary. There are, of course, further research tools that would be extremely useful. Helmut Gneuss' catalogue of manuscripts written or owned in England before 1100 will provide many answers when it is finished; it is already essential even in its present brief form.[9] Good glossaries and good editions are invaluable to lexicographers, and there are still not a few Old English texts which could be better edited. There are thousands of unsolved problems with some of the difficult glosses. Word studies based on the use of vocabulary throughout the corpus as a whole can save entry-writers hours and days, and greatly improve the quality of the Dictionary; by making the concordances and the corpus available we hope to facilitate and encourage work on semantic studies. A lemmatized concordance, where all the spellings of each word are brought together under a headword form, would be extremely helpful, and will be a by-product of the Dictionary itself. Sorting the less common homographs from the high-frequency words — separating *ac* 'oak' from *ac* 'but' — will be an early priority in this work.

A dictionary is perhaps the most basic research tool for any scholarly investigation involving linguistic records. Important questions in almost every discipline turn on the interpretation of words. Since the Dictionary of Old English will be based on evidence which was not systematically available to earlier lexicographers of Old English, it should be both more comprehensive and more authoritative than earlier dictionaries. Someone looking up an individual word should find more useful and more accurate information than he would in an earlier dictionary. I am far from sure now whether he will find the materials that would make a literary history of Old English straightforward, or whether vocabulary will offer important clues to dating, as I hoped seven years ago, or whether we will understand the Old English language — its orthography, its morphology and syntax — in a different way after consulting the Dictionary; the material will provide us with complex evidence not easily reduced to simple schemas.[10] Our first year of entry-writing does suggest some things. The listing of all attested spellings of a word is likely to be of great interest to philologists, especially for a word like *deofol*, with over a hundred widely varying spellings of stem and endings; such a list will also serve as an index to relevant citations in the *Microfiche Concordance*. In cataloguing grammatical information about our entries we have been struck by how much less regular inflections are than the grammars suggest: weak 1 and weak 2 verbs fall together frequently in the eleventh century, and many verbs are attested in both forms, or in a strong and a weak form. Nouns frequently vary in gender, and the use of strong and weak inflectional endings in adjectives is far from regular. Many words seem to occur with by-forms: we have *ge-daf(e)nian, ge-dæf(e)nian, ge-deaf(e)nian, ge-deofenian,* and *ge· daflian* for the verb 'to be fitting', or the different verbs *dryppan, dropian, droppettan, drypan* from the root 'to drop', *drencan, drinclian, druncian, druncnian, drincan* from the root 'to drink'. The question of compounding becomes extremely complex since some inflected collocations seem to function as compounds (*dæges eage* 'daisy'; *domesdæg* 'doomsday') while others (*dyran ceapa* 'at a high price') do not, and many compounds have parallel collocations (*dægtid, dæges tid*). The charter material in particular has many compounds unrecorded in previous dictionaries, but a number of these may be place names.

Some very preliminary conclusions can be drawn from our work on the letter *d*. We have approximately 900 headwords beginning with *d;* older dictionaries, with duplicate entries and extensive cross-referencing, have more: 1000 in Clark Hall and Meritt, about 1800 in Bosworth, Toller, and Campbell. But we have 65 words, or about 7% of our total, which are not recorded at all in previous dictionaries or which are only listed as elements of compounds. Many of these words are predictable: they are *ge-* prefixed forms of words attested as simplexes, or vice-versa, nouns in *-nes* or verbs in *-ian*, adjectives in *-lic* or adverbs in *-lice* where another form of the word was already attested, and so forth.[11] The other new words fall into several classes. Some are Latin or Greek loans which were omitted in previous dictionaries, like *dellium* 'bdellium', *diptongon* 'digraph' or 'diphthong', *disciplin* '(monastic) discipline', *dominus* 'Lord'. Others are twelfth-century words, allowed in by late cut-off, like *duran* 'to endure, to last' or *deafian* 'to grow deaf'. Others arise from the extensive charter vocabulary, like *dalland* 'shared arable land', *dicheafod* 'one end of a ditch', and *dyngelandscear* (of uncertain meaning). Some are combinations of well-known words: *deofolfremednes* 'acquiescence by the will in a sin already desired', *dilesæd* 'dillseed', *domagende* 'possessing *dom*, authority'.

Particular entries may carry special excitement. *Dohter* appears as a gloss for *Rabboni* in the Rushworth Gospels, John 20:16, and from its spelling and context there seems to be no reason not to regard it as the earliest attestation in English of *doctor* 'teacher, master'. The appearance of *cam* spellings for *camp* may suggest how the *Beowulf* scribe, looking at *cain* (which would be indistinguishable from *cam*), came to write *camp*.[12] *Dreorig*, the Old English reflex of Modern English *dreary*, has traditionally been taken as 'bloody, blood-stained', but an examination of the seventy-odd instances suggests that the word may already have weakened to its later, impressionistic sense, 'sad'.

Still other research tools may logically grow out of work on the Dictionary — a lemmatized concordance, a student's dictionary, a Latin-Old English dictionary; and other research tools, chief among them other dictionaries, will be used in its creation. The Dictionary, like any academic work, will both depend on the research current in its day and add to it. We ask in turn that scholars using the tools the Dictionary has provided let us know of errors that they find so that we may correct them and make the Dictionary itself as accurate and useful a research tool as possible.

UNIVERSITY OF TORONTO

Notes

1. N[eil] R. Ker, *Catalogue of Manuscripts Containing Anglo-Saxon* (Oxford, 1957); N[eil] R. Ker, "A Supplement to *Catalogue of Manuscripts Containing Anglo-Saxon,*" *ASE*, 5 (1976), 121-31; P[eter] H. Sawyer, *Anglo-Saxon Charters: An Annotated List and Bibliography* (London, 1968); H[ertha] Marquardt, *Die Runeninschriften der Britischen Inseln,* Vol. I of *Bibliographie der Runeninschriften nach Fundorten,* Abhandlung der Akademie der Wissenschaften in Göttingen, phil.-hist. Klasse, 3rd ser., No. 48 (Göttingen, 1961); R[ené] Derolez, *Runica Manuscripta: The English Tradition* (Brugge, 1954); R[aymond] I. Page, *An Introduction to English Runes* (London, 1973); Elisabeth Okasha, *Hand-List of Anglo-Saxon Non-Runic Inscriptions* (Cambridge, 1971).

2. Roberta Frank and Angus Cameron, eds., *A Plan for the Dictionary of Old English* (Toronto, 1973).

3. Ker, *Catalogue,* p. xix. Ker notes that British Library Cotton Claudius D.iii was omitted in error (p. xix, n. 2).

4. Stanley B. Greenfield and Fred C. Robinson, *A Bibliography of Publications on Old English Literature to the End of 1972* (Toronto, 1980).

5. Richard L. Venezky and Antonette diPaolo Healey, *A Microfiche Concordance to Old English* (Toronto, Newark, Delaware, 1980).

6. Richard L. Venezky and Sharon Butler, *A Microfiche Concordance to Old English: The High Frequency Words* (Toronto, 1985).

7. Angus Cameron, Allison Kingsmill and Ashley Crandell Amos, *Old English Word Studies: A Preliminary Author and Word Index* (Toronto, 1983).

8. Bruce Mitchell, *Old English Syntax* (Oxford, 1984).

9. Helmut Gneuss, "A Preliminary List of Manuscripts Written or Owned in England up to 1100," *ASE*, 9 (1981), 1-60.

10. Ashley Crandell Amos, *Linguistic Means of Determining the Dates of Old English Literary Texts* (Cambridge, 1980), p. 169.

11. Examples are *davidisc, ge-dæghwamlic, dearflice, deriendnes, ge-dic, drædlic, drifennes, dyrstlic.*

12. The *cam* for *camp* spellings occur in glosses [*cā* for *cam(p)*, *gecā* for *gecam(p)* in AldV 7.3 (Meritt) 162 and 23, and in compounds (*cādō* for *cam(p)dom* in BenRG1 2.14, *cālicere* for *cam(p)licere* in AldV 2.3.1 (Napier) 156, *comstidi* for *com(p)stede* in CollGl 35.1 (Steinmeyer-Sievers) 5, and *camwerod* for *cam(p)werod* in HomU 6 (FoerstVercHom 15) 149]. The abbreviations are those used in *A Microfiche Concordance to Old English.* The preliminary entries for *camp* have been written by Antonette diPaolo Healey; the parallel to the *Beowulf* passage was suggested by E. G. Stanley.

The Index to Iconographic Subjects in Anglo-Saxon Manuscripts: A Research Tool

THOMAS H. OHLGREN

I. Introduction

In the fields of interdisciplinary studies, where scholars often consider evidence from collateral disciplines and media, there is a pressing need for access to the visual dimensions of culture. This need for pictorial or iconographic documentation is particularly evident in Anglo-Saxon studies, a field in which, given the relative paucity of surviving written documents, art is an important reflection of the values, attitudes, and tastes of early English society. Because of the ravages of time, neglect, censorious zeal, and later restoration, the monumental art forms—wall painting, sculpture, embroidered tapestries, and stained glass—are often mere shadows of their former selves, if they survive at all. Manuscripts, by contrast, frequently preserve in excellent condition smaller-scale illustrations which offer to researchers in many disciplines a visual encyclopedia of Anglo-Saxon culture. Access to the iconographic content of early English illustrated manuscripts has until now been hampered by the lack of a systematic, complete, and portable finding aid.

II. Survey of Manuscripts Illuminated in the British Isles

In the field of early English manuscript illumination, a major step toward producing a comprehensive inventory was taken in 1975, 1976, and 1978 with the publication by Harvey Miller of J. J. Alexander's *Insular Manuscripts 6th to the 9th Century,* Elżbieta Temple's *Anglo-Saxon Manuscripts 900–1066,* and C. Michael Kauffmann's *Romanesque Manuscripts 1066–1190.* Altogether the three volumes list 317 manuscripts located in at least 71 libraries scattered around the world. Each manuscript entry begins with codicological information such as library, shelfmark, title or type of manuscript, date, place of origin, and size. Next follows a narrative section giving descriptions and stylistic analyses of selected illustrations, initials, and decorated borders. Each entry also contains a brief section on the provenance of the manuscript and a select bibliography. Finally, the three volumes reproduce 1100 photographs of selected illuminations. Temple's volume on *Anglo-Saxon Manuscripts* and the Alexander and Kauffmann volumes will no doubt be standard references in the field.[1]

Owing to space limitations and other editorial considerations, however, the Harvey Miller volumes do not include complete descriptions of the illustrations in every manuscript. Instead, selected iconographic identifications are embedded in narrative paragraphs devoted mainly to stylistic analysis. Consequently, it is often difficult for readers to determine the precise iconographic subjects and the sequence of pictures in the manuscript. In addition, the pictorial contents of a large number of manuscripts are omitted altogether. Among the important manuscripts not systematically described in the Temple volume, for example, are the *Marvels of the East* (T52: London, British Library Cotton Vitellius A.XV; and T87: British Library Cotton Tiberius B.V), the *Psychomachia* by Prudentius (T48: Cambridge, Corpus Christi College 23; T49: London, British Library Cotton Cleopatra C.VIII; T50: Munich, Bayerische Staatsbibliothek CLM. 29031b; and T51: London, British Library Additional MS. 24199), the *Herbal* by Pseudo-Apuleius (T63: London, British Library Cotton Vitellius C.III), the *Harley Psalter* (T64: British Library Harley 603), the *Grimbald Gospels* (T68: London, British Library Additional MS. 34890), the *Bury Psalter* (T84: Vatican City, Biblioteca Apostolica Vaticana Reg. lat. 12), and Ælfric's *Hexateuch* (T86: London, British Library Cotton Claudius B.IV). Another problem is the absence of an index to iconographic contents. Such an index is needed to guide researchers to specific representations of persons, scenes, and themes. It is not now possible, for instance, to locate quickly the four depictions of the unusual Disappearing Christ. To find the manuscripts in which this iconographic variant appears the reader must skim through Temple's entire volume.[2]

III. The Index to Iconographic Subjects in Anglo-Saxon Manuscripts

To remedy the above mentioned limitations, a Project Group composed of art historians, codicologists, historians, and literary scholars is in the process of undertaking the following five steps.[3]

1. *Compilation of iconographic material in Anglo-Saxon manuscripts.* The Project Group is compiling from various sources, including the Harvey Miller volumes and a large number of other published works, a complete and systematic listing of the iconographic contents of all manuscripts illuminated in the British Isles during the Insular and Anglo-Saxon periods, from the early seventh century to ca. A.D. 1100. Although a final count of the relevant manuscripts has not been made, a draft version of the *Index* contains main entries for 223 manuscripts, including 78 Insular manuscripts, 133 Anglo-Saxon manuscripts, and 12 early Romanesque manuscripts. To this number we shall add an unknown but probably small number of manuscripts omitted from the Harvey Miller volumes. In her review of Temple's volume, for instance, Linda Brownrigg noted the omission of two Anglo-Saxon illuminated manuscripts: Cambridge, University Library MS. Gg.5.35 and Rouen, Bibliothèque municipale MS. A.337.[4] Furthermore, an Evangelist portrait of St. Mark on fol. 42^v of Saint-Lô, Archives de la Manche 1 is probably Anglo-Saxon in origin.[5] In addition to including these three manuscripts, we have also deleted manuscripts of Continental origin, such as the Valenciennes Apocalypse (A64: Valenciennes, Bibliothèque municipale MS. 99) and the Otbert Gospels (T30 xiii: New York, Pierpont Morgan Library M. 333). For those manuscripts not adequately described in the Harvey Miller *Survey,* we are consulting not only the original manuscripts themselves but a large number of published sources, including scholarly books, monographs, dissertations, journal articles, and facsimiles. For example, we consulted Robert M. Harris' 1960 Princeton dissertation for detailed descriptions of the fifty illustrations in the *Bury Psalter* (Vatican City, Biblioteca Apostolica MS. Reg. 12). Similarly, we consulted C. R. Dodwell's listing of the 403 illustrations of British Library Cotton Claudius B.IV in *The Old English Illustrated Hexateuch,* EEMF, 18 (1974). Finally, for those manuscripts not previously described in published sources, we have invited contributions from scholars with first-hand knowledge of the manuscripts.

2. *Codification of codicological data.* Because of the inconsistent treatment of codicological data in the Harvey Miller volumes, Charles Wright has recommended that we revise this information to conform to the system proposed by Helmut Gneuss in "A Preliminary List of Manuscripts Written or Owned in England up to 1100" (*ASE*, 9 [1981], 1–60). We are following Gneuss' method of listing titles, authors, dates and origins: for example, his use of plus-signs and asterisks, to indicate when a text is in Old English; his dating scheme (ix in.; ix^1; ix. med.; ix^2; ix ex.); and his use of parentheses to indicate Irish or Continental origin.

3. *Preparation of iconographic descriptions.* We are standardizing the iconographic descriptions gathered from a number of different sources according to uniform descriptive standards. To this end, we have emulated the subject terms employed at the Index of Christian Art and the Warburg Institute in London. During my visit to London in the Fall of 1981, I received permission from Michael Evans to photocopy the subject-headings used in the Photographic Collection of the Warburg. This encyclopedic listing of subjects, focusing on secular iconography (with nine major subdivisions), social life (with twenty-five subdivisions), and magic and science (with thirteen subdivisions), will be an invaluable guide to the description of secular subjects in early English manuscripts. In Fall 1981 we also received permission from Isa Ragusa, then acting director of the Index of Christian Art, to obtain a complete microfilm copy of their Editor's File, comprising some 60,000 title cards. This comprehensive list of subjects will also be very useful in helping us to create the broad cross-references needed in the iconographic index. Such a referential network, consisting of broad subject-headings, and "*see*" and "*see also*" references, will enable researchers perhaps unfamiliar with specialized iconographic terminology to locate specific illustrations relevant to their individual fields of study. Finally, in August, 1983, I spent a week at the Princeton Index where I painstakingly compared the iconographic descriptions in the draft version against the main entry cards at Princeton. After discussing the project with Nigel Morgan, the new director of the Princeton Index, I decided that we will emulate Princeton's more detailed descriptive method, and upon my return to Purdue, I revised the iconographic descriptions of many of the illuminations, our goal being to produce a uniform, controlled vocabulary exhibiting consistency of specification and depth.

4. *Coding for computerized data entry.* In view of the large quantity of information to be collected, verified, edited, and indexed, it is only practical to

use modern word-processing techniques. To gain total editorial control over the massive amount of data, we entered the data into the Word–11 System at Purdue. This powerful system, which operates on a PDP 11/70 microcomputer, provides standard word-processing functions such as creating, editing, merging, and printing, as well as more sophisticated list-processing functions which were employed to create the indexes. Using this system, we are confident that we can produce photo-ready copy for the publisher. The technical advisor for this project is William I. Bormann, Systems Programmer at the Purdue University Computing Center.

Coding operations for this project involved the creation of a structured record for each manuscript in the inventory. Each main entry in the inventory (Fig. 1) consists of two parts: 1) the heading, and 2) the iconographic content.

The heading includes the following categories of information:

(a) A main entry number (a unique number assigned to each manuscript).

(b) A cross-reference to the corresponding entry in the appropriate Harvey Miller volume (i.e., A2, T55, K10).

(c) A bibliographic reference to present location of the manuscript, by city, library, and shelfmark.

(d) The author (if known) and title (or type of manuscript).

(e) The place of origin or provenance.

(f) The date of the manuscript, followed, when relevant, by the date of the illuminations.

(g) The size in millimeters.

(h) Comment, usually a citation of a modern edition of the text illustrated, or acknowledgment of the source of the iconographic description.

(i) Cross-references, as appropriate, to: P. McGurk, *Latin Gospel Books from A.D. 400 to A.D. 800* (Paris, Brussels, 1961); Helmut Gneuss, "A Preliminary List of Manuscripts Written or Owned in England up to 1100" (*ASE*, 9 [1981], 1–60); and N. R. Ker, *Catalogue of Manuscripts Containing Anglo-Saxon* (Oxford, 1957).

The iconographic content of each main entry represents a systematic, folio-by-folio listing of iconography and major decorative features of each manuscript. The inclusion of decorative features, such as initial pages, carpet pages, canon tables, and borders, may seem to complicate the project unnecessarily, but after due consideration we decided to include these features particularly for the early Insular manuscripts in which iconographically significant material is minimal. As we discovered, the so-called decorative pages often contain figural representations, such as the masturbating (?)

MANUSCRIPT INVENTORY SAMPLE

182   (T77)   London, British Library MS Cotton Titus D. XXVI and D. XXVII.
Collectar; Litany; Prayers; Calendar; Aelfric, De temporibus anni*; Offices; etc.
Winchester, New Minster
xi[1]
128 x 93 mm.
[Gneuss 380; Ker 202]

1 f. 19^v (Titus D. XXVI)
Apostle: St. Peter. Within draped architectural frame, monk (Aelfwine) wearing habit, book in left hand, right hand extended toward Peter, tonsured, pearled nimbus, seated on arc, feet on footstool, open book on left knee, key in right hand.
[Ill. 243; also, Wormald, *English Drawings,* pl. 16b; Dodwell, *A-S Art,* pl. 9]

2 f. 65^v (Titus D. XXVII)
Christ: Crucifixion. Christ, cross-nimbed, bearded, head inclined, long loin cloth, four nails, on Cross with suppedaneum and inscribed titulus; Hand of God at top of Cross; Personifications of Sun and Moon above arms of Cross; Virgin Mary, nimbed, and Evangelist John, nimbed, writing in open book; inscriptions.
[Ill. 246; also, Rice, pl. 82a; Rickert, pl. 37b; Millar, pl. 24a]

3 f. 75^v (Titus D. XXVII)
Trinity or Quinity: within a circular Glory, God the Father, holding an open book, (right) and God the Son, holding a closed book (left), both cross-nimbed and bearded, sit on the firament and converse. On the left, the Virgin, crowned, with the nimbed Holy Dove perching on her head, holds the cross-nimbed Christ Child, holding an open book. Beneath God the Son's feet, Satan, nude and bound, is used as a footstool. Below, is a Hell-mouth. On either side, Arius and Judas, names inscribed, Judas holding bent spear or hook.
[Ill. 245; also, Rice, pl. 82b; Wormald, *English Drawings,* pl. 16a; Kantorowicz, fig. 1; Dodwell, *Canterbury School,* pl. 13c; Millar, pl. 24b]

Fig. 1.

figure in the central column of the Canon Table on folio 1 of the *Barberini Gospels* (Vatican City, Biblioteca Apostolica MS. Barberini Lat. 570) (Alexander, Illustration 173). Furthermore, the addition of major initial pages often gives a picture of the structure of the manuscripts, particularly for Gospel books and psalters. Although the decorative features will be listed in the inventory of pictorial content, they will not be separately indexed. The compilation of an index to decoration in Anglo-Saxon manuscripts is also needed, but it is beyond the scope of this project.

The iconographic part of each entry therefore consists of the following elements:

(a) An item number, which together with the main entry number uniquely identifies each illustration. It is to these numbers that the numerical codes following each index entry refer.

(b) The iconographic description of each illustration. As mentioned above, although we focused our attention primarily on iconographically identifiable figures, we have included brief descriptions of major decorative features. Every attempt is also being made to ensure consistency of description. We are striving to achieve sufficient depth of description to avoid the listing of 25 undifferentiated Crucifixions. The subject-headings and full descriptions obtained from the Index of Christian Art will guide us in this instance, just as the Warburg list will help us in the description of secular iconography. Neither of these sources, however, offered us detailed descriptions of every illumination in our inventory. What they did contribute were models of classification and description, which were emulated in the creation of new descriptions. Once the Princeton "method" of description was mastered, for example, we were able to apply it on our own to the production of detailed descriptions of illuminations.

(c) A verse or line reference to a modern edition of the text illustrated, or a Biblical citation.

(d) A photographic reference either to a plate in the appropriate Harvey Miller volume or to another published source. Our goal is to locate at least one published photograph of each illumination in the inventory. The references will enable researchers to locate in their own university libraries both reproductions of a large number of illustrations and scholarship on the manuscripts. While a short author/title reference will appear after each iconographic description, the full bibliographic references will be found in the *Photo-Bibliography*. Carl Berkhout has kindly agreed to complete this part of the project. In addition, with the help of Daniel Burton, we are assembling at Purdue a complete file of published photographs of Anglo-Saxon illumination.

5. *Creation of indexes.* Creation of the five indexes is being accomplished in part by means of the Word-11 list-processing system. However, upon producing a draft version of the indexes we discovered that machine indexing has severe limitations. As a result, each index had to be extensively edited by manual means to produce the results obtained to date. We have learned that although machine sorting and indexing are beneficial for the preliminary processing stages, human intervention is needed to refine the results. The indexes are as follows:

(a) Index to Manuscripts (Fig. 2): an alphabetical listing of cities, from Antwerp to York, followed by names of libraries and the shelfmarks for each manuscript. The numbers attached to each entry are the main entry numbers of manuscripts in the inventory.

(b) Index to Authors and Titles (Fig. 3): an alphabetical list of authors and titles or types of manuscript.

(c) Index to Origins (Fig. 4). As Linda Brownrigg has pointed out, it is not always clear whether the references in the Harvey Miller volumes are to the manuscripts or to the illustrations which may have been added to an existing manuscript. Brownrigg has also noticed a hidden thesis in Temple's volume concerning the importance of Canterbury scriptoria. She recommends that many of these attributions need to be re-examined.[6] We have attempted to rectify these problems by adopting the places of origin and provenance proposed by Gneuss in "A Preliminary List of Manuscripts Written or Owned in England up to 1100." As Gneuss notes, his listing "indicates the place or places where a manuscript was written and where it was owned for a part or the whole of the Anglo-Saxon period if this is known or can fairly safely be assumed."

(d) Index to Dates (Fig. 5). As with places of origin, we have adopted Gneuss' system of dating. Since he dates the manuscripts on paleographical grounds, we have included dates for illustrations that were executed at a later time.

(e) Index to Iconographic Contents (Fig. 6). This index consists of iconographically significant figures arranged in alphabetical order, from Aaron to Zodiac Signs. The listing exhibits the limitations of alphabetizing: the entry must begin with the prime search term; key terms are often buried within phrases; and hierarchical relationships among concepts are not expressed. These limitations can be somewhat overcome, however, by superimposing an extensive cross-reference system on the alphabetically arranged prime terms. In addition, the prime terms must be carefully selected to reflect the search strategies of users in a wide variety of disciplines. The iconographic index in the draft version represents therefore a rudimen-

INDEX TO MANUSCRIPTS

Antwerp
    Museum Plantin-Moretus
        MS M. 17. 4 65

Berlin
    Staatsbibliothek
        MS Hamilton 553 ... 14

Besançon
    Bibliothèque Municipale
        MS 14 ... 181

Boulogne
    Bibliothèque Municipale
        MS 10 ... 88
        MS 11 ... 149
        MS 82 ... 117
        MS 189 ... 132

Cambridge
    Clare College
        MS 30 ... 215

    Corpus Christi College
        MS 23 ... 153
        MS 41 ... 186
        MS 57 ... 127
        MS 183 ... 84
        MS 197B ... 12
        MS 198 ... 193
        MS 326 ... 100
        MS 389 ... 141
        MS 391 ... 214
        MS 411 ... 145
        MS 421 (pp. 1-2) ... 187
        MS 422 (pp. 27-586) ... 209

Fig. 2.

INDEX TO AUTHORS AND TITLES

Aelfric, Colloquy ... 205
Aelfric, De temporibus ... 182, 192, 205, 211
Aelfric, Grammar ... 206
Aelfric, Hexateuch ... 191
Aelfric, Homilies ... 134, 179, 187, 193
Aethelstan Psalter ... 83
Aethicus Ister, Cosmographia ... 122
Alcuin, Epistolae ... 159
Aldhelm, Aenigmata ... 120, 190
Aldhelm, Carmen de virginitate ... 97, 162
Aldhelm, De laude virginitatis ... 80, 82, 97, 100, 101, 102, 105, 128, 144, 162
Aldhelm, Epistola ad Heahfridum ... 82, 102, 128
Amalarius, De ecclesiasticis officiis ... 109, 117
Anglo-Saxon Chronicle C ... 135
Anhalt-Morgan Gospels ... 150
Apocalypse ... 64
Apuleius: see Pseudo-Apuleius
Arator, Historia apostolica ... 121, 139
Arenberg Gospels ... 161
Augustinus, Enarrationes in Psalmos ... 217
Augustinus, Enchiridion ... 118
Barberini Gospels ... 36
Beda, De die iudicii ... 123
Beda, De natura rerum ... 69
Beda, De temporibus ... 69
Beda, De temporum ratione ... 69, 220
Beda, Historia ecclesiastica ... 19, 33, 87, 186
Beda, Vitae S. Cuthberti ... 84, 98, 124
Benedictional ... 95, 111, 112, 113, 140, 195
Benedictional of Archbishop Robert ... 112
Benedictional of St. Ethelwold ... 111
Bible ... 7, 207
Boethius, De consolatione philosophiae ... 108, 125, 129, 137, 142
Boethius, Institutio arithmetica ... 137
Book of Armagh ... 53
Book of Cerne ... 66
Book of Deer (Gospel extracts) ... 72
Book of Dimma ... 48
Book of Durrow ... 6
Book of Kells ... 52

Fig. 3.

INDEX TO PLACES OF ORIGIN AND PROVENANCE

Note: The information about places of origin and provenance is based upon Helmut Gneuss' "A Preliminary Handlist." The listing "indicates the place or places where a manuscript was written and where it was owned for a part or the whole of the Anglo-Saxon period if this is known or can fairly safely be assumed" (Gneuss, p. 4).

Abingdon	102, 127, 135
Barking	144?, 164
(Brittany)	56?
Bury, St. Edmunds Abbey	156?, 180, 189, 222
Canterbury	110, 129?, 158?, 177?, 187, 201?
Canterbury, Christ Church	20, 30, 90, 92?, 99, 100, 101, 103, 104, 105, 106?, 107, 113, 120, 123, 124, 125, 128, 132, 133?, 140?, 142, 153?, 154, 161, 162, 163?, 166?, 167?, 168?, 169, 170?, 171, 172, 173, 174, 175, 176, 179, 180?, 189?, 202?, 205, 206, 207, 211, 217, 218, 219
Canterbury, St. Augustine's	29, 30?, 32, 91?, 93?, 98, 108, 109, 118, 119?, 121, 122, 141, 142, 143, 144, 145, 159?, 160, 190, 191, 219, 221
Cerne	66
Chester-le-Street	9, 10, 81, 84
(Continent)	23?, 27?, 49?, 60, 64, 90, 190
Crediton	195
Crowland	184
Durham	5, 9, 10, 16, 17, 84, 167, 196
(Echternach)	24, 25?, 26?, 28?
Ely	106?
England, north	22
England, south	31, 33, 34
Exeter	95, 107, 109, 131, 142, 186, 187, 213

Fig. 4.

INDEX TO DATES

Note: The dates listed below are derived from Helmut Gneuss' "A Preliminary Handlist." They refer in all cases to the dates of the manuscripts, not necessarily to the illustrations. Also, when Gneuss gives more than one date for each manuscript, the first date is listed here.

vii in.	1, 2, 3?, 4?
vii med.	5
vii^2	6
vii/ viii	9, 11, 12
viii	10, 14, 16
viii in.	7, 8, 13, 22, 24, 25, 26
viii^1	15, 18, 20, 21, 23, 29
viii med.	17, 19, 27, 28?, 31
viii ex.	30, 33, 34, 37, 38, 39, 42, 51, 55
viii^2	36, 43?, 44, 45, 46, 47, 49, 50
viii^2/ viii ex.	48
viii/ ix	41, 52?, 56, 57, 58, 59?
ix	32, 69, 70
ix in.	53, 54, 62, 64, 65, 66
ix^1	60?, 61, 63, 67
ix med.	40, 68
ix^2	70
ix ex.	71, 79
ix/ x	80, 90, 190
x	72
x in.	81, 85, 86, 87
x^1	73, 82, 84
x med.	88, 92, 93, 97, 98

Fig. 5.

Thomas H. Ohlgren

INDEX TO ICONOGRAPHIC CONTENTS

Aaron: anointed ... 169(104), 191(309)
Aaron: communicating with God ... 191(340)
Aaron: death ... 191(344)
Aaron: miracle of manna ... 191(289)
Aaron: miracle of rods ... 191(252)
Aaron: plague of flies ... 191(260)
Aaron: plague of frogs ... 191(256-257)
Aaron: plague of lice ... 191(258)
Aaron: speaking to Israelites ... 191(247)
Aaron: see also Moses
Aaron and Miriam: rebuked by God ... 191(328)
Abel: birth ... 163(25)
Abel: crying from the ground ... 163(26)
Abel: making offering ... 83(5), 163(26), 191(20)
Abel: tending flock ... 163(26), 191(19)
Abel: see also Cain
Abimelech: dream ... 191(114)
Abimelech: restoring Sarah to Abraham ... 191(115)
Abimelech: treaty with Abraham ... 191(122-123)
Abraham ... 169(70)
Abraham: angels departing ... 191(101)
Abraham: approaching Haran ... 163(48)
Abraham: as Ancestor of Christ ... 149(18)
Abraham: battle against Kings ... 191(81-83)
Abraham: blessed by Melchizedek ... 191(85)
Abraham: building altar ... 191(66)
Abraham: burial ... 191(133-134)
Abraham: communicating with God ... 163(48-50), 191(64), 191(77), 191(86-87), 191(90), 191(96), 191(125)
Abraham: departure to Canaan ... 163(49)
Abraham: driving away fowls ... 191(88)
Abraham: dwelling at Bersabee ... 191(124)
Abraham: Eliezer taking oath ... 191(129)
Abraham: entertaining the three angels ... 191(97-99)
Abraham: feasting ... 191(117)
Abraham: greeting the three angels ... 153(6), 154(4), 156(4)
Abraham: Hagar sent away ... 191(118-119)
Abraham: Hagar taken ... 191(91)
Abraham: infancy ... 191(57)
Abraham: instructing Sarah ... 191(68)
Abraham: journey to Egypt ... 163(51), 191(65), 191(67)
Abraham: journey to Sodom with three angels ... 191(100)
Abraham: messenger tells of Lot's capture ... 163(52), 191(80)
Abraham: moving tents to Hebron ... 191(78)

Fig. 6.

tary stage of development, and should not be taken as representing the final product. An important step taken to resolve some of these problems includes the production of a concordance to the iconographic data file, using the Oxford Concordance Program which Purdue has recently acquired.

IV. Progress to Date and Future Activities

Substantial progress has been made on the project during the last year. A draft version of the *Index* to 223 manuscripts was produced, duplicated, and disseminated to a group of about twenty advisors and contributors in April, 1983. As a provisional effort, the draft version made no claim to absolute accuracy or completeness. The distribution of the list at that time was intended to elicit comments, suggestions, and especially contributions from scholars in Anglo-Saxon manuscript studies. Some of the responses received have already been incorporated into a revised draft version, but several important contributions are still outstanding at this writing.

To summarize, the major changes include: a) the adoption of Gneuss' system for listing the codicological information; b) the revision of many iconographic descriptions using the entries from the Index of Christian Art; c) the modification of the alphabetically arranged Index to Iconographic Subjects, employing the Editor's File from the Index of Christian Art; and d) the addition of three Anglo-Saxon illuminated manuscripts omitted from Temple's volume. It should be remembered, finally, that this project continues to evolve. In view of the fact that some ten to twenty new publications on Anglo-Saxon manuscripts appear yearly, any printed version of the *Index to Iconographic Subjects* will be in part out of date. We do plan, however, to maintain the data base and to release periodic updates of the Index.[7]

V. Postscript

Subsequent to the 1983 Kalamazoo Symposium and the writing of this paper, a number of important activities have taken place. As a result of publicity received at both the 1983 and 1984 meetings of the Symposium, a number of scholars have submitted contributions, ranging from additions to the Photo-Bibliography and corrections of existing entries to descriptions of new miniatures. In addition, we have added another manuscript to the inventory (Rouen, Bibliothèque municipale A.337, fol. 20 with an historiated initial depicting Paulinus, bishop of Nola, offering himself as a slave to the Vandals), bringing the total to 227 manuscripts. In 1984 we received support in the form of two travel grants from the National Endowment for the Humanities and the J. Paul Getty Trust, which enabled me to travel to the Index of Christian Art at Princeton and to the British Library, Warburg Institute, and the University of London Library in London. I also reported on the project at the Second International Conference on Automatic Processing of Art History Data and Documents in Pisa, Italy. Finally, the book-length manuscript, entitled *Anglo-Saxon Illuminated Manuscripts: An Iconographic Catalogue,* is scheduled for publication in late 1985 by Garland Publishing.

PURDUE UNIVERSITY

Notes

1. See Thomas H. Ohlgren, rev. of *Anglo-Saxon Manuscripts 900–1066,* by E. Temple, *Speculum,* 55 (1980), 178–80.

2. In contrast, by turning to the *Index to Iconographic Subjects* the researcher will be able to locate quickly the relevant scenes. Of the six Ascensions listed, four are of the Disappearing type (Rouen, Bibliothèque municipale MS. 274, fol. 81^v; Vatican City, Biblioteca Apostolica MS. Reg. lat. 12, fol. 73^v; London, BL Cotton Caligula A.XIV, fol. 18; and BL Cotton Tiberius C.VI, fol. 15). In addition, the Translation of Enoch (p. 61 of Bodleian MS. Junius 11) is rendered as a Disappearing type. Closely related too is the Ascension on fol. 85 of Pierpont Morgan M. 333, the Continental Otbert Gospels. The new image consists of two elements: the body of Christ disappears into a cloud with only the legs or feet showing; and the perspective or point of view is that of the earthly spectators, the Apostles, below. See Meyer Schapiro, "The Image of the Disappearing Christ," in *Late Antique, Early Christian and Medieval Art: Selected Papers* (New York, 1979), pp. 266–87.

3. The Project Group comprises the following individuals: Carl T. Berkhout (Arizona), Mildred Budny (London), John Contreni (Purdue University), John B. Friedman (Illinois), Robert Harris, (Smith College), John Higgitt (Edinburgh), Louis Jordan (University of Notre Dame), Lister Matheson and Ann Shannon (Michigan), William Voelkle (Pierpont Morgan Library), and Charles Wright (Texas Tech University). Advisors to the project include: Bruce Barker-Benfield (Bodleian Library), Robert Deshman (Toronto), Michael Kauffmann (Victoria and Albert Museum), Nigel Morgan (Princeton Index of Christian Art), Joseph Trapp (Warburg Institute), and David Wilson (British Museum).

4. Linda Brownrigg, "Manuscripts Containing English Decoration, 871–1066,

Catalogued and Illustrated: A Review," *ASE,* 7 (1978), 256–57.

5. Nigel Morgan of the Princeton Index of Christian Art kindly directed our attention to this manuscript, which Temple omitted from *Anglo-Saxon Manuscripts.* The miniature is reproduced by C. R. Dodwell in *The Canterbury School of Illumination* (Cambridge, 1954), Pl. 6b.

6. Brownrigg, "Manuscripts Containing English Decoration," pp. 255, 263.

7. This paper has also been published in Vol. I of the *Papers* of the Second International Conference on Automatic Processing of Art History Data and Documents (Pisa, 1984), pp. 367–85.

The Corpus of Anglo-Saxon Stone Sculpture

ROSEMARY CRAMP

The *Corpus of Anglo-Saxon Stone Sculpture* is a multi-volume work that will provide the first comprehensive catalogue of the stone sculpture which survives from the pre-Conquest period in England. Previous attempts to publish this material have been frustrated by the quantity and inaccessibility of the material and by the problem of constructing a satisfactory descriptive grammar for its extremely diverse ornamental repertory. A new system of description has been developed to deal with the form and ornament of the material, and this system will be applied throughout the entire series.

Work has been in progress for twenty years, and under the direction of Rosemary Cramp, who is General Editor of the series, a national archive has been compiled and is housed at the University of Durham. The project has been funded by the British Academy since 1977, and a team of authors to cover the country, region by region, has now been assembled.

Each volume will be prefaced by an Introduction which places the sculpture within its historical context and discusses the significance of its distribution. This is followed by general discussion of the stylistic groupings and "schools" in the region under consideration in that volume. The catalogue entries provide a detailed description of each stone and a discussion of its connections in art history and its date, together with a full bibliography. Each piece is also provided with comprehensive photographic coverage. In the first three volumes these are largely the work of one photographer, Mr. Tom Middlemass.

Much of the material in these volumes is concerned with those monuments which are distinctive of the British Isles in the pre-Conquest period, i.e., the stone crosses; and many of these are well illustrated for the first time. Recent excavations on ecclesiastical sites have however revealed other types of funerary monument and a wealth of architectural sculpture and furnishings, much of which has not hitherto been described in print.

Volume I covers the pre–1974 counties of Durham and Northumberland — the heartland of the old Northumbrian kingdom of Bernicia. The volume is divided into two parts, each of 264 pages, including 406 illustrations, and incorporates the sculpture from the well-known early monastic houses of Lindisfarne, Hexham, Wearmouth, and Jarrow. From the last two sites, the Corpus catalogue includes a considerable amount of recently excavated material. The sculpture from the later period of the ninth and the tenth to eleventh centuries includes the important collection from the See of Durham and its dependencies, as well as the outstanding Anglo-Viking sculpture from Sockburn. Volume I was published early in 1984.

Volume II — Cumbria, written by Richard Bailey and Rosemary Cramp — was scheduled to go to press in 1985. This volume includes some of the most outstanding crosses from Northumbria and includes a re-evaluation of the Bewcastle Cross by Rosemary Cramp with a commentary on the runic inscriptions by R. I. Page. Richard Bailey's work includes a lengthy commentary on the Gosforth Cross and a discussion of the western "schools" of Viking-Age ornament.

Volume III — York and the East Riding, by James Lang — includes the important new material from Viking-Age York; and succeeding volumes for the southeast and southwest of England will include new architectural sculpture from the important Anglo-Saxon excavations at Winchester and Gloucester.

These volumes will be a useful source of information for the student of Anglo-Saxon civilization and art, and prints of the photographs (which in the publications are not as large as ideally one could have wished) can be obtained from the University of Durham. For students of the language, there may be some interest in the series of photographs of inscriptions.

We hope then that this series will provide a research tool for a wide range of scholars working in this period.

UNIVERSITY OF DURHAM

A Handlist of Anglo-Saxon Manuscripts

HELMUT GNEUSS

In order to draw up an inventory of all texts available to Anglo-Saxon readers, various types of evidence will have to be examined. Among These, the extant manuscripts written in Anglo-Saxon England or known to have reached England before A.D. 1100 are an extremely important source of information. It is intended to provide a comprehensive survey of these books and fragments in a "Handlist of Anglo-Saxon Manuscripts" (the title is provisional), with special emphasis on the contents of these manuscripts and on a bibliographical record of work done on them. It will thus become possible to compile an inventory of texts known to the Anglo-Saxons and still extant in contemporary manuscript copies. At the same time, work with such manuscripts will be facilitated by offering a fairly complete record of studies concerned with individual books or groups of them; at present, very few libraries holding such books can provide such a service to their readers.

The scope of the "Handlist" will be the same as that outlined in *Anglo-Saxon England,* 9 (1981), 2–3: All manuscripts which were certainly written in England up to 1100, and manuscripts written outside Anglo-Saxon England, if they certainly or very probably reached England before 1100, will be included. Single-leaf documents and manuscripts that were written or annotated by Anglo-Saxon scribes on the Continent will not be considered. Work on the project is to proceed in the following stages:

1. "A Preliminary List of Manuscripts Written or Owned in England up to 1100" was published in *Anglo-Saxon England,* 9 (1981), 1–60. This was intended as a brief and tentative inventory of Anglo-Saxon manuscripts, and as a search-list; as a result of its publication, specialists in various fields have supplied me with important addenda and corrigenda. All further information of this kind will be most welcome and will of course be acknowledged in print when it is used.

2. A number of articles meant as supplements to the "Preliminary List" are to be published in the near future:
   a. "Addenda and Corrigenda to the Preliminary List of Manuscripts Written or Owned in England up to 1100"; about 50 manuscripts or fragments to be included as addenda have come to my knowledge, and further items in this category are to be expected.
   b. An index to the liturgical manuscripts in the "Preliminary List," including addenda appearing in *Learning and Literature in Anglo-Saxon England: Studies Presented to Peter Clemoes on the Occasion of His Sixty-fifth Birthday*, ed. Michael Lapidge and Helmut Gneuss (Cambridge, 1985) pp. 91–141.
   c. An index to the contents (i.e., all texts written in Latin) of the manuscripts recorded in the "Preliminary List." This will comprise all items in these manuscripts, so far as they have been identified; it is intended to serve a purpose similar to that of the "Preliminary List."
3. A brief provisional handlist of Anglo-Saxon manuscripts, giving the contents of each manuscript (except for minor fragments and short, unidentified pieces), as well as bibliographical references to one or two important descriptions or discussions of the manuscript. (This stage may be omitted.)
4. The Handlist in its final form.
   The projected "Handlist of Anglo-Saxon Manuscripts" (stage 4) is to contain, for each manuscript known to have been written or owned in Anglo-Saxon England at any time up to 1100:
   a. Information on date, origin and provenance, with additional notes in doubtful or difficult cases;
   b. A note on the type of script and on codicological peculiarities; the "Handlist" will not however provide detailed treatments of the paleography and codicology of the manuscripts;
   c. A full list of contents, giving for each item references to authoritative editions (inclusive of unpublished theses) and to relevant work on textual criticism. References to editions will include a statement as to whether the manuscript has been used as the basis for the printed text, whether it has been collated for the critical apparatus, or whether the manuscript has not been utilized at all;
   d. For texts in Old English: a note on what is known about the dialect

characteristics of its phonology, morphology, and vocabulary;

e. A note on the decoration of the manuscript;

f. A full bibliography of all work done on the history, paleography, and codicology of the manuscript, and references to recent work on its illumination (not yet listed in the volumes of the Survey of Manuscripts Illuminated in the British Isles edited by J. J. G. Alexander and E. Temple) as well as to all studies of the manuscript as a whole. References to facsimile reproductions of the manuscript or parts of it will also be given so far as possible; unpublished dissertations will be taken into account. The bibliography will not include historical, literary and other studies dealing with the texts contained in the manuscript, apart from those mentioned above under "c."

Books and fragments that have been fully described in N. R. Ker's *Catalogue of Manuscripts Containing Anglo-Saxon* will be treated in a somewhat briefer form, but all references to editions and works to be listed under section "f" will be as full as possible for the period after Ker's *Catalogue* was published.

The "Handlist" will contain indices for texts, authors, places of provenance, etc., and two appendices, of which one is to record manuscripts known to have survived into modern times but now lost or untraced, while the other will list those early books in Insular script which, according to expert opinion, were written either in England *or* in a Continental scriptorium.

Enquiries concerning the project should be directed to

Institut für Englische Philologie
Universität München
Schellingstr. 3
D-8000 München 40
West Germany

UNIVERSITY OF MUNICH

Dictionary of Medieval Latin from British Sources

DAVID R. HOWLETT

In 1913 the British Academy received a proposal for a dictionary of Medieval Latin which would replace Du Cange's *Glossarium Mediae et Infimae Latinitatis,* published in 1678 and supplemented in 1733 and 1766. In 1920 the *Union Académique Internationale* accepted this vast project with the co-operation of the British Academy, which in 1924 appointed two committees to extract quotations from British and Irish sources. The first fruit of their work was a *Medieval Latin Word-List from British and Irish Sources,* published for the British Academy by Oxford University Press in 1934 and reissued five times. In 1965 a *Revised Medieval Latin Word-List* was edited by R. E. Latham, who began in 1967 to edit an historical dictionary from British sources only, since in 1968 the Royal Irish Academy undertook a separate dictionary of Hiberno-Latin.

The *Dictionary of Medieval Latin from British Sources* enjoys the financial support of the British Academy and the hospitality of two great institutions which house it, the Public Record Office in Chancery Lane, London, and the Bodleian Library in Oxford. Besides direct access to the treasures of the P.R.O. and the Bodleian its resources include:

- all the unprinted quotations collected for the *Oxford Latin Dictionary* (from the beginnings to A.D. 200), now completed by P. G. W. Glare;
- an extensive collection of quotations from Late Latin sources (200–600);
- about 750,000 quotation slips from Medieval Latin sources from the sixth century to the sixteenth, from Gildas to Camden;
- a growing archive of machine-readable texts and computer-produced concordances;

an archive of bibliographical material for printed and manuscript Medieval Latin literature;

access to the archive assembled for revision of Liddell and Scott's Greek Lexicon now being edited by P. G. W. Glare.

Fascicule I (A–B) appeared in 1975, Fascicule II (C) in 1981, two years after the present editor had succeeded Latham. Fascicule III (D–E, with a completely revised Bibliography) is expected to appear in 1986. Editorial staff are working on Fascicule IV (F–G–H).

The *Dictionary of Medieval Latin from Celtic Sources* enjoys the financial support of the Royal Irish Academy. The first of its ancillary publications, *A Bibliography of Celtic-Latin Literature 400–1200*, by Michael Lapidge of the University of Cambridge and Richard Sharpe, Assistant Editor of the British *Dictionary*, is at press. A series of concordances (printed and microfiche), reprints of inaccessible editions of texts, and new editions of badly edited and previously unedited texts is in preparation. The entire corpus to be cited by this *Dictionary* is being made machine-readable under the supervision of Mr. Anthony Harvey at the Royal Irish Academy in Dublin and is archived at Queen's University in Belfast.

OXFORD

Abbreviations and Short Titles

ASE	*Anglo-Saxon England* [cited as a periodical by volume and year]
ASPR	*Anglo-Saxon Poetic Records*, in six volumes edited by G.P. Krapp and E.V.K. Dobbie [New York, 1931–42; 2nd printing 1958–65]
BL	British Library, London (in citations of manuscripts)
BN	Bibliothèque Nationale, Paris (in citations of manuscripts)
CCCC	Cambridge, Corpus Christi College (in citations of manuscripts)
CCSL	*Corpus Christianorum Series Latina* cited by volume
CSEL	*Corpus Scriptorum Ecclesiasticorum Latinorum* cited by volume
CUL	Cambridge, University Library (in citations of manuscripts)
EEMF	Early English Manuscripts in Facsimile
EETS	Early English Text Society [cited in the various series: OS, Original Series; ES, Extra Series; SS, Supplementary Series]
MGH	*Monumenta Germaniae Historica*, cited by subseries and volume
PG	*Patrologia Graeca* ed. J.P. Migne [Paris, 1857–67], cited by volume and column
PL	*Patrologia Latina* ed. J.P. Migne [Paris, 1844–91], cited by volume and column

List of Manuscripts Cited

[N.B. See also: 1) the list of manuscripts appended to Thomas Bestul's "Continental Influences on Anglo-Saxon Devotional Writing," pp. 124-26; 2) the general Index under the traditional or customary title of a codex.]

Angers
	Bibliothèque Municipale 477(461): 62n15
Antwerp
	Plantin-Moretus Musaeum 190: 58
Autun
	Bibliothèque Municipale 54: 264
Bamberg
	Staatsbibliothek
		—A.II.42: 283
		—A.I.47: 133-38, 142-46 passim
		—B.II.10: 107-08
Berlin (East)
	Deutsche Staatsbibliothek Phillipps 1716: 84
Bern(e)
	Bürgerbibliothek 318: 327, 334-36
Brussels
	Bibliothèque Royale 8558-63: 61n3
Cambrai
	Bibliothèque Municipale
		—MS 386: 295
		—MS B 822(727), 89n47

Cambridge
    Corpus Christi College
        —MS 23: 314n29, 324, 416
        —MS 41: 90
        —MS 57: 282n46
        —MS 162: 78
        —MS 163: 62n13
        —MS 183: 322
        —MS 214: 57
        —MS 272: 115
        —MS 276: 62n19
        —MS 391: 115-16, 118, 290
    Pembroke College
        —MS 23: 89n55
        —MS 24: 89n55
        —MS 25: 85
    Trinity College
        —B.11.2(241): 62n9
        —B.16.44: 53
        —O.3.7: 58-59
        —O.7.41: 54
    University Library
        —Ff. 1. 23: 228
        —Ff. 4. 43: 282n46
        —Gg. 5. 35: 417
        —Kk. 3. 21: 57
        —Kk. 5. 32: 62n18
        —Ll. 1 .10: 103-15

Cologne
    Dombibliothek 106: 107

Dublin
    Trinity College
        —A.I.6: 284, 295
        —E.4.2: 106

El Escorial
    Real Biblioteca E.II.1: 58

Etschmiadzen
    Monastery Library 229: 369

Florence
    Biblioteca Medicea Laurenziana Ashburnham 10: 115

Frankfurt am Main
    Stadtbibliothek Cod. Ausst. 68: 283

Geneva
    Bibliothèque Publique Bodmer Collection C.B. 175: 58

Gloucester
 Cathedral Library 35: 25
Hague
 Koninklijke Bibliotheek 70 H 7: 133, 142
London
 British Library
  —Add. 49598: 261-68, 272-73, 277, 279n31, 341n31
  —Add. 24199: 314n29, 416
  —Add. 34890: 416
  —Add. 57337: 54
  —Arundel 155: 115-16, 124n82
  —Cotton Caligula A.XIV: 309 pl. 22, 310 pl. 23, 316n54, 429n2
  —Cotton Claudius B.IV: 228, 308 pl 20, 316n54, 416-17
  —Cotton Cleopatra C.VIII: 314n29, 315n47, 416
  —Cotton Faustina B.III: 62n8
  —Cotton Galba A.XIV: 115, 124n82
  —Cotton Galba A.XVIII: 109, 115, 117, 267-72, 279n13
  —Cotton Julius E.VII: 25
  —Cotton Nero C.IV: 283, 317n56
  —Cotton Otho B.X: 25
  —Cotton Tiberius A.III: 62n8
  —Cotton Tiberius B.V: 308 pl. 20, 316n54, 320-38, 416
  —Cotton Tiberius C.II: 315n45
  —Cotton Tiberius C.VI: 303, 429n2
  —Cotton Titus D. XXVI-XXVII: 116, 303, 420
  —Cotton Vespasian A.I: 124n82
  —Cotton Vitellius A.XV: 320-38, 416
  —Cotton Vitellius C.III: 416
  —Egerton 3763: 110
  —Harley 603: 295, 416
  —Harley 863: 115
  —Harley 2965: 103, 112, 114
  —Harley 6258B: 408
  —Harley 7653: 103
  —Royal 2 A.xx: 60, 63n33, 103-05, 109-10, 112, 114-15, 117
  —Stowe 944: 303
Lyons
 Bibliothèque Municipale 447(376): 79, 80
Munich
 Bayerische Staatsbibliothek
  —clm. 835: 340n16
  —clm. 29031b: 416
  —clm. 14276: 78, 80, 86n12, 87n15, 92-100
  —clm. 14277: 80

List of Manuscripts Cited

New York
    Pierpont Morgan Library M. 333: 417, 429n2
Orléans
    Bibliothèque Municipale
        —MS 342(290): 101
        —MS 184: 106, 115
Oxford
    Bodleian Library
        —Auct. F.1.15: 57-59
        —Auct. F.4.32: 54
        —Bodley 579: 290-93, 303, 316n54
        —Bodley 614: 320
        —Digby 211: 133, 142
        —Douce 296: 116
        —Junius 11: 295, 298-303, 429n2
        —Selden Supra 30: 103
    Corpus Christi College 74: 63n25
Paris
    Bibliothèque Arsenal 610: 316n50
    Bibliothèque Nationale
        —Lat. 943: 62n13
        —Lat. 1153: 105
        —Lat. 6401: 58-59
        —Lat. 6401A: 57-59
        —Lat. 8824: 316n54
        —Lat. 9377: 62n15
        —Lat. 9428: 283
        —Lat. 11561: 80, 86n12, 87n15, 92-100
        —Lat. 13388: 106, 108-09
        —Lat. 14380: 58
        —Lat. 17814: 58
Rouen
    Bibliothèque Municipale
        —MS 274(Y.6): 429n2
        —MS A.337: 417, 428
        —MS 368(A.27): 62n13
        —MS 1385(U.107): 61n7
St. Gall
    Stiftsbibliothek
        —MS 908: 79
        —MS 869: 107
St. Lô
    Archives de la Manche 1: 417
St. Omer
    Bibliothèque Municipale 716: 89n47

Salzburg
>Studienbibliotek Sign. V. I. H. 162: 314n30

South Bend, Indiana
>Notre Dame University Library 4: 340

Trier
>Stadtbibliothek 31: 295

Urbana, Illinois
>Univ. of Illinois Library DeRicci 140: 340n16

Utrecht
>Rijksuniversiteit
>>—MS 32: 295, 303, 327, 334–36

Valenciennes
>Bibliothèque Municipale 99: 417

Vatican City
>Biblioteca Apostolica Vaticana
>>—Barberini lat. 570: 421
>>—Chigi C VI: 173
>>—Graec. 752: 284
>>—Lat. 84: 110
>>—Lat. 3363: 44
>>—Pal. Lat. 67: 120n3
>>—Reg. Lat. 12: 124n82, 228, 267, 289n27, 416–17, 429n2
>>—Reg. lat. 76: 78–79, 80, 90–100
>>—Reg. lat. 1650: 48n23

Index

(mainly to persons and titles)

Ælfric of Eynsham, 8-9, 12-13, 15, 18-19, 29, 37, 42, 60, 80, 228, 268, 279n19, 290, 346, 348-49
Ælfwold, king, 162
Æthelbert, 169
Æthelstan [see Athelstan]
Æþelwold of Abingdon, 29, 30, 113, 261, 273-74, 277
Æþelwold, bishop of Lindisfarne, 104, 111
Abecedarian form, 109-10
Abraham, 10, 306
Adam, age at creation, 79
Adamnan [see Adomnan]
Adana medallions, 369
Adelard, 276
Adelinus, 322
Adomnán (alt. Adamnán), 157, 159, 161, 167, 193, 196
Adrian and Ritheus, 79
Advent lyrics, 272-73, 277-78
Aed, 167
Aetheria, 345-46
Agnus Dei, as depicted on Ruthwell and Bewcastle crosses, 377-78
Alan of Farfa, 85
Alchfrith, 105, 111, 116

Alcuin, 18-19, 55, 107, 109-13, 162, 348-49; works, life of Martin, 85; *Officia per Ferias,* 107, 113; *De Psalmorum Usu,* 107
Aldhelm, 55, 108-09, 293, 321-22
Alexander the Great, 319-20
Alexander, J.J.G., 114, 415-16, 435
Alfred the Great, 37-45 passim, 117, 162, 171, 346-47, 353n11; account of Orpheus, 41; and biblical style, 132; his *Boethius,* 37, 42; his *Soliloquies,* 37, 45
Allegory, 8
Altar, image of, as cornerstone, 272
Amalarius of Metz, 54-55
Ambrose, 53, 71, 167-68
Amos, Ashley Crandell, 20n
Anderson, Marjorie, 169
Andreas, 8-9,
Andreas cross, 54
Anglian style, 244
Anglo-Saxon art, 214, as source for "gripping beast," 211
Anglo-Saxon Chronicle, 37, 40, 48n27, 346
Anglo-Scandinavian, as a term, 244
Animal ornament (generally), in early medieval art, 203-05

Annals of Ulster, 196
Annunciation, depicted on Ruthwell Cross, 358, 361, 369
Anselm of Canterbury, 116, 156
Anskar (St.), 163
Antiphonary of Bangor, 105, 111
Ant(h)ony the hermit, 29 [see Paul and Anthony panels]
ap Llywelyn, Gruffudd, 166
Apocrypha, 8
Apollonius of Tyre, 37
Apuleius, 35
Arator, 108
Arbman, Holger, 204
Arno of Salzburg, 107
Arnulph, ciborium of, 283
Arnulph of Milan, prayerbook of (= BL Egerton 3763), 110
Aspatria hogback, 248
Athanasius, his *Life of Antony,* 30, 348
Athelstan (alt. Æthelstan), king, 115, 117, 166, 177n29, 322
Athelstan Psalter (= BL Cotton Galba A.XVIII), 109, 115, 117, 267-72, 279n13
Atwood, E. Bagby, 21n
Augustine, 19, 53, 154, 349; works: *De Civitate Dei,* 38-39, 82, 284; *Confessiones,* 104, 108; *De Consensu Evangelistarum,* 67; prayers attributed to him, 109, 112-13; *Soliloquia,* 7, 43, 45, 104, 108-09, 113; *De Trinitate,* 7, 55, 104, 108
Augustinus Hibernicus, 65

Bailey, Richard, 248, 252, 432
Balaam's ass, 80
Balinderry gaming-board, 246
Bamberg Apocalypse (= Staatsbibl. A.II.42), 283
Bamburgh, 192,
Bannerman, John, 169
"Baroque Master," 207, 214
Barrow, Geoffrey, 169

Bartlett, Robert, 171
Bately, Janet, 83
Battle of Degastan, 185
Beatus Apocalypse, 284
Bede, 18-19, 55, 65-73, 81, 84, 154, 185, 193, 348-49, 370, 385-86, 388, 393-94; and the *Chronicle,* 37; and Romanism, 70; as subject of *Epistola Cuthberti,* 142-44; works: *De Arte Metrica,* 111; Ascension Hymn, 14; *Historica Ecclesiastica,* 40, 46n 12, 55, 65, 71-72, 106, 107; hymn to Ætheldryd, 107; hymns and prayers (various), 108-10; hymns on the psalms variously entitled in mss., 106, 107; "Laudate altithronum pueri," 109; *De Natura Rerum,* 80; "O deus aeterne mundo," presumed author, 106; paraphrase of Psalm 83, presumed author, 106; "Tu enim es domine spes mea," 106
Beltain (festival), 153
Benedict Biscop, 195
Benedict (St.) of Nursia, his *Rule,* 276, 382
Benedictine reform, 29, 113, and its propaganda, 261-78, 306
Beowulf, 154, 164-65, 167, 290, 319, 321, 324; and *Aeneid,* 35-36; and Cain, 82
Berht, 185
Berkhout, Carl T., 421
Berne *Physiologus,* 327, 334-36
Bernicia, 199, 431-32
Bewcastle Cross, 345, 349, 352, 358, 370-74, 377-79; multivalence in "Agnus Dei" panels, 391-99; multivalence in "Christ over the Beasts" panels, 379-90
Bible, as source, 7; ten rules of style, 131-32; writers employing biblical style, 132
Biblical exegesis (see Exegesis)
Billfrith, 193
Binchy, Daniel, 152, 157, 169, 172

Index

Bischoff, Bernhard, 54, 65–66, 68–69, 78, 81
Bishop, Edmund, 105, 109–10
Blathmac, 16–17
Bleeding Cross/Tree (motif), 16–18
Blemmyae, 324–27
Blunt, C.E., 214
Boethius [see also Alfred], his *Consolation of Philosophy*, 7, 42–43, 55, 57, 59
Bonner, Gerald, 377
Book of Armagh, 157, 166
Book of Cerne (= Cambridge, University Library Ll.1.10), 103–15
Book of the Devil, 284–87, 303
The Book of Enoch, 82–83
Book of Kells (= Dublin, Trinity College A.I.6), 284, 295
Book of Nunnaminster (= London, BL Royal 2 A.xx), 60, 63n33, 103–05, 109–10, 112, 114–15, 117
Book of Rights, 167
Book of Settlements (*Landnámabók*), 290
Bormann, William I., 419
Borre style, 214, 217, 220, 227–28, 236, 238, 244–46, 254
Bóruma Laigen, 164
Bradley, S.A.J., 11, 21n
Brehons, 153, 157, 164
Brendan (St.), presumed author of prayers, 105
Brewer, Charlotte, 33n
Brian Boru, 166
British Academy, 431, 437
Broa, 204
Brompton cross, 246–48, 252–54
Brownrigg, Linda, 417, 422
Brunet, A., 32n
Brussels Cross, 347, 353n11
Bryan, W.F., 20n
Burlin, R.B., 12, 21n
Bury St. Edmunds Psalter (= Vatican Reg. Lat. 12), 124n82, 228, 267, 289n27, 416–17, 429n2
Butler, Sharon, 409
Byrhtferth of Ramsey, 275

Byrne, Francis John, 151, 153, 164

Caedmon, 9, 26
Caedmon manuscript (= Oxford, Bodleian Library Junius 11), 295, 298–303, 429n2
Caesarius of Arles, 85
Cain, 81–82
Cambrai Apocalypse, 295
Cameron, Angus, 407–08
Cammin casket, 248
Cancellarius, 166
Canmore, Malcolm, 170
Canterbury, and dissemination of Greek, 58–59
Canticle of Habbakuk, 383–88, 401n21, 402n28
Canticles, 112
Carileph, 232
Carlisle, 192
Carney, James, 16, 21n
Carnicelli, Thomas A., 45
Carolingian art, 214, 220, 336–38; and depiction of the devil, 284; as source for "gripping beast," 204, 207
Carolingian innovations in hymns, 116–17
Carolingian Renaissance, 151
Cassian, 82
Cassiodorus, 351; his *Institutiones*, 55
Castledermot, 252
Célí Dé, 348
Chadwick, H.M., 153, 164–65
Charlemagne, 103, 112; and Alcuin, 107
Charles the Bald, 30, 117
Chaucer, 20n
Chester, 198
Chester-le-Street, 199
Chiasmus, feature of biblical style, 129–32, 142–46
Christ, figure of, 262; and the Beasts, 372–74, 375n6, 378–90; as Judge and Saviour depicted on the Ruthwell Cross, 368; and Mary

Magdalene depicted on the Ruthwell Cross, 361, 370
Christ I, 4, 10–15, 18–19
Christ II (see also Cynewulf), 4, 6, 10–11, 13–15, 18–19
Christ III, 4, 10–11, 15–19
Christ and Satan, 4, 290
Christ Church, Canterbury, 114, 116, 295, 324
Christian literature, 7–8, 35, and devotional literature, 104
Church (Ecclesia), theme, 261–78
Churches, construction of, 193–94
Church fathers, and Greek, 54–56
Church history, 7
Classen, Peter, 175n14
Classical authors and OE writers, 41
Classical texts, 35–45 passim
Clonenagh, 155
Clonmacnoise, 155
Clovis, 163–65
Cnut (alt. Knut), 227, 306
Cofractio Panis, 370
Cogitosus, 167
Coleridge, Samuel Taylor, 32n
Collectio Psalterii, 112
Collingwood, W.G., 246
Columba, 155
Columban(us), 66, 72, 112; works, "Domine deus, destrue quicquid" (prayer), 105; *Regula Monachorum*, 104
Comgall (St.), presumed author of hymns, 105
Comitatus, 163
Commentaries, 53, 65–73 passim, 78, 81
Connacht, 166
Constantine, 164, 347
Constantinescu, Radu, 107, 110
Cook, Albert S., 11–13, 21n
Cormac, 168
Cornerstone, image of, 272, 276, 280n20, 280n27
Corpus of Anglo-Saxon Stone Sculpture, 238, 244; described, 431–32
Crafts, at secular sites, 194; at Jarrow, 196, 198
Cramp, Rosemary, 220, 258, 358, 368, 377, 395, 397, 432
Crith Gablach, 168
Croft-on-Tees, 207
Cromwell, Oliver, 84
Cross, as cosmological symbol, 349–50, 352; and pilgrimages, 350–52
Cross, J.E., 46n1, 71
Cross Canonby, 246
Cross of Muiredach, 284–87, 303
Cross of Scriptures (Flann's Cross), 284–87
Crosses, silver, 224; stone, 431
Crozier ferule from the River Bann, 246
Cruachain, 158
Crucifixion, 421; depicted on Ruthwell Cross, 358, 386
Cumberland, 244
Cumbria, 214, 227, 243, 432
Cummianus (Cummean), 69, 156
Cuthbert, (= Cuth?) 106, 110; his *Epistola Cuthberti de obitu Baedae*, 132–47
Cuthwine, 142
Cwicwine, 198
Cynecephali, 315n36, 321, 327
Cynewulf, 6 [see *Elene*]
Cyprian, 104, 348
Cyril of Jerusalem, 345, 348
Cyril of Scythiopolis, 32n

Dál Cais, 165
Dalriada, 186
Danelaw, 217
Dating, problems of 3–4,
David I (king of Scotland), 159, 170
Davies, Wendy, 151, 157
De abbatibus, 198
Deira, 192, 199
de Man, Paul, 24

Index 449

Dembowski, Peter F., 25–29, 33n
Demonic imagery, 283–312 passim, 312n1, 312n2, 313n14; three elements of, 284
Dempster, Germaine, 20n
Deor, 190
De Ordine Creaturarum Liber, 80, 82
Derrida, Jacques, 24
de Saussure, Ferdinand, 24
Descent into Hell, 4
"Deus delicti" (hymn), 107, 112
"Deus inaestimabilis misericordiae" (hymn), 118
"Deus universitatis conditor" (hymn), 113,
Diadema Monachorum, 276
Diamond, Robert E., 11, 20n–21n
Dictionary of Medieval Latin from British Sources, described 439–40
Dictionary of Old English, *d* entries in, 411–12; and other dictionaries, 407; and other research tools, 407–10
Dinas Powys, 189
Dioscorides, 60
Doane, A.N., 9, 20n
Dobbie, E.V.K., 132–33
Dodwell, C.R., 190, 417
Doherty, Charles, 151, 168
"Domine Deus meus qui non habes dominum" (hymn), 115
"Domine deus omnmipotens, spei insertor," prayer in *Vita Julianae,* 107
"Domine exaudi orationem meam quia iam cognosco quod tempus meum prope est" (hymn), 115
"Domine Iesue Christe, adoro te in cruce ascendentem" (hymn), 114
"Domine Iesu Christe qui de hoc mundo" (prayer), 109
"Domine iustitiae te deprecor" (prayer), 109
Donestre, 320, 327–334
Dream of the Rood [see also Ruthwell and Bewcastle crosses] 4, 18, 119, 345, 347, 349–52

Drogo Sacramentary (= BN lat. 9428), 283
Druids, 155
Dublin, 198, 252
Du Cange, C., 437
Duleek, 193
Dún Ailline, 158
Duncan, Archie, 158
Duncan, Henry, 357
Dunstan, 161, 167, 276, 290
Durham, 199, 431; crozier from, 232

Eadsige, 274–75
Ealdormen, 166
Ealhswith, 113, 117
Earle, John, 32n
Easter controversy, 69, 71, 156
Ecclesia (theme) [see Church]
Ecclesia Primitiva, 370
Ecgfrith, 185–86
Einhard, 117, 153–54
Elene, 345, 347, 351–52
Elias/Elijah, 386, 388
Elmswell, 188, 190–91
Emain Macha, 158–59
Emerson, O.F., 81
Ephraim the Syrian, 111, 118
Epistola Alexandri, 320–21, 324
Eric Bloodaxe, 243
Eucharist, and Ruthwell and Bewcastle Crosses, 391, 393–97, 432
Eusebius-Rufinus, 107
Evangelists, figures of, 262
Evans, Michael, 418
Evernew Tongue (motif), 18, 78
Excavations, relevant to Northumbria and Ireland, 188
Exegesis, 7, Hiberno-Latin e. 65–73
Exeter Book (= Exeter Cathedral Library MS 3501), 272, 277–78
Exodus, and Ruthwell and Bewcastle Crosses, 391

Fadda, A.M. Luiselli, 84
Farrell, Robert T., 377, 382–83, 385, 388–90, 400n15

Feis, 159
Fifteen Signs of Judgment, 16
Filid, 154–55, 157–58, 170–72, 176n20, 176n22
Flambard, 232
Flann's Cross, see Cross of Scriptures
Flavigny Gospels, 262
Fleury, and Oswald of Ramsey, 276; and Anglo-Saxon painting, 341n36
Flight into Egypt, depicted on Ruthwell Cross, 369–70, 395
Flodoard of Reims, 25, 32n
Flores Psalmorum, 112, 117
Florilegia, 70
Florus, 39
Flower, Robin, 350
Fortunatus, 108
Foucault, Michel, 24
Foundation, image of, 272
Franks Casket, 190
Frazer, Sir James, 151
Freeman, Edward A., 170
Frese, Dolores Warwick, 21n
Fuglesang, Signe Horn, 252
Fulda, 109

Gabriel, depicted on Ruthwell Cross, 361, 369
Galsted, silver fibula, 287
Garryduff, 189, 192, 194
Gaut, 254
Gelasian sacramentary, 110–11, 401n22
General Assemblies of the Church of Scotland, and Ruthwell Cross, 361
Genesis A, 11, 298
Genesis B, 290, 298
Gerald of Wales, 158–59, 170
Gildas, 72, 132, 159, 437
Glare, P.G.W., 437–38
Glastonbury, 167, 290, 303
Glendalough, 155
Glossaries, Latin-Old English and OE writings, 41–42, 44
Gloucester, 432

Gneuss, Helmut, 84, 410, 418–19
Godden, Malcolm, 21n
Goði, 163
Golden Legend, 25
Good Friday rites, 346, 385–90, 391
Gosforth Cross, 214, 244–46, 432
Gosforth hogback, 248
Gotland, 204
Gradon, Pamela, 83
Great Chronicle of London, 160
Great Fishing Stone, 217
Greek literature, prayers: 109
Greenfield, Stanley B., 4, 20n, 408, 410
Gregory the Great, 72, 82, 109, 111, 290, 378, 398, and Greek, 56; works: Ascension homily as source of *Christ II,* 6, 14; *Cura Pastoralis,* 84; *Dialogues,* 56, 59, 84
Gregory of Tours, 154
Grendel, 290, 313n18, 321
Grid patterning, 252–58
Griesser, Bruno, 68
Gripping beast (motif), 204, 211
Grosjean, Paul, 71
Gubreth, 168
Gumbalda, 204
Gunhild Cross, 306
Gutenberg, 24
Guthlac B, 19

Hadrian's Wall, 370
Hagiography, 8–9, 71
Halfdan, 243–44
Handlist of Anglo-Saxon Manuscripts, described, 433–35
Harald Finehair, 163, 165
Harley Psalter (= BL Harley 603), 295, 416
Harris, Robert M., 417
Haseloff, Gunther, 204
Havelock, Eric, 24, 29, 32n
Haymo of Auxerre, 85
Healey, Antonette diPaolo, 409
Hedeby, 224
Heggen vane, 227

Index

Heimann, Adelheid, 293
Helgö, 188, 191
Hell-mouth, 298, 314n24
Henderson, George, 370, 395, 399n3
Henderson, Isabel, 198
Henry VIII, 84
Henry, Françoise, 189, 284, 287
Herefordshire, Scandinavian inluence in, 232; snake carving, 236
Herzfeld, Georg(e), 81
Hexham, 432
Hilary of Poitiers, 108, 111
Hilda, abbess, 194-95
Hildebert of Lavardin, 25, 33n
Hill, Archibald A., 21n
Hill, Thomas D., 21n, 350
Hogbacks, 227, 246-48, 252
Homiliaries, 85
Homily, 8
Homo dubius, 327
Honorius I (Pope), 111
Hostes, 324-27
Hoveringham, slab, 369; tympanum, 232
Hrabanus Maurus, 85
Hughes, Kathleen, 71, 105, 151
Huppé, Bernard F., 20n
Hygbald, (prob.) abbot of Lindsey, 105
Hywel Dda, 168

Ildefonsus of Toledo, 110
Inauguration rituals, 158-62
Index of Christian Art, 418, 421, 428
Index to Iconographic Subjets, and Harvey Miller Survey, 415-18, 421-22; described, 417-23; progress of 428-29
Instructions of Cormac mac Airt, 168
Insular, idea of, in sources, 15-19, 70, 113; Psalter form, 106
Intertextuality, 24, 31-32
Iona, 192-93, 196, 201n22
Iosephus Scottus, 66
Ireland, as "source" of Anglo-Saxon civilization, 151

Irish Christianity, 104-05: influence of, 106
The Irish Reference Bible, 78-81, 92-100 (text)
"Irish symptoms," 79
Isidore of Pelusium, 80
Isidore of Seville, 72, 161, 336; works: *Chronicon,* 38; *Etymologies,* 40, 45, 55, 82; *Synonyma,* 108, 111; *De Viris Illustribus,* 43
Isle of Man, 214
Iteration, 127-31
Iudex aequitatis, 380, 390, 395-96
Iugulatio, 161
Ivarr, 243

Jackson, Kenneth, 154
Jarrow, 194-98, 370, 432
Jeffrey, Christopher, 84
Jelling, 220
Jellinge style, 214, 217, 224, 227-28, 236, 238, 244, 254
Jenkins, Dafydd, 169
Jerome, 53, 55, 82, 111, 168, 385, 387; works: *Eusebius's Chronicle,* 80, letter to Damasus, 81, *Life of Paul,* 30
Jevington church, 232
John, Eric, 282n51
John the Baptist, figure of, 262; depicted on Bewcastle and Ruthwell Crosses, 377, 391
John of Beverley, 348
John Chrysostom (St.), 345
John Scotus Erigena, 66
Judgment Day (motif), 15
Judgment Day I and *II,* 4
Judith (empress), 117
Julian of Toledo, 18
Juliana, 290
Juvenal, 39
Juvencus, author of *Evangelica Historia,* 107; 108-09

Karlsson, Lennart, 246, 258
Kaske, Robert E., 82, 350

Kauffmann, C. Michael, 415-16
Kells cross, 248
Kells crozier, 248
Kemble, John Mitchell, 153, 163
Kendrick, Thomas, 220, 228
Ker, N.R., 435; his *Catalogue* and the Dictionary of Old English, 407-08
Kildare, 155, 167
Kilpeck, snake carving, 236
King, various terms for, 163, 180n62
Kingston-on-Thames, 160, 178n42
Kirkleavington, 252
Knut, 227, 306
Kuypers, A.B. 111

Lacan, Jacques, 24
Lagore, 189, 194
Laidcenn, author of *Lorica*, 104-05, 107, 111-12
Lamech, 81
Lanfranc, 156
Lang, James, 432
Lantfred, 274-76
Lapidge, Michael, 151, 438
Lastingham cross, 246-48
Last Judgment, and Ragnarok, 214, 283, 287
La Tène metalwork, 188
Latham, R.E., 437
"Laudate altithronum dei" (hymn), 107
Laws of Æthelbert 7, 190
Laws of Ine 63, 190
Lazarus, 306
Lees, Clare, 86n1
Legendaries, 85
"Legimus in ecclesiasticis historiis" (text), 85
Leinster, 192
Leitch, Vincent B., 32n
Leofric Missal (= Bodleian, Bodley 579), 290-93, 303, 316n54
Leofric Psalter (= BL Harley 863), 115
Lertex, 324
Letter of Alexander to Aristotle, 37
Lévi-Strauss, Claude, 24

Lex Salica, 163, 169
Libellus precum, 103
Liber hymnorum, 106
Liber monstrorum, 321-22, 336-38, 340n13
Liber de numeris, 82
Liber Ordinum, 104
Liber Regalis, 160
Liber Vitae, 284, 303
"Libri IV de laude dei et de confessione orationibusque sanctorum collecti ab Alcuino," 107
Life of St. Cyriacus, 25
Life of St. Guthlac, 290
Life of St. Mary of Egypt see *Vita Mariae*
Life of St. Philibert, 192
Limes, 188
Lindau book binding, 204, 220
Lindisfarne, 192-93, 198-99, 432
Lindisfarne slab, 220
Lisbjerg Altar, 232
Literary History, problems of, 3-4
Liturgy, 7; Good Friday, 54; and Ruthwell and Bewcastle crosses, 380-90
Liutger, 306
Livy, 39
Localizing, problems of, 3-4
Lord, A.B., 24, 32n
Lorica, see Laidcenn
Lough Erne reliquary shrine, 248
Louis the Pious, 112
Lowe, E.A., 351
Lucan, 39
Luce Bay, 189
"Luce videt Christum" (hymn), 111

Mac Aedo, Domnall, 161
Macahaoi (St.), 189
Mac Alpin, Kenneth, 170
Mac Cana, Proinsias, 170
Mac Cerbaill, Diarmit, 159, 161
Mac Cuillennáin, Cormac, 162
MacDonald, Aidan, 196
Mac Gabráin, Aedán, 170

Index

McGuire, Martin, 55
McGurk, P., 419
McLuhan, Marshall, 24, 32n
Mac Murchada, Diarmait, 166, 170
NcNally, Robert E., 67–68, 78
McNamara, M(artin), 88n38
Mac Neill, Eoin, 172
Macregol Gospels, 257
Macrobius, 38, 55, 59.
Magi, 190
Majestas Domini, 397
Mammen style, 220
Manaig, 193, 199
Man Born Blind, as depicted on the Ruthwell Cross, 361
Manchianus, 71
"Mane cum surrexero" (prayer), 110
Marian the Scot, 54
Marinus (Pope), 346–47, 353n11
Martianus Capella, 55
Marvels of the East, 319–38, 339n1, 339n9
Mary Magdalene, 29; depicted on the Ruthwell Cross, 361, 369
Mass of the Presanctified, 390
Mayr-Harting, Henry, 70
Mellinkoff, Ruth, 82
Mercia, 110
Metalwork, 224–227, 232
Metz book cover, 283
Metz ivory casket, 262
Meyvaert, Paul, 357–58, 368, 399n3
Michael the archangel, 232, 284–87
Middlemass, Tom, 252, 431
Middleton Cross, 217
Milfield, 191
Millefiori, 198
Miller, J. Hillis, 24
Mirabilia [see also Marvels of the East], as catalogues, 320, 322
Mitchell, Bruce, 33n
Moelcaich, 396
Morecambe Bay, 198
Morgan, Nigel, 418
Morris, William, 30–31

Moses, 386, 388
Moucan, 105, 109
Mucking, 190–91
Multivalence, and interpretations of Ruthwell and Bewcastle crosses, 379–99 passim
Myredah (Muirdach), 199

Nativity, image of, 262
Nelson, Janet, 160
Nendrum, 189, 194
Newgate slab in York, 224
Nicholson, Lewis F., 20n
Nicolson, W., 358
Niðuðr, 204
Niederdollandorf, gravestone, 287
Noah's ark, and the cross, 350–51
Noonday demon, 314n32
Norman Conquest, 169–70, 183n119
Norse mythology, 204, 214–17
Northumbria, 186, 431–32; and devotional writing, 109, 111; evangelization of, 72; and Viking settlement, 243–44
Northumbrian manuscript decoration, 220
Norwich Cathedral cloister, 232
Notker, 117
Nunburnholme cross, 252
Nydam Bog, silver handle, 287

"O andreae sanctae" (prayer), 124n73
O'Brien kings, 168–69
"Obsecro te domine" (prayer), 124n73
"Obsecro te Iesu Christe filius dei vivi per crucem tuam" (prayer), 110
Ó Carragáin, Éamonn, 368
O'Connor, inauguration of, 159
Ó Corráin, Donnchadh, 151, 162, 166, 168
Ó Cróinín, Daibhi, 69
O'Donnell, Manus, 157
O'Dwyer, Peter, 349
Oenachs, 169, 192
Offa of Mercia, 165

Officium divinum, 380
Ogilvy, J.D.A., ix, xiin, 46n5
Ohlgren, Thomas H., 298
Okasha, Elisabeth, 397
Old English Martyrology, 46n12, 80–82
Old English Newsletter, ix
Old English Orosius, 37–45 passim
Old Latin version of Habbakuk, 383–84
Olsen, Glenn W., 370
Ong, Walter, 24, 29, 32n
Opus dei, 380
Oral literature, 24
Orosius, 39–44 passim
Orpen, G.H., 170, 172
Orpheus, 37
Oseberg style, 207, 220
Ostmen, 166
Oswald of Ramsey, 275–76
Otley, 227, art at 244, 252–54
Ottonian art, 232
Otto the Great, 160
Ovid, 38–39, 41
Owen, Olwyn, 232
Ox, speaking ox of Rome, 88
Oxford Concordance Program, 428

Page, R.I., 432
Pan, 293–95
Panoti, 324–27
Papebroche, Daniel, 30
Paphnutius, 29
Parallelism, feature of biblical style, 128–32, 142–46
Paris Psalter, 327
Parry, Milman, 24
Passio Andreae, 111
Passion (Christ's), 16–18, 111–12
Patrick (St.), 66, (presumed) author of hymns, 105, 112
Patrick, bishop of Dublin, 80
Patrologia Latina, as source, 8
Paul and Anthony panels, and Ruthwell and Bewcastle Crosses, 380, 390, 393–94, 396–98
Paul the Deacon, 55, 85, 154

Paul of Naples, 25, 30, 32n, 33n
Paulinus of Nola, 108, 111
Pelagius, 70, 108
Pharasmanes, 320–21
Phillips, Derek, 244
Phoenix, 8–9, 19
Picts, 186, annals, 193
Piers Plowman, Z-text, 32
Pitney brooch, 232
Polycarp, prayer of, "Deus dilecti et benedicti," 107, 112
Pope, John C., 21n
Porus, 320
Pottery, 189
Prayers, 103–19 passim
Primasius, 67
Procopius, 163
Proindtech, 196
Propaganda, and Benedictine reform, 261–78 passim
The Prose Solomon and Saturn, 79
Prosper of Aquitaine, 108
Prudentius, 324
Prudentius of Troyes, 112
Psalm 90, 372, 381–85, 387, 400n15, 401n18, 402n26
Psalm 135, 387
Psalter of Nonantola (= Vat. lat. 84), 110
Pseudo-Apuleius, 60
Pseudo-Athanasius, 80
Pseudo-Augustine, 84–85
Pseudo-Bede, 370
(Pseudo-)Hilary, 68
Pseudo-Isidore, 78
Pseudo-Jerome, 22n, 68–69, 272

"Quinity" of Winchester, 116, 303
"Quoit brooch style," 191

Ragnarok, 214, 244
Ragusa, Isa, 418
Ramsbury, 220
Rath of the Synods, 188
Ravenna throne, 369

Index

Ray, Roger, 65, 72
Reask, 195
Reception of text, 9,
Regularis Concordia, 54, 114-15
Reichenau, 227
Repoussé, 188-89
The Resurrection of Christ, 293
Return from Egypt, 390, 397
Rigg, A.G., 33n
Ringerike, 227-28, 238
Robinson, Fred C., ix, xiin, 33n, 408, 410
Roesdahl, Else, 224
"Rogo te beate patre" (prayer), 124n73
Romanesque, 228-32, 236, 283-84
Roman Wall, 186
Royal collection of prayers (= BL Royal 2 A.xx), 60, 63n33, 103-05, 109-10, 112, 114-15, 117
Rufinus, translator of Eusebius, 107
Runes, 54, 372, 377, 432
Ruthwell Cross, 345, 347, 352, 377-79; construction, 361-64; history, 357-60; iconography, 368-74; incongruous fragment of, 365-66; multivalence in "Agnus Dei" panels, 391-99; multivalence in "Christ over the Beasts," 377-90

Sacrality, of Irish kings, 153, 159-62, 163; of others, 174n7
Sagas, and Irish kingship, 155, 160, 167
St. Conan's bell, 246
St. Nicholas in Ipswich, carved stones, 232
Sallust, 38
"Salve sancte crux" (hymn), 111
Samain (festival), 153
"Sancta Maria gloriosa dei genetrix" (hymn), 116
Sarre, 192
Satan, 290, 295, 298-303, 313n19
Saxl, Fritz, 369-70, 372, 379-80
Sawyer, Peter, 163
Scandinavian influence in art, 227

Schaefer, Kenneth, 86n1
Schapiro, Meyer, 370, 372, 379-80, 382-83
Scottish Chronicle, 169
Scragg, D.G., 119
The Seafarer, 77
Secular sites, in Northumbria, 194
Secular subject matter in art, 319
Sedulius, 108-09; prayer "Alma fulget," 110; prayer "A solis ortus cardine," 109
Sedulius Scottus, his *Liber de Rectoribus Christianis,* 162
Segene of Iona, 69
Seneca, 42
Servius, 38, 40
Seven Sins of Cain (motif), 81, 91
Seventh heaven (motif), 78, 90
Sextus Placidus, 60
Sharpe, Richard, 438
Sheerin, Daniel, 274
Shetelig, Haakon, 257
Shobdon, snake carving, 66
Sigeric, 324
Sign of the Cross, 347-49, 352
Sims-Williams, Patrick, 66
"Singularis meriti sola sine exemplo" (hymn), 116
Skaldic verse, 217
Skeat, Walter W., 32, 33n
Skellig St. Michael, 192
Smalley, Beryl, 65
Smaragdus, 85, his *Diadema Monachorum,* 276
Smiths (craftsmen), 189-90, 198
Smyth, Alfred, 165-66, 171, 181n80, 185, 192
Snake motifs, 236
Sockburn, 432; warrior, 248-52
Soiscel Molaise, 246, 254
Sollsted horse yokes, 254-56
Sophronius, 25, 29, 32n, 33n
Source criticism, issues of and in: 4-10, 19-20, 23-24, 38, 47n14, 66-73 passim, 77-79, 83, 113-14; and art,

203–04, 238, 261, 277–78, 306–08, 398–99
Southampton, 192
Southwell, tympanum, 232
Spanish influence on Anglo-Saxon literature, 105–06
Speculum Historiale, 25
Sphaera Apulei, 290–92, 303–06
Spinning, 195, 201n28
Stancliffe, Clare, 86n13
Stanley, E.G., 9, 20n
Statius, 36
Stegmüller, F., 81
Stone of Scone, 158,
Stowe Missal, 156, 395–96
Stubbs, William, 153, 163–64
Style, biblical, 127–47
"Succure mihi domine antequam moriar" (hymn), 11
Sutton Hoo, 154, 164, 191, 287
Swanton, Michael, 369
Swithun (St.), 261–62, 272–78, 280n30
Sybil, 284
Symons, Thomas, 114
Szarmach, Paul E., 20n

Tabus, and kingship, 153, 160
Tacitus, 42, 163
Táin Bó Cuailnge, 154, 165, 167
Talmud, 82
Tara, 156, 158–59, 188
Tech Mor, 196
Templates, use of, 248–54 passim
Temple, Elzbieta, 415–16, 428, 435
Tendril patterns, 254
Tertullian, 347
Testament of Morand, 156, 160, 162, 168
Textual integrity, and biblical style, 146
Textus Roffensis, 182n106
Theobald, Lewis, 32n
Thirlings, 195
Thomas the Apostle, 287
Thomas of Cantimpré, 321
Thomson, Derick, 169
Thor, 217

Tiberius Psalter (= BL Cotton Tiberius C.VI), 303, 429n2
Timber structures, 196
Tolkien, J.R.R., 172
Toronto microfiche concordance, 40, 409–11
Translation, in Alfred's works, 37
Traprain Law, 186
Trefoil brooches, 220, 224
Trier, 227
Trier Apocalypse (= Stadtbibl. 31), 295
True Cross, 8, 345–47, 353n11
Tselos, Dimitri, 295
Tuath, 157
Tune, 217
Twelve Abuses, 161–61, 168
Typology, 10, 15, 20

Uilberch, 144
Uí Néill, 157, 159, 165–66,
Ulster Cycle, 165
Ultan, 198
Ulysses, 41
Uppland, 228
Urnes style, 228–36
Utrecht Psalter (= Rijkuniversiteit 32), 295, 303, 327, 334–36

Varby, 220
Venantius Fortunatus, 347
Veneration of the Cross, 346
Venezky, Richard L., 409
Verbal detail, in sources, 9
Vercelli Book, 119, 345, 357
Vercelli Homily 19, 79
Vespasian Psalter, 114, 116, 119, 384
Vézelay tympanum, 338
Via negativa, 31
Vikings, 199, settlements of, 243
Vincent of Beauvais, 25, 33n
Virgil, 321, his *Aeneid:* 35–36, 41
Virgil of Salzburg, 78
Visitation, as depicted on the Ruthwell Cross, 365
Vita Julianae, 112

Index

Vita Mariae, 25–32
Vita Oswaldi, 275–76
von Schlegel, Friedrich, 32n

Wack, Mary, 84
Walcher, 232
Wallace-Hadrill, J. 162
Walsh, Maura, 69
Wanderer, 36, 77
Warburg Institute, 418, 421
Wearmouth, 194–96, 432
Weaving, 191, 195, 201n28
Weland (alt. Weyland), 43, 190, 204
Whitby, 195, and Hackness estate, 194
Whitelock, Dorothy, 9–10, 20n, 81
Whithorn, 199
Widukind, 154
Wife-giver, 327–44
Willard, Rudolph, 78, 84
Williams, David, 82
Willis, G.G., 393
Wilmart, André, 81
Wilson, David, 190, 214, 220, 232, 238
Winchester, 432; and hymns, 116; manuscripts of, 228, 303–06, 322, 324, 334
Winchester Benedictional (= BL Add. 49598), 261–78, 272–73, 277, 279n13, 341n31
Winchester Psalter (= BL Cotton Nero C.IV), 283, 317n56
Wittig, Joseph, 38
Wonders of the East, 37, 46n10
Wormald, Jenny, 183n118
Wrenn, C.L., 36
Wright, Charles D., 22n, 418
Wulfila, 163
Wulfstan, his *Portiforium* (= Cambridge, Corpus Christi College 391), 115–16, 118, 290
Wulfstan cantor, 273
Würzburg gloss on kings, 169

Yeavering, 191, 195–96, 200n17
Yerkes, David, 83–84
"Ymnum dicat turba" (hymn), 111
"Ympnarius Edilwaldi," 109
York, 192, 198, 224, 243, 432
"York Master," 252
York Minster, 217, 244, 257
Yorkshire, Scandinavian influence in, 227, 232; snake carving, 236
Young, Edward, 32n

Zettel, Patrick, 83
Zosimus (alt. Zosimas), 26–31